Midwest Studies in Philosophy
Volume XIII

MIDWEST STUDIES IN PHILOSOPHY

EDITED BY PETER A. FRENCH, THEODORE E. UEHLING, JR., HOWARD K. WETTSTEIN

EDITORIAL ADVISORY BOARD

ROBERT AUDI (UNIVERSITY OF NEBRASKA)
JONATHAN BENNETT (SYRACUSE UNIVERSITY)
PANAYOT BUTCHVAROV (UNIVERSITY OF IOWA)
RODERICK CHISHOLM (BROWN UNIVERSITY)
DONALD DAVIDSON (UNIVERSITY OF CALIFORNIA, BERKELEY)
KEITH DONNELLAN (UNIVERSITY OF CALIFORNIA, LOS ANGELES)
FRED I. DRETSKE (UNIVERSITY OF WISCONSIN, MADISON)
GILBERT HARMAN (PRINCETON UNIVERSITY)
RUTH BARCAN MARCUS (YALE UNIVERSITY)
JOHN R. PERRY (STANFORD UNIVERSITY)
ALVIN PLANTINGA (UNIVERSITY OF NOTRE DAME)
DAVID ROSENTHAL (CITY UNIVERSITY OF NEW YORK
    GRADUATE CENTER)
STEPHEN SCHIFFER (UNIVERSITY OF ARIZONA)
MARGARET WILSON (PRINCETON UNIVERSITY)

Many papers in MIDWEST STUDIES IN PHILOSOPHY are invited and all are previously unpublished. The editors will consider unsolicited manuscripts that are received by January of the year preceding the appearance of a volume. All manuscripts must be pertinent to the topic area of the volume for which they are submitted. Address manuscripts to MIDWEST STUDIES IN PHILOSOPHY, Box 601, Notre Dame, IN 46566.

The articles in MIDWEST STUDIES IN PHILOSOPHY are indexed in THE PHILOSOPHER'S INDEX.

Forthcoming Volumes.

Midwest Studies in Philosophy Volume XIII Ethical Theory: Character and Virtue

Editors
PETER A. FRENCH
Trinity University
THEODORE E. UEHLING, JR.
University of Minnesota, Morris
HOWARD K. WETTSTEIN
University of Notre Dame

University of Notre Dame Press • Notre Dame, IN

Published by the University of Notre Dame Press
Notre Dame, IN 46566
Printed in the United States of America

Library of Congress Cataloging-in-Publication Data

Ethical theory : character and virtue / editors, Peter A. French,
    Theodore E. Uehling, Jr., Howard K. Wettstein.
        p.   cm. — (Midwest studies in philosophy ; v. 13)
    ISBN 0-268-01369-1,   ISBN 0-268-01370-5 (pbk.)
    1. Ethics. 2. Virtue. 3. Character. I. French, Peter A.
II. Uehling, Theodore Edward. III. Wettstein, Howard K.
IV. Series.
BJ1012.E8835   1988
170—dc19   88-20570

Midwest Studies in Philosophy
Volume XIII
Ethical Theory: Character and Virtue

Midwest Studies in Philosophy
Volume XIII

Sōphrosunē: How a Virtue Can Become Socially Disruptive

ALASDAIR MACINTYRE

It has recently been argued that an adequate ethics of the virtues requires a functionalist, but not a teleological account of what a virtue is. So Edmund L. Pincoffs has characterized the virtues of persons and actions as qualities of their functioning well in a way which is "appropriate to the common life," a common life within which different individuals and groups will pursue a range of different ends *(Quandaries and Virtues,* Lawrence, Kans., 1986, pp. 6–7 and pp. 97–99). On Pincoffs' view, "as tendencies within common life or within the organization of common life change through history or across cultures, then what counts as a virtue or vice will change. But there are limits." Some qualities will be accounted virtues in all times and places, because they are functional to, necessary to the good functioning of any form of common human life. Other qualities will be accounted virtues in some social and cultural orders, but not in others. Pincoffs' examples of the former include justice and courage.

Pincoffs' central theses clearly presuppose that the qualities which we individuate as virtues are individuated in much the same way in different cultural and social orders. His bold sociological and historical generalization that justice, for example, is accounted a virtue in every form of common life evidently presupposes that what is identified as justice is always, at least in salient respects, one and the same. It is this claim which I want to put in question by arguing that there are important transformations both in the concepts of particular virtues and in the concept of a virtue, so that although, for example, it may be true that in most, perhaps even in all social and cultural orders there is something which it is appropriate to name by our word 'justice' or by some relevantly cognate expression, it is not thereby true that one and the same quality or one and the same set of qualities is being accounted a virtue.

The cases to which I want to appeal however are not drawn from the history which runs from the archaic Greek *'dikē'* to contemporary *'justice'* (in part because this history receives book-length treatment in my *Whose Justice? Which Rationality?* Notre Dame, Ind., 1988), but from the history of the transformations of *'sōphrosunē'*, into *'temperantia'* and thence again into our 'temperateness'. That history, so I shall argue, provides grounds for doubting the truth of another thesis, one entailed by Pincoffs' assertions. It follows from what he asserts that no one can truly judge a particular quality to be a virtue, in the light of the best account of the virtues available within his or her culture, and also judge truly that that quality is dysfunctional in respect of the type of common life which he or she inhabits. Against this I shall suggest that those qualities which have the best claim to be accounted virtues may be and are dysfunctional to and disruptive of certain types of social and cultural order. The virtuous person may be committed to overthrowing rather than sustaining the established forms of social life. *Sōphrosunē,* so often thought of as a conformist virtue, for that very reason provides an excellent test case.

1.

'*Saophrosunē*' names originally in its root meaning the quality of being of sound mind. When it becomes the name of a more specific quality in archaic Greek, it does not always name the same quality, but at an early stage it becomes the name of a virtue which it is especially appropriate for women to possess. In the society portrayed in the Homeric poems a virtue is a quality which enables someone to discharge his or her established social role well; and knowing her place and the limitations imposed on the occupants of that place is peculiarly important for women. Penelope became the literary exemplar of this virtue (see Helen North, *Sophrosyne,* Ithaca, N.Y., 1966, p. 21, a book to which I am generally indebted). The male counterpart virtue was *andreia,* manliness or courage.

Pincoffs' thesis that what are accounted virtues are those qualities which enable some form of common life to function successfully is confirmed by the example of the society portrayed in the Homeric poems. That society is a cooperative order of clearly defined and interdefined, hierarchically organized social roles, and the way in which the virtues enable and facilitate the activities of the common life is unproblematic. Yet just because this is so, insofar as later Greek thinkers criticize Homeric attitudes and roles, they put in question the Homeric conception both of particular virtues, such as *sōphrosunē,* and of the functioning of the virtues. For Euripides' Phaedra, *sōphrosunē,* still conceived in Homeric terms, is insufficient to perform its allotted function (North, op. cit., pp. 86–88); it is unable to contain and inhibit the expression of irrational passion in wrong action. Those who confronted this kind of critique of the Homeric conception had two alternatives. They might have concluded either that *sōphrosunē* was not after all a virtue or instead that the Homeric understanding of *sōphrosunē* was inadequate. It was the latter view which found support in the enquiries of Plato and Aristotle.

Their discussions of *sōphrosunē* and of the character of the person who is *sōphrōn* correct earlier understandings of that virtue in two different ways: first by the accounts which they develop of its relationship to other virtues and secondly by their accounts of what *sōphrosunē* consists in. Plato sets the central problem in the *Charmides:* what is the relationship of *sōphrosunē* to *epistēmē* ? His answer to this question and correspondingly his account of *sōphrosunē* change. What is said in the *Republic* is not the same as what is said in the *Laws,* and passages in the *Phaedrus* and the *Statesman* suggest what the problems may have been which led Plato to develop his views. In the *Republic sōphrosunē* is presented as a virtue which it is possible for an individual to have without his or her having or as yet having *sophia,* wisdom, and that knowledge of the forms which wisdom requires. *Sōphrosunē,* which is defined as "a certain order and a mastery of certain pleasures and desires" (430E) is said to exist both among the rulers of the Republic, who possess wisdom, and the ruled, who do not (431E). And it is a quality already to be looked for in those whose philosophic nature qualifies them for admission to a philosophical education (485E), and hence once more is something which can be possessed prior to and independently of a knowledge of the forms.

Sōphrosunē, thus understood, is a virtue whose possession and exercise seems to be independent of any knowledge and intelligence except that of knowing where the boundaries of appropriate behavior set limits to the satisfaction of desire. It was *sōphrosunē* thus understood which Euripides had criticized and it was this understanding which seems to have become problematic for Plato in both the *Phaedrus* and the *Statesman.* In the *Phaedrus* Plato remarks upon two very different kinds of person in whom *sōphrosunē* has two very different kinds of effect, the difference being a matter of what other qualities *sōphrosunē* is accompanied by. When it is united to the affections of a non-lover (256E), it issues in a kind of narrowness taken to be virtue by the multitude. Yet when allied to "divine madness" in the soul of a lover (256B), it seems to be equated with genuine virtue.

The *Phaedrus* is of course one of the least straightforward of Plato's dialogues. The rhetoric which deploys arguments for and against the same thesis in rival types of speech allows Plato to explore possibilities in a way which leaves the final outcome of the argument open. We should also note that while in the *Phaedrus sōphrosunē* is indeed defined in terms of restraint upon pleasures and desires, it at the same time retains its original meaning of 'soundness of mind'. So that one kind of *sōphrosunē* is a sanity which happily coexists with a certain type of madness. *Sōphrosunē* is also contrasted with *hubris* (237E–238A), the suggestion clearly being that *hubris* is itself a kind of madness. Moreover when the soul achieves a limited vision of the realm of what is, *sōphrosunē* is to be found there, along with *dikaiosunē* and *epistēmē.*

Plato thus seems to have been moving towards a systematic account both of different types of *sōphrosunē* and of different ways in which someone may be *sōphrōn,* and this interpretation is reinforced by a passage in the *Statesman* (208B–C) where Plato entertains the possibility that *sōphrosunē* and *andreia* may on occasion be not complementary or allied, but antitheses, so that what is from the standpoint of *sōphrosunē* appropriate restraint is from that of *andreia* cowardice, while what *andreia* enjoins as courage is from the standpoint of *sōphrosunē* a lack of restraint. But since Plato was deeply committed to the view that in the soul genuinely possessed by virtues, those virtues cannot be in conflict, once again there was a problem.

It is in the *Laws* that alternative ways of understanding the virtues in their interrelationship are seriously investigated. There are first of all the ways in which the virtues are understood in actual Greek city-states in the fourth century. So the Spartan conception of courage as the comprehensive virtue is shown to require that courage discharge the functions usually assigned to *sōphrosunē* (633D). Secondly there is the civic virtue of the ruled in the well-devised *polis,* those whose passions have been molded by the prospect of pleasure and the fear of pain (644C–D). Such a citizen is habituated so that he or she calculates in terms of pleasure or pain (645A) and from this habituation there emerges (648E) a person who is *sōphrōn.* But this civic *sōphrosunē* is certainly not that *sōphronein* which is a virtue of the gods (900D) as well as of the rulers whose souls possess godlike virtues. We thus have to distinguish what are actually praised as virtues in various cities both from the civic virtue of the citizen whose external conformity to the norms of the virtues is the outcome of a form of conditioning imposed by those who are genuinely virtuous, and from the virtues of the genuinely virtuous themselves which require *epistēmē.* Versions of *sōphrosunē* occur at all three levels.

The evaluation of Pincoffs' thesis about the virtues as qualities enabling persons to function well within some form of common life is a more complex matter when it is posed in Platonic rather than in Homeric terms. Certainly in actual Greek city-states the conception of particular virtues, such as *sōphrosunē,* is connected to some conception of what serves the common life in that particular *polis.* But since such conceptions are not founded upon *epistēmē,* they may involve various kinds of error. The true civic virtue of the ruled, molded in accordance with Plato's anticipations of Bentham, more obviously exemplifies Pincoffs' thesis. But it is important that such is only a *simulacrum* of that genuine virtue which is a product of knowledge rather than of fear and shame.

The person who possesses genuine *sōphrosunē* of this highest kind, along with the accompanying virtues and *epistēmē,* while well fitted as a ruler to promote the common life of the kind of *polis* devised in the *Laws,* would in many actual Greek city-states be a disruptive influence of just the kind that Socrates was at Athens. Thus a counter-thesis to Pincoffs' emerges: that genuine virtues are dysfunctional to any but the best form of common life. This is of course a thesis unacceptable not only to Pincoffs, but also to Aristotle, and it is important therefore to ask what, in this respect as in others, Aristotle makes of the virtue of *sōphrosunē.*

2.

Aristotle's portrait of the virtuous person is of one who is able to be at home in a number of different types of *polis,* albeit finding more scope for the civic exercise of his virtues the more nearly his *polis* approximates the best kind of *polis.* It is indeed by the exercise of the virtues that he will perform well in serving the *polis* in various ways, during his military service, as a member of juries, and in a range of public offices. So that the virtues, as political virtues, serve the common life of the *polis* but would not function similarly in a barbarian society. What it is to exhibit a given virtue varies with one's place in the *polis* and the *household.* The virtue of a ruler is not the same as that of one of the ruled, and "the *sōphrosunē* of a woman is not the same as that of a man, nor are their *andreia* and *dikaiosunē* the same, as Socrates thought" *(Politics* 1.1260a21–22).

Within the Aristotelian scheme of the virtues, *sōphrosunē* was assigned a narrower, more specialized and better defined place than it had possessed in either the

Homeric or the Platonic schemes. The specific character of the person with *sōphrosunē* is that he (Aristotle's masculine pronoun, not mine) acts in accordance with the mean in respect of bodily pleasures and pains *(Nicomachean Ethics* 2.1107b4–8; 3.1117b27–1118a27), but not even all of these but only those which we share with other animals. One can, in a way analogous to that in which one is *sōphrōn* with respect to such bodily pleasures, be guilty of either excess or defeat in respect of other pleasures, such as aesthetic pleasure in paintings, and in respect of other desires, such as ambition for public office. But *sōphrosunē* itself has this more restricted place. Two aspects of its importance need to be noted.

Sōphrosunē is no longer to be thought of as concerned only with the control of or restraint upon the desires for certain pleasures. *Enkrateia* is the quality of self-control and *sōphrosunē* is more and other than *enkrateia.* The *sōphrōn* takes pleasure in and is pleased by the right things in the right way and to the right degree *(NE* 3.1118b21–27). His capacities for pleasure and pain have been educated. The *sōphrōn* has come to find enjoyable an abstinent mode of life that would be burdensome to the profligate person *(NE* 2.1105b5–7). He finds unpleasant what the profligate finds enjoyable *(NE* 3.1119a11–15). Aristotle indeed uses this as an example of how more generally it is what we take pleasure or pain in which reveals the character of our settled dispositions to act in one way rather than another, of our virtues and vices. This is why, for Aristotle, pleasures or pains cannot by themselves provide us with any standard of goodness or badness. For what we take pleasure in or are pained by varies with and is secondary to the state of our moral education and development.

A second aspect of the importance of *sōphrosunē* is the double character of its relation to *phronēsis.* On the one hand in order to be *sōphrōn* one must know how to value bodily pleasures at their true worth in relation to other goods, as right reason *(orthos logos)* enjoins *(NE* 3.119a18–20). The exercise of right reason is exhibited in right *prohairesis* and that in turn depends on the possession of *phronēsis.* So that there can only be *sōphrosunē* where there is also *phronēsis.* But on the other the exercise of *phronēsis* will not be possible if one is distracted or corrupted by addiction to bodily pleasures or too great fear of bodily pains. Hence there can only be *phronēsis* where there is also *sōphrosunē.* What happens to those without *sōphrosunē* is that they lose sight of the first principle of right action, that *telos* for the sake of which everything ought to be undertaken *(NE* 4.1140b12–20). Aristotle accompanies this thesis with an ingenious but false etymology for *sōphrosunē,* according to which its original meaning was that which preserve *phronēsis* (1140b11–12).

By connecting *sōphrosunē* and *phronēsis* in this double way Aristotle provided himself with the means for distinguishing between genuine *sōphrosunē* and inferior versions of it, although he never explicitly addressed this issue. But he did, in his account of *andreia,* distinguish genuine courage from such inferior versions of it— called by the name of *'andreia'* in ordinary language—as that exhibited by those who do what the courageous person would do, but from fear of doing otherwise and not because they are in fact courageous. Such is the quality of the well-drilled soldier compelled into battle by his superior officers *(NE* 3.1116a15–1116b3). It would be easy to construct a parallel account for *sōphrosunē* in which genuine *sōphrosunē* was contrasted with that version of *sōphrosunē* referred to by Plato, which is in fact no more than a certain narrowness, taken to be virtue by the masses. And more generally the problems posed by Plato's references to *sōphrosunē* can be responded to from the standpoint provided by Aristotle's account. On one such issue Aristotle makes peculiarly relevant remarks.

Plato had in the *Statesman* (208B–C), as I noted, considered whether from the standpoint of *andreia* the restraint of the *sōphrōn* might not have to be characterized as cowardice. Aristotle points out *(NE* 2.1108b23–6) that what is called courageous by the courageous person will not be the same as what is called courageous by the rash or cowardly person. Judgments as to what is virtuous or vicious vary with whether the person making the judgment is virtuous or vicious. It follows from what Aristotle says that we should expect some people to call the restraint of the *sōphrōn* cowardly, but they would be themselves rash, and not courageous persons. Hence there would be no conflict between genuine *andreia* and genuine *sōphrosunē.*

It is therefore misleading to read Aristotle's catalogue of the virtues as a listing of those qualities generally held to be virtues. There is in the background a conception of the relationship of the virtues to each other and more especially of each to *phronēsis,* in the light of which the choices and preferences of the virtuous person differ systematically from those of the vicious and from those of the person still in the course of moral education. It follows that from an Aristotelian standpoint, it can never be right to weigh preferences in such a way that everybody counts for one and nobody for more than one. And it would be as fundamental a mistake to try to maximize the satisfaction of the preferences of all the members of a given society. For this would be to give the same weight to the preferences of the vicious, the *akratic,* and the undeveloped as to the preferences of those possessing the intellectual and moral virtues, from an Aristotelian standpoint a political and moral absurdity.

Yet just this absurdity is often presented as a basic principle in the common life of modern liberal democratic societies. And it is perhaps no accident that such societies are consumer societies in which *sōphrosunē* is not generally accounted a virtue anymore. I do not mean by this that moderation in the pursuit of bodily pleasures is not often praised and prescribed in such societies; but it is characteristically praised and prescribed as a means to longevity, to contemporary fashions in physical attractiveness, and to career success rather than as a prerequisite for *phronēsis* and thus for the achievement of the good and the best.

Two points relevant to Pincoffs' functionalist thesis emerge. The first begins from the fact that *sōphrosunē* as understood by Aristotle, both in itself and in its relation to other virtues, is functional in respect of some modes of common life and dysfunctional in terms of others; and this was also the case with *sōphrosunē* as understood by Homer and by Plato. This suggests that there are some grounds for asserting three closely related generalizations. A first is that, when any virtue has been specified with sufficient adequacy to provide guidance for moral practice and moral education, it will turn out to be functional in respect of some forms of political and social life and dysfunctional in respect of others. A second generalization is that debate and conflict as to the character of *sōphrosunē,* debate as to which rival account of it is the best, must therefore be inescapably linked to political debate and conflict as to which forms of social and political life merit our allegiance. A third correlative generalization is that any account of the virtues which made it plausible to suppose that a certain virtue was functional to *any* form of common life, will be one in which that virtue has been inadequately characterized and in which instances of various inferior versions of that virtue or of simulacra of it are being treated as examples of that virtue in a way that does not distinguish them from genuine instances of the exercise of that virtue at its best.

The truth of these three generalizations is compatible with, indeed would be paradigmatically exemplified by, the occurrence of a state of affairs which is certainly incompatible with Pincoffs' functionalism, namely one in which it is simultaneously the case that there is a socially and politically determinate form of common life, that within that common life certain persons and perhaps groups exhibit genuine virtues and that, just insofar as those persons and groups exhibit these virtues, they are put in conflict with the forms of the common life in serious and long-term ways. In other words, what Pincoffs' thesis rules out is the possibility of there being forms of social and political life in which the practice of the virtues is at revolutionary odds with those forms, so that one can only be virtuous by being in systematic conflict with the established order.

It may be retorted that the virtuous in such a society will of course tend to make common cause and to share a form of common life with each other; and this is undeniable. But Pincoffs' functionalism is a significant thesis just because it commits those who accept it to affirming not merely that the virtuous will characteristically enter into relationships with each other and that the virtues will be functional to *this* form of common life, but rather that it is in respect of the common life as such, the overall forms of political and social order, that the virtues are functional. That it is possible to specify a state of affairs incompatible with Pincoffs' thesis is a strength of that thesis, not a weakness. It shows that it possesses empirical content, that it is falsifiable. It exhibits its character as a thesis at once philosophical and sociological. What would damage Pincoffs' thesis is not that such a state of affairs is possible, but that it actually obtains. Does it?

Before suggesting what would need to be done to answer that question, let me point out another kind of difficulty for Pincoffs' thesis which is raised by the history of *sōphrosunē* from Homer to Aristotle. Pincoffs' thesis about the virtues denies their teleological character. But on an Aristotelian account the only way in which a virtue such as *sōphrosunē* can be characterized adequately, either for the purposes of moral precept and education, or so that an answer can be provided to the theoretical questions raised by Plato's discussions, is by relating it to the *telos,* both directly and through its relationship to *phronēsis.* Remove the teleological aspects from the characterization of *sōphrosunē* and what will remain will be an account too bare and impoverished for us to pass a verdict upon its status as a virtue, let alone upon whether as a virtue it is functional or dysfunctional to any particular form of common life.

It may be remarked that to say this is to say no more than that Pincoffs is in disagreement with Aristotle; it is to say nothing about who is in the right. And certainly from the skeletal outline history of *sōphrosunē* which I have sketched so far not much more than this can be derived. But something can, and something which undermines Pincoffs' identification of the virtues. For Aristotle's account is in central respects a more adequate account than that provided by either the archaic Greek conception or the Platonic. At each successive stage in the history of *sōphrosunē* problems raised at earlier stages are to a significant degree resolved. What Aristotle shapes and gives direction to has received definition as a tradition both of enquiry into the nature of the virtues and of moral practice.

There were of course rival traditions of moral theory and practice in the ancient world, in Asia and in Europe, as well as other rival traditions in later periods. But what each rival tradition presents to us, what all moral practice presents to us, are not the claims of a set of virtues, specified adequately for practical purposes without any reference to the theory of the virtues, about which we may then, if we are so minded, go on to construct a theoretical account, as some additional, morally supererogatory task. What we are always in fact presented with are the claims of virtues already understood in specific theory-presupposing ways. The theory of the virtues, Aristotelian or otherwise, has thus generally been to some large degree internal to that understanding of them which is required for practice—generally, but not universally. For in the moral culture peculiar to modernity, the use of the virtue-words has often become detached from the various backgrounds of theoretical belief in terms of which they were originally deployed. And since the moral idiom of modernity is a *collage* of fragments from a variety of heterogeneous traditions, so the collection of expressions used in the languages of modernity to express evaluations of persons are a multifarious, not always mutually compatible, set. Hence lists of such expressions, such as Pincoffs supplies (p. 42, pp. 76–77, p. 85) need to be sorted out and identified in terms of their historical antecedents, Christian, Stoic, Epicurean, Enlightenment or whatever, in order for their present coexistence in use to be intelligible.

Virtues, that is to say, are conceptions of personal qualities, each of which has a history of transformations such that, at later stages in that history, those who employ one variety of conception rather than another express in so doing their allegiance to or dissent from those past schemes of evaluation of which that virtue has been a part. To use the virtue-words in as near as possible complete detachment from their past, as the tradition-deprived inhabitants of modernity do for the most part, involves a repudiation of all those schemes of the virtues from the past which did involve a commitment to systematic, theoretical belief and to those institutionalized forms of cultural, social, and political order which either incarnated or presupposed such belief. So that the particular set of virtue-words and virtues with which Pincoffs is concerned, specified as they are without adequate reference to their history, provide inadequate data either for conceptual analysis or for empirical generalization.

3.

When *sōphrosunē* was translated by the Latin *'temperantia'*, there was awaiting it in the moral practice of the later Roman republic no single virtue which was the counterpart to what *'sōphrosunē'* had named for Greeks (North, op. cit., ch. 8). Cicero invoked *temperantia* in his oratory when attacking a disparate set of vices, all of them forms of self-indulgence which prevented a Roman citizen from giving primacy to the duties owed to his household and his city, and Cicero's moral theory also adapted *temperantia* to specific Roman norms and situations. *'Temperantia'* as used in both contexts corresponded neither to those broader Greek uses, in which *'sōphrosunē'* came close to naming virtue as such, nor to such narrower uses as Aristotle's in which its province was restricted to that of the bodily pleasures and pains.

In other authors' texts *'temperantia'* remained a translation of *'sōphrosunē'*, as *'sōphrosunē'* had been used by Greek moral theorists, and when Christian moral theory became systematic in a way which owed a great deal to Plato, and was then translated into Latin, *'temperantia'* became the name of a single virtue, in practice as well as theory, with a well-defined place within the scheme of the virtues. At the same time looser and more generalized uses of *'temperantia'* persisted and, when French and English equivalents of *'temperantia'* appeared, this same dual set of uses survived: *'temperantia'* and its heirs on some occasions named a highly specific cardinal virtue, understood in Platonic or Aristotelian terms, and on others a more generalized quality of restraint from self-indulgence. One way of classifying later moral philosophers is by reference to whether it is the former or the latter set of uses which they treat as paradigmatic. The most notable member of the former class is Aquinas, of the latter Hume.

Aquinas follows Aristotle closely in his *Commentary on the Nichomachean Ethics* (III lect. 19–22), laying stress upon the difference between what the temperate person enjoys and what the intemperate (lect. 20). His psychological elucidations, although brief, emphasize how the patterning of enjoyment differs in the two cases and so how the temperate person is not someone imposing restraint upon precisely the same desires as one felt by the intemperate, but someone with transformed desires. In his *Commentary on the Politics* (I lect. 10) he treats the difference between Aristotle and Socrates over whether *sōphrosunē* and other virtues are the same in women as in men not as a disagreement, but as a matter of level of specificity in the characterization of the virtues. The virtues, characterized generally, are the same for all humans; but what their practice in specific detail amounts to varies with political and household roles. Aquinas was thus able to reconcile Aristotle not only with Socrates, but also with Clement, who had, as a Christian, asserted the sameness of *sōphrosunē* in women and in men *(Paidagogos* 14.10,2).

As with Aristotle, there is an assertion of the same double relationship of *sōphrosunē* to rational prudence. *Temperantia* guides and prescribes to the relevant desires in accordance with the norms of reason (*Summa Theologiae* II-II q. 141, a. 1; III q. 8, a. 2); and it is required, if the other virtues, including *prudentia,* are to play their due part (*ST* I–II q. 58, a. 5; II–II q. 141, a. 2, 7). But Aquinas gives a much more systematized account of the virtues than does Aristotle, identifying their character and relationships in terms of a psychology of reasons, passion, and the will (the latter, of course, a notion alien to Aristotle). Correspondingly Aquinas' account of the kind of transformation of personality which is involved in the development of the virtuous person is also more systematic. As with Aristotle, the virtuous person fails if he or she does not enjoy what it is reasonable to enjoy. Aquinas is as much a critic of a false asceticism as he is of any other type of refusal to develop the appetites and passions in accordance with reason (*ST* II–II q. 142, a. 1). So to have the virtue of *temperantia* is to enjoy and to be pained by quite other objects than he or she who lacks it enjoys and is pained by.

Hume's account of temperance gives it a quite different place in the catalogue of the virtues. Temperance involves no transformation of what pleases us, but merely a restraint upon the kind of indulgence which will "draw ruin upon us, and incapacitate us for business and action" (*Treatise* III, iii, 4). The virtues in general are those qualities which human beings, almost universally, find pleasant or useful: temperance restrains overindulgence in pleasure for the sake of utility (*Enquiry Concerning the Principles of Morals* IX, ii). It follows that to put restraint upon what pleases, as people in general are pleased, and what is also accounted useful, as people in general reckon utility, is not a virtue, but a vice. "Celibacy, fasting, penance, mortification, self-denial, humility, silence, solitude, and the whole train of monkish virtues; for what reason are they everywhere rejected by men of sense, but because they serve to no manner of purpose . . . ?" (*Enquiry* IX, i). Aquinas' reply would have been that one can only rightly discern purposes if one acquires those qualities which Hume called 'monkish', qualities which are all aspects of or closely related to the virtue of *temperantia*.

Hence in a society organized to secure those reciprocities of pleasure and utility which, on Hume's view, are embodied in the relations of virtuous persons, any follower of Aquinas would exhibit virtues which are dysfunctional to the common life. And in a society organized so that the practice of the virtues, understood as Aquinas understood them, may achieve the common good, understood as Aquinas understood it, any systematic Humean would be a dysfunctional deviant. Nor is this merely a matter of moral theory. There may only have been small-scale societies within which Aquinas' moral philosophy and theology have found adequate expression; but Hume represented in theoretical terms the dominant order of the eighteenth-century United Kingdom. And within that order the virtues Thomistically understood could only have been disruptive.

So we have here two examples of ways of understanding the virtues in theory and practice which are at home in some kinds of social order and disruptive in others. But this by itself leaves open a response for a defender of Pincoffs' functionalist generalization. For all that I have shown, it may be said, is that what have been taken to be virtues in certain times and places by certain theorists and their followers are not functional in respect of the common life. But these theorists may well have been mistaken; what are taken to be virtues may well in fact not really be virtues at all. So that perhaps my counter-examples, drawn from the history of *sōphrosunē* and its successors, are not genuine counter-examples to Pincoffs' thesis, which concerned what are in fact the virtues and not what have been falsely supposed to be virtues. Indeed at the outset I said that I would show that those qualities which have the best claim to be accounted virtues may be dysfunctional to certain forms of the common life, whereas I have so far provided no reason for asserting either that it is the virtues as characterized by Aristotle or the virtues as characterized by Aquinas or the virtues as characterized by Hume which have the best claim to be accounted genuine virtues. If I am to make good my claim, must I not at least justify the thesis that one of these accounts is the best account which we have? Happily a simpler line of argument is open to me.

For any account of the virtues, both incompatible with and in those respects superior to that of, say, either Aquinas or Hume or both, will have to specify a set of virtues allegiance to which will be incompatible with and the practice of which will be in conflict with allegiance to or the practice of at least either the virtues as understood by Aquinas or the virtues understood by Hume. But in that case the practice of the virtues understood in this third way would be disruptive of and dysfunctional to the common life of a Thomist order or the common life of a Humean order. So that we do not need to argue for the superiority of Aquinas' account to Hume's or *vice versa* in order to reach the conclusion that on the best account of the virtues we have, whatever it turns out to be, the virtues will be disruptive of and dysfunctional to the common life of *some* social order. And to have reached this conclusion is not unimportant. For on Pincoffs' view it does seem that the practice of the virtues in any order will always be fundamentally conservative, preservative of the functioning of that order. That his functionalist generalization is false opens up the possibility that being virtuous may require one to be at odds with the established modes of the common life in radical ways. The virtue of *sōphrosunē*, like other virtues, can be a virtue of revolutionaries.

The Virtue of Love

ROBERT C. SOLOMON

In a famous—or infamous—passage, Kant off-handedly dismisses one of the most essential elements in ethics:

> Love out of inclination cannot be commanded; but kindness done from duty—although no inclination impels us, and even although natural and unconquerable disinclination stands in our way—is *Practical,* and not *Pathological* love, residing in the will and not of melting compassion.[1]

In the *Symposium,* on the other hand, Phaedrus offers us one of many contrasting comments by Plato in honor of *erōs:*

> That is why I say Love is the eldest of the gods and most honored and the most powerful for acquiring virtue and blessedness, for men both living and dead.[2]

This paper has two aims: to understand erotic (romantic, "pathological") love as itself a virtue, and to broaden our view of ethics.

1. *ERŌS* AND ETHICS

> It (love) does not hesitate to intrude with its trash. . . . It knows how to slip its love-notes and ringlets even into ministerial portfolios and philosophical manuscripts. Every day it brews and hatches the worst and most perplexing quarrels and disputes, destroys the most valuable relationships and breaks the strongest bonds. . . . Why all this noise and fuss? . . . It is merely a question of every Jack finding his Jill. (The gracious reader should translate this phrase into precise Aristophanic language.) Why should such a trifle play so important a role?[3]

Love as a virtue? Well, hardly. Motherly love, certainly; patriotism, perhaps. The love of humanity, to be sure, but romantic love? Sexual love? The passion that makes fools of us all and has led to the demise of Anthony, Cleopatra, young Romeo, Juliet, and King Kong? Love is nice, but it is not a virtue. Maybe it is not even nice. Hesiod in the *Theogony* warned against *erōs* as a force contrary and antagonistic to reason. Sophocles and Euripides both denounced *erōs*, in *Antigone* and *Hippolytus* respectively, and even Virgil had his doubts. Schopenhauer, much more recently, thought all love to be sexual and damnable, and today we are much more likely to invoke the cynical wit of Oscar Wilde or Kingsley Amis than the saccharine pronouncements of our latter-day love pundits. Indeed, running through the history of ideas in the West one cannot but be struck by the ambivalence surrounding this central and celebrated concept. It is cursed as irrational and destructive and praised as the origin of everything. *Erōs* is famous for its foolishness and at the same time elevated and venerated as a god, albeit at first a rather minor one, but by the time of early Christianity, nothing less than God as such.

Today, we find ourselves torn between such mundane considerations as dependency and autonomy, security and the dubious freedom to remain 'uncommited'. It is hard to remind ourselves, therefore, that the history of love is intellectual warfare between bestiality on one side and divinity on the other. The word 'love' has so often functioned as a synonym for lust that it is hard to take it seriously as a virtue. It has just as long been raised to cosmological status, by Parmenides, Empedocles, and Plotinus, for example, and it therefore seems somewhat small minded to reduce it to a mere source of human relationships. Most modern philosophers have, accordingly, ignored it, Schopenhauer here as elsewhere being a bit eccentric, while moralists have had a field day playing the one side (lust) against the other (divine grace, piety, and contempt for all bodily functions, but particularly those that are best when shared).

In any discussion of love as a virtue, it is necessary, if by now routine, to mention some different 'kinds' of love. (The notion of 'kinds' may already be question begging here, for the more difficult issue may be what links, rather than distinguishes, e.g., friendship, sexual love and parental affection.) In particular, it is essential that we distinguish *erōs* and *agapé*, the former usually translated as sexual love, the latter as selfless and certainly sexless love for humanity. The distinction is often drawn crudely. For instance, *erōs* is taken to be purely erotic and reduced to sexual desire, which it surely is not. Or *agapé* is characterized as selfless giving, opposed by *erōs* which thus becomes selfish taking (or at least craving). *Agapé* is idealized to the point where it becomes an attitude possible only to God, thus rendering it virtually inapplicable to common human fellow-feelings. *Erōs* by contrast is degraded to the profanely secular and denied any hint of spirituality. To think of love as a virtue, therefore, is first of all to expand (once again) the domain of *erōs*. (Romantic love, I am presuming, is one historical variant of *erōs*.) One need not deny the desirability (or the possibility) of altruistic *agapé* to insist that erotic *erōs* shares at least some of its virtues.

Erōs, and what we now call 'romantic love', should also be distinguished (carefully) from other forms of particular affection—for example, motherly, fatherly, brotherly, or sisterly love and friendship. I think that Schopenhauer was partly right when he suggested (with Freud following him) that all love is to some extent sexual. But to make this point one obviously needs a generously enlarged conception of sex and sexual desire, and I often fear that this insight is motivated as much by its titillating implications as by the impulse to clarify the nature of human bonding. A more modest thesis is that *erōs* (not sex) encompasses almost all intimate, personal affections. What characterizes *erōs* in general, we might then suggest, is an intense quasi-physical, even "grasping," affection for a particular person, a Buscaglian "urge to hug" if you will. (Plato often uses such desire-defined language in talking about *erōs,* even when he is reaching for the Forms.) In romantic love, sexual desire is undeniably a part of this affection, though it is not at all clear whether this is the source of the affection or rather its vehicle. *Erōs* differs from *agapé* in the prevalence of self-interested desire, but it is not thereby selfish and the desire is not just sexual. It also includes a much more general physical desire to "be with," such personal desires as "to be appreciated" and "to be happy together," such inspirational desires as "to be the best for you" and such "altruistic" desires as "to do anything I can for you." As laRochefoucauld once put it, "in the soul . . . a thirst for mastery; in the mind sympathy; in the body, nothing but a delicately hidden desire to possess, after many mysteries."[4]

It is a common mistake to think of the other person in sex as a mere 'object' of desire, which leads to the idea that *erōs* too is degrading and seeks only its own satisfaction. Consider Kant on the matter:

> Because sexuality is not an inclination which one human being has for another as such, but is an inclination for the sex of another, it is a principle of the degradation of human nature, in that it gives rise to the preference of one sex to the other, and to the dishonoring of that sex through the satisfaction of desire.[5]

But surely the question (as Plato raised it 2300 years earlier) is *what* one desires when one sexually desires another person. In the *Symposium,* Aristophanes suggested that one desires not sex but permanent (re-)unification with the other; Socrates insisted that one really wants the Forms. Even if we consider such goals too fantastic for *erōs,* it is clear that the Greeks—as opposed to Kant and many moderns—saw that sexual desire was much, much more than desire for sex and not at all opposed to virtuous desire. At the very least, it is clear that sexual desire is some sort of powerful desire *for* the other person *through* sex. The question is: a desire *for what?* And by no means should we assume from the outset that the answer to this question has anything to do with sexual *objects.* Indeed, taking our clue from Hegel and Sartre, we might suggest rather that it has everything to do with the sexual *subject,* and subjects by their very nature cannot be wholly sexual.

The most obvious difference between erotic (romantic) and other particular forms of love is the centrality of sexual (do not read "genital") desire, but there are two other differences that, philosophically, are much more illuminating. The first, though quite controversial, is the prerequisite of *equality* between lovers. This may seem odd in the light of modern accusations against love as a vehicle for the degredation and oppression of women (Shulamith Firestone, Marilyn French), but in historical perspective it becomes clear that—however far we may be from real equality—romantic love emerges only with the relative liberation of women from traditional subservient social and economic roles. Romantic love emerges only when women begin to have more of a choice about their lives—and about their lovers and husbands in particular. One thinks of John Milton's Adam, created early in the era of romantic love, who specifically requested from God not a mere playmate or companion or a mirror image of himself but an *equal,* for "among unequals what society/

Can sort, what harmony or true delight?"[6] Or, paraphrasing Stendhal, we might say that love tends to create equals even where it does not find them, for equality is as essential to romantic love as authority is to parenthood—whether or not this is adequately acknowledged or acted upon.

One other difference between *erōs* and other loves is that romantic love, unlike familial love, for example, is unprescribed and often spontaneous. ("Romantic friendships" are especially worth noting in this context.) Critical to erotic, romantic love is the sense of *choice*. Family love, in this sense, is always prescribed. The love between husband and wife, or what such authors as de Rougemont call 'conjugal love', might be considered prescribed in this sense too, including its sexuality. This is emphatically not to say that married love cannot be romantic, or that romantic love is characterized only by its novelty or by the excitement and anxiety consequent to that novelty. It is a common mistake to take the exhilaration of love as love—without asking what that exhilaration is *about*. Love and marriage often begin together even if they do not always remain together, and to separate them is just to say that love can be unhitched just as horses can, while carriages sit unmoving.

What could be virtuous about *erōs?* One might rationalize sexual love as the slippery slope to marriage, but this faint praise only reinforces our image of romantic love as something in itself childish, foolish, and a kind of conspiracy of nature and society to trick self-consciously rebellious adolescents into maturity. One might celebrate *erōs* as the often unrecognized source of many of our most beautiful creations, from Dante's poetry to the Taj Mahal, but this too is to demean love as a virtue and see it merely as a means, as Freud once saw anal retention as a means to great art. But it seems to me that *erōs* is not considered a virtue for three general sorts of reasons:

(1) *Erōs* is reduced to mere sexuality, and philosophers, insofar as they deign to dirty their minds with sex at all *(qua* philosophers, of course), tend to see sexuality as vulgar and not even a candidate for virtue. Part of this is the common perception of sex as either a form of recreation or a means to procreation, but in any case a set of desires constrained by ethics but hardly of ethical value in themselves.

(2) Love is an emotion and emotions are thought to be irrational, beyond our control, merely episodic instead of an essential aspect of character, products of 'instinct' and intractible in the face of all evidence and objective consideration. Even Aristotle, one of the few friends of the passions in the history of philosophy, insisted that only states of character, not passions, can count as virtues.

(3) *Erōs* even insofar as it is not just sexual is self-love and the self-indulgence of desire, while an essential characteristic of the virtues is, in Hume's phrase, their utility, their being pleasing to others and based on such sentiments as compassion and sympathy. Romantic love, far from being "pleasing to others," tends to be embarrassing and sometimes harmful to others and self-destructive. It tends to be possessive, jealous, obsessive, antisocial, even "mad." Such drama is not the stuff of which virtue is made.

I obviously believe that each of these objections to erotic love as a virtue is just plain wrong, but it will take most of this paper to spell out an alternative view. Simply, for now, let me state that these objections demean and misunderstand the nature of sexuality, the nature of emotions, and the nature of love in particular. So that I do not appear overly irrationalist and romantic here, let me draw Plato to my side. He clearly saw *erōs* as a virtue, and every one of the speakers in the *Symposium* agrees with this. Even Socrates, by far the most effete of the speakers, celebrates *erōs* not as the disinterested appreciation of beauty and wisdom (as many Oxford commentaries would make it seem) but rather as a 'grasping' sensuality, perhaps of the mind rather than the body, but erotic none the less for that. (Why did he so distrust beauty in art but yet celebrate it in *erōs?*) In Plato's thinking, *erōs* was a virtue just because it was (in part) a passion, filled with desire and—in that peculiarly noble Socratic sense—self-obsessed as well.

2. ETHICS AND SUBJECTIVITY

One more word against Kant as a *moralist*. A virtue must be *our own* invention, *our* most necessary self-expression and self-defense; any other kind of virtue is a danger . . . "Virtue," "duty," the "good in itself," the good which is impersonal and universally valid—chimeras and expressions of decline, of the final exhaustion of life. . . . The fundamental laws of self-preservation and growth demand the opposite—that everyone invent *his own* virtue, his *own* categorical imperative.[7]

A single paradigm of rationality has retained hegemony in ethics since the Enlightenment. In the shadow of this paradigm, there is less difference than similarity between Kant and the utilitarians: moral philosophy is nothing if not objective, rational, based on principles, and exclusive of particular self-reference and mere personal perspectives. What is shocking is what the paradigm leaves out: most emotions and love in particular (except insofar as these might motivate duty or serve "the greatest good for the greatest number"). The persistence of this paradigm (which I will call "Kantian") has turned the most exciting subject in philosophy—or so it would seem from novels, the newspapers, soap operas, and ordinary gossip—into the dry quasi-legal tedium that we find in some philosophy journals. And worse, it has proved to many people—including many philosophers—that ethics has little to do with the intricate realities of human behavior. The elegant observations of Hume are shunted aside in favor of *policy* decisions. The neglect of personal inclinations in favor of legalistic universal principles leaves out the substance of the ethical, which is not principles but feelings. Bernard Williams points out that it would be "insane" to prefer an act of kindness born of principle rather than personal affection, as Kant recommends.[8] When one thinks of the myriad delights, affections, and felt obligations in love, one cannot help but decide that, given a choice between insisting that love is amoral (at best) and retaining the Kantian paradigm, one's preference is quite clear. Kant's line that we quoted from the *Groundwork* about "pathological love," even on the most generous interpretation (as "pathos" rather than "diseased"), dismisses romantic affection as wholly irrelevant to moral worth, and with this eliminates most of what we—and most of Kant's more romantic colleagues—take to be the very heart of morality.

Richard Taylor once wrote that he found Kantian ethics basically offensive, so much so that he insisted that he would have the same attitude toward a true Kantian that he would toward a person who "regularly drowned children just to see them squirm."[9] This is extreme, and it ignores many recent attempts to "humanize" Kant,[10] but the Kantian position is offensive, and one of the reasons for this is its resistance, if not rejection, of any inclusion of personal, particular feelings in moral evaluation. We find similar resistance in many modern Kantians, for instance, in Bernard Gert's *The Moral Rules* where he dismisses feelings as morally worthless and insists instead that "feelings are morally important only insofar as they lead to morally good actions."[11] It seems to me, on the contrary, that nothing is more important to our evaluation of a person's moral character than feelings, and not just because of our reasonable expectation that actions generally follow feelings. The worth of our feelings is not parasitic on the desirability of our actions. In love, the worthiness of our actions depends on the feelings they express. Generous and even heroic actions may follow from love, but the virtue of love stands quite on its own, even without such consequences (Socrates' criticism of Phaedrus in the *Symposium*). We may think Othello foolish and tragic but we still admire the motive, while Victorian literature is filled with Kantian gentlemen acting on their principles who are utterly repulsive (for instance, Mr. Collins in Jane Austin's *Pride and Prejudice*). Not only is it desirable to love, but those who have not loved (if not lost), or fear they cannot, rightly worry not only about their character but about their completeness as human beings—quite apart from any questions about action or performance. Love itself is admirable, quite apart from its effects and consequences.

Why is the tradition so opposed to love and other feelings as essential, even primary ingredients, in morality? The opposition is all the more surprising given the heavy emphasis on love (though as *agapé*) as the supreme virtue in the New Testament—and it is just this oddity that Kant is trying to explain away in the passage quoted. There seem to be several reasons for Kant's antagonism to feelings in moral evaluation. First and foremost, he seems to believe that only that which can be "commanded" is morally obligatory, and love as a passion cannot be commanded. This particular claim has been admirably disputed in Ed Sankowski's 1978 paper on "Love and Moral Obligation," where, in particular, he argues that we at least hold people responsible for fostering or evading the conditions that breed love.[12] One might challenge as well the claim that only that which can be commanded is moral; much of what goes into "good character," while it can be cultivated, cannot be commanded. One might also argue—as I have often—that the emotions are far more voluntaristic and under our control than we normally believe, and not just in the sense that we can foster or avoid the conditions in which they typically emerge. This is not to say that an emotion such as love can simply be produced, by an act of will or volition, as one might now produce a thought or a movement of one's finger. There may be, in Danto-esque phrase, no "basic action" where love is concerned. But there are lots of intentional actions of both mind and body that are not basic, and to insist that love can be produced *de nihilo* by a volition is surely to place an unreasonable demand on its moral virtue.

Second, on the Kantian paradigm, it is always the universal that is in question, never the particular. Here Kant is once again in agreement with New Testament ethics, for *agapé* could be argued to be universal (or, one might also say, indiscriminate) love, and not love for any particular person. (It is worth noting that Christian psychology did hold people responsible for their feelings, did believe that love could be commanded, and, in just the phrase disputed by Kant, demanded it.) But on many interpretations Christian love, as love, is emphatically the love of particulars—even if of every particular and not just of the universal (God, humanity) as such. Love—especially erotic or romantic love—is wholly particular. It is the elevation of one otherwise ordinary person to extraordinary heights with extraordinary privileges. The idea of a categorical imperative in such instances is laughable. On the Kantian model, the particularity of love would seem to be a form of irrationality—comparable to our tendency to make "exceptions" of ourselves, in this case, making exceptions of persons close to us. In love the particular is everything. The virtue of love is and ought to be entirely preferential and personal. The lover who gives special preference to his love (though not, of course, in a bureaucratic or departmental position) is virtuous. A lover who insisted on treating everyone including his or her lover the same would strike us as utterly repulsive.

Third, because morality is a matter of reason, the irrationality of the emotions (in general) is good enough reason not to make them central to ethics. The alleged irrationality of emotions is something more than their supposed involuntariness and particularity. Kant thinks that emotions are irrational, Bernard Williams suggests, because they are capricious. One might add that they also seem to be intrusive, disruptive, stubborn, stupid, and pointless. These are very different accusations, but they are often levied together against emotions in general and love in particular. As "feelings," it is often said that emotions are *non*rational (not even smart enough to be *ir*rational.) Or, granting emotions a modicum of aims and intelligence, it is insisted that emotions *(sui generis)* have limited ends and (at best) inefficient means. Against the 'disruptive' view of emotions it should be argued that they do not always intrude or disrupt life but often (always?) define it and define the ultimate ends of rationality as well. Against the view that emotions are stupid, one could argue at length how emotional 'intuition' is often more insightful and certainly more strategic than many of the ratiocinations of abstract moralizing, and against the view that emotions are aimless it should be said that all emotions have their aims, even if rather odd and sometimes limited. On the other hand, it should be commented that some emotions—among them love—have the most grandiose aims, far grander than the surely limited desire to be "reasonable." Consider Hegel:

> Love neither restricts nor is restricted; it is not finite at all . . . love completely destroys objectivity and thereby annuls and transcends reflection, deprives man's opposite of all foreign character, and discovers life itself without any further defect.[13]

The most common accusation against the emotions, and love in particular, is that they confuse or distort our experience (Leibniz called them "confused perceptions"). What is in question here is the infamous resistance of emotions to canons of consistency and evident facts, their alleged lack of "common sense" and tendency to bias perception and judgment, their apparent tolerance of contradiction (which Freud made one of the hallmarks of "the Unconscious"), their refusal to conform to obvious considerations of objectivity. In love, this is embarrassingly obvious. A homely lover looks longingly at his equally plain love and declares, "you are the most beautiful woman in the world." How are we to understand this? Self-deception? Insanity? Surely not "blindness" (which would be plain ignorance), for the problem is not that he cannot see. Indeed, he might well claim to see much *more* than we do, or more deeply. Impolitely pressed, our enraptured lover may resentfully concede the point, perhaps doing a phenomenological retreat to, "Well, she's the most beautiful woman in the world *to me!*" but we know how such qualifications are treated in philosophy—with proper epistemological disdain. In love one makes a claim, and it is a claim that is demonstrably false. Beauty is not in the eye of the beholder, perhaps, but is this an argument against love?

Consider in the same light the accusation of "intractability" that is thrown at the emotions as a charge, supposedly separating them from reason and rationality. (Amelie Rorty, for example, develops this charge at length in her "Explaining Emotions."[14]) It is worth noting that Kant rejected the emotions not because they were stubborn but because they were capricious, even though such a suggestion goes against the obvious—that emotions can be durable and devoted, even stubborn and intractable. In love, in particular, it is notoriously difficult, when one has been in love, to purge that emotion, even though it now has become an intolerable source of pain and not at all a source of pleasure. But is this an accusation against the emotions, or is it rather part of their virtue? It is passing fancy that we criticize, not unmovable devotion. It is sudden anger that we call irrational, not long motivated and well-reasoned animosity (which is not to say, of course, that sudden anger is always improper or inappropriate, or that long-term outrage is not sometimes irrational and even insane). It is true that the emotions are stubborn and intractable, but this—as opposed to much less dependable action in accordance with principle—is what makes them so essential to ethics. Principles can be easily rationalized and reinterpreted. One trusts a person fighting in accordance with his passions far more than one fighting for abstract principles. (It is remarkable how principles can always admit convenient exceptions and amendments.) Intractability is a virtue of the emotions as rationalization is to reason a vice. Indeed we might even say that the "truth" of emotions is their intractability, their resistance to every attempt to change them.

Objectively, what love sees and thinks is mostly nonsense, and what it values is quite contrary to everything that philosophical ethics likes to emphasize—objectivity, impersonality, disinterestedness, universality, respect for evidence and arguments, and so on. And yet, it seems to me that such irrationality is among our most important and charming features. We care about each other prior to any evidence or arguments that we ought to. We find each other beautiful, charming, and desirable, seemingly without reference to common standards. We think less of a lover if his or her love alters when it alteration finds, or if one bends to the opinions of friends. Love *ought* to be intractable, we believe, even if this same stubbornness causes considerable pain once the love is over. We are thoroughly prejudiced, to use a jaundiced word, thoroughly unreasonable. "Why do you love *her?!*" is a question that need not be answered or even acknowledged. Indeed, we even think it admirable, if also foolish, to love someone totally undeserving (from someone else's point of view). Love itself is the virtue, a virtue so important that rationality itself pales in importance.

Ultimately, the charge against the emotions—and against love in particular—is that of "subjectivity." Subjectivity is a notoriously slippery notion in philosophy which is often opposed to contrastingly tidy concepts of rationality and objectivity. The charge of "subjectivity" typically turns into an accusation of bias and unreasonableness. But, on the other hand, there is a complementary charge against objectivity, against impersonal, merely abstract ratiocination. There is that sense of 'objectivity'—pursued by Camus and Thomas Nagel, for example—in which we are all infinitesimal specks in the galaxy, our lives no more significant than the lives of trees or sea polyps, our bodies nothing but the stuff of physiology, our sex a dubious advancement on the reproduction of bacteria, our speech nothing but noise, our lives meaningless. It is what Nagel calls "the view from nowhere," and in its extreme forms it is as undesirable as it is impossible. But such a viewpoint tends to dominate ethics and value theory as well, if in a more humane or anthropocentric scope. Most of contemporary ethics is still framed not as personal but as policy—to be applied, one suspects, by some imagined philosopher-king. The emphasis is not on being a "good person" but rather a just and fair administrator (being a good person is presumably the same). The model, thinly disguised by the evasive logic of "universalizability," is the bureaucrat, who treats everyone the same and has no relevant personality of his or her own. Love is thus unethical, for against all principles of ethics it has the audacity to view one other person as someone very special and does not, as Mill insisted, count "everyone as one and only one" at all.

3. ON LOVE'S VIRTUES: PLATO'S *SYMPOSIUM* REVISITED

It is, in fact, just a love story. . . . Alcibiades, asked to speak about eros, cannot describe the passion or its object in general terms, because his experience of love is an experience that happened to him only once, and in connection with an individual who is seen by him to be like nobody else in the world.[15]

The classical text on the virtue(s) of erotic love is, of course, Plato's *Symposium*, and Plato (not Socrates) provides us with a portrait of *erōs* as a virtue which is quite appropriate to our modern concept of romantic love. Let us begin by saying very quickly that the concept of *erōs* there discussed is not the same as our concept of romantic love, that Greek love is assymetrical love between man and youth rather that our symmetrical romance between man and woman, that Plato is doing much in that dialogue which is by no means evident or easily comprehensible to the modern nonclassicist reader. That said, we can remind ourselves that the subject of the dialogue is the nature and the virtues of love. Each of the various speeches can be interpreted as a substantial theory. It is worth noting that Socrates objects to Phaedrus' speech, in particular, because he stresses only the virtues of love—we might say love's good social consequences—instead of the emotion itself, while Aristophanes would give us an account of the nature of love without giving us an adequate account of its virtues. I think that Socrates is right on both counts: virtues are not virtues by virtue of their consequences (against Hume, for example), and an analysis of love that does not tell us how important it is—not just why we are obsessed with it—is inadequate. But we might also note that the usual characterization of the dialogue is extremely misleading, that is, as a ladder of relatively forgettable speeches leading up to a culmination—the speech by Socrates that tells us exactly what love is. The usual assumption that Socrates acts here as the spokesman for Plato's own view seems utterly unsupportable. In this dialogue, even the minor speeches portray essential aspects of love. For example, the banal speech of Eryximachus the physician clumsily captures today's obsession with love as a physiological phenomenon with health as its virtue. Most important, however, is the fact that in this dialogue, Socrates does not have the last or the best word. Martha Nussbaum, Michael Gagarin, and others have shown, convincingly, I believe, that Alcibiades' tragi-comic description of Socrates at the end of the dialogue is essential, if not the key, to the *Symposium*.[16] Indeed, one might even make the case that Plato is partially opposed to Socrates and uses Alcibiades as his argument. Socrates' speech makes love virtuous but only by ignoring or denying most of its essential features—its sexual passion, its interpersonality, its particularity, and its apparent irrationality. *Erōs*, in short, becomes excitement about philosophy. It is impersonal, indifferent to any particular person, 'above' bodily desire. In contrast, Alcibiades emphasizes the very personal, passionate, irrational, physical aspect of love, the love for a particular, incomparable human being, not a desexed universal. A similar foil for Socrates is the delightful story by Aristophanes, once he has gotten over his hiccups, in which we are all imagined to be the offspring of perfect (spherical) ancestral beings, split in two by Zeus, twisted around and now desperately looking for our other halves. This explains the "infinite longing" that every lover knows, which includes the longing for sexual union but by no means can be satisfied just with that. Aristophanes is about to continue his story near the end of the dialogue—perhaps completing the account by telling us about virtue—when he is interrupted by Alcibiades, wholly drunk, who launches into his paean for Socrates, contradicting everything Socrates has just been arguing. Socrates is sandwiched between Aristophanes and Alcibiades and it must be said that the conclusion of the debate is that Socrates is weird. Here, I think, is Plato's own voice, not as Socrates *via* Diotima, but as Alcibiades, presenting love as it is against the perhaps admirable but admittedly inhuman efforts of Socrates to say what it should be ideally. I think that this is important for our concern here, because the problem with understanding love as a virtue is not just its undervaluation as sex and emotion; it is also its excessive idealization as something more—or completely different from—sexuality and personal passion. If we think that the virtue of love is nothing less than the virtues of divinity itself, then love may be virtuous but it will have little to do with us and our petty particular affections. If love is a virtue in the sense that I want to defend here, it must apply to Alcibiades as well as Socrates. Socrates gives us a noble sense of the idealization that is part and parcel of *erōs* but I think that we can safely say that he goes too far in abandoning the eroticism of the particular.

4. THE HISTORY OF LOVE

Having said all this, we may now agree that the Western concept of love (in its heterosexual and humanistic aspects) was—if not 'invented' or 'discovered'—at least developed in the twelfth century as never before. Only at that late date was man able to begin thinking consecutively about ways of harmonizing sexual impulses with idealistic motives, of justifying amorous intimacy not as a means of preserving the race, or glorifying God, or attaining some ulterior metaphysical object but rather as an end in itself that made life worth living.[17]

The virtues, according to Alasdair MacIntyre, are historical. They perform different functions in different societies, and one would not expect the virtues of a warrior in Homeric Greece to be similar to those of a gentleman in Jane Austen's England. Love as a virtue is also functional and historical. Sexuality "fits" into different societies in different ways, and conceptions of love and marriage vary accordingly. However 'obvious' the universal function of uninterrupted and unhampered heterosexual intercourse may be in the preservation of every society, sexual desire is virtually never limited to this end, and the myriad courtship rituals, mores, and emotions invented by human cultures attest to the variety of ends to which this basic *ur-lust* can be employed. The virtues of love, accordingly, are the intrinsic ends which *erōs* serves, one of which may be, as Stendhal used to argue, its existence for its own sake.

Sexual desire may seem like something of a constant through history, but the objects of desire (obviously) and the source, nature and vicissitudes of that desire vary as much as societies and their philosophies. Love is defined not primarily by sex or the libido but by ideas, and romantic love, which is a very modern (eighteenth century) concept, involves certain specific ideas about sex, gender, marriage, and the meaning of life as well as the perennial promptings of biology. Strictly speaking, there is nothing in the *Symposium* (or anywhere else before the seventeenth century) about romantic love. Romantic love is part and parcel of Romanticism, a distinctively modern movement. It presupposes an unusually strong conception of privacy and individual autonomy, a relatively novel celebration of the emotions for their own sake, and a dramatic metaphysics of unity—of which sexual unity in love is a particularly exciting and tangible example. (Compare Hegel, "In love the separate does still remain, but as something united and no longer as something separate," or Shelley, "one soul of interwoven flame.") The speakers in Plato's *Symposium* praised courage, education, and wisdom as the virtues of love, but they had little to say of the virtues of heterosexuality (apart, of course, from its function of producing more Athenians). Charity, devotion, and chastity were praised as virtues of Christian love, but there was too little to say about the joys of sexuality. (Consider the classic seventeenth-century preface: "Let virtue be rewarded, vice be punished, and chastity treated as it deserves.") Romantic love has among its virtues the metaphysical legitimization of sexual desire, the motivation for marriage, and the equalization of the sexes, surely no part of Greek love and doubtful in traditional Christian love. (Contemporary Christian concepts of love, of course, have adopted and incorporated much of the romantic ideology.) Romantic love has as its virtue the expansion of the self to include another, hardly necessary in societies in which citizenship and other memberships provided all of the shared identity one could possibly imagine. Romantic love has as a virtue the expression of what we opaquely call 'the inner self', again not a virtue that would have been understood in less psychological and more socially minded societies. To put the matter bluntly (and without argument), romantic love came of age only when newly industrialized and increasingly anonymous societies fostered the economically independent and socially shrunken ("nuclear") family, when women as well as men were permitted considerable personal *choice* in their marriage partners, when romantic love novels spread the gospel to the multitude of women of the middle class (whereas courtly love had been the privilege of a few aristocratic heroines), and, philosophically most important, when the now many centuries old contrast between sacred and profane love had broken down and been synthesized in a secular mode (like so many ideas in the Enlightenment). Romantic love depended on what Robert Stone has called "affective individualism," an attitude to the individual and the importance of his or her emotions that did not and could not have arisen until modern times.

It is essential that we keep the historical character of love in mind so that we do not get seduced by an idea that might well be prompted by the seeming timelessness of the *Symposium* or the always familiar (and cynical) view that love is nothing but hormonal agitation coupled with the uncertainties and frustrations of courtship—or as Freud put it, "lust plus the ordeal of civility." This idea is that love is itself something timeless and universal, a singular phenomenon which varies only in its culturization and interpretation but is otherwise universally the same. In fact, even the *Symposium* provides us with no fewer than half a dozen conceptions of love, and it is not clear to what extent these are disagreements about the true nature of *erōs* or different kinds of *erōs*. Socrates, in particular, is certainly giving us a new conception, a "persuasive definition." Historically, we find these variations played out on a grand scale, with Socrates setting the stage for an ethereal concept of love that comes of age with Christian theology, Alcibiades displaying the "languor" and its imagery that would come to characterize late Medieval courtly love, and Aristophanes anticipating modern romantic love. But paganism, even in Plato, cannot begin to capture the range and complexity of romantic conceptions of love in modern times. To understand erotic love as we know it, it is necessary to appreciate the power of the long, if often antagonistic, history of Christian conceptions of love.

The history of erotic love has been determined not only by the fact that Christian thought demeaned sexual love as such but also by the Christian emphasis on the 'inner' individual soul and the importance of such emotions as faith and devotion. The genius of Christianity was that it coopted erotic love and turned it into something else, still the love of one's fellow man and even perhaps the love of one's wife or husband, but no longer particularly sexual, no longer personal, no longer merely human. In its positive presentation, love became a form of idealization, even worship, an attempt to transcend not only oneself and one's own self-interests but also the limited self-interests of an *egoism-a-deux*. It did not have to deny the sexual or the personal so much as the Christian conception of love aimed always "higher," toward not just virtue or happiness but perfection itself. On the negative side, it must be said (and often has been) that the Christian conception of love was also brutal and inhuman, denying not only our "natural" impulses but even the conception of a loving marriage as such. Saint Paul's advice, "better to marry than to burn" was one of the more generous sentiments governing this revised concept of love. Tertullian was not alone in insisting that even to look on one's wife with lust was a sin. Aristophanes' thesis that lovers experience that "infinite longing" which manifests and only momentarily satisfies itself in sex would be lost here. Indeed all such desires become antithetical to love, not an expression of it. To Nietzsche's observation that Christianity is Platonism for the masses we might add that because of Christian psychology, we now have psychoanalysis.

Christian theology may have encouraged and revered love above all else, but it was not erotic love that flourished. Alternative names for love—*"caritas"* and *"agapé"*—may have clarified the scholarship but not the phenomenology of the emotion. When one looked lovingly at another, who could say whether the feeling was divine *caritas* or nasty *erōs,* except that one knew that one *should* feel the former. An entire literature grew up, from which some of our favorite first date dialogues are derived, distinguishing loving from sexual desire as if these were not only always distinguishable but even opposed. By the fourteenth century, this confusion had become canonized as Platonic love, for which Plato (or at least Socrates) is indeed to blame. Platonic love dispensed with Agathon, Aristophanes, and the others, took Diotima (whose name means "honor the god") at her word, and substituted Christian faith for pagan wisdom. Love had become even more idealized than Socrates had urged, but what had been gained in spirituality was more than lost in the denial of the erotic passions and the importance of happy human relationships for their own sake.

It was in reaction to this insensitivity to human desires and affections that courtly love was directed in the twelfth century. Romantic love is often identified historically with courtly love—which is rightly recognized as its significant late Medieval predecessor. But the two are quite distinct, as Irving Singer has argued in his *Nature of Love.*[18] The two are often conflated (e.g., by Denis de Rougemont, in his much celebrated but dubious study of the subject[19]), and courtly love, in particular, is often reduced to the ridiculous image of the horny troubador singing pathetically before the (very tall) tower of some inevitably fair but also unavailable lady. The name "courtly love," it should be noted, was not employed by the participants themselves but rather was applied much later—in the romantic period—by Gaston Paris, who used it to refer to the hardly frustrated or separated couple of Lancelot and Gueneviere. Indeed, the paradigm of courtly love began not as chaste and frustrated (if poetic) desire but as secret, adulterous, and all-embracing illicit love. (C. S. Lewis continues this paradigm well into this century.)

Socially, courtly love was a plaything of the upper class. It was as much talk (and crooning) as action, and, perhaps most important, it was wholly distinct from, even opposed to, marriage. (It is not surprising that the texts and theories of the male troubadors—Andreas Capellanus, especially—were typically drawn from the adulterous advice of Ovid. But their female counterparts—Eleanor of Aquitaine, for example—did not take love and marriage any more seriously, in part because they were almost always already married.) What is often said of courtly love—that it rarely resulted in consumation—is not true. Indeed, if anything, one might say that courtly love was *more* obsessed with sex than contemporary romantic love. The fact that consumation came slowly and after considerable effort does not eclipse the fact that consumation was the explicit and sometimes single end of the endeavor.

Much of the history of our changing conceptions of love has to do with the effort to bring together and synthesize the idealization suggested by Plato and Christian love with the very real demands and desires of a couple in love. The virtue of "courtly love" was its effort to carry out this synthesis and at the same time introduce some sexual and aesthetic satisfaction into a world of arranged marriages based wholly on social, political, and economic considerations (thus the separation—if not opposition—between courtly love and marriage). It is courtly love that also introduces the essential romantic conception of erotic love as good in itself, a conception that one does not find in the teleology of the *Symposium* and certainly does not find in Christian concepts of love. In his study, Singer formulates five general features of love that characterize the courtly: (1) that sexual love between men and women is *itself* an ideal worth striving for, (2) that love ennobles both lover and beloved, (3) that sexual love cannot be reduced to mere libidinal impulse, (4) that love has to do with courtship but not (necessarily) with marriage, and (5) that love involves a "holy oneness" between man and woman.[20] It should be clear, as Singer goes on to argue in great detail, how courtly love constituted an attempt to synthesize both pagan and Christian conceptions of love, incorporating both ethical ideals and sexual desire. The first feature signals a radical challenge to the traditional Christian view of love, while the third is a rebuke of the vulgar view that love is nothing but sexual desire. It is worth noting that the last feature listed is very much in tune with much of Christian theology, and indeed, the Aristophanic notion of love as a "union" would continue to be one of the central but most difficult (and therefore often "magical" or "mystical") themes of love through the romantic period. I shall try to develop this idea more literally in the following section.

The distinction between love and marriage is of particular interest in the history of love, and it is worth noting that these have not always been linked so essentially as "horse and carriage," as one popular song would have it. In Plato, for obvious reasons, the question of marriage did not even arise in considerations of *erōs* (at least, for that form of *erōs* that was worthy of philosophical consideration). Ovid considered love and marriage as opposites, although the marriage of one's intended did provide a challenging obstacle and thereby an additional source of excitement. The long history of marriage as a sacrament has little to say about sexual love and sometimes has much to say against it, and by the time of courtly love, courtship typically provided an alternative to loveless marriage rather than a prelude to marriage or—almost unheard of—the content of marriage itself. Gaston Paris and C. S. Lewis's paradigm of Lancelot and Gueneviere may have represented excessive antagonism between love and all social and religious institutions and obligations, especially marriage, but courtly love cannot be conceived—whatever else it may have been—as a prelude to or a legitimate reason for marriage. Indeed, the idea that marriage is the culmination of love becomes popular only in the seventeenth century or so, as exemplified in Shakespeare's plays, especially in the comedies. And compared to the rigid ethos of Jane Austen's novels, for example, it must be said that our current understanding of love and marriage is quite in flux and confused.

Romantic love, we may now say, is the historical result of a long and painful synthesis between erotic pagan love and idealistic Christian love or, ahistorically, between Aristophanes and Alcibiades on the one hand and Socrates on the other. It is not just sexual, or even primarily sexual, but an idealistic up-dating of the pagan virtues of cultivation and sensuousness and Christian devotion and fidelity in the mod-

ern context of individual privacy, autonomy, and affectivity. To think that romantic
love is without virtue is to grossly mistake romance with sexual recreation or unrealistic idealization and ignore the whole historical development that lies behind even
the most ordinary love affair. But it is time to say something more about the nature
of romantic love as such.

5. WHAT IS ROMANTIC LOVE?

Love is the expression of an ancient need, that human desire was originally one
and we were whole, and the desire and the pursuit of the whole is called love.[21]

Romantic love, we may need to remind ourselves, is an emotion—an ordinary and
very common emotion. It is not a "force" or a "mystery." Like all emotions, it is
largely learned, typically obsessive, peculiar to certain kinds of cultures with certain
brands of philosophy. I will not here rehearse once again my usual analysis of emotion as a complex of judgments, desires, and values. Let me just claim, without argument, the weaker thesis that every emotion presupposes, if it is not composed of, a set
of specifiable concepts (e.g., anger as offense, sadness as loss, jealousy as the threat of
loss) and more or less specific desires and values, such as revenge in anger, care in sadness, possessiveness in jealousy. Love, accordingly, can and must be analyzed in
terms of such a set of concepts and desires, some of which are obvious, the more interesting perhaps not so. It is evident enough that one set of desires in romantic love
is the desire to be with, the desire to touch, the desire to caress, and here we are immediately reminded of Aristophanes' lesson: that which manifests itself as a sexual urge
in love is actually something much more, a desire to be reunited with, to be one with,
one's love. From this, I want to suggest what I take to be the dominant conceptual in-
gredient in romantic love, which is just this urge for *shared identity,* a kind of *onto-
logical dependency.* The challenge, however, is to get beyond this familiar idea (and
its kindred characterizations as a "union," "a merger of souls," etc.) and explain exactly what "identity" could possibly mean in this context. Aristophanes' wonderful
metaphor is still a metaphor, and whether or not we would want Hephaestus to weld
the two of us together, body and soul, the image does not do our understanding much
good. Aristophanes claims that we want the impossible, indeed the unimaginable; he
does not give us any indication of how we might in fact share an identity, over and
above brief and not always well-coordinated unifications of the flesh.

More to the point, one might well quote Cathy's climactic revelation in *Wuth-
ering Heights:* "I *am* Heathcliff—he's always, always in my mind—not as a pleasure,
anymore than I am always a pleasure to myself—but as my own being." Here we have
more than a hint of what is involved in shared identity, not a mystical union nor a
frustrated physicality but a sense of presence, always "in mind," defining one's sense
of self to one's self. Love is just this shared identity, and the desires of love—
including especially the strong nonphysiological desire for sexual intercourse—can
best be understood with reference to this strange but not at all unfamiliar concept. I
cannot do justice to this challenge here, but let me at least present the thesis: Shared
identity is the intention of love, and the virtues of love are essentially the virtues of

this intended identity. This is not to deny or neglect sex but to give it a context. Nor does this give away too much to marriage (which is a legal identity) but it does explain how romantic love and marriage have come so close together, the latter now considered to be the culmination of the former.

Before we say any more, however, let me express a Socratic caveat: I think that it is necessary to display love as it is by itself, without confusing it with all of the other Good Things we would like and expect to go with it—companionship, great sex, friendship, someone to travel with, someone who really cares, and, ultimately, marriage. Of course we want these things, and preferably all in the same package, but love can and must be understood apart from all of them. Without being depressing, let us remind ourselves that love often goes wrong, that love can be unrequited, that love can interfere with or at least it does not assure satisfying sex, that love and friendship are sometimes opposed, that love can be very lonely, that love can be not only obsessive but insane. Not that love must be or often is all of these, but it can be, and so let us look at the virtues of love itself, as Socrates insisted, not in terms of its consequences or its most desirable embellishments.

The nature of identity in love, briefly described, is this. (You will note, no doubt, a certain debt to Hegel and Sartre in what follows.) We define ourselves, not just in our own terms (as adolescent existentialists and pop-psychologists may argue) but in terms of each other. The virtues, in a society such as Aristotle's, are defined and assigned communally; the idea of "private" virtues would be incomprehensible. But we distinguish public and private with a vengeance, and we typically value our private, personal character more highly than our public persona, which is sometimes thought to be superficial, impersonal, "plastic," and merely manipulative, instrumental. A person's character is best determined by those who "really know him," and it is not odd to us that a person generally known as a bastard might be thought to be a good person just on the testimony of a wife, a husband, or a close friend. ("But if you knew Johnny as I do, you would see that . . . . ") In a fragmented world so built on intimate privacies, love even more than family and friendship determines selfhood. Love is just this determining of selfhood. When we talk about "the real self" or "being true to ourselves," what we often mean is being true to the image of ourselves that we share with those we love most. We say, and are expected to say, that the self we display in public performance, the self we present on the job, the self we show to acquaintances, is not real. We sometimes take great pains to prove that the self we share with our family (a historical kind of love) is no longer the self that we consider real. Nor is it any surprise that the self we would like to think of as most real is the self that emerges in intimacy, and its virtues are the typically private virtues of honesty in feeling and expression, interpersonal passion, tenderness, and sensitivity.

The idea of an Aristophanic union—the reunification of two halves that already belong together—is charming and suggestive, but it is only half of the story. The other half starts with the fact of our differences and our stubborness, and how we may ill fit together even after years of compromise and cohabitation. The freedom of choice that allows us virtually unrestricted range for our romantic intentions also raises the possibility—which was one of the suppositions of courtly love as well—that our choice will often be difficult, if not socially prohibited. (Who was the one girl in Verona that young Romeo should not have chosen? And the one woman wholly forbidden to Lancelot?) The process of mutual self-identification runs into conflict with one of its own presuppositions—the ideal of autonomous individualism. The selves that are to merge do not have the advantage of having adjusted to and complemented each other when the self was still flexible and only partially formed—as in societies where families arrange marriages between children who have grown up together. And whatever the nostalgic popularity of "first love" and the Romeo and Juliet paradigm, the truth is that most of us fall in love well advanced in our development, even into old age, when the self is full-formed and complementarity is more often an exercise in compromise. The development of love is consequently defined by a *dialectic,* often tender but sometimes ontologically vicious, in which each lover struggles for control over shared and reciprocal self-images, resists them, revises them, rejects them. For this reason, love—unlike many other emotions—takes time. It does not make sense to say of love, as it does of anger, that one was in love for fifteen minutes but then calmed down. But neither is this to say that there is no such thing as unrequited love, or that unrequited love is not love, for the dialectic, complete with resistance and conflict, can go on just as well in one soul as in two. Granted that the drama may be a bit impoverished, but as Stendhal often argued, the imagination may be enriched thereby. Or as Goethe once said, "If I love you, what business is that of yours?"

6. IN PURSUIT OF A PASSION (CONCLUSION)

True love, whatever is said of it, will always be honored by men; for although its transports lead us astray, although it does not exclude odious qualities from the heart that feels it—and even produces them—it nevertheless always presupposes estimable qualities without which one would not be in a condition to feel it.[22]

Love, briefly summarized, is a dialectical process of (mutually) reconceived selfhood with a long and varied history. As such, it is much more than a feeling and it need not be at all capricious or unintelligent or disruptive. But the idea that love is concerned with selfhood might suggest that love is essentially self-love, casting love in the role of a vice rather than a virtue. And the suggestion that love is essentially the reconception and determination of oneself through another looks dangerously similar to some familiar definitions of narcissism. But self-reference entails neither cynicism nor narcissism. Although one does see oneself through the other on this analysis, and although as in narcissism the idea of "separation of subject and object" is greatly obscured, love as mutual self-defining reflection does not encourage either vicious or clinical conclusions. Unlike narcissism, love takes the other as its standard, not just as its mirror, which is why the courtly lovers called it "devotion" (as in devoting oneself to God) and why Stendhal—himself an accomplished narcissist—called "passion-love" the one wholly unselfish experience. Love is not selfless but it is nevertheless the antithesis of selfishness. It embodies an expansion of self, modest, perhaps, but what it lacks in scope it more than makes up for in motivation.

The virtues of love can be understood in terms of this sense of this limited but passionate self-expansion. In a fragmented and mobile society, romantic love allows us to forge intensive ties to others, even to strangers. There is much talk in ethics today of "communitarian" as opposed to individualistic frameworks, but the fact is that passionately united community larger than a small circle of carefully chosen friends strikes most of us as oppressive if not dangerous. One may well lament the lack of public virtues or the priority of private virtues, but the fact is that the primacy of privacy is where we must now begin. Nor should one in Kantian enthusiasm for the universal ignore the dramatic importance of the modest move from caring only about oneself to caring about someone else. The expansion of selfhood in love may be modest but, in today's climate of personal greed and "self-fulfillment," it is for many successful citizens today one of the last virtues left standing.

Romantic love is a powerful emotional ally—far better than communal indignation and shared resentment—in breaking down the isolating individualism that has become the dubious heir of some of our favorite traditional values. But we remain staunch individualists, and the extent to which we will allow our virtues to be publically determined remains limited indeed. But too many authors in recent years have simply dismissed such intimacies as love as not virtuous at all, when a more just judgment would seem to be that love is a particularly appropriate virtue in a society such as ours. With this it is essential to revise our concept of virtue. Some important virtues are not public, so we can no longer use Aristotle, nor even Hume, as our guide. Being virtuous does not mean for us "fitting into" the community; good character is rather privately determined by loving and being loved. This may make (some) virtues subjective, but subjectivity here does not mean capricious, incommensurable, eccentric, or "merely emotional"; it rather means private and personal. Our presumption is that a good person is not a public figure but a private one. Perhaps the accompanying assumption, no doubt false, is that a person who is loving in private will be a good person in public too.

There are other virtues of love, beyond this minimal self-expansion. We might, for instance, mention the sense of self-awareness that goes along with this dramatization of self and the often described sense of self-improvement that is its consequence, something argued by the early speakers in the *Symposium* and often propounded by some of the courtly troubadors. To love is to be intensely conscious of one's own "worth" and greatly concerned with one's virtues (not only charms) where being in love is already considered the first great step in the teleology of self-realization. ("Love me as I am" is not an expression or an instruction of love but rather a defensive reaction.) We might mention, too, the healthy and positive outlook on the world that often accompanies love, a form of generalized idealization that—while it might not take on the cosmic form suggested by Hegel in his early writings—nonetheless counters the cynicism and suspicion that have become the marks of wisdom in our society.

So too we might mention the fact that love is a remarkably inspirational and creative emotion—though one might somewhat cynically speculate that envy and resentment may be its betters in this regard. (It was not just Iago's intelligence that made him more than a match for Othello; he had his envy to motivate him.) The inspirational qualities of love and its impulse to creativity do not just refer, of course, to those who are particularly gifted, for we find at least attempts at poetic self-expression in even the most philistine lovers. Indeed, regardless of the quality of the products of such inspiration, one might argue—following Stendhal—that the exhilaration and inspiration of love is itself its greatest virtue, a virtue that is often ignored in the age-old over-appreciation for philosophical *apatheia*. I too would want to argue that romantic love is a virtue just because it is exciting. One rarely finds philosophers taking excitement as a virtue (Nietzsche being the most obvious exception), but I think many of us do in fact take energy, vitality, being "turned on" as virtuous, whatever might result and however exhausting. I think we ought to wonder about the frequent if implicit emphasis on dullness as a prominent feature of the virtues.

So too we might note the low esteem of sexuality in discussions of virtue. Romantic love is sexual love, and here too we can appreciate the resistance of traditionally modest moral philosophers. Sex, in the history of ethics, has been treated as a biological urge, a force (often an inhuman force) to be controlled. So treated, it is hard to see any virtue in it. Ethical questions about sex tend to focus on its restriction, and sexual love is offered at best as a legitimization of sex but still hardly a virtue. So too we should vehemently reject that picture of sex, evidently held by chaste Kant, which takes intercourse to be either a biological function (reproduction or, sanctioned by God, "procreation") or mere recreation—what Kant considered mutual masturbation. Either way, sex loses any status in ethics and, more mysteriously, loses its immediate connection with love (the conceptual problem that faced courtly love). But sex, I would argue, ought to be viewed not as an urge and neither as procreation nor recreation but rather as expression, defined neither by physiology nor by pleasure but rather circumscribed by ideas and what is expressed. In particular, sex is (or can be) an expression of love, though this is just part of the story (as Sartre in particular has gruesomely argued). But the point that should be made here is that love is a virtue in part because of and not despite of its sexuality. My Nietzschean premise (though one can find a sublimated version of it in Spinoza) is that the virtues can be exhilarating, and this is (in part) what makes them virtues.

The foregoing points would be greatly misunderstood if they were taken to suggest that erotic love is some sort of "trump" virtue, more important than any others. Virtues can conflict, and any one virtue may be but a negligible exception in an otherwise wholly flawed or pathological character. To pretend that the private joys and obsessions of love raise no questions in terms of public engagement, to move from the objection that love has been neglected in ethics to the insistence that such personal emotions take the place of policy decisions in the public sphere, would be irresponsible. But the example of love makes it evident that the traditional objections to subjectivity in ethics, that appeal to emotions is whimsical, not serious and not subject to criticism, will not bear scrutiny. And against much of recent "virtue ethics," love seems to show that virtues should not be understood as traits (for no matter how "loving" one may be, the only virtue in love is actually loving), nor are all virtues instantiations of universal principles, as Frankena, for example, has argued.[23] It has too long been claimed without argument that subjectivity and emotion in ethics inevitably means selfishness, prejudice, chaos, violence, and destruction, but the truth is that the nature of love, at least, is quite the opposite, not at all selfish, often tender, and creative. Indeed, against the obsessive emphasis on objectivity and impersonal equality in ethics, the aim of love is to *make* a single person extraordinary and to reconceptualize oneself in his or her terms, to *create* an escape from the anonymity of the Kantian moral world and thrive in a world *a deux* of one's own. Of course, to deny that love can go wrong—against the cumulative evidence of ten thousand romantic novels—would be absurd. It can destroy as well as conjoin relationships, and it can ruin as well as enhance a life. Yes, love can be dangerous, but why have we so long accepted the idea that the virtuous life is simple and uncomplicated rather than, as Nietzsche used to say, a work of romantic art? For love is a virtue as much of the imagination as of morals.

Notes

1. I. Kant, *The Groundwork of the Metaphysics of Morals,* translated by H. J. Paton (New York, 1964), 67 (p. 13 of the standard German edition).
2. Plato, *The Symposium,* translated by W. Hamilton (London, 1951), 43.
3. A. Schopenhauer, *The World as Will and Representation,* translated by E. Payne (New York, 1958), quoted in *Sexual Love and Western Morality,* edited by D. Verene (New York, 1972), 175.
4. laRochefoucauld, *Maxims,* translated by J. Heayd, no. 68.
5. I. Kant, *Lectures on Ethics,* translated by L. Infield (Indianapolis, 1963), 164.
6. J. Milton, *Paradise Lost* (New York, 1969), Book 8, lines 383–85.
7. F. Nietzsche, *The Antichrist,* translated by H. Kaufmann (New York, 1954), sect. 11.
8. Bernard Williams, "Morality and the Emotions," in *Problems of the Self* (Cambridge, 1973).
9. Richard Taylor, *Good and Evil* (New York, 1970), xii.
10. Barbara Herman, "The Practice of Moral Judgment," *Journal of Philosophy* 82, no. 8 (1985).
11. Bernard Gert, *The Moral Rules* (New York, 1973), 143.
12. Edward Sankowski, "Love and Moral Obligation" and "Responsibility of Persons for their Emotions" in *Canadian Journal of Philosophy* 7 (1977): 829–40.
13. G. W. F. Hegel, *Early Theological Manuscripts,* translated by T. Knox (Philadelphia, 1971), 305.
14. Amelie Rorty, "Explaining Emotions" in *Explaining Emotions* (Berkeley, 1980).
15. M. Nussbaum, "The Speech of Alcibiades," *Philosophy and Literature* 3, no. 2 (1979).
16. Ibid., and Michael Gagarin, "Socrates' Hubris and Alcibiades' Failure," *Phoenix* 31 (1977).
17. I. Singer, *The Nature of Love,* vol. 2 (Chicago, 1986), 35–36.
18. Ibid.
19. Denis de Rougemont, *Love in the Western World* (New York, 1974).
20. Singer, *Nature of Love,* 22–23.
21. *Symposium,* 64.
22. J. J. Rousseau, *Emile,* translated by A. Bloom (New York, 1979), 214.
23. William Frankena, *Ethics* (Engelwood Cliffs, N.J., 1973), and in a recent newsletter to University of Michigan Philosophy Department alumni.

Non-Relative Virtues:
An Aristotelian Approach

MARTHA C. NUSSBAUM

All Greeks used to go around armed with swords.
Thucydides, *History of the Peloponnesian War*

The customs of former times might be said to be too
simple and barbaric. For Greeks used to go around
armed with swords; and they used to buy wives from
one another; and there are surely other ancient customs that are extremely stupid. (For example, in
Cyme there is a law about homicide, that if a man
prosecuting a charge can produce a certain number of
witnesses from among his own relations, the defen-
dant will automatically be convicted of murder.) In
general, all human beings seek not the way of their
ancestors, but the good.
Aristotle, *Politics* 1268a39 ff.

One may also observe in one's travels to distant
countries the feelings of recognition and affiliation
that link every human being to every other human
being.
Aristotle, *Nicomachean Ethics* 1155a21–22

I

The virtues are attracting increasing interest in contemporary philosophical debate. From many different sides one hears of a dissatisfaction with ethical theories that are remote from concrete human experience. Whether this remoteness results
from the utilitarian's interest in arriving at a universal calculus of satisfactions or
from a Kantian concern with universal principles of broad generality, in which the
names of particular contexts, histories, and persons do not occur, remoteness is now
being seen by an increasing number of moral philosophers as a defect in an approach
to ethical questions. In the search for an alternative approach, the concept of virtue is

playing a prominent role. So, too, is the work of Aristotle, the greatest defender of an ethical approach based on the concept of virtue. For Aristotle's work seems, appealingly, to combine rigor with concreteness, theoretical power with sensitivity to the actual circumstances of human life and choice in all their multiplicity, variety, and mutability.

But on one central point there is a striking divergence between Aristotle and contemporary virtue theory. To many current defenders of an ethical approach based on the virtues, the return to the virtues is connected with a turn toward relativism—toward, that is, the view that the only appropriate criteria of ethical goodness are local ones, internal to the traditions and practices of each local society or group that asks itself questions about the good. The rejection of general algorithms and abstract rules in favor of an account of the good life based on specific modes of virtuous action is taken, by writers as otherwise diverse as Alasdair MacIntyre, Bernard Williams, and Philippa Foot,[1] to be connected with the abandonment of the project of rationally justifying a single norm of flourishing life for and to all human beings and with a reliance, instead, on norms that are local both in origin and in application.

The positions of all of these writers, where relativism is concerned, are complex; none unequivocally endorses a relativist view. But all connect virtue ethics with a relativist denial that ethica, correctly understood, offers any trans-cultural norms, justifiable with reference to reasons of universal human validity, with reference to which we may appropriately criticize different local conceptions of the good. And all suggest that the insights we gain by pursuing ethical questions in the Aristotelian virtue-based way lend support to relativism.

For this reason it is easy for those who are interested in supporting the rational criticism of local traditions and in articulating an idea of ethical progress to feel that the ethics of virtue can give them little help. If the position of women, as established by local traditions in many parts of the world, is to be improved, if traditions of slave holding and racial inequality, if religious intolerance, if aggressive and warlike conceptions of manliness, if unequal norms of material distribution are to be criticized in the name of practical reason, this criticizing (one might easily suppose) will have to be done from a Kantian or utilitarian viewpoint, not through the Aristotelian approach.

This is an odd result, where Aristotle is concerned. For it is obvious that he was not only the defender of an ethical theory based on the virtues, but also the defender of a single objective account of the human good, or human flourishing. This account is supposed to be objective in the sense that it is justifiable with reference to reasons that do not derive merely from local traditions and practices, but rather from features of humanness that lie beneath all local traditions and are there to be seen whether or not they are in fact recognized in local traditions. And one of Aristotle's most obvious concerns is the criticism of existing moral traditions, in his own city and in others, as unjust or repressive, or in other ways incompatible with human flourishing. He uses his account of the virtues as a basis for this criticism of local traditions: prominently, for example, in Book II of the *Politics,* where he frequently argues against existing social forms by pointing to ways in which they neglect or hinder the development of some important human virtue.[2] Aristotle evidently believes that there is no incompatibility between basing an ethical theory on the virtues and defending the singleness and objectivity of the human good. Indeed, he seems to believe that these two aims are mutually supportive.

Now the fact that Aristotle believes something does not make it true. (Though I have sometimes been accused of holding that position!) But it does, on the whole, make that something a plausible *candidate* for the truth, one deserving our most serious scrutiny. In this case, it would be odd indeed if he had connected two elements in ethical thought that are self-evidently incompatible, or in favor of whose connectedness and compatibility there is nothing interesting to be said. The purpose of this paper is to establish that Aristotle does indeed have an interesting way of connecting the virtues with a search for ethical objectivity and with the criticism of existing local norms, a way that deserves our serious consideration as we work on these questions. Having described the general shape of the Aristotelian approach, we can then begin to understand some of the objections that might be brought against such a non-relative account of the virtues, and to imagine how the Aristotelian could respond to those objections.

II

The relativist, looking at different societies, is impressed by the variety and the apparent non-comparability in the lists of virtues she encounters. Examining the different lists, and observing the complex connections between each list and a concrete form of life and a concrete history, she may well feel that any list of virtues must be simply a reflection of local traditions and values, and that, virtues being (unlike Kantian principles or utilitarian algorithms) concrete and closely tied to forms of life, there can in fact be no list of virtues that will serve as normative for all these varied societies. It is not only that the specific forms of behavior recommended in connection with the virtues differ greatly over time and place, it is also that the very areas that are singled out as spheres of virtue, and the manner in which they are individuated from other areas, vary so greatly. For someone who thinks this way, it is easy to feel that Aristotle's own list, despite its pretensions to universality and objectivity, must be similarly restricted, merely a reflection of one particular society's perceptions of salience and ways of distinguishing. At this point, relativist writers are likely to quote Aristotle's description of the "great-souled" person, the *megalopsuchos,* which certainly contains many concrete local features and sounds very much like the portrait of a certain sort of Greek gentleman, in order to show that Aristotle's list is just as culture-bound as any other.[3]

But if we probe further into the way in which Aristotle in fact enumerates and individuates the virtues, we begin to notice things that cast doubt upon the suggestion that he has simply described what is admired in his own society. First of all, we notice that a rather large number of virtues and vices (vices especially) are nameless, and that, among the ones that are not nameless, a good many are given, by Aristotle's own account, names that are somewhat arbitrarily chosen by Aristotle, and do not perfectly fit the behavior he is trying to describe.[4] Of such modes of conduct he writes, "Most of these are nameless, but we must try . . . to give them names in order to make our account clear and easy to follow" *(NE* 1108a16–19). This does not sound like the procedure of someone who is simply studying local traditions and singling out the virtue names that figure most prominently in those traditions.

What *is* going on becomes clearer when we examine the way in which he does, in fact, introduce his list. For he does so, in the *Nicomachean Ethics,*[5] by a device whose very straightforwardness and simplicity has caused it to escape the notice of most writers on this topic. What he does, in each case, is to isolate a sphere of human experience that figures in more or less any human life, and in which more or less any human being will have to make *some* choices rather than others, and act in *some* way rather than some other. The introductory chapter enumerating the virtues and vices begins from an enumeration of these spheres *(NE* 2.7); and each chapter on a virtue in the more detailed account that follows begins with "Concerning X . . . " or words to this effect, where "X" names a sphere of life with which all human beings regularly and more or less necessarily have dealings.[6] Aristotle then asks: What is it to choose and respond well within that sphere? What is it, on the other hand, to choose defectively? The "thin account" of each virtue is that it is whatever it is to be stably disposed to act appropriately in that sphere. There may be, and usually are, various competing specifications of what acting well, in each case, in fact comes to. Aristotle goes on to defend in each case some concrete specification, producing, at the end, a full or "thick" definition of the virtue.

Here are the most important spheres of experience recognized by Aristotle, along with the names of their corresponding virtues:[7]

SPHERE	VIRTUE
1. Fear of important damages, esp. death	courage
2. Bodily appetites and their pleasures	moderation
3. Distribution of limited resources	justice
4. Management of one's personal property, where others are concerned	generosity
5. Management of personal property, where hospitality is concerned	expansive hospitality
6. Attitudes and actions with respect to one's own worth	greatness of soul
7. Attitude to slights and damages	mildness of temper
8. "Association and living together and the fellowship of words and actions"	
a. truthfulness in speech	truthfulness
b. social association of a playful kind	easy grace (contrasted with coarseness, rudeness, insensitivity)
c. social association more generally	nameless, but a kind of friendliness (contrasted with irritability and grumpiness)
9. Attitude to the good and ill fortune of others	proper judgment (contrasted with enviousness, spitefulness, etc.)

10. Intellectual life	the various intellectual virtues (such as perceptiveness, knowledge, etc.)
11. The planning of one's life and conduct	practical wisdom

There is, of course, much more to be said about this list, its specific members, and the names Aristotle chooses for the virtue in each case, some of which are indeed culture bound. What I want, however, to insist on here is the care with which Aristotle articulates his general approach, beginning from a characterization of a sphere of universal experience and choice, and introducing the virtue name as the name (as yet undefined) of whatever it is to choose appropriately in that area of experience. On this approach, it does not seem possible to say, as the relativist wishes to, that a given society does not contain anything that corresponds to a given virtue. Nor does it seem to be an open question, in the case of a particular agent, whether a certain virtue should or should not be included in his or her life—except in the sense that she can always choose to pursue the corresponding deficiency instead. The point is that everyone makes some choices and acts somehow or other in these spheres: if not properly, then improperly. Everyone has *some* attitude and behavior toward her own death; toward her bodily appetites and their management; toward her property and its use; toward the distribution of social goods; toward telling the truth; toward being kindly or not kindly to others; toward cultivating or not cultivating a sense of play and delight; and so on. No matter where one lives one cannot escape these questions, so long as one is living a human life. But then this means that one's behavior falls, willy nilly, within the sphere of the Aristotelian virtue, in each case. If it is not appropriate, it is inappropriate; it cannot be off the map altogether. People will of course disagree about what the appropriate ways of acting and reacting in fact *are*. But in that case, as Aristotle has set things up, they are arguing about the same thing, and advancing competing specifications of the same virtue. The reference of the virtue term in each case is fixed by the sphere of experience—by what we shall from now on call the "grounding experiences." The thin or "nominal definition" of the virtue will be, in each case, that it is whatever it is that being disposed to choose and respond well consists in, in that sphere. The job of ethical theory will be to search for the best further specification corresponding to this nominal definition, and to produce a full definition.

III

We have begun to introduce considerations from the philosophy of language. We can now make the direction of the Aristotelian account clearer by considering his own account of linguistic indicating (referring) and defining, which guides his treatment of both scientific and ethical terms, and of the idea of progress in both areas.[8]

Aristotle's general picture is as follows. We begin with some experiences — not necessarily our own, but those of members of our linguistic community, broadly construed.[9] On the basis of these experiences, a word enters the language of the group, indicating (referring to) whatever it is that is the content of those experiences. Aristotle gives the example of thunder.[10] People hear a noise in the clouds, and they then refer to it, using the word "thunder." At this point, it may be that nobody has any concrete account of the noise or any idea about what it really is. But the experience fixes a subject for further inquiry. From now on, we can refer to thunder, ask "What is thunder?" and advance and assess competing theories. The thin or, we might say, "nominal definition" of thunder is "That noise in the clouds, whatever it is." The competing explanatory theories are rival candidates for correct full or thick definition. So the explanatory story citing Zeus' activities in the clouds is a false account of the very same thing of which the best scientific explanation is a true account. There is just one debate here, with a single subject.

So too, Aristotle suggests, with our ethical terms. Heraclitus, long before him, already had the essential idea, saying, "They would not have known the name of justice, if these things did not take place."[11] "These things," our source for the fragment informs us, are experiences of injustice—presumably of harm, deprivation, inequality. These experiences fix the reference of the corresponding virtue word. Aristotle proceeds along similar lines. In the *Politics* he insists that only human beings, and not either animals or gods, will have our basic ethical terms and concepts (such as just and unjust, noble and base, good and bad), because the beasts are unable to form the concepts, and gods lack the experiences of limit and finitude that give a concept such as justice its point.[12] In the *Nicomachean Ethics* enumeration of the virtues, he carries the line of thought further, suggesting that the reference of the virtue terms is fixed by spheres of choice, frequently connected with our finitude and limitation, that we encounter in virtue of shared conditions of human existence.[13] The question about virtue usually arises in areas in which human choice is both non-optional and somewhat problematic. (Thus, he stresses, there is no virtue involving the regulation of listening to attractive sounds or seeing pleasing sights.) Each family of virtue and vice or deficiency words attaches to some such sphere. And we can understand progress in ethics, like progress in scientific understanding, to be progress in finding the correct fuller specification of a virtue, isolated by its thin or "nominal" definition. This progress is aided by a perspicuous mapping of the sphere of the grounding experiences. When we understand more precisely what problems human beings encounter in their lives with one another, what circumstances they face in which choice of some sort is required, we will have a way of assessing competing responses to those problems, and we will begin to understand what it might be to act well in the face of them.

Aristotle's ethical and political writings provide many examples of how such progress (or, more generally, such a rational debate) might go. We find argument against Platonic asceticism, as the proper specification of moderation (appropriate choice and response vis-à-vis the bodily appetites) and the consequent proneness to anger over slights, that was prevalent in Greek ideals of maleness and in Greek behavior, together with a defense of a more limited and controlled expression of anger, as the proper specification of the virtue that Aristotle calls "mildness of temper." (Here Aristotle evinces some discomfort with the virtue term he has chosen, and he is right to do so, since it certainly loads the dice heavily in favor of his concrete specification and against the traditional one.)[14] And so on for all the virtues.

In an important section of *Politics* II, part of which forms one of the epigraphs to this paper, Aristotle defends the proposition that laws should be revisable and not fixed, by pointing to evidence that there is progress toward greater correctness in our ethical conceptions, as also in the arts and sciences. Greeks used to think that courage was a matter of waving swords around; now they have (the *Ethics* informs us) a more inward and a more civic and communally attuned understanding of proper behavior toward the possibility of death. Women used to be regarded as property, bought and sold; now this would be thought barbaric. And in the case of justice as well we have, the *Politics* passage claims, advanced toward a more adequate understanding of what is fair and appropriate. Aristotle gives the example of an existing homicide law that convicts the defendent automatically on the evidence of the prosecutor's relatives (whether they actually witnessed anything or not, apparently). This, Aristotle says, is clearly a stupid and unjust law; and yet it once seemed appropriate—and, to a tradition-bound community, must still be so. To hold tradition fixed is then to prevent ethical progress. What human beings want and seek is not conformity with the past, it is the good. So our systems of law should make it possible for them to progress beyond the past, when they have agreed that a change is good. (They should not, however, make change too easy, since it is no easy matter to see one's way to the good, and tradition is frequently a sounder guide than current fashion.)

In keeping with these ideas, the *Politics* as a whole presents the beliefs of the many different societies it investigates not as unrelated local norms, but as competing answers to questions of justice and courage (and so on) with which all the societies (being human) are concerned, and in response to which they are all trying to find what is good. Aristotle's analysis of the virtues gives him an appropriate framework for these comparisons, which seem perfectly appropriate inquiries into the ways in which different societies have solved common human problems.

In the Aristotelian approach it is obviously of the first importance to distinguish two stages of the inquiry: the initial demarcation of the sphere of choice, of the "grounding experiences" that fix the reference of the virtue term; and the ensuing more concrete inquiry into what appropriate choice, in that sphere, *is.* Aristotle does not always do this carefully, and the language he has to work with is often not helpful to him. We do not have much difficulty with terms like "moderation" and "justice" and even "courage," which seem vaguely normative but relatively empty, so far, of concrete moral content. As the approach requires, they can serve as extension-fixing labels under which many competing specifications may be investigated. But we have already noticed the problem with "mildness of temper," which seems to rule out by fiat a prominent contender for the appropriate disposition concerning anger. And much the same thing certainly seems to be true of the relativists' favorite target, *megalopsuchia,* which implies in its very name an attitude to one's own worth that is more Greek than universal. (For example, a Christian will feel that the proper attitude to one's own worth requires understanding one's lowness, frailty, and sinfulness. The virtue of humility requires considering oneself *small,* not great.) What we ought to get at this point in the inquiry is a word for the proper behavior toward anger and offense and a word for the proper behavior toward one's worth that are more truly neutral among the competing specifications, referring only to the sphere of experience within which we wish to determine what is appropriate. Then we could regard the competing conceptions as rival accounts of one and the same thing, so that, for example, Christian humility would be a rival specification of the same virtue whose Greek specification is given in Aristotle's account of *megalopsuchia,* namely, the proper way to behave toward the question of one's own worth.

And in fact, oddly enough, if one examines the evolution in the use of this word from Aristotle through the Stoics to the Christian fathers, one can see that this is more or less what happened, as "greatness of soul" became associated, first, with Stoic emphasis on the supremacy of virtue and the worthlessness of externals, including the body, and, through this, with the Christian denial of the body and of the worth of earthly life.[15] So even in this apparently unpromising case, history shows that the Aristotelian approach not only provided the materials for a single debate but actually succeeded in organizing such a debate, across enormous differences of both place and time.

Here, then, is a sketch for an objective human morality based upon the idea of virtuous action—that is, of appropriate functioning in each human sphere. The Aristotelian claim is that, further developed, it will retain virtue morality's immersed attention to actual human experiences, while gaining the ability to criticize local and traditional moralities in the name of a more inclusive account of the circumstances of human life, and of the needs for human functioning that these circumstances call forth.

IV

The proposal will encounter many objections. The concluding sections of this paper will present three of the most serious and will sketch the lines along which the Aristotelian conception might proceed in formulating a reply. To a great extent these objections are not imagined or confronted by Aristotle himself, but his position seems capable of confronting them.

The first objection concerns the relationship between singleness of problem and singleness of solution. Let us grant for the moment that the Aristotelian approach has succeeded in coherently isolating and describing areas of human experience and choice that form, so to speak, the *terrain* of the virtues, and in giving thin definitions of each of the virtues as whatever it is that consists in choosing and responding well within that sphere. Let us suppose that the approach succeeds in doing this in a way that embraces many times and places, bringing disparate cultures together into a single debate about the good human being and the good human life. Different cultural accounts of good choice within the sphere in question in each case are now seen not as untranslatably different forms of life, but as competing answers to a single general question about a set of shared human experiences. Still, it might be argued, what has been achieved is, at best, a single discourse or debate about virtue. It has not been shown that this debate will have, as Aristotle believes, a single answer. Indeed, it has not even been shown that the discourse we have set up will have the form of a *debate* at all, rather than that of a plurality of culturally specific narratives, each giving the thick definition of a virtue that corresponds to the experience and traditions of a particular group. There is an important disanalogy with the case of thunder, on which the

Aristotelian so much relies in arguing that our questions will have a single answer. For in that case what is given in experience is the definiendum itself, so that experiences establish a rough extension, to which any good definition must respond. In the case of the virtues, things are more indirect. What is given in experience across groups is only the *ground* of virtuous action, the circumstances of life to which virtuous action is an appropriate response. Even if these grounding experiences are shared, that does not tell us that there will be a shared appropriate response.

In the case of thunder, furthermore, the conflicting theories are clearly put forward as competing candidates for the truth; the behavior of those involved in the discourse suggests that they are indeed, as Aristotle says, searching "not for the way of their ancestors, but for the good." And it seems reasonable in that case for them to do so. It is far less clear, where the virtues are concerned (the objector continues) that a unified practical solution is either sought by the actual participants or a desideratum for them. The Aristotelian proposal makes it possible to conceive of a way in which the virtues might be non-relative. It does not, by itself, answer the question of relativism.

The second objection goes deeper. For it questions the notion of spheres of shared human experience that lies at the heart of the Aristotelian approach. The approach, says this objector, seems to treat the experiences that ground the virtues as in some way primitive, given, and free from the cultural variation that we find in the plurality of normative conceptions of virtue. Ideas of proper courage may vary, but the fear of death is shared by all human beings. Ideas of moderation may vary, but the experiences of hunger, thirst, and sexual desire are (so the Aristotelian seems to claim) invariant. Normative conceptions introduce an element of cultural interpretation that is not present in the grounding experiences, which are, for that very reason, the Aristotelian's starting point.

But, the objector continues, such assumptions are naive. They will not stand up either to our best account of experience or to a close examination of the ways in which these so-called grounding experiences have in fact been differently constructed by different cultures. In general, first of all, our best accounts of the nature of experience, even perceptual experience, inform us that there is no such thing as an "innocent eye" that receives an uninterpreted "given." Even sense-perception is interpretive, heavily influenced by belief, teaching, language, and in general by social and contextual features. There is a very real sense in which members of different societies do not see the same sun and stars, encounter the same plants and animals, hear the same thunder.

But if this seems to be true of human experience of nature, which was the allegedly unproblematic starting point for Aristotle's account of naming, it is all the more plainly true, the objector claims, in the area of the human good. Here it is only a very naive and historically insensitive moral philosopher who would say that the experience of the fear of death or the experience of bodily appetites is a human constant. Recent anthropological work on the social construction of the emotions,[16] for example, has shown to what extent the experience of fear has learned and culturally variant elements. When we add that the object of the fear in which the Aristotelian takes an interest is death, which has been so variously interpreted and understood by human beings at different times and in different places, the conclusion that the "grounding experience" is an irreducible plurality of experiences, highly various and in each case deeply infused with cultural interpretation, becomes even more inescapable.

Nor is the case different with the apparently less complicated experience of the bodily appetites. Most philosophers who have written about the appetites have treated hunger, thirst, and sexual desire as human universals, stemming from our shared animal nature. Aristotle himself was already more sophisticated, since he insisted that the object of appetite is "the apparent good" and that appetite is therefore something interpretive and selective, a kind of intentional awareness.[17] But he does not seem to have reflected much about the ways in which historical and cultural differences could shape that awareness. The Hellenistic philosophers who immediately followed him did so reflect, arguing that the experience of sexual desire and of many forms of the desire for food and drink are, at least in part, social constructs, built up over time on the basis of a social teaching about value that is external to start with, but that enters so deeply into the perceptions of the individual that it actually forms and transforms the experience of desire.[18] Let us take two Epicurean examples. People are taught that to be well fed they require luxurious fish and meat, that a simple vegetarian diet is not enough. Over time, the combination of teaching with habit produces an appetite for meat, shaping the individual's perceptions of the objects before him. Again, people are taught that what sexual relations are all about is a romantic union or fusion with an object who is seen as exalted in value, or even as perfect. Over time, this teaching shapes sexual behavior and the experience of desire, so that sexual arousal itself responds to this culturally learned scenario.[19]

This work of social criticism has recently been carried further by Michel Foucault in his *History of Sexuality*.[20] This work has certain gaps as a history of Greek thought on this topic, but it does succeed in establishing that the Greeks saw the problem of the appetites and their management in an extremely different way from the way of twentieth-century Westerners. To summarize two salient conclusions of his complex argument, the Greeks did not single out the sexual appetite for special treatment; they treated it alongside hunger and thirst, as a drive that needed to be mastered and kept within bounds. Their central concern was with self-mastery, and they saw the appetites in the light of this concern. Furthermore, where the sexual appetite is concerned, they did not regard the gender of the partner as particularly important in assessing the moral value of the act. Nor did they identify or treat as morally salient a stable disposition to prefer partners of one sex rather than the other. Instead, they focused on the general issue of activity and passivity, connecting it in complex ways with the issue of self-mastery.

Work like Foucault's—and there is a lot of it in various areas, some of it very good—shows very convincingly that the experience of bodily desire, and of the body itself, has elements that vary with cultural and historical change. The names that people call their desires and themselves as subjects of desire, the fabric of belief and discourse into which they integrate their ideas of desiring, all this influences, it is clear, not only their reflection about desire, but also their experience of desire itself. Thus, for example, it is naive to treat our modern debates about homosexuality as continuations of the very same debate about sexual activity that went on in the Greek world.[21] In a very real sense there was no "homosexual experience" in a culture that did not contain our emphasis on the gender of the object, our emphasis on the subjectivity of inclination and the permanence of appetitive disposition, our particular ways of problematizing certain forms of behavior.

If we suppose that we can get underneath this variety and this constructive power of social discourse in at least one case—namely, with the universal experience of bodily pain as a bad thing—even here we find subtle arguments against us. For the experience of pain seems to be embedded in a cultural discourse as surely as the closely related experiences of the appetites; and significant variations can be alleged here as well. The Stoics already made this claim against the Aristotelian virtues. In order to establish that bodily pain is not bad by its very nature, but only by cultural tradition, the Stoics had to provide some explanation for the ubiquity of the belief that pain is bad and of the tendency to shun it. This explanation would have to show that the reaction was learned rather than natural, and to explain why, in the light of this fact, it is learned so widely. This they did by pointing to certain features in the very early treatment of infants. As soon as an infant is born, it cries. Adults, assuming that the crying is a response to its pain at the unaccustomed coldness and harshness of the place where it finds itself, hasten to comfort it. This behavior, often repeated, teaches the infant to regard its pain as a bad thing—or, better, teaches it the concept of pain, which includes the notion of badness, and teaches it the forms of life its society shares concerning pain. It is all social teaching, they claim, though this usually escapes our notice because of the early and non-linguistic nature of the teaching.[22]

These and related arguments, the objector concludes, show that the Aristotelian idea that there is a single non-relative discourse about human experiences such as mortality or desire is a naive idea. There is no such bedrock of shared experience, and thus no single sphere of choice within which the virtue is the disposition to choose well. So the Aristotelian project cannot even get off the ground.

Now the Aristotelian confronts a third objector, who attacks from a rather different direction. Like the second, she charges that the Aristotelian has taken for a universal and necessary feature of human life an experience that is contingent on certain non-necessary historical conditions. Like the second, she argues that human experience is much more profoundly shaped by non-necessary social features than the Aristotelian has allowed. But her purpose is not simply, like second objector's, to point to the great variety of ways in which the "grounding experiences" corresponding to the virtues are actually understood and lived by human beings. It is more radical still. It is to point out that we could imagine a form of human life that does not contain these experiences—or some of them—at all, in any form. Thus the virtue that consists in acting well in that sphere need not be included in an account of the human good. In some cases, the experience may even be a sign of *bad* human life, and the corresponding virtue, therefore, no better than a form of non-ideal adaptation to a bad state of affairs. The really good human life, in such a case, would contain neither the grounding deficiency nor the remedial virtue.

This point is forcefully raised by some of Aristotle's own remarks about the virtue of generosity. One of his points against societies that eliminate private ownership is that they have thereby done away with the opportunity for generous action, which requires having possessions of one's own to give to others.[23] This sort of remark is tailor-made for the objector, who will immediately say that generosity, if it really rests upon the experience of private possession, is a dubious candidate indeed for inclusion in a purportedly non-relative account of the human virtues. If it rests upon a "grounding experience" that is non-necessary and is capable of being evaluated in different ways, and of being either included or eliminated in accordance with that evaluation, then it is not the universal the Aristotelian said it was.

Some objectors of the third kind will stop at this point, or use such observations to support the second objector's relativism. But in another prominent form this argument takes a non-relativist direction. It asks us to assess the "grounding experiences" against an account of human flourishing, produced in some independent manner. If we do so, the objector urges, we will discover that some of the experiences are remediable deficiencies. The objection to Aristotelian virtue ethics will then be that it limits our social aspirations, getting us to regard as permanent and necessary what we might in fact improve to the benefit of all human life. This is the direction in which the third objection to the virtues was pressed by Karl Marx, its most famous proponent.[24] According to Marx's argument, a number of the leading bourgeois virtues are responses to defective relations of production. Bourgeois justice, generosity, etc. presuppose conditions and structures that are non-ideal and that will be eliminated when communism is achieved. And it is not only the current *specification* of these virtues that will be superceded with the removal of deficiency. It is the virtues themselves. It is in this sense that communism leads human beings beyond ethics.

Thus the Aristotelian is urged to inquire into the basic structures of human life with the daring of a radical political imagination. It is claimed that when she does so she will see that human life contains more possibilities than are dreamed of in her list of virtues.

V

Each of these objections is profound. To answer any one of them adequately would require a treatise. But we can still do something at this point to map out an Aristotelian response to each one, pointing the direction in which a fuller reply might go.

The first objector is right to insist on the distinction between singleness of framework and singleness of answer, and right, again, to stress that in constructing a debate about the virtues based on the demarcation of certain spheres of experience we have not yet answered any of the "What is X?" questions that this debate will confront. We have not even said very much about the structure of the debate itself, beyond its beginnings—about how it will both use and criticize traditional beliefs, how it will deal with conflicting beliefs, how it will move critically from the "way of one's ancestors" to the "good"—in short, about whose judgments it will trust. I have addressed some of these issues, again with reference to Aristotle, in two other papers,[25] but much more remains to be done. At this point, however, we can make four observations to indicate how the Aristotelian might deal with some of the objector's concerns here. First, the Aristotelian position that I wish to defend need not insist, in every case, on a single answer to the request for a specification of a virtue. The answer might well turn out to be a disjunction. The process of comparative and critical debate will, I imagine, eliminate numerous contenders—for example, the view of justice that prevailed in Cyme. But what remains might well be a (probably small) plurality of acceptable accounts. These accounts may or may not be capable of being subsumed under a single account of greater generality. Success in the eliminative task will still be no trivial accomplishment. For example, if we should succeed in ruling out conceptions of the proper attitude to one's own human worth that are based on a notion of original sin, this would be moral work of enormous significance, even if we got no further than that in specifying the positive account.

Second, the general answer to a "What is X?" question in any sphere may well be susceptible of several or even of many concrete specifications, in connection with other local practices and local conditions. For example, the normative account where friendship and hospitality are concerned is likely to be extremely general, admitting of many concrete "fillings." Friends in England will have different customs, where regular social visiting is concerned, from friends in ancient Athens. And yet both sets of customs can count as further specifications of a general account of friendship that mentions, for example, the Aristotelian criteria of mutual benefit and well-wishing, mutual enjoyment, mutual awareness, a shared conception of the good, and some form of "living together."[26] Sometimes we may want to view such concrete accounts as optional alternative specifications, to be chosen by a society on the basis of reasons of ease and convenience. Sometimes, on the other hand, we may want to insist that this account gives the only legitimate specification of the virtue in question for that concrete context; in that case, the concrete account could be viewed as a part of a longer or fuller version of the single normative account. The decision between these two ways of regarding it will depend upon our assessment of its degree of non-arbitrariness for its context (both physical and historical), its relationship to other non-arbitrary features of the moral conception of that context, and so forth.

Third, whether we have one or several general accounts of a virtue, and whether this account or these accounts do or do not admit of more concrete specifications relative to ongoing cultural contexts, the particular choices that the virtuous person, under this conception, makes will always be a matter of being keenly responsive to the local features of his or her concrete context. So in this respect, again, the instructions the Aristotelian gives to the person of virtue do not differ from one part of what a relativist would recommend. The Aristotelian virtues involve a delicate balancing between general rules and the keen awareness of particulars, in which process, as Aristotle stresses, the perception of the particular takes priority. It takes priority in the sense that a good rule is a good summary of wise particular choices and not a court of last resort. Like rules in medicine and in navigation, ethical rules should be held open to modification in the light of new circumstances; and the good agent must therefore cultivate the ability to perceive and correctly describe his or her situation finely and truly, including in this perceptual grasp even those features of the situation that are not covered under the existing rule.

I have written a good deal elsewhere on this idea of the "priority of the particular," exactly what it does and does not imply, in exactly what ways the particular perception is and is not prior to the general rule. Those who want clarification on this central topic will have to turn to those writings.[27]

What I want to stress here is that Aristotelian particularism is fully compatible with Aristotelian objectivity. The fact that a good and virtuous decision is context-sensitive does not imply that it is right only *relative to,* or *inside,* a limited context, any more than the fact that a good navigational judgment is sensitive to particular weather conditions shows that it is correct only in a local or relational sense. It is right absolutely, objectively, from anywhere in the human world, to attend to the particular features of one's context; and the person who so attends and who chooses accordingly is making, according to Aristotle, the humanly correct decision, period. If another situation ever should arise with all the same morally relevant features, including contextual features, the same decision would again be absolutely right.[28]

Thus the virtue-based morality can capture a great deal of what the relativist is after and still lay claim to objectivity. In fact, we might say that the Aristotelian virtues do better than the relativist virtues in explaining what people are actually doing when they scrutinize the features of their context carefully, looking at both the shared and the non-shared features with an eye to what is best. For as Aristotle says, people who do this are usually searching for the good, not just for the way of their ancestors. They are prepared to defend their decisions as good or right, and to think of those who advocate a different course as disagreeing about what is right, not just narrating a different tradition.

Finally, we should point out that the Aristotelian virtues, and the deliberations they guide, unlike some systems of moral rules, remain always open to revision in the light of new circumstances and new evidence. In this way, again, they contain the flexibility to local conditions that the relativist would desire, but, again, without sacrificing objectivity. Sometimes the new circumstances may simply give rise to a new concrete specification of the virtue as previously defined; in some cases it may cause us to change our view about what the virtue itself is. All general accounts are held provisionally, as summaries of correct decisions and as guides to new ones. This flexibility, built into the Aristotelian procedure, will again help the Aristotelian account to answer the questions of the relativist, without relativism.

VI

We must now turn to the second objection. Here, I believe, is the really serious threat to the Aristotelian position. Past writers on virtue, including Aristotle himself, have lacked sensitivity to the ways in which different traditions of discourse, different conceptual schemes, articulate the world, and also to the profound connections between the structure of discourse and the structure of experience itself. Any contemporary defense of the Aristotelian position must display this sensitivity, responding somehow to the data that the relativist historian or anthropologist brings forward.

The Aristotelian should begin, it seems to me, by granting that with respect to any complex matter of deep human importance there is no "innocent eye"—no way of seeing the world that is entirely neutral and free of cultural shaping. The work of philosophers such as Putnam, Goodman, and Davidson[29]—following, one must point out, from the arguments of Kant and, I believe, from those of Aristotle himself[30]—have shown convincingly that even where sense-perception is concerned, the human mind is an active and interpretive instrument and that its interpretations are a function of its history and its concepts, as well as of its innate structure. The Aristotelian should also grant, it seems to me, that the nature of human world-interpretations is holistic and that the criticism of them must, equally well, be holistic. Conceptual schemes, like languages, hang together as whole structures, and we should realize, too, that a change in any single element is likely to have implications for the system as a whole.

But these two facts do not imply, as some relativists in literary theory and in anthropology tend to assume, that all world interpretations are equally valid and altogether non-comparable, that there are no good standards of assessment and "anything goes." The rejection of the idea of ethical truth as correspondence to an altogether uninterpreted reality does not imply that the whole idea of searching for the truth is an old-fashioned error. Certain ways in which people see the world can still be criticized exactly as Aristotle criticized them: as stupid, pernicious, and false. The standards used in such criticisms must come from inside human life. (Frequently they will come from the society in question itself, from its own rationalist and critical traditions.) And the inquirer must attempt, prior to criticism, to develop an inclusive understanding of the conceptual scheme being criticized, seeing what motivates each of its parts and how they hang together. But there is so far no reason to think that the critic will not be able to reject the institution of slavery or the homicide law of Cyme as out of line with the conception of virtue that emerges from reflection on the variety of different ways in which human cultures have had the experiences that ground the virtues.

The "grounding experiences" will not, the Aristotelian should concede, provide precisely a single language—neutral bedrock on which an account of virtue can be straightforwardly and unproblematically based. The description and assessment of the ways in which different cultures have constructed these experiences will become one of the central tasks of Aristotelian philosophical criticism. But the relativist has, so far, shown no reasons why we could not, at the end of the day, say that certain ways of conceptualizing death are more in keeping with the totality of our evidence and with the totality of our wishes for flourishing life than others; that certain ways of experiencing appetitive desire are for similar reasons more promising than others.

Relativists tend, furthermore, to understate the amount of attunement, recognition, and overlap that actually obtains across cultures, particularly in the areas of the grounding experiences. The Aristotelian in developing her conception in a culturally sensitive way, should insist, as Aristotle himself does, upon the evidence of such attunement and recognition. Despite the evident differences in the specific cultural shaping of the grounding experiences, we do recognize the experiences of people in other cultures as similar to our own. We do converse with them about matters of deep importance, understand them, allow ourselves to be moved by them. When we read Sophocles' *Antigone,* we see a good deal that seems strange to us; and we have not read the play well if we do not notice how far its conceptions of death, womanhood, and so on differ from our own. But it is still possible for us to be moved by the drama, to care about its people, to regard their debates as reflections upon virtue that speak to our own experience, and their choices as choices in spheres of conduct in which we too must choose. Again, when one sits down at a table with people from other parts of the world and debates with them concerning hunger or just distribution or in general the quality of human life, one does find, in spite of evident conceptual differences, that it is possible to proceed as if we are all talking about the same human problem; and it is usually only in a context in which one or more of the parties is intellectually committed to a theoretical relativist position that this discourse proves impossible to sustain. This sense of community and overlap seems to be especially strong in the areas that we have called the areas of the grounding experiences. And this, it seems, supports the Aristotelian claim that those experiences can be a good starting point for ethical debate.

Furthermore, it is necessary to stress that hardly any cultural group today is as focused upon its own internal traditions and as isolated from other cultures as the relativist argument presupposes. Cross-cultural communication and debate are ubiquitous facts of contemporary life. Our experience of cultural interaction indicates that in general the inhabitants of different conceptual schemes do tend to view their interaction in the Aristotelian and not the relativist way. A traditional society, confronted with new technologies and sciences, and the conceptions that go with them, does not, in fact, simply fail to understand them or regard them as totally alien incursions upon a hermetically sealed way of life. Instead, it assesses the new item as a possible contributor to flourishing life, making it comprehensible to itself and incorporating elements that promise to solve problems of flourishing. Examples of such assimilation, and the debate that surrounds it,[31] suggest that the parties do, in fact, recognize common problems and that the traditional society is perfectly capable of viewing an external innovation as a device to solve a problem that it shares with the innovating society. The parties do, in fact, search for the good, not the way of their ancestors; only traditionalist anthropologists insist, nostalgically, on the absolute preservation of the ancestral.

And this is so even when cross-cultural discourse reveals a difference at the level of the conceptualization of the grounding experiences. Frequently the effect of work like Foucault's, which reminds us of the non-necessary and non-universal character of one's own ways of seeing in some such area, is precisely to prompt a critical debate in search of the human good. It is difficult, for example, to read Foucault's observations about the history of our sexual ideas without coming to feel that certain ways in which the Western contemporary debate on these matters has been organized, as a result of some combination of Christian morality with nineteenth-century pseudo-science, are especially silly, arbitrary, and limiting, inimical to a human search for flourishing. Foucault's moving account of Greek culture, as he himself insists in a preface,[32] provides not only a sign that someone once thought differently, but also evidence that it is possible for *us* to think differently. Foucault announced that the purpose of his book was to "free thought" so that it could think differently, imagining new and more fruitful possibilities. And close analysis of spheres of cultural discourse, which stresses cultural differences in the spheres of the grounding experiences, is being combined, increasingly, in current debates about sexuality and related matters, with the critique of existing social arrangements and attitudes, and with the elaboration of a new norm of human flourishing. There is no reason to think this combination incoherent.[33]

As we pursue these possibilities, the basic spheres of experience identified in the Aristotelian approach will no longer, we have said, be seen as spheres of *uninterpreted* experience. But we have also insisted that there is much family relatedness and much overlap among societies. And certain areas of relatively greater universality can be specified here, on which we should insist as we proceed to areas that are more varied in their cultural expression. Not without a sensitive awareness that we are speaking of something that is experienced differently in different contexts, we can nonetheless identify certain features of our common humanity, closely related to Aristotle's original list, from which our debate might proceed.

1. *Mortality*. No matter how death is understood, all human beings face it and (after a certain age) know that they face it. This fact shapes every aspect of more or less every human life.

2. *The Body*. Prior to any concrete cultural shaping, we are born with human bodies, whose possibilities and vulnerabilities do not as such belong to one culture rather than any other. Any given human being might have belonged to any culture. The experience of the body is culturally influenced; but the body itself, prior to such experience, provides limits and parameters that ensure a great deal of overlap in what is going to be experienced, where hunger, thirst, desire, the five senses are concerned. It is all very well to point to the cultural component in these experiences. But when one spends time considering issues of hunger and scarcity, and in general of human misery, such differences appear relatively small and refined, and one cannot fail to acknowledge that "there are no known ethnic differences in human physiology with respect to metabolism of nutrients. Africans and Asians do not burn their dietary calories or use their dietary protein any differently from Europeans and Americans. It follows then that dietary requirements cannot vary widely as between different races."[34] This and similar facts should surely be focal points for debate about appropriate human behavior in this sphere. And by beginning with the body, rather than with the subjective experience of desire, we get, furthermore, an opportunity to criticize the situation of people who are so persistently deprived that their *desire* for good things has actually decreased. This is a further advantage of the Aristotelian approach, when contrasted with approaches to choice that stop with subjective expressions of preference.

3. *Pleasure and pain*. In every culture, there is a conception of pain; and these conceptions, which overlap very largely with one another, can be plausibly seen as grounded in universal and pre-cultural experience. The Stoic story of infant development is highly implausible; the negative response to bodily pain is surely primitive and universal, rather than learned and optional, however much its specific "grammar" may be shaped by later learning.

4. *Cognitive capability*. Aristotle's famous claim that "all human beings by nature reach out for understanding"[35] seems to stand up to the most refined anthropological analysis. It points to an element in our common humanity that is plausibly seen, again, as grounded independently of particular acculturation, however much it is later shaped by acculturation.

5. *Practical reason.* All human beings, whatever their culture, participate (or try to) in the planning and managing of their lives, asking and answering questions about how one should live and act. This capability expresses itself differently in different societies, but a being who altogether lacked it would not be likely to be acknowledged as a human being, in any culture.[36]

6. *Early infant development.* Prior to the greatest part of specific cultural shaping, though perhaps not free from all shaping, are certain areas of human experiences and development that are broadly shared and of great importance for the Aristotelian virtues: experiences of desire, pleasure, loss, one's own finitude, perhaps also of envy, grief, gratitude. One may argue about the merits of one or another psychoanalytical account of infancy. But it seems difficult to deny that the work of Freud on infant desire and of Klein on grief, loss, and other more complex emotional attitudes has identified spheres of human experience that are to a large extent common to all humans, regardless of their particular society. All humans begin as hungry babies, perceiving their own helplessness, their alternating closeness to and distance from those on whom they depend, and so forth. Melanie Klein records a conversation with an anthropologist in which an event that at first looked (to Western eyes) bizarre was interpreted by Klein as the expression of a universal pattern of mourning. The anthropologist accepted her interpretation.[37]

7. *Affiliation.* Aristotle's claim that human beings as such feel a sense of fellowship with other human beings, and that we are by nature social animals, is an empirical claim, but it seems to be a sound one. However varied our specific conceptions of friendship and love are, there is a great point in seeing them as overlapping expressions of the same family of shared human needs and desires.

8. *Humor.* There is nothing more culturally varied than humor, and yet, as Aristotle insists, some space for humor and play seems to be a need of any human life. The human being was not called the "laughing animal" for nothing; it is certainly one of our salient differences from almost all animals, and (in some form or other) a shared feature, I somewhat boldly assert, of any life that is going to be counted as fully human.

This is just a list of suggestions, closely related to Aristotle's list of common experiences. One could subtract some of these items and/or add others. But it seems plausible to claim that in all these areas we have a basis for further work on the human good. We do not have a bedrock of completely uninterpreted "given" data, but we do have nuclei of experience around which the constructions of different societies proceed. There is no Archimedean point here, and no pure access to unsullied "nature"—even, here, human nature—as it is in and of itself. There is just human life as it is lived. But in life as it is lived, we do find a family of experiences, clustering around certain foci, which can provide reasonable starting points for cross-cultural reflection.

VII

The third objection raises, at bottom, a profound conceptual question: What is it to inquire about the *human* good? What circumstances of existence go to define what it is to live the life of a *human being,* and not some other life? Aristotle likes to point out that an inquiry into the human good cannot, on pain of incoherence, end up describing the good of some other being, say a god, a good, that on account of our circumstances, it is impossible for us to attain (cf. *NE* 1159a10–12, 1166a18–23). Which circumstances then? The virtues are defined relatively to certain problems and limitations, and also to certain endowments. Which ones are sufficiently central that their removal would make us into different beings, and open up a wholly new and different debate about the good? This question is itself part of the ethical debate we propose. For there is no way to answer it but ask ourselves which elements of our experience seem to us so important that they count, for us, as part of who we are. I discuss Aristotle's attitude to this question elsewhere, and I shall simply summarize here.[38] It seems clear, first of all, that our mortality is an essential feature of our circumstances as human beings. An immortal being would have such a different form of life, and such different values and virtues, that it does not seem to make sense to regard that being as part of the same search for good. Essential, too, will be our dependence upon the world outside of us: some sort of need for food, drink, the help of others. On the side of abilities, we would want to include cognitive functioning and the activity of practical reasoning as elements of any life that we would regard as human. Aristotle argues, plausibly, that we would want to include sociability as well, some sensitivity to the needs of and pleasure in the company of other beings similar to ourselves.

But it seems to me that the Marxian question remains, as a deep question about human forms of life and the search for the human good. For one certainly can imagine forms of human life that do not contain the holding of private property—and, therefore, not those virtues that have to do with its proper management. And this means that it remains an open question whether these virtues ought to be regarded as virtues, and kept upon our list. Marx wished to go much further, arguing that communism would remove the need for justice, courage, and most of the bourgeois virtues. I think we might be skeptical here. Aristotle's general attitude to such transformations of life is to suggest that they usually have a tragic dimension. If we remove one sort of problem—say, by removing private property—we frequently do so by introducing another—say, the absence of a certain sort of freedom of choice, the freedom that makes it possible to do fine and generous actions for others. If things are complex even in the case of generosity, where we can rather easily imagine the transformation that removes the virtue, they are surely far more so in the cases of justice and courage. And we would need a far more detailed description than Marx ever gives us of the form of life under communism, before we would be able even to begin to see whether this form of life has in fact transformed things where these virtues are concerned, and whether it has or has not introduced new problems and limitations in their place.

In general it seems that all forms of life, including the imagined life of a god, contain boundaries and limits.[39] All structures, even that of putative limitlessness, are closed to something, cut off from something—say, in that case, from the specific value and beauty inherent in the struggle against limitation. Thus it does not appear that we will so easily get beyond the virtues. Nor does it seem to be so clearly a good thing for human life that we should.

VIII

The best conclusion to this sketch of an Aristotelian program for virtue ethics was written by Aristotle himself, at the end of his discussion of human nature in *Nicomachean Ethics* I:

So much for our outline sketch for the good. For it looks as if we have to draw an outline first, and fill it in later. It would seem to be open to anyone to take things further and to articulate the good parts of the sketch. And time is a good discoverer or ally in such things. That's how the sciences have progressed as well: it is open to anyone to supply what is lacking. *(NE* 1098a20–26)[40]

Notes

1. A. MacIntyre, *After Virtue* (Notre Dame, Ind., 1981); P. Foot, *Virtues and Vices* (Los Angeles, 1978); B. Williams, *Ethics and the Limits of Philosophy* (Cambridge, Mass., 1985) and Tanner Lectures, Harvard, 1983. See also M. Walzer, *Spheres of Justice* (New York, 1983) and Tanner Lectures, Harvard, 1985.

2. For examples of this, see Nussbaum, "Nature, Function, and Capability: Aristotle on Political Distribution," circulated as a WIDER working paper, and forthcoming in *Oxford Studies in Ancient Philosophy,* 1988, and also, in an expanded version, in the Proceedings of the 12th Symposium Aristotelicum.

3. See, for example, Williams, *Ethics and the Limits,* 34–36; Stuart Hampshire, *Morality and Conflict* (Cambridge, Mass., 1983), 150 ff.

4. For "nameless" virtues and vices, see *NE* 1107b1–2, 1107b8, 1107b30–31, 1108a17, 1119a10–11, 1126b20, 1127a12, 1127a14; for recognition of the unsatisfactoriness of names given, see 1107b8, 1108a5–6, 1108a20 ff. The two categories are largely overlapping, on account of the general principle enunciated at 1108a16–19, that where there is no name a name should be given, unsatisfactory or not.

5. It should be noted that this emphasis on spheres of experience is not present in the *Eudemian Ethics,* which begins with a list of virtues and vices. This seems to me a sign that that treatise expresses a more primitive stage of Aristotle's thought on the virtues—whether earlier or not.

6. For statements with *peri,* connecting virtues with spheres of life, see 1115a6–7, 1117a29–30, 1117b25, 27, 1119b23, 1122a19, 1122b34, 1125b26, 1126b13; and NE 2.7 throughout. See also the related usages at 1126b11, 1127b32.

7. My list here inserts justice in a place of prominence. (In the *NE* it is treated separately, after all the other virtues, and the introductory list defers it for that later examination.) I have also added at the end of the list categories corresponding to the various intellectual virtues discussed in *NE* 6, and also to *phronesis* or practical wisdom, discussed in 6 as well. Otherwise the order and wording of my list closely follows 2.7, which gives the program for the more detailed analyses of 3.5–4.

8. For a longer account of this, with references to the literature and to related philosophical discussions, see Nussbaum, *The Fragility of Goodness* (Cambridge, Mass., 1986), chap. 8.

9. Aristotle does not worry about questions of translation in articulating this idea; for some worries about this, and an Aristotelian response, see below sections IV and VI.

10. *Posterior Analytics,* 2.8. 93a21 ff.; see *Fragility,* chap. 8.

11. Heraclitus, fragment DK B23; see Nussbaum, *"Psuche* in Heraclitus, II," *Phronesis* 17 (1972): 153–70.

12. See *Politics* 1.2. 1253a1–18; that discussion does not deny the virtues to gods explicitly, but this denial is explicit at *NE* 1145a25–7 and 1178b10 ff.

13. Aristotle does not make the connection with his account of language explicit, but his project is one of defining the virtues, and we would expect him to keep his general view of defining in mind in this context. A similar idea about the virtues, and experience of a certain sort as a possible basis for a non-relative account, is developed, without reference to Aristotle, in a review of P. Foot's *Virtues and Vices* by N. Sturgeon, *Journal of Philosophy* 81 (1984): 326–33.

14. See 1108a5, where Aristotle says that the virtues and the corresponding person are "pretty much nameless," and says "Let us call . . . " when he introduces the names. See also 1125b29, 1126a3–4.

15. See John Procope, *Magnanimity* (1987); also R.-A. Gauthier, *Magnanimité* (Paris, 1951).

16. See, for example, *The Social Construction of the Emotions,* edited by Rom Harré (Oxford, 1986).

17. See Nussbaum, *Aristotle's De Motu Animalium* (Princeton, N.J., 1976), notes on chap. 6, and *Fragility,* chap. 9.

18. A detailed study of the treatment of these ideas in the three major Hellenistic schools was presented in Nussbaum, *The Therapy of Desire: Theory and Practice in Hellenistic Ethics,* The Martin Classical Lectures 1986, and forthcoming.

19. The relevant texts are discussed in Nussbaum, *The Therapy,* chaps. 4–6. See also Nussbaum, "Therapeutic Arguments: Epicurus and Aristotle," in *The Norms of Nature,* edited by M. Schofield and G. Striker (Cambridge, 1986), 31–74.

20. M. Foucault, *Histoire de la sexualité,* vols. 2 and 3 (Paris, 1984).

21. See the papers by D. Halperin and J. Winkler in *Before Sexuality,* edited by D. Halperin, J. Winkler, and F. Zeitlin, forthcoming (Princeton).

22. The evidence for this part of the Stoic view is discussed in Nussbaum, *The Therapy.*

23. *Politics* 1263b11 ff.

24. For a discussion of the relevant passages, see S. Lukes, *Marxism and Morality* (Oxford, 1987). For an acute discussion of these issues I am indebted to an exchange between Alan Ryan and Stephen Lukes at the Oxford Philosophical Society, March 1987.

25. *Fragility,* chap. 8, and "Internal Criticism and Indian Rationalist Traditions," the latter co-authored with Amartya Sen, in *Relativism,* edited by M. Krausz (Notre Dame, Ind., 1988) and a WIDER Working Paper.

26. See *Fragility,* chap. 12.

27. *Fragility,* chap. 10, "The Discernment of Perception," *Proceedings of the Boston Area Colloquium in Ancient Philosophy* 1 (1985): 151–201; "Finely Aware and Richly Responsible: Moral Awareness and the Moral Task of Literature," *Journal of Philosophy* 82 (1985): 516–29, reprinted in expanded form in *Philosophy and the Question of Literature,* edited by A. Cascardi (Baltimore, 1987).

28. I believe, however, that some morally relevant features, in the Aristotelian view, may be features that are not, even in principle, replicable in another context. See "The Discernment," and *Fragility,* chap. 10.

29. See H. Putnam, *Reason, Truth, and History* (Cambridge, 1981); *The Many Faces of Realism,* The Carus Lectures, forthcoming; and *Meaning and the Moral Sciences* (London, 1979); N. Goodman, *Languages of Art* (Indianapolis, 1968) and *Ways of World-Making* (Indianapolis, 1978); D. Davidson, *Inquiries into Truth and Interpretation* (Oxford, 1984).

30. On his debt to Kant, see Putnam, *The Many Faces;* on Aristotle's "internal realism," see Nussbaum, *Fragility,* chap. 8.

31. C. Abeysekera, paper presented at Value and Technology Conference, WIDER 1986.

32. Foucault, *Histoire,* vol. 2, preface.

33. This paragraph expands remarks made in a commentary on papers by D. Halperin and J. Winkler at the conference on "Homosexuality in History and Culture" at Brown University, February 1987. The combination of historically sensitive analysis with cultural criticism was forcefully developed at the same conference in Henry Abelove's "Is Gay History Possible?," forthcoming.

34. C. Gopalan, "Undernutrition: Measurement and Implications," paper prepared for the WIDER Conference on Poverty, Undernutrition, and Living Standards, Helsinki, 27–31 July 1987, and forthcoming in the volume of Proceedings, edited by S. Osmani.

35. *Metaphysics* 1.1.

36. See Nussbaum, "Nature, Function, and Capability," where this Aristotelian view is compared with Marx's views on human functioning.

37. M. Klein, in Postscript to "Our Adult World and its Roots in Infancy," in *Envy, Gratitude and Other Works 1946–1963* (London, 1984), 247–63.

38. "Aristotle on Human Nature and the Foundations of Ethics," forthcoming in a volume of essays on the work of Bernard Williams, edited by R. Harrison and J. Altham (Cambridge). This paper will be a WIDER Working Paper.

39. See *Fragility*, chap. 11.

40. This paper was motivated by questions discussed at the WIDER conference on Value and Technology, summer 1986, Helsinki. I would like to thank Steve and Frédérique Marglin for provoking some of these arguments, with hardly any of which they will agree. I also thank Dan Brock for his helpful comments, and Amartya Sen for many discussions of these issues.

MIDWEST STUDIES IN PHILOSOPHY, XIII (1988)

Ancient Wisdom and Modern Folly

RICHARD TAYLOR

The Oxford edition of Aristotle's *Nicomachean Ethics* includes a detailed table of contents wherein every topic touched upon in the work is noted in outline. Nowhere there does one find reference to any distinction between right and wrong, nor to duty or obligation. Certain Athenian practices, moreover, which a modern reader might suppose would have involved ethical issues deserving of a philosopher's attention, such as slavery and infanticide, are likewise not alluded to.

How come? Is it not surprising that this great treatise on ethics which, together with Kant's writings on the subject, stands as one of the most important contributions to moral philosophy that our culture possesses, should entirely disregard concepts that one would think lie at the very foundation of the subject?

The explanation is that the philosophers of antiquity did not think of ethics as having to do with moral right and wrong. It was religion, and the advent of Christianity in particular which, for better or worse, injected that distinction into philosophical ethics. The moral philosophy of the ancients revolved, instead, around the concepts of virtue, happiness, and justice. But to this one must immediately add that their understanding of these three concepts was vastly different and profounder than ours—so different, in fact, that it is difficult for a modern reader to study the ancient moralists without thorough misunderstanding. And this is true not only of philosophical novices. Indeed, I have seen philosophers of standing, who earned their livelihood teaching that subject, who supposed, for example, that Aristotle, in his application of the doctrine of the mean, was trying to draw a distinction between right and wrong!

Our misunderstanding of the ancients thus arises from two sources. The first is that we read into their writings our own conceptions of ethics, which have a religious rather than a philosophical origin. We thus suppose them to be addressing themselves to questions which were remote, not only from their interests, but from their comprehension. The profoundly unfortunate result of this is that we tend to think of the writings of the ancient moralists as primitive, as mere adumbrations of a subject that awaited sophisticated development by modern thinkers. I call this profoundly unfortunate because it blinds us not only to the treasures that this classical literature contains, but to the worthlessness of most modern ethics. It is the modern efforts at philosophical ethics that are primitive and vacuous, and we have no chance of improving upon the ancients without at least first understanding them.

The other source of our misunderstanding is, of course, that the basic concepts upon which the moral philosophies of the ancients rested have become so trivialized in our thinking that we have little appreciation of what they were talking about. This is especially true of the concepts of virtue and happiness. Most persons today, for example, even including philosophers, would find nothing terribly incongruous in saying of some man that, while he might be uneducated and poor, and unable to point to any significant personal achievement, he might nevertheless be a *good* man—a description that would have been totally incomprehensible to Aristotle. Similarly, most persons today, including even philosophers, would probably see nothing inherently funny in describing a child, or even a moron, as *happy*. Indeed, there are even philosophers who speak of happiness as if it were a *feeling*. And so, equipped with no better understanding than this, it is no wonder that the profundity of the ancients should be so largely lost to us.

I shall now undertake three tasks.

First, I shall explain the basic meanings of virtue, happiness, and justice, as these figured in the writings of the ancients, and note how watered down the first two of these ideas have become.

Second, I shall explain the basic meanings of the terms right and wrong, and indicate how the idea of moral right and wrong found its way into philosophy. In doing so, I shall suggest that this distinction is quite worthless and offers no hope for enlightenment in the area of philosophical ethics.

And finally, I shall enter a plea for the ancients, urging that we not merely try to understand and appreciate their moral philosophies, but that we resume what they undertook. More precisely, I shall urge that we once and for all expunge from our thinking the ideas of moral right and wrong, ideas that have led and will continue to lead to nothing but darkness and vain meddling in the affairs of other people and cultures, and turn instead to the ideas of virtue and happiness. The third idea from antiquity, that of justice, I shall leave aside, first because it seems to me, as I think it did to the ancients, the less important one, and second, because people today, including philosophers who are supposed to be wise, seem incapable of talking about justice without infecting the idea with those very moral overtones which I have urged that we get rid of.

The concept of virtue.—Virtue to the ancients meant personal excellence, that is, individual strength or superiority. Thus a virtuous man was not, as we tend to think of him, one who merely fits in with or accommodates himself to others, or who poses no kind of threat. He was, on the contrary, someone who stands out as superior to others, someone who is quite literally better than others, uncommon, noble, and therefore deserving of honor in a sense in which others are not. We, unlike the ancients, think of virtue as the expression of a benevolent will, such that a virtuous person is marked by selflessness and kindness. He is one who puts the interests of others equal to his own, great virtue being a devotion to the interests and needs even of strangers or, sometimes, even of enemies. Such personal meekness comes very close to being the antithesis of the virtue of the classical moralists. For them virtue was the expression, not of a good heart, but of a good mind, such that a virtuous man is identified by his resourcefulness, his powers of achievement, his stature as a thinker and planner or, in a word, his rationality in the broadest sense. A man of virtue was to the ancients a man of special worth, and was to be contrasted, not with the vicious, as we would think of him, but with the worthless. Thus while our model of a person bereft of virtue would most likely be a criminal, the type of person most likely to occur to the ancients would be the slave, the "living tool," as Aristotle described him, the worthless person.

Misunderstanding of the ancients is thus especially acute with respect to their concept of a *good man*. These words instantly evoke in us a certain image, together with an automatic approval, but the image is quite the opposite of what would be intended by the writer if he were a Greek. Contemporary people would have no difficulty in pointing to masses of the meek, ignorant, and dispossessed and saying, with sincerity, that each and every one might be just as good as the best of us and every bit as deserving. Indeed, modern moralists are quite capable of declaring that they want nothing for themselves which they do not also want for others, even for the least among them. This would have seemed to the Greeks, if not self-contradictory, then at least sick and perverse. To see this, imagine Aristotle's reaction if someone were to point to his slaves and say, with a straight face, that each and every one of them is as good a human being as Aristotle himself. I believe one has to dwell on this image for awhile in order to appreciate its absurdity.

Aristotle's *Nicomachean Ethics* abounds with illustrations of the points just made, but so do the philosophies of the Stoics and the portrayals exhibited in Plato's *Dialogues*. To cite a small but revealing example from Aristotle,[1] it will be recalled that he reserves his third kind of friendship, friendships of "the good," to men of outstanding virtue, and declares such friendships to be rare, precisely because those capable of it are so few. Common people are incapable of such friendship because, being common, they lack the requisite excellence. When Aristotle says of such friends that each must be "good," the modern reader almost automatically misunderstands him to be speaking of how such men treat each other, which is a total distortion. When we see what Aristotle does mean by "a good man," we see how difficult it was for him to imagine establishing any kind of friendship with a slave or any person who is not, in his sense, *good*.

The same point arises in connection with Aristotle's famous description of the proud man, as one disdainful of common things and contemptuous of ordinary people, a man who believes, correctly, that he is deserving of great honors, but is willing to accept them only from those who are themselves of sufficient worth to render them worthy of such bestowal. Modern readers, infused with the Christian concept of virtue as including humility, tend to look upon Aristotle's description of pride as an aberration, when in fact it is simply a logical consequence of the Greek conception of virtue which seemed to him obvious.

The Stoic philosophy, which had such a profound and enduring impact on the thinking of the ancients, exhibits the same idea of virtue, that is, personal excellence.

For the Stoic this virtue was simply the only thing that mattered. Virtue was within the reach only of a truly rational man and, once he possessed it, he could not be divested of it, not even by the most calamitous misfortune. The Stoics did, to be sure, speak sometimes of duty, but if you look closely you see that this is always duty to oneself. The Stoic who comes upon the distraught man, weeping over his calamities, comforts him, but not from any prompting of the heart. He does it to prove his own goodness, once more, to himself. The virtuous man was, to the Stoic, a man whose life was so totally rational that feelings had almost no place in it.

Again, when Diogenes, confronted by Alexander the Great, asked the king whether he was "good or bad," and Alexander replied that he was "good, of course," we are tempted to read into this our own watered down conception of goodness. Alexander certainly did *not* mean that he was benevolent and kindhearted.

The Greek ideal of virtue, so different from our own, is also abundantly exhibited in the Platonic dialogues. When Socrates repeatedly wonders why the sons of virtuous men are not themselves virtuous, it is worth noting what kind of men he is referring to.[2] He is not speaking of the common run of honest and decent Athenians. Similarly, when Callicles identifies virtue with strength, that is, with personal ability and resourcefulness,[3] Socrates never really repudiates that image. Instead, he leads Callicles to the discovery that the description of such virtue is not as simple as he had supposed.

To illustrate this idea further would only be, I think, to belabor it. It is enough to say that this idea inspires virtually every page of the classical moralists' writings that have come down to us. We must not approach these writings having in mind the concept of virtue embodied in the Beatitudes. The meek and the poor in spirit were never imagined by the Greeks to be among the blessed. They were quite rightly seen as the wretched and the antithesis of any ideal of virtue that the pagan moralists were capable of imagining.

The idea of happiness.—The Greek *eudaimonia* is always translated "happiness," which is unfortunate, for the meaning we attach to the word *happiness* is thin indeed compared to what the ancients meant by *eudaimonia*. *Fulfillment* might be a better translation, though this, too, fails to capture the richness of the original term. I shall follow custom and use the term *happiness,* noting, however, how this word must be understood if it is to capture the meaning of *eudaimonia.*

The ancient moralists thought of personal happiness as something that is rare, ill-understood, and indescribably precious. It was the aim of every classical moralist to discover what this elusive happiness consists of and to point out the path to its attainment. The different post-Socratic "schools" were distinguished from each other by how they resolved these two issues. Most of the classical moralists simply assumed, quite plausibly, that nothing can be of greater importance to anyone. They further supposed that the path to this goal is a long and difficult one, filled with pitfalls, and the pursuit of it the work of a lifetime. Thus did Aristotle, expressing an attitude characteristic of the classical moralists, raise the question whether any man can really be called happy until he is dead.[4] This did not mean, of course, that the dead might be happier than the living, but that happiness is to be thought of as the blessing of one's whole lifetime. It is not something ephemeral that might be gained one day, lost the next, regained another day, lost once more, and so on. I believe it is no exaggeration to say that one cannot even begin to understand the classical moralists without an appreciation of the place of this idea in their thinking.

The concept of happiness in modern philosophy, as well as in popular thinking, is superficial indeed in comparison. Even J. S. Mill, whose strange, almost grotesque utilitarianism rests so heavily on the concept of happiness, does not bother to explore what it is. At times he even treats it as being nothing but the feeling of pleasure! Having introduced the *word,* he then hastens on, almost childishly, to try to derive from it some rule of moral obligation—a proceeding which would have left even the hedonists of antiquity totally baffled.

Nor is Mill by any means alone in this superficiality. I cannot offhand think of a single philosopher of the modern era who has even attempted what the ancient moralists took to be their paramount responsibility, namely, to ascertain the nature and conditions of personal happiness. It seems to be assumed that, since the word is in such common use, its meaning must be well understood, and hence, that it must be known by all what happiness is and how it is achieved. The fact that most people, including most of those who are envied, live out wasted lives and go to their graves never having known the kind of personal fulfillment sought by the moralists of antiquity should raise doubts whether the knowledge of what happiness is can be considered common. Nor does the fact that most persons would, if asked, probably declare themselves happy, change this. One's own happiness or lack of it is perhaps the easiest thing one can be deluded about.

Thus people speak of happy feelings, or bid each other to have a happy day, with no awareness that a valuable idea is thus trivialized. Similarly, no incongruity is seen in describing a child or even some worthless person as happy. There have even been philosophers who have spoken of happiness as if it were a feeling. Sometimes the same philosophers speak glibly of "maximizing" happiness, and think they have made a meaningful utterance, even without the least hint of what personal happiness might be, or how its achievement in even a single individual is to be ascertained. Along with this superficiality has gone a tendency to deem it presumptuous for anyone to instruct another person in such a subject. Each person, it is sometimes thought, must be the ultimate judge of his own happiness, of what it consists of and how it is attained. It would be difficult to imagine a presupposition more deadening to a spirit of inquiry, for it appears to rule out the very asking of the question most ancient moralists considered to be at the heart of all their reflections. By assuming such a position, a philosopher eliminates in advance the possibility that people might erroneously think they have achieved personal happiness. If someone sincerely declares that he has met his goal of personal happiness, then we are somehow supposed to simply take his word for it. Thus, for example, if we are shown someone who has succeeded overwhelmingly in the honest attainment of power and wealth, and who declares himself totally satisfied with what he has done and judges his life to have been happy, then we are somehow not allowed even to raise the question whether his life has not, unbeknown to him, been badly spent after all, even though this might be quite obvious to anyone of minimal wisdom. The question, "Who's to judge?" comes almost automatically to the lips of those who have not learned to reflect, who have, indeed, been taught that the quest for wisdom in this area is somehow improper. Thus do the opinions of fools come to be vested with the same importance as the profoundest and clearest reflections of the wisest men of the ages. The silliest among us thereby achieves, as if by right, the stature of an Aristotle in the realm of moral philosophy.

The idea of happiness was seldom far from the center of ancient reflections on ethics, even when the topic under consideration would seem only loosely related to it. Thus Plato's *Republic* is concerned with the nature of justice, but Plato regarded it as a potentially fatal flaw in his analysis that the guardians might fail to be happy, or that the state itself might fail in this respect.[5] In meeting that challenge he presented his own, characteristically Greek, conception of happiness as the rule of reason, both in the individual and the state. And, also characteristically, that conception of happiness coincides almost exactly with the Greek conception of virtue, giving clear meaning to the claim that happiness is not after all the reward of virtue, but virtue itself.

Aristotle identified happiness as that which all things seek,[6] but he did not imagine that he had thereby given any real content to the concept of it. To do this he resorted to an illation familiar to us from Socrates; namely, that happiness is a kind of fulfillment and, more precisely, the fulfillment of one's function as a person.[7] Not surprisingly, this again turns out to be the fulfillment of one's function as *rational,* in the Greek sense of the term; that is, as intellectual, contemplative in the ancient sense, capable of thought, reflection, creativity, and knowledge. But once again, Aristotle is not content with abstract description.[8] He describes the state of personal happiness in great detail, notes the role of "externals" in its achievement, describes how it is related to pleasure, and then finally describes at length what a genuinely happy life consists in. To do this he does not, of course, merely record the testimony of those who believe, perhaps erroneously, that they are happy. He instead describes what fulfillment must consist of for a rational being, much as a physician might describe, in terms of the idea of function, what health must consist of.

The Stoic philosophy proceeded in much the same way, but pushed to an extreme the Socratic injunction to perfect one's own soul or inner life. It is hard, Epictetus said, to combine the industry of one who values externals with the apathy of one who does not, but it is not impossible. For otherwise, he adds, it would be impossible to be happy. The Stoic happiness, like the Aristotelian and the Platonic, then turns out to be one and the same as virtue, and once attained it is secure forever quite regardless of fate.

Of course even a brief allusion to the Greek ideal of happiness would be incomplete without reference to the Epicureans. Epicurus' question was the same as that of all the ancient pagan moralists, namely: How can I make myself happy? But he departed from most moralists by identifying happiness with the cultivation of pleasant sensations and the avoidance of painful ones. The perfection of virtue and the cultivation of justice and honor were made subordinate to this. His moral philosophy thus consists of an extensive manual of instruction on how happiness, thus conceived, can be won.

One cannot fail to see that the Epicurean conception of happiness, while having some plausibility, is shallow in comparison with that of the other ancient moralists. But it is also worth noting that this ancient hedonism is not as shallow as its most famous modern version, that of J. S. Mill. Epicurus did at least undertake, through many instructive pages, to tell us how his goal might be achieved. Mill did nothing of this kind at all. He merely made the abstract claim that it is good, said almost nothing about what it consists of beyond declaring it to be pleasant, said almost nothing about how it can be won, but instead simply deduced, as he imagined, an abstract and implausible moral rule that it is our duty to increase it. It is not very clear how he convinced even himself of this strange injunction, other than by a kind of play on words, much less how he thought it would persuade anyone else.

The concept of justice.—The ancient idea of justice is far too complex for adequate discussion here, besides which it is the least important of the three concepts around which the moral philosophies of the ancients revolved. Virtue and happiness were central themes for all the classical moralists, but justice emerges in the thinking of some of them, such as the Cynics and Stoics and even the Epicureans, only as a subordinate or derivative one.

In general, the ancients entertained two quite dissimilar ideas of justice. The first was justice considered as a virtue, and the other, justice considered as custom, particularly the customs governing the sale and exchange of property.

The first idea, that of justice considered as a virtue, is well exhibited in Plato's *Republic,* where justice is identified with a certain harmonious condition of the soul. By extension, it is identified with a similar harmony within the parts of the state, or rather, of a just, good, or virtuous state. Little is said in the *Republic* concerning what the laws should be, other than identifying their source in those persons, the guardians, who embody the virtue of justice most perfectly.

The second idea, of justice considered as customary rules, is perfectly expressed by Gorgias in the Platonic dialogue named for him.[9] Gorgias, it will be recalled, defines rhetoric as the art of persuasion in matters of justice and injustice, and casually notes that the youthful students who come to him for instruction in this art can of course be presumed to know what justice is. That assertion shocked Socrates, as it does us, but probably no other Athenian of that day would have seen anything odd in it. All Gorgias was saying was that young men of good families can be presumed to know the customs of the Athenians. Socrates understood him, or rather pretended to understand him, to be ascribing to callow youth a knowledge of some ultimate and *natural* principle of justice, something which Socrates certainly made no claim to know and which he doubted anyone knew. But that idea of justice, as something fixed, true, binding on all, and having no origin in human fabrication, which is also how we tend to think of justice today, was not very familiar to the Greeks. Eventually it evolved into the idea of natural law, which is still to this day a fond notion in some quarters of philosophy and jurisprudence.

This second idea of justice as custom was also well expressed by Protagoras, who while he rhetorically ascribed its origin to "the gods," described it simply as consisting of those arts and rules, varying from one place to another, which men follow in order to make social life possible or, when the practices are good ones, which enable social life to thrive.

Again, Aristotle perfectly expresses this second idea of justice when he remarks that the gods have no concern for justice, explaining that the gods have no interest in contracts, the exchange of property, and so on.[10]

How very far modern ethical thought has departed from the thinking of the ancient moralists, and how very much it has, in my opinion, degenerated from that of our remote philosophical ancestors, is illustrated by the history of this idea. If one takes the classical Greek view of justice, so perfectly expressed by Protagoras, identifying it with the laws and practices of a given state, then it will immediately follow that justice is as variable and relative as those laws and practices themselves. One will then not be entitled to describe any such laws and practices as *unjust*. The only question that can arise concerning them is how well they work for those who live under them, or in other words, whether the laws and customs of a given society enable it to prosper and thrive. That is a kind of question that admits of a verifiable answer, but it will not enable one to villify the society in question as "unjust." Such a conception of justice, then, provides no excuse for waging war, except in defense. No nation, under this conception, can stand in moral judgment of another. Today, however, people think it perfectly acceptable to villify other nations and to threaten war against them, even when those nations pose no threat to their interests, and for no other reason than that their laws and practices are deemed somehow "unjust." We have, in other words, taken those practices and principles which suit us, and which we identify with justice, and treated them as *natural* principles, to which other nations must bend, whether they suit them or would even work for them or not. The result is nothing but mischief and the prospect of bloodshed.

Modern ethics.—Let us finally look briefly at the ideas of right and wrong around which all modern ethical philosophy resolve and which, as we have noted, are so significantly missing from the reflections of the pagan moralists of antiquity.

To speak of an action as *wrong* is to say that it is in some sense or other forbidden—for example, that it violates some rule, law, or moral principle. To say of one that it is *right* is to say that it is not in any such sense forbidden, or in other words, that it is permitted by such rules, laws, or principles. And to say that a given action is *obligatory* is to say something different still; namely, that some rule, law, or principle requires that it be done.[11]

This is, I think, perfectly obvious with respect to actions that are governed by man-made laws and customs. There can be no legal wrong that violates no actual law, nor can one have a legal obligation which no law of man imposes. In the absence of a criminal statute one can commit no crime, no matter what else might be said in condemnation. And in the same way are legal obligations, such as the obligations to pay taxes or to perform covenants, created by laws, whether these are found in the common law or in enacted legislation. In the absence of legal prohibitions one can commit homicide, but not murder; one can enter upon, but not trespass; can occupy, but not own; can take, but not steal. All such pairs of actions differ, it is obvious, *only* with respect to the existence or non-existence of laws prohibiting them.

It is the same with respect to the usually unwritten laws of custom. Mendacity, for example, is wrong even in those instances which cannot be prosecuted, for it violates a rule of custom that is valuable, imposed in non-legal ways, and generally accepted. Similarly, the obligation imposed by a pledge, such as a pledge to a church or a charity, derives from a rule of custom and is considered to be binding even when it is neither enforceable by law nor imposed by any moral rule other than custom.

So long, then, as we confine ourselves to rights, wrongs, and obligations that are merely legal or customary, keeping aside any that might be thought to be moral as well, it does seem fairly obvious that they are intelligible only as the creation of rules of some sort, that is, actual laws, or rules of custom. No sense can be made of the suggestion that someone trespasses in the absence of any law of real property, or that one can be guilty of bigamy in a society whose laws permit plural marriage, or that one can commit murder in taking a human life under conditions that are permitted by law, as in abortion.

No great acumen or philosophical reflection is necessary to see that the same must hold of *moral* right and wrong; namely, that these are relative to rules too, although here we are talking not about mere man-made custom or law, but rather moral law or, as it is more commonly called, moral principle. Even though this should be quite evident to anyone who will reflect upon it, it is probably the commonest error of contemporary ethical philosophy to disregard it. Philosophers are sometimes heard to declare, for instance, that such things as war, or enslavement, or abortion, are somehow morally *wrong,* imagining that they have said something meaningful and significant even in the absence of any reference to any moral principles that forbid them. No one would fail to see the absurdity in someone's asserting the existence of a *legal* obligation in the absence of any actual law that would impose it. Why, then, is the absurdity less apparent when one moves to the level of moral obligations and rules? Suppose, for example, someone claiming to be versed in the law were to suggest that people have an obligation to file income tax returns even in a society, such as Saudi Arabia, whose laws impose no such taxes. Such a suggestion would surely be met by laughter. Without the rule, there can be no corresponding obligation. Why then, one wonders, does a philosopher imagine that he can speak of some *moral* obligation—such as, for instance, some presumed obligation to make other persons happy—without feeling any need to justify or even refer to any moral principle that might yield such an obligation? Yet this does constantly happen. Persons well versed in philosophy are sometimes heard rendering moral judgments upon this and upon that, out of thin air, without hint of any reference to any moral rules. They seem to expect those around them simply to nod agreement, when the appropriate response would again be laughter.

If this is so—that is, if moral judgments are meaningful only in the context of moral rules or principles—then any philosopher approaching ethics in this way has got to tell us what those moral principles are *and* where they come from. We know where laws come from, namely, from human legislators, and there are established ways of discovering what those laws are. Similarly, we know where customs originate. They are human inventions sometimes, but not always, created in response to certain needs. They are then transmitted by acculturation and constitute the foundation of the popular or conventional ethics familiar to all. But with respect to the moral rules and principles that are supposed to transcend both human laws and customs, I believe it is fair to say we do *not* know where they are supposed to come from, or how they are to be known. It was once generally believed that they come from God, conceived as a supreme lawgiver. The classical moralists did not entertain such a view, but the Christians who followed them did, and many religious persons throughout the world still do. Such people have no difficulty giving meaning to the ideas of moral right and wrong. Modern philosophical moralists do not trace such distinctions to divine command, however, and in the absence of any other source it is difficult to see how the moral laws or principles upon which such distinctions must rest can be presumed to exist at all. It is therefore doubtful whether there is or can be any such thing as philosophical ethics, as that subject is understood today. Philosophers can, to be sure, *make up* moral principles, to their hearts' content, and have in fact done so with great abandon. The result is that we have a wide selection from which to choose, ranging from the categorical imperative of Kant to the greatest happiness principle of Mill. Or we can do what these authors have done and fabricate some new rule of our own, one that will enable us to praise as "morally right" those actions we happen to approve of and to condemn as "wrong" those we happen to dislike. But to note this is, I believe, equivalent to saying once more that there is no such thing as philosophical ethics, if that discipline is supposed to be concerned with the ideas of moral right and wrong and moral obligation. A subject matter whose content differs according to what philosophical author one happens to read, who can do no more in the defense of his favorite rule of morality other than to enunciate it, is hardly a discipline worthy of being taken seriously.

Shall we, then, abandon ethics as an area of philosophical inquiry? Hardly. We need only abandon the vain and pointless philosophical ethics that concerns itself with such empty concepts as moral right and wrong and moral obligation. But there still remains the ethics of virtue, which is philosophical ethics in its original form. It is an area of inquiry that is vast and profound. The ancients wrote thoughtfully and incisively on such things as happiness, virtue, honor, pride, friendship, and, in general, the rational life. I suggest that it is way past time to return to themes such as these, with the hope that philosophers might again live up to their name as lovers of wisdom.

Notes

1. *NE* 8.1156b.
2. *Protagoras* 320; *Meno* 93.
3. *Gorgias* 483.
4. *NE* 1100a10.
5. *Republic* 419–420.
6. *NE* 1097a15–30.
7. Ibid., 1095b15–30, 1098a5–15.
8. Ibid., 1097a20–30.
9. *Gorgias* 460.
10. *NE* 1178b10.
11. It is the lasting value of Kantian ethics to have insisted that obligations are derivative from rules, commands, or "imperatives."

The Structure of Virtue

R. B. BRANDT

We think a man's virtue may (partially) explain his action. "He would not have done this if he had not been courageous"—or compassionate, and so on. A virtue, then, is often, if not always, some feature of a person which, at least partially, can *explain* his intentional behavior (often also his emotions and thoughts). Aristotle says "virtue . . . is a state of character concerned with choice."[1] In what follows I want to defend a part (only) of Aristotle's spelling out of his view on this. A virtue, he says, is a settled state of the person which is *manifested* in emotions (he mentions desire, anger, fear, confidence, joy, friendship, etc.[2]), some of these involving an appetitive element (e.g., fear involving a desire for safety[3]), the emotions being "in a mean . . . determined by a rational principle" which a person of practical wisdom would identify.[4] Again, he says that virtuous *acts* must be chosen for their own sakes and "proceed from a firm and unchangeable character."[5] I omit the part about emotions and virtue being in a mean. What I want to defend is his view that a virtue is a (certain kind of) relatively unchanging disposition to desire an action of a certain sort (e.g., helping one in distress, not stealing) for its own sake.[6]

Before trying to answer our question what a virtue is, let us look at the picture of the determinants of action with which motivation theory and common sense provide us.

I. A SKETCH OF THE DETERMINANTS OF BEHAVIOR

Let me preface my account of this theory by observing that, while this theory is widely accepted by writers on the theory of motivation (and in other social sciences) as an empirical supposition (and not a thesis about what is rational), it may be only an approximation to the truth: further knowledge about the physiology of the brain, and more detailed knowledge of the phenomenology of action may require modifications and additions. Moreover, the theory is only partially quantitative, and hence does not compare with physics for confirmability. However, the theory at present stands as follows:

First, the theory holds that intentional (not reflex or "instinctive" or habitual) behavior is restricted to options the agent thinks, at the time of choice, are open to him. Second, action is influenced by the agent's view, at that time, of the consequences of his behavior (counting the kind of act as itself a consequence—and one consequence could be the deviation of an action from preexisting intention), and how likely these consequences are, given the act. Third, the action is a function of the "valence" (being desired or aversive), at the moment of decision or action, of the complex act-plus-consequences, that is, of the intensity of the desires (or aversions) toward members of this complex, including the force of any already established intentions. Finally, it is influenced by the salience of one or more features of the situation as apprehended, whether clearly before the mind, or only dimly so. We might break all this down as follows.[7]

Say that an agent's *tendency,* at a given time, to perform a given act is a sum: the sum of the intensity of his desire/aversion toward any consequence of that action (as explained above), reduced by the subjective improbability of its occurring if the action is performed, and reduced again by the lack of salience of that consequence and its relation to action in the awareness of the agent—the sum over all the anticipated consequences of the act. Then we can affirm that what an agent actually does is adopt whichever option is the one he has, at that time, the strongest *tendency* to adopt—for which this sum is greatest.[8]

This is not to say that an action follows automatically, according to this function, from all the agent's *dispositional* beliefs roughly at the time of action. To say this would be to ignore the fact that dispositional beliefs may not all be before the mind at the time of choice, and, among other things, to overlook the role of deliberation. Usually one option open is to postpone decision and reflect further. The deliberation which follows may eliminate some options for one reason or another. When more deliberative procrastination has become aversive, one chooses among the remaining alternatives on the basis of the salient beliefs about them—in consciousness or in short-term memory, and salient—at the moment of decision, and the valences (at the time) of the expected consequences (including the action itself). There is reason, however, to doubt that all choice-reflection is that simple.[9] Whether the valences are always consciously represented is doubtful; at least it seems hard to deny the influence of unconscious desires.

Many philosophers who would not question the above as a piece of psychology would want a good many details filled into the above sketch. What the details should be is controversial. But something like the following is probably as near as we can get to an agreed view. First, it will be said that the tendency to adopt a particular course of action strongest for a person (in view of all the factors described above) will *result* in the formation of an *intention*—acquisition of a disposition to follow a relevant plan of action. (Some philosophers have said that an intention *is just* an everything-considered preference or pro-attitude toward an action plan, as compared with alternatives;[10] but others would insist that formation of an intention is more than this, partly because intentions persist and mold future plans.[11]) This intended plan of action will presumably fix when it should be executed, and when that time is (believed to be) *now* the agent will (possibly partly just because of the intention, but also supported by the underlying desire for the outcome and possibly antecedent intentions) begin to execute the plan by trying, or willing, to bring about an initial *basic* bodily action (one he can bring about without it being caused by some other bodily action)—a "willing" sometimes thought of as being the focusing of attention on the prospective basic action or a prescription of it ("Do so-and-so now!"), and perhaps involving an image of the sensations characteristic of the intended movement, any of which will, with the cooperation of the nervous system, cause the intended action. This basic action will set an appropriate next stage of the action, or even produce the wanted outcome.[12] (If one wants more light in the room, the act of pulling the drapes aside will be enough.) The intention will, unless there is a change of mind, remain through the period necessary for reaching the desired outcome, monitoring the sequence of actions in view of the feedback resulting from earlier members of the sequence, and other information.

All of the foregoing can be construed in a way compatible with the major theories of the relation of body and the mental. It appears, however, to be an analytic reduction of what it is for "the self" to act. All of this is consistent with holding that, directly or indirectly, acts are caused by a complex of beliefs and desires/aversions.

How might virtues possibly fit into such an account? Obviously, it could be that a virtue is a relatively permanent *desire or aversion* (or complex of these) directed at some action-type and/or some expectable kind of consequence of an action (which can be included in the description of the action, e.g., helping the distressed), with a strength up to a certain (acceptable) level, and furthermore being good in some sense.

But what are desires and aversions? These are (unlike longing) not primarily introspectible "felt" items of experience. A person is said to "desire" some situation S if his belief that S will occur if he does a certain thing will increase his tendency to do that.[13] This proposal may seem to render analytic the above statement that a person's tendency to act is a function of his desires/aversions; but in fact it does not, in view of the fact that the above statement says, not that a tendency to act is a function of one's desires/aversions simply, but only of these in conjunction with subjective probability judgments and degree of salience. In any case there are other features of a desire which suffice to make the statement synthetic. For example, when one thinks of something one wants, the thought of it tends to have an attractive aura.[14] Or, if a desire is frustrated (and its intensity above a certain level), one will experience some discomfort, like thirst, what Karl Duncker called "the sorrow of want."[15] Again, if one wants a given situation but has been in doubt whether it will occur, information that it will occur (provided the desire has a certain level of intensity) will cause joy. Conversely, if one has believed that the situation will occur, but then hears that it will not, she will (provided the desire is strong) feel disappointed. Moreover, the occurrence of a desired event of the kind E, or the belief that it has occurred, tends to be pleasant. Again, if one desires E, one will tend to notice possibilities for getting it, maybe daydream pleasantly about its occurrence. Further, at least in the case of physical desires (hunger, thirst, sex, etc.) there is a satiation effect: when an event of the kind E occurs, all the symptoms of the desire vanish, for a time (to recur after a certain time interval), and indeed desires for related states of affairs are diminished—as, for instance, when consumption of some item of food reduces interest in other kinds of food. This last feature is not wholly limited to physical desires: it seems that a desire for the company of others, and a desire for expressions of approval or admiration by others, also vanish after satiation, and recur after an interval (varying with the individual person).[16]

Aversions are a bit different: an aversion to S is not exactly a desire for *non-S*, although a person is said to have an aversion to S if his belief that S will occur if he does a certain thing will increase his tendency *not* to do that thing. (We should note that one can find an experience like a shock or a bad odor aversive now, but one can also have an aversion now to some kind of event *as mentally represented,* occurring in the future or elsewhere.) An example is having an aversion to one's child being injured or to being thought stupid. To some degree, the concept of aversion is the mirror image of the concept of desire, except that desires aim at a target, whereas aversions are aimed at just getting away from something, anywhere.[17] If one thinks of an event occurring to which one has an aversion, one may feel repugnance at the idea (not an "attractive aura"); but in the case of aversion it appears there is no parallel to the "sorrow of want" which occurs when there is frustrated desire. If one has been in doubt whether an aversive event will occur, and one learns that it will not, one will feel relief (provided the aversion is strong)—not be pleased, as would be true if there were a desire for *non-S*—but the aversion is not a desire for this feeling of relief. If one has been expecting it wouldn't occur, but learns that it will, one will be (provided the aversion is strong) disturbed. But, different from the case of desire, one normally does not reflect on what might produce any one of various possible aversive events, or daydream (unpleasantly) about them. (One could, if some one of highly aversive events is threatening; but there is normally not motivation to have unpleasant daydreams.) And there is no satiation effect reducing aversions toward events of the same general kind, when an aversive event has occurred (though repetition reduces dislike, and there is some recovery of the dislike after a time-lapse[18]).

With this contrast in mind, it might make sense to say that an agent may have an *aversion* to acting dishonestly, or deceptively, but less obviously a positive desire to act honestly and truthfully. The virtue of benevolence might be a *desire* to give to others, and the virtue of compassion might be a desire to help—or to see others help—those in severe need. (Alternatively, one might say one has an *aversion* to other persons suffering, and hence a tendency to help relieve it—perhaps arising out of the emotion of pity, along a line suggested by Aristotle.) Again, one might have an *aversion* to unfairness: failure to adhere to standards of truthfulness in a trial, or lack of correspondence between merit and reward, or of equal consideration of persons, and so on. A virtue might be a desire for some action or state of affairs just for itself and not for any further reason—in that sense an intrinsic desire—and so like a desire for achievement or for human company; or it could be an aversion to some state of affairs like stealing, or telling lies, also for no further reason; and it could be both. (We might speculate that when Kant spoke of acting out of "respect" for the moral law, what he should have had in mind was an intrinsic *aversion* to acting in disconformity with moral law.)

The strength of these desires/aversions will presumably vary from one person to another. As we shall see, such desires/aversions will not be called "virtues" unless they are thought good in some sense, and their strength reaches a certain acceptable level.

If we speculate that what are usually regarded as virtues can, at least some of them, be so conceived, we can ask about the corresponding vices. It would seem that, in the case of at least some of the aversions, the corresponding vice is just *lack* of the aversion; for instance, dishonesty or mendacity seems to consist in just lack of an aversion to theft or deception. Dishonest people normally do not desire dishonesty for itself, only behavior expected to lead to wanted outcomes, which they know is dishonest. And in the case of compassion, again lack of aversion to the suffering of others seems enough—a person is said to be "lacking in compassion." However, in the case of benevolence the vice would seem to be a contrary desire: malevolence, a desire for others to be unfortunate. (A person might, however, be thought to have a vice if he merely wholly lacks benevolence.) Things are more complex with the virtues of courage and self-control, as we shall see.

Most of these motivations are concerned in some way with interactions with other persons. But there are other relatively unchanging motivations: for instance, ambition. "Ambitious" might be explained, following the Random House Dictionary, as "eagerly desirous of obtaining power, superiority, or distinction." This concept is obviously motivational.

There are some interesting personality traits, affecting action or at least a style of behavior, which do not obviously fit easily into this pattern: gentleness, grouchiness, sulkiness. The behavior patterns characteristic of these traits are obvious enough, but it is not clear what the motivation is. Possibly these are not dispositions having to do with *intentional* action, but are just traits of personality (not of character), dispositions of some other kind.

Somewhat the same may be said for intelligent behavior, behavior showing at least an average ability to be aware of a full range of options, an ability to identify their probable consequences with a justified belief about the likelihood of the consequences on the agent's evidence, an ability to represent all this vividly. This capacity cannot be analyzed motivationally. Intelligence in behavior instantiates a *capacity,* one which to some extent can be learned. (There may be, of course, motivation to think, to try to balance valenced consequences, etc.) Aristotle was right in distinguishing intellectual from practical virtues. (He would also classify wisdom as an intellectual virtue; I shall discuss wisdom below.) Let us call such qualities "intellectual excellences."

So much, initially, for the concept of a motivational analysis of various nonintellectual kinds of virtue.

II. IS SELF-CONTROL A MOTIVATIONAL VIRTUE?

According to G. H. von Wright, virtues are not dispositions at all, hence not dispositions of the kind desires/aversions (roughly) are. The master virtue is "Self-control . . . [which is] a feature of character which helps a man never to lose his head, be it for fear of pain or for lust after pleasure, and always lets his action be guided by a dispassionate judgment as to that which is the right thing for him to do."[19] Von Wright does not explain what he means by "character," not considering, apparently, that a motivational theory of character is possible. What is self-control? Perhaps, as we shall see, it can be given a motivational analysis.

A more restricted proposal is made by R. C. Roberts, to the effect that at least *some* virtues are *capacities* whereby to "resist adverse inclinations."[20] "The most important distinction between kinds of virtues is that between the virtues of will power and those that are substantive and motivational"[21] (the latter, including honesty and compassion, being those of which roughly a desire/aversion account can be given). The virtues of will power are "capacities to manage our inclinations,"[22] are "skills of self-management." Exercise of these is a matter of the agent's own "achievement, his own choice, and thus reflects credit on him as an agent."[23] That they are skills is shown by the fact that they can be learned, by instruction, as a child learns self-control by being advised to put off minor gratifications for a short period of time, gradually enlarging the time-span and the scope.[24] Emotions can be controlled by learning to act contrary to their behavioral impulses, and by "self-talk," e.g., "the power of positive thinking."[25] (But, as we shall see, desires/aversions can also be learned, and the details about how to do so can be fitted into a belief-desire framework.)

Similarly, Stephen Hudson says that a virtuous person "must be principled and must have the capacity, the strength of will, to act as he should despite temptations."[26]

Again, James Wallace says some virtues are tendencies or *capacities,* that are *not* skills, to act in ways that constitute living well as a human being.[27] They involve a "positive capacity for acting rationally when certain motives are apt to incline us to do otherwise."[28] Thus courage is a capacity or tendency to overcome excessive (disabling) fear, as temperance (self-control) is a capacity or tendency to overcome disabling indulgence in easy pleasures. But, *in contrast,* some virtues like honesty, veracity, fidelity, and fairness are intrinsic (in the sense of not being for any further reason, such as self-interest) desires/aversions, different from just a desire to maximize one's own benefit, toward certain forms of behavior—so fitting in with a motivation theory. There are other clearly motivational virtues: of kindness, generosity, humaneness, and compassion—all involving a direct concern for the happiness and well-being of others.

The question I wish to raise about these writers is whether their conception of the relation of self-control (and courage) to motivation is probably correct. Can the former be explained in terms of the latter? Let us consider self-control.

There are various areas in which we think self-control is often called for: to restrain indulgence too often or inappropriately in eating, liquor, sex, and watching television; to avoid losing control of oneself in emotional states like anger, grief, or fear; to avoid self-gratifications like those involved in boasting or putting other persons down; to overcome a tendency to daydream or be distracted when trying to work. Persons are often so aware of deficiency in self-control in these areas that they seek therapeutic advice.

We should notice that there is motivation here, even in those dissatisfied with the degree of their self-control—enough to seek therapy and try to follow a constructive program. The motivation is usually specific: to overcome bad eating habits, alcoholism, losing one's temper.

Since there is motivation here, why is therapeutic advice necessary? The answer seems to be that goals, like that of being self-controlled or even weighing only 115 pounds, being either remote in time or abstract, are not, relatively, strongly motivating. Whether this is a basic fact, or a result of difficulty in visualizing vividly, we need not try to decide. (Psychologists seem not to have an opinion on this.) Much more is this the case with a recollection that one has judged a constrained line of action to be "the best thing to do," in some sense or other—a situation which is essentially the problem of "akrasia." Even if it is supposed that "is best" serves, as the internalist will have it, to express an overall preference for that course of action, a judgment that some action "is best" may be "remote" in the sense of being a recollection of an *earlier* judgment. If the "is best" judgment, in the suggested internalist sense, is made *now,* then what is judged best may of course be done, but the fact of experience, that we sometimes fail to do something at the very moment we are judging that it would be "best," is some evidence that "is best" at most expresses a strong motivation but not an overall preference.

What does the therapist do to help? The kind of "treatment" recommended varies somewhat depending on the particular problem. To control eating habits, it is agreed that there should be adoption of a program of sub-goals, one for each day, and, if possible, involvement of others (in a "weight-watchers" group) and making a pledge to them to submit periodic progress reports. Moreover, the plan should include daily evaluations of how well one is succeeding, and rewards for oneself, for success, either by some indulgence (going to a movie to celebrate) or at least by congratulating oneself verbally. How does all this work? Well, first, motivation to abstain may not be strong enough to adhere to a long-range program, but possibly be sufficient for success just today; moreover, this motivation will be supported by one's explicit resolution and the pledge to others (not to mention the anticipated shame in having to confess one's failure). Moreover, reinforcement by rewards will enhance motivation to adhere to the program, including the long-range target. Furthermore, the agent will often have sought therapy because he is convinced he cannot manage on his own, and if he is convinced there is something he cannot do, the motivation to do it will be less effective (the goal seeming not probable). The day-to-day success, however, will change this view, being replaced by the thought that he can cope with the problem.[29]

For other problems, like loss of temper, a slightly different regimen may be recommended. First, it is suggested that the agent take two or three deep breaths, when he gets angry, before doing anything. (It is not too much to be motivated to do this.) This gives time to think. Second, the agent is invited to notice the internal talk that tends to arise in such situations, such as "He's trying to push me around again, and I'm not going to stand for it!" which raise the level of anger. The agent is urged, after having noticed this, to substitute different thoughts: about what the problem really is, what actions he can take, how well he will like the probable consequences of each. He is then to adopt a plan of action. (His desire to vent his anger may not be strong enough to prevent these steps from being taken.) In all this, he will be motivated by the thought of self-censure if he fails. And, afterwards, he will evaluate how successful he has been in following the adopted plan. If he has been successful, he will reward himself, as in the previous case, and have his sense of ability to cope enhanced.

After a time, the self-rewards can be "faded," the meetings with weight-watchers dropped. So what is the resulting motivational situation? This seems unclear: perhaps the temptation of suboptimal behavior has lessened, or perhaps the moving power of one's motives not to overeat, or to avoid losing one's temper, has been strengthened.[30] (My own experience is that the attractiveness—in prospect, not necessarily enjoyment of the act—of consuming chocolates diminishes after three or four weeks.) Whichever it is, it appears that the "problem" calling for self-control has been abolished: "temptations" are no longer stronger than the desire to reduce, not to give vent to one's anger, etc.

Will such regimens tend to establish a *general* trait of "self-control"—adequate motivation, in case one recognizes *any* inclination to an immediate and pleasurable good which conflicts with beliefs about what one "ought" to do or is "best" for one to do, to do the latter? Some psychologists doubt whether such a general trait develops, wondering how much *generalization* there will be as a result of the "training"; but there is some suggestion that the idea of self-control may become a part of a person's ego-ideal.[31] Of course, it is possible that a person master the temptation to eat, but not master the temptation to watch television when he knows he should be working. So he can act akratically in one area, but not in another. We might say a person is not akratic, but self-controlled, if he is not akratic *in as many types of situations* as the average person is.

The writers cited above seem to be right in distinguishing the role of motivation in "self-control" from motivations such as manifest truthfulness or sympathy. How much difference is there? One difference is in the specificity of the target: in the latter cases one is motivated to avoid telling lies, and to help other people. In the former, there is initially inadequate motivation to do what the agent thinks he "ought" to do, followed by adoption of a plan for specific situations, with rewards, and then development of motivation so that the problem calling for self-control does not exist (and possibly generalization to a general motive of self-control). So there is some difference between the type of *plural* motivation (plural in the sense of relatively stronger motivation to this, and that) characteristic of "self-control" and that of these other virtues; but it is not true that self-control is not "motivational"—there has been learned a total motivational situation so that motives effective in controlling specific kinds of situations have been established.[32] Incidentally, the other virtues may be somewhat more like such self-control than at first appears: e.g., if sympathy is stronger for some types of situations than for others where it does not lead to helping behavior.

There seems to be phenomenological support for a further observation about self-control (and other virtues). For there are things we want, like sensory pleasures, the company of other people and their respect, and it is easy to think of desire for these things as controlling behavior. We actually seem to feel the pull of such opportunities.[33] The same for many states of affairs to which we are averse. We do not like electric shocks, or drinking castor oil, or visiting a dentist. Here, again, we seem to feel an aversive push. But there are also things we do not do by inclination, where, as

James said, we seem to be acting "in the line of greatest resistance."[34] I want to eat a sweet, but control my impulse by reflection on the undesirability of more weight. I want to go to a party, and can hear the good time everyone is having; but I do not because I know I need a good night's sleep in order to be in shape for demanding tasks tomorrow. I want to help myself to another piece of cake, but desist because I know other guests will be arriving later. These cases seem very different from refraining to act because I have an aversion to shocks, castor oil, or public criticism. In the latter cases I may feel a "pushing" inclination to avoid imminent personal discomfort. In the former cases this is not true: at least there is nothing aversive or uncomfortable *now,* or in some cases even a personal loss at all, about later getting too little sleep, putting on more weight, and allowing late-arriving guests to go without goodies. There is no "felt" desire involved.

Nevertheless this phenomenon has been stated too simply. When self-control (courage, etc.) is involved, a choice is being made between two options. If we assume the main idea of the belief-desire theory of motivation, we shall hold that a person always does (roughly) what he *prefers* to do. How is it possible that a person *prefer* (viz., be *more motivated* to do, or get) something that does not promise enjoyment, or the avoidance of pain, now, to something which does? How is it possible for one's own long-range good, or the well-being of others, to be a motivating consideration? Well, presumably there is some brain *representation* of a future state of affairs—expressible in either images or concepts—that is motivating. (The representation may be of outcomes of a kind of action, or the kind of action itself.) So one can ask, must a representation be of something that is an immediate or pleasurable good (or an immediate or unpleasant bad), and be *felt* as an inclination, in order to be motivating? If not, if behavior can be otherwise motivated, then we have to say that *felt* inclinations are not all that important as indicators of effective causal processes, and of course we shall want a story about how this is.

How in particular can we be averse to acting dishonestly—perhaps with no felt aversive push at all, of the sort we feel when we consider drinking castor oil? The most plausible view is that the *representation* has become motivating as a result of conditioning by prior pleasant or unpleasant (or other) experiences. Take, for example, the case of giving aid or avoiding lies. The best explanation seems to be that, for evolutionary-survival reasons, young children are *natively* motivated to relieve the perceived distress of others—and the cries of distress are distressful to them. When they relieve the distress, the relief of their own distress reinforces the behavior of relieving the distress of others—representation of the goal of relief of distress becomes more strongly motivating. This motivation is supported by the praise of others (or criticism if the individual ignores the distress of others); and there is further support from observation of others with whom the agent identifies. Then, as a result perhaps of parental explanations, the motivating force of relieving distress spreads, by conditioning, to bring about intrinsic motivation not to lie, or act dishonestly, in view of the fact that these behaviors are normally hurtful.[35] So there is a proliferation of aversions—a result of conditioning by association—supported by praise or blame, and by identifications. The development of sympathy (and empathy), then, has a major role to play in the development of moral aversions.[36] (Of course, response to categories like truthfulness—"That would be deceptive"—requires development of corresponding concepts.) Thus we can see how it can be that the idea of certain behavior or its consequences is attractive—the representation of that behavior, or its consequences, motivating—even though the representation is not of some pleasant or immediate good or ill, and there is possibly no felt pull of inclination at all.[37]

This phenomenon needs to be unpacked a bit further. When some representation of an option for action is aversive enough so that the individual "prefers" to act in a self-controlled way, nevertheless there may be left a feeling of regret for the pleasures, or safety, foregone; *that* is why we feel, in James' terms, that we are "acting in the line of greatest resistance."[38] This feeling makes us think we are *not* doing what we *prefer* to do, but what is shown is simply that such feelings are not necessarily a guide to what is really motivating.

This view, and the foregoing account of how one "learns" self-control may be contrasted with that of Aristotle (and St. Thomas[39]), to the effect that virtues are learned by habit—perhaps by parents inducing a child to act in a certain way, with the effect that he finds acting in that way pleasant (perhaps we should say, more accurately, not irksome[40]), and then in some sense sees the point of it all—that such a life is best.[41]

It can be that two persons may have differing degrees of self-control or sympathy although both are called "self-controlled" or "sympathetic." But the success of one person may be less frequent than that of another, owing to the different degrees of strength and the specific directions of the motivation.

III. ARE ALL THE VIRTUES MOTIVATIONAL?

We have noticed that various writers agree that some traits naturally invite a motivational analysis, that is, invite the view that to have the trait is for the person to be motivated positively or negatively toward a represented situation. Thus for sympathy/compassion, generosity, honesty, veracity, promise-keeping, apparently justice and conscientiousness. These are what R. C. Roberts called "substantive" virtues.[42] But I concede that other virtues, at least at first glance, appear to be different: virtues like self-control, and perhaps courage, patience, reliability, perseverance, industry, tolerance. I have now made a general proposal to the effect that the virtue of "self-control" can be viewed as motivational—a (plural) motivation to abstain in the face of contrary motivations, of sexual desire, appetite, or whatever. But let us look now at some others from these apparently nonmotivational virtues, and see how they may be construed, whether like compassion, or like self-control, or different from both.

Let us begin with courage, which Random House defines as "the quality of mind that enables one to encounter difficulties and dangers with firmness or without fear." Courage is obviously a quality one shows in situations that are thought to be dangerous. Is courage a matter of confidence? If confidence means confidence in one's own skills, it would seem not; for if one is a skilled boxer he knows that there is not really danger if he gets involved in a street-fight; so courage is not called for. It is, however, clear that we all have an aversion to death, being wounded, loss of status to a significant degree, or a significant risk of these. In the case of some persons, this aversion is so strong that it overcomes any desire for a course of action which risks the danger, however important doing so is for personal or social well-being. Such persons are cowards. This is not to say that a person is courageous if he sets *no* store at all by the safety of his person or status; a person who sets no store by safety is simply foolhardy or insensitive. How much store can a courageous person set by safety? The answer seems to be that the coward sets more store by personal safety than we think proper, although one person might identify a "satisfactory" level of concern for safety differently from another. A courageous man is one whose aversion to danger and risk of disaster is not all consuming; at least his concern for important things, such as principles, duty, the protection of his family, his own long-term goals, and so on, are sufficiently strong, and his aversion to danger relatively sufficiently weak, that he faces the danger and risk nevertheless (when it is worth it).

But perhaps this sketch is too unspecific, and there is no *one* trait (or motivation) which distinguishes the courageous from the cowardly. Perhaps courage is a trait only in the sense in which there is a (plural) trait of self-control, and which we acquire in much the way depicted above for self-control—and courage might be viewed as a *form* of self-control. I speculate that in fact this is the case, and that many of the phenomena we noted about self-control and learning it have parallels for the case of courage—although there are differences, because fear is not an appetite like desire for chocolate, but an emotionally qualified aversion to danger.

We know that some people fear high places, being in a crowd, giving a talk in public. How do people get to overcome these fears, when they do? Work done by psychologists to overcome fear seems restricted to situations that, in fact, are not dangerous, whatever the patient may think. Such persons are motivated to go to psychologists, either because they dislike fear or because it is disabling, for instance if a person is unable to go to his job because of agoraphobia. So there is motivation to overcome fear all right. Now the therapist does not simply give stern injunctions to behave properly. He proceeds by stages. If the person is, say, afraid of snakes, he may be encouraged to watch someone else fearlessly handle snakes, from a safe distance. Then, maybe next day, he is brought closer. Until finally he himself picks up a large snake, and has the exhiliration of feeling the movement of its muscles and looking it in the eye at close range. This regimen convinces a person that snakes are not dangerous, in a way no lecture could. So his fear has been reduced, and his approach has been strongly rewarded. The individual has overcome his disabling fear of snakes. Much the same for agoraphobics. They are currently treated in groups, and may board a bus as a group and ride around London. While free to leave, they remain aboard through the dynamics of group interaction. As in the case of snake-fear, they learn that being in a crowd is not harmful and can reward themselves for surviving in a crowd. There is also mutual support among members of the group. The agoraphobia gradually becomes manageable. Or, if a person is terrified at the thought of making a speech in public, again there is training by stages. First the person is trained to relax his body. When he has learned to do this, he is then instructed to imagine himself preparing to make a speech, going on the platform, and so on. The thought is that the relaxation will associate with the image of speech-making conditions, and that this will carry over—as it seems to—to the real-life situation. So, these people have gradually come to be more relaxed in these formerly disturbing situations, having learned through rewards, support from other persons, association with a relaxed bodily state, and finding that, with this training, it is possible to "cope." These methods, then, have succeeded in dissociating fear from these situations, and the person is no longer disabled by it. Obviously, however, such persons hardly qualify to be called "courageous" in general.

Suppose there is real danger, say to a soldier who is exposed to mortar fire. How does he overcome his natural fear? (I know of no psychological literature on this.) I speculate that, as in the foregoing examples, the soldier may notice that relatively few individuals are hurt by mortar fire, and will reflect that if he is hurt he will be given good care and a vacation behind the lines. He may say to himself that he will be unharmed unless "his number comes up." This somewhat less worried attitude will be strengthened by the behavior of those around him, going about their business apparently without much concern (except to take cover if the fire comes too close), and by their giving him moral support. He will discover that he can "cope"—do his work despite the threat of harm. If he is given the responsibility of being a leader, this will strengthen his attitudes—the feeling he is being depended upon. So he may become able eventually to lead an infantry charge effectively. Then is he courageous?

Unfortunately, the fears he has mastered may be specific. He may be terrified if confronted by a bayonet charge—or if not at that, too terrified to phone the attractive woman he met last night and ask her out, or to report someone's dereliction of duty to a commanding officer, or to ask for a promotion. So, just as a person may have overcome his appetite for chocolates, but not for drink or sex or self-glorification, so his "training" may enable him to carry on in the face of mortar fire, but not to do what he thinks is best for him in confronting a young lady on the telephone. How much *generalization* will there be from such learning to overcome fears of various dangers? Can a person come to a stage where, despite risks, he effectively does *whatever* he thinks is his duty, or is best for him to do? Perhaps we do not know.

Thus courage may be a "plural" virtue, like self-control. Perhaps no one is courageous in all areas, but we might say one person is more courageous than others if he faces, with firmness, more situations normally fear-arousing, than most. His motivation is strong enough to overcome his fears, as they are after treatment or experience. We do not call a person a coward if there are only some situations in which he is fearful and performs poorly, especially if they are unimportant. For all this, need we introduce some nonmotivational concept of "character-trait"?

Some of the other virtues do not obviously yield to even the foregoing kind of complex motivational analysis, possibly because it is far from clear what kind of motivation is typical of a person with the virtue: e.g., patience, perseverance, reliability. *O.E.D.* defines "patience" as "the quality or capacity of suffering or enduring of pain, trouble, or evil with calmness and composure." For those of us for whom patience is called for in nothing more than being caught in a traffic jam, it is hard to imagine what it is like to suffer pain "with composure." Perhaps what is behind this "composure" is the awareness of the disutility of crying out or complaining—reactions one knows are only annoying or disturbing to others, or looked upon by them as a sign of weakness. One could also develop a kind of stoic ideal: be motivated to avoid what disconforms with that ideal, or to do what will be disturbing to others or what will be viewed by them as weaknesses. In either case, the "composure" behavior seems motivated either by positive desire for an ideal or by aversion to the results of non-composed behavior. At least the suggestion is sensible.

What is it to be reliable? *O.E.D.* defines this as that in which "reliance or confidence may be put." Of course, this is only the case if one is talking of a general trait of character. If someone says I am not a reliable guide to the geography of the State of Michigan, he may have nothing at all in mind beyond the fact that I frequently give mistaken advice when asked questions. Matters seem different if we are speaking of someone as a reliable (or responsible) person. Here it seems not improper to think of motivation to do what others properly expect of one: that one do one's job. Or, we might say it is aversive motivation toward failing to do one's job, or what others properly expect.

IV. MORAL AND NON-MORAL VIRTUES

When should we call one of these intentional-action-explaining traits a "virtue"? I suggest that the answer is *roughly* that the trait must be one *normally and importantly favorable* either for the well-being of society (or some group thereof) or for the flourishing of the agent (or those dear to him, e.g., his family).

Of course, the term "virtue" is sometimes used very broadly, to apply to non-actional traits or even to characteristics of non-persons: for instance, we might say that it is a virtue of a certain make of automobile that it starts easily in winter, or that it is a virtue of a certain drug that it gives fast relief. And we might say of a teacher that one of her virtues is that she is an extremely lucid lecturer. What is correctly or incorrectly called a "virtue" is a subtle question of linguistic sense; but we do well in the present context to follow Aristotle and view virtue as a disposition having to do with intentional action. Only thus would we be able to regard a virtue as a trait of *character.*[43]

But what counts as a *moral* virtue? *O.E.D.* takes as the primary use of "virtue" the moral use: a disposition to conform one's conduct with principles of morality, or of recognized standards of morality such as chastity. I think we might approach the notion better by utilizing a concept of J. S. Mill. He said that when we call anything "wrong" we mean to imply "that a person ought to be punished in some way or other for doing it—if not by law, by the opinion of his fellow creatures; if not by opinion, by the reproaches of his own conscience."[44] We can drop the part about law, and say that a moral virtue is some level of some kind of desire/aversion, having to do with intentional action, manifestation of the absence of which ought to be (Mill means, it is *desirable* that it be) punished [on utilitarian grounds], either by the disapproval of others, or by the reproaches of the agent's own conscience. I should prefer to say a virtue is moral if manifestation of its absence would be punished, in this way, by a moral system a rational person would support for a society in which he expected to live. This definition, however, is a bit restrictive in explaining "moral virtue" only as motivation to produce *required* behavior. We should loosen it, I think, by adding desires/aversions the manifestation of which a rationally preferable moral system would *reward* by admiration/praise, and *encourage* self-reward by the agent in feeling pride.[45]

Normative theories, e.g., rule utilitarianism, purport to show us which motivations are moral virtues, and how relatively strong they should be, perhaps by showing that a justified moral system would require certain motivations, and admire/praise others, with an ordering of strength, because of the utility of such a system.

It is possible that different moral virtues will motivate conflicting forms of behavior, in response to a particular situation. In that case the "strongest" one will dominate action. McDowell has suggested that what happens is that one virtue "silences" the others,[46] although he should concede that the virtues which are "silenced" may well reappear in feelings of compunction (to use a term employed by Ross).[47] Such a conflict may also motivate a good deal of reflection about the situation, partly about just what its features are, but also including reflection on what the relative weight of the different virtues (desires/aversions) should be.[48]

How are the moral virtues—at least those of them which can be analyzed in motivational terms, like sympathy and honesty—related to the agent's moral commitments or principles? Lester Hunt has proposed that traits of character are dispositions to act "on principle," because of beliefs "about what is in some sense right or good" (not good only as a means). Hence, someone has a trait of character "insofar as he holds the corresponding belief and holds it on principle; insofar, that is, as he believes it and acts on it consistently.[49] For instance, he holds that a courageous action is one which is done "from the principle that one's own safety, in general, has no more than a certain level of importance."[50] A great deal depends, of course, on what is meant by a "belief about what is good or right," a concept which Hunt does not explain. Now suppose someone, in saying that something is morally obligatory, is expressing some degree of motivation to do that thing for itself and not from some personal interest, plus a disposition to feel guilty if he does not and to disapprove of others if they are not so motivated, and a belief that these attitudes are justified. Then if to have a moral belief is to have such an attitude/belief complex, one will be motivated accordingly. If one is not motivated accordingly, one does not have the "principle." So construed, we can agree with Hunt that a virtue is a disposition to act consistently in accordance with a certain principle.

But shall we say, then, that for a person to have the *virtue* of compassion is *identical* with his being motivated (etc.) with respect to the principle of aiding those in need? I think not, for two reasons. In the first place, I suggest that a virtue is *purely* motivational; one can have the virtue of sympathy without necessarily having a disposition to feel guilty if one is not motivated in a sympathetic way, or to disapprove of others who are not, or to think one's attitude is justified. (But some psychologists think there is a *causal* connection.[51]) So to say someone has a certain virtue is to say less than that the corresponding principle is part of his moral code. But second, a person can have a principle in his moral code, but only weakly. He is somewhat disposed to give aid to those who need it, but not very strongly—not enough really to put himself out. I suggest that for a person to have a certain virtue is for him, in a *normal* frame of mind, to show corresponding moral motivation up to an acceptable level.

("Acceptable" does not mean "average.") A judgment about whether a person has a given trait to an acceptable degree must take into account how the individual perceives a situation, e.g., as dangerous to him. With this, and doubtless other adjustments, we judge whether a person's trait is in the acceptable class by considering whether his behavior is acceptable in standard situations. So having a virtue is more demanding than simply to have a moral principle in the suggested sense. Of course, what is judged acceptable may differ from one person to another, and exactly what people mean by, e.g., "sympathetic," will differ accordingly. I have discussed this more in detail elsewhere.[52]

The question may be raised whether it is possible to have too much of any virtue, e.g., to be generous "to a fault"? One might say that a virtue like generosity is not to count as a virtue when it goes beyond a certain point, perhaps because there are other virtues, say justice and prudence, and too much generosity might conflict with one of these. The same with veracity, which can conflict with sympathy—unnecessarily telling someone hurtful truths. Can even conscientiousness—concern to do one's duty—go too far? It would seem that one can at least be too much concerned with it, say, always wondering what is one's duty in rather trivial situations. Or, one could let one's spontaneous following of desirable motivations be swallowed in concern to do exactly what is one's duty. In that sense there could be too much.

So much for the moral virtues. How about the non-moral ones, such as industry? I propose we use the term "nonmoral virtue" for a relatively permanent desire or aversion which is normally beneficial for any agent (or those dear to him—or for some special group, or in his job) for him to have, which adds to his (their) "flourishing."[53] Thus a given desire/aversion (virtue) might qualify as both moral and nonmoral. If one held that it is always best for any agent to act morally, the moral virtues would seem to qualify also as nonmoral, in my sense. And, if one held that industry—and, in general, features that contribute to the well-being of the agent—is itself morally obligatory, at least some nonmoral virtues would qualify as moral. (It is also true that a rational person would *regret* the absence of one of the nonmoral virtues, perhaps feel ashamed on account of a defect in one, and feel some pity for others who lack them.) But a more standard (and more acceptable) view is that the classes of moral and nonmoral virtues are not extensionally equivalent. Ambition, enviousness, patience, persistence, and industry are normally good (or bad) qualities for an agent to have, and often it is desirable that one (not) have them, from the point of view of society; but it is not clear that a rationally chosen moral system would *require* their presence or absence, or praise (admire) them.[54]

The relation between a person's moral code and his nonmoral virtues is not very close. A moral commitment need not put one at all on the way to having a nonmoral virtue; there just may be no nonmoral virtue corresponding to a given moral commitment. Take a commitment not to be deceptive. Is there a nonmoral virtue corresponding—a disposition of advantage to the flourishing of the agent? Perhaps not. Moreover, a person might have a nonmoral virtue like ambition or curiosity, and have no disposition to feel guilty for behavior not manifesting it, or to feel resentment or indignation at others whose behavior does not manifest it.[55] Shame or pity, perhaps, but not remorse or indignation. So much for the nonmoral virtues.[56]

I suggest that we so use the term "character" (as contrasted with "personality") so that all the virtues/vices (in the foregoing senses), both moral and non-moral, count as traits of *character*.

What should we say about wisdom? Is it a virtue at all, and if so, is it moral or nonmoral? I suppose there is no agreed conception of what it is. It seems to be at least in part a cognitive achievement: of what one would want if one were fully and vividly informed about relevant facts, and of what kind of morality one would choose if one were so informed. I believe it would be thought that one is not really wise if there is not a favorable concern for what one would so want, or for the so identified morality. So, if all virtues are *purely* motivational, wisdom is not a virtue. Furthermore, if condemnation or praise will hardly change it,[57] it is not a property which there would be point in society expecting to bring about, fully, by teaching, or by criticism or praise. So, what is its status? Why not say, with Aristotle, that it is an intellectual *excellence*, a quality of mind it is a good thing for people to have, for action, both from their own point of view and from that of society?

V. VIRTUES AND ACTION

What will a virtuous person do in a particular situation? The answer is that, if only one virtue is relevant to the situation, he will do what that virtue motivates him to do (provided temptations are not too strong). But in a great many cases more than one virtue will be involved, and they will motivate in contrary directions. What then does one do? The answer: whatever the strongest virtue—or the combined force of several virtues all motivating in the same direction—motivates one to do. This fact makes it necessary to emphasize that different virtues have different degrees of strength. But reflection on this situation also indicates a need to make our conception of a virtue more subtle. Take for instance a conflict between the virtues of fidelity to promise and that of compassion, for helping or at least not injuring. Evidently it makes a difference what kind of promise it is: how much failure to perform will damage or inconvenience others, whether the promise was casual and impulsive, or deliberated and made before a "cloud of witnesses," whether it was made long ago in circumstances different from those now obtaining. Similarly, there is the question of what kind of benefit, and to whom. Is the benefit to one's self? Is it a matter of giving emergency aid, or at any rate aid essential to saving a person from a disastrous situation? Evidently, for guidance in real life situations we need something more specific than abstract properties like those called "fidelity" and "benevolence/compassion," but rather a complex set of motivations, of differing strengths, pertinent to the particular problems which may arise. In this sense having a virtue like honesty or veracity, just as such, abstractly, can hardly be a guide to life except in very simple situations.

If a person already has the "right" set of complex virtues built in, we might say that what he ought to do is simply what these relevant virtues motivate him to do. But suppose one comes to doubt whether one's built-in set of virtues is "right." Then what is one to do? A conscientious person will want to perform the act that is morally right—he has an overriding motive to do that. In this case he needs to reflect on what the relative weights of his motives *ought to be,* and it is not clear just how to discover this. It is here that a person's normative moral theory will come into play. For instance, one may hold that the (moral) virtues one ought to have are those it would be most beneficial for everyone to have, everything taken into account (including the social cost of teaching them) and with just the strength it is optimal for them to have. One may reflect on which these are, and one's conclusions may activate the motive of conscientiousness.[58]

Notes

1. *Nicomachean Ethics* 1106b36, translated by W.D. Ross, in *The Works of Aristotle,* edited by W. D. Ross (Oxford, 1915).

2. *NE* 1105b20–25.

3. See J. O. Urmson, "Aristotle's Doctrine of the Mean," *American Philosophical Quarterly* 10 (1973): 224, 226, 229. Urmson proposes this interpretation as a possible one.

4. *NE* 1107a1–2.

5. *NE* 1105a30–35.

6. *NE* 1105a30 ff.

7. There is criticism of the theory in Albert Bandura, "Self-Regulation of Motivation and Action Through Goal Systems," forthcoming.

8. Readers who suspect there are no experimental data bearing on these matters should consult Douglas G. Mook, *Motivation: The Organization of Behavior* (New York, 1987), chaps. 5, 7, 9–11. I have reviewed the evidence for the theory in *A Theory of the Good and the Right* (Oxford, 1979), chaps. 2 and 3. See also A. I. Goldman, *A Theory of Human Action* (Englewood Cliffs, N.J., 1970), chaps. 3, 4, 157–69; D. Davidson, *Essays on Actions and Events* (Oxford, 1980), chaps. 1, 3, 5; and W. P. Alston, "Wants, Actions, and Causal Explanation," in *Intentionality, Minds, and Perception,* edited by H. N. Castaneda (Detroit, 1967).

Some philosophers would reject this type of causal conception of human action altogether. See R. M. Chisholm, "The Agent as Cause," in *Action Theory,* edited by M. Brand and D. Walton (Dordrecht, 1975), 199–212; "He Could Have Done Otherwise," in *The Nature of Human Action,* edited by M. Brand (Glenview, Ill., 1971), 293–301; "On the Logic of Intentional Action," in *Agent, Action, and Reason,* edited by R. Binkley et al. (Toronto, 1971), 38–69;and "The Struc ture of Intention," *Journal of Philosophy* 67 (1970): 633–47; also Richard Taylor, *Action and Purpose* (Englewood Cliffs, N.J., 1966). For a critique, see I. Thalberg, "How Does Agent Causality Work?" in *Action Theory,* 213–38.

I do not accept the account of maximizing behavior offered by David Wiggins in "Weakness of Will," *Proceedings,* The Aristotelian Society (1978–79): 271–72.

9. See, for example, Albert Bandura, *Social Foundations of Thought and Action: A Social Cognitive Theory* (Englewood Cliffs, N.J., 1986), 231, 465, 473, 477. Experimental data show that individuals do not very reliably estimate the probabilities of outcomes, given their evidence. Moreover, we are not equipped with any summing device which enables us to know which sum comes out highest, as is obvious to anyone who has bought a car or even a sandwich. There are all sorts of strategies individuals use to solve this problem, and all sorts of proposals what these strategies are. See Mook, *Motivation,* and various review articles in the *Annual Review of Psychology:* J.R. Bettman, "Consumer Psychology," 37 (1986): 257–89; G.F. Pitz and N. J. Sachs. "Judgment and Decision," 35 (1984): 139–63; H. J. Einhorn and R. M. Hogarth, "Behavioral Decision Theory: Processes of Judgment and Choice," 32 (1981): 53–88, especially 69–77; and P. Slovik, B. Fischhoff, and S. Lichtenstein, "Behavior Decision Theory," 28 (1977): 1–39. Also see D. Kahneman and A. Tversky, "Prospect Theory: An Analysis of Decisions under Risk," *Econometrica* 47 (1979): 263–91.

10. Davidson, *Essays on Action and Events,* 98–100. For more clarification of this view, see the following note on his reply to Bratman, and pp. 220 f.

11. See Michael Bratman, "Davidson's Theory of Intention," in *Essays on Davidson: Actions and Events,* edited by B. Vermazen and M. Hintikka (Oxford, 1985). Also his forthcoming

(Harvard) *Intentions, Plans and Practical Reason;* and his "Taking Plans Seriously," *Social Theory and Practice* 9 (1983): 271–87. Davidson replies lucidly in *Essays on Davidson,* 195–201.

12. See, for example, Bruce Aune, *Reason and Action* (Dordrecht, 1977), chaps. 1, 2, and 137–42; A. I. Goldman, *Theory of Human Action* and "The Volitional Theory Revisited," in Brand and Walton, *Action Theory;* Hugh McCann, "Volition and Basic Action," *Philosophical Review* 83 (1974): 451–73; L. H. Davis, *Theory of Action* (Englewood Cliffs, N.J., 1979), 38 ff., 59–93; John Searle, *Intentionality* (Cambridge, 1983): 83–135; Wayne Davis, "A Causal Theory of Intending," *American Philosophical Quarterly* 21 (1984): 43–54; G. A. Miller, E. Galanter, and K. H. Pribram, *Plans and the Structure of Behavior* (New York, 1960), especially chap. 4; William James, *The Principles of Psychology* (New York, 1913), II 487–92; A. G. Greenwald, "Sensory Feedback Mechanisms in Performance Control: With Special Reference to the Ideo-Motor Mechanism," *Psychological Review* 77 (1970): 73–101.

13. See Mook, *Motivation,* 59.

14. See Goldman, *The Theory of Human Action,* 49–50, 94; Karl Duncker, "On Pleasure, Emotion, and Striving," *Philosophy and Phenomenological Research* 1 (1941): 416; J. C. B. Gosling, *Pleasure and Desire* (Oxford, 1969), 97, 105, 121, 124.

15. Duncker, "On Pleasure, Emotion, and Striving," 417–18.

16. For instance, R. Eisenberger, "Is there a Deprivation-Satiation Function for Social Approval?" *Psychological Bulletin* 74 (1969): 255–75.

17. See Mook, *Motivation,* 172, 310.

18. R. B. Zajonc, "Attitudinal Effects of Mass Exposure," *Journal of Personality and Social Psychology* 9 (1968), monograph supplement; and S. P. Grossman, *A Textbook of Physiological Psychology* (New York, 1973).

19. *The Varieties of Goodness* (London, 1963), 149.

20. R. C. Roberts, "Will Power and the Virtues," *Philosophical Review* 93 (1984): 227–84.

21. Ibid., 228.

22. Ibid., 233.

23. Ibid., 234.

24. Ibid., 243.

25. Ibid., 245 f.

26. Stephen Hudson, "Character Traits and Desires," *Ethics* 90 (1980): 539–49.

27. James D. Wallace, *Virtues and Vices* (Ithaca, N.Y., 1978), 40 ff.

28. Ibid., 61.

29. See Bandura, *Social Foundations* and the paper mentioned as forthcoming.

30. See Douglas Meichenbaum, "Teaching Children Self-Control," in *Advances in Child Clinical Psychology,* edited by B. Lahey and A. Kazden (New York, 1986); also D. Meichenbaum, *Cognitive-Behavior Modification: An Integrative Approach* (New York: 1977); and Albert Bandura, *Social Foundations,* chap. 8.

31. Bandura, *Social Foundations,* 240 ff.

32. Contrast much of the foregoing with David Wiggins, "Weakness of Will, Commensurability, and the Object of Deliberation and Desire," *Proceedings,* The Aristotelian Society (1978–79): 251–78, especially 255–58.

33. See Alexander Pfaender, *Phenomenology of Willing and Motivation,* translated by Herbert Spiegelberg (Chicago, 1967): 17.

34. James, *Principles of Psychology,* 549.

35. See Martin Hoffman, "Moral Development," in *Carmichael's Manual of Child Psychology* II, edited by P. Mussen (1970), 261–359.

36. Jonathan Bennett, "The Conscience of Huckleberry Finn," *Philosophy* 49 (1974): 123–34. And various early figures.

37. See notes 35 and 51.

38. James, *Principles of Psychology,* 534, 549.

39. *Summa Theologica* q. 51, a. 2; q. 52, a. 3.

40. Gabriele Taylor and Sybil Wolfram, "Virtues and Passions," *Analysis* 31 (1971): 82.

41. See M. F. Burnyeat, "Aristotle on Learning to be Good," and Richard Sorabji, "Aristotle

on the Role of Intellect in Virtue," both in *Essays on Aristotle's Ethics,* edited by A. O. Rorty (Berkeley, 1980).

42. Roberts, "Will Power and the Virtues," 227–48, especially 229 ff.

43. E. L. Pincoffs *(Quandaries and Virtues* [Lawrence, Kans., 1986]) explains "virtue" more broadly than I have done. He says virtues and vices are "dispositional properties that provide grounds for preference or avoidance of persons" (82). So he includes carefulness, cheerfulness, cleverness, civility, courtesy, dignity, serenity, nobility, grace, wit, and liveliness. This is certainly different from motivations to intentional action. However, he distinguishes various types of virtue, and could distinguish sets like the one I recognize, as sub-classes. Perhaps the disagreement is largely semantic; but his "virtues" turn out to be a very heterogeneous collection.

44. J. S. Mill, *Utilitarianism,* chap. 5, Library of Liberal Arts edition (Indianapolis, 1957), 60.

45. See Aristotle, *NE* 1103a10 and 1129b15–20.

46. John McDowell, "Are Moral Requirements Hypothetical Imperatives?" *Proceedings,* The Aristotelian Society (supplementary volume, 1978).

47. This point was called to my attention by Allan Gibbard.

48. This might be what Aristotle had in mind in *NE* 1103b29–1104a9.

49. Lester Hunt, "Character and Thought," *American Philosophical Quarterly* 15 (1978): 183.

50. Lester Hunt, "Courage and Principle," *Canadian Journal of Philosophy* 10 (1980): 289.

51. Martin L. Hoffman, "Development of Prosocial Motivation: Empathy and Guilt," in *The Development of Prosocial Behavior,* edited by N. Eisenberg (New York, 1982) and "Empathy, Justice and Moral Development," in *Empathy and its Development,* edited by N. Eisenberg and Janet Strayer (Cambridge, 1987).

52. R. B. Brandt, "Traits of Character: A Conceptual Analysis," *American Philosophical Quarterly* 7 (1970): 36–37.

53. This is a distinction different from that drawn by G. Taylor and S. Wolfram, in "The Self-regarding and Other-regarding Virtues," *Philosophical Quarterly* 18 (1968): 238–48, especially 244 ff. Their view is that what distinguishes courage, temperance, etc., is the nature of the temptation not to do something which the agent thinks there is overriding reason to do. The temptation may be fear or danger or indulgence in pleasures. I am drawing a different distinction, between motivations which it is desirable for society to require or praise and beneficial ones outside of this category.

54. Professor E. L. Pincoffs has a somewhat different way of classifying virtues, and a different way of defining "virtue." See his *Quandaries and Virtues,* 78–92.

55. For a fuller discussion, see my "W. K. Frankena and Ethics of Virtue," *The Monist* 64 (1981): 271–92 *passim.*

56. Lester Hunt, in "Character and Thought," lists various traits which he says are "all examples of traits of character." Among them he includes obedience, gentleness, and impulsiveness. The first two seem neither to be required by an optimal moral system, nor to be normally important for the agent's flourishing. (Do we even want a general trait of obedience among adults?) As for gentleness, it would seem that as a dispositon for intentional action, traits like kindness and consideration cover the same ground. Gentleness strikes me as a stylistic trait of personality. My intuition is to exclude these. Impulsiveness is a harder case. I would think it implies action without awareness of options, consequences, etc. "Think first!" may be a disposition which is usually both socially and personally beneficial.

57. See Burnyeat, "Aristotle on Learning to be Good," and Sorabji, "Aristotle on the Role of Intellect in Virtue."

58. I am grateful to Marcia Baron and William Frankena for criticisms of an earlier draft.

Flourishing and the Failure
of the Ethics of Virtue

SARAH CONLY

I. The Need for a New Ethical Theory

The ethics of virtue has achieved a popularity among contemporary moralists which speaks tellingly of disillusionment with traditional Kantian and utilitarian ethical theories. Philosophers discuss their intention to take a new and more fruitful approach to ethics in general, one sensitive to nuances of human life which debates about the content of duty do not capture. Central to these discussions are those who want an account of good character that is not derivative of an account of good deeds.

This desire makes sense. There are two problems associated with duty-based ethics and their evaluation of the person according to her fulfillment or nonfulfilment of duty. First is the syndrome of the irritating saint. We are all familiar with the picture of nasty do-gooders whom we hardly admire, do not want to emulate, and whose company we avoid, even while admitting the merit of their actions. In contrast to this we have the picture of those whose concerns do not lead to a life of perfect fulfillment of duty but who attract us by the strength, purity, and sensitivity of their characters.[1] Second, there is the more pervasive problem of integrity.[2] It is a fact of common experience that attention to moral duty can be felt as an intrusion in one's life, taking time and attention away from one's more heartfelt concerns and subordinating them to the stern impartial demands of moral law. Moral goodness, then, is held by some to be bought at the price of internal harmony and wholeness. The proponent of ethics of virtue, on the contrary, hopes to bring about a rapprochement of meaning and morality. A virtue is generally held to be a part of one's character, and thus something within the person. The possession of a virtue thus provides an internal impetus to action which is not at odds with the general orientation of the person. It may on this account be a set of virtuous desires, dispositions, and traits which generate the unifying goals that make a life integrated and meaningful. Since one is good because of good character arising within, rather than because of obedience to laws imposed from without, being good should not rend the texture of one's life. The ethics of virtue has, then, much to offer, in rehabilitating moral theory and making moral evaluation palatable. The problem is whether this ethics of virtue can be made sense of—whether there is any plausible account of why character is or should be prior in our evaluation of selves or others.

I will argue that there is no such account. We need, as philosophers, not only an attractive picture of an ethics but a theory which makes coherent our judgments in that area, and it is this theory which is lacking in the attempt to make character the basis for moral evaluation.[3] We need an account which gives at least rudimentary understanding of the criteria used in designating one trait a virtue and another a vice, or the whole effort to recast our ethical approach will be a dead end. I will argue that, unfortunately, the most successful attempt to provide a basis for evaluating character prior to deeds, the Aristotelian and neo-Aristotelian notion of flourishing, is not and cannot be successful in providing a criterion of virtue and vice. An account of flourishing specific enough to support claims about what traits will or will not contribute to it will itself be unacceptable; an account broad enough to be acceptable will be too broad to entail that any specific traits will contribute to, or detract from its achievement. The idea of flourishing will not provide a standard that successfully distinguishes virtue from vice. While this does not entail that no account can be given which will provide a way of evaluating character without reference to actions, it should, at the least, make us wonder whether the attempt by this new age ethics to reorient our approach to moral evaluation is misguided.

II. WHAT AN ETHICS OF VIRTUE IS

One's first impression on reviewing contemporary literature on virtue is that here, more than most places in philosophy, anything goes. Virtues may be learned like skills, or natural; unreflective desires (such as spontaneous promptings of affection) are considered as virtues; introspection and autonomy (presumably arrived at only through reflection) are considered as virtues. Virtue may or may not involve acting in accordance with rules one believes in. The virtuous person may or may not have an idea of the good. The desire to do what is right, as such, may be either the quintessence of or totally unrelated to virtue. And so forth.

These different approaches seem to be explained not so much by disagreement as by quite different ideas of what an ethics of virtue will do for morality that other theories cannot. There seem to be three different, general theses debated here (of course, there may be more, but these appear the most important): (1) that reason is means-end only, where ends are determined by some kind of desire; (2) that desires and emotions, and actions motivated by desires and emotions, can be morally evaluated as praiseworthy or blameworthy; (3) that states of character, somehow independent from actions, are central to moral evaluation. Now, none of these entails any other, although some are good companions. The first is the familiar Humean thesis about rationality and motivation, which argues that while there may be different types of desire—some unconsidered appetites, some reflectively tuned, some first-order, some second-order—it is always the force of (contingent) desire, not the force of reason, which ultimately determines one's goals. Thesis (2) maintains that desires can be morally evaluated, despite their contingent nature, and their possible immunity to direction by a free will.[4] One might argue this whether or not one endorses (1): it is certainly possible to believe that *both* reason and desire are sources of motivation and believe that both can be morally evaluated (with supplementary argument). And, one might believe (1) without believing (2): one might believe that desire is the source of all motivation, that desires cannot be morally evaluated, and that consequently humans cannot be morally evaluated as agents.

Theses (1) and (2) can be (and frequently are) argued from within familiar moral theoretical frameworks. While neither is compatible with classical Kantianism, they are both, of course, compatible with consequentialism, and just such issues have contributed to much of the substantive disagreement between Kantian and consequentialist theories. A debate over these issues, then, does not necessitate a departure from the traditional approach which takes evaluation of actions and their right-making characteristics as basic. So, neither thesis (1) nor (2), nor their combination, entails (3).

Thesis (3) is more radical. The proponent of (3) argues that the emphasis on right-making characteristics of actions is misplaced, and that there is an independent basis of evaluation in the character a person has. What aspect of character should be evaluated is debated, but proponents of (3) agree that it is these internal states of character which matter when we call a person a good person. Of course, character typically is reflected in action, but the idea is that it is the character that determines the goodness of the action. We would then say that an act is courageous (and thus *ceteris paribus* good) insofar as it is the action of a courageous person, just as it is the product of a just person, and so forth. It is thesis (3) which is the most thoroughgoing ethics of virtue and which seems to be the object of the greatest attention. Our orientation in evaluation is to be internal rather than external.[5]

How is the priority of internal character a departure from other sorts of ethics? It is, after all, common practice for most ethical theories to consider the internal state of a person when evaluating an action that person does. Even utilitarianism evaluates differently someone who consciously tries to benefit others and someone who maliciously tries to hurt them, even where both fortuitously succeed in producing the same amount of utility. And, for Kant, where the consequences do not matter at all, the basis of our judgment seems to be entirely a state internal to the agent—the rational process that agent went through in determining how to act. The answer to the question above seems to be that the internal state the proponent of this ethics of virtue wants to evaluate must not be connected in the way these other theories are to right-making characteristics. While common Kantian and consequentialist theories evaluate character, they make their evaluation derivative of their evaluation of actions. In the case of utilitarianism this is clear: while we praise the benevolent person more than the malicious even when the outcomes of their acts are the same, this is because we have reason to believe benevolence will in general produce more utility than will malice. That is, it is the actions it will normally result in that make benevolence superior. Kantianism is harder to explain, but it is clear that proponents of the ethics of virtue do not propose the *Groundwork* as an early manifesto of their views. Why?

It appears that not just any kind of internal state will qualify as the basis of a virtue ethics. While Kantianism does take an internal state to be crucial to the value of an action, and of an agent, the state in question is one in which one concerns oneself with the rightness of a proposed action. That is, the mental state which is judged is one in which one considers the universalizability of an action, with the understanding that it is this universalizability which makes the act right. Hence while it is true for Kantians that it is not merely the external action itself which is the basis of moral evaluation, the mental process which is so evaluated is one which assesses the rightness of actions, so that there is a sense in which right-making characteristics take a primary role. This at least seems to be what the proponent of an ethics of virtue is driven to if the theory is to be distinct from other theories. For, after all, not only consequentialism and Kantianism but just about any moral theory will consider the mental state of the agent in some way relevant in assessing the value of an action. If ethics of virtue is to be a novel approach it must reject these as insufficient.

III. FLOURISHING

A. Narrow conceptions of flourishing

The question which naturally arises is what criterion will in fact be used to evaluate character. If it is not doing or intending morally right action which makes a character good, what does? For the ethics of virtue to be useful, we need an account which (1) provides a unifying principle telling what it takes to be a virtue (i.e., the necessary and sufficient conditions, or as close to these as we may come); (2) explains the desirability of a virtue (why we approve of these traits); and (3) captures at least a fair number of our beliefs about what traits are virtues (that is, gains intuitive recognition by giving an account that either does include courage, sympathy, etc., or explains comprehensibly why these were mistaken for virtues). Given this, we can fruitfully explore the ramifications of an ethics of virtue.

The notion of flourishing has provided the best grounds for such a theory. The idea that there is a kind of life in which the organism is doing well, and that virtues are the traits which contribute to this state of well-being, is understandably attractive in its promise of a comprehensible explanation and beneficial recommendations. The fullest development of the idea of flourishing is in Aristotle, where, as we know, eudaimonia is the goal of human striving. In Aristotle the idea is that we may understand whether a thing is a good thing of its kind if we understand what it is to be a thing of that kind. To be a leaf is to be a device for shading fruit; to see if this is a good leaf we see how well it does its shading job. The virtues of the leaf are those traits which allow it to achieve this flourishing state, perhaps its strength or shape. Philippa Foot uses the same device: if we understand what a knife, a cactus, a farmer, *is*, we will understand how one should be judged. It is neither our choice nor our approbation which sets the standard but the nature of the object itself.[6] As a knife is for cutting, a good knife is one which cuts well. Of course, what it is to cut well bears further discussion; one might sacrifice the strength of the blade for its greater sharpness, weight for maneuverability, and so forth, but the general standard, the neo-Aristotelian will say, is clearly defined by the function of the thing we evaluate.

The difficulty in this account arises, of course, when we come to human beings. In order to say when a human is flourishing we need to say what, in a relevant sense, a human being is, and this is not easy.

Aristotle's familiar answer is that a human being has a function *(ergon)*, which is to reason. Hence, human flourishing will involve reasoning, and reasoning well. This answer, while initially plausible, is, of course, not very specific. Almost all waking human (and some sleeping) activities involve some sort of reasoning, and to say flourishing involves reasoning well in doing some or all of these does not enlighten us much as to what we ought actually to be, what traits we ought actually to cultivate. Aristotle himself is ready with an answer: the kind of reasoning we should engage in is that purest of rational activities, contemplation.[7] While Aristotle is never as specific about what contemplation consists in as we would like, he does tell us enough to suggest its parameters. Aristotle differentiates between the activity of contemplation and other activities; contemplation is distinct, as an activity and in value, from the whole life of emotion, work, and even the practice of justice. Even within the intellectual realm contemplation is a rarefied and exclusive activity. Inquiry, the search for truth, is not as good as contemplation, since it involves seeking what one has not got. In contemplation one needs nothing more; the activity spins on its own axis, a self-absorbed sphere, and divine.

Contemporary proponents of ethics of virtue generally do not, however, endorse this conclusion. However acceptable they may find the Aristotelian strategy, the particular answer Aristotle offers seems simply wrong. The problem lies in the narrowness of Aristotle's picture of flourishing. Many of the experiences and occupations we regard as intrinsically valuable are, on his account, either not valuable or valuable only as a means to making contemplation possible. Even the moral virtues, whose cultivation is discussed at length, turn out in the end to be only second best—it is not in courage or justice that flourishing lies but in the intellect. There seems even less room for basketball, first kisses, promotions, or lying lazily in bed while someone else makes coffee. Yet, these or other such minutiae seem to play strong roles in the individual sense of flourishing. While contemplation in Aristotle's sense may be a pinnacle of human achievement, it is not clear that we want to or should live our lives on a pinnacle. This is not just a philistine inertia. The quintessentially human life seems to us to be more variously textured. While Aristotle reasonably thinks that we will engage in some noncontemplative activities, this is a matter of practical necessity not to be rejoiced in. Aristotle's position is intelligent and nicely constructed. It is, however, simply inconsistent with our impressionistic but strongly rooted picture of what a human being is and what human flourishing will consist in. While this does not show it to be false, it dissuades us from remodeling our ethical theories to its standard.

The problem with Aristotle's suggestion is not just in what he chose to be the human function but in the argument that any one activity, however well done, could capture all of what we see as constituting a good life and good character. Had he suggested that having a just soul, and that alone, is intrinsically worthwhile we would reject his account just as surely. We recognize too many kinds of traits and activities as intrinsically worthwhile to limit ourselves to any unitary account of flourishing. Consequently, any account which is to be plausible will have to be one which sets up parameters within which different combinations of traits may constitute flourishing —so that baseball players as well as philosophers, revolutionaries as well as Athenian gentlemen, have hopes of living the good life.

B. Collective notions of flourishing

The most natural response to the classical Aristotelian position is one that attempts to eliminate its unattractively narrow focus, while preserving its foundation of virtue in function. The argument is that Aristotle's approach through the characteristic function of an organism is a sound one, but that he has concentrated too exclusively on a human being's intellectual potential. To understand flourishing properly, we must understand that humans have a wider range of characteristic activities, with their concomitant excellences. We will arrive then at a collectivity of constituents to flourishing.

How viable is this solution? It has obvious appeal, in that on this account we can recognize the multiplicity of human interests. At the same time, we satisfy our intuitions about the good life by taking characteristic human activity to include all and only those activities which seem to the evaluating eye to be genuinely worthwhile. The picture of a human it presents is a more rounded and more interesting one—the metaphysical equivalent of the Renaissance man.

The problem, of course, is in supporting any particular collection of activities and virtues one proposes for human flourishing. Typically, a person articulating the virtues that must make up an intuitively appealing picture of flourishing will mention the classical moral virtues of justice, courage, etc.; throw in some reference to roughly Bradleyesque notions of self-realization, include some Kantian idea of respect for persons as ends in themselves, and add that the flourishing life must, furthermore, be pleasant for the person who lives it. The difficulty in this potpourri of dispostions, activities, and sensations is, of course, in its justification. There does not seem to be an accessible notion of what it is to be human which will yield this collection of virtues; nor, indeed, any similar collection. We do not, after all, want to adopt a circular argument by saying that the characteristic functions of a human are whatever yield what we have antecedently assumed to be virtues. We want here an independent explanation of function—but how are we to obtain it?

The collectivity theory of flourishing has two options. Either all these virtues (the experience of pleasure, self-realization, etc.) are founded in one human characteristic, of which they are all the excellence, or the different virtues rest on different characteristics, each with its respective excellence. The first of these is awkward. It is difficult to imagine a single characteristic function upon which such diverse virtues could be founded; they vary even as to type, since some involve beliefs, some emotional dispositions, and some perhaps just good luck in the receipt of life's goods. It is hard to see how one function could involve both, say, respect for rights and the sensation of pleasure.

If, however, as seems more likely, we base the different virtues on distinct characteristic functions, different problems arise. First, and most obviously, any given selection of functions is apt to appear ad hoc. Why should self-realization be thought more characteristic than the systematic nullification of one's consciousness? The appeal of the collectivity view seems to rest on the picture of a life it yields, but given this, the danger that we will circularly choose as functions those activities that yield what we have preconceived to be virtues is clear. Second, the very idea of a being possessed of multiple functions is a somewhat peculiar one. The concept of flourishing rests on the idea that there is a characteristic activity which sets an internal standard by whose performance that organism's well-being can be measured. As that organism is described by reference to more than one function, it takes on, however, a relatively fractured appearance. It is not that a thing cannot have more than one characteristic function—we know the example of the combination corkscrew and bottle-opener[8]— but that this bifurcation can undercut the unity of the organism in a way that presents us with two objects, however inseparably yoked, rather than one. The corkscrew-bottle-opener has, after all, as its basic function simply to open containers, typically of liquid, and is thus fairly unified and comprehensible. If a person is identified with the very diverse functions the intuitively appealing collective view seems to attribute to it, though, the picture we get is rather more like a combination corkscrew-carburetor: it is hard to imagine what constitutes a good one.

C. Broad conceptions of flourishing

It is for these reasons presumably that what we get in contemporary Aristotelians is a third conception of flourishing. Here we find an account of flourishing which allows a collection of dispositions and correlative activities as its constituents, justified by reference to a function which, however broad, is at least conceptually unified. Even the most influential of these accounts (Williams, MacIntyre) tend to be rather impressionistic in the specification of necessary and sufficient conditions for flourishing, but a common underlying theme is apparent. What we have is an account which bases the standard of flourishing in the development of a robust sense of one's individuality, and the activities in which that expresses itself.

While the development of this sense of oneself as an individual may not be quite Aristotle's idea of function, it serves its purpose: it provides an account of the prerequisites for humanity. These thinkers argue that one can see in the effect of modern deontological and consequentialist theories that they have ignored the essential component of a flourishing life: not autonomy, conscientiousness, or even benevolence, but the development of a cohesive sense of self. This requires several things. A person needs to develop desires which are relevantly consistent, so that her deep-seated dispositions reflect general unity in what she likes and in what she values. She must avoid what is sometimes called schizophrenia[9]—a radical split within herself, within her whole orientation, which undercuts the unity of her identity. And, she needs to recognize her own unity of character, in a way that gives her a sense of herself as an individual. This involves in turn seeing one's life as a unified whole; as having, as MacIntyre puts it, narrative structure.[10] This is possible only insofar as one sees the activities and events of that life as natural concomitants of one's own character rather than random and disparate intrusions. If it is to be my life its events must not be foreign to my nature.[11] Lastly, for this sense of internal coherence to endure we need the internal requisites for action on these cohesive dispositions; the practical wisdom to figure out what kinds of means suit one's ends and the self-control to act when it is practically feasible.[12] These coherence conditions are necessary for a strong identity, and we can see how without such an identity human flourishing, in any recognizable sense, is hardly possible.

Obviously, many kinds of dispositions, attachments, projects, and ambitions are compatible with this picture. What it sets up is in a sense a suitable background, a setting, in which different varieties of character may develop well. It suits our pluralistic notions of human good in a way that no single, exclusive notion can. As a notion of flourishing, then, it is prima facie acceptable, and to that extent preferable to Aristotle's. The problem arises when we try to use this idea of flourishing to establish a theory of virtue and vice. Flourishing is to help a theory of virtue and vice in this way: when we understand what flourishing is, we can see what traits contribute to it and what detract from it. From this we derive knowledge as to which traits are virtues. Now, the question is whether a plausible notion of flourishing will actually be able to designate some traits as virtues and some as vices. It is difficult to see how, on a plausible conception of flourishing, any particular traits are ruled in, or that any particular traits are ruled out. When we have a picture of flourishing as specific as Aristotle's, we have or can derive a specific picture of what traits of character are consistent with this. We can see that a boorishly sensual temperament detracts from the achievement of flourishing, that taking pleasure in the intellect is necessary, and so forth. When we have so broad a picture of flourishing as that presented above, however, it is hard to see what traits in particular will contribute to or detract from it. We cannot tell a vice from a virtue, since almost any trait is compatible with flourishing. The attraction of the broad account of flourishing is that it is not arbitrarily selective; the problem is that given this, it is too broad to serve as a foundation for a theory of virtue and vice.

Let us take, for example, courage. Courage is regarded as very solidly a virtue. It is almost universally admired (unlike, e.g., piety or prudence, which to many have unpleasant connotations); it seems to rest on an internal motivation distinct from recognition of laws or duties, and thus need not be derivative, in the mind of the courageous person, from beliefs about right-making characteristics;[13] and, there is a general consensus about what constitutes a courageous act and who the courageous person is. A courageous person is willing to risk (some degree of) her personal safety (whether the safety of her body or her peace of mind) through a recognition that there are things more important than her security.

Now, does the plausibly broad neo-Aristotelian account of flourishing show why we should be courageous? Consider the following scenario from science fiction.[14] In a futuristic world we find many species, with, as one might suspect, many different characteristics. There are extremely aggressive, warlike species, who kill unless there is good reason not to, and who welcome early death. There are species who balance aggression and prudence. And, there is a species of cowards. These are beings who believe that in all cases the dominant consideration is personal security. The puppeteers (as the species is called) fear injury above all else. They act on this disposition consistently and perspicaciously, planning ahead to avoid dangers years away. Anyone who risks his own safety, for whatever reason, is regarded as insane and exiled.

Can these people flourish? They seem to. The puppeteers know precisely what to expect of themselves and each other. A puppeteer makes only those plans which are consistent with his own well-being. Nor does he feel hemmed in by his own lack of adventurousness, any more than I feel constricted because my lack of adventurousness keeps me from even wanting to be a race-car driver. His plans are consistent with his desires, and, given the strength of these desires, a whole culture has been built around them. Puppeteers need not be deprived of affection, for example, merely because one will not sacrifice his safety for another. I believe I genuinely care for my family, but I cannot sincerely promise I would undergo extensive torture for their sake. The puppeteer is different only in degree—he will not undergo any injury for others. But, like us, his peers do not make insane sacrifices the price of love.

As a society, as well as individually, the puppeteers flourish. This is important, since it is generally agreed that humans, social creatures, normally need a stable society, both for material and psychological needs. Certainly within his own culture there is no problem: each knows what to expect of the other, and acts accordingly. Far from making cooperation impossible, this makes it simple, since behavior is completely dependable. And, society is peace-loving and law-abiding, since no one would risk his safety for possible gain. Since our scenario includes other, aggressive species we might conjecture that the timid puppeteers would be wiped out, but this disregards the puppeteers' prudence. They have, for example, developed a technology which allows them to trade advantageously. And, they have developed a reputation and a rule that insures their safety: Anyone who kills a puppeteer will be the subject of a disastrous economic boycott, which allows the puppeteers to retaliate from a safe distance.

It seems that the proponent of radical ethics of virtue must say either that the puppeteers do not flourish, or that they are courageous, and either of these is a difficult claim to make.[15] Not only do they flourish according to the broad criteria of integrity, cohesion, and social success, but also by our own parochial standards of economic stability and social mobility (they can, as far as we know, choose their own careers, etc.). It begs the question to say they do not flourish simply because they are cowards.

The alternative view is that the puppeteers are courageous. They do show certain behavior associated with courage—the ability to reason and plan what to do about potential dangers rather than simply panicking. This collectedness, though, does not appear sufficient for courage. Collectedness is possible as one foreswears one's true beliefs for the sake of popularity; as one leaves one's comrades-in-arms in the lurch for the sake of one's own safety; as one forsakes one's role as captain in abandoning the sinking ship. While self-possession may be necessary for courage, it is clearly not sufficient without that risking of the self for others which the coward does not have. And yet, given the right means, cowards may flourish.

Consider, second, justice. Justice is also traditionally a cardinal virtue. It involves respect for others and a proper estimation of their worth, and acting in a way which reflects this. It is important that the person who is truly just must truly appreciate others; the person who wishes to give others their due, but consistently estimates their worth to be nothing, is unjust. It is important, too, that the just person act on his correct estimation; if he believes the right thing but does not reflect it in his actions he is again unjust rather than just. Justice is a complex virtue, in that it requires a cohesion of true belief and action.

Can we flourish without justice? If circumstances are suitable, it seems we may. Virtues like justice, indeed, have always posed a problem for flourishing accounts. That is, if virtue is what allows an organism to reach a flourishing state, it is not clear why traits that entail particular regard for and treatment of *others* should be virtues. This is a problem Foot broaches in her discussions of justice. She first argues that if justice does not benefit the person who is just it is not a virtue.[16] Granting that justice may well not benefit oneself, she later argues that a virtue need *not* benefit the person who has it but may benefit anyone.[17] This emendation, however, does not sit well with the idea that virtues are derivative of the natural state of flourishing of the organism. To borrow Foot's example: if we know what a farmer is (someone who grows a crop), we know what a good farmer is (someone who does this successfully). Benefiting others, though, may not make him flourish. If a farmer overextends and goes bankrupt, this trait may well benefit the farmers around him (who get his machinery at a low price); but we can hardly say this trait makes him a better farmer. That is, his benefit of others hardly contributes to his flourishing. To be consistent in their derivation of virtue, someone who holds the flourishing account must show that traits like justice actually, however indirectly, are necessary to the flourishing state of the person who exercises them if they are to be virtues.

Can an individual flourish without justice? Can the society needed to nourish individual flourishing exist without justice?[18] Again, it seems that on the neo-Aristotelian account both can.

We may see this pointedly in an individual. Take Lorenzo the Magnificent. If Florence in the Renaissance was great it is largely Lorenzo who made it so. Astute and ambitious, he navigated the labyrinthine difficulties of fifteenth-century Italian politics with dexterity, establishing himself securely as tyrant. Under his rule, industry, commerce, and public works made enormous progress, leading Florence to unequaled prosperity. At the same time, Lorenzo was not only a great patron and appreciator of the arts, but extremely creative himself, "an elegant prose writer, and likewise a poet of real originality."[19] He seems, indeed, to have done everything well. And while we are not privy to Lorenzo's personal experience, there seems good reason to believe that, successful in all he undertook, he was happy. Yet, there is no doubt that Lorenzo was an extremely unjust person. He trampled the liberty of Florence underfoot, he lied, he spied, and he assassinated his enemies with abandon. Ruthless and pitiless, concern for the rights of others seems never to have crossed his mind. Yet, while incontrovertibly unjust, he seems certainly to have flourished. Indeed, not only did Lorenzo flourish while unjust, it looks as though just character and just behavior would have prevented him from flourishing. One simply could not become ruler of Florence with a strict regard for the rights of others. A just person might, perhaps, have flourished in some more self-effacing role, but he would not flourish as Lorenzo the Magnificent. The two simply are not compatible.

Nor is this an isolated example. An individual can hone his skills, develop his talents, cultivate his tastes, and be happy without a sense of justice. A society with no concept of justice can succeed, and its citizens can flourish, in a sphere where a sense of justice is not expected of them. It is when we do expect justice that we are confused to find it lacking; in areas we do not expect it, we adjust. (Consider Boston drivers: they seem to enjoy a ruthless dash across four lanes to gain their exit. It is the timid visitor from Iowa, waiting courteously for a gap in traffic, who causes the traffic jam.) From a historical perspective we can see that widespread concern for justice is a very modern and local phenomenon, but surely it would be parochial to insist that no society other than our own has ever flourished. Considerations other than justice may inform the life of an individual or a community in a way that is a perfectly good basis for flourishing. As in the society of cowards, individuals guide their behavior and their expectations according to experience.[20]

What seems to be needed, more than the cultivation of any particular disposition, is a kind of general stability of character. For an individual to flourish in a community he needs to be able to predict the behavior of those around him with some accuracy, so that expectations can be raised and generally met. This makes coordination possible, since I can plan around your action, whether just or unjust, cowardly or courageous. And, of course, I need a certain stability in my own dispositions, so that I can plan well the implementation of my desires. Perhaps this stability of disposition might itself be called a virtue; but it is important to note that it does not in itself predilect one in any one particular direction as to likes and dislikes, actions and reactions. Whatever one's approach, what matters within that approach is consistency within oneself and the (relative) dependability of one's society.

The point then is not that courage and justice are improperly called virtues, and that there are other dispositions which would consistently play a greater role in flourishing. The point is that an account of flourishing which is broad enough and neutral enough to suit human activities as such must necessarily allow latitude for many kinds of traits. The neo-Aristotelian account wants to be intuitively acceptable, and it wants to base itself around the actual nature of humans. Human nature is sufficiently broad, however, that its flourishing state—flourishing in terms of a cohesive, integrated, socially successful life—will not require any particular trait in all cases. It gives us no basis for generalizing, for saying this disposition is a virtue, that is a vice. If we are to have a substantive notion of virtue, it will not come from flourishing.

IV. THE PROBLEM

We feel, granted, a continuing dissatisfaction with these examples. We are inclined to think, simply, that virtuous people do not treat others as do those in the examples. Virtue has for us a positive connotation, and these people seem unattractive. Yet, if these people are flourishing, and if flourishing people are ipso facto virtuous, these people are virtuous—and that is hard to swallow. The question, however, is where to cut the line of inference.

What our discomfort shows, I think, is that there is a fundamental dissatisfaction with the idea that we may discover the nature of virtue by looking at flourishing alone. That is, the inference from X's flourishing to X's virtuousness is unjustified. It seems that we hold to be virtues those traits in particular which support a kind of treatment of other people, which is not required by the individual's own flourishing. While an individual, to flourish, needs a community of a certain order, it does not look as though his own flourishing requires his supporting the community in the way we would consider just, or courageous, or even kind. These traits are considered virtues because of the actions they induce in our behavior toward others. What kind of treatment do the traditional virtues support? It may be that we consider virtues those dispositions whose possession maximizes utility, or it may be that we consider virtues those traits which make it easier for us to act only on those maxims which we could will to be universal law. Or, it could be that our regard for these traits is a mixture of concern for utility with concern that one respect others as ends in themselves. The precise determination of the roots of our regard for virtue is, fortunately, beyond the scope of this paper. What seems certain is that (1) it is not the idea of flourishing which provides us our idea of a virtuous disposition, and (2) probably the root is in right-making characteristics of action, so that a virtuous character is the one which tends to produce the most right actions.

V. IMPLICATIONS

What does this say about the ethics of virtue? It depends on what aspect of ethics of virtue we mean. In section I above we saw that there are three independent claims made by proponents of ethics of virtue: (1) that reason is means-end, and so does not ultimately determine the objects of motivation; (2) that desires and emotions can be morally evaluated, and (3) that states of character, not actions, are central to moral evaluation. Now, it is true that if flourishing cannot provide an account of virtue there is some argument against (3), since flourishing has seemed the account most likely to provide criteria for the moral evaluation of character. There is no argument here, however, against claims (1) and (2). As has been pointed out, these claims are compatible with the claim that it is actions which are prior in moral evaluation, and that character assessment is derivative of the actions a person does or would produce. We have in (1) and (2) a theory about agency and its evaluation which does not entail that the evaluation of agency be independent of the evaluation of actions in terms of right-making characteristics.

And, it should be noted that many of the motivations which contribute to the popularity of ethics of virtue can be addressed by a view which includes only theses (1) and (2), and says nothing about the priority of right-making characteristics.[21] Concern that traditional ethics is not sufficiently sensitive to the whole person—that duty is an alien force, intrusive to the integrity of the individual, and that character is too often ignored—can all be met by a theory which recognizes the degree to which feeling is involved in one's moral behavior. The stronger claim, that the character per se would be the primary object of evaluation, does not need to be made simply to provide ethics with adequate scope.

However enticing the ethics of virtue, then, to our worn sensibilities, there is some reason to reject it. Until we can explain the nature of that virtue which it takes as its basis, its promise of insight is necessarily misleading; and a theory's sensitivity should, after all, be measured by the elucidation it brings.[22]

Notes

1. Of course, many proposed irritating saints of the Eddie Haskell variety turn out not to be saints at all by realistic standards of duty. This is a problem in Susan Wolf's "Moral Saints" *(Journal of Philosophy* 79, Aug. 1982); her "saints" are such caricatures that the desirability of genuine sainthood is not convincingly questioned.

2. Bernard Williams has made this a philosophical household word in "A Critique of Utilitarianism," in *Utilitarianism: For and Against,* edited by J. Smart and B. Williams (Cambridge, 1973); "Persons, Character, and Morality," in *The Identities of Persons,* edited by Amelie Rorty (Berkeley, 1976), and other influential writings. For a discussion of Williams, see Conly, "Utilitarianism and Integrity," *Monist* 66 (1983), 298–311.

3. Harold Alderman, "By Virtue of a Virtue," *Review of Metaphysics* 36 (1982), 127–53 (reprinted in Kruschwitz and Roberts, *The Virtues* [Belmont, Calif., 1987]) argues that paradigmatically virtuous characters are indisputably and transculturally recognizable as such, so that, apparently, no theory is needed to tell us what is a virtue and what a vice. This approach has the advantage of standard intuitionism in appealing to our primitive and pleasing belief in the universality of our own inarticulate opinions. It has, alas, the same disadvantages: its lack of explanatory force, its breakdown in the face of disagreement, and its general philosophical indefensibility make it an uninteresting approach to the ethics of virtue.

4. The desires discussed are obviously distinct from Kant's obligatory ends, the ends arrived at by reason, in which the rational agent must take an interest.

5. Consider Frankena's classic account: "It [an ethics of virtue] would, of course, not take deontic judgments or principles as basic in morality . . . instead, it would take as basic aretaic judgments like 'That was a courageous deed,' 'His action was virtuous', or 'Courage is a virtue', and it would insist that deontic judgments are either derivative from such aretaic ones, or can be dispensed with entirely. Moreover, it would regard deontic judgments about actions as secondary and as based on aretaic judgments about agents and their motives or traits . . . " W.F. Frankena, *Ethics,* (2nd ed., Princeton, N.J., 1973), 63.

6. Foot, "Goodness and Choice," in her *Virtues and Vices* (Berkeley, 1978).

7. This, it seems to me, is Aristotle's considered view, as expressed in *Nicomachean Ethics* 10.7. I am naturally aware that some favor the comprehensive interpretation of Aristotle, where contemplation is just one among other constituents of eudaimonia. The particular interpretation of Aristotle one favors doesn't matter to the thesis of this paper.

8. Thomas Nagel, "Aristotle on Eudaimonia," in *Essays on Aristotle's Ethics,* edited by Amelie Rorty (Berkeley, 1980), discusses this and human function in general.

9. Michael Stocker, "The Schizophrenia of Modern Ethical Theories," *Journal of Philosophy* 73 (1976), 453–66; reprinted in Kruschwitz and Roberts, *The Virtues.*

10. Alasdair MacIntyre, *After Virtue* (Notre Dame, Ind., 1981), esp. chaps. 14 and 15.

11. A pervasive theme in MacIntyre and Williams.

12. Philippa Foot emphasizes these in her discussions of virtue. See *Virtues and Vices.*

13. Of course, it is possible one can act courageously out of regard for duty, moving to save the child from the burning house because one thinks one ought; the point is the act need not rest on such a considered opinion, so that courage fits neatly into an ethics of virtue as described in thesis (3) of section II.

14. Larry Niven, *Neutron Star* (New York, 1968).

15. A third alternative is, of course, to say that courage is not a virtue, but, as discussed above, courage is so central to our idea of virtue that to argue this suggests that the account is dealing with something distinct from what we mean by virtue.

16. Foot, "Moral Beliefs," in *Virtues and Vices.*

17. Foot, "Virtues and Vices," in *Virtues and Vices.*

18. It may be argued that while an individual in a generally just society can live unjustly and flourish, an individual (just or unjust) in a generally unjust society cannot flourish. It seems, though, that while it is no doubt true that an individual needs a society where cooperation is possible, this may be achieved by systems of coordination distinct from justice. Imagine a religious

community, where action is governed by obedience to divine law. This community might have no consideration at all for human rights or human value, and yet achieve a social coordination which would allow the individual to flourish perfectly well. Justice involves a specific kind of recognition of others, and is not the only source of coordinating rules.

19. *Encyclopaedia Britannica,* 11th ed., article on the de Medeci's, by Pasquale Villari.

20. It is sometimes argued that the flourishing of a society entails that it is just. One explanation of virtue is that it is social in origin, in that a society determines the content of virtue to be simply whatever aids that society to flourish. If this is correct, then a society could not, logically, flourish without the virtues. If justice is a virtue, it contributes to the flourishing of a society. Whatever the merits of this position, however, it is quite distinct from the one we are debating, where virtue is to be grounded in the nature of an individual, and so is not relevant to this discussion.

21. See Conly, "The Objectivity of Morals and the Subjectivity of Agents," *American Philosophical Quarterly* 22 (Oct. 1985), 275–86, for a detailed discussion.

22. I would like to thank David Cummiskey, Roseanne Ducey, Mark Okrent, and Charlotte Witt for their comments on this paper.

Common Sense and Uncommon Virtue

NANCY SHERMAN

*"If I was a princess—a real princess," she murmured, "I
could scatter largess to the populace. But even if I am only
a pretend princess, I can invent little things to do for people. Things like this. She was just as happy as if it was largess. I'll pretend that to do things people like is scattering
largess. I've scattered largess."*
                    Frances Hodgson Burnett, *A Little Princess*

Recently Marcia Baron has argued persuasively for a de-emphasis within ethical
theory of the category of the supererogatory.[1] Commonly understood, supererogatory actions are actions that are good, but not morally required; they are beyond
the call of duty. Briefly put, Baron's objections to the notion are that it detracts from
the actions of ordinary morality, it emphasizes isolated act-types apart from context
and ongoing character traits, and it confuses the admirable with what is right. Her
proposal is to return to Kant's fertile notion of imperfect duties, to the notion, that is,
of fulfilling duties of virtue or end. Within this notion, due regard can be given to the
agent who goes the extra mile, "who does far more to fulfill an imperfect duty than do
many others who themselves cannot be faulted for having too legalistic or minimalist
a conception of what they ought to do."[2]

I want to pursue this line of inquiry from an Aristotelian point of view. In particular, I want to consider just what role Aristotle assigns to the uncommon or spectacular moral act. While it would be peculiar to claim that Aristotle has or needs a
notion of the supererogatory (since there is no narrow notion of what is morally required which the supererogatory would be needed to supplement), he nevertheless
does single out for special attention the idea of spectacular moral acts and the specific
character traits from which they emanate. I have in mind his account of the grand
scale virtues of magnificence and magnanimity.[3] Here the sort of worries that can be
raised against the supererogatory surface. I shall address these concerns and suggest
that Aristotle's discussion of the grand scale virtues obscures what is especially noteworthy about exemplary virtue. For that, we must turn to the more ordinary virtues,
and the notion of stably and reliably acting from them.

My remarks divide as follows: After showing how right action is for Aristotle
inseparable from character, I defend his conception of character against certain views
of perfectionism. However, his account remains problematic in its inclusion of the

grand scale virtues. In indicating the defects, I suggest more plausible Aristotelian criteria for accounting for exemplary virtue.

1. FINE AND RIGHT ACTION

It is reasonably clear that Aristotle's notion of fine and right action (i.e., action that is for the sake of *to kalon* and that is *to deon*—what one ought to do) goes well beyond any narrow interpretation of obligation.[4] It goes beyond a narrow construal of what is morally required if by that is understood action that is accidentally right, but in spirit or motive unworthy or unmeritorious. To act in a way that is fine and right is to act from virtue and from a commitment to specific virtuous ends of character. More precisely, it is to act knowingly, from a firm and stable character, choosing virtuous actions for their own sake (1105a26ff.). Action fails to be *hōs dei* if it is performed out of fear or desire for self-gain. To refrain from bribery merely because of the political advantage of a clean image is to act *ou dei*—contrary to what is required and what is most fine (1142b24, 1112b17) even though from the point of view of action there has been no wrongdoing.

The Aristotelian notion of right action thus captures, as we would expect, something more than deontically right action. It probes motives relative to the circumstances as well as long-term character states (cf. 1137a4–25). Admittedly, Aristotle recognizes certain actions, the performance or omission of which are socially and legally enforceable, independent of motive (cf. 1134a15–22, 1136a9–25). Proscriptions against murder, theft, and adultery require such omissions; what is required is not a policy or end, but the nonperformance of a specific action. But still the notion of juridical (perfect) duties exacted from another, independent of motives or character states, does not hold an especially important place in his account. Civic law, Aristotle tells us, ultimately derives from the considerations of virtue as a whole *(apo tēs holēs aretēs)* and has to do with living that is productive of it *(poiētika tēs holēs aretēs, 130b22–26).*[5]

Action that is right and fine goes beyond obligation in another way related to the issue of motive.[6] So, for example, I may act permissibly in refusing to participate in an important political poll for the thin reason that I would rather resume my conversation with my friend; or again omit no obligation when I rudely cut short a rights activist at the front door, explaining that I have a book to finish and a pot of beans overboiling on the stove. These specific actions of goodwill or generosity are not required; the omissions are permissible. But I do seem, nonetheless, to lack virtue *at such moments* and, in an Aristotelian sense, fail to do what is required of virtue. I fail to act as the ideally virtuous character would, giving time if one has it, making donations for good causes relative to one's means, at the very least giving excuses that are less callous, that express one's concern even if one is now unwilling to act on it. To the extent that I embrace the ideals in question, and believe that *now,* all things considered, however harried my life, acting on them is the best and finest thing, I am akratic. If I consistently refuse my time or money for these sorts of solicitations, giving the reason that the pot is still boiling or the book is still on the back burner, then I am chronically akratic, or what seems to come to the same thing, dispositionally deficient in the requisite motives. Given my past performance, it is just self-deceiving to think that I am, in fact, a generous person who given the right occasion will give readily. The record invalidates that. Whether the lapse is chronic or occasional, the agent fails to hit the mean, fails to act *hōs dei*—as one ought given the requirements of virtue. And this is so, even though from a more minimalist notion of obligation, the agent acts permissibly.

The notion that right action requires seriousness of commitment has further implications. In particular, it entails that choice *(prohairesis)* embraces a policy that goes well beyond the boundaries of a given intention or even performance. This is to say, for Aristotle, choice reveals character. To make a choice requires both preparedness at the front end (e.g., requisite skills and education) as well as a willingness at the time of action to follow through, to do what one can to bring about the desired outcome. Consequently, there is no easy sense in which one can say: "I've made the right choice and now I'm finished" in the way in which one is at least tempted to say: "I've done my duty, and now I'm off the hook."

In this regard, contrast a few cases. Consider first the National Security Agency official who notices that his superior is involved in illicit fundraising, questions him several times about the propriety of his actions, and though doubtful of the sincerity of his answers, feels satisfied that he has spoken up and voiced the concerns of his conscience. He has done his duty to probe the matter, and now turns to other business. Contrast this with the whistle blower in the Pentagon, who notices that contractors have doctored their bills, charging $500 for an ash tray or $600 for a toilet seat. He brings it to the attention of several superiors who express surprise at the irregularity and pledge to investigate, but never do. Unflinchingly, he exposes the scandal, at the cost of his job and considerable risk to his career.

The issue here is not consequences nor that the worth of one's good efforts is measured by success in bringing about planned results. The most unlikely impediments can botch the best plans of the most perservering agent. For those sorts of failures an agent cannot be criticized, though he may feel defeat and, indeed, unhappiness.[7] Rather, the issue has to do with commitment to an end. What distinguishes the two agents is that the second does not stop with initial efforts or actions, but views them as part of a greater policy to fight political corruption and dishonesty. It is this end that motivates his choices *(prohaireseis),* and continues to motivate him through sustained deliberation about what to do next, about how to pick up the pieces if one plan fails. His resourcefulness is an indication of the seriousness of his commitment. In its relation to an end of character, then, or what Aristotle calls a *boulēsis,* choice-making requires not one-time, isolated efforts, but a sustained chain of actions that can be brought within an agent's power *eph'hēmin).* The end requires some agenda about how to proceed from here and about how to be prepared for the future.[8] Part of that preparation includes a readiness to seek counsel when one's own efforts fail or are limited. Thus, choice may be that of a single agent or a group of collaborators, whose advice and counsel extend the deliberative point of view and expand "what is within an agent's power" to do and see.[9] In this sense, the excuses: "I don't know how to go on," "There is nothing left for *me* to do" must come after, not before exhausting the available resources of experts and friends. But the main point is that virtuous agency requires more than good intention. To choose well is to show a persistent interest to do what one can to promote an end.

The various examples point to the thinness of legalistic morality in the assessment of action. When the child or adult says "let's divide things down the middle so we each have an equal share," and one party rightly feels put off by the proposal because she has greater need for more, or the objects in question mean more to her because they are her own work or have greater personal value, good will and kindness seem to require not standing on one's rights, but yielding and responding to the other's needs. And this is so even though the party who favors the equal share is within her rights, not guilty of *pleonexia*—an overweening grasp for more than her fair share; in a certain sense, she can without impunity say, "I'm just demanding my fair share, no more, no less." But that defense, Aristotle argues, betrays a defect in character, even if justice in the narrow sense has not been violated.[10]

This is implicit in the synonym Aristotle adopts for the good person. The good person is *epieikēs*—decent, considerate, equitable.[11] Not a stickler for justice (an *akribodikaios,* literally, one who is exacting as to his rights), he is willing to forgo what is strictly speaking his due out of forgiveness and sympathy *(eugnōmosunē),* or the recognition of another's greater need. "Having law on his side," he nonetheless chooses to take "less of his share" (1138a1–3). He is fair-minded *(suggnōmonikos),* willing to make allowances (cf. *MM* 1198b21ff.). In assigning less to himself, he commits no injustice, though in assigning less to others, he of course does.

The conception of equity *(epieikeia)* borrows from its more local usage in the judicial sphere where it indicates interpretation and judgment of law truer to its spirit than letter.[12] In fitting unqualified law to the exigencies of the case, equity embodies a superior form of justice, "superior to the error resulting from the rule being stated unconditionally" (1137b24–5, b9). Equity takes many forms. Its focus on context and circumstance sometimes requires judgment by decree rather than statute; other times, arbitration rather than the stricter and less flexible methods of litigation.[13] The general assumption is that abstraction from the particulars of circumstance, motive, and past performance distorts assessments of culpability:

> Equity considers not so much the action of the accused, but the choice, not this or that part of the account but the whole story, not merely what the agent is like now, but what sort of person he has been or is usually. *(Rhetoric* 1374b13–16)

So stated, the concerns of equity are in direct tension with the underlying principles of corrective justice which looks not to agent, but only to act and the cancellation of its damage.[14] Behind such a veil, damage and gain may find parity. But Aristotle now suggests that such a veil may both obscure the degree to which an injurious action is voluntary, as well as mask the unreasonable demand that a transgressor, given his resources and means, pay the full penalty. Thus, a failure to deliver contracted and paid for goods may be explained by extenuating circumstances which the equitable jurist recognizes as grounds for diminution of damages. A similar interest in the spirit rather than letter of morality moves the equitable and decent agent. Indeed, here, in the negotiations and judgments that are made privately without jurists, it is the concerns of decency, not rights, that are most compelling: "Decency bids us to remember benefits rather than injuries and benefits received rather than benefits conferred; it requires us to be patient when we are wronged" *(Rhetoric* 1374b16–17).[15]

2. PERFECTION

My remarks thus far have reinforced the uncontroversial view that to the extent that Aristotle has a notion of what is right and ought to be done *(to deon),* it requires reference to character and motive (cf. 1106b21–23). In pointing to excuses that show defects of character but no wrongdoing, we see how thin, by comparison, a minimalist morality of right action can be. But this seems to invite only the familiar objection from the other side, that moral theory based on virtue is too excessive, too perfectionist. It requires too much good samaritanism and too little delimitation of the claims others can make against self. While it might be correctly argued that the supererogatory is not the right solution to minimalist morality for it makes goodness too much of a one-time affair, the alternative, of putting the emphasis on virtue, seems to do just the opposite—make good action never ending and unattainable. If the supererogatory tends to encourage moral laxity in more routine moral matters, the problem with virtue is that its work never ends.

But an objection to perfectionism is misplaced if it is the moral saint that is the worry.[16] (At least it is misplaced as an objection against Aristotle, though not necessarily against Kant, though I won't pursue *that* matter here.) Thus, perhaps it bears reminding that the virtues which the Aristotelian agent cultivates are not exclusively "moral virtues," in the intuitive sense of other-regarding or altruistic. Rather, the virtues refer to excellences of character and intellect. To the extent that the full list of character excellences includes such traits as proper pride, a sense of humor, wit, tact, and affability, we can easily see emerging an ideal character that is necessarily more well-rounded than the moral saint is popularly imagined to be.

Consider first the role of humor and wit in the good life *(NE* 4.8). They are traits, Aristotle says, necessary for the leisure and amusement, which the good person values as legitimate pursuits (4.8. 1128b3, 1129b33). These traits have their place in the overall constellation of character just as the more obviously altruistic virtues of courage, generosity, and justice do. Their presence implies that the individual who is so relentless at her moral labors that she no longer enjoys or pursues more trivial pursuits, who does good doggedly but humorlessly, without a trace of lightness or wit, falls short of the ideal. Thus the person who fails to notice the absurd side of life, who forgets to laugh at such moments, has in a sense forgotten how to live. A temporary lapse in humor is one thing, but when one gets the joke (i.e., is not culturally or linguistically handicapped) yet dispositionally fails to laugh, then something valuable seems to be missing. It is not just that such a person is a bore and a drag to be with, or even downright rude. All that may be true. What is more lamentable is that the person does not *really* notice how silly and imperfect human beings can look when compromised in certain circumstances.

In this vein the child who learns for the first time how to make a joke, how to be clever with words, how to spot something incredibly silly in someone else enjoys a power of communicating, a sense of the absurd that is stunning. To forget *that* human pleasure is to be dead somewhere inside. Indeed, the elderly, Aristotle mockingly implies, may already be dead in just that way. Hardened by life's misfortunes, for them the absurd is cause not for sarcasm, but for resignation. Peevishness supplants humor, cynicism replaces hope *(Rhetoric* 2.13). Given these general considerations, it seems reasonable for Aristotle to insist that humor within boundaries—humor that is neither excessive nor tasteless, neither abusive nor overly manipulative, neither buffoonish nor slavishly dependent upon audience—is a human good that we ought to care deeply about. The individual who does good with a rapier wit, who educates through judicious ridicule, deserves some place in the Aristotelian cast of good characters.

The unnamed virtue of friendliness in the list of excellences (4.6) further enriches the portrait of the good person. The good person, Aristotle argues, conveys appropriate pleasures as well as annoyances to others with whom he comes in casual contact. This may include the niceties of civil behavior: of acknowledging another with a smile and meeting of the eyes, of offering the proper greetings and casual banter. But equally, it may include showing displeasure when it is warranted; for example, letting another know that you are fed up with her stupidity or tactlessness. It suggests that an overly tolerant response to repeated tactless but intended insults is not something we necessarily admire or would hold up as exemplary behavior to our children. Rather, the person who can say, "I have had enough; I find this offensive" (even when the offense falls short of wrongdoing) displays a certain honesty and emotional candor that seems on the whole worth cultivating.

The general point is that Aristotle's conception of perfection casts a wider net than does the blander notion of benevolence or kindness. When Aristotle says we must "strain every nerve to do the noblest deeds" (1169a8; Ross trans.), strive toward perfection in our lives, it is not moral perfection narrowly understood that he is urging us to realize. It is human perfection which includes excellences more diverse and rich than those requisite for altruistic behavior. Admittedly, the overall thrust of the full complement of virtues must be toward just and decent dealings with others *(NE* 5.2); but *how* one dispenses that altruism, through such traits as humor and emotional candor, is part of overall perfection.[17] In this regard, Aristotle would not deny that greater efforts and forfeitures are more, rather than less, deserving of praise. The claim is that these, in the absence of some sense of how to pace one's efforts, and how to proceed without being obnoxious, boorish, tactless, or gruff, or on the other hand, insipid, dull, humorless, or flat, fall short of what is humanly best.

3. VIRTUE ON A GRAND SCALE

But can't it now be objected that the Aristotelian puts too much emphasis on style and manner? While we may have no objections to conviviality and wit (and indeed believe that morality fares better with them than without), there are other marks of Aristotelian virtue that seem harder to accept as part of even a broad portrait of goodness. These emphasize, for example, the aesthetically handsome, the skillful, what is physically strong or politically and economically powerful. They are, we might argue, the holdovers from an age of Homeric heroism that lay too much emphasis on the lottery of natural and social endowments. As factors outside an agent's control, they ought to have little to do with morality, little to do with what an agent "is himself somehow responsible for" (1114b3). Indeed isn't what Aristotle hails as the ornament *(kosmos)* of the virtues, namely magnanimity (1124a1), as well as its companion virtue magnificence,[18] evidence of just the sort of grandeur and position that is neither here nor there when it comes to morality? There are two objections implicit in this charge that I want to untangle. The first has to do with the dependence of these virtues upon goods outside an agent's control. Call this the non-autonomy thesis. The second has to do with the notion that acting from the grand scale virtues exempts an agent from ordinary moral service. Call this the exemption thesis. It is the second thesis that interests me more, though I shall begin with some remarks about the first.

The virtue of magnificence makes most perspicuous, perhaps, the dependence of virtue upon external goods and resources. Magnificence is a grand scale version of liberality (or generosity). It is large scale benefaction. To be magnificent, and *a fortiori* to be able to make the choices that the magnificent typically make, requires wealth. Indeed, the surplus required to be able to spend in a magnificent way—for public building, to support the arts, to fit a trireme, to placate the gods (1122b22)—seems restricted to those with wealth: "Hence a poor person cannot be magnificent, since he lacks the means necessary for spending large sums in a fitting way" (1122a25). As the remarks suggest, expenditure alone is not sufficient for magnificence.[19] One must have the taste and judgment that go with knowing how to manage large sums. It is the judgment we associate with public patronage, with those who sponsor civic building, or have brilliant receptions for foreign dignitaries, or underwrite public festivals, or make large benefactions for the homeless. Both the exquisiteness of taste and ampleness of resources point to the members of a privileged class. In its focus on status, magnificence is precisely the sort of virtue Kant would reject and does reject in *The Doctrine of Virtue:*

> The ability to practice beneficence, which depends on property, follows largely from the injustice of the government, which favours certain men and so introduces an inequality of wealthy that makes others need help. This being the case, does the rich man's help to the needy, on which he so readily prides himself as something meritorious, really deserve to be called beneficence at all? [20]

Although Aristotle, himself, in his account of generosity is all too aware that the fineness of giving is relative to holdings, that greater holdings do not equal greater virtue (1120b7–10), in the account of magnificence that concern is eclipsed.

Magnanimity too is a privileged virtue. It is the preserve of those who have the wealth and political position to gain great honor and public recognition for their service (1124a21–24). Their deeds are visible because their position is. Though position alone does not yield excellence and in many cases is a positive deterrence (1124a25–b7), still, for those inclined toward virtue, the opportunities are there for greatness of deed.

In an obvious way, then, the grand scale virtues are exclusive and raise serious questions about their accessibility to otherwise virtuous agents. Their inaccessibility suggests that Aristotle's requirement of the unity of virtues—that to have one virtue implies having them all (1144b33–45a2)—may be overly stringent.[21] The inconsistency between the requirements of generosity and magnificence points to this.

There are various ways to minimize the impact of these virtues. Aristotle can argue that just as cowardice is less reproachable than intemperance since opportunities for its exercise are less ubiquitous than occasions for temperance (1119a25), analogously a defect of magnificence is less blameworthy than the defect of generosity, since its conditions and equipment are less widely available. In fact, Aristotle does not explicitly argue this way here, though it is an option available to him. Instead, applying his notion of the mean, he discusses the absence of magnificence in terms of extreme responses to the same external conditions. Thus the deficiencies relative to magnificence are vulgar spending and niggardliness (1123a20–32). Both presuppose that the agent has more or less the proper resources but simply uses them inappropriately and without taste. The vulgar benefactor will outfit a comic chorus in garish purple or give a small party on the scale of a wedding banquet; the niggardly will routinely calculate how he could have spent less. Both dispositions are defects, though none too serious or disgraceful; they involve no harm to others (1123a23). Overall virtue is not grossly marred.

Alternatively, Aristotle can argue that the grand virtues are not specific virtues within the full complement, but a more personal style of virtue that supervenes on an already complete complement. To be deficient in style is less serious than to be deficient in a specific virtue. Thus, it is not like being courageous yet dishonest, but more like being courageous but not very dashing or charming. It is not as serious a failing. There is partial support for this line of reply in the *Eudemian* and *Nicomachean*. In the *Eudemian* Aristotle distinguishes between a general and a special sense of magnanimity. The former, unlike the latter, is not a separate virtue with a distinct sphere but is an aspect of character "that accompanies all the virtues" (1232a32; b26). Similarly in the *Nicomachean* 1123b30 and 1124a3 Aristotle suggests that magnanimity is supervenient upon the other virtues; it presupposes them and amplifies them. It is an ornament or crown, "for it makes each virtue greater." On this view, the person who lacks the grand style of virtue may still have all the virtues and thus be good, even if in a less spectacular and exquisite way.

But the thrust of these arguments misses the general point that even if the grand scale virtues can be given a more optional role in the account of the virtues, the worry about the dependence of virtue upon external goods, upon power, wealth, experience, and opportunity does not disappear. And by this worry, I do not mean simply that happiness (as the unimpeded *exercise* of virtue) depends upon favorable conditions and equipment, but that goodness itself does. That is, being capable of making choices adequate to the circumstances, indeed of construing the circumstances correctly, requires external equipment and experience. Thus, as we said earlier, choice or *prohairesis* as it reveals good character is not a mere intention to act well, but a decision that concretely exemplifies virtue in a specific context. As such it requires that virtuous choices be informed and embrace the knowledge and experience requisite for the moment. This is implicit in Aristotle's notion of practical *nous* as a kind of inductive experience, constitutive of virtue, that enables an agent to discern successfully the particular circumstances of action.[22] This sort of discernment and correct choice is required, whether the end in question is friendship and the problem how to act as a friend ought in these trying times, or magnificence and how to contribute to the gods in a way that will ensure the city's honor.

The requirement that one have adequate experience is a tall order, and I cannot discuss here ways in which it might be ameliorated. The point now is to indicate that the dependence of virtue upon external goods—power, wealth, friends, experience, technique, and equipment for correct perception and choice—is hardly specific to the possession of the grander virtues. It is not in this way that these virtues raise special *aporiai*.[23]

But in what sense, then, is the portrait of the grand virtues, especially magnanimity, odd? In what sense does it pull apart from the more general account of virtue? In what sense is it deficient as an account of superlative virtue? What is odd is its suggestion that the magnanimous will, as it were, store up efforts for great and spectacular moments, discern as due occasions for response just those from which persons of more ordinary virtue would hesitate or recede. But it is not merely that the magnanimous are willing to perform heroic and dangerous actions, or can act with a graciousness and ease at moments when others face too much internal noise. Rather, it is that their performance at such moments seems to *excuse* them from more ongoing and persistent concern for the welfare of others. It is as if, as Baron charges against the supererogationist, doing *now* what is more than others would do cancels out previous debts for undone moral requirements. This is what I have called the exemption thesis. This sort of charge bears directly on the following description Aristotle offers of magnanimity:

> And it is characteristic of the magnanimous person not to go for common honors or those things in which others excel; and to be inactive and sluggish except where the honor or deed is great, and to be a person of few deeds, but great and notable ones. (1124b23–26)

As I have said, my worry is not that Aristotle is operating with some implicit notion of supererogation; there is no sense of minimal morality that supererogation is needed to supplement. To the contrary, there is ample room within the notion of good character for degrees of perfection and moral progress, just as there is a place for different degrees and kinds of defects. Thus, there are motives that are vicious and intend injury to others, as well as those that are merely foolish or insensible or self-deprecatory; to have certain defects rather than others mars overall virtue in different ways. Rather my concern is with the underlying notion that one can buy one's way out of a more attentive and ongoing concern for the fine, that one can afford to be only intermittently active if one compensates through infrequent but brilliant displays. That one might be able to, it might reasonably be thought, is of a piece with a heroic and status-centered ethics. Whatever the resolution to that general issue, I want to argue that the notion is anomolous, at least within Aristotle's account.

Before making the case, though, it might be contended, and indeed has been by commentators, that Aristotle's above remarks ought not be accorded serious theoretical weight.[24] Along with the description of the voice and gait of the magnanimous person at 1125a13, they are part of the more graphic and "miscellaneous details" of an already overly psychologized portrait:

> And it seems to be characteristic of the magnanimous person to have a slow walk, and a deep voice and a calm speech; for the person who takes few things seriously is not likely to be hurried, nor the one who thinks nothing great to be impetuous, while a shrill voice and a rapid gait are the results of hurry and excitement. (1125a13–16)

In this emphasis on detail, the account stands apart from the character sketches of the other virtues, which on the whole remain more abstract; it is even distinct from the *Eudemian* account of magnanimity in which this sort of concrete portrait is noticeably absent.

There might be reason to dismiss worries if the notion of exemption from more regular moral service occurred only in this psychologized portrait. But it is suggested again in *Nicomachean Ethics* 9.8, when Aristotle remarks that the good person prefers "one great and fine action to many smaller ones," "a year long fine existence to many years that are more ordinary" (1169a22–25). Here, again there is the sense of choosing exceptional feats over more common ones, of giving them a higher priority ranking. Moreover, there is the implication that a record of such feats may permit exemptions from more routine moral matters and from more regular, steady engagement. Greatness of spirit (magnanimity) seems to involve a certain selective detachment from action.

In light of the evidence, then, I think the remarks Aristotle makes in the sketch of magnanimity ought to be taken seriously. Nevertheless, as I shall now argue, there are strong independent reasons for ultimately rejecting their impact on the overall account of virtue.

4. THE INCONGRUITY OF MAGNANIMITY WITHIN THE OVERALL ACCOUNT

That Aristotle's remarks are not fully at home with the rest of his account can be seen from several related considerations. From these will emerge reasons why magnanimity, by Aristotle's own lights, should not be regarded as superlative virtue.

(1) Aristotle lays down as a substantive criterion of the good life that it be a life of *sustained* virtuous activity *(energein sunechōs,* 1170a6). It is for this reason, Aristotle argues, that companionship with virtuous friends is so desirable. For such friends, as collaborators in our projects, help to stimulate and sustain our virtuous interests; as ubiquitous others in our lives, they provide the occasions and objects for good action. This does not mean, as we have said, that an agent must strive to make *every* action an embodiment of virtue, moral or otherwise. But certainly an agent who is inertial most of the time except for highly sporadic spurts of brilliant though selfless activity violates the spirit of that criterion. Thus, the agent who jumps into burning houses and freezing ponds to come to the rescue of others, but who is systematically

unmindful of the milder calls of distress of those around him—of a child who has top-
pled down the stairs or a neighbor who out of loneliness needs someone to talk to every now and again—violates the criterion. His virtue is not *monimos* and *bebaios*—
dependable and reliable.

(2) Not only is such an individual's activity too uneven and bumpy, but it is
lacking in overall responsiveness and sensitivity. It lacks the due regard for other's
distress—great or small—that characterizes an overall sense of justice and decency
(cf. 1129b17–1130a10). To overlook certain ethical problems in favor of those that require (and show off) more exceptional fortitude or grace seems simply too callous and
calculated.

In this regard, consider the following two examples. Lenore is a neighbor who
can be counted on to keep a watchful eye on the block and the person to whom you
would turn in an emergency. She is responsive and friendly, and is careful to remind
you of her standing offer to help if you are in a pinch. You have taken her up on the
offer several times. Megan, in contrast, is a more aloof neighbor, most would agree.
She has never made such offers—to you or others—nor in general would you dream
of asking her for help, though she too is about the neighborhood a lot and apparently
available. On one occasion, though, she came through, unsolicited. Noticing your
struggle with an assailant as you started out for a jog, she warded him off using defense
techniques learned for just this sort of urban combat. The act was at considerable risk;
the dangers real and present. To this day you are not sure why she acted with such
courage on behalf of someone who seems to matter so little in her life. But that the act
was courageous you have no doubt. You feel enormous gratitude and have expressed
it in heartfelt ways. But still, you would not dream of asking her for aid, nor does she
ever ask it of you.

What are we to say about virtue in these two cases? Certainly Megan came
through in an emergency which you have no reason to believe Lenore would have responded to, at least so valiantly. Moreover, it was a helping act that averted considerable emotional and physical injury, possibly even death. The act was heroic,
admirable, morally admirable, that is; and for this you have enormous moral praise.
But there is still something contemptuous about Megan's character, about the not so
invisible sign she seems to wear which says "Don't ask for help unless you really are
up against a wall." Her record suggests she means it, and this makes you feel very uneasy, vulnerable, as if you do not have a neighbor at all. The restriction of her good
deeds to the gravest emergencies earns her your gratitude, but not your trust as someone whom you could reliably count on for her good will and generosity.

I think Megan shares certain similarities with the magnanimous character and
gives us some test of what our response to it might be. There is no denying that Megan's action is morally praiseworthy, and notches above a more lukewarm, less courageous response from others. To have people willing to do such things is desirable and
valuable. But this style of valor does not sit well with other characteristics we admire
in people, like neighborliness, a sense of trust, sympathy, a certain accessibility and
willingness to give of one's time; it seems to squeeze these out. In this sense, her character is not one we would recommend *overall*. It is not the kind of model we hold up
as a moral exemplar for ourselves or our children.

(3) The focus of magnanimity on the spectacular also sits uneasily with Aristotle's formulaic remark that what hits the mean is relative to the individual, and to the circumstances and resources at hand (1107a1). Indeed, the idea of ranking lives, of saying without equivocation that the person who tends to perform certain actions rather than others has the best character, goes against the Aristotelian grain. Thus, in a duly famous passage (1109a15ff.; cf. 1126b4) Aristotle insists that the degree of praise and blameworthiness of an agent is a matter of contextual judgment, a matter of perceiving the circumstances that the agent faces, and of assessing the agent's choice given the alternatives in those circumstances; as he says, the discernment (or judgment) *(krisis)* rests in perception. This entails not only that the manner and degree to which a particular virtue is exemplified must be contextually judged, but equally that the appropriateness of this virtue (as opposed to some other) is, in part, a matter of context. The notion of giving pride of place to one virtue over the others suggests that some advance preview can be given to a life and a determination made as to which virtue the opportunities in that life will favor. This is absurd.

Admittedly, there is a special place in Aristotle's taxonomy of virtues (as there still seems to be in our own) for the sort of greatness *(megalopsuchia)* and courage that comes with the sacrifices of the battlefield (e.g., 1115a33). But how strictly Aristotle would want to defend this ranking is open to debate. The bravery of war has to do with the severity of the risks, the nobleness of the end, and the opportunities for hope, that is, for thinking one's efforts will make a difference (1115b1).[26] The battlefield may exemplify these conditions, but it is not the only place in which they are displayed. To argue that it is, is simply to restrict too narrowly the kinds and contexts of fine actions, indeed even of altruistic self-sacrifices, of which humans are capable. Thus, there is much to be said for the hero in Urmson's example[27] who, new to a unit (and so without motives of friendship), throws himself on a live grenade in order to save the others in the cadre; there is also something to be said for the mother who pleas to have her own life taken, by brutal torture, in place of the torture of her three children. The issue here is not merely the narrow one—that motives of attachment are not *a priori* excluded from the Aristotelian account of moral motives as they are from some other ethical accounts.[28] Rather, my point is the more general one, that elevating certain sorts of act types and traits above others is simply too unresponsive to the variety of circumstances and histories that are the fabric of actual lives, whether of men or women.[29]

The requirements of context recall Aristotle's repeated methodological warnings against transforming ethical theory into a practical *science (epistēmē,* e.g., 1084b13–27, 1098a25ff.). While the philosophical temperament may aspire to make more precise and systematic the data of moral life, theory is ultimately misguided if it seeks the sort of precision that characterizes practical reason and judgment. The best that theory can do is to give a general specification of the kinds of goods that should be included within the best life. This itself will provide some practical aim and target for choice (1094a22–24; *EE* 1214b8). But the actual placement and overall fit of goods in an integrated life is the task of practical reason and *nous;* it is the task, that is, of ethical perception, emotional sensitivity, and choice. It cannot be done in the abstract.

(4) Aristotle's resistance to reify a particular style of life as the best also emerges from his discussion of friendship. For even those equally committed, virtuous individuals who are companions for life will thrive on their differences. Thus, contrary to the popular opinion that Aristotelian virtue companions are duplicate images of each other's virtue, closer scrutiny of his account suggests that the critical sense of self each offers the other depends upon cultivated differences and different points of view. Even here in the closely orchestrated life of shared interest and consensus *(homonoia)* there is no demand for consensus about the portrait of the true *phronimos.*[30] A diversity of style and strength, a differing emphasis on certain virtues rather than others as a result of accident or choice, may peacefully coexist within the Aristotelian friendship of virtue.

But in response to all this, it might be argued that the problem with magnanimity is much more innocuous than we have made out. What has exercised us may not be something peculiar to magnanimity, but rather a symptom of Aristotle's general tendency to offer separate character sketches of the individual virtues apart from their operation in an integrated life.[31] It is only a dull imagination that prevents us from seeing the trait as a *part* rather than the *whole* of a good life. When painted within a more comprehensive character portrait, magnanimity can find a proper balance and place. There is something to this thought, some good reason to be cautious about letting magnanimity swallow up the whole of an agent's character. But having said this, I think Aristotle intends us to view the virtue as expansive and as justifying a certain systematic neglect for the circumstances salient to other virtues—to occasions for gratitude, small scale generosity, routine kindness and favors. It is just this attitude of exemption from more ordinary virtue that is the problem.

5. WHAT THEN OF EXCEPTIONAL VIRTUE?

Aristotle has good reason to want to reject the idea of ranking virtuous lives. But still we should expect that his theory leaves some room for the notion of exceptional virtue and gives some general account of it. If the magnanimous person is not the one we should think of as exceptionally virtuous, then who is? Common sense suggests great virtue has something to do with the willingness to make sacrifices and forfeitures, though not in the calculated or self-indulgent way the magnanimous person exhibits that capacity. Thus, to be ready to act for others at considerable cost to self is a mark of serious moral commitment. Aristotle endorses these intuitions in *Rhetoric* 1.9. There he identifies acting for the sake of the fine with altruistic action and suggests that motive increases in fineness to the degree to which it aims at benefit to others without advantage to self:

> Fine also are those actions whose advantage may be enjoyed after death, as opposed to those whose advantage may be enjoyed during one's lifetime; for the latter are more likely to be for one's own sake only. Also all actions done for the sake of others, since these less than other actions are done for one's own sake; and all successes which benefit others and not oneself; and services done to one's benefactors, for this is just; and good deeds generally, since they are not

directed to one's own profit . . . And those qualities are fine which give more pleasure to other people than to their possessors. (1367a1–20; revised Oxford transl. I have replaced "fine" for "noble" in the rendering of *ta kala.)*

The view needs to be more carefully qualified as to what counts as justified forfeiture. Certainly not all acts of beneficence justify sacrifices of personal goods or self; some such acts would seem gratuitous, futile, insensible, or self-deprecating. Aristotle makes these qualifications in the *Nicomachean Ethics.* The overly generous or lavish person is foolish *(elithiou)* in overlooking her own needs (1121a25, 1120b5); her benefactions exceed her own resources and are indiscriminate in the selection of beneficiary (1121a30–b15). Equally, the soldier who is overly ready to face dangers and sacrifice his life "at too little gain" inadequately appreciates the worth of life and limb (1117b20); he is contrasted with the person of real courage who knows the true pain of ending a worthwhile life (1117b10–15). Again, some sacrifices betray a fundamental contempt for self, and thus constitute, on Aristotle's view, injustices (1138a9–14).[32]

But what I presently want to consider is the suggestive idea in the *Rhetoric* that a conception of altruistic action requires the absenting of the agent from the state of affairs which he intends. When we imagine a world in which the desired state of affairs obtains *without* the agent having to be present ("after his lifetime" as it were) we conceptually distill the notion of acting for a beneficiary rather than for self. Aristotle's conception recalls Williams' notion of a "non-I desire."[33] Briefly, an I-desire is one whose propositional content requires I or related expressions; a non-I desire does not. So for example, when I desire to help Libby out of true concern, what matters is not that *I* help her, but that she be helped, whoever happens to do the helping; my desire is not cancelled if I cannot be the one who helps. Similarly, if the desire is "that she be helped" I need not be there to witness the helping or to gain any advantage for myself from the helping.[34] That should not matter to me or be part of my motivation. Now actually untangling these motives is another question, and it does not seem to be a part of Aristotle's remarks (nor Williams') that an agent can always tell which motive is in fact operative and doing the work. The implication is rather that exemplary virtue requires the possibility of this sort of motivation.

Now in the *Nicomachean* the conception of altruism is somewhat different. While the focus is still on willingness to make forfeitures, there is not the same eagerness to remove the agent from the circumstances of action or the state of affairs that results: self-sacrifice is often for *my* friend and *my* country; and in the act of self-sacrifice, the agent may gain, just as the beneficiary does. But the satisfactions of each are different: the agent derives the intrinsic pleasure of fine activity, of making himself the seat of excellence; the beneficiary gains the satisfactions of external goods, of the sort of things one can give another without robbing the other (or self) of rational agency. While such intrinsic pleasure is not the reason for acting, there is still the acknowledgment, lacking in the *Rhetoric,* that virtuous performance may bring with it agent-specific pleasures:

> And it is true of the good person that he does many things for the sake of his friends and his country, and if necessary would die for them . . . And they

will throw away wealth on condition that their friends gain more; for while a person's friend gains wealth, he himself gains fineness; and he thus assigns the greater good to himself. And it is the same way concerning honors and office; for these are things one will sacrifice to a friend, for this is fine and praiseworthy for oneself. It is right, then, that such a person be thought good who chooses what is fine in place of all other things. And he may even give up actions to a friend, for it may be finer to be the cause of a friend's acting than to act himself. And in all actions that are praiseworthy, the good person appears to assign to himself more of what is fine. (1169a18–1169b1)

Now there is a sense in which this removal of self from the pool of external goods is precisely what is missing in the portrait of magnanimity. There is all too conscious and priggish a selection of the sort of occasions that are a worthy match for the magnanimous person's fortitude or grace. They are the sort that typically reap honor, that will befit his position and importance. He does not easily surrender the moments for such display. Though he surely would not vie with others to exploit such moments, they are the ones that appeal to *his* sense of virtue. In this sense, the scope of his desire to help is restricted. While it is unlikely that his desire to help would be voided if he could not be the one to act, what he takes to be an occasion for action is too bound up with the thought of his own agency and his self-image. In the selection of circumstance he projects too strongly his own role. To this it might be replied that we *all* make certain arbitrary selections in the assignment of our aid. We cannot help everyone, we cannot give to everyone, and so we make certain discriminations. But there are some grounds for discrimination which exclude for the wrong reasons. I have been suggesting that the magnanimous person's disregard for the smaller, more everyday kindnesses, in favor of those that show off his stature, is that sort of bias.[35]

Notes

1. "Kantian Ethics and Supererogation," *Journal of Philosophy* 84 (1987): 237–62.
2. Ibid., 258.
3. These are discussed in *Nicomachean Ethics* 4.2, 3; *Eudemian Ethics* 3.5, 6; and *Magna Moralia* 1.25, 26. For a different conception of superlative virtue, see Aristotle's brief remarks at *Rhetoric* 1374a25.
4. The term *dei* and its cognates are etymologically the source of our term "deontology," and through Latin, the source of the term "obligation." The relation of the term to moral obligation has been explored by Gauthier, vol. II.2, pp. 568–74 of his commentary to *L'Ethique à Nicomaque* (Louvain, 1970), and more recently by T. Irwin in "Aristotle's Conception of Morality," in *Proceedings of the Boston Area Colloquium in Ancient Philosophy,* edited by John Cleary, vol. I (Lanham, Md., 1985), 115–50.
5. "For the majority of lawful acts are those acts prescribed from the point of view of virtue in general. For the law prescribes living in accordance with each virtue and prohibits living in accordance with each vice" (1130b22–24; cf. 1129b20–25). Laws involve an education *(paidia)* concerned with the virtues requisite for the common good (1130b26). Aristotle's distinction between cases involving assault and those involving hubris draws attention to the importance of motive in the determination of justice, cf. *Rhetoric* 1374a13–15, 1378b23–25.
6. I am indebted in this paragraph to Gregory Trianowsky's discussion "The Autonomy of the Ethics of Virtue," *Journal of Philosophy* 83 (1986): 16–40.
7. See 1135a25ff., 1136a5–10; also *Rhetoric* 1374b4–10.

8. See Sherman, "Character, Planning and Choice in Aristotle," *Review of Metaphysics* 39 (1985): 83–106.

9. "What is in our powers *(di'hēmōn)* in a sense includes what our friends achieve for us, since the originating principle *(archē)* is in ourselves," 1112b27–28; cf. 1112b10–11.

10. Thus Aristotle distinguishes between a narrow and general sense of justice and injustice. Narrow injustice has to do with unfair gain, i.e., *pleonexia;* general injustice has to do with vice in general, and indicates that any one of the virtues requisite for the full complement, e.g., generosity, courage, etc. is lacking. See *NE* 5.1, 2.

11. 1126b21, 1128b21, 1132a3f., 1169a3, a16.

12. See the discussions in *NE* 5.10 and *Rhetoric* 1.13.

13. 1137b29–32, 1374b20–23; *Politics* 1268b7–17.

14. So Aristotle remarks: "For it makes no difference whether a good person has robbed a bad person or a bad person a good one, nor whether it is a good or bad man that has committed adultery; the law looks only at the different amounts [of damage] in the injury" (1132a3–24).

15. There is of course a sense in which one may undersell one's self, give up too much of what is rightfully one's own by being "too decent." I consider Aristotle's view of these sorts of forfeitures in the last section.

16. Cf. Susan Wolf, "Moral Saints," *Journal of Philosophy* 79 (1982): 419–39 and Robert Adams' reply in the *Journal of Philosophy* 81 (1984): 392–401.

17. The list need not be fixed with these; other socially attractive features might be added or amended, in keeping with the Aristotelian dictum of allowing time to be "co-partner" and "co-discoverer" of a more accurate account (1098a22). But some collection of these sort of traits is part of the account of good character.

18. For a very useful, selective review of the literature on Aristotle's conception of magnanimity, see W. F. R. Hardie, " 'Magnanimity' in Aristotle's Ethics" *Phronesis* 78: 63–79. Cf. D. A. Rees " 'Magnanimity' in the *Eudemian* and *Nicomachean Ethics"* in *Untersuchungen zur Eudemischen Ethik,* edited by P. Moraux and D. Harlfinger (Gruyter, 1970), 231–43. I agree with Hardie in rejecting Gauthier's contention that the magnanimous person is intended as a portrait of the self-sufficient philosopher. See R. A. Gauthier, *Magnanimité* (Paris, 1951) as well as the relevant section of the commentary of Gauthier and Jolif, *L'Ethique à Nicomaque,* Commentaire vol. II.1 (Louvain,1970), 272ff. Stewart also finds in the account of magnanimity an emphasis on the notion of moral autonomy, and indeed likens the account to a portrait of the ideality of Kant's good will. J. A. Stewart, *Notes on the Nicomachean Ethics,* vol. 2 (Oxford, 1892), 336. In what follows, I offer reasons for rejecting such a resemblance.

19. Thus, Gauthier and Jolif see a shift in the account from a focus on merely quantitative differences between magnificence and liberality to qualitative ones, (vol. II.1, p. 271.). It is not the size of expenditure which is crucial, but the brilliance of the work which results. As Aristotle himself remarks, even a cheap baby present, if exquisite in taste can be evidence of magnificence (1123a15). While I agree that the difference between magnificence and liberality is not merely one of degree, even so, the *primary* instances of magnificence are those in which both expenditure is large and aesthetic judgment is impeccable.

20. *The Doctrine of Virtue,* translated by Mary Gregory (Philadelphia, 1964), 122 [454]. I am grateful to Marcia Baron who cites this passage in "Supererogation."

21. This is the primary concern of Irwin's paper, "The Unity of Aristotelian Virtue," to appear in *Oxford Studies in Ancient Philosophy* (1988) (from the Oberlin Colloquium of 1986).

22. On the notion of practical *nous,* see the notoriously difficult passage at 1143a35–b5 as well as Aristotle's remarks about ethical perception at 1142a23–30. The former passage has been given extensive commentary recently by Norman Dahl, *Practical Reason, Aristotle, and Weakness of the Will* (Minneapolis, 1984), Appendix I, 227–36. See also M. Nussbaum's pertinent piece, "The Discernment of Perception: An Aristotelian Conception of Private and Public Rationality" in *Proceedings of the Boston Area Colloquium in Ancient Philosophy,* 151–201. I discuss this also in the chapter, "Discerning the Particulars" of my forthcoming book, *The Fabric of Character* (Oxford, 1989).

23. It still needs to be conceded that the vulnerability of goodness is not a thesis which Ar-

istotle embraces without some ambivalence. Commentators standardly point to the recommendation of the self-sufficient comtemplative life in *NE* 10.6–8 as evidence of the internal tension. But equally, it emerges in the account of magnanimity. The magnanimous person is on the one hand an individual who has status and position requisite for publicly noteworthy action, and who seeks and enjoys the acclaim for accomplishment afterward. He is a person of pride who puffs up with honor that is his due (1123b16–24a26). But on the other hand, he is one who does exceptionally well in cramped conditions, whose virtue shines through both when he has to make do at the front end and when his luck runs out midstream (NE 1.1100b31–1101a6; cf. *Rhetoric* 1367b15). In fact he has a disdain for fortune and for benefaction from others (1124a14–20, 24b9–19) and has an almost sage-like mentality that one can do well with little, however adverse the conditions (1125a11).

Some of the ambivalence is relatively superficial. The disdain is for honor from unworthy sources, from those whose opinion cannot be trusted; honor from highly esteemed and respected sources is quite a different matter (1124a5–11; cf. *Rhetoric* 1384a25–35, b23). Equally, the magnanimous person's disdain for favors and more reliable memory of his record as benefactor than beneficiary (1124b13) seems less objectionable and less like ingratitude when put within the context of Aristotle's more general thesis that we derive greater pleasure from being agents than patients, from actively exercising our excellences than from being activated upon externally. (Cf. especially *NE* 9.7, though these remarks still jar with Aristotle's contention in *Rhetoric* 1374a21–25 and 1374b16–17 that goodness and decency require showing gratitude to benefactors.)

Still, other ambivalences are deeper and harder to eradicate. On the one hand, there is the general preoccupation of the magnanimous person with honor (albeit from the right sources) as a litmus test of his worth; yet on the other, the sense that he, above all others, has an accurate assessment of his character, that he knows *for himself,* from his *own* deeds, his true self-worth. His self-knowledge is central to the portrait; and in his ability to neither under- or overestimate his resources and capacities, he achieves just what the more humble and vain lack (1125a21–30). Yet all the same, Aristotle implies that his self-importance is tangled up with honor and acclaim, and his relish for it. Here it is instructive to contrast the attitude toward honor in Gyges' myth *(Rep.* II). According to the myth, the true test for the individual committed to virtue is to do well but to be uniformly misunderstood, to have self-knowledge of one's fine worth but to be held in ill-repute and disgrace by all. The challenge to Socrates is to show that for this individual, robbed of external acclaim, indeed, whose goodness is invisible to all but himself, virtue still pays. In constructing the portrait of magnanimity, Aristotle seems tempted by the model, though is ultimately unwilling to embrace it. He appreciates full well that genuine honor is parasitic upon fine action, that the good is in the action, and only derivatively in the honor *(NE* 1.5). But unlike Plato, he also appreciates that self-knowledge and self-esteem require fundamentally, as common sense confirms, external support *(Rhetoric* 1384a25–35, 1384b23–27). To have self-consciousness and self-knowledge requires what is extrinsic to self. Though he would agree virtue pays even if robbed of reward, he would deny that one could sustain a sense of shame or self-respect *(aidōs)* without others. On the relation of these claims to Aristotle's views on friendship, see Nancy Sherman, "Aristotle on Friendship and the Shared Life," *Philosophy and Phenomenological Research* 47 (1987): 589–623.

24. Thus Dirlmeier, in *Nikomachische Ethik* (1956), 249. Grant too seems to be dismissive about the details, especially in his claim that the portrait is an idealized sketch of what is "essentially not a human attitude," Alexander Grant, *The Ethics of Aristotle*, essays and notes, vol. 2 (London, 1885), 72. Rees, on the other hand, concedes philosophical importance to most of the details (240).

25. Contrast however the remark in 9.8 that virtue requires "being especially busy with fine actions" *(diapherontōs spoudazontas,* 1169a6) with the more restricted remark in 4.3—that the magnanimous person is busy with few things *(ho peri oliga spoudazōn,* 1125a15).

26. The battle against sickness, Aristotle thinks, lacks the last element, as does death at sea, when one has reason to give up hope for safety (1115a34–b6).

27. J. O. Urmson "Saints and Heroes" in A. I. Melden, ed. *Essays in Moral Philosophy* (Seattle, 1958).

28. Indeed Aristotle says friendship is among the finest circumstances for virtuous action (1154b30, 1169b12).

29. My remarks should not obscure the male bias in Aristotle's ethics, of which, no doubt, the honors of the battlefield are a part. Rather, it is to suggest that the subordination of female virtue (cf. *Politics* 1260a12–30; *NE* 1162a22–27) like the elevation of male virtue and its typical contexts, is overly restrictive of full human possibilities.

30. See *EE* 1245a30–34 for the acknowledgment that a virtue friend need not realize all of one's ends or interests.

31. Pears cites this as a general problem in Aristotle's presentation of the virtues, "Courage as a Mean" in A. O. Rorty, *Essays on Aristotle's Ethics* (Berkeley, 1980), 187.

32. Strictly speaking, the wrongdoing is not against self, (as it would be for a Kantian), but against the state. Aristotle's reasoning here, perhaps overly simplistic, has to do with consent—that one cannot commit an injustice against another if it has been voluntarily consented to. The state, though not the self, fails to give consent to the injury against its citizen.

33. "Egoism and Altruism" in *Problems of the Self* (Cambridge, 1973), 260–85.

34. Williams correctly notes that the class of non-I desires is wider than that of altruistic desires; thus, in his wonderful example, the cranky eccentric not believing in life after death may write in his will that he wants a chimpanzee party to be held in the cathedral, not so that he can witness it, but "just because it would be such a striking event" (263). His main point, though, is that altruistic non-I desires do not carry with them impersonal demands, that is a desire that others—"everyone" promote the benevolent end. In this sense, altruism does not entail a (Kantian) universalizability criterion. Aristotle, it is worth noting, does not argue for such a criterion in this passage or elsewhere.

35. See Aristotle's suggestive remarks at 1109b1ff. indicating that the virtuous person should be able to correct for such distortions in perception. I would like to thank Marshall Presser for his comments and support in the writing of this paper. I am also grateful to the American Council of Learned Societies under whose auspices this paper was completed.

Character and Ethical Theory

JOEL KUPPERMAN

Ethical philosophy has provided two very different models of choice. In one, an agent encounters a situation in which two or more alternative courses of action are available. He or she then tests these against a rationally derivable theory. If the theory is Kantian, this means that each alternative is to be tested against the categorical imperative: Can the agent will the maxim embodied by the alternative to be a universal law? Does it treat other rational beings as ends instead of means? Could it play a part in an ideal moral realm? If all options pass the test, then any one of them is morally licit. If "imperfect duties" are involved, then moral grounds are still relevant to a decision; in the more frequent case in which imperfect duties are not involved, the decision has to be made on grounds that lie outside of morality and outside of Kant's theory. Any option that fails the test of the categorical imperative is immoral. If there are two options and one fails, then the other is our duty.[1] In the decision procedure of consequentialism (one form of which is the classical utilitarianism associated with Jeremy Bentham and John Stuart Mill), one compares the likely consequences of the various alternatives or of the policies they represent. The strategy is to maximize value: One should choose the action, or follow the policy, that is likely to lead to the greatest value in the world.[2]

In the other model, an agent is assumed either to have a formed character or to be in the process of forming one. Thus choice takes place against a background of habits, inhibitions, and patterns of satisfaction with certain kinds of behavior. The agent either has the desire (or lack of desire) to become a certain kind of person, or has the satisfaction (or lack of satisfaction) in being a certain kind of person. When difficult choices present themselves, character is crucial. Thus, if given a ring of invisibility that made it possible to do anything with impunity, most people would behave badly, according to Plato; but someone whose virtue is not a matter of habit only, who "has philosophy," can choose a good life.[3] Aristotle suggests, as the test of whether someone really possesses a virtue, that what is crucial is whether he or she enjoys behaving in the manner corresponding to that virtue.[4] In the *Analects* of Confucius the suggestion is made, even more sharply than in the works of Plato and Aristotle, that for

115

someone who has developed the right kind of character, a pattern of conduct can be subsumed naturally under pre-established decisions about character.[5]

It is important to stress that the two models I have presented do not directly conflict. It is possible, that is, to hold that the second model, which is dominant both in classical Greek and classical Chinese philosophy, gives the best account of how someone can be prepared to make ethical choices and can integrate these into a sense of self, and also to hold that the first model is correct in pointing out that a rationally derivable theory is needed for the actual decision making. Thus one can be Aristotelian or Confucian about the role of character in decision making and also be a Kantian or a consequentialist.[6]

Despite this, it is clear that the two models pull in opposite directions. The first model, with its emphasis on rationally derivable theory, tends to lead to portrayal of ethical decision as largely a matter of deployment of appropriate theory, which itself then gets viewed as impersonal and available equally to all. Despite the opposition between Kantians and consequentialists, it is easy for someone who is reading some of the works of either school to get the picture of an essentially faceless ethical agent who is equipped by theory to make moral choices that lack psychological connection with either the agent's past or future. This may be accentuated in the case of Kantian theory by Kant's belief that pure reason both makes possible rational moral choice and is outside of time.[7]

In this paper I will argue for the primacy of the second model of ethical decision, which takes character or the process of character formation as crucial. By the "character" of an agent I will mean a complex that includes the presence or absence of dispositions to recognize certain situations as ethically problematic (as calling for ethical decision, possibly decision that requires reflection) and dispositions to treat certain factors as having special weight in ethical decision, and, more fundamentally, the presence or absence of concerns for certain things thought to matter and commitments (to people, organizations, causes, and/or values) such that these commitments provide a connecting thread among different moments of the agent's life.[8] Having argued for the ethical primacy of character, I will then say something about what is left for ethical theory.

1

Let us assume for the sake of argument that there is an entirely correct, rationally derivable ethical theory, T. We can leave it open what T is, but bear in mind that Kantian and consequentialist theories are the main candidates.

At this point the temptation is great to assume that two elements only are required for correct ethical choice. One is that an agent has learned T well enough to remember it on short notice and to understand what it means. The other element is a good will: the agent must will to choose what T dictates. There can be no "backsliding" or *akrasia*.

This is naive. Any acceptable ethical theory is likely to be abstract and highly general, and certainly the two leading candidates have been presented as abstract and highly general. Thus, inevitably, an agent has the problem of mediating between theory and the case at hand. As Kant points out, moral laws "require a power of judgment sharpened by experience, partly in order to decide in what cases they apply and partly to procure for them an access to man's will and an impetus to their practice."[9] The first step in approaching any problematic case is to have a sense of what is ethically salient.[10]

We must bear in mind two facts about ethical life that are easily overlooked. The first is that someone who makes ethical decisions characteristic of a good person cannot make them constantly.[11] Life would be unbearable if every moment of every day were treated as calling for an ethically problematic choice. Hence the first step in qualifying as a good person is to have a sense of when a situation is ethically problematic, and of when it is appropriate to stop to think. This in turn requires a perception such that some features of the situation or of one or more of the available alternatives jump out, as it were, at one, or trigger an ethical mode of thought. It is easily assumed that people who behave immorally have thought about their conduct and decided badly, or through weakness of will have not acted on what had been a correct decision; but there is much to suggest that such people in many cases do not think at all about what they are doing, simply taking it not to be problematic.

The second fact is that even if X views situation S as ethically problematic, X will need some way of structuring S in order to think effectively about it. In the real world ethically problematic situations typically include objects with colors, shapes, masses, velocities, etc., and people with hopes, fears, dreams, toothaches, etc.; if everything is relevant, there is nowhere to begin. In a situation in which dozens of objects and people are in motion, and one of them is taking your wallet without your permission, it requires a certain perception of things for the last-mentioned fact to leap out as being of special relevance to ethical judgment. The sciences began to make progress when (among other steps toward rigor) scientists rigorously excluded many features of the world (e.g., the colors of the balls rolling down the inclined plane, the smell of nearby flowers) from consideration. Something like this must be true also of ethics. How can X structure situation S in order to think about it ethically in an effective way?

One answer is that traditional moral rules, the kind we were taught as children, not only are prescriptive but also are guides to perception.[12] It is important to make this point partly because it has become a commonplace that ethical "rigorism" is unacceptable, that traditional moral rules all or almost all have imaginable exceptions; and many philosophers are tempted to conclude from this that traditional moral rules have no usefulness for intelligent adults. But even if there are imaginable cases in which someone, say, should steal or should lie, it may be useful that traditional moral rules govern people's perceptions so that situations in which one of the alternatives involves stealing or lying leap out as ethically problematic and also so that this aspect seems especially salient. It may be useful, in addition, that mature, thoughtful people who believe that there are imaginable situations in which one should steal or lie also have generalized inhibitions about stealing or lying.[13]

The role of traditional moral rules in Kantian ethics is so obvious that it is easily overlooked. Maxims are the crucial intermediaries between the categorical imperative and specific cases: the categorical imperative tests maxims rather than specific decisions. When Kant does give examples, it is clear that maxims are drawn from the familiar world of traditional morality and are formulated in terms of either keeping or violating a traditional moral requirement. A twentieth-century reader may wonder "Why are the maxims given in the *Foundations of the Metaphysics of Morals* so simple? Why not allow for much more complicated and qualified maxims?" The *Metaphysical Principles of Virtue* suggests that it is by no means clear what Kant's answer to this would be. But a more radical suggestion is that, whether simple or complicated, the maxims presuppose the structure provided by a moral tradition, and that for someone totally outside that moral tradition the maxims to be tested could look very different indeed. It is not clear that someone who has not been influenced by any moral tradition could begin the process of Kantian ethical reflection at all; this point is not merely of theoretical significance.[14]

Moral traditions also must play a crucial role in any viable consequentialist decision procedure. On the face of it, this might seem preposterous, especially in relation to the simplest form of consequentialism, act consequentialism. If we are to weigh the values likely to be produced by various alternatives, and we are to choose the alternative that produces the most favorable balance of what is good over what is bad, what need is there for moral tradition?

The answer can be appreciated only in relation to the controversies surrounding consequentialism. One objection to consequentialism is that, however plausible it may sound in the abstract, it simply is unworkable: we never can know the consequences of any action.[15] Other objections found widely in the literature are that the recommendation of actions which all or almost all of us would consider immoral can be derived from consequentialist theory: e.g., hanging an innocent person so that riots will not occur, or torturing an innocent person to the delight of a large number of sadists. The response frequently made by consequentialists to these latter objections is to doubt that their theory would indeed endorse what is alleged. When side-effects are considered, including the effects on people's dispositions that play a part in their future choices, and including effects on people's faith in various protective institutions, is it really clear that hanging the innocent man, or whatever, would have on the whole good consequences? It may be suggested that the actions which intuitively seem immoral are generally likely to have bad consequences, especially if we look to the long run and bear in mind facts that are not likely to change about people and about social organizations.

This may well be true, but it also may be that in some cases it is wishful thinking: we cannot rule out the possibility that an act most of us would consider vicious could turn out to have some exceptionally good, not entirely unforeseeable consequences. In my opinion it is reasonable to assume that unless there are reasons of special weight and character to the contrary, the long-run consequences of an action are likely to be good or bad to roughly the degree of the short-run consequences. This assumption is weaker than a claim to virtual certainty about the degree of goodness of long-run consequences. It is far from clear that in the great majority of cases we can claim virtual certainty even about the goodness of the short-run consequences of actions. In some cases, especially those that involve a startling or unusual action (e.g., hanging the innocent man to avoid a riot), it would appear that we have very little ground for confidence of judgments even of short-run consequences. At the other end of the spectrum, when X decides capriciously or out of spite to run someone over with his automobile, we can be virtually certain that the short-run consequences will be bad.

How can someone who holds a consequentialist theory respond to the difficulties of predicting consequences? A part of any reasonable response is to admit that there are cases of moral choice in which, given a consequentialist theory, we cannot be said to know what is morally right. A great many public policy decisions might fall in this category. The admission that one does not know which of the possible policies will have the best consequences in the long run is consistent with having grounds for confidence that one policy will have better consequences than another, if these grounds for confidence are not so strong that one can be said to know which policy will have the best consequences. There are advantages indeed in political discourse to one's being able to advocate a policy on moral grounds without necessarily having to condemn proponents of rival policies as immoral. But take the case in which one has grounds for confidence that hanging the innocent man will have bad consequences on the whole, without these grounds being such that one knows this. Here it may look as if a moral theory which did not offer assured moral condemnation of hanging the innocent man was not doing the job we expect of a moral theory. And indeed, if we were to say that we do not *know* whether in the long run the consequences of hanging the innocent man would be bad or not (although we have grounds to think that they will be), and if we then went on to say that we do not know whether hanging the innocent man would be morally wrong, the consequences of this limp moral stance could themselves be predicted to be bad.

Consequentialist theories are generally taken by their proponents to be prescriptive as well as rationally justified; hence they must be useful as well as well-founded and consistent. To provide systematic moral guidance of the sort required of a usable moral theory, consequentialist theories must offer definite and assured answers even in some cases in which we cannot attain virtual certainty for the short run, or much ground for confidence for the long run, as to which option will have the best consequences. The only way such a theory can do this is to fall back on a mechanism other than estimation of consequences of actions for determining what we should do. The most plausible mechanism is the appeal to established moral rules. A good example of its use is to be found in G. E. Moore's *Principia Ethica,* where it is suggested that we never are in a position to be confident, in any particular case, that "neglect of an established rule will probably be the best course of action possible."[16] A somewhat similar appeal is found in recent work of R. M. Hare.[17] The point is not just that established moral rules can function as "rules of thumb," but also that there are generally good consequences when members of society are prepared to follow the rules in all cases to which they apply, except for those in which there are unusually strong grounds for confidence that an exception to the rules would have optimal consequences. This stance is consistent with the realization that some of the established moral rules of a society may be inadequate, and that conscience may turn out to have been a poor moral guide.[18] Consequentialist theory can help us over time move away from social roles whose general consequences are on balance not optimal; it can help us not to cling to pointless virtues and not to condemn harmless vices.

Do moral rules by themselves then provide what is needed in order to apply Kantian or consequentialist ethical theory? Clearly there must be still more to the story. Three factors especially stand out. First, even if moral rules function effectively in a number of cases as ways of alerting us that a situation is ethically problematic and as guides to our perception of the ethically problematic situation, there are cases in which they are unlikely to perform that role effectively. These are cases in which what is at stake, while important, is also subtle and psychological, concerning the feelings, attitudes, policies, or life plans of other people or, for that matter, of ourselves. A moral rule to the effect of "Do not hurt other people" or "Do not damage other people's lives," while acceptable to both Kantians and consequentialists, is unlikely to carry us very far toward noticing the ways in which our actions might cause psychological harm to others or to ourselves. It simply is easier, in the general run of cases, to be aware that something would count as stealing or killing than to be aware that something would count as damaging another person's life. In many cases it helps considerably to be a sensitive person.

The second factor is that depth of concern must be an element in any reliably effective perception of features of situations as ethically salient. It is, of course, not enough to notice that an action would count as stealing, killing, or damaging another person's life; one must care that it has this characteristic. Concern is required, at least minimally, if it is to count against an action that it would be killing or damaging to another person's life. More than minimal concern is required so that one takes such a fact seriously in the face of what may be considerable temptation. Someone who makes ethical choices reliably well must be committed to certain values and forms of behavior, and there must be some forms of behavior that he or she will be prepared to dismiss out of hand. One of the signs of strong character is when a person says flatly of a possible course of action of type X, "I do not do X."

Finally, much virtuous conduct has to do with projects continued and realized over time, or with relationships (friendship, marriage, etc.) in which the relationship can take on meaning in someone's life that transcends the meaning of any of its episodes. Ethical decisions in relation to matters of these sorts are especially interconnected and not readily isolated from one another. Hence a factor crucial to virtue is what has been called "commitment," which involves an integrated long-term loyalty to projects, persons, and/or values.[19]

This last point looms large in the Confucian analysis of what gets translated as "sincerity."[20] A little thought shows that sincerity cannot require merely that what one says or how one presents oneself corresponds to what one is thinking at that very moment. Reliability over time is required, so that what one says or how one presents oneself corresponds to continuing features of what one is. It can be argued, further, that self-knowledge, as the phrase is normally used, presupposes a decision to maintain such continuing features, or at least the absence of a decision to reject them.[21]

The points that we have just been making add up to the following conclusion: If there is a correct ethical theory T, one needs in addition to it:

(1) A mechanism to pick out situations that are ethically problematic,

(2) A mechanism for perceiving ethically problematic situations in such a way that certain features seem salient,

(3) Sensitivity to features that are important but are not picked out by (2),

(4) Concern, so that what is picked out as ethically salient matters,

(5) Commitment, so that there is integrated long-term loyalty to values, projects, etc.

These factors fall under the heading of character, as it was defined at the beginning of this paper. Hence good character is required for reliably correct ethical choice. This is not only the obvious point that one must have a good will as well as the knowledge of what is right. Someone who lacks an adequate set of perceptions, concerns, and commitments cannot be relied upon to know what is right. Sometimes he or she can get the correct ethical answer as it were by luck; but in many cases the correct answer will disappear into the huge, unmediated gap between theory and particular case.

2

Someone who has accepted the argument thus far might turn the question around: What need is there for ethical theory? It would appear that someone who had good character but was innocent of philosophical ethics could lead a virtuous life. Ethical theories, such as Kant's or utilitarianism, provide us with a mechanism for evaluating maxims, policies, or courses of action, and also provide an interpretive framework within which we can make sense of familiar rules. But surely, it will be said, someone who has good character, who is well brought up and kind, can be virtuous without a need for a special mechanism for evaluating maxims, policies, or courses of action, and without viewing his or her virtuous behavior in some special interpretive framework.

Part of my answer is that, while it is possible to behave virtuously without any tincture of ethical theory, ethical theories have so much to contribute to the process by which virtues are formulated that any group of people is in a much better position to behave virtuously if they are armed with a good ethical theory than if they are not. I will merely outline the reasons for this part of my answer; to go into more detail would be to enter the debate about what an optimal ethical theory would be like—a subject which falls outside the limits of this paper. My view is that there is more than one ethical theory that is better than no theory at all.

Indeed it has been widely noticed that leading ethical theories are closer in their dictates for conduct than they might seem in the abstract. Something like this has been true for theories in other areas; one might recall the difficulty of finding an experimental test that would distinguish between Einstein's Theory of Relativity and Newtonian physics, and the crucial role that the observations of the orbit of the planet Mercury played in resolving this. Not all ethical philosophers are happy with "desert island" examples; but anyone who has tried to construct cases in which it was entirely clear that Kantian ethics and act utilitarianism would yield different injunctions can only admire J. J. C. Smart's adroitness in creating an example, which was, of course, a desert island case.[22]

If leading ethical theories all tell us that in general we should not break promises, steal, torture, etc., what do they contribute that goes beyond the combination of traditional morality and a disposition to be kind? Part of the answer is that traditional morality can be faulty and a disposition to be kind can be directed in a less than ideal way. One has only to think of slavery or the subjection of women to apprehend the permanent possibility that "nice" people, under the guidance of traditional morality, can acquiesce in atrocious or unworthy practices. Within such a framework, kindness can be directed toward the comfort, but not toward respecting the dignity, of those who are worst off.

One of the functions of an ethical theory, such as Kantian ethics or utilitarianism, is to facilitate the criticism of existing practices. Now it would be naive in the extreme to suppose that moral awakenings, in say, the last hundred and fifty years, can be credited to armies of Kantians or utilitarians or to representatives of other ethical theories. My claim is a more modest one. Both Kantian ethics and utilitarianism, which can be taken as paradigms of ethical theories, are marked by an attempt to make moral judgment systematic and comprehensive, by going beyond assortments of familiar moral rules in order to find the elements that unify and justify them. My claim is, first, that the moral pioneers who helped to change general thinking on such matters as slavery, the subjection of women, or the entitlements of the very poor had, at the least, theory-like elements in their thinking. They saw that all of the moral considerations that applied to whites also applied to blacks, that those which were applicable to men were applicable to women, and that the general thrust toward the prevention of misery which links many elements of familiar morality had special relevance to the plight of the very poor. No doubt these theory-like elements were in many cases not well-formulated, and no doubt also it was not uncommon to find the same person combining elements that might seem to belong to different theoretical orientations, or mixing what we would now consider moral sophistication with backwardness. My claim is, second, that there is no plausible way in which a group of people can begin to criticize an established morality except by means of such theory-like elements. If one's moral universe consists solely of an assortment of familiar rules, with no attention given to connecting and underlying elements, where is criticism to begin? Third, to the extent that getting behind familiar rules is desirable for moral progress, someone who has the systematic sense of justifications and connections that is provided by an ethical theory ought to be in a better position to engage in the necessary reflection than someone whose thinking is marked merely by half-developed theoretical elements. Thus one can see the great usefulness of ethical theory in facilitating the criticism of existing practices. One can claim this without claiming that all advocates of an ethical theory will use it in the same way or will use it well: the discussion in the first part of this paper should have made this obvious.

Part of the usefulness of ethical theories also is this. We have pointed out that awareness of a situation as ethically problematic and also awareness of factors in a situation as salient, both require a structuring of experience that can be provided by a moral tradition. Some matters can best be judged, however, if we eschew immediate response, and instead choose to reflect on the facts of the case. Reflection, like perception, needs to be structured in order to be effective: we need to know what considerations require further examination, and how we are to weigh against each other facts that seem to lead us in opposite directions. Again we might ask: Is there any systematic way in which we can do this without what amounts to at least the beginnings of ethical theory? There are many ethical issues, including most matters of public policy, and also the issue of how we are to regard the putative rights of children and of animals, which cannot be solved either by straightforward application of traditional morality or by a resolve to be good-hearted. In cases in which, whatever we do, some will benefit and others will pay in various ways, simple good-heartedness may be at a loss; in the case of the rights of children, e.g., a determination to adopt policies that are good for children may be fairly worthless if we cannot reflectively arrive at a judgment of what those policies would be.

Thus we need theory. My contention is not only that we need theory to be in a good position to criticize existing practices, and that we need it effectively to structure reflection, but also that theory contributes to character. The question with which this section of the paper began "What about someone who has a good character without any tincture of ethical theory?" rests on the misleading assumption that theory and goodness of character are entirely unrelated. Recall, however, that important ingredients of character are concerns and commitments. What it is that we think and care about, and how we think and care about it, matter to character, even if what we do is the major ultimate test. Ethical theories, however, can change what are the objects of our concern, and also affect (typically to a much greater degree) the ways in which we think and care about them. Thus a person who accepts and thinks along the lines of an ethical theory will not normally have exactly the same character as he or she would have had while innocent of ethical theory.

There is a wide variety of ethical theories, and even within Kantian theory and consequentialism there is an enormous variety of forms. But we can say as a broad generalization that a convinced Kantian is more likely than the average person to focus on whether one treats oneself as an exception to a generally valid rule; we also might expect a Kantian to focus on whether some conduct under consideration respects people's dignity, and whether it is the kind of thing that could have a place in an ideally moral world. We would expect consequentialists, of whatever stripe, to be unusually concerned about the foreseeable results of their actions, and to be preoccupied with a person's responsibility not only for what is done but for what predictably follows from it. These are crude generalizations; the important point is, again, that ethical theories are not merely rarified decision procedures but are also (much more importantly) ways of structuring our experience of and reflection on our moral life. At a minimum, adherence to an ethical theory makes one talk differently to oneself about matters of importance. Someone who genuinely accepts an ethical theory comes to be, to a degree, a different person.

Thus the primacy of character does not mean that there is no room for ethical theory. Much attention has been paid to the early stages of the formation of character, to the habits and inculcated moral rules of youth. Ethical theory plays a part at a more advanced stage.[23]

Notes

1. The basic structure of Kantian moral theory is set out in the *Foundations of the Metaphysics of Morals,* translated by Lewis White Beck (Indianapolis, 1959). Complications emerge in *The Metaphysical Principles of Virtue,* translated by James Ellington (Indianapolis, 1964).

2. The term 'consequentialism' has gained currency as the generic term for theories whose primary emphasis is on the evaluation of consequences. Utilitarianism is the best known, but not the only, species of consequentialism. Cf. Richard W. Miller, "Marx and Aristotle: The Unity of Two Opposites," *Proceedings of the American Political Science Association* (1978); Joel Kupperman, "Vulgar Consequentialism," *Mind* 89, no. 355 (July 1980) and "A Case for Consequentialism," *American Philosophical Quarterly* 18, no. 4 (October 1981); Samuel Scheffler, *The Rejection of Consequentialism* (Oxford, 1983); and Michael Slote, *Common-Sense Morality Consequentialism* (London, 1985).

3. For the ring of invisibility, see Plato's *Republic,* Book II, 359–360. The discussion of habit and philosophy is in the context of the Myth of Er, *Republic,* Book X, 619.

4. Cf. *Nicomachean Ethics* 2.3.1104b. See also J. O. Urmson, "Aristotle on Pleasure," in *Aristotle,* edited by J. M. E. Moravscik (New York, 1967).

5. This is brought out nicely by Herbert Fingarette in *Confucius—The Secular as Sacred* (New York, 1972), chap. 2, "A Way Without a Crossroads." See also Joel Kupperman, "Confucius and the Problem of Naturalness," *Philosophy East and West* 18, no. 3 (July 1968).

6. Some philosophers in recent years have combined consequentialism with decision procedures that take account of the role of character. See R. M. Hare, "Ethical Theory and Utilitarianism," *Contemporary British Philosophy, Fourth Series,* edited by H. D. Lewis (London, 1976), and *Moral Thinking* (Oxford, 1981). See also Joel Kupperman, *Foundations of Morality* (London, 1983). Nothing in this essay should be taken to suggest that consequentialist theory cannot be combined with an emphasis on character as the crucial determinant in ethical choice for those of us who do not fit into the category of what Hare calls 'archangels'.

7. Cf. *Critique of Pure Reason,* translated by Norman Kemp Smith (New York, 1965): A 550–51 and B 579–80, 474–75.

8. It is easy to confuse character with what we call 'personality', which has more to do with superficial factors of presentation. Cf. Anthony Quinton, "Character in Real Life," *Thoughts and Thinkers* (New York, 1982), 21–26.

9. *Foundations of the Metaphysics of Morals,* 5.

10. For a provocative discussion of salience as a factor in ethical judgment, see John McDowell, "Virtue and Reason," *Monist* 62, no. 3 (July 1979).

11. This point is made for act utilitarianism by J. J. C. Smart in "Benevolence as an Over-Riding Attitude," *Australasian Journal of Philosophy* 55, no. 2 (August 1977).

12. Cf. Julius Kovesi, *Moral Notions* (London, 1967).

13. Cf. Kupperman, "Inhibition," *Oxford Review of Education* 4, no. 3 (1978).

14. Much of what is presented as moral education in American schools, influenced by Lawrence Kohlberg, misses this point. See Joel Kupperman, "Educating Character as the Integration of Choice," *Content, Character and Choice in Schooling* (Washington, 1986).

15. Cf. Alan Donagan, *The Theory of Morality* (Chicago, 1977), 199 ff.

16. Cf. *Principia Ethica* (Cambridge, 1903), 162. Moore is not a rule utilitarian: he appeals to established moral rules as indispensable rules of thumb.

17. This is to be found in his distinction between two levels of moral thinking. Cf. "Ethical Theory and Utilitarianism" and *Moral Thinking,* chaps. 2 and 3. Hare's view is more sophisticated than Moore's (among other respects) in that he allows for the possibility of cases in which someone does have strong grounds for confidence that an action that violates an established moral rule will have better consequences than adherence to the rule would have. However infrequent such cases may be, it is not clear that Moore is justified in ruling out their possibility.

18. For the possible inadequacy of established moral rules and unreliability of conscience, see Jonathan Bennett, "The Conscience of Huckleberry Finn," *Philosophy* 49, no. 188 (April 1974).

19. One of the strengths of Nancy Sherman's "Character, Planning, and Choice in Aristotle," *Review of Metaphysics* 39, no. 1 (September 1985), is her emphasis on this. See also her "Aristotle on Friendship and the Shared Life," *Philosophy and Phenomenological Research* 47, no. 4 (June 1987).

20. Cf. *The Doctrine of the Mean, The Chinese Classics* vol. 1, translated by James Legge (New York, 1870).

21. Cf. Joel Kupperman, "Character and Self-Knowledge," *Proceedings of the Aristotelian Society* 85 (1984–5).

22. Cf. J. J. C. Smart, "Extreme and Restricted Utilitarianism," *Philosophical Quarterly* 6, no. 25 (October 1956).

23. I have benefitted from comments on a first version of this paper made by Jonathan Bennett, R. M. Hare, Loren Lomasky, Lynn Paine, Henry Rosemont, Jr., L. W. Sumner, Gong Qian, and Tim Elder.

Radical Virtue Ethics

KURT BAIER

When von Wright, in his Gifford Lectures *(The Varieties of Goodness,* 1963) claimed that virtue and the virtues were a seriously neglected topic in contemporary ethics, he made an important and entirely justified criticism of Anglo-American ethics at the time. Since then, however, there has appeared a stream of publications trying to remedy the neglect. As was to be expected with such a renewal of interest, the assessment of exactly what were the important matters that had been neglected and what was the exact import of that neglect has varied enormously. I do not have the space nor the knowledge to attempt a survey of the major positions on this question. I merely want to explore two opposing strands in the revival of virtue ethics, both concerned with the implications for mainstream ethical theory of the long neglect of the virtues. I shall call one "the moderate" thesis, and the other "the radical" thesis.

The moderate thesis claims that mainstream contemporary ethics has ignored the important question 'What constitutes a virtue, what a vice?' and with it a whole slew of questions arising from it, such as 'What is character—as opposed to temperament and personality?' 'Are all character traits either virtues or vices?' 'Do the virtues form a unity or is there an irreducible diversity among them?' 'What is the relation between being virtuous and having one or all of the virtues?' 'Are there non-moral as well as moral virtues and if so, what makes some moral?' 'What is the relation between being a virtuous person and doing the right thing?' and others.

At the same time, the moderate thesis does not claim that the neglect of these questions necessarily undermines, invalidates, or distorts the answers mainstream ethics has given to the question on which it has concentrated, namely, 'What morally speaking ought we to do?' The moderate thesis regards contemporary ethics as lamentably incomplete but not radically wrongheaded. For it thinks that the question it has tried to answer is logically independent of, or indeed, logically prior to the questions neglected. We can know what we morally ought to do independently of knowing what virtues and character are and how a particular person's character or performance is to be morally assessed, and indeed, some moderates think, we cannot answer these neglected questions unless we have answers to the main question moral philosophers have recently concentrated on.

The radical thesis, by contrast, maintains that the neglect of these virtues-related questions invalidates the answers to the question examined. On this view, we cannot determine what is morally incumbent upon us or what it is morally desirable that we do independently of what are virtues and vices, without knowing from what motives the morally good or virtuous person acts. Hence, the radical claims, the neglect of virtue ethics is much more serious than the moderate acknowledges. In the absence of a clear understanding of the virtues and of properly moral motivation, it is impossible to determine what is morally incumbent on us or morally desirable for us. The attempts by mainstream ethicists to answer this question are therefore wrong-headed and indeed unsound.

In the remainder of the paper I want to examine three authors who have advanced such radical theses. Of course, I do not claim that they represent all strands of radical virtue ethics, let alone all versions and aspects of virtue ethics. Far from it. All I claim on behalf of these authors is that they have interesting and challenging things to say and that the first two, at any rate, have attracted much attention and support.

1

In her widely discussed and much admired paper, "Modern Moral Philosophy" *(Philosophy* 33:1–19, reprinted in *Ethics,* edited by J. J. Thomson and G. Dworkin, [New York, 1968], 186–210), Professor Elizabeth Anscombe argues that mainstream Anglo-American ethicists attempt to answer the question what we are to do, morally speaking, in terms of the concepts 'morally wrong', 'moral obligation', and 'moral duty', which are legal notions and so presuppose a moral legislator without, however, wishing to assign this role to God, who naturally and traditionally has been assigned it, and without being able to find a tenable alternative source of such legislation. All suggested substitutes—society, conscience, nature, social contract—face insuperable problems. Anscombe concludes that moral philosophers should abandon this model of providing a source for moral norms and adopt instead the Aristotelian model of the virtues. This model sets out from the idea of human flourishing, "and essentially the flourishing of a man *qua* man consists in his being good (e.g., in virtues); but for any *X* to which such terms apply, *X* needs what makes it flourish, so a man needs, or ought to perform only virtuous actions; and even if, as it must be admitted may happen, he flourishes less, or not at all, in inessentials, by avoiding injustice, his life is spoiled in essentials by not avoiding injustice—so he still needs to perform only just actions." (Thomson-Dworkin, p. 209).

I shall not examine whether Anscombe's Aristotelian approach is able to escape from the well-known difficulties it faces—say, the problem of convincing a judge in a dictatorial regime that by refusing to give an unjust verdict of guilty against a political enemy of the regime he will flourish less only in inessentials, if it involves losing his livelihood or facing a trial and prison or death; nor whether and why it is thought impossible to find a defensible substitute for the divine legislator. Instead, I want to argue that the concepts 'wrong', 'obligation', and 'duty' do not imply a moral legislator or moral authority whose say-so is the basis of moral norms, and that, therefore, there is no need to assume a divine legislator or find a suitable substitute for him.

It is simply a mistake to think that the notions of 'right', 'wrong', 'duty', and 'obligation' presuppose a moral legislator whose authoritative say-so creates the moral norms by reference to which moral wrongs, duties, and obligations are determined. The initial plausibility of this erroneous view disappears the moment we distinguish between moral obligation or duty, on the one hand, and conventionally established requirement, on the other, and similarly between moral wrong, on the one hand, and conventional prohibition on the other. The existence of a legal requirement to return an escaped slave to his legal owner may imply the existence of a legal (what else?) legislator whose authoritative say-so has created the legal requirement. But the fact that it is wrong for me to kill or lie, or that it is my moral duty to help the man in the bus next to me who has fainted, or that I have a moral obligation to do what I can to provide for the child I have fathered does not imply that there exists a special moral legislator different from but analogous to the ordinary legislator, one whose authoritative say-so creates moral wrongs, duties, and obligations the way the ordinary legislator's say-so creates legal requirements and prohibitions. The frequent use of the expressions 'legal duty' and 'legal obligation' to mean the same as 'legal requirement' helps to foster the confusion between the conventional and the moral realms.

The fact that there are these wrongs, duties, and obligations implies merely that (i) there is adequate moral reason for me to do and no adequate moral reason for me not to do, that is, "compelling" moral reason for me to do these things, and (ii) that there is adequate reason for society "to insist," that is, set up suitable social pressures to ensure that its members follow these compelling moral reasons (for, obviously, the mere existence of such compelling moral reasons does not actually compel people).[1]

It may, of course, be true, as Anscombe claims, that the correct way to find out what we are to do is to determine what is required for human flourishing. But this may involve the existence of a social order designed to ensure that all its members flourish, and this in turn may require that the members not interfere in one another's lives, that they assist one another when they need help, and that they cooperate with one another in various mutually beneficial enterprises. But this in turn may require that the society spell out for its members what is due from whom to whom and that it organize suitable sanctions to ensure that, as far as possible, everyone gives to and so everyone receives from everyone what is his due. And if this is done in a morally acceptable way, people are not merely conventionally required but morally obligated to do these things; it is their moral duty to do them; it would be wrong for them not to do them.

Note that this does not imply the existence of a conventional authority whose say-so creates these obligations, duties, and wrongs. This is obvious where the social system is one of custom as opposed to law, since societies governed by custom lack an institutional rule-maker and changer. But even if the system is a legal one, there is no *moral* legislator, in the sense of one that creates moral norms by his say-so. Of course, if the legal system passes moral muster—this is the crucial point—then the ordinary (the "legal") legislator is a moral one, as opposed to an immoral (but not to a non-moral, e.g., legal) one. In other words, the divergence between legal and moral norms does not imply the existence of two corresponding legislators. If there is a legislator at all, it is the ordinary legal one, but he does not create separate moral norms; his norms are moral norms if they pass moral muster; the conventional norms he creates by his say-so are moral norms if and only if they pass moral muster. And if there are certain norms, say a norm forbidding killing, such that if they became part of the sanctioned conventional order, they would pass moral muster, then these are moral norms even if they have not become part of the system. Of course, the fact that they are not part of the system makes an important difference to how we assess the moral worth of people on account of following or not following them. If slavery is part of the legal system, we assess the moral worth of judges and others who do not treat slaves as having equal rights differently than we would if slavery were not part of the legal system. I conclude that Anscombe's approach may yield valuable suggestions about how we can arrive at an answer to the question of what is our moral duty. But her arguments do not succeed in showing that all or most or indeed any of contemporary ethics is confused, incoherent, or vitiated because it operates with an incoherent conception of wrongness, duty, and obligation. Nor do they show that we should give up trying to answer this basic moral question and concentrate instead on what is a virtue or that this neglected question is independent of the first. Thus, insofar as Anscombe presents a version of radical virtue-ethics, she is mistaken, but she may have acceptable things to say if she is construed as a moderate.

2

Another paper that indicts the whole of contemporary ethics and that has received a great deal of attention is Michael Stocker's "The Schizophrenia of Modern Ethical Theories" *(Journal of Philosophy* 73 [August 1976]: 453–66). Stocker draws attention to an important type of human relationship, such as love or friendship, in which the question of what it is our duty to do and what the virtuous person would do seem to be related in a way different from that assumed by the bulk of contemporary ethicists including those who urge moderate versions of virtue ethics. Stocker's important example is this:

"The standard view is that a morally good intention is an essential constituent of a morally good act. This seems correct enough. On that view, further, a morally good intention is an intention to do an act for the sake of its goodness or rightness. But now suppose you are in a hospital, recovering from a long illness. You are very bored and restless and at loose ends when Smith comes in once again. You are now convinced more than ever that he is a fine fellow and a good friend—taking so much time to cheer you up, travelling all the way across town and so on. You are so effusive with your praise and thanks that he protests that he always tries to do what he thinks is his duty, what he thinks will be best. You at first think he is engaging in a polite form of self-deprecation, relieving the moral burden. But the more you two speak, the more clear it becomes that he was telling the literal truth: that it is not essentially because of you that he came to see you, not because you are friends, but because he thought it his duty, perhaps as a fellow Christian or Communist, or whatever, or simply because he knows of no one more in need of cheering up and no one easier to cheer up."

This is an important and valid point against certain interpretations of Kantian ethics. As is generally agreed, Kant's answer to the question of what, morally speaking, we ought to do, is that we must always do our duty, as determined by the Categorical Imperative. But whereas the discharge of one kind of duty—a duty of justice—is compatible with any motive, the discharge of another kind—a duty of virtue—involves action from a certain motive, namely, *aus Pflicht,* which is translated as either "from" or "for the sake of" duty. His answer to the second question is that an act has moral worth if and only if it is the performance *of* a duty of either kind, *from* duty. Although we can perform our duties of justice from non-moral motives and so do *what,* morally speaking, we ought to do, such acts according to duty but not done from duty can have no moral worth. Given a very common and natural interpretation of what Kant meant by 'from duty' or 'for the sake of duty', i.e., acting from a sense of duty, the visitor in Stocker's example acts in a way which must, indeed, be disappointing to the friend he visits. He makes it clear to her that he visits her not because it is she who is ill, but because he finds himself in a situation in which it happens to be his duty to visit her. If his duty had been to visit someone else or not to visit anyone but instead, say, to participate in a protest march, he would have done that. Or more disappointing still, if *(per impossibile?)* he had had no duty at all at this time, he would (perhaps) have watched television or gone to a football match.

Stocker says about this case: "Surely there is something lacking here—and lacking in moral merit or value." And he concludes from this that moral value, moral merit, or moral worth cannot depend on acting for the sake of duty and that if it depends on acting from a moral motive, acting for the sake of duty cannot be the only moral motive. He also concludes from this that, since "the reasons, values, justifications of ethical theories should be such as to allow us to embody them in our motives and still act morally and achieve the good" (462), ethical theories which construe the moral motive as the motive to do one's duty for the sake of duty, cannot account for important parts of our morality, for example, that concerned with intimate personal relations, such as love and friendship.

However, I believe the conclusion does not follow and is, in fact, unsound. For, in the first place, one need not interpret Kant in the way indicated or, if that really is what Kant meant, one can refuse to follow Kant in this particular detail, without having to reject his deontological approach. One could interpret or modify Kant's view to read that the peculiar moral worth of an act lies in its being one that is the doing of *what* (one has adequate reason to believe) is morally required, or *what* is morally desirable, or *what* is morally permissible, and would not be done unless and insofar as (one has adequate reason to believe) it is so.[2] In other words, a moral motive is indeed one that involves knowledge or belief of what is morally required, desirable, or permissible, but may be only a "regulative" or "constraining" motive, one that keeps a check on one's "natural," "premoral" motives. On this interpretation, the visitor acts from a moral motive as long as it is true that he would not visit his friend if he thought it morally required of him not to do so but to do something else. The visit may not lack this specific moral worth even if the visitor would not visit his friend unless he thought it morally required or desirable to do so. Of course, if he felt no wish to visit her although they were supposed to be friends and if he wanted to maintain the appearance of this friendship perhaps in order to be able gradually to rebuild its reality (that is, reciprocal instead of one-sided affection), then it would be inept of him (or worse) to tell her that he came *only* because he thought it his duty.

However, it should be noted that it is only in cases where the relationship is such that it is the moral duty of the partners to develop or preserve love and affection for each other, as in the case of parents and children, or husband and wife, or where it is morally desirable for them to do so, as in the case of friends, that the action of the visitor lacks the peculiar moral worth. If, from moral or religious motives, I visit lonely old people who are strangers to me and with whom I cannot establish a lasting personal relationship, then this may well be a case in which it is neither my moral duty to have nor even morally undesirable not to have such love and affection for them. And if this is so, then my visiting them from moral or religious motives alone, and not from love or affection for them, would not necessarily lack all moral worth, though undoubtedly it would have more moral worth if I could at least feign concern, compassion, and interest, for that would presumably provide greater consolation and reduce the loneliness of the visited, which is what I am aiming at.

To accommodate Stocker's points, we need to introduce only two minor additions to the received Kantian framework. We need, in the first place, to add a third kind of duty beyond the two distinguished by Kant, namely, the kind in which its performance requires a certain *non-moral* motive over and above the merely regulative moral motive. In such cases, one ought to do what Kant said could not be done, namely, act from pathological love, or whatever. If Kant is right, as I think he is about the impossibility of doing so "at will," as we say, then what we are morally required to do in these cases is to cultivate or develop or preserve such feelings to the extent we can do so.

We should note that even in such a case where the visitor visits because the convalescent is his friend whom he loves and wants to visit, he nevertheless can be said to do so *from* duty (though not *for the sake of duty*), if it is a fact that he would not visit her if he thought he had a duty not to do so. And if she is herself a moral person, she would not hold that fact against him in those cases in which he had a moral duty not to—e.g., a morally more stringent commitment to his family or his students. But she would rightly hold it against him if he did not visit her despite its being morally permissible though not required for him to do so, for that would reveal a lack of love and concern on his part. But where such love is not itself morally required or desirable, the failure in this case to visit does not show the non-visitor to be lacking in specifically moral worth, merit, or value.

The second addition is a distinction between what it is a moral duty (obligation) to do, or a wrong not to do, and what it is morally desirable that we do but goes beyond the call of duty. Both are subclasses of the morally desirable, but the former, as we saw, are those things that are so desirable that there is compelling reason for society to insist on their being done. In the case of the latter this is not so. Doing someone a favor, contributing to charity, visiting the sick and lonely, is something desirable but it is beyond the call of duty, not something that there is compelling or even adequate reason for society to insist on. Kant's and the traditional distinction between perfect and imperfect duties are unsatisfactory in various ways, the most important being that it creates duties, the imperfect ones, concerning which it is impossible to tell whether and when a person has discharged them and so is "off the moral hook."

There is, of course, a great deal more to be said about Stocker's challenging paper, but I believe his initially most persuasive piece of evidence, the example of the visitor, cannot support his radical conclusion.

3

I now turn to a view, developed by N. J. H. Dent in his *The Moral Psychology of the Virtues* (1984), which straddles my distinction between the moderate and the radical theses. Dent is a moderate in that unlike Anscombe and Stocker, he does not think of all or most of contemporary ethics as radically misguided, but he goes beyond the moderate by claiming that mainstream contemporary ethics does not merely neglect, but cannot account for, an important part of our moral life or experience. He agrees with mainstream ethics that the basic question in ethics is what sorts of acts are morally required or morally desirable. But he then distinguishes three major approaches to the question of why a certain sort of act is morally required or morally desirable (32)—the deontological, the consequentialist, and the aretaic—and claims that only the aretaic approach, which has recently been ignored, can account for all of the moral virtues, i.e., "such qualities as generosity, sympathy, patience, fortitude, kindness, love, gentleness, tact, discretion, candour, responsiveness, reverence, and so on" (28, 31). The deontological approach must reduce all the virtues to dutifulness/conscientiousness, and the consequentialist to benevolence/beneficence, but the virtues of generosity, kindness, patience, compassion, and tact, for instance, cannot be so reduced.

Dent attempts to clinch this point with regard to kindness and, more elaborately, to generosity. Since the arguments adduced are essentially the same, I shall consider only the case of generosity. Against the deontological approach, Dent makes two major points. The first is that a deontologist must explain the virtue of generosity as the disposition to follow rules or principles spelling out "the class of act-kinds by performing which, with the right motive, a man shall have exemplified the virtue of generosity" (29) but that there can be no such principles. For generosity "comprises no set forms or formulas, but transcends all such, spilling over the customary pathways which are 'standard' ways of giving and helping" (30). The second point is that the generous person is not one who promotes the good of others from a sense of duty, but who does so from a non-moral motive, namely, sympathy, fellow-feeling, or compassion.

But these objections can be met by a deontologist. We have already seen, in the previous section, that even a Kantian—on a certain interpretation—can hold that a person can be kind and generous "from duty" without doing so for the sake of duty. He can do so from natural inclination so long as he follows that inclination only to the extent he has adequate reason to think it to be within the limits of the morally desirable or at least permissible, and so long as he cultivates such an inclination as far as it is morally required or desirable. He can allow that among the things that are morally required or desirable is the having of certain feelings, sentiments, or attitudes. Of

course, he must provide reasons for saying that these are morally desirable or required, but such reasons are not difficult to find. Plainly, a person who has the appropriate feelings and sentiments will be more likely to attain these ends than one who
has to battle against his inclinations, and one who shows these sentiments will promote the others' well-being more satisfactorily than one who does not, and one who
actually has them is more likely to be able to show them than one who does not have
them.

Even a hide-bound Kantian can meet the first objection, for Kant himself distinguishes between maxims of acts (which spell out act-kinds, e.g., promise-keeping)
and maxims of ends (which spell out ends without specifying the act-kinds by which
they are to be attained, e.g., self-perfection or the happiness of others). Hence the
Kantian can accept Dent's analysis of generosity as "an ever-inquiring, ever-
developing, creative attitude, seeking new ways of helping and giving to another as
chances occur or can be contrived" (29–30). He can subscribe to the maxim of ends,
to promote other people's well-being; and such a maxim need not spell out the act-
types by which this end is to be attained, but leave it to the creative ingenuity of individuals to recognize or create the opportunities for promoting this end.

There is therefore no insuperable problem for the deontologist to give an
account of generosity and of kindness along the lines of Dent's analysis of these two
virtues. And for the same reasons, there is no problem for the consequentialist. The
consequentialist can, of course, adopt the same principle of promoting other people's
well-being and include the agent's having certain feelings, sentiments, or attitudes
among the things that are morally required and desirable, and precisely for the same
reasons that the deontologist can embrace. Both the deontologist and the consequentialist, therefore, need not ignore "the inestimable worth of the virtues which have regard to men's relations one with another" since they need not "see the value in these
as reposing only in the intent to procure, or the actual production of, benefit for another through action" (29).

It might, of course, be said, on behalf of Dent that even if everything I have said
is sound, it might still be important and interesting to follow the aretaic approach
rather than the deontological or consequentialist. However, I believe the aretaic approach is not independent of the other two, but presupposes them. Since we have
come to interpret justice, benevolence, courage, temperance, dutifulness, and the others as moral virtues, and especially if we accept the doctrine of the unity of the virtues
(none of them ever amounting to a vice, e.g., benevolence amounting to breach of
duty), then these character traits imply that the virtuous person will not follow her
generous, courageous, kind, patient, etc., impulses (or even regard these impulses as
generous, etc.) when she thinks that it would be wrong or undesirable to follow them.
But then she needs to know when it would be wrong or undesirable to do so, and this
brings us back to the question of what it would be wrong or undesirable to do, hence
to the deontological or consequentialist answer to the question of what sorts of acts
are morally required or forbidden, what morally desirable or undesirable. We cannot
without circularity answer this question in this context by the aretaic approach. We
cannot say this sort of act is morally required or desirable because it is the sort of act
typical of a certain moral motive, an act of the sort that it would be natural to a good

(in this case, a generous) person to do. One is not a generous person unless one constrains one's inclinations in light of one's judgment of what is morally required or desirable. Generosity, when interpreted as a moral virtue, is not simply the disposition to promote other people's well-being, *perhaps to a fault;* it is this natural inclincation regulated by moral judgment. But Dent's aretaic approach cannot provide any basis for that judgment. I believe this is a serious difficulty for any aretaic approch, such as Dent's, or Aristotle's whose approach he follows, which construes the moral virtues as character traits in which certain natural inclinations are developed, regulated, and controlled in light of independent moral judgments.

I conclude that, despite the many important insights to be found in Dent's book, the central thesis that the mainstream of contemporary ethics is unable to account for important sectors of our moral life is unsound.

4

However, I do not wish to and I need not end on a negative note. Our examination of the various more or less radical theses in virtue ethics have brought to light an important vagueness or error in mainstream ethics. My attempt to give a deontological or consequentialist account of generosity and similar virtues has shown that the primary and fundamental question in ethics is not what the mainstream, and incidentally also Dent, has taken it to be, namely, 'what sorts of *acts* are morally required or desirable?'—for generosity, kindness, and similar virtues involve the question 'what sorts of feelings, sentiments, attitudes, motives are morally required or desirable?' Thus, mainstream ethics has neglected not only the secondary questions involving moral assessment of character and a person's performance on a particular occasion, but also a part of the primary question, 'what is morally required or desirable?' namely, 'what feelings, sentiments, etc., are morally required or desirable?' It would, therefore, be better to formulate the two main questions in ethics as follows: (i) 'What is morally permissible to, or wanted of, us?' This does not imply that the answer must refer to behavior only, but can include such things as character, motives, virtues, feelings, and perhaps more. Nor does it imply that what is so wanted of us is a duty or obligation—it may be merely desirable. (ii) 'How has this or that person performed under these two kinds of moral norm?' This retains the relationship of dependence of (ii) on (i), but allows that a person's moral worth, praiseworthiness, or desert depends not solely on what he has done, but also on the spirit in which he has done it and on the extent of his effort to develop the virtues and avoid or eradicate any vices he may be prone to. This also makes clear that the moral virtues and vices appear in both questions. In the first as a task set to all of us, in the second as a criterion of the moral performance of particular persons.

It should also be borne in mind that individual variations in people's innate motivational endowment and their childhood environment, which largely determines what they will make of this innate endowment, may create for different individuals moral tasks of very different difficulty. We should therefore distinguish, as Kant suggested, between those whose nature and upbringing have produced a moral character from those who have had to struggle for it once they reached the age of reason and responsibility. We prefer the company of those who have a moral character to those who do not, even if a given person who does not has worked much harder on coming closer to it than another who does have it; but we give credit or pay moral tribute to the latter. The famous difference between Aristotle and Kant on the question of moral value or worth would seem to be due to the fact that Aristotle thought mainly of the finished product, irrespective of the effort that led to it, whereas Kant thought mainly of the effort, irrespective of the outcome. It is, therefore, a mistake to ask the question, 'who has greater moral worth or value, the person who is benevolent and beneficent from natural inclination, or the person who is so for moral reasons and in the teeth of opposed natural inclination?' The reason why we are torn between accepting one or the other is that we are dealing with two different questions. Aristotle's question is about the finished moral product. A person is nearer moral perfection if he has achieved, by whatever effort, a character such that he does what is morally required and desirable from natural inclination and takes pleasure in doing it. Kant's question is about the moral credit, the brownie points, the commendation a person deserves for transforming the endowment nature gave him in the morally required or desirable direction. Since people are not responsible for what nature—in some instances generous, in others niggardly—gave them, fairness requires that we consider not only what a person has achieved or failed to achieve in the way of character-building but also what it took or would have taken to achieve it. In choosing friends, associates, or partners we are free to consider only Aristotle's question. In meting out punishment and condemnation, we must also as far as possible consider Kant's question.

Notes

1. This is simply a slightly modified version of J. S. Mill's account of moral duty, obligation, and wrongness in chap. 5 of *Utilitarianism.* I substitute social *insistence* for Mill's *exacting,* which is too specific, since exacting is only one very strong form that insistence may take; public condemnation is another. Social insistence, even in its weaker forms, is stronger than social weighting as by a tax. To spell out what exactly is involved would take us too far afield here.

2. It would be natural, but misleading to put this point by saying 'and is done only because and insofar as it is so'. For that would suggest that the moral consideration is the *only* motive from which it is done. Note that if the moral consideration is moral permissibility, it cannot be the only motive, for the permissibility of doing something is not a motive for doing it.

Virtues and Their Vicissitudes

AMELIE O. RORTY

When does a set of habits, skills, or dispositions qualify as a virtue? What assures —or can assure—that such dispositions are well and appropriately exercised?

The somber answer to the first question is that character traits are classified as virtues whenever they are admired or thought beneficial, even though they sometimes conflict with one another and often fail to secure individual thriving. There is considerable social pressure to acquire and exercise such traits—sets of voluntary and discriminating dispositions, habits, capacities, and skills—even though they are not always directly rewarding or rewarded. Typically such traits are admired when they are the expression of a cultural ideal that is thought to be relatively difficult to realize, an ideal that usually involves modulating some natural tendencies such as self-protection or the desire for whatever conduces to one's own happiness. They are regarded as beneficial when they are thought to serve social welfare, especially when doing so appears to involve some cost to oneself. A culture can of course be mistaken about the traits that serve its thriving, failing to identify characteristics that are central to social welfare and admiring those that damage it. Entrepreneurial traits might, for example, be valued in the mistaken belief that they tend to improve the standard of living, which itself might erroneously be believed essential to a culture's (conception of its) thriving.

But at least sometimes the dark answer has a bright side: there is some relation between socially prized traits and flourishing, if only because social esteem is one of the goods of life. With moral and political luck, the connection is stronger: traits that are socially prized are often—though certainly not necessarily—connected to at least some aspects of social and individual flourishing. That connection is sufficiently strong so that both moral philosophers and those who on the whole want to live well can at least initially be guided by social conceptions of virtues. But where there is good luck, there is also bad luck: the connection between socially recognized virtue and flourishing is also generally sufficiently weak to allow the indignant and the visionary grounds for reformist proposals. Even though individual conceptions of thriving are largely socially formed and individual thriving is socially controlled, individual and social thriving can conflict.[1]

The somber answer to the second question is that nothing can *assure* that the traits constituting the virtues are always well and appropriately used, except by the strategic, unilluminating maneuver of not counting typically virtuous traits as *virtues* in a person unless they *are* well and appropriately exercised by that person.[2] But the merit of such a strategy is largely limited to the benefits of elegant theory construction; it leaves us in the dark about what assures or even conduces to the appropriate use of such traits.

However skeptical we are about the pretentions of purely philosophical ethical theory to serve as a guide for action, we nevertheless do want a philosophic ethics that does more than propose a general theory about *right, good, duty, virtue.* There are implicit practical constraints and directives on normative ethical theories: they should be capable of being psychologically and educationally action-guiding in structuring and restructuring our practices toward living well, and—since failure is nearly as common as success in this area—they should also explain why it is sometimes so difficult for even the best of us to succeed.

I. CHARACTER AND THE CONTEXT OF VIRTUE

The virtues hunt in packs.

Before moving to the large and difficult problems we have set for ourselves, we first need to describe how those traits which we call virtues function in forming actions. When a set of dispositions constitute a virtue, the thoughts and categorial preoccupations that are central to that virtue form interpretations of situations; they focus the person's attention and define what is salient, placing other concerns in the background. To act well, and to do so reliably, a person must perceive and interpret situations appropriately, and do so reliably. Without appropriate cognitive structures—thresholds of attentiveness that are sensitive without being hypersensitive, habits of salient focusing that are corrigible without being distractible, imaginative habits of association that elicit relevant material without being volatile—good will remains empty.

The cognitive dispositions that partly constitute the virtues are tropic or magnetizing: perceptions and interpretations of situations elicit the responses that are immediately appropriate to them. Significantly, they also generate scenarios—sequences of events—that require the further exercise of the virtues. Because they generate situations that manifest the continued need for the exercise of strongly entrenched virtues, such cognitive dispositions are self-reinforcing. *Dispositions of interpretation* structure patterns of salience and importance: they organize the dominant proper descriptions of situations. Without waiting to be called upon, a generous person is perceptively and interpretively sensitive to needs, even when such needs are unacknowledged by others. Where some might perceptively focus on relations of power, or on aesthetic compositions, a generous person notices how she can correct what is wanting. *Tropic dispositions* lead a person to gravitate to the sorts of situations that predictably elicit prized character traits. Often avoiding situations where she might herself require aid, a strongly generous person tends to move toward situations in which her contributions might be useful, even when she has no desire to find herself in such situations and would prefer to be somewhere else, doing something else. Tropic dispositions can often work independently of, and sometimes in conflict with, a person's strong desires. *Self-activating dispositions* promote or create the occasions that require their exercise. A heroic figure, for example, can sometimes structure his foreign policy and his personal relationships in such a way that others predictably come to depend upon and even to require his bold, imaginative leadership.

When the virtues are esteemed and rewarded, they ramify to develop and exercise associated supportive traits, while inhibiting other, often highly beneficial traits. In situations of conflict, publicly recognized virtues tend to determine priorities, sometimes at the cost of highly functional, but unacknowledged traits. The magnetizing dispositions of centrally organizing virtues are focal and expansive in a person's character: focusing on what is salient blurs what is in the background.[3] (The persistent and tenacious are not, for example, normally sensitive to the ironies of the contingencies of practical life; rarely delighting in ludicrous turns of chance, they are often so intent on their purposes that they are not responsive to the unexpected.

Traits do not, of course, form actions in isolation. Individual virtues underdetermine appropriate actions. They only function within a supportive, directing, and sometimes oppositional network. The attribution of any trait is made against the background of *ceteris paribus* assumptions about an interrelated network of standard operating functions. Some of the interrelations among the virtues arise primarily from their cognitive components, others from the consequences of the actions they standardly generate. *Artificially,* solely for the purpose of exposition, and not because they are psychologically separable, we can distinguish the cognitive combinatorial properties of the virtues from those that are normally formed by the dynamics of their habitual exercise in action.

The cognitive components of the virtues carry the whole range of combinatorial logical and psychological properties: logically, their cognitive contents presuppose and entail one another; complex virtues contain simpler virtues as ingredients; they can be contraries, and even contradictories. Psychologically, their associations can be law-like; the development of the cognitive components of one virtue can presuppose, enhance, or block another; they can reinforce or inhibit each other; they can combine in new virtues and form cyclical patterns of vacillation and ambivalence.

The virtues are also strongly, dynamically interconnected in socially structured narratives.[4] There are culturally fixed and socially controlled expectations that promote and then replace the sequence of virtues, as appropriate to age and to role. The virtues of youth are sometimes seen as dangers in the middle-aged, those of age as inappropriate to youth. Sometimes the successes of one virtue generate situations which require not only the replacement, but also the checking of the original virtue. For instance, the bold, inventive entrepreneurial traits of an early mercantile society can so change material and social conditions that the original virtues are reclassified as vices unless they are strongly checked by prudential and sometimes even cautious calculation. Obviously, these relations and changes do not necessarily occur smoothly or automatically. Early virtues can continue to operate even when they are judged no longer appropriate; counterpoised virtues do not always achieve an appropriate balance.

II. VIRTUE AND VIRTUES

No virtues without virtue;
no virtue without virtues.

With this characterization of the structures and relations among the virtues in mind, we are better equipped to return to our original question: What assures the virtue of the virtues?

(1) The most radical solution is that of *contextualizing* attributions of virtue: since the same set of dispositions can sometimes be appropriately and sometimes inappropriately exercised, even by the same person, traits qualify as virtues only when they have been appropriately exercised. While this solution is elegant, it appears to make the attribution of virtue redundant, reiterating—in the form of a pseudo-explanation—the judgment that the action is meritorious. In any case, this is a solution provided for and by a problem in theory construction: it sets the conditions for attribution virtue without providing the analysis of its conditions.

(2) The strictest solution is the introduction of a condition for *self-modulation:* no set of dispositions qualifies as a virtue unless it includes its own appropriateness-assuring conditions. To qualify as a virtue, a set of traits must be discriminatingly, *internally* self-regulating to determine the appropriate occasion, extent, and manner for its exercise (true courage does not lapse into bravado, generosity does not lapse into wastefulness). Significantly, it must also be *externally* self-regulating to determine the appropriate balance with other, sometimes competing sets of traits.

But while this solution is philosophically ingenious in defining conditions for identifying the virtues, it is not psychologically illuminating, or, for that matter, psychologically convincing. In practice, while the individual virtues, characterized as a set of intellectual and practical dispositions to typical actions, are internally self-regulating, they are rarely externally self-regulating. When the action claims of various virtues compete, individual virtues do not themselves determine the appropriate *balance.* While kindness might be self-regulating in situations in which no other virtues compete with its action-claims, what is it about *kindness* that checks its exercise when it competes with truthfulness? The claim that the requirements of kindness and those of truthfulness must in the end always coincide has all the air of denying the phenomena to save the theory.

(3) The most familiar and the most thoroughly explored solution is the *master virtue* solution. Since definitions of the various individual virtues do not by themselves give rules for determining their appropriate relative priority, an independent external condition, a regulative master virtue such as *phronesis* or *caritas* or Kantian good will—virtues that unite the practical and intellectual traits required to determine the priority and balance among the several virtues—seems also to be necessary. Since the master virtue solution has been developed in some detail, we should look at some of its most refined presentations.

It was because he thought that wisdom provides the necessary and sufficient condition for the development and the proper exercise of the various virtues that Socrates argued for the unity of the virtues in knowledge. No virtues without virtue, and no virtue without knowledge. To defend this intellectualist account of virtue, Socrates had to introduce non-intellectualist conditions on wisdom: the wise must not only apply what they know in argument and discussion, but also in the minutiae of action and practice.[5] Notoriously, the Socratic condition is circular: the various traits that assure wisdom are both intellectual and practical. The wise are both good and clever: besides giving each dialectical inquirer the *logos* appropriate to his understanding, they also teach by good example. None but the wise are virtuous; yet none but the virtuous qualify as wise. A good formula, perhaps also true, but not really helpful for those of us who need to know how to become wise and good.

It was because he thought that the proper exercise of presumptively virtuous traits requires both cognitive and character dispositions—well-formed, discriminating habits directed to good ends, appropriately understood—that Aristotle located the master virtue in *phronesis*. The internal self-regulation assured by locating each of the virtues in a mean defined by *logos* does not automatically assure the appropriate exercise of *that* virtue, in relation to all others, all things considered. But *phronesis* is an umbrella term for a wide range of independent traits that enable a person to see, and to actualize the goods that can best be realized in extremely varied, particular contexts. While Aristotle avoids some of the problems of the Socratic solution, he only postpones others. Since *phronesis* combines a range of independent intellectual and character traits—ingenuity, insight, perceptual sensitivity, acuity in inference, a sound sense of relevance, an active understanding of the relative importance of heterogeneous and sometimes incommensurable ends, allocating different priorities to the various components of *phronesis* could sometimes lead to different action outcomes. A *phronimos* whose ingenuity was more acute than his sense of relevance, might form different actions from those performed by a *phronimos* with a somewhat different balance of traits. How does *phronesis* assure that the individual virtues— including those that compose and constitute it—are appropriately exercised, in the right way, at the right time?

It was because he thought that only a good will could assure that the various virtues would be rightly exercised, that Kant held that the only thing good in itself, without qualification, is a good will, that is, an autonomous, rational will. Kant hoped to avoid Aristotle's difficulties in determining the priority among the various traits that compose *phronesis* by showing the unity of the rational good will. While in principle, the conditions that assure the will's freedom can be distinguished from those that assure its goodness, Kant attempts to secure the autonomy of the will by identifying its conditions with those for practical rationality. Because the will *is* reason in its practical employment, it is self-legislative, free of external determination when it conforms to the requirements of rationality. And since rationality requires self-legislated impartiality, practical reason assures both the freedom and the goodness of the will. Because Kant proposed to give an analysis of the conditions that make morality possible, he was concerned to locate the unconditioned origin of action, the absolute locus of responsibility. While his preoccupations were quite different from those of Socrates, his solution to the problem of assuring the virtues is nevertheless a variant of the Socratic solution: Kant's claim that the commands of practical rationality *are* the claims of morality is parallel to Socrates' identification of knowledge with virtue.

The analogue of the Socratic solution inherits an analogue to the Socratic problem: as Kant himself was the first to acknowledge, the condition that assures morality is judicial rather than generative. Acting from a good will requires testing the rationality, the universalizability, of maxims of action; but practical rationality neither develops the motives nor discovers the appropriate empirical maxims for any given action. While a good will assures the possibility of acting purely from a conception of the moral law, it does not by itself determine actions or, for that matter, empirical motives.

Both Socrates and Kant extend their views by including the individual virtues within virtue. As the Socratically wise are also temperate, courageous, and just, so too Kant's *person* of good will actively commands himself to possess the individual virtues. In doing his duty for its own sake, the moral agent does what each duty rationally commands. Consistent rationality recognizes that in order for a moral intention to issue in well-formed actions, the will must necessarily be supported by the virtues. Since Kantian morality commands the acquisition of the several virtues, Aristotle's problems reappear within the Kantian frame; something like *phronesis* is required to assure the appropriate connection between the purity of the moral intention and the appropriateness of a particular action.

It is because she hopes to combine the advantages of Aristotle's complex psychology with Kant's strict account of responsibility that Philippa Foot distinguishes the virtues from other practical dispositions and skills: they are, she says, controlled by the will, directed toward what is good.[6]

But the virtuous cannot assure the appropriate use of their traits by willing good ends. A villain and a good citizen can, and often do, will the same ends. To begin with, they have the same species-defined ends; they are constituted so as to have at least some of the same central needs and desires whose satisfaction constitutes thriving. Besides the necessities and comforts of life, they want esteem and friendship, and want their friends and families to thrive. The virtuous and the vicious can be ambitious for fame, respect, and fortune; they can even sometimes have virtually identical intentional descriptions of their general aims; and both can be prudently courageous in pursuing their ambitions. Nor is the difference that the good citizen is reliable, while the cad is not; they can both be counted on to behave in character. Sometimes it is just their *petites habitudes*—the configuration of their ends and traits, the *way* they are courageous, prudent, tactful in pursuit of their common ends—that differentiate the cad and the good citizen.

Although each of the familiar versions of the master virtue solution encounters somewhat different difficulties, we can generalize that there are roughly three major problems with that solution. There is, first, the problem of selecting among the serious candidates for the master virtue, particularly since each can, in principle, command different patterns of dominance and recessiveness among the various virtues. When there is uncertainty and conflict in action, *phronesis* might well form different priorities from those proposed by *caritas,* envisaged by magnanimity, commanded by the good will, or assured by justice. Is there a master master virtue?

Second, there is the problem of regression: If the master virtue is to be action guiding in particular, variable, contingency-ridden contexts, it does not act from, nor is it characterizable by, a set of rules. But then just how does the master virtue regulate or check competing first-level virtues? How does it fuse intellectual and practical traits to guide its determinations? Just identifying the will as reason in its practical application does not help us understand how that identity works, particularly if the will could in principle fail to affirm what rationality commands. Even if there are some very general principles that define *right* or *good,* what determines the appropriate application of these principles through the contingencies and vagaries of particular situations?

Third, there is the problem of determining the appropriate balance among the component dispositions that themselves constitute the master virtue. *Phronesis*—or good sense, magnanimity, *caritas,* or justice—are each composed of a complex set of skills, capacities, and traits. The primary candidates for the master virtue involve an appropriate level of acuteness and precision in perception, the ability to focus—and stay focused—on what is important, despite irrelevant attractions. They also involve impartiality, a capacity to form well-structured, valid inferences, ingenuity and tact, and the open-minded traits required for corrigibility combined with firmness of purpose. Because the master virtue itself encompasses a wide variety of potentially counterpoised intellectual and character traits required to coordinate first-order virtues, all the problems about the appropriate coordination of virtue-assuring dispositions reappear. The regulative intellectual and character virtues are also action-forming; and first-order virtues can sometimes also function as regulative master virtues. The distinction between first- and second-order virtues appears to be a context-dependent difference in functional role rather than a distinction between types or traits.

Indeed, it seems as if the master virtue is not one trait, not even one *way* of appropriately coordinating capacities, dispositions, traits: it is *nothing in particular,* over and above having a well-constructed character that tends to act well and appropriately. If excellence of character is assured by anything, it is assured by an appropriate configuration of traits, rather than by a single trait or by a conjunction of traits. But since each situation requires a slightly different configuration of traits to produce an appropriate action, and since different people might require different configurations in different situations, the appropriate configuration of virtue-assuring traits cannot be specified.

The difficulties with the master virtue solution suggest another, less familiar solution to the problem of assuring the virtues. (4) The next solution might be described as a checks-and-balances solution, for it locates the virtues in a system of supportive and tensed traits. A set of traits qualifies as a virtue only when it is supported and balanced against other traits in an appropriate pattern or configuration. The traits that constitute the virtues hunt in role-differentiated packs, not only requiring one another to determine particular actions, but also, darkly and significantly, to modify, to check and balance, one another's exercise. Long after moral philosophers abandoned Socratic theories of the unity of the virtues, they still retained the Platonic assumption that the various virtues form a harmonious system directed to the same general ends. However differentiated in function, the virtues were assumed either to coincide in forming the same extensionally identified action or—more frequently—typically to coordinate and support one another's exercise and action outcomes.

By contrast, the check-and-balances solution does not assume that the virtues form a mutually supportive, harmonious system directed toward realizing compatible ends. On the contrary, according to this solution, at least some of the virtues are assured because their typical cognitions and actions are dynamically opposed to one another.[7] Virtues can check one another in a number of ways. (1) When the cognitive component of the traits that constitute them are contraries or contradictories, they will constrain each other. (The cognitive set of a particular devotion or commitment can, for instance, sometimes be contrary to that of impartiality.) (2) Virtues can check each other when the traits that compose them are typically exercised in actions whose outcomes standardly undermine or frustrate one another's intention, direction, or satisfaction. (The habits of consensual sociability are, for instance, tensed against those exercised in strong independence.) (3) The development of one set of traits can typically inhibit the development of another. (The habits developed in the service of a rule-bound bureaucracy tend to block those required for improvisatory resourcefulness.) (4) The exercise of one set of traits can produce conditions that require the exercise of an opposed set. (The combative soldierly virtues that sometimes bring peace can endanger the fragile trust on which the preservation of that peace depends.)

It is of course not possible to give a general rule or principle to determine the proper *measure* of any particular balance among tensed or opposed virtues. Sometimes one virtue might entirely and appropriately block another; sometimes two virtues modulate or diminish one another's force; sometimes one virtue appears recessively within the action determined by another, modifying the way the dominant virtue is expressed, hesitantly or ambivalently. The whole range of combinatorial properties of the cognitive and habit-based traits are brought into play.

Unfortunately, despite the advantages of its dark and rare truthfulness, the checks-and-balances solution seems as regressive as the master virtue solution and nearly, but not quite, as uninformative as the contextualizing solution. Since there is no general rule or principle to determine it, what assures the appropriate balance in each situation? To make matters worse, there seem to be competing criteria for a well-ordered appropriate configuration, which varies with the weight assigned to each virtue. Do the difficulties of the system of checks and balances lead back to the master virtue solution in order to evaluate competing criteria for appropriate balance— which in turn requires a system of checks and balances among the various components of the master virtue?

While there are undeniable problems for the checks-and-balances solution, I believe that it nevertheless presents an advance over the other solutions. For one thing, it is psychologically truthful; for another, it presents some rudimentary heuristic guidance for maintaining the virtue of their virtues by locating them in a logical and psychologically dynamic field.

But here we are, once again, in the old familiar circle. Nothing in particular seems to assure virtue—nothing less than the whole of a virtuous character, well formed in a system of checks and balances, so as to assure its proper activity, acting appropriately as the situation requires, i.e., acting virtuously. Where can we go from nowhere?

III. COMMUNITY AS THE CONTEXT OF CHARACTER

No action without interaction;
no interaction without politics.

But perhaps our somber reflections are premature. Perhaps we have been looking at the wrong place. Virtue is, after all, primarily and fundamentally an attribute of humans rather than of actions or sets of traits. It is the man, Aristotle remarks, who is the source of action: the regression of traits that assures the appropriate balance of the virtues stops at the *person,* the total configuration of character, rather than at a master regulatory virtue or principle.[8] But if the man is the source of action, we need to understand what forms the man, what leads to his being the sort of person who is capable of virtue. According to Aristotle, a certain sort of psycho-physical constitution is required, as well as appropriate economic and socio-political conditions and the good fortune of a person's early models. The assurance of a person's virtues cannot occur in a social or political vacuum.

Action takes place in a social world. It is, in the end, our social and political relation to others that keeps our virtues in whatever precariously appropriate balance they have. Minimally the cooperation and esteem we require from our fellows elicit the appropriate balance among supporting and opposing virtues. Significantly, our actions have their sense, their meaning, and their direction in a public, interactive world. This is not just a consequence of the fact that political institutions shape our attitudes and social structures form our views, although this is of course true. Nor is it solely a consequence of the fact that our actions often so change our social and political circumstances, that they in turn require us to change, although this is of course also true. In addition, we have been culturally influenced by the ideal of offering a social justification of the principles that guide our actions.

More to the point of the assurance of the virtues, our actions are dramatically and substantively formed by our minute interactions with others. The details of most of our actions are determined through a subtle process of interaction. Think of the way in which a conversation, a real conversation, a common investigation rather than a comforting ritual or an exchange of monologues, takes place. In a real conversation, the participants do not know, ahead of time, what they will say, or even sometimes what they think. To be sure, there are constraints: interlocutors want (among many other things) to arrive at what is true, and they are guided by what they presently believe is true. But at any moment in the conversation, there are an indefinite number of relevant, consecutive true things they could say and think. Closure is given by the minutiae of interactions: the look of puzzlement on an interlocutor's face, the excitement of common pursuit, an ironic remark. The more subtly partners in a conversation understand each other—the more they are familiar with one another's gestures, facial expressions, and reactions—the more condensed and improvisatory their conversation is likely to be. Like jazz musicians, they sometimes lapse into a familiar riff for a little rest, finding something in that riff that leads them in a new direction. Not only conversations and music-making, but many of our central actions—designing a playground or a curriculum, cooking a meal, selecting a Supreme Court Justice, hanging paintings for an exhibition—take this form. Even when we act in solitude or in character, from our deeply entrenched traits, the actions we perform emerge from an interactive process that sometimes takes place *in foro interno*. Some of our interactive partners elicit our (very own) boldness, others elicit our (very own) caution. The configuration of a person's traits—the patterns of dominance and recessiveness—that emerges in any given situation is affected by her interactive company.[9]

We characteristically respond to a skeptical interlocutor in one way, to a confirming interlocutor in another, to a co-explorer in yet another. The views we form as a result of our common investigations—views that each interlocutor genuinely holds as her own—are, in their fine grain details, co-produced, even when the interlocutors end with markedly different views.[10] As with views, so with the balanced pattern of our virtues. Character, in all its constitutional and socio-political configuration, regulates the particular virtues; and community regulates character. It is these that, taken together, hold the virtues in check. But then it is these that, taken together, can also lead to vice.

Obviously, the interactive context of the formation of action cannot assure virtue, cannot determine the appropriate configuration of our typically virtuous traits. Even the shiningly virtuous are sometimes corrupted rather than supported by the company they keep. Nevertheless, once we know the patterns of our interactions, we can—bearing in mind our patterns of contrariness—strengthen an appropriate configuration of traits by being careful of the company we keep. But since we can also voluntarily erode what we take to be a relatively virtuous configuration, all the problems of assuring the virtues are again postponed. What determines the company we choose to keep? Have we returned to *phronesis?* Or to a checked-and-balanced cycle of dominance and recessiveness in the configuration of traits, this time extended to the company to which we gravitate, a characteristic cycle of high-minded and low-life company, or of solitude and random sociability? More soberly, does the interactive social determination of the checks and balances of the virtues throw us into the power politics of the control of the virtues? Aren't we playthings of the moral luck of our political and social situation, the luck of the draw of our interactive community? After all, we are subject to the power of charisma and of interest groups all contending to define the dominance and recessiveness of their prime candidates for our virtues: there is no assurance that the outcome of such struggles issues in an appropriate balance.

It is indeed just for this reason that some moral philosophers attempted to replace theories of virtue with theories of rules and principles. Complex, pluralistic, and dynamic societies with genuinely opposed needs, values, and interests are likely to have competing models of virtue. Acknowledging the motto "No virtues without virtue," they add: "No virtue without rules and principles." Sometimes, when such societies recognize that they require a variety of opposed models, they succeed in formulating general procedural rules and principles to adjudicate among the claims of competing models by placing them in a system of checks and balances. But there is no guarantee that there will be agreement on such procedural principles: when there are competing models for the proper balance of the virtues, there is also usually disagreement about principles, including those procedural principles regulating the adjudication of disagreement.[11] Finding an overlapping consensus on rules for adjudicating disagreement introduces justice as the master virtue. A set of principles governing procedures for adjudicating disagreements appears to have the special advantages of being self-referentially capable of arbitrating competing claims about its own formulation. But the self-referential closure of procedural rules and principles is broken when there are competing claims about their priority and formulation, particularly when differences in formulation and priority among procedural principles would issue in distinctive policies and actions, or form a different community. Although it seems initially to be a liberating solution, the attempt to provide procedural rules and principles for resolving conflicts has all the advantages and disadvantages of the master virtue solution.

It seems that we have, despite everything, returned full circle to the somber answers to our original questions. Traits are called *virtues* when they are culturally regarded as admirable or beneficial, when there is social pressure to develop and exercise them. When—as is normally the case in complex and dynamic societies—there are competing and sometimes conflicting models of benefit and admirability, we can attempt to find or form a consensus on procedural principles of justice, or develop a solidly operating system of checks and balances among the contending models of virtue. Nothing can assure that competing models of virtue in a polity will be appropriately balanced, rather than merely determined by the accidental play of power politics. We can try to characterize the master virtue and the particular system of checks and balances among the virtues that, given existing conditions and dominant motivational structures, are most likely to assure the appropriate exercise of the various virtues. The proposal to make procedural justice the master virtue is just such an attempt.

But sometimes there just *is* no appropriate way to assure the balance among virtues. At worst, the emergent balance is determined by the power of charisma and the power of interest groups. With luck, the distribution of power is so structured as to produce a cycle rotating the benefits of each model of virtue.

These dark conclusions have led many moral theorists to elect to do programmatically normative moral theory, arguing that before we can direct operative psychological processes for assuring the appropriate balance of the virtues, we must determine the most general conditions of appropriateness. Unfortunately, the constraints set by characteristic social and psychological process—the laws describing the conditions and effects of various power relations, for instance—directly enter into the determination of the criteria for appropriateness. The constraints of applicable practicability, of psychological and political realizability, appear *within* the determination of appropriateness. The difficulties of defining the appropriate balance among competing virtues reappear as difficulties in arbitrating among competing normative moral theories.

Reconstructivist moral philosophers who propose to assure virtue by offering either rules for or an imitable model of acting well tend to bracket the contingencies that affect moral luck: the luck of a person's constitutional and intellectual traits; the luck of having appropriate formative models to imitate; the luck of living in historical, economic, and socio-political conditions that are consonant with one's own dispositional directions; the luck of good company. But it is just the strength of practical, descriptively oriented virtue theories that they acknowledge the pervasive presence of moral luck. The virtues are, among other things, the range of skills that enable a person to cope with luck, to deal with the contingencies and vagaries of the particular situations.

It seems we end where we began, recognizing that although there is much to be said about the details of the appropriate balance of checked and opposed traits, there is nothing in particular that assures virtue in general. Another equally sober reflection emerges from our investigation. Even action-guiding practical theories cannot—and indeed should not—provide moral solutions where virtuous moral agents have moral problems. The more practical an ethical theory, the more it reflects the sorts of difficulties that virtuous agents have, and the more clearly it locates and explains our failures. Ethical theories designed to be practical and action-guiding cannot reasonably be expected to provide salvation where none is to be had.[12]

Notes

1. Cf. Michael Walzer, *Interpretation and Social Criticism* (Cambridge, Mass., 1987); Jonathan Lear, "Moral Objectivity," *Objectivity and Cultural Divergence*, edited by S. C. Brown (Cambridge, 1984).

2. Philippa Foot, "Virtues and Vices," *Virtues and Vices* (Berkeley, 1978), 7 ff. Following this strategy, Foot says, "The villain's courage is not a virtue in him."

3. Cf. "The Two Faces of Courage," *Philosophy* (1986): 5ff.

4. Cf. Michael Slote, *Goods and Virtues* (Ithaca, NY, 1983), chap. 2; Alasdair MacIntyre, "How Virtues Become Vices."

5. "The Limits of Socrates' Intellectualism: Did Socrates Teach Virtue?" *Proceedings of the Boston Area Colloquium in Ancient Philosophy*, vol. 3, edited by John Cleary (1986).

6. Foot, "Virtues and Vices."

7. There is a tradition according to which virtue is assured by the balance among opposed virtues. That tradition is represented by Plato, in *The Statesman* 311B-C: "Those who are careful, fair and conservative—those of a moderate temperament—are not keen; they lack a certain sort of quick, active boldness. The courageous on the other hand are far less just and cautious, but they are excellent at getting things done. A community can never function well . . . unless both of these are present and active . . . woven together by the ruler." Cf. also Hume, *Treatise of Human Nature* II. 2. 1-12 and Spinoza, *Ethics* III Scholia and Definitions, for detailed accounts of the ways in which the passions function within a dynamic system of support and opposition. The opposition of virtues is explored in Book III of *The Fairy Queen* where Spenser describes a duel between the Knight of Temperance against the Knight of Chastity.

8. I am grateful to Alasdair MacIntyre for stressing this point.

9. Stephen White pointed out to me that it might seem that interactive action formation could be analyzed as a sequence of microactions. M says x in manner f, which serves as a stimulus for N to say y in manner g, which serves as a stimulus for M to say z in manner h. While a conversation or an improvisation could be analyzed in that way, such an analysis would miss the formation of the action as a whole. Of course any action can be broken down into a series of microactions: not only such complex actions as emigrating, undertaking to follow a course of study, but also swimming across or walking around a pond can be decomposed into micromovements. But while such an analysis might explain the details of each micromovement, it would not explain the form of the sequence, taken as a whole, in relation to other action sequences, taken as a whole. To understand the structured sequence of microactions as forming a complex whole, we refer to a shared general intention that integrally encompasses the interactive process: partners making music together or having a conversation.

10. David Wong pointed out to me that it might seem as if the greater the role assigned to the interactive structuring of actions, the less of a role does the configuration of character play

in acting well. It is true that we often not only have different types of conversations with different interlocutors, but even different types of conversations on the same subject. The emergent details of a person's views on a topic are strongly influenced by the views and the characters of her interlocutors. But both are required: a particular interactive response is drawn from a person's repertoire of character traits and it is, as we say, characteristic. Cf. Jonathan Adler, "Moral Development and the Personal Point of View," *Women and Moral Theory.*

11. Cf. John Rawls, "The Idea of an Overlapping Consensus" and "The Priority of Right and Ideas of the Good in Justice as Fairness." See also Jürgen Habermas, *The Theory of Communicative Action* (Boston, 1987).

12. This paper grew out of many conversations, held over a long period of time: Rudiger Bittner, Larry Blum, Sissela Bok, Owen Flanagan, Genevieve Lloyd, Alasdair MacIntyre, Georges Rey, William Ruddick, Michael Slote, Stephen White, and David Wong have helped shape it, as did the participants in a colloquium at the University of Maryland.

Morality and the Morally Informed Life

R. Z. FRIEDMAN

I

A pervasive aspect of the present mood in moral philosophy is the sense that it is too narrow an enterprise to do justice to the diverse nature of practical life. The moral dimension of life is thought to have been too narrowly conceived while the non-moral dimension has been left unexplored and the question of the unity of the moral and the non-moral not even raised. This narrowness is a consequence of understanding morality to be concerned with social conduct and indeed only with one dimension of social conduct, variously understood as those actions which limit self-interest and contribute to the harmony of society, those actions which insure a fair distribution of society's resources and opportunities, those actions which contribute to the greatest good, or those actions one must refrain from doing lest one treat others as means and not ends. But morality conceived in this way says little about the nature of one's involvements as such. It is concerned to articulate the nature and the range of the moral agent's responsibilities to others but has little if anything to say about the character, texture, and color of those relationships. Someone may respect his parents but not listen to them, love his children but not give them a sense of their importance, appreciate his wife but lose a sense of her as a person. Moral theory as we have inherited it allows us to imagine someone who is on the one hand morally worthy and, on the other, distant, uncomprehending, and insensitive.

This difficulty is even more obvious in the case of non-social, self-regarding concerns. Moral philosophy has had little to say to the moral agent who surveys his own life without regard to his moral responsibilities to others. To give the problem a traditional form: Does the single individual on the desert island have moral obligations? The received answer is "No." And with this answer the concern of moral philosophy, indeed of philosophy in general, with individual life has ended. But what is an individual to make of the fact that although he is, in general, not a moral monster, he has yet managed to make wrong choices of a monumental kind—sent out wrong messages to friend and foe alike, made the wrong career choices, chose to do what he wanted rather than what he was most talented for, made and kept the wrong friends for the wrong reasons, wore all the social masks of his generation, including the one that decries the use of masks. Although his life is not obviously morally unworthy, the individual might feel there is much that is "wrong" about it which may cause him to feel not guilt, as one might in the case of moral failure, but sadness and regret. The experience Dante relates in the opening lines of the *Divine Comedy* of finding himself lost and in need of a fundamental reexamination is certainly a common if not universal experience. I am struck by how often I hear and, indeed, feel the force of Dante's question and how infrequently I hear the Kantian question, "What ought I to do?" More of us, I think, feel the failure of what we have not become than moral failure.

In "The Importance of What We Care About," Harry Frankfurt makes an important contribution to the expansion of philosophical inquiry into practical life beyond the parameters of morality. Frankfurt argues that in addition to the epistemological concern with what is to be believed and the traditional concern with behavior there is another as of yet ignored "cluster of questions which pertain to another thematic and fundamental preoccupation of human existence—namely, *What to care about.*"[1] Where ethics is concerned with interpersonal conduct, with the distinction between right and wrong, with moral obligation, this "third branch of inquiry" is concerned with non-moral but important considerations, i.e., "what [we are] to do with *ourselves*" and in turn "what is *important* or rather, what is *important to us.*"[2]

According to Alasdair MacIntyre in his response to Frankfurt's paper, in the modern period the question "What is it important to care about?" replaces the question "What ought we to desire?" much as the question "What is the meaning of life?" replaces "Does God exist?"[3] In MacIntyre's view, "care" and "importance" are the wrong issues. They reflect concerns unleashed by the Romantic backlash against the tough line that Kant and his followers took on the passions. The Aristotelian tradition, MacIntyre believes, includes and can deal with these issues within its moral theory, but the Kantian tradition cannot; hence the emergence of a new branch of inquiry to deal with non-moral practical concerns.[4] For MacIntyre, both the question concerning the treatment of others and that concerning care require the answer to a more fundamental question, "that most fundamental of questions, 'What sort of person am I to become?' "[5]

But does MacIntyre's "fundamental question" provide an explanation for each of the two practical questions which Kant and Frankfurt raise? In this paper I shall argue that the Kantian analysis is not flawed, at least in the way that MacIntyre thinks it is, that indeed without Kant's distinction between the moral and the non-moral there can be no adequate explanation of morality. I shall argue this point in section 2. Frankfurt's question serves to point out the most serious weakness in Kant's moral philosophy—its treatment of non-moral practical interests. Kant pushes these interests beyond the parameters of philosophy, and, rightly, Frankfurt would have us retrieve them. In section 3, I argue the case for an objective consideration of non-moral practical interests and offer four questions as a tentative way of organizing and developing our views on this heterogeneous and amorphous area. In section 5, I develop a question which is broader and more inclusive than either the moral question or the non-moral question and which allows these questions to be seen in relation to each other.

II

To support his contention that care may be a more important or more weighty cause of action than moral considerations, Frankfurt observes:

> If a mother who is tempted to abandon her child finds that she simply cannot do that, it is probably not because she knows (or even because she cares about) her duty. It is more likely because of how she cares about the child, and about herself as its mother, than because of any recognition on her part that abandoning the child would be morally wrong.[6]

MacIntyre makes much of this example, countering that if we insist on the distinction between care and what is morally wrong, that contemporary legacy of the great Kantian distinction between duty and happiness, we fragment the image of the truly developed moral agent, we lose "any portrait of the mother as moral agent *qua* mother." He continues:

> To be a mature moral agent is to have educated one's feelings appropriately. It is to care the right amount for the right people and things in the right way at the right time and place. So that a mother who is a mature moral agent will have learned how to care about her child and its good; for her the contrast between her duty *qua* mother and what *qua* mother she cares about will not arise. Indeed the appearance of such a contrast in her moral reasoning and judgment would signal some defect in her moral education. If this is right, then there must be something mistaken about Frankfurt's initial classification, since just this point is what it obscures from view.[7]

The classical tradition brings together psychological, moral, prudential, and educational categories. The "mature moral agent" is one who has "educated [his] feelings appropriately" and who as a result "cares" but cares "the right amount for the right people and things in the right way at the right time and place." This analysis provides for a unity in the moral agent and in that agent's conduct. Deliberation, evaluation, internal struggle, decision making are not the stuff of the mature moral agent. He wants to do the right thing, he knows what the right thing is, he does it, he produces the best that his situation allows. This portrayal of the moral agent evokes the figure of Socrates, with that special sense of resoluteness and confidence, that sense of always knowing what to do and never hesitating to do it. Kant would have us believe, and I do believe it, that this classical archetype is the model of the successful person—the actor who knows what to do as if by instinct, who knows how to make things happen, and who seems to do everything well. But he is not for these reasons a morally admirable person. Kant's analysis draws our attention to the inside of the action, to the impulse that moves and animates the choice for the action. Success belongs to those who effectively master their situations, including those elements necessary for the effective presentation of the self. But moral worthiness is not to be found in this sort of mastery; it lies in the mastery over the will. This is not a denial of the value of success but a denial of the view that success is the content of morality.

Using Frankfurt's example, let us ask what would cause the mother to refrain from abandoning the child and how we would judge the moral worthiness of each decision. Let us begin with the instance of the mother who refuses to abandon her child and who does so not out of regard for moral considerations but because of her care for the child. Might we not ask whether the mother's care reflects a concern for her child as such or whether this concern is limited to a particular child among, let us say, the several children she has? What would we say of the mother if we knew that she had made her choice on the basis of her care for the child in question but that this caring did not extend to her other children, and indeed if she appeared prepared to abandon them? We would say, I think, that the mother is making a decision which is emotional, subjective, and arbitrary.

One can imagine a decision which allows for the inclusion of all of the mother's children as being objects of her concern. But this might be a very "primitive" form of caring, for the mother may care about those things she believes to be *hers* and care about them *because* they are hers. "These children are mine," she might say, "and nobody takes what is mine and I don't give anything of mine away, these children included." One might imagine a decision of a similar sort based not on an interpretation of children as property but on family or even tribal loyalty. "We stick together," the mother might say, "united against those forces outside of us that would undermine our unity." Primitive loyalty recognizes the distinction between people and things, but this sort of loyalty is hardly what we mean by mature responsibility.

One can easily imagine a more acceptable decision. "I will not abandon this child because this is my child," the mother might say. "I am its mother; I brought it into the world and I am responsible for it." Emphasis here falls on the mother's perception of what sort of conduct is consistent with her role as mother. Self-esteem may be a higher rung on the ladder than loyalty because it involves the idea of a role which may have objective modes of conduct associated with it, but performing in the role is not the same thing as respecting one's objective responsibilities to the child.

Of course it is possible to imagine an explanation of caring for the child that does allow this important element in moral decision making to surface. The mother might say, "This is my child. My decision to have this child was a decision not simply to bear a child but to raise that child. And I will do so." Here the role implies certain objective relationships between the mother and the child; that is, the mother accepts the fact that there are things which she, *qua* mother, can and cannot do. The role has precedence over her needs, feelings, and self-esteem, and the role involves certain responsibilities which run (under normal circumstances) counter to the idea of abandonment. In the first example above, the mother makes her decision based on her care for her child; in this instance the mother makes her decision based on an acknowledgment of objective considerations.

We can also imagine a mother who would refrain from abandoning her child because she would not abandon any child. "All children are my concern," she might say, "not because they are *my* children but simply because they are *children.* "This position moves beyond the notion of objective responsibilities based on role to a notion of the child as an entity who has certain rights *per se.* Here the rights of the child are acknowledged to have primacy over the idea or concept of "mine," whether my possessions, my feelings, my loyalties, my role, my self-esteem, or even my perfection and self-realization. My care is not *my* care; it is my objective recognition of my responsibilities to the child by virtue of the fact that the child is a human being. When care becomes universal it becomes rational, and rational care is, I would say, what Kant means by reverence.

The intentional structure of reverence is different from that of wanting, desiring, caring, perfection, or self-realization. It involves the recognition of a value independent of the moral agent such that the form of his intention is "I do this not because it realizes even the best in me but because of the value in it that requires me to do it." We might say that success is the result of the ability to make good things happen while morality is the choice that recognizes the intrinsic goodness of the person. We must, then, distinguish between success and morality, between desire and reverence, between the non-moral and the moral good.

Kant, of course, makes much of this distinction, and I do not see how there is to be a satisfactory understanding of morality which does not recognize this point. Now if I am told that the Aristotelian formula actually includes this point within its analysis of the moral agent who knows the right thing and how to do it, who does the right thing with regard to the right person in the right way, to the right degree, at the right time and place, I would reply that this sounds deserving of Hegel's criticism of Schelling's philosophy, that it is "a night in which all cows are black."[8]

Morality requires the distinction between the moral and the non-moral good. The failure of the classical tradition is that it does not make this distinction. If I read Kant correctly, however, he believed that in Stoicism is found the highest achievement of classical moral thought, an achievement which in terms of moral philosophy in general stands just beneath his own. The Stoics, according to Kant, understood the principle of morality as embodying obligation. Their mistake was to link that principle to the attainment of happiness, a move made possible, in Kant's view, by a misinterpretation of happiness as moral contentment, as satisfaction with one's moral performance rather than satisfaction with the course of one's life generally. For instance, in the *Gorgias* Socrates is at great pains not only to demonstrate that justice is of great benefit as a condition without which human happiness could not be achieved, but to demonstrate as well that with the achievement of justice necessarily comes the prize of happiness. Ironically, although Socrates argues for the identity of morality and happiness, his own experience serves to point out the need to distinguish between the two. Socrates is an instance of the tragic collision of the just man with a hostile society. Socrates, however, does not see it that way; for him, real tragedy is to do wrong, for doing wrong not only makes a person morally unworthy it invites sickness into the soul, and this, Socrates argues, is the worst of all possible fates. But is it? Is it worse than being "put on the rack?" There are, I believe, fates worse than sickness of the soul. But even if the doing of evil and the sickness of the soul were worse than the rack, this "worse" must refer to something other than well-being, fulfillment, and happiness. And with this Socrates' position comes apart. Kant believes that the fidelity to principle which may bring one to the rack is not the same as that which contributes to one's self-realization. What is required is a notion of two goods, one concerned with realization and happiness, the other with morality and virtue. Without this distinction, morality is lost.

I think, however, that, while right on this score, the Kantian interpretation misses the meaning of Stoicism. Stoicism is the claim that the individual makes or determines his fate through his control over himself, that self-mastery is mastery not only over oneself but over one's fate as well. But is Socrates the author of his fate? Socrates presents himself in this way, an incredible position for a man in his situation, but he does appear confident that he is living his reward—a certain kind of life which is indeed the best. But I wonder whether Plato saw it that way. For Plato, Socrates is a tragic figure, his life that of the philosopher who returns into the cave, there to suffer his inevitable fate. The Stoicism that Plato sees in the life of Socrates is not the Stoicism Socrates espouses; it is not that buoyant, self-confident Stoicism that makes self-mastery the key to control over one's fate. Rather, it is a Stoicism of defeat, a Stoicism that has retreated to a position that claims that self-mastery does not control the events of one's life but only one's attitude to those events. Socrates is not the man who got what he deserved; he thought he deserved the crown of the Olympian hero but received death instead. His power was not that of making his fate but simply of rising to it. His lot in life was not happiness but nobility. His error was to argue that nobility *is* happiness rather than that nobility is not happiness but worth more than happiness. Had he argued this latter position, he would have been the moral hero who also had the right theory of morality.

III

MacIntyre's question, "What sort of person do I wish to become?" is not the fundamental question of practical life. This question gives the moral agent a number of choices. In an Aristotelian context, for example, it asks whether I would choose the ordinary life of pleasure, the more respected life of government, or the life of philosophy. I must decide what I want, and what I want is a life which best realizes the things that I want. Kant's fundamental point, with which I am in agreement, is that moral concerns are not generated out of such a question. A thing is not morally good because it fulfills my needs; it is morally good independent of my needs. It is not a product of my will; my will acknowledges it.

But Kant not only makes the distinction between moral and non-moral practical interests, he argues that philosophy has no role with regard to non-moral interests, for these are a matter of pleasure and what makes for pleasure varies from person to person and from time to time within the life of each person. Consequently, non-moral practical interests do not allow for objective standards. Philosophy and these interests, therefore, pass like the proverbial ships in the night.

Not surprisingly, then, Kant has little to say about the psychological dimension of the subject. However, philosophy after Kant not only builds more interesting psychological structures, it builds them on Kantian foundations. Kant's morally inspired duality becomes the basis of the dialectical self in Hegel, who brings together this duality with a traditional teleology and produces brilliant descriptions of human life and culture along a historical continuum from mind subsumed in nature to mind at its pinnacle, mind's knowledge of itself as absolute. Kierkegaard's view of human life as three stages also reveals the strong influence of the Kantian duality of the finite and the infinite, of nature and reason, but as is the case with Hegel, this view is included in a more unified and developmental view of the self, a view which owes much to Hegel. In Kierkegaard I find a modern Dante who narrates a complex, at least in part Kantian-inspired, journey through the self. The Kantian duality and the moral psychology it is based on need not be a dead end. Indeed, as the examples of Hegel and Kierkegaard point out, they have not been.

I do not accept Kant's hedonistic interpretation of the non-moral good or his conviction that all non-moral practical interests are completely relative. The two spheres do have different subject matters but each is open to philosophical reflection. The task is to find the method appropriate to each. Frankfurt's paper is a significant contribution to this task. His question, "What is it important to care about?" addresses individual, personal, and subjective concerns and attempts to integrate them within philosophical reflection alongside moral concerns.

I find it difficult to believe that *any* one question can adequately encompass an area as diverse and heterogeneous as non-moral practical interests. I suggest the following four questions as a way of organizing the concerns that characterize the non-moral good. This list of questions is tentative, designed to suggest a line of inquiry, not to gather all the material that inquiry will require.

1. What is the impact of morality on character and personality?
2. What kind of person is emerging from my life and activity?
3. What is important to me as a distinct person?
4. What are the things that are important in general in terms of the non-moral good?

It is with the first question that the strength of the classical tradition is most apparent; it insists on the unity of the subject. Nowhere is this better demonstrated than in the moral-psychological portrait of Callicles in the *Gorgias*. The life of Callicles shows how immorality can produce not only unworthiness but frustration in terms of the achievement of the non-moral good. Callicles is hopelessly divided against himself, contemptuous of reason and philosophy, and eager to cultivate his own needs and their gratification. As an individual involved in politics, Callicles brings strife to public life, a consequence he justifies by arguing that human society is really a jungle where the strong fight for control over the weak. Immorality produces discord and strife. This in turn produces what might be called instability and volatility in the character of the individual, and this is externalized into the social arena as aggression and hostility. Wounded in character, the immoral individual loses the power of thought, objective deliberation, and discussion. His horizons narrow; his world becomes smaller as he becomes more single-minded.

Now it may well be the case that moral worthiness does not enable the individual to transcend fate. We might even say that the example of Socrates helps to prove this point. But, we may ask, is moral worthiness integral to a healthy psychological development? Does the performance of morality or immorality simply involve discrete choices and acts which have no determining power on future choices? Or do these choices contribute to the formation of a discernible path and a firmly developed character, for example, the life and personality of Callicles? I believe that these are not moral questions as such but questions about the impact of morality on character and personality. I think that in Plato's description of Callicles we find good reason to believe that this connection between morality and personality does exist.

The second question "What kind of person is emerging from my life and activity?" is directed not at my fidelity to morality or even to morality's impact on my life, but at myself in the broad, one might say psychological, sense. Am I becoming more distant and remote? Am I becoming the kind of person who does his duty and who may be said to have a social conscience but who steps back from any demanding or compelling personal involvements? Am I becoming narrow, less willing to be involved with new things, less willing to invest time and energy in things that I used to think were very important? Do I find myself thinking of all my social relationships as "responsibilities to others" and everything that is not my work as "entertainment"? Has my life led me down increasingly narrow paths with the result that I have myself become narrow and self-concerned? Who, I might ask under the direction of the second question, is emerging from my life and activity? And is this the person I wanted to become?

The third question draws on the fact that each of us is a distinct and unique individual. I have a specific history and experience. I live in a place that imposes certain political, social, and economic facts. My physical constitution is what it is. I have certain talents and interests and not others. These conditions and many more constitute my given, what Sartre would call my "facticity." It may not determine me, but it does much to define the parameters within which my thought about what sort of person I wish to become will be conducted. Appreciation of my facticity may allow me to identify and realize those things which I think to be important about me as a distinct individual.

The fourth question raises a more general issue, What is important as such? What are those things worth wanting? Where should one place one's past in planning for the future? Should continuity be a more important factor than change? How is friendship to be made compatible with family relationships? How are responsibilities to children and to parents to be balanced? Is it more important to do scientific research than to write poetry, more important to do medicine than art? Should "career choices" be guided by talents, needs, or by social utility? Can these responsibilities and values be made specific and ranked? The fourth question asks how the tangle of human relationships, traditions, talents, needs, loyalties, which constitute human life are to be sorted out and ranked in terms of importance.

IV

Kant does not accept, as I do, either the objective character of non-moral considerations or the contention that activity within the moral sphere has an impact on character and personality. The fundamental distinction between the moral and the non-moral, however, which underlies discussion in the preceding section remains Kantian. And even Kant does not accept the distinction between the moral and the non-moral as being ultimate. He contends that their complete separation would serve to undermine morality. The question of the relation of the two is expressed in the third of Kant's three questions, "What can I hope?" What I can hope, Kant reasons, indeed, what I must hope is that if I do what I ought, a matter which lies solely within my control, the events of my life upon which my happiness depends but over which I have no control will produce happiness to the extent to which I am worthy of it. This hope is no capricious need or hedonistic inducement to morality but a rational need of morality itself. Furthermore, it requires the acceptance of the existence of God as that condition without which this hope could not be realized. There is then, in Kant's view, a connection between the moral and the non-moral, but it is external to the subject and is mediated by an omniscient and omnipotent ruler of the universe who insures the hegemony of the moral order over the natural. This external connection is consistent with Kant's denial of Stoicism, which is really the affirmation of a connection internal to the subject. That is, Stoicism understands the subject to make himself happy through moral activity, and since this activity is solely within his power and control he can make himself as happy as he can make himself good, a conviction to which Kant seems consistently hostile.

In this section, I shall not argue the case for Kant's external connection, which I think is profound and compelling but which I have elucidated in other contexts, or further argue the internal connection advanced in the previous section. Rather, I wish to raise yet another question, one which does not establish a synthesis of the moral and the non-moral or even a causal integration of the two, but one which indicates a larger framework, enabling the subject to think about his life from a more inclusive point of view. The question is, "How can I understand my life?" Not, "What ought I to do?" Not "What can I hope?" But "What can I make of a life in which these other questions emerge and operate?"

When Kant considers the three questions which unify his work, he is asking something like the question I have in mind, although the emphasis of my question is essentially practical. How do these various pieces fit together, and what am I to make of a life of which they are the essential elements? The opening lines of the *Divine Comedy* provide one example of what this question means: "Midway in the journey" of this life, the author finds himself lost in "a dark forest," and "the right path" is not to be found.[9] Finding it involves a complex journey through the self. Dante's question is not "What will make me happy?" or "What ought I to do?" but something like "What can I make of my life? How am I to understand it?"

Kant would appear to have little if anything to say in a discussion of this question. The moral law is the moral law, he seems to say; the law is the content of moral life and, basically, moral life is life. This is a very limited, negative view of Kant's work, although one familiar enough in the literature. In this view, Kant sees the moral law as that principle which all human beings ought to use in their attempt to determine what morality expects of them. There is certainly much, especially in the *Groundwork*, to support this view of Kant. But there is another view, found for instance in A. R. C. Duncan,[10] according to which the moral law is first and foremost a critical principle. As such, the moral law becomes the fundamental element in an extensive philosophical investigation which traces the law to its source, i.e., an activity of reason; this in turn requires the assumption of freedom of the will. The moral law, in this latter view, is not a first-order principle but a meta-ethical principle which allows us not simply to be accurately guided in our moral deliberations but furthermore to more fully and completely understand the enterprise of morality as such and the relationship of this enterprise with theoretical inquiry in both its empirical and speculative aspects. It is from this perspective that I wish to make two points about Kant's analysis.

(1) There is more to Kant's analysis of practical life than the moral law. Indeed there is more to Kant's analysis of *moral life* than the moral law. The moral law is a part of a larger whole, a larger view of life. Hence Kant's position *can* address the question, "How can I understand my life?" for morality is not simply a limit which must occasion the positive question "What is it important to care about?" but an enterprise which gives us things to care about. Morality is not simply an enterprise which limits and routinizes life; it is an enterprise which *informs* life. Morality is not only a law but an ethos.

(2) When I follow the law from the point of view of a critical inquiry I am following a principle which is one of discovery. In Kant, this discovery proceeds from the "Ought," which surfaces in the context of ordinary rational knowledge of morality, through to freedom, which is the unconditioned condition of the Ought and which must be accepted as a "supersensuous causality" lest it contradict natural determinism. The principle of morality allows for the discovery of freedom as a supersensuous causality. One can also say that this principle is one of discovery for the individual himself. It gives him a path to follow in order to know himself insofar as that knowledge is possible. This, too, indicates the ability of Kant's thought to respond to the question, "How can I understand my life?"

Assuming these two points, let me sketch an answer to my question from a Kantian point of view. (1) My understanding of myself begins with the Ought, with the presence within me of a moral fact, a value, which cannot be understood in terms of the natural condition of my existence. I know the Ought, and while this is sufficient to do the Ought, I may also take the Ought and the principle which expresses it as a route of discovery about myself and my situation in the world. (2) I discover conscience, that knowing the Ought as something within me implies that I know the difference between right and wrong, good and evil. This means that I do not require the assistance of religious and political institutions in the determination of my moral responsibilities. Indeed, conscience implies that I am to resist those institutions and forces in society which seek to impose their knowledge on me. Morality tells me that I am bound, but bound morally to a principle which is a synthetic *a priori* principle. The exercise of this principle requires the affirmation of myself as religiously and politically free. (3) Through morality I discover a non-idiosyncratic, non-pathological appropriation of myself and others. I am not a thing for use but a creature of worth and dignity. I am not permitted to exploit myself, to allow others to exploit me, nor, of course, to exploit others. Humanity is not a means to an end but an end in itself.

Morality, one might argue, does not merely demand that I not misuse another individual, it connects me to him, not through the mechanisms of like and dislike but through the rational recognition of the other as a creature of worth and dignity. Furthermore, this recognition extends to social arrangements built on mutual respect, on moral facts, a kingdom of ends. (4) Through morality I discover that I am the author of my own action. My conduct is not an effect, the result of causes over which I have no control, but is, rather, the direct result of my choices. I come to realize as a result of this that although everything else in the world must be understood to be determined, I and all other moral creatures must be free. I am *in* the natural world but not *of* it. (5) I discover that there is more to my situation than I can see. I must assume myself to be part of a moral order. I understand that I must do what I can about what is under my control. There can be no escape from my responsibility. But my fate is not really under my power, especially when one realizes that the cultivation of one's fate requires survival and benefit while fidelity to morality demands virtue and worthiness. I am not free to abandon myself to despair for that would undermine morality, and I am not free to adopt Stoicism, for that confuses the issue of my control over my fate. Even a posture of tragic acceptance would have the effect of reducing morality to an idiosyncracy of the human mind. I discover that there is a moral order in existence which assures at least the rational possibility of the success of the moral enterprise. That it will succeed is not certain, but we can and must hope that it will.

"How can I understand my life?" As a life not merely bounded by morality but *informed* by it. My life is not a lonely process of self-denial and purification, passion circumscribed by a straight-jacket of "don'ts." It is a bridge to what is common and great in man, his ability to reject what *is* in the name of what *ought to be*. My lot is the struggle of the David of morality against the Goliath of nature, a good cause with an uncertain ending.

V

In this paper I have argued, contrary to MacIntyre, that the Kantian fragmentation of practical life into moral and non-moral spheres is necessary if morality is to be made intelligible. I have argued, however, that the non-moral sphere is inadequately dealt with if simply dismissed as subjective, beyond the realm of philosophy. This sphere is more diverse and heterogeneous than the moral sphere but hardly less worthy of philosophical study. Philosophy, I think, must develop the tools and methods appropriate to this study. I see Frankfurt's essay as a step in that direction.

I have suggested a number of questions to help focus discussion in this area. I have concluded with yet another question, "What am I to make of life generally, of a life which includes these moral and non-moral concerns?" The strength of the classical position is in the way it searches for the unity of practical life, a unity which MacIntyre rightly believes the Kantian view fragments. But unity is not alien to this Kantian tradition. Hope is Kant's answer to the question of unity. My answer is the morally informed life.

Let me end with another allusion to Dante. Life is understood as a journey; it may have one goal, one destination, but it does not have only one part. It has different parts; Hell is not Purgatory and Purgatory is not Paradise. Each part must be understood on its own and in relation to other parts, but the differences among them must not be lost. The unity of practical life is not to be found in a view that espouses the sameness of all aspects of practical life. Rather it is to be found in that view which preserves the differences among the parts while insuring their place in a more inclusive whole.

Notes

1. Harry Frankfurt, "The Importance of What We Care About," *Synthese* 53 (1982): 257–72.

2. Ibid.

3. Alasdair MacIntyre, "Comments on Frankfurt," *Synthese* 53 (1982): 291–94.

4. Ibid., 293.

5. Ibid., 292.

6. Frankfurt, 268.

7. MacIntyre, 292.

8. G. W. F. Hegel, *Phenomenology of Spirit,* translated by A. V. Miller; analysis and forward by J. N. Findlay (Oxford, 1977), 9.

9. Dante, *The Divine Comedy,* translated by Laurence Binym, notes by Paolo Milano (New York, 1960), 3.

10. A. R. C. Duncan, *Practical Reason and Morality* (Edinburgh, 1957).

The Dog that Gave Himself
the Moral Law

CORA DIAMOND

Thirty years ago, Elizabeth Anscombe published "Modern Moral Philosophy." In it, she urged that moral philosophy be stopped until it could be done with some profit, and that we should get rid of what are the central notions of much moral thinking. Moral philosophy went on, but not as before. My paper, which involves a story about a dog, is a tribute to "Modern Moral Philosophy."

I

That legislation can be 'for oneself' I reject as absurd; whatever you do for yourself may be admirable; but is not legislating. (Anscombe 1981, 37)

Vicki Hearne tells a (true) story, which she says "is a clear case of a dog's giving himself the moral law" (Hearne 1986, 207). But if no one can give himself the moral law, neither can a dog. The case is perhaps less clear than Miss Hearne says it is, the dog Fritz being more Greek than Kantian. But I will not get to Fritz until section 10. I need first to say what Professor Anscombe was doing.

She was arguing that we ought, if possible, to get rid of the notion of the moral 'ought', of what is morally right and wrong, of moral obligation and moral duty. She argued that these concepts were unintelligible, since their intelligibility depends on a particular framework of thought, and the notions are used outside that framework; "they are survivals . . . from an earlier conception of ethics which no longer generally survives, and are only harmful without it" (26). At the heart of her argument is a division of ethical thought into some that makes sense and some that may seem to but does not. I shall try to make clear where that boundary lies, and where to put the story about Fritz.

Her argument must be understood to be about the survival of concepts or notions, not about the survival of words or expressions. A claim like hers, but about the survival of words, would clearly be untenable, as can be seen by considering one of her examples. She suggests that the use among us of notions like 'moral obligation' is as if "the notion 'criminal' were to remain when criminal law and criminal courts had been abolished and forgotten" (30). There would be nothing at all peculiar about the *word* "criminal" surviving, and coming to express some other concept. But that is not the sort of possibility she asks us to consider.

It may seem as if there is a dilemmatic argument that can be used against her. We are concerned either with the survival of words or with the survival of notions. If we are concerned with the survival of a word, there can be no problem about its surviving the disappearance of a framework of thought necessary for the concept it once expressed; for the conclusion then would simply be that it had come to express something else. On the other hand, if we are supposedly to concern ourselves with the survival of a concept outside the framework of thought that makes it intelligible, we must ask what is meant by the survival of that very concept. Take Professor Anscombe's example of the notion 'criminal'. If we consider a pattern of use of a term, which is not tied to anything at all like criminal proceedings or criminal law, what does it mean to say that the term is for the notion 'criminal'? The argument here is that Professor Anscombe has asked us to think of a case in which a notion survives the disappearance of a framework of thought essential to its intelligibility, but, in trying to imagine such a case, what we come up with is not anything we should think *was* the survival of the original notion. For without the survival of the framework there is no such thing as a pattern of use of a word or phrase closely similar to that of whatever term originally expressed the notion, hence no such thing as the survival of the notion.

I presented that dilemma, not to raise an objection to Professor Anscombe's argument, but because we can move forward if we see what escape is possible between the horns of the dilemma.

Here then is what I shall do. I shall describe a particular notion of divine law, and look at its supposedly unintelligible descendant notion. There are various notions of divine law, and some of them may be quite unlike the particular ones (Jewish, Christian, Stoic) which Professor Anscombe has in mind. I shall focus, in what follows, on the notion of divine law in the Pentateuch, and in Deuteronomy in particular. It may be said that other notions of divine law are higher or more profound. All very well; but it is irrelevant to what I shall be arguing. That is, although I shall refer to the notion of Yahweh's law as a notion of divine law, the applicability of the word "divine" is not significant for the argument. "Yahweh" is a proper name; and I shall be speaking about a part of the use of that name. If that use departs from what we take to be appropriate to divinity, those departures or differences may raise all sorts of interesting questions, none of which concerns me here except so far as the differences may make it hard for us to see what Professor Anscombe meant. (On the differences and the questions they raise, see Miskotte 1967.)

II

The notion of divine law in the Pentateuch has much in common with the notion of a divine command to do some particular act, like leaving some place, or eating some food with your sandals on, in a hurry, or starting to call your wife by a new name. These divine commands to do particular acts have two important features. First, it makes sense to say of Yahweh that he has commanded someone to do something which that person would otherwise have had no reason to do, or even to do something (as in the case of the command to sacrifice Isaac) which that person had every reason not to do. Yahweh may also, of course, be said to command of someone something that he did have other reason to do. It is not then the case that the recognition of a particular act as commanded by Yahweh depends on recognition of the need or desirability that the thing be done. There may indeed be other notions of divine command to do particular acts, in which the recognition of divine command comes from the force of the recognition of the desirability or need that the thing be done. But that is not the notion we can see in the Pentateuch.

Secondly, if a person is commanded by Yahweh to do a particular thing, he may say, because of the command (perhaps in telling someone else about it), "This is what I have to do," or "This is what I am obliged to do." Why the person commanded has a reason for doing the thing, and why it is supposed to be good that he do it, I cannot examine in detail because it depends on a complicated story. But the story involves (as Professor Anscombe implies, although in arguing a different point) a reference to the person's trust and to Yahweh's promises (42). Why he should trust Yahweh, what it would mean for him to obey or disobey, these have to be understood in relation to Yahweh's doings with the man himself (as in the case of Abraham) or with the people to which he belongs. There is a tie to a notion of human virtue, but it comes through that story, and not in connection with the kind of act that is commanded (as is especially clear in the case of Abraham's willingness to sacrifice Isaac). Again, there may be other notions of divine command, in which understanding why one should do the thing commanded depends on the character of the thing commanded, and not on what disobedience to this particular person would be, given the character of the relation to him. But that is not the notion in the Pentateuch.

The difference in the Pentateuch between a particular divine command and a divine law lies in the generality of the latter and in its being addressed to a people for its future life as a people, not to an individual or people for a particular occasion. The statutes ordained by Yahweh have two characteristics, corresponding to the two, just summarized, of particular divine commands. First, it makes sense to say of a divine law that it requires a kind of act which people would otherwise have no reason to regard as necessary. It makes sense to say that Yahweh requires circumcision, whether or no it is desirable independently of Yahweh's commands. What is required by divine law may be such things as not misdirecting the blind (which there are other reasons for condemning) or such things as circumcision (and here the only reason for doing the sort of thing may be Yahweh's having instituted the practice as one of the ways he chooses to distinguish his people).

The person who believes that some act is prohibited by divine law may say "I must not do this," meaning that the law obliges him not to. The divine laws prohibiting various kinds of injustice or hardness add to whatever reasons there are for not doing the prohibited things, reasons like those given by Yahweh's command to someone to do some particular act. Those, I suggested, are not reasons tied to the character of the act, but to the relation between the person and Yahweh. We can see why Yahweh's command to do a particular act gives the person commanded reason to do the thing, if we look at his and his people's relation to Yahweh: we can see what it would be, what breach of trust, what ingratitude, what kind of pride and folly, to refuse to obey. What is striking in Deuteronomy is the repetition in it of an argument why the people to whom the divine statutes have been given must obey them all. The account looks backwards and forwards: backwards to what Yahweh has done in his caring for this people as "the apple of his eye," bearing them away from troubles, like an eagle bearing them on its pinions; and forwards to what is promised, blessing and curse. The pattern of argument looking backwards and forwards echoes the reasons Abraham was given for obedience and trust: this is what Yahweh has done for you, this is what he promises.

These features of the Pentateuch notion of divine law are not shared by every notion of divine law; and some criticisms of Professor Anscombe's piece stem from attention to a different sort of notion. Thus Peter Winch argues that the understanding of a divine law requiring something to be done is a development from understanding of particular acts simply that they *must be done* (e.g., that we must help this person in need). Winch is speaking about how we reach an understanding of "divinity and its laws" (Winch 1987, 161; also Winch n.d., 5) but what he says fits only some notions of 'divinity'. In the particular case of the Pentateuch notion of divine law, the logical relation to "I must" is different from what Winch speaks of. The notion of divine law that Winch has in mind has little more than a superficial analogy to the command by a patriarch to his children; the Pentateuch idea of Yahweh's law has a deeper relation to that notion. Winch's notion of God is not one capable of being used to explain why "one thing rather than another has happened" (Winch 1972, 224; contrast Miskotte 1967, 62–63, 68); but Yahweh's acts and choices do figure in such explanations, and that they can do so is essential to the Pentateuch idea of his law. With Winch's notion of divine law (as developed from our independent grasp of certain things as what we must do) there is no room for a question how obeying God's law is connected with the needs, or the good, of the people under the law, but the Pentateuch treats that question as making sense and as answerable, not just by showing what kind of stubborn, prideful invitation to disaster disobedience is, but also by tying obedience and disobedience to such virtues as gratitude and trust, and such vices as filial impiety. (See also Anscombe, 42, also Hearne, 42–76, on the relation between consequences and coherence of command. Yahweh's relation to the people Israel is analogous to that of a trainer to a 'hard dog', a dog that tests the coherence of the trainer's authority: is the trainer committed, all the way, to *meaning it?* The Pentateuch account of Yahweh's actions shows him taking on meaning what he said, all the way, in the face of Israel's attempts to 'prove' him, making clear by the consequences of obedience and disobedience the authority with which his commands are given.)

Someone might object to my discussion of divine law and divine command in the Pentateuch that I have left it unclear whether, when Yahweh commands someone to do something, it is *morally obligatory* to do so, or merely prudent (and it may seem as if I have suggested that it would be the latter). But the idea that such a question makes sense is what I am discussing, and it is no accident that I have not provided an answer. The confusion that reflects itself in the question comes out sharply in what might be called a moralizing conception of the virtues exhibited by Abraham or Moses. We tend to think that disobedience to Yahweh might be *morally wrong* in that it involves ingratitude to a benefactor, and gratitude is (we may think) morally required. But (the same line of reasoning continues) it is mere imprudence to ignore the threats to do harm with which a command was accompanied. But Deuteronomy treats the self-destructive folly of ignoring Yahweh's promised blessings and curses as a badness or vice in the people Israel, just as Israel's perverse ingratitude is a badness or vice. Appropriate hope and fear in relation to the consequences of obedience and disobedience to Yahweh's law are a part of the Pentateuch notion of virtue. The notion of virtue here is not shaped by anything resembling our notion of the moral.

III

So far I have discussed only a notion of divine law, not a divine law theory of ethics. What it is to have such a theory, Professor Anscombe says, is "to hold that what is needed for conformity with the virtues failure in which is the mark of being bad *qua* man (and not merely, say *qua* craftsman or logician)—that what is needed for *this*, is required by divine law" (30).

I have claimed that, on the Pentateuch notion of divine law, a kind of action can be divinely enjoined (or divinely prohibited), even if there is no independent reason for thinking of that action as a good (or, in the case of prohibitions, bad) kind of thing to do. So if it is said that justice is a virtue, failure in which is a mark of being bad *qua* man, and that Yahweh enjoins just actions, their being enjoined by him is a distinct matter from their being just or from justice's being a virtue failure in which is a mark of being bad *qua* man. "Is prohibited by Yahweh" is something that can intelligibly be said of unjust acts and also of acts which there would be no reason to avoid apart from Yahweh's choosing to prohibit them. Indeed, William Blake's idea that no virtue can exist without breaking the ten commandments is perfectly intelligible, whatever else one may think about it.

IV

Once used within the framework of a divine law theory of ethics, a notion might, after the disappearance of that framework, leave behind various kinds of survivor notions. And these would not necessarily be unintelligible.

Consider the notion of being an act contrary to one of the virtues failure in which is a mark of being bad *qua* man (see Anscombe, 30). If we were to use the word "illicit" for this idea, to say of an act admittedly unjust that it was illicit in this sense would add to the description of it as unjust only what was contained in saying that justice is a virtue failure in which is a mark of being bad *qua* man; and the notion of such a virtue could not be defined, without circularity, in terms of what was illicit in this sense. As Professor Anscombe points out in relation to a similar case (38), there is an objection to such a use of the word "illicit": it is misleading, since the word, thus used, has no connection with law of any kind. But there need be nothing incoherent or unintelligible in the notion. Because I have said nothing about how we are to understand the predicate "is a virtue failure in which is a mark of being bad *qua* man," I have not actually specified a *single* notion: understanding that predicate in different ways would give us different notions.

Notions originally in place within a divine law theory of ethics may be used figuratively after the framework has gone, and are not made unintelligible by its absence. I shall look briefly at a case in which not a notion of divine law but a related notion is used. On a visit to the workhouse in West Derby, Nathaniel Hawthorne was followed about by a quite repulsive little child, wretched and sickly, "underwitted" and apparently unable to speak. The child then stood in front of Hawthorne, smiled at him and, holding up its hands, insisted on being picked up. In his notebook, Hawthorne wrote that

> its face expressed such perfect confidence that it was going to be taken up and made much of, that it was impossible not to do it. It was as if God had promised the child this favor on my behalf, and that I must needs fulfill the contract. (Hawthorne 1891, vol. 2, 184–85)

The language of God's having promised on his behalf is used by Hawthorne to make clear both the force of the "must" and its tie to a conception of the child's hope as sacred. I shall discuss later the use of the modal terms in Hawthorne's account. They are connected (implicitly in his notebook, explicitly in his fictionalized version of the incident) with his understanding how failure to pick up the child would have been connected to badness *qua* man.

It is possible to use "It is as if God had commanded this" or "It is as if God had prohibited this" in something like the way Hawthorne uses "It was as if God had promised on my behalf" to give the force of a "must." Professor Anscombe's arguments are not directed against terms used as "must" or "impossible" are in cases like Hawthorne's. Although there may be objections that some ways of introducing figurative references to what God requires, or figurative references to law, may be misleading, that is not the use of language at which her criticisms are directed. She does object to an emphatic use of "ought"; but the emphasis she is concerned with is the peculiar emphasis given to "morally ought." It is not an objection to emphatic modals in general.

V

What now about the notion 'morally wrong' that Professor Anscombe criticizes, the supposedly unintelligible descendant notion? To bring out the features of this notion, Professor Anscombe asks us to think about cases of admittedly unjust actions, where the applicability of "unjust" depends on some factual description.

I shall look at a case of a particular kind of injustice: taking advantage of those who are specially vulnerable. The case is an actual one described in Laura Ingalls Wilder's *The Long Winter*. At great risk, two young men manage to get some wheat into their community, which has been cut off by blizzards for months; people are desperately hungry and have no other hope of food. The storekeeper Loftus, who put up the money for the wheat, now wants to make an enormous profit at the expense of his neighbors, who are close to starvation. That his intention makes him despicable is brought home to Loftus; he gives it up and sells the wheat, not even at a fair profit, but for no more than what it cost.

I want to imagine this case, first as it might be thought about with the notion of divine law, and then as it might be thought about with the notion 'morally wrong'.

Suppose first that we have a storekeeper who, unlike Loftus, thinks in terms of a divine law prohibiting what is unjust, or prohibiting this particular kind of injustice. (I call him "Legg" for legal.) But there is also a resemblance to Loftus. What Loftus came to see, though only with difficulty, Legg recognizes too: to charge all he could would be a despicable act of injustice, which would be shameful even if the victims were not one's neighbors, but they are, and that makes it worse. So Legg might say—if the suggestion were made to him that he take a huge profit—that he could not do such a thing. I want a term for this "could not"; I shall call it Aristotelian, but without implying anything about Aristotle's actual views about extortion or his views about how virtues and vices are related to particular actions or wants. I am alluding rather to Professor Anscombe's discussion of the language available to Aristotle (30, 32–33). Terms not only like "unjust" but also like "disgraceful," "impious" are available to him; his use of such terms does not depend on a framework involving law. I shall clarify my use of the term "Aristotelian" in sections 6–11.

To get back now to Legg's response to the suggestion that he charge all he can. If he not only believes, as Loftus came to, that that would be despicable, but also that divine law prohibits such extortion, and if, as he understands the prohibition, it has the logical features of divine law which I described in section 2, then he may say, because of that prohibition, that he must not do such a thing; he has an obligation under divine law to eschew such acts (Deuteronomy 15:7–11).

The first modal, the Aristotelian "could not," which has nothing to do with divine law, points to the relation between the character of the particular act (not as disobedient but as unjust) and a kind of badness *qua* man. The "I must not do that," tied to the obligation under divine law, points in a different direction. Charging the high price is indeed prohibited because it takes advantage of the desperation of people who are close to starving, but the fact of its being prohibited, i.e., the fact that doing it is disobedience to divine law, leads us to a quite distinct understanding of what would be involved in doing it, of what goes against even considering it, the mad pride or folly of thinking one could in stubbornness of heart disobey, and that all would nevertheless go well with one. (See Deuteronomy 29:19; I have combined two translations. Compare Anscombe, 42.)

Professor Anscombe's criticisms of the moral "ought," of the notion of the morally wrong, of moral obligation, can be understood if we imagine that we keep the idea of going beyond the kind of considerations which lead Loftus to give up his intention, keep (that is) the idea of a non-Aristotelian use of modal terms (non-Aristotelian in the sense in which Legg's "I must not (am obliged not to) do that" is non-Aristotelian), but drop the notion of a divine law with the logical features described in section 2. We can put this in terms of a second imaginary storekeeper, whom I call Morrell. Morrell knows perfectly well that selling the wheat at a terribly high price would be cashing in on the starvation of his neighbors. But he does not pursue the issue in Aristotelian terms. He wonders whether it is morally permissible to go ahead and demand the high price, since he paid for the wheat, and it is after all his own, his own to charge what he chooses for; and, since the value of the wheat is, as he tells himself, measured by the effective demand for it, would it actually be morally wrong to charge a very high price? Surely he cannot be morally obliged to sell it at less than its (presently extremely high) value. And it cannot be unjust for him to do what he has no moral obligation not to do. (Here "unjust" is untied from factual description and made dependent on the notion 'moral obligation'.)

What we see in Morrell's case is a use of "morally wrong" which shares with "prohibited by divine law" (where the latter is understood as having the features described in section 2) that it goes beyond such factual descriptions as "taking advantage of those who are specially vulnerable"; it is so used that there is a question: "Is this morally wrong?" even when we are clear that what we would be doing is cashing in on the starvation of our neighbors. Whether "morally wrong" goes beyond a description like "unjust" depends on how the latter is used. It does not go beyond "unjust" as Morrell uses it: thus used, "unjust" cannot apply to what is held on other grounds not to be morally wrong. But Morrell need not have used it that way; he might have admitted that charging a high price was unjust, in that to do so is to take advantage of those who are specially vulnerable. If he still went on to ask whether it was morally wrong to charge the high price, "morally wrong" would go beyond "unjust" so used. This going beyond has nothing to do with the conclusion Morrell reaches. He might have come to think that it was after all morally wrong to take advantage of the specially vulnerable. Here, too, the term "morally wrong" goes beyond the description "taking advantage of those who are specially vulnerable" and beyond "unjust," so used that to take advantage of the specially vulnerable is one kind of unjust act.

Morrell's use of "morally wrong" is not like the use of "illicit" that I described in section 4. When he raises the question whether charging the high price is morally wrong, he is not asking whether it is contrary to a virtue failure in which shows a man to be bad *qua* man.

There is also Morrell's notion of what one is *morally obliged* to do; we need to see how it is like and how unlike Legg's being *obliged by divine law* to do something. The "I must not" or "I am obliged not to" arising through divine law is distinct from the Artistotelian "I could not do such a thing," which Legg comes up with when he considers charging the high price, not as contrary to divine law, but simply as despicable or shameful. Morrell's "morally obliged" is like Legg's recognition of obligation under divine law in not being Aristotelian. "Morally obliged" does not (as Legg's Aristotelian "could not" does) point to the relation between the character of the particular act (as unjust or as a particular kind of injustice) and what it is to be bad *qua* man. It is, however, unlike Legg's recognition of the obligation under divine law not to do the act. Not only is there no giver or enforcer of a law, but there is no characterization of the act tying it to a distinct range of considerations against doing it, to an understanding of what it would be to do it as (in Legg's case) exhibiting perverse ingratitude, failure of filial piety and the folly of inviting disaster. If Legg's talk of obligation under divine law points away from the relation between the act as unjust and human badness, we can say what it points *to*, what other characterizations of the act, what other relation between the act and human badness; Morrell's talk of moral obligation resembles Legg's in pointing away from the relation between the act as unjust and human badness, resembles it in pointing to something else, taken to be extremely weighty. But the weight is provided in Legg's case by what he takes God to have done, what he takes God to have said, and meant, that he will do, and what it means to ignore all that. The weight is supposed still to be there in Morrell's case (it may now be supposed to be different in kind), although God's statutes, his past doings and his promises are all removed, and, with that removal, there has also been removed the connections to consequences and to human vice and virtue important for Legg's understanding of obedience and disobedience. Is Morrell making sense any more, or is he using the expressions "morally obliged," "morally wrong" with mere mesmeric force?

VI

We can now see why the dilemmatic argument of section 1 is no objection to Professor Anscombe. Her argument about the unintelligibility of notions like 'morally wrong' and 'moral obligation' depends on two claims about these notions: (1) that they share certain features of at least some notions of what is prohibited or required by divine law (these are the features in which Morrell's talk of moral obligation resembles Legg's talk of obligation under divine law), and (2) that we use the suspect moral notions outside the framework of thought essential to the intelligibility of any notion with those features. You cannot keep talking as much like Legg as Morrell does, and drop as much as he does of Legg's thought about God's law.

It follows that there are only two ways in which her argument can be disputed: one must show either that notions *with the features* that she thinks 'moral obligation' and its relatives have are coherent, or that no notion with those features bedevils moral thought. It will be no objection to her that such-and-such a notion used in moral thinking is intelligible, unless that notion has the features of which she complains. No notion is the supposedly objectionable 'moral ought' if, in its use, it is what I have called an Aristotelian 'ought'. But its not being an Aristotelian 'ought' is not by itself sufficient for it to be an 'ought' of the type Professor Anscombe claims is incoherent. Her claim is not that moral thought of what I have called a non-Aristotelian sort is incoherent if it is detached from the framework provided by divine law. She gives an example of how the idea of the universe as a sort of legislator might be connected with an intelligible use of the notion of obligation, outside the framework of divine law. While such a notion is not unintelligible, it is, she says, hardly likely to lead to anything good (37). And, indeed, Morrell's rationalization of what he wants to do could very easily be conducted in terms of such a notion. (Professor Anscombe's claim is not that if we stay away from unintelligible notions, we shall be unable to give bad defences of bad actions.) In general, non-Aristotelian uses are intelligible, if connected with *some* appropriate framework. What we are said to be required to do, when talk of 'requirement' *is* connected with such a framework, may or may not then be good to do.

At this point I turn aside from what may appear to be the most pressing question: is she right that thought like Morrell's (including much ethical theorizing) sounds like sense but is not? I am concerned in this paper with a different and prior question: What boundary does her argument draw between ethical thought that makes sense and ethical thought that does not? I have drawn that boundary using the term "Aristotelian" but not explaining it. So I have not made that boundary clear.

I introduced the term "Aristotelian" to distinguish between Legg's two different sorts of response to the suggestion that he treat the desperate hunger of his neighbors as an opportunity for great profit. The term alludes to Professor Anscombe's comment that we do not need to do ethics using terms which depend for their sense on a framework of thought involving law. That we can do ethics without such notions is shown, she says, "by the example of Aristotle" (32–33). As I used the term "Aristotelian," it was not tied to any of Aristotle's actual ethical views, nor to any particular account of what it is to do ethics without dependence on legal or quasi-legal notions; and about that absence of a tie, something needs to be said. The structure of Professor Anscombe's argument will be misunderstood if we treat as part of the argument itself any particular account of what it is to do ethics without dependence on legal or quasi-legal notions.

Here is why. On the suspect side of the boundary drawn by Professor Anscombe, there lies ethical thought which, although it is what I have called non-Aristotelian, is used outside a framework of thought of the type required for the intelligibility of non-Aristotelian uses: Morrell's thought serves as an example. On the other side of the boundary lie both Aristotelian thought and varieties of non-Aristotelian thought used within an appropriate framework. Suppose that the term "Aristotelian" were taken to be tied to some particular account of what it is to do ethics without dependence on legal or quasi-legal notions; suppose that it were understood as tied to some particular account of how Aristotelian uses of modal terms in connection with moral subject matter were related to good or wants or needs. In that case, the term would have two distinct definitions. It will then look as if objections can be raised to Professor Anscombe's basic argument, objections which are in fact not relevant to it. Thus, e.g., one might construct some example and say of it:

> Here is a kind of ethical thought which is not tied in the required way to good or wants or needs. So it is not Aristotelian. But it is not a non-Aristotelian use tied to the sort of framework Professor Anscombe says is necessary for such uses. So, since it is not Aristotelian, nor one of the allowable sorts of non-Aristotelian modes of ethical thinking, it counts on her view as unintelligible. But it is intelligible. So her argument must be wrong.

The mistake in that argument lies in the first two sentences, in taking the term "Aristotelian" to be tied to some particular account of how ethical terms are related to notions of good or wants or needs. If you want to argue against Professor Anscombe by saying "She treats x's as unintelligible, but here is an x that is intelligible," you must show that your x is a case of moral thought to which is essential some legal or quasi-legal notion, like that of obligation.

VII

In sections 8–11, I describe a variety of cases included in what I have been calling Aristotelian uses. The cases are intended to meet and thereby to explain a constraint suggested by Professor Anscombe's remarks. In this section, I explain the constraint in a preliminary way.

If I am explaining to a foreigner the difference between a Yield sign and a Stop sign on the road, I may say that one has to stop at the latter, but need not at the former. Here "has to," "needs to" mean "is required to by law." I might add that, although the law requires one to come to a *complete* stop at a Stop sign, one need not actually do so, since the requirement is not enforced, and sometimes one *should not*. Or I might say, of a particular Yield sign, that one ought to stop there, or that, to be safe, one really has to. In these latter cases, the modal terms "need not," "should not," "ought," "has to," do not relate to what is required by law. Professor Anscombe says, of modals like those, that they "relate to good and bad"; they do so whether or no they are used in connection with a moral subject matter. She distinguishes such a use of modal terms, in connection with a moral subject matter, from modal terms used in a supposed special 'moral' sense (29). In suggesting the variety of cases covered by my term "Aristotelian," I limit myself to cases in which the modal terms are used in the way she describes: i.e., they "relate to good and bad," and are not like "have to" in "You have to, are required by law to, stop at such-and-such kind of sign."

It is obvious that "relates to good and bad" covers a variety of kinds of case. "The plant needs water," "The soup needs salt," "We need coffee, we're nearly out," have three different relations to good. And, of the four modals relating to good and bad in my examples about driving, three bear on what it is to be a good driver, and the other on the avoidance of penalties. It is useful to note that emphatic words like "really" with modal terms often serve to distinguish the use of modal terms in which they relate to good from the use in which they are tied to a law or to a rule of a game or something similar. Thus "What I *really* need to do is to dump the queen of spades fast; unfortunately I have to (am obliged by the rules to) discard this diamond."

The distinction between modals that "relate to good and bad" and those that are tied to a law or rule of some kind should not be confused with the distinction between categorical and hypothetical imperatives. Hypothetical imperatives are dependent in their application (dependent in some way) on what is wanted (in some sense). But modal terms which "relate to good and bad" are not in general dependent on wants. It may be true of me that I need a rest, whether or no I want a rest, or want something that a rest would provide.

There is a point of Professor Anscombe's that may be misunderstood. She says that thought about what something (e.g., a plant) needs affects your actions only through your wants. This does not imply that modals concerned with what I *must* or *ought* to do (if they are modals that "relate to good and bad") depend in general for their sense or their application to me on my wants. There are here two sorts of case:

the good to which the first person modal relates may be another's good or my own. Suppose it is the good of others. There are clear cases in which such modals are independent of my wants: "I ought to spend more time on Locke with this bunch, but I don't want to." It may be said that the application of such modals to me depends on my acceptance of a role. (See Foot 1978, 163.) To that there is a double reply. First, even when a role has initially been accepted, modals connected with it may apply to someone regardless of any further choices on his part; he cannot, in the face of the application of a modal to people in this role, now say that he opts out of the role. That reply would need argument; the second should not. I cannot get out of being a daughter, and there are things a daughter ought to do if her parents need or want such-and-such or will suffer if so-and-so. The "ought" relates to good and bad, and is as categorical as an "ought" can be. People without the notion of moral obligation can express such 'ought's perfectly well. Judgments, based on someone else's needs, that I must or ought to do something involve perfectly ordinary modals. Sometimes the actions which are the subjects of such judgments are dull and ordinary, sometimes they are as noble or courageous as human actions can be; but the character of the act does not affect the type of use the modal term has.

Consider now first person modals, related to my own good. "I ought to get so me rest," "I have to get some rest," may be used in just the way their surface grammar suggests, viz., as the first person statements corresponding to "You ought to get some rest," "She has to get some rest," said of me. The first person modal does not depend for its truth or sense on my wants any more than do other modals. In whatever grammatical person the judgment is made, its relation to my wants may be this: if I act in a way I know will get me some rest, and if my understanding that rest is good for me, or that I need it, belongs to the sense of what I am doing, it may be possible to ascribe to me, purely as a consequence, a desire for the good that I know will be secured by my resting. (See McDowell, 1978.) Nothing in that story affects the question whether "I ought to get some rest" is a modal relating to good and bad. One may be unwilling to accept a first person modal (relating to one's own good or relating to that of another) if one is unwilling to do what one should or must; but the unwillingness to accept a modal does not make it inapplicable. Professor Anscombe's point that thought relates to action only through your wants leaves "I ought" perfectly applicable to you, whatever your wants.

VIII

Take another version of the Storekeeper's Tale. A third imaginary storekeeper, Fearful by name, gives up the idea of overcharging, thinking "I had better not do it, they'll burn my store down some dark night." Here everything is simple: the store's being burnt down is a disaster he wants to avoid, and his "I'd better not overcharge" relates to the danger of that disaster. The point of the example is only that it should not be taken as a guide to what all Aristotelian uses of modal terms are like. We can contrast it with Legg's case. He takes it to be contemptible to treat the desperate hunger of his neighbors as an opportunity for great profit, and says that such a thing is not to be thought of. How do the modals he may use relate to good and bad? Clearly not in the same way Fearful's do; the difference is brought out by "Try it and see." "Try it and see, perhaps they won't burn your store down" may be bad advice, but it makes sense. "Try it and see, maybe it won't turn out to be despicable injustice" makes none.

Here it may be said against what I am arguing that the difference between the two cases is indeed great, but so great that the second is not a case of *modals related to good and bad* in Professor Anscombe's sense. That is (this is the suggestion), the despicableness lies in doing something which one *must,* for very strong moral reasons, *not do;* the badness is not logically prior to the judgment what one must do.

The suggestion itself depends on a false idea: that if an action is non-contingently related to some good or evil, then the judgment that one must do the thing or must not, or ought to or ought not to, is not concerned with what needs to be done to avoid something bad or to achieve some good. It is a great mistake to take it that purposive action with respect to good and bad always shares the logical structure exemplified by Fearful's case. I shall argue that point, using two different kinds of example.

(1) On Christmas Day I had a violent scene with Father, and Father told me to get out of his house, the sooner the better. I have never been in such a rage in my life; I said that I thought their whole system of religion horrible. . . . Father had said if I wanted money he would lend it to me; but this is impossible now. (Adapted from Van Gogh 1958, vol. 1, 294–95)

Vincent cannot take money from his father, given what has happened between them. Fine; but that modal, in just those circumstances, can relate to good in *several* ways. It may be that self-respect rules out Vincent's approaching his father for money. But it might equally be said that he cannot because it would be incompatible with respect for his father. One might judge that he cannot, and have in mind both those goods, or possibly some other. Since there are *various* goods that "I can't do that" might relate to, it follows that the relation of "I can't" to good and bad in this case is not that the good and bad simply lie in doing or failing to do what one has to do. Neither self-respect, nor respect for his father, is contingently related to Vincent's not asking his father for money in the circumstances described. It follows that there is no general truth that if there is a non-contingent relation between some action and good or bad, modal judgments about the action are prior to an understanding of the good or bad that the action brings.

(2) Suppose that I want to be a good teacher, and come to recognize that I am too impatient, and (among other things) interrupt students far too often. If, listening to a boring student struggle to formulate a question, and feeling on my lips the question cleanly put, I tell myself that I must not interrupt, this "must not" relates to good and bad, and is concerned with my purposes, although the case is very different from Fearful's. Not interrupting the student does not stand to my wants as not over-charging stands to what Fearful wants.

It is a mistake to think of all means-end reasoning as having the same logical structure. (See MacIntyre 1981, 139–41, 172.) It would be impatient of me to interrupt, and what I want is to be more patient; I want *that* because I want to be a better teacher. But the relation between not acting impatiently on this occasion and becoming the kind of teacher I want to be does not allow the "Try it and see" that is in place where the relation is of the kind we most usually think of as causal. My understanding of what it is to be a good teacher develops through experience; but experience does not just give us knowledge of Humean causal relations. I am denying this idea: that to be a good teacher is to be an efficient producer of something, and *patience* would then be desirable for being a good teacher if it increased the efficiency of production of that something; and not interrupting on this occasion would then be a means to my becoming more patient if it altered my psychological mechanisms, as a course of treatment perhaps might, and made the mechanisms produce patient behavior in the future. On the contrary, the relation between being a good teacher and not interrupting is not contingent; but despite the non-contingency of the relation, not interrupting is directed to a purpose of mine, that of becoming a better teacher. The non-contingency of the relation between the good aimed at and not interrupting does not mean that the modal is prior to an understanding of the good to which it relates.

It might be objected that what is necessary to being a good teacher *is* purely a matter of what causes certain developments in the students. But that is wrong; being a good teacher is incompatible with (for example) betraying one's students to the secret police. In general, how being a good teacher may demand courage (or any other virtue) cannot be told from any crude instrumental account.

But now it may seem as if, by avoiding the last objection, I have caught myself in a different trap. How, it may be asked, does one learn that being a good teacher is incompatible with betraying one's students? The idea urged against me is that the teacher who recognizes the necessity not to betray *thereby* comes to have a deepened understanding of all that can be meant by "good teacher": the "must" deepens the notion of 'good teacher' and is not dependent on a prior understanding of that notion. It is not; but, for all that, the objection fails, so far as it is meant to suggest that the only good or bad to which "must" in such cases relates is the *consequent* good or bad of doing or failing to do the thing one quite independently 'must' do. What is at stake in cases of this sort is patterns of relation of goods and evils in one's life; and the "must"s and "cannot"s relate to these patterns rather than to a single good. These cases are explored in literature, most usually in fiction. (See also Taylor 1976.) But I will give a crude summary of one case, to bring out simply that the "must" in such cases is not an independent 'moral' "must." In Zbigniew Herbert's poem, "The Power of Taste," the "I cannot obey" that refuses the demands of the totalitarian state is related to the good of *taste,* to the ugliness of what is resisted. The situation is one in which possibilities in *taste* are revealed, in which its connections with life are understood differently. The "cannot" in question has to be understood in relation to the good of taste and not as an independent moral "cannot." Who knows what would have happened if we had been better and more attractively tempted? The poem places itself an ironic distance from any Kantian view of genuinely moral resistance to evil. Considered with Herbert's other poems, the point is that love of beauty, love of truth, take on different significance in relation to what he can call our politics and our history. For my purposes, though, the point is simpler. The fact that a modal term cannot be understood in relation to some good as we had previously grasped that good does not imply that there is no good, newly understood here, to which the modal term relates; it does not imply that the modal term is understandable independently of its relation to good.

It should be added that one may *think* a "must" or "ought" or "cannot" without articulating the relation to good and bad. On such later possible articulation of what is involved in a thought, see Wittgenstein on "It'll stop soon," especially *Philosophical Investigations,* §§682 and 684.

IX

In section 4, I quoted Hawthorne's account of his visit to an English workhouse. He described the child who wordlessly appealed to him to be picked up, and said that it was "impossible not to do it." What sort of modal is this? He does not want to pick the child up, he could hardly want anything less. And so it may seem as if, when he picks the child up, he acts in accordance with a moral imperative which properly silences his wants.

But the imposition of Kantian concepts distorts Hawthorne's thought. I shall explain briefly how the modal relates to good and bad, to notions of vice and virtue, and to ideas about human nature and human need; to do so I shall place the story with some similar material.

In "The Old Cumberland Beggar," the beggar is someone we may be tempted to scorn, to sweep off to a workhouse out of view. But he has still a vital connection to us, lying in his hope that he will be given food or the money he needs for it. Wordsworth tells us to

> Reverence the hope whose vital anxiousness
> Gives the last human interest to his heart.

Confronted by the vital anxiousness of the beggar's hope, or confronted by the pathos of the child's confidence that it will get what it hopes for, we may recognize that this is something we must not scorn. For Wordsworth as for Hawthorne, the modal terms we may use when we see someone with such a hope for some simple thing which it is in our power to give are tied to a teleological conception of being human. Just as there are judgments I may properly make about what I ought to do, given the fact of my mother's needing something or other, so (the notion 'human being' having, for Wordsworth and Hawthorne, a logical character analogous to 'daughter') there are judgments we may properly make about what we ought to do, given the fact of the vital anxiousness of a hope like that of the Cumberland beggar or the workhouse child.

The modal language Hawthorne uses is not dependent on his wants. But we should see how his needs fit into the story. He used the incident some time afterwards in *Our Old Home.* There it is told as an incident involving a reserved Englishman

> afflicted with a peculiar distaste for whatever was ugly, and, furthermore, accustomed to that habit of observation from an insulated stand-point which is said . . . to have the tendency of putting ice into the blood. (Hawthorne 1891, vol. 1, 352–53)

The phrase "ice in the blood" helps us understand Hawthorne's own act in those circumstances, his sense of what refusal of the child means, what it would be for him to cut himself off in that way from her and her pathetic neediness.

Hawthorne's understanding of the situation can be tied to much nineteenth century exploration of a group of related vices, vices of unconnectedness to human suffering, need and mortality, of denial of solidarity in neediness. The metaphor of ice in the blood in connection with insulatedness from humanity echoes Dickens's earlier use of that metaphor in a similar connection in *A Christmas Carol:* Scrooge carries his own low temperature with him, ices his office in the dog days, is unwarmable by any external heat. Hawthorne, Dickens, Dostoyevsky, Tolstoy, Wordsworth, Conrad in different ways show what kind of trouble a human being is in if his acts put him into the soul-state of isolation. The power of the phrase "ice in the blood" expresses the depth of failing in us, as Hawthorne saw it. This failing, and, more generally, the significance of this group of vices, are understood by what Professor Anscombe once spoke of as "a mystical perception" (Anscombe 1972, 25).

It is not obvious, then, that we have in Hawthorne's story a moral "must" of the sort to which Anscombe objects. The modal terms Hawthorne uses are ordinary modals; they relate to good and bad; the good and bad are not explicable only as doing or failing to do what is (independently) morally required.

In the original notebook version of the incident, Hawthorne says that it was as if God had made a promise to the child on his behalf. So it is as if he had the obligation that would thus be created, as if what made refusing impossible were that promise. But an as-if obligation is not an obligation; and its being as if what made refusing impossible were God's promise is not its being the case that what makes refusing impossible is that promise.

Figures of speech attached to modal language cannot in general show what kind of use the modal term has. Metaphors of divine command may be connected to metaphors of obligation, but such metaphors, or figurative speech more generally, do not settle whether the modal terms are used in what I am calling an Aristotelian way, do not settle whether the modal terms are dependent on legal or quasi-legal notions. The Hawthorne case suggests that we may have modal terms so used that they relate to good and bad, whatever figurative language they are tied to.

X

What now about the dog that gave himself the moral law? Here is the story as Vicki Hearne tells it. Fritz the Doberman worked with Philip Beem, a policeman too ready to take might (his own) to be right.

> One night, Officer Beem stopped a young black woman for jaywalking and started clubbing her with his nightstick, for the sheer fun of it as near as anyone could make out. . . . Fritz attacked—not the woman, but his policeman partner, and took his club away from him emphatically.
>
>   Now Fritz was not only by nature a good dog, he was well trained and had a keenly developed sense of what his job entailed, what did and did not belong in this particular little dog-human culture. Sitting by while people got beat up for no good reason was not part of his job, it simply didn't belong. While it

would not be exactly wrong to interpret this story by saying that Fritz was moved by compassion or a sense of rescue or protectiveness, it wouldn't be quite right, either. He simply knew his job, had his own command of the law in a wide sense of "law", and was putting his world back in order. (Hearne 1986, 208)

Vicki Hearne says the story is "of a dog giving himself the moral law." But the Kantian language does not fit. Fritz has his relation to, command of, the law, but the story does not involve us in thinking about him as *under* a law he himself makes. He may use his teeth in the service of something we can call law, but in the story there is no idea of Fritz as *possibly disobeying* a law he is imposing on himself. Whether or no "legislation for oneself" is absurd, the temptation to use such language comes from a more complex relation to law than Fritz's. He acts to put his world back in order, Vicki Hearne says. But there is nothing that suggests that for him it is a matter of obeying an order to do so: not an external order, and thus one he gives himself.

A pre-Socratic description of Fritz is better than a Kantian one, and is indeed suggested by Vicki Hearne's discussion of training. Coherent training gives a dog a "new cosmology." The world comes to be understandable by the dog as one in which breaches of the world's order by things the dog might do, like digging a hole in the garden, are met by claps of doom, by terrible events. The world is one in which if you do not sit when she says to, something terrible happens. But the acts of the trainer, the trainer as Vicki Hearne describes her, contain a love for, an attachment to, the order she enforces with her own 'teeth', with the corrections she gives. And because that attachment is in those corrections, because they are not (this is an ideal trainer now) corrupted by ego in various ways, the training can lead the dog, too, into attachment to the order, a sense of its good, of what disaster its being broken is. With that picture of training in the background, can we now describe Fritz as a pre-Socratic dog? The order of things is broken: "Phil Beem is beating up this woman, and I, Fritz, am sitting by. *No one* is giving me a command to set things back into order. But *I am commanded*": here it is as if the cosmos itself were demanding to be set right.

That version of Fritz's story, while it is an improvement over the Kantian one, still does not get Fritz's relation to the law, his command of it, right. Fritz, through training, has become *kosmios* (as habitual obedience to law was supposed to make a man *kosmios*): that is, he knows and attends to his job and leads a disciplined life. (See Jones 1956, 74.) He is "putting his world back in order." There are two vital elements in what he does: one of attachment, a sense of what is good (the to-be-restored order of his world); one of knowledge, that teeth may be needed to establish or re-establish that order. The good order, the order to which he is attached, he knows only as made through law enforced with 'teeth'. He acts, then, with his teeth, for the sake of a good to which a notion of law, law with 'teeth', is internal: the good is the restoration of eunomia.

XI

So what? What comes out of that version of the story?

It is not an incoherent story by Professor Anscombe's arguments. There is a virtue: attachment to the good ordering of the dog-human world, and Fritz's sitting by and doing nothing is contrary to that virtue. The virtue is part of being good *qua* dog (and not, e.g., *qua* tracking dog). Fritz has a sense of what he needs to do in the circumstances, and this use of "needs" relates to good.

At the end of section 9, I argued that the use in connection with a moral subject matter of legal or quasi-legal terms, or of the notion of divine command, does not itself show that the context is non-Aristotelian, for the terms may be used figuratively. But Fritz's case is different. If we think of his action as embodying an understanding of what he *needed* to do, the need can be related to good and bad only via the notion of law or of a quasi-legal order. So Fritz's case forces a choice on me. Either I must give up my rough-and-ready specification of Aristotelian uses of modal terms, or I must treat Fritz's case as non-Aristotelian. The former course is right.

The difficulty arises because, in non-Aristotelian uses of modal terms, the modal term may be related to good and bad, but the good or bad can be explained in terms of doing or failing to do what is legally or quasi-legally required. The right, as it is said, is prior to the good. In the Aristotelian cases, the modal term relates to good and bad, and, as I have tried to show, the relation may be of various kinds; but in all the cases except Fritz's, the good and bad to which the modal term relates are not dependent on legal notions.

If Fritz had actually been given a command, by someone with authority over him, to bite or snap at Beem or take away his club, or if attacking such people had been what he was trained to do, attacking would be obedient, and obedience in such circumstances might then be good (whether obedience *is* good depends on various things). But the good to which Fritz's act relates is not obedience to a command, nor is it the good of doing what he was trained to do. It is the good of a kind of life for man and dog, a life he has come to understand the good of through experience, and a good which has internal to it the authoritative enforcement by 'teeth' of good order.

I am adding Fritz's case to the variety of cases that explain what I mean by an Aristotelian use of modal terms. If there is a good order which we can understand or imagine only through the use of legal notions, and if acts may be done out of attachment to such an order, or a sense of what it means for the life of us-as-dog or us-as-man, modal terms relating to *that* good are Aristotelian.

Some of what is significant in Kantian moral thought, so far as it reflects attachment to such an order, can thus be expressed without recourse to non-Aristotelian uses of language. Those elements of Kantian moral thought are, however, thereby tied to an unKantian notion of virtue; and, further, put into such a context, they lose what Kant took to be essential: the absolute necessity of the moral law. All that is left is what Fritz needed, what we need.

XII

The strength of Professor Anscombe's argument can be judged only in light of the variety of thought about moral subject matter which counts, given those arguments, as intelligible. To see the cogency of her argument, we have to see not only the logical relations between non-Aristotelian notions and the framework of thought on which their intelligibility depends, but also that our real needs in ethics are met by what counts, on her view, as intelligible. The force of her arguments can be appreciated only when we recognize for what they are our wishes for something we do not need.

References

Anscombe, G. E. M. 1972. "Contraception and Chastity." *The Human World* 7: 9–30.

Anscombe, G. E. M. 1981. "Modern Moral Philosophy." In *Ethics, Religion and Politics*, 26–42. Minneapolis.

Foot, Philippa. 1978. "Morality as a System of Hypothetical Imperatives." In *Virtues and Vices*, 157–173. Oxford.

Hawthorne, Nathaniel. 1891. *Our Old Home* and *English Note-Books*. Boston and New York.

Hearne, Vicki. 1986. *Adam's Task*. New York.

Herbert, Zbigniew. 1985. "The Power of Taste." In *Report from the Besieged City*. New York.

Jones, J. Walter. 1956. *The Law and Legal Theory of the Greeks*. Oxford.

McDowell, John. 1978. "Are Moral Requirements Hypothetical Imperatives?" *Proceedings of the Aristotelian Society*, Supp. Vol. 52: 13–29.

MacIntyre, Alasdair. 1981. *After Virtue*. Notre Dame, Indiana.

Miskotte, Kornelis H. 1967. *When the Gods are Silent*. London.

Taylor, Charles. 1976. "Responsibility for Self." In *The Identities of Persons*, edited by Amelie Rorty, 281–299. Berkeley.

Van Gogh, Vincent. 1958. *The Complete Letters*. Greenwich, Connecticut.

Wilder, Laura Ingalls. 1940. *The Long Winter*. New York.

Winch, Peter. 1972. "Ethical Reward and Punishment." In *Ethics and Action*, 210–228. London.

Winch, Peter. 1987. "Who Is My Neighbour?" In *Trying to Make Sense*, 154–166. Oxford.

Winch, Peter. N.d. "Professor Anscombe's Moral Philosophy."

Moral Minimalism and the Development of Moral Character

DAVID L. NORTON

Three recent books in ethics—Alasdair MacIntyre's *After Virtue,* Richard Taylor's *Ethics, Faith, and Reason,* and Edmund L. Pincoffs's *Quandaries and Virtues*[1]— have, each in its own way, contrasted modern ethics and classical ethics as very disparate modes of ethical theorizing, and each has offered arguments for the superiority of the classical mode. It is my intent in what follows to contribute to their theses, both of the radical disparity of the two modes, and of the superiority of the classical mode in important respects. Specifically I will argue that modern ethics is typically minimalist (a) with respect to the kinds of situations and choices that count as moral, and (b) in its conception of moral character, and that its minimalism in these respects removes from moral consideration factors that cannot be disregarded without the dilution of moral thought and moral life. I will begin by attempting my own characterizations of modern and classical ethics.

MacIntyre calls the modern mode of moral thought "Nietzschean," and the classical mode "Aristotelian"; Richard Taylor contrasts the modern "ethics of duty" with the classical "ethics of aspiration"; and Edmund Pincoffs characterizes modern "quandary ethics" against classical "ethics of virtue." Each of these pairings has indicative force, but the contrast I want to highlight can best be represented under the headings, "ethics of rules" and "ethics of character." By "ethics of rules" I refer to what I suggest has been the dominant mode of ethical theorizing since Thomas Hobbes. By "ethics of character" I intend to refer in general to ethical theory in classical Greece and Rome, whose fullest and soundest formulation I take to be the eudaimonism of Socrates, Plato, and Aristotle.

My attempted characterizations must be prefaced by a caveat. As for MacIntyre, Taylor, and Pincoffs, so for me, the modern-classical dichotomy must be understood not as "hard" but as "soft," and in two senses. In the first place the modern and the classical modes do not stand with respect to each other as mutually exclusive, but rather as a transformative difference in emphasis. Thus modern "rules morality" is not devoid of the concern for the development of moral character but gives remarkably less attention to it, and attends to it in the light in which it appears when rules are the paramount concern. Conversely, "character morality" does not altogether neglect rules, but subordinates them to the development of moral character and views them instrumentally with reference to that end. Secondly, the dichotomy is "soft" in the sense that historical exceptions are to be recognized: there are "character" ethicists in modernity (notable among them Nietzsche, Emerson, Henry Thoreau, and the Scottish "moral sense" school—e.g., Hutcheson, Hume, Adam Smith—and including brilliant flashes from John Stuart Mill), but they are a distinct minority and relatively lacking in influence; and "rules" ethics was by no means unknown in the ancient world, but was, so to speak, the moribund residue of ethics of character.

We will begin the study in contrast by observing that "rules ethics" and "character ethics" start with different primary questions. For modern moral philosophy the primary question is: "What is the right thing to do in particular (moral) situations?" and it is answered by finding the rule that applies to the given situation and acting in accordance with it. Thus if I am driving my car and collide with another vehicle, I am obligated by law to describe the event, and morality (here backed by law) holds me to the rule, "always tell the truth." Within this framework what we refer to as "contemporary moral problems"—e.g., abortion, euthanasia, compensatory preferential hiring—are problems for which the covering rule(s) is unsettled and in dispute. The point, however, is the unquestioned assumption that such problems are to be solved by arriving at the covering rule.

The accepted agenda of modern ethics is to formulate (discover; devise and contractually agree upon) a supreme and universally applicable moral principle—Hobbes's natural right of self-preservation, Kant's categorical imperative, Bentham's "greatest happiness of the greatest number," and Rawls's two principles of justice are famous examples—together with criteria for distinguishing moral from non-moral situations, criteria for recognizing relevantly different kinds of moral situations, and, as far as practicable, a complete list of rules representing the application of the supreme principle to all possible types of moral situations, or a set of rules for applying the supreme principle to particular situations. Then moral conduct is the conduct that best accords with the applicable rules in given moral situations. What is meant by a "prima facie duty" is a duty to obey a rule that is held to prevail in appropriate moral situations unless contravened by a higher rule.

By contrast, classical morality begins with the question, "What is a good life for a human being?" (Socrates: "But we ought to consider more carefully, for this is no light matter: it is the question, what is the right way to live?"[2]) It leads directly to the problem of the development of moral character, because any adequate description of a good human life will necessarily include attributes that are not manifest in persons in the beginning of their lives, but are developmental outcomes. The attributes on which classical ethics focuses are the moral virtues, and here it is enough to name the famous four of Plato's *Republic*—wisdom, courage, temperance, and justice—to recognize that none of them can be expected of children, but only of persons in later life, and only in the later life of persons in whom the requisite moral development occurs.

In the classical understanding the virtues are excellences of character that are objective goods, of worth to others as well as to the virtues-bearer (for example, the courage of our friend enhances the assistance he or she renders to us, just as it strengthens his or her pursuit of independent ends). Second, the manifestation of a virtue is understood to be the actualization of what was theretofore not totally absent in the person, but present in the form of a potentiality.[3] In other words, to be a human being is to be capable of manifesting virtues, and the problem of moral development is the problem of discovering the conditions for the actualization of qualities that are originally within persons as potentialities.

Classical ethics endeavors to answer the question, "What is a good life for a human being?" but to deepen our understanding it is important to consider first the prior question, "What sort of a being is it to which the question of the good life is posed?" The eudaimonistic answer is famously expressed by Plato in his image of the human soul as chariot, charioteer, and two contrary-minded horses *(Phaedrus):* distinctively, human being is problematic being; to be a human is in the deepest sense to be a problem to oneself, specifically an identity problem. It is the problem of deciding what to become and endeavoring to become it. The problem of deciding what to become is the problem of learning to recognize ideal goods and choosing among them which good to aim at as the goal of one's self-fulfilling and objectively worthy life. The problem of endeavoring to become the person one chooses to become is the problem of acquiring the resourcefulness and force of character to overcome external and internal obstacles. In the eudaimonistic view, human freedom has its ground in the absence in human beings of the metaphysical necessity that characterizes all other kinds of being, and in virtue of which they cannot be other than they are. But the absence of metaphysical necessity in the individual human being must be compensated for if his or her chosen end is to be achievable, and the compensatory necessity, because it must itself be chosen, is termed moral necessity. Here is the "fire" that Prometheus steals from the gods to equip man—left naked and helpless in the world by the negligence of Epimetheus—for survival. Despite conventional misinterpretation it is not physical fire but spiritual fire. In the myth we are told that it is the god's most precious possession, and, indeed, it is nothing less than the power of creation *(Eros)* by which man is equipped to carry out the unfinished work of making himself. Persons in whom moral necessity is lacking are described by Thoreau as "thrown off the track by every nutshell and mosquito's wing that falls on the rails."[4] Moral necessity is the "I must" of the dedicated and resourceful person. As against "I wish to," "I hope to," and even "I will," it bespeaks the strength of character to overcome the inevitable obstacles in the world, as well as vagrant impulses and ordinary apprehensions within the self.

Deciding what to become requires knowledge of the good, which is wisdom, and endeavoring to become it requires moral necessity. Connecting these two sides of the problem that every person is to him- or herself is the virtue of integrity, consisting in integration of the separable and initially disordered aspects of the self-faculties, desires, interests, roles—such that they complement rather than contradict one another, and each contributes to the realization of the chosen good.

It will be evident that the classical themes briefly touched upon above have taken us a good distance into the development of moral character, for alike, moral necessity, wisdom, and integrity are developmental outcomes, possessed *ab initio* by persons not as manifest capacities but as unactualized potentialities. What now requires to be noticed is that modern ethics, in its dominant mode that I have termed "rule" ethics, is notable for its relative disregard of the problems pertaining to the development of moral character. This is an important respect in which modern morality is "minimalist" in comparison to classical morality—it makes minimal demands upon the intelligence and developed moral character of moral agents, requiring little or nothing of them in the way of wisdom, courage, or integrity. It is also minimalist in a second sense, namely that it delimits the arena of moral choice to but a small sector of human experience. We shall say something about each of these instances of minimalism, beginning with the delimitation of moral choice.

It has often been observed that modern ethical theory typically works with a threefold classification of actions from the standpoint of moral meaning—right actions, wrong actions, and morally indifferent actions. This classification is coupled with a distinction between moral and non-moral situations, which accounts for the restrictive stipulation in what we earlier offered as the foundational question of modern ethics, "What is the right thing to do in particular *moral situations.*" The restriction is not to be found in classical ethics because the distinction does not exist. For classical ethics nothing in human experience is without moral meaning, and "the moral situation" is the life of each person in its entirety. If these contentions appear extreme, support for them will be offered shortly. Meanwhile it can readily be recognized that some situations typically adjudged non-moral in modern terms are importantly moral in classical terms.

An example of a situation that is generally understood to be non-moral by modern standards is the situation of vocational choice. Suppose, for instance, that my supreme moral principle is Kant's categorical imperative, and I decide to become a chemical engineer. I obviously cannot will that everyone in my situation, i.e., the situation of vocational choice, decide to become a chemical engineer, yet it is entirely conceivable that this choice is the right choice for me. This problem might be handled in a number of ways, but modern ethics is typified by the simple expedient of agreeing to regard the situation of vocational choice as normally a non-moral situation. Then to say that my choice is the "right" choice for me is to use the word "right" in one of its non-moral senses.

The same categorial distinction expels from the domain of the moral countless other types of choice that human beings characteristically make, e.g., of what friends to cultivate, what avocations to pursue, what books to read. Indeed, John Stuart Mill, in his utilitarian voice, says that "ninety-nine hundredths of all our actions are done from other [than moral] motives, and rightly so done if the rule of duty does not condemn them."[5] He is obliged to thus delimit the workings of the utilitarian principle in order to preserve any vestige of individual autonomy under utilitarianism. Were we at all times obliged to seek to produce the greatest happiness of the greatest number (with its correlative rule on diminishing pain), we would be morally culpable in reading a book, writing a poem, or attending to the needs of our children, for in these cases there are many things we might do instead that would better serve to alleviate human misery in the world. (That we are thus culpable appears to follow from "strong" versions of utilitarianism, the best known of which are those of Bentham, Moore, and

Peter Singer, that afford no non-moral domain of refuge. If I am correct, "strong" utilitarianism is an anomaly in modern ethics, and an untenable one. Later I will undertake to show that eudaimonism's contention for the ubiquity of moral meaning does not entail the sacrifice of individual autonomy, and does not have the other untenable implications of "strong" utilitarianism.)

The distinction of moral from non-moral situations affords to persons, institutions, and practices the opportunity to pitch their tents on non-moral turf, and it is difficult to find arguments or incentives that will induce them to move to moral ground. One class of arguments to this end is conspicuously circular, resting on premises that the outlander is under no obligation to accept, while another, by offering non-moral incentives to moral conduct (e.g., prudence, happiness), appears to "degrade and prostitute virtue,"[6] setting it in the service of non-moral ends.

Two such non-moral campouts that have decisively shaped modern history are science and business management. Modern science gained its immunity on the ground of the supposed gulf between facts and values, description and prescription; its devotion to facts was thus at the same time its claim to be "value-free." And for approximately the past hundred years, business management has sought to claim for itself the status of applied social science on the bridge of economics, availing itself of moral exemption (except with respect to the "my station and its duties" type of code that no practice can be without) on the fact-value distinction. The prevailing spirit of management theory and practice is succinctly captured by management scholar Neil W. Chamberlain: "Employees are being paid to produce, not to make themselves into better people. Corporations are purchasing employee time to make a return on it, not investing in employees to enrich their lives. Employees are human capital, and when capital is hired or leased, the objective is not to embellish it for its own sake but to use it for financial advantage."[7]

The proliferation of non-moral domains of refuge from morality comes home to roost when the so-called private sector, which Mill (in his eudaimonistic voice) fought for as a sanctuary for the self-development of moral character, becomes regarded instead as an arena for the gratification of desires that are relieved of any obligation to answer for their worth. Self-development is arduous (albeit deeply rewarding) work, and private life has become, for many, the playground for mindless diversions from the public workplace. The modern rise to predominance of both science and business appears to be accounted for on the basis of powerful a priori human incentives—the love of truth on one side, and the desire for material gain on the other. But to this I believe the following consideration should be added. On any viable conception of human nature, *aspiration* is a definitive human characteristic. (I mean nothing heroic by this, but only that in order to understand any human being's present conduct, we must know the sought-for future toward which present conduct is meant to be contributory.) The effect of modern moral minimalism is to afford to moral life little space for aspiration; it is a small room with a low ceiling and not much of a view. In particular, it calls for little in the way of developed moral character—our second sense of modernity's moral minimalism. I believe an important consequence of this has been to redirect human aspirations away from the confines of morality and toward the apparently limitless horizons afforded by the laboratory and the market.

By contrast to modern ethics, classical ethics gives a central place to ideals, and it is characteristic of ideals that they are capable of enlisting the full measure of human aspiration. The function of ideals in classical ethical theory and moral life is to guide moral development, transforming random change in the lives of individuals and societies into the directed change that deserves to be called moral growth. Central to the development of moral character that constitutes moral growth is the achievement of integrity, by which all of an individual's faculties, desires, choices, dispositions, courses of conduct, and roles are alike expressive of him or her, and contribute to the chosen end. It is a common misconception of modern ethics that ideals are inappropriate *res gestae* of moral obligations because they make extravagant demands that the average person is unable and/or unwilling to accept. The partial truth that this misconception rests upon is the fact that ideals, by their very nature (as perfections) can never be fully actualized, hence the very best human conduct falls short of its ideal. The reason it is nevertheless a misconception is that under the guidance of an ideal, what counts *now* is the next step. The fact that each next step invokes another, and thus no step can be final, does not bespeak the impracticability of ideals per se, for next steps are always possible for a human being, which is to say that for a human being moral growth is always possible. Another modern misconception of the place of ideals in moral life has engendered discomfort over the supposed likeness of the moral idealist and the fanatic. It is true, as Hare observes,[8] that a moral idealist may cleave to his ideals at the expense of his present interests, but to understand this as "fanaticism" is to condemn an important way by which "interests" are moralized. (The ex-alcoholic's personal ideal of sobriety must override what for a considerable time is his immediate desire to have a drink.) With respect to the moral idealist's stance toward others, it may be true that some seek to impose their ideals upon others,[9] but that some moral idealists do not so conduct themselves is evidence of the contingency of such conduct. Eudaimonism's insistence on the autonomy of moral agents as the basis of respect is the requirement for consent by whomever an ideal affects, and condemns the imposition of the ideals of one person, or community, or party, or nation, upon resistant or unwitting others.

It will be immediately obvious that choices which were earlier cited as typically non-moral in the modern understanding of morality are moral choices in the classical understanding. This is because choices of vocation, of avocations, of friends to cultivate and books to read (our previous examples), have a direct bearing on the development of moral character. In the matter of vocation, for example: if it is the fundamental moral responsibility of every person to discover his or her innate potential worth and progressively actualize it in the world, then vocational choice is clearly one of the important means for such actualization, and *vocation* has thematic moral meaning beneath the periodic "moral situations" that arise in it. This is why Socrates, Plato, and Aristotle refused to categorially divorce vocational skills from moral virtues (and not, as some modern commentators have hastily assumed, because they failed analytically to recognize the difference). Indeed, classical thought integrates the vocation and the life of the individual by the understanding that the true work of each person is his or her life, to which vocation and all other dimensions should be contributory. Were it possible here to pursue the implications of vocation as moral choice, I would argue for vocation as a foundational form of generosity, for by identifying with, and investing themselves in their vocations, persons are endeavoring to give the best of themselves to others in the products of their work, including their own developed traits of character.

Similarly friendship is inseparable from the moral work of self-discovery and self-actualization, and the long section given to it by Aristotle in the *Nicomachean Ethics* is not, as many modern moral philosophers have supposed, a diversionary ramble. According to Socrates in the *Lysis* and Aristotle in the *Nicomachean Ethics*, true friends, willing the best for one another, furnish reciprocal aid toward worthy living. Socrates says that friends, to be of such use to one another, must be alike in pursuing the good, but different and complementary in the kind of good that each pursues, each contributing something of worth to the other that the other cannot self-supply. Though I cannot develop the point, it is worth noting that Socrates is here working out a conception of individual autonomy that is compatible with interdependence, rather than implying a total self-sufficiency that would belie the social nature of humankind.

We have cited key instances of choices that are typically non-moral by modern parameters but moral in classical understanding. However our earlier contention that for classical ethics nothing in human experience is without moral meaning requires that we go further. Specifically we must speak to the trivial desires, choices, and acts which fill a considerable portion of our days. The answer, however, is the same: even our trivial desires, choices, and acts have moral meaning because they have some effect—no matter how small— on the person we are in process of becoming. To modern moral theory they appear to be devoid of moral meaning because they have no direct effect upon others, but classical morality is concerned with their effect upon the self, and quite clearly the kind of person one is in process of becoming has its effects upon others. But suppose that it did not and could not affect others? An individual marooned upon a desert island with no prospect of rescue would be relieved of all moral responsibility under the sort of theory that restricts moral meaning to the effects of a person's conduct on others. By contrast, under eudaimonistic theory such an individual would be nonetheless responsible for doing the utmost that circumstances allowed to manifest his or her potential worth. Because this worth is objective it is meant to be appreciated and utilized by (some) others, but the fact that in the desert island situation this is impossible is a contingency that does not abolish the moral responsibility to (as far as possible) actualize one's potential worth.

It is common in modern theory to distinguish prudential conduct from moral conduct (Kant is a notable example), but eudaimonism recognizes prudence as a necessary conditon of worthy living and therefore a moral responsibility.

Returning to our trivial desires, choices, and acts—the virtue of integrity represents the integration of all dimensions of the self, such that each complements all others, and all contribute to the end of the worthy life that is one's own to live. It is an inclusive virtue, leaving nothing out, and an extraneous desire, choice, or act, however minor, is an inner disorder and in some degree (however small) an impediment. Granted, integrity as thus described is an ideal that, as such, cannot be fully realized. Granted also, our very finitude obliges us to adopt measures of economy, included among which is the measure of disregarding truly minor desires, choices, and acts in order to attend to larger ones (as, if asked to describe the features of the room in which I now sit, I would confine myself to conspicuous ones while recognizing that description in infinite detail literally could not be concluded in a lifetime). But notice that this policy of economy is but a plea *de minimus,* ignoring moral meaning that it acknowledges to exist.

If morality is coterminous with human life and unrestrictedly pervasive within it, then individuals are afforded no non-moral domain of refuge, and no human institution, practice, or discipline can claim exemption from morality's ultimate concern—the good life for human beings. Plato expresses this for state government when he says *(The Republic),* "Can anything be better for a commonwealth than to produce in it men and women of the best type?"[10] Mill is a modern spokesman for this view when he says, "The most important point of excellence which any form of government can possess is to promote the virtue and intelligence of the people themselves."[11] And John Dewey puts the same principle by saying, "Democracy has many meanings, but if it has a moral meaning, it is found in resolving that the supreme test of all political institutions and industrial arrangements shall be the contribution they make to the all-around growth of every member of society."[12]

By classical principles the physical sciences, the social sciences, business, and indeed all disciplines, institutions, and practices are ultimately to be judged by their contribution to the good life for humankind. It will perhaps be objected that this understanding would put an end to the so-called "pure research" that constitutes the leading edge of the physical and the social sciences. But "pure research" (presuming for purposes of argument that it exists or is possible) is not precluded by the classical moral picture. It can be sustained by arguments to show that the inalienable responsibility for improving the quality of human life is furthered by pure research. What *is* disallowed is the claim by entire disciplines (e.g., the "pure" sciences, business management) to be exempt from moral demands.

The other "minimalist" delimitation of modern morality that we have identified is the limited demands it makes upon developed moral character. The reason for this delimitation is that modern morality is built upon what Edmund Pincoffs terms the "Hobbesian truism"[13] that in the absence of recognized rules and generally rule-abiding conduct, the lives of persons would be unbearable. On this foundation morality is paired with law in the interest of the preservation of social order. This interest requires the observance by (almost) everyone of rules that are understood and acknowledged as authoritative by (almost) everyone. For this to be the case, the rules must be very simple and straightforward, and acting in accordance with them must require very little in the way of developed moral character. This accounts for the tendency of modern modes of normative ethics—contractarianism, deontology, utilitarianism, intuitionism, ideal observer theory, agent theory—to devolve (from their ultimate and far from simple principles) upon simple rules of the sort as, "Do not lie," "Do not steal," "Keep your promises," "Do not commit murder," etc., and to introduce exceptions and complications with great reluctance.

One consequence of directing morality to the preservation of social order is that morality becomes very difficult to distinguish from law; moral requirements are framed as rules, moral rules serve the same basic purpose as civil and criminal statutes, and moral judgments are modeled on judicial decisions in terms of impartiality and impersonality. Impartiality and impersonality mean that rightly made moral judgments will be made identically by whomever is called upon to judge, and will be applied identically to different persons in relevantly similar circumstances. We say of such judgments that they are "universalizable," typically meaning that what is right for any person in given circumstances is right for every person in relevantly similar circumstances. But there is an internal disparity here, for of the two principal factors in the formula—circumstances and persons—only the former is qualified by "relevantly similar."[14] The reason that differences among persons typically are disregarded or disallowed is that universalizability is intended to thwart the inherent propensity of individuals to regard themselves as the exception to any rule. The effect of this disregard is to preclude recognition of differences among persons in respect to levels of the development of moral character, and this in turn means that only such moral rules can be recognized as make no demands upon moral capacities that (almost) everyone cannot be expected to possess. In sum, the universalizability criterion, by the internal disparity just noted, is obliged to confine its demands upon moral character to the barest minimum.

Granted, the just noted internal disparity is not present in universalization formulations by Sidgwick, Marcus Singer, and David Lyons. Thus Lyons, for example, poses the criterion as the question, "What would happen if every *similar* person did a *similar* thing under *similar* circumstances?"[15] But the effect has been slight upon universalization advocates generally, in part, perhaps, because Sidgwick, Singer, and Lyons do not pursue the practical effects of the qualifications "relevantly similar" as applied to persons. And in theory, because none of them considers the question of moral development in reference to relevant similarities and differences among persons, the above noted correlation of moral demands to minimal moral development is unchanged.

To be sure, this bare minimum is not nothing; it includes the ability to understand simple moral rules and recognize the situations to which they apply, together with the ability to act in accordance with them and the will to do so. Edmund Pincoffs gathers these abilities under the terms "conscientiousness" and "rule responsibility." He extends the requisite minimum capacities by using an analogy between rule-morality demands and military imperatives. Among the latter a distinction is recognized between "commands" and "orders." "A command tells us what to do or refrain from doing in such explicit terms that there is either no or very little room for variation in the way in which it is obeyed or disobeyed. An order, on the other hand, does not so much specifically tell us what to do as what to accomplish or at what we should aim. 'Report at 10.00' is a command; 'Provide protective screen for the convoy' is an order. There can, of course, be general and standing orders and commands. A general command would be 'All hands report at 10.00 tomorrow morning', and a general standing command would require all hands to report every morning at 10.00. 'Exercise extreme caution when in enemy waters' can serve as a general standing order.'[16] On this analogy, Pincoffs notes that moral rules that resemble general standing orders require for compliance more in the way of developed individual capacities than do rules resembling general standing commands. Nevertheless what is required remains characterizable under "conscientiousness" or "rule responsibility," which, as the single virtue (or closely interrelated set of virtues) implicated by the modern mode of ethical theorizing, neglects most of the developed moral capacities recognized as moral virtues in classical thought. This prompts Pincoffs's comment that "The attempt to reduce moral character to any given trait by philosophical fiat is open to suspicion."[17]

The question of what "rule responsibility" requires in the way of developed moral character has not often been addressed by modern ethical theorists, but an attempt at adequate description would have something to gain, for example, from John Rawls's "Two Concepts of Rules" and R. M. Hare's "Universalizability,"[18] among other contributions. (Hare points out that by the universalizability criterion we are not told what to do, but must propose hypothetical acts and submit them to the touchstone of the criterion.) What makes an attempt at adequate description unnecessary for our purposes is that by assigning responsibility for preserving social order to morality, modern ethics (as noted earlier) has been obliged to make minimal demands on developed moral character, whatever the precise description of the requisite character may prove to be. Urmson captures this decisively when he says in his essay, "Saints and Heroes": "If we are to exact basic duties like debts, and censure failure, such duties must be, in ordinary circumstances, within the capacity of the ordinary man. It would be silly for us to say to ourselves, our children, and our fellow men, 'This and that you and everyone else must do', if the acts in question are such that manifestly but few could bring themselves to do them, though we may ourselves resolve to try to be of that few."[19]

To summarize what has here been said about modernity's moral minimalism in the second of the two respects we have identified: modern ethics either disregards, or treats inadequately, "good" or "right" acts that make large demands upon developed moral character in individuals.

It may be supposed that Mill and Kant, as dominant figures in modern ethical theory, furnish decisive counterexamples to our thesis that modern ethics makes minimal demands upon developed moral character, and I will speak briefly to each case. It is true that Mill gives great importance to the "sympathetic feelings" in chapter 3 of *Utilitarianism,* and calls for their deliberate cultivation by the "influences of education." But his reason for this is that it is through sympathetic feelings that human beings are induced to act on the principle of "the greatest happiness of the greatest number." This is to say that character development is here conceived by Mill as instrumental to rule-adherence, which subsumes it under Pincoffs's "conscientiousness," and fits our description of "rules morality" offered at the outset.

Similarly Kant's preoccupation with "the good will," which is dutiful solely for duty's sake, is a "conscientiousness" that considers character development only insofar as it procures "rule responsibility." Otherwise he treats moral virtues, not as developed traits of character, but as "a matter of temperament," and of no moral importance. Kant does indeed (in his monograph *Education)* treat "moral culture" as the part of education intended to develop moral character, but for Kant moral character is the "readiness to act in accord with 'maxims' " which precisely subsumes it under Pincoffs's "conscientiousness."[20]

In the matter of conduct that makes large demands upon developed moral character we can effectively contrast the modern and classical perspectives by means of Urmson's "Saints and Heroes," which calls attention to the deficiency of modern moral theory in this respect, but then tries to rectify it in a distinctly modern—and, I believe, unsatisfactory—manner.

Urmson criticizes the three-part classification of actions by most ethical theorists—acts that are morally obligatory, acts that are morally forbidden, and acts that are morally indifferent—for its inability to handle supererogation, understood as the class of acts that are good to do but not wrong not to do. Using "saintly" and "heroic" acts as his paradigms, he says "It would be absurd to suggest that moral philosophers have hitherto been unaware of the existence of saints and heroes and have never even alluded to them in their work. But it does seem that these facts have been neglected in their general, systematic accounts of morality."[21] He thinks it possible to revise the theories he specifically considers (Kantianism, utilitarianism, and intuitionism) "to accommodate the facts," but adds that "until so modified successfully they must surely be treated as unacceptable, and the modifications required might well detract from their plausibility."[22]

A saint acts for the good in contexts in which inclination, desire, or self-interest would prevent most people from so-acting; a hero acts for the good in contexts in which terror, fear, or a drive to self-preservation would prevent such action by most people. Both the saint and the hero act "far beyond the limits of [their] duty,"[23] but Urmson indicates that the class of acts that ethical theory must be rectified to include begins with acts that exceed the limits of duty in the least measure, e.g., acts that are even "a little more generous, forebearing, helpful, or forgiving than fair dealing demands," and all cases of "going the second mile."[24] Because "basic duties" are uniformly obligatory for everyone they must make minimal demands on developed moral character, and Urmson (as we have seen in a previous citation) argues for retention of their minimalist character. The case he makes is for the revision of ethical theory to include the category of supererogation as "higher flights of morality [to be] regarded as more positive contributions that go beyond what is universally to be exacted." He says of these "higher flights" that while they are not to be "exacted publicly," they are "clearly equally pressing *in foro interno* on those who are not content merely to avoid the intolerable."[25]

The problems in Urmson's position to which I want to call attention are two. In the first place he has acknowledged a continuum of what might be called "degrees of difficulty" between basic duties and the "higher flights" of morality, which means that wherever the line is drawn between basic duties and acts that exceed basic duties (acts of supererogation), it will be prone to the appearance of arbitrariness. Second, Urmson acknowledges that saints and heroes regard their saintly and heroic deeds as their duty ("There is indeed no degree of saintliness that a suitable person may not come to consider it to be his duty to achieve"[26]), yet Urmson is in the position of contending that their deeds are in truth "far beyond the limits of [their] duty," and it is unclear by what authority Urmson contradicts the saint or hero.

At bottom, Urmson is beset by the same dilemma that is responsible for the deficiency he calls attention to in the ethical theories he cites. If impartiality precludes consideration of relevant differences among persons, then either moral heroism is obligatory for everyone, or moral duties are confined to what Urmson terms the "rock-bottom" minimum, and moral conduct that exceeds the minimum is the duty of no one. In the latter case there will be nothing *admirable* in moral conduct; ("the admirable" is what deserves to be "looked up to," whereas minimal moral demands are groundlevel); in the former case everyone will be morally responsible for conduct that lies beyond the developed capacities of most, and which it is therefore unreasonable to expect of them. To avoid this consequence, Urmson opts for restriction of duties to "rock-bottom" minimum, to which he adds the category of supererogation. The supererogatory is what is morally good to do but not morally obligatory. The problem here is that by his fidelity to impartiality and universality, Urmson is obliged to conclude that whatever is supererogatory, i.e., whatever is in the least beyond minimum "rock-bottom" duties, is not morally obligatory for anyone. But he acknowledges that heroes perceive their heroic conduct as their duty.

Urmson's key mistake, I think, lies in minimizing the significance of the hero's or saint's own conception of his or her moral duty. Noting that only the saint or hero can thus identify his or her duty, and that he or she characteristically attributes this duty to no one else, Urmson says it is *not* "a piece of objective reporting."[27] This propensity to minimize the saint's or hero's own sense of moral responsibility is widespread in modern ethics. Thus Michael W. Jackson says it is "modesty" or "genuine confusion" when Dr. Bernard Rieux, in Albert Camus's *The Plague,* or Cornielle's El Cid, refer to their heroic conduct as their duty.[28] But on the contrary, I think that both Camus and Cornielle are astute in the matter of the psychology of heroism, and that this psychology accurately reflects the facts. The seeming warrant of Urmson's denial of objectivity to the hero's self-judgment is the equation of objective human responsibilities with universally distributed human responsibilities, but this ignores the objective fact of moral development—a morally developed individual possesses greater capabilities than does an individual of lesser development, as a skilled swimmer can accomplish a deep-water rescue that would be beyond the capabilities of a novice swimmer. The recognition that the moral life of individuals is a development is the recognition that moral demands continually increase, and this is corroborated by the testimony of "heroes" (Cornielle's, Camus's, Urmson's) that they demand more of themselves than they expect of most persons, and more than they expected of themselves at prior levels of development. Drawing upon eudaimonistic ethical theory, what we must add to this is the inalienable moral responsibility of every human being for continuous moral development. This cuts off the populist resort of contending that a handful of persons are "born heroes," while nothing but moral mediocrity is to be expected of the rest of us.

In sum, eudaimonism's thesis is that some of what is obligatory at later stages of moral development is supererogatory with respect to prior stages of moral development. This is a continuity-thesis concerning what exceeds or is included within the moral obligations of persons at given times. But the distinction between duty and supererogation is not arbitrary—it is grounded in the objective fact of moral development.

We have referred to the "Hobbesian truism" that for life to be tolerable (almost) everyone must conform to basic moral rules, which entails that demands upon developed moral character must be minimal. To this I will counterpose what I will term the "Socratic truism." It is the proposition that any person may in the course of his or her life encounter one or more ultimate tests in which to pursue the course of life that he or she has chosen to live is at the risk of life or well-being (Socrates, *Apology:* "This is the truth of the matter, gentlemen of the jury: wherever a man has taken a position that he believes to be best, or has been placed by his commander, there he must I think remain and face danger, without a thought for death or anything else, rather than disgrace"). My leave to call this a truism rests in well-recognized cases, for example, when citizens are called upon to risk their lives in defense of their country; or again, when a parent is called upon to risk his or her life to save his or her child. Similarly we recognize, I think, that were we residents of a Nazi-occupied country in WW II, our humanitarian principles would demand of us that we attempt to shelter Jews from Nazi genocide. In general, we know that we cannot live lives that are worthy in our own estimation if we abandon our commitments at the first sign of trouble. Our supreme test may or may not come, but because it may, we must prepare ourselves for it. The Hobbesian truism tells us that minimally acceptable conduct is required of everyone; the Socratic truism tells us that moral heroism may be required of anyone. The demands implicit in the Socratic truism are universalizable because the opportunity of moral growth is in principle universalizable. On the question of universality this is to say that eudaimonism holds the demand for moral growth in individuals to be universal, but holds that morally obligatory conduct in "relevantly similar" situations will differ among persons by virtue of differences in the levels of moral development that they have achieved.

Urmson is surely correct in holding as a paramount criterion of normative ethical philosophy that "our morality must be one that will work,"[29] (this follows from the definition of normative ethics as "practical reason") but modern ethical philosophy is mistaken in supposing this to entail moral minimalism. Large moral demands are practicable when they are proportional to moral development, and when moral development of individuals is a social undertaking. And until morality is understood to include the higher reaches of moral development (as represented by the classical virtues), it is so impoverished as to be unable to enlist human aspiration. The following, by mountaineer Reinhold Messner, will do metaphoric service here: "Striding along, my body becomes so highly-charged it would be quite impossible for me to stop. It feels as if something wants to break free, to burst from my breast. It is a surge of longing that carries me forward as if I were possessed."[30] It is a reflection recorded by Messner during his ascent of K-2 in the Karakoram Himalaya, and would not be likely to have visited him in the flatlands. Moral thought and moral life require their upper reaches if they are to enlist human aspiration lifelong, and ethical theory is bound to accommodate them. But we must recognize that, like the mountain, the upper reaches of moral character can only be attained by starting from where one is, and ascending in steps, and for this one must know how to climb. What happens when lofty goals are posed but nothing is done about learning to climb is illustrated by "strong" utilitarianism, which I earlier referred to as in some respects an anomaly in modern ethical theory, and which I will speak to briefly in conclusion.

Urmson judges utilitarianism to be the (modern) normative ethical theory that is most amenable to the inclusion of the category of the supererogatory. He says that this is because "Utilitarians, when attempting to justify the main rules of duty in terms of a *summum bonum,* have surely invoked many different types of utilitarian justification, ranging from the avoidance of the intolerable to the fulfillment of the last detail of a most rarified ideal."[31] In other words, utilitarianism can be formulated in such a way as to include the "higher flights" of morality. The trouble is that when it is so formulated, it results in making out "the most heroic self-sacrifice or saintly self-forgetfulness [to] be duties on all fours with truth-telling and promise-keeping."[32] And Urmson concludes that because the saintly and heroic are "too far beyond the capacity of the ordinary men or ordinary occasions . . . a general breakdown of compliance with the moral code would be an inevitable consequence."[33]

It is "strong" versions of utilitarianism that Urmson has in mind, as distinguished from "weak." The latter seek to obviate the problem that Urmson cites by placing limits of one kind or another on utilitarian responsibility. Accordingly, in our earlier citation Mill contended that "ninety-nine hundredths of all our actions are done from other [than moral] motives, and rightly so done if the rule of duty does not condemn them." What Mill may safely be supposed to have in mind as the principal category of the "ninety-nine hundredths" is conduct in the private sector that he maps in *On Liberty,* consisting in conduct that either does not affect others, or does not affect others directly. But the problem here is that identification of a private sector does not, as Mill supposes, deactivate the utilitarian principle and its derivative responsibilities. The reason for this is that human beings can exchange their situations. It is true enough that if I am alone in my apartment, my decision whether for the next hour to read a book, watch TV, or develop photographic film in my darkroom is unlikely to have direct effect upon others—but why am I not, say, out on the street finding shelter for the homeless? The utilitarian principle mandates that I *always* act for the greatest good of the greatest number. To be sure, the qualification "within the limits of human possibilities" is to be understood (e.g., I must eat and sleep), but it cannot grant exemption to Mill's private sector of individual experience for the reason just given.

This leaves us with "strong" utilitarianisms, e.g., Bentham's version and the formulation by Moore that Urmson brands unworkable. But the most interesting in this category is that of Peter Singer. With Mill, Singer perceives that on the face of it the utilitarian principle makes moral demands upon persons that most are going to perceive as extravagant, and by the touchstone of which almost all human lives must be judged morally wanting. But unlike Mill, Singer's response is unequivocal acceptance—indeed, insistence—upon these entailments. In his words, "if it is in our power to prevent something bad from happening, without thereby sacrificing anything of comparable moral importance, we ought, morally, to do it."[34] He contends that considerations of distance and proximity are disallowed, and argues that it is irrelevant whether we are the only person who could possibly help, or one among millions. The effect is that suffering anywhere in the world is every person's moral problem, and because suffering in its concrete forms (starvation, malnutrition, disease, etc.) is the exigent moral problem, the only way any of us is at any time relieved of responsibility to be contributing to the alleviation of suffering in, say, Bengal (the best publicized example when Singer wrote), is by contributing to the limit of his or her ability to the alleviation of suffering elsewhere. The amount of resources (energy, money, skill, etc.) each is to contribute is "at least up to the point at which by giving more one would begin to cause serious suffering for oneself and one's dependents— perhaps even beyond this point to the point of marginal utility, at which by giving more one would cause oneself and one's dependents as much suffering as one would prevent in Bengal."[35]

By persons who accept the utilitarian principle as the supreme moral principle Singer is, I think, difficult and perhaps impossible to refute. Moreover from the standpoint of classical ethics, Singer is to be commended for reintroducing the moral mountain without which ethical theory becomes an arid flatland. But how can it be other than futile to present a mountaineering demand to flatlands-dwellers without reckoning with the problem that they are devoid of climbing skills? It is precisely in its recognition that learning to climb must come first that the classical mode of ethical theorizing demonstrates its superiority to prevailing modern modes. Supposing that Singer's argument for the preemptive status of the moral problem of physical suffering is decisive and irrefutable, it is nevertheless a fallacy of anachronism to suppose that it will be recognized and responded to if prior attention is not given to the discovery and establishment of the conditions that conduce to generalization of moral development in individuals. To distill the thesis of the present essay, it is by giving priority not to one contemporary moral ill or another, but to the neglected problem of the development of moral character, that we gain prospect of generalizing the dedication of persons in substantial numbers to the realization of moral ends.

Notes

For critical comments on earlier drafts of this essay, I am grateful to John Kekes, Edmund L. Pincoffs, William G. Scott, and Mary K. Norton. This should not be understood to imply their unqualified or qualified endorsement of the present version.

1. Alasdair MacIntyre, *After Virtue: A Study in Moral Theory* (Notre Dame, Ind., 1981); Richard Taylor, *Ethics, Faith, and Reason* (Englewood Cliffs, N.J., 1985); Edmund L. Pincoffs, *Quandaries and Virtues: Against Reductivism in Ethics* (Lawrence, Kans., 1986). My *Personal Destinies* (Princeton, 1976) attempted to outfit classical eudaimonism for current service. Bernard Williams shows some favor for the classical model of ethical theorizing in *Ethics and the Limits of Philosophy* (Cambridge, 1985). In addition it will be recognized that interest in "the virtues" has been mounting rapidly among ethical theorists for a decade or more, e.g., Philippa Foot, *Virtues and Vices* (Berkeley, 1978); James D. Wallace, *Virtues and Vices* (Ithaca, N.Y., 1978). First-rate work on virtues, coupled with the recognition that this emphasis is at home in the classical mode of ethical theorizing, is to be found in essays by Lester H. Hunt, John Kekes, Lawrence C. Becker, and R. W. Hepburn.

2. Plato, *Republic*, translated by F. M. Cornford (New York, 1945), 37.

3. A recent and thorough consideration of the concept of potentiality is Israel Scheffler, *Of Human Potential* (Boston, 1985).

4. Henry D. Thoreau, *Walden*, edited by J. Lyndon Shanley (Princeton, 1971), 97.

5. John Stuart Mill, *Utilitarianism* (Indianapolis, 1957), 23.

6. F. H. Bradley, *Ethical Studies*, cited in Peter Singer, *Practical Ethics* (Cambridge, 1979), 209.

7. Neil W. Chamberlain, *The Limits of Corporate Responsibility* (New York, 1973), 92. I am indebted to Prof. David K. Hart for this reference.

8. See R. M. Hare, *Freedom and Reason* (Oxford, 1965), 176. In his subsequent *Moral Thinking*, Hare believes he solves the problem that fanaticism poses to his universal prescriptivism, but he retains the definition of the fanatic that is offered in *Freedom and Reason*, and it is the definition I am questioning.

9. This criticism is one of several directed against moralities consisting in "the self-conscious pursuit of moral ideals" by Michael Oakeshott in "The Tower of Babel," *Rationalism in Politics* (Totowa, N.J., 1977), 59–79.

10. Plato, *Republic*, 154.

11. John Stuart Mill, *Considerations on Representative Government* (Indianapolis, 1958), 25.

12. John Dewey, *Reconstruction in Philosophy* (Boston, 1957), 186.

13. Pincoffs, *Quandaries and Virtues*, 58.

14. See David Norton, "On an Internal Disparity in Universalizability-Criterion Formulations," *Review of Metaphysics* 33, no. 3 (1980): 519–26.

15. Henry Sidgwick, *The Methods of Ethics* (London, 1907), 209, 379; Marcus George Singer, *Generalization in Ethics* (New York, 1961), esp. chap. 2; David Lyons, *Forms and Limits of Utilitariansim* (London, 1965), the citation is from p. 31.

16. Pincoffs, *Quandaries and Virtues*, 24–25.

17. Ibid., 31–32.

18. John Rawls, "Two Concepts of Rules," in *An Introduction to Ethics*, edited by Robert E. Dewey and Robert H. Hurlbutt III (New York, 1977), 259–66. R. M. Hare, "Universalizability," in *Essays on the Moral Concepts* (Berkeley, 1972), 13–28, esp. 19–20.

19. J. O. Urmson, "Saints and Heroes," in *Reason and Responsibility*, edited by Joel Feinberg (Belmont, Calif., 1985), 520.

20. For a fuller development of Kant's thinking on this point, see Lester H. Hunt, "Character and Thought," *American Philosophical Quarterly* 15, no. 3, (1978): 180–81.

21. Urmson, "Saints and Heroes," 518.

22. Ibid., 519.

23. Ibid., 516.

24. Ibid., 518.

25. Ibid., 522.

26. Ibid., 517.

27. Ibid.

28. Michael W. Jackson, *Matters of Justice* (London, 1986), 126, 122.

29. Urmson, "Saints and Heroes," 520.

30. Reinhold Messner and Alessandro Gogna, *K-2, Mountain of Mountains* (New York, 1980), 78.

31. Urmson, "Saints and Heroes," 522.

32. Ibid., 518.

33. Ibid., 521.

34. Peter Singer, "Famine, Affluence, and Morality," in *Reason and Responsibility*, edited by Feinberg, p. 523. I here neglect Singer's weakened version of his principle—"If it is in our power to prevent something very bad from happening, without thereby sacrificing anything morally significant, we ought, morally, to do it"—as less interesting and more problematic than his strong version.

35. Ibid., 524.

Moral Exemplars:
Reflections on Schindler, the Trocmes, and Others

LAWRENCE A. BLUM

In *The Sovereignty of Good*[1] Iris Murdoch berated Anglo-American philosophers for failing to describe a moral ideal which is of unquestionable excellence and which has the power to inspire us to be better than we are. Murdoch assumed that such a task would involve a fuller moral psychology than the resources of philosophy had at that time been able to provide.

While the beginnings of such a moral psychology have begun to show themselves in work done within virtue theory, at the same time there has been an attack on moral excellence itself, an attack which has had two sources. The first questions the traditional view that moral considerations—generally associated with an impersonal, impartial, and universal point of view—take automatic precedence over any other action-guiding considerations. Thomas Nagel and, more radically, Bernard Williams argue that considerations of personal satisfaction or self-realization should in some circumstances be allowed to outweigh moral considerations (as defined by an impersonal point of view), while Philippa Foot argues more generally that moral considerations do not always override non-moral ones.[2]

This attack on the priority of the moral has spawned a second, more direct, attack on moral excellence itself, that is, on the supreme value of a morally excellent life. A weaker form of this attack has it that since many human goods—for example, aesthetic, scientific, athletic—lie outside morality, lives devoted to morality exemplify only one of the many types of human good, and one which cannot be given a general priority over all others. A stronger form of the attack on moral excellence has questioned the human worth of a life centered on moral concerns itself, and has suggested that such a life involves various important deficiencies. Both these lines of argument have been taken by Susan Wolf in her influential article "Moral Saints," but they have been echoed by others as well.[3]

These criticisms of moral excellence raise Murdoch's challenge once again.

196

They remind us how devoid of attempts to articulate the contours of an admirable and worthy life most recent moral theory has been since Murdoch lodged her challenge in the late 1960s. Utilitarianism, and to some extent contemporary Kantianism, while purporting to defend the supremacy of moral considerations in a human life, have given surprisingly little indication of what a person would actually be like who lived a life according to their recommendations. It is especially striking that utilitarianism, which seems to advocate that each person devote his or her entire life to the achievement of the greatest possible good or happiness of all people, has barely attempted to provide a convincing description of what it would be like to live that sort of life.[4] Wolf's article, though largely critical of utilitarianism, has provided more in this direction than have most utilitarian theorists themselves.

This paper attempts a beginning of a psychology of moral excellence, with the ultimate goal of showing that moral excellence is worthy of our highest admiration and, appropriately understood, our aspiration. I will argue here that morally exceptional persons—whom I will call "moral exemplars" or "moral paragons"—are of irreducibly different types (some of which share features in common); and that a recognition of these differences is the first step in a realistic moral psychology of excellence. In the first section of the paper I will consider in some detail one example (Oskar Schindler) of a type of moral paragon or exemplar which I will call the "(moral) hero." The second section will examine the complexities of determining "unworthy motives" and their relationship to moral excellence. The third section will distinguish from the moral hero another type of exemplar I will call the "Murdochian exemplar." The fourth section will consider the role of risk and adversity in the determination of moral excellence, primarily in connection with the hero and the Murdochian. The fifth section will distinguish two more types of moral exemplar—the "idealist" and the "responder." (None of the distinctions among types of moral exemplars is meant to be exhaustive, and the discussions will point to other varieties as well.) The sixth section will briefly raise some questions, based on the types of moral exemplar developed in previous sections, for Susan Wolf's description and assessment of moral excellence. The final section discusses the extent to which ordinary persons can and ought to imitate, emulate, and learn from moral exemplars.

In partially defending moral excellence against various charges of deficiency and unattractiveness, I will not, however, be disputing the reservations which Foot, Williams, Nagel, and Wolf have expressed concerning traditional Kantian and utilitarian assumptions about the supremacy of the impersonal point of view. Rather I will want to show that some of the reason why Wolf is able to depict moral paragons as unappealing and unworthy is because she, like Williams and Nagel, too fully accepts the identification of morality with an impersonal, impartial, and universalistic point of view. I will thus be suggesting that the conception of morality in terms of which the different types of moral exemplar are seen to be excellent is *not,* or not primarily, that of Kantianism or utilitarianism.

SCHINDLER AS MORAL HERO

I will first discuss in some detail a fascinating character whom I take to be an example of a "moral hero"—Oskar Schindler, portrayed in Thomas Keneally's book *Schind-*

ler's List.[5] Schindler was a German industrialist who ventured to Poland in the late 1930s as an agent of the German intelligence service, in order to avoid duty in the German Army, and with the intention of going into business there. During the Nazi occupation of Poland (1939–1945) Schindler saved the lives of thousands of Jews, at great personal risk to himself (he was arrested several times), and with the ultimate result of losing the entire personal fortune which he had made, primarily from his war-related businesses. Schindler accomplished this feat primarily through employing Jews as workers in his enamelware factory; by cajoling and tricking Nazi officials, he managed to employ many more Jews than were in any way necessary to production, and also to keep them in reasonably good health. He thereby protected all of them.[6] In addition, toward the end of the war Schindler managed to keep his own workers from being shipped to death camps, while also securing the release of three hundred other Jews from Auschwitz, the largest and most notorious of the concentration camps.

This description alone means that Schindler accomplished something morally notable and extraordinary. But accomplishing a great good or preventing a great evil, such as the death of many people, even at great risk to oneself, is not sufficient for moral heroism or excellence. During the war some Jews were saved by Poles who sheltered them in exchange for payment.[7] While humanity can be grateful for those choosing to take this path rather than (what a much larger number did) to denounce Jews to the Nazis or to fail to provide any help whatsoever when they were in a position to do so, such activity does not constitute moral heroism or excellence, no matter how many endangered Jews an individual saved in this manner (which did generally involve substantial risks). Because the rescue effort was carried out primarily from the motive of self-interest our moral approval of the act does not lead to a judgment that the agent was morally heroic in performing it.[8]

Oskar Schindler was different from these financially benefiting rescuers in that he saved Jews because he cared about the Jews—at least about the particular Jews he came to know—and because he believed the Nazi policies abhorrent. These sentiments and moral attitudes, rather than any expectation of reward, prompted his actions.

Yet more seems necessary for moral heroism than accomplishing a great good at great risk to oneself and from morally worthy motives, as we can see by contrasting Schindler during the later period of the Nazi occupation of Poland with the Schindler of 1939 and 1940. In those early years, while Schindler already wanted and intended to help Jews, he did not think that such efforts would result in great losses and risk to himself. Failing (along with many others) to grasp the extraordinary power and evil of the Nazi regime, Schindler seemed to have believed that he would be able to help the Jews *and also* make a great fortune from his manufacturing operations, and that he would escape from the war unscathed. Though Schindler's acts of helping Jews during this period were morally motivated and morally praiseworthy ones, he was not then, or yet, a moral hero. For all one could tell at that point, Schindler might *not* have engaged in a rescue effort if he had realized its financial consequences for himself. Moral excellence seems to require, in addition to a morally worthy motive, some degree of depth of moral commitment, in relation to other desires, dispositions, and sentiments operating in the person's psychological economy. Even though there was no definite point at which Schindler's desire to save Jews did become paramount in his motivation—far outweighing any concern with his own fortune—by the final two years of the war his commitment to saving Jews had certainly attained the requisite depth and centrality in Schindler's scheme of commitments. The morally good rescue efforts of the earlier years had turned into full-fledged moral heroism.[9]

Our discussion of Schindler so far has yielded three criteria of 'moral heroism': (1) a moral project—bringing about a great good or preventing a great evil; (2) morally worthy motivation; and (3) deep rootedness of that morally worthy motivation in the individual's system of motivation. But what counts as "morally worthy motivation"? I cannot give a full account here, but want to make clear that I am rejecting a purely Kantian conception of that catagory, which restricts it to "doing what is right because it is right" or "acting from (a sense of) duty." The sense of duty seems to me insufficiently broad to encompass the full range of moral motivation involved in morally excellent activities and lives. I want to suggest that other morally worthy motives include: direct concern for the well-being of individual persons or groups of persons; personal and communal ideals not (necessarily) seen as duties.[10]

In addition to these three criteria, a fourth seems involved in the form of moral excellence which Schindler seems to exemplify—the facing of risk or danger. It is not only that the facing of risk can be one way of testing for the presence of the third criterion—depth of moral motivation.[11] But there seems, in addition, an element of admiration attached in its own right to the doing of good in the face of risk, an admiration captured, as J. O. Urmson suggested in his seminal article on this subject, by the notation of "hero."[12]

UNWORTHY DESIRES

The portrayal of Schindler so far may seem to omit what to many readers of Keneally's book is one of its most striking features—the moral *ambiguity* of its central character. There are aspects of Schindler's life and character which could be thought to render him less than morally excellent or exemplary. Discussing some of these will help us to examine Schindler in light of the second criterion (morally worthy motives), and also to confront a fifth criterion of moral heroism, namely "faultlessness," or the relative absence of unworthy desires, sentiments, and attitudes. Moral exemplars must have not only morally good desires as their primary motives, but must also *not* possess too much in the way of unworthy states of consciousness, to some extent independent of their direct motivational role. Discussing Schindler's possible faults and foibles will help us to see how far from moral faultlessness or purity of consciousness someone must be for us no longer to regard him or her as a moral exemplar.

I shall discuss five aspects of Schindler's behavior or motivation which arguably detract from his moral excellence: (1) Schindler's love of pleasure, especially sex and drink; (2) his unfaithfulness to his wife; (3) his ready ability to lie, when doing so furthered his ends; (4) his adventurousness or attraction to taking risks; and (5) his apparent attachment to his power and self-image as a kind of "savior-father" of the Jews in his factory.

(1) Keneally portrays Schindler as a *bon vivant,* almost a libertine. He was a sensual man, and seemed entirely unashamed of his devotion to sex and the pleasures of food, drink, and fast cars. These features certainly do not sit well with a common understanding of what it is for someone to be "highly moral," or a "very moral person." For many persons the notion of "moral" excludes a full sensuality (or perhaps much sensuality at all), and especially excludes a valuing of sexual pleasure purely for its own sake, in no particular connection with marriage.[13]

As Alasdair MacIntyre and others have pointed out, the notion of "moral" encompasses several traditions of thought; and we are familiar with one which connects it intimately with sexual prohibitions.[14] I would suggest, however, that such a denial of sensuality and sexuality would be difficult to further justify in terms of the broader perspective of concern for human well-being characteristic of other traditions and elements within our honorific concept of "moral."

(2) Schindler's infidelity to his wife Emilie is another matter, though as Keneally describes it (and this aspect is not really much discussed in the book), Schindler's open sexuality was closely connected with his seeming lack of concern for sexual fidelity. It is difficult not to regard this as a moral deficiency in Schindler—it certainly appeared to cause his wife some degree of pain—though one would have to know more about the specific nature of Emilie and Oskar's relationship (as well as his relationships with his two mistresses in Poland) to know precisely how to assess it. There is no suggestion that Oskar mistreated Emilie, and it is relevant that they lived apart during Oskar's years in Poland, and that when Oskar returned to Germany in the final year of the war Emilie worked closely with him in his rescue activities.

This infidelity certainly renders Schindler less of a moral paragon than he would otherwise be; but he remains, I think, a moral hero.

(3) Schindler's lying and deception were integral to his project of saving Jews. He could succeed in the complex and risky project of inefficiently and wastefully employing more and more Jews and keeping them reasonably healthy and out of the clutches of the Nazis only by a deep and continually maintained deception that he was devoted to production for the war effort. When inspectors came to visit his factory "he would play the somber, baffled, manufacturer whose profits were being eroded."[15] Schindler was clearly aware of his ability to strike up relationships with all sorts of people and make them think him an affable fellow. He had to maintain a semblance of friendship with morally repulsive characters, such as Amon Goeth, the head of the local labor camp, who would shoot inmates at random. While all would agree that even paragons of honesty ought to lie to Nazis if this is necessary to save lives, only certain kinds of personalities could have pulled off the sort of vast and intimately maintained deception that Schindler did; and a person considered to be devoted to truthfulness would probably not have been one of this kind.[16]

It is significant, however, that there is no suggestion that Schindler was a generally dishonest or untrustworthy person, for example, in relationships with those he respected or from whom he needed nothing for his rescue efforts, nor that he enjoyed deception for its own sake (though he may have enjoyed deceiving the Nazis). Thus, while it might be that Schindler lacked the highest embodiments of the virtue of honesty, it would not be true to say that Schindler's lying and deception to the Nazis constitute a moral *deficiency,* and certainly not one which detracts from his moral heroism. What this indicates (contrary to a strong "unity of the virtues" view) is that not all virtues can be combined within one person in all situations, and that moral excellence does not require possession of every virtue; further, it suggests that there will be irreducibly different types of moral excellence.

(4) In his study of some Christian rescuers of Jews, Perry London finds a "spirit of adventurousness" in many of them;[17] one certainly sees this in Schindler. Such a spirit may draw some people to the risky activity of rescue of threatened persons or refugees (e.g., in the 'underground railroad' at the time of slavery, or currently [1987] in regard to sanctuary for Central American political refugees).

To assess this 'attraction to risk', we must distinguish between a person who gets positive gratification from risky activities, and one who does not but who is not so *averse* to such activities that she is unable to engage in them when she has a strong moral impulse to do so. Schindler certainly falls within the former category, but the distinction is important, since it might be a psychologically necessary condition of engaging in risky, long-term rescue operations that one not be too averse to taking risks, that one can accept risk. We can perhaps put this point by saying that one must have a "spirit of adventurousness" to *some degree* in order to exemplify that form of moral excellence.

Further, among those who, like Schindler, possess that spirit of adventurousness not minimally but more fully, one must distinguish between the spirit of adventurousness being motivationally *necessary* to get the rescuer to act, and it being an element of attraction of the endeavor but not actually necessary to get the rescuer to act. Yet this distinction begins to break down somewhat in regard to long-term activities such as Schindler's. Certainly his primary motives in *planning to undertake* rescue of Jews seemed entirely moral ones (concern for those Jews, belief that the Nazi policies were wrong); there is no suggestion that love of adventure or risk constituted a distinct, initial, direct motivation toward the activities in question. Nevertheless what motivates the initiating of a long-term project is different from the various motives which over time sustain the complex activities which constitute that project. Perhaps this can be put by saying that for Schindler the concern for Jews' lives was a necessary condition for his spirit of adventurousness playing a motivational role for him in sustaining his risky activities of rescue; without the former the latter would not have moved him toward rescue at all.

If this is right about Schindler, then his love of adventure seems to me not to be a moral deficiency, nor to detract from his being a moral hero. "Love of adventure" is not itself a morally *unworthy* motive, and if it is not playing an autonomous motivational role, then I suggest its presence should not be seen as a moral deficiency.

Accepting this, however, one might yet say that love of adventure is not itself a positively morally *worthy* motive; so Schindler represents a less 'pure' case of moral excellence than someone for whom moral projects are animated by purely moral motives. Such a purer case of moral excellence seems represented by Magda Trocme, described in Philip Hallie's book, *Lest Innocent Blood Be Shed.*[18] Magda was one of the two guiding spirits of an extraordinary rescue effort during the Nazi occupation of France. Under the leadership especially of Magda's husband André, the French Protestant village of Le Chambon sheltered thousands of refugees (mostly Jews) from the Nazis during the war years; Hallie claims that Le Chambon was the safest place for Jews in Europe. During that time Magda Trocme worked tirelessly in caring for the refugees who arrived at Le Chambon. She exhibited great courage and resourcefulness in finding shelter for them and helping to sustain the village's system of rescue; she fed them and took some into her own home. These were all very risky activities for her; yet there is no suggestion of a substantial attraction to risk itself such as was involved in Schindler's courage in facing similar risks.

At the same time Magda Trocme managed to hold together her family—her husband and four children—with love and understanding, and with attention to their individual needs, in the midst of the tension and danger occasioned by the rescue effort. Her husband Andrè thought of her thus, "Here is a person who cares for others on their own terms, not in order to parade her own virtues, but in order to keep them well. . . . She cared for others . . . both emotionally and in action" (64–65). There is no suggestion in Magda Trocme of any less than morally worthy motive, such as one sees in Schindler.

Magda Trocme does seem a more admirable character and a purer case of moral excellence than does Schindler. She combines the bringing about of a great good or the prevention of great evil, at risk to herself, performed from moral motives rooted deeply in her character, and with an absence of less than morally worthy motives. (Magda Trocme will be discussed further below.) But it does not follow from this that Schindler's love of adventure (in the particular role it played in his motivation) either disqualifies him from moral excellence (of the morally heroic sort), or constitutes an actual moral deficiency.

(5) Schindler's attitude toward his own role as the central figure in the rescue effort presents a more complex matter. Schindler was able to help the Jews who worked for him only because of his position of power, his contact with various German officials (locally and in the Armaments administration), and his ability to pull strings. While in itself this fact does not detract from his moral accomplishment, Schindler's attitude toward that power is significant. There is some suggestion at various places in the account of Schindler's life that he was a bit too taken with his role as savior of his Jews.

There are some parallels here to our discussion of the spirit of adventurousness. Schindler's attachment to his power is not an autonomously operating motive; it is only his power *as a helper* that he is attached to. So the concern to save the lives of Jews is a necessary condition for that motive to operate. Nevertheless there seems an important moral distinction between the two motives. For while love of risk or adventure seems morally neutral, attachment to power seems morally unworthy. Thus the degree of this motive's role in Schindler's motivational system seems a significant issue for determining his moral excellence.

A full treatment of this complex point is not possible here. Because of Schindler's unique situation, it is very difficult to discern the degree to which his desire that-Jews-be-saved-by-him corrupted his desire that-Jews-be-saved. But it is relevant to note that Schindler deeply respected several of the Jews with whom he worked closely in the financial and administrative end of the enamelware company; he was clearly aware of his reliance for the success of his projects on these Jews and their own virtues of courage, resourcefulness, and moral strength. Moreover, it seems significant that when the Allied armies finally gained control of the German territory where Schindler had moved his operations, roles were completely reversed, and Schindler became entirely dependent on the Jews to protect him from being killed or taken prisoner. While Keneally does not delve into Schindler's emotions at the time, Schindler did seem to accept this situation of dependency, and continued throughout the rest of his life to remain in personal and emotional contact with several of his former workers. These events suggest, though by no means conclusively, that Schindler's attachment to his sense of power over the Jews did not run nearly as deep as his concern for their welfare.

I claim, then, though acknowledging uncertainty about this, that Schindler meets the five criteria for the moral hero: (1) bringing about a great good (or preventing a great evil); (2) acting to a great extent from morally worthy motives; (3) substantial embeddedness of those motives in the agent's psychology; (4) carrying out one's moral project in the face of risk or danger; and (5) relative "faultlessness," or absence of unworthy desires, dispositions, sentiments, attitudes.

MURDOCHIAN MORAL EXEMPLARS

We have no trouble seeing Magda Trocme and (though perhaps to a lesser extent) Oskar Schindler as living morally worthy lives, as being extraordinarily admirable. And yet there exists a very different picture of the moral exemplar in the history of moral thought. This is a picture articulated, though somewhat sketchily, in Iris Murdoch's writings, including her novels but especially the philosophical essays in *The Sovereignty of Good*. It is a picture of the good, humble, selfless person, an inheritor of a familiar Christian conception, and one perhaps closer to what people mean when they refer to "saints," taking this term in a not necessarily directly religious sense, and yet a sense strongly influenced by that religious heritage.

An example of the Murdochian paragon can be drawn (with one significant variation, which will be discussed below, note 26) from the character of Ed Corcoran in Mary Gordan's *Men and Angels*.[19] Ed has a young son and a wife with a terrible disease, contracted during her pregnancy with their son, which has distorted her body, made her generally unable to take proper care of herself, and unbalanced her mentally. Rose Corcoran says horribly embarrassing and hurtful things in front of other people; she is evidently a terrible trial to live with; yet Ed seems to care for her without resentment or bitterness, yet also without illusion. Rather than dwelling on how terrible her condition is, Ed chooses to view her in relation to the progress she has made since an earlier time, when for example she could not even walk. Ed's admirable character is shown also in his relationship with his son, for whom he is the primary parent and whom he takes with him when he does electrical work in people's houses. Ed has managed through his love and understanding of his wife and his child to shield the boy, at least to some extent, from his mother's terrible behavior and to help him to be reasonably happy. Ed treats other people too (though in the book one sees only the people he works for) with kindness and respect. He is generous and warm-hearted, where one might have expected bitterness, resentment, and envy. He is responsible and conscientious. He leads an admirable life in the face of a great tribulation. He exemplifies many significant virtues and appears to lack what Murdoch calls "the avaricious tentacles of the self": self-pity, envy, overconcern with the opinion of others, self-absorption, concern for power.

In contrast to the moral hero, the Murdochian moral exemplar is not necessarily engaged in a "moral project," a bringing about of great good or preventing a great evil. That there can be this sort of moral excellence is especially significant in light of Susan Wolf's portrayal of what she calls the 'moral saint'. Wolf gives two different descriptions of that figure—first, that the person has the virtues or excellences of character to an extraordinary degree; and second, that the person is devoted to maximizing the good of others or of society. It is the second of these descriptions—maximizing overall good—which in fact plays the larger role in Wolf's argument, though she implies that the two descriptions correspond. But as Robert Adams points out in his reply to Wolf,[20] these two descriptions are by no means identical. A person who has the virtues to an extraordinary extent is not necessarily someone devoted to doing good (much less to *maximizing* the amount of good in the world). The converse is true as well; as the example of Schindler shows, a person sincerely devoted to a moral, good-producing project can well lack certain important virtues.

(From this point on I will, for stylistic reasons, sometimes refer to the Murdochian paragon as the "saint," attempting to use this concept without its religious overtones, without the connotations of self-sacrifice which it often carries in common parlance, and also as distinct from Wolf's characterization, especially those aspects connected with Kantianism and utilitarianism.)

The moral saint and the moral hero share three features in common—they are animated by morally worthy motives, their morally excellent qualities exist at a deep level of their personality or character, and they meet the standard of relative absence of unworthy desires.

But there is another difference between them besides the absence of "moral project" in the Murdochian paragon: the standard of "absence of unworthy states of consciousness" is more stringent for her than for the moral hero. In a sense the moral project of the moral hero can be seen (as in the case of Schindler) as counterbalancing a somewhat less-than-pure consciousness. For the saint, by contrast, it is precisely the higher standard of faultlessness which is salient, though this does not mean that the moral saint is to be pictured as, so to speak, spiritually excellent but remote from engagement with the world of action. Part of severing this notion of saint from its religious roots is to ensure that the sense of excellent motivation and excellent form of moral consciousness in the Murdochian paragon not be seen on the model of a purely inner spiritual purity, but that it precisely concern the way one acts within the world of other persons. It is the greater absence of unworthy or suspect elements of consciousness, not a greater remoteness from the world, which distinguishes the saint from the hero.

So far I have discussed the moral hero and the moral saint as if they were entirely parallel types of moral exemplar. But there is an important disanalogy between them, though the difference is perhaps only one of degree. To call someone a moral hero is not necessarily to refer to more than a specific, time-limited (though necessarily substantial) slice of her life. Thus (as we will discuss further below) Schindler's heroism lasted only the length of the war. He did not seem to continue being "morally excellent" after that. The notion of moral heroism allows for that time limitation; the notion of moral saint, or Murdochian paragon, does not. A person cannot be a Murdochian paragon for three or four years, reverting then to moral mediocrity. While the moral commitments and relatively faultless motivation characteristic of the moral hero must also be deeply rooted, they do not need to be *as* deeply rooted in the moral hero's character as in the Murdochian paragon's. The Murdochian paragon must be more resistant to change. If someone who appears to be a 'saint' begins to act, and continues to do so, in a morally non-excellent manner, this generally indicates that we were wrong to think her a saint in the first place.

But this does not mean that the Murdochian paragon's character must be *totally* resistant to change or undermining. In very extraordinary situations, under extreme sorts of pressures, a person who is good can become mediocre, or even bad, without this showing that she was never really good in the first place. Where to draw this line is a difficult matter, and little can be said about it in general; hence distinguishing cases of change of character from variations within the same character will be a difficult task.[21]

The positive features of the saint and hero can be combined in one individual. Magda Trocme appears to exemplify someone who meets the Murdochian's standard of faultlessness, yet who also brings about a great good. Obviously such a person is rarer than either of the single types alone.

The absence of a single picture of the moral exemplar may in part be a reflection of the different traditions of moral thought mentioned earlier. According to ordinary usage it may even be more natural to see the Murdochian paragon than the moral hero as "very moral" or "morally virtuous." It would be intelligible to say that Ed Corcoran was a "better person" than Oskar Schindler. Certainly a recognizable tradition within our own thinking does in fact connect the term "moral" more closely with an excellence and purity of inner motivational state than with the bringing about of good. In a certain sense this is a point on which the Kantian emphasis on inner motivation comes together with the Aristotelian emphasis on individual character, virtue, and motivational state, despite their differences in other important respects. Both contrast with a tradition such as the utilitarian which, while requiring appropriate motivation in its assessment of character, connects moral excellence more closely with the production of good. Schindler's form of moral excellence might more naturally be expressed by saying that his *life* exemplifies moral excellence, or that he led a *morally exemplary life,* than by locutions (such as "morally virtuous") which emphasize *state of character,* and apply more naturally to the moral saint.

Apart from these considerations, is there more to be said about whether we should attach more value to the moral saint or to the moral hero? There is one popular tradition of thought ("charity begins at home") which would aver that virtue in one's personal and domestic life is more fundamental than concern for those unrelated to oneself; this tradition might, for that reason, accord greater moral merit to Ed Corcoran than, say, to Schindler. But the overly privatized vision of morality expressed in that sentiment may itself be a socially and historically limited one; a society and moral culture in which (unlike our own) concern with the wider communities of city, nation, and humanity in general are seen as fundamental to a morally responsible life would reject such a prioritizing of the 'private' to the 'public' (which is not to say that it would *reverse* that prioritizing).

In light of this argument, can one say that the more privatized moral saint (such as Ed Corcoran) cannot be morally exemplary if, while generous, loving, courageous, and understanding toward those close to him, evinces no concern for wider communities of persons? Both Bishop Butler and J. S. Mill appear to vindicate, if not actually to justify, the more limited scope of moral concern, by saying that many, even most, people are never or virtually never in a position to take the public good as their province.[23] But modern civilization has undercut the support for that position; there are now ways for most individuals to have an impact on their wider communities, and even on the world as a whole, unimagined in the periods when those philosophers lived.

At the same time, it would be going too far in the other direction to say that a person who evinces no concern for the wider community cannot be a moral exemplar. Whether some such individual can be depends very much on the particular circumstances, the degree of exposure of the individual to the concerns of the wider community, the ethos of the person's own community, and the like.[24] But I think we have to allow that often we properly do have great admiration for the Ed Corcorans of the world, and regard them as moral exemplars.

Thus, both moral heroes and Murdochian moral paragons seem to be exceptionally admirable and exemplary persons, and are so in a way recognizably 'moral'— as opposed, say, to exemplifying non-moral excellences, such as artistic talent, personal charm, athletic ability, physical beauty, theoretical intelligence.[25] Both involve morally excellent motivation as well as good action in the world; but the differences between them may reflect an irresolvable difference in understandings of notions of morality or different interests involved in what it is to assess someone as 'morally excellent'.

RISK AND ADVERSITY

I have described the Murdochian exemplar without mentioning the element of "risk," which was central to the merit of the moral hero. Urmson distinguished a "saint" from a "hero" in that the former performed great morally worthy actions at great *cost* or *sacrifice* to himself, while the latter performed these actions in the face of *danger* or *risk* to himself. Urmson was correct to link our idea of 'heroism' to danger and risk, and to distinguish it from another kind of moral excellence which did not involve these elements. But was Urmson correct to see 'cost' or 'sacrifice' playing an analogous role in the saint? Certainly the adversity constituted by Ed Corcoran's wife's illness, and Corcoran's ability to live with this honorably, is an important element in the exceptional merit which we see in Corcoran's character and life.

But while adversity in the saint's life can play an analogous role to risk in the moral hero's, adversity cannot be identified with sacrifice and cost. 'Sacrifice' and 'cost' are concepts to a significant degree (though by no means entirely) internal to or relative to a particular person's conception of value in his or her life; this is much less true for adversity and risk. While there can be no doubt that Ed Corcoran's wife's illness constitutes 'adversity' for him, Ed's own sense of identity and value may well be so bound up with his marriage to her, with his sense of the value of marriage and faithfulness, and with his family, that the notion of Ed's sacrificing himself for his wife, or the marriage involving a 'cost' to him, seems not the best way of expressing the fact that there are possible goods in life which Ed cannot pursue because of this marriage.[26]

Thus, contrary to Urmson, 'cost' and 'sacrifice' do not play the same role with regard to saints (Murdochian paragons) as risk and danger do with regard to heroes. But in addition, while the one example we have given of the Murdochian paragon (Ed Corcoran) does involve adversity, and while that adversity is part of its moral excellence, in fact confronting adversity can by no means be seen as a *requirement* of this form of moral excellence. A person's motivational system can be built around morally worthy motives without her really facing any siginficant adversity. A person can be exceptionally generous, caring, honest, and kind in the absence of adversity. (However some virtues—such as courage—seem by definition to require adversity.) This does not mean that such a person would never face some kind of temptation to act contrary to those virtues—that situation is unimaginable. But conflicts from various personal interests or inclinations are not the same as genuine adversity, and in fact many persons' lives, including Murdochian paragons, can be fortunately spared adversity such as Ed Corcoran's.

Something analogous is true of risk as well. A person can exhibit the form of moral excellence (to which we have not given a name) which is like moral heroism but without the element of facing risks. A person can have the required depth of moral commitment to a moral project, act from worthy motives, and have the requisite degree of absence of unworthy ones, without facing serious risks or adversity. This is very nicely illustrated in John Berger's *A Fortunate Man,*[27] a non-fiction account of a doctor, John Sassall, who chooses to establish a medical practice in a poor remote village in the north of England. Sassall is acutely aware that the villagers have few resources to develop themselves, and his choice of where to set up his practice stems importantly from an ideal of "service" to the needy villagers. At first he is attracted by the excitement of emergency medicine (and is somewhat impatient with patients presenting lesser complaints) and by its sense of concrete accomplishment. But gradually Sassall comes to realize that in order to attend fully to the health of the villagers, he must understand them as whole human beings, beyond their "medical condition" narrowly defined, and must expand—one might say "morally expand"— his sense of what it means to be a doctor in that village. Berger describes how Sassall comes to care for the villagers in a fuller way than the ideal of "service," admirable as that is.

While occasionally frustrated and despondent at what he is unable to do to make the lives of the villagers better, Sassall retains a belief in the worth of each life he tends. He emerges from the book an excellent man (at least in relation to the villagers—Berger does not deal with his family life at all), exemplifying many virtues, and bringing great benefit to his patients and to the village in general. And we learn how Sassall came to develop his greater depth of moral character in the process of his work. We can think of Sassall as (or as close to being) a moral exemplar (though neither a hero nor a saint).

Yet the burden of the title of the book—"a fortunate man"— is that Sassall is a man for whom life has worked out very well. In contrast to most of the people in the village, he has had options and has ended up with what he knows that he values; and he lacks few goods that he genuinely wants. He is part of a community within which he has an honored and meaningful place. In contrast to Schindler, Magda Trocme, and Ed Corcoran, Sassall does not face serious risks, danger, or adversity; in a straightforward sense he has much more in the way of well-being than they. Yet like them he is morally excellent.

Thus it is possible for morally excellent qualities to exist and inform a good part of a life, yet without being tested in the face of grave adversity or risk. This is not to deny that we may feel of some persons that their lives have been too sheltered to count them as exceptionally virtuous, even though they give evidence of being so. And there may be persons of whom we think that if they *did* face certain moral challenges they would be unable to meet them, and that this counts against saying, now, that they are exceptionally good persons. Nevertheless, it cannot be a *general* test of the attribution of virtue, or of exceptional virtue, that one be confident that it not weaken in the face of various situations the person has not faced and is not likely ever to face. This is partly because, as I have tried to indicate, there are different kinds of moral excellences; and while it is unlikely that Schindler would have maintained the virtue of an Ed Corcoran in the sort of situation Ed faced, this does not count against Schindler's being himself morally excellent.[28]

"IDEALIST" AND "RESPONDER"

Another distinction among moral exemplars, which cuts across that of hero and Murdochian paragon, I will call "responder" and "idealist"; as in the case of saint and hero the difference may not be a sharp one, and is also not meant to be exhaustive. The idealist is someone who consciously adopts general moral values and principles, ones which, from the outside, can be regarded as high or demanding moral standards (though they need not be seen that way by the idealist herself); she then goes about attempting to live up to these ideals, and searches for ways to implement them. To be an idealist, the agent must see these ideals as more than merely personal goals or a personal conception of the good. They must be formulated as general values, and regarded by the agent as having some kind of intrinsic worth or general validity.

The idealist must in some way believe that it is *possible* for her ideals to be implemented in the world, or at least possible for the world to be made to correspond substantially *more* to these ideals than it does currently. Thus the idealist is characterized by a quality of hopefulness. A person who guided her life by general and honorable values but did not really believe that the world could in any significant way be brought more into line with these values would not be an 'idealist' (though she might be admirable, and even a moral exemplar). The idealist's life has a quality of conscious self-creation and self-direction; the idealist chooses her ideals and explicitly guides her life according to them.

Even assuming that the idealist meets other requirements of moral exemplariness, an idealist as so far defined is not necessarily a moral exemplar. Only a successful idealist—one who truly lives her ideals—is a moral exemplar. But there can be persons who genuinely hold worthy ideals and (what is not the same thing) attempt conscientiously to live up to them, but who do not succeed in doing so. Such persons may be in some ways admirable, but they are not moral exemplars (or anyway, not the sort of moral exemplars I mean by 'idealist').

A fine example of an idealist moral exemplar is André Trocme, Magda's husband and the pastor of the village of Le Chambon. Prior to his arrival in Le Chambon, André came to develop, adopt, and live out a moral outlook centered on the principles of resistance to evil, of non-violence, and of the cherishing of each individual human life. In his years at Le Chambon, André continually looked for ways to implement these ideals. He wanted to go beyond helping refugees who happened to arrive in the town, conceived of turning the village into a haven for refugees, and organized the town in this endeavor. This rescue effort manifested André Trocme's ideals; it was a form of resistance to the Nazi evil which, in contrast say to the armed resistance (with whom André had an uneasy relationship), could remain non-violent; and it involved the cherishing of refugee and other lives through sheltering them from likely death.

In contrast to the idealist, the 'responder' moral exemplar does not, prior to confronting the situations in which she manifests her moral excellence, possess a set of moral principles which she has worked out explicitly, committed herself to, and attempted to guide her life by. Nevertheless the responder responds to the situations she faces and to individual persons in a morally excellent way. While the idealist is concerned to ensure that her behavior meet a predetermined standard or principle (which does not, however, require that she consult the principle on every occasion), the responder just, as it were, *does* the morally good thing, without having the further project of ensuring that she live up to specific standards.

This does not mean, however, that the responder acts impulsively, irrationally, inconstantly, or unreliably. His or her behavior manifests a perceptive understanding of particular situations. Consistency of moral behavior is no less correlated with responderness than with idealism.[29] To be *morally excellent,* both idealists and responders must act from dispositions, sentiments, and traits of character which lie at a fairly deep level of their psychological economy.

Schindler illustrates the 'responder'. His awakening to the plight of the Jews was wholly surprising and (morally) unprepared for. In the 1930s Schindler seemed entirely morally unexceptional, and for a time even flirted with the Nazi party, though not from any firm convictions but simply because it was opportune to do so. While, prior to his coming to Poland, Schindler had already become leery of Nazism, he gave no evidence of seeking to resist it, or of trying to do anything morally good with his own life. He sought only to wait out the Nazi period and make a fortune in some business venture.

But when Schindler came to see what was happening to the Jews in Poland—

the seizure of property, the raids, then the ghettos, then the round-ups for the camps—he *responded* to the situation. As related earlier, he showed exceptional powers of perceptiveness and imagination in figuring out how to shelter substantial numbers of Jewish workers. Nothing in Schindler's previous life would have led one to expect this from him.

Schindler *never* really formulated an explicit moral outlook to anything like the extent that someone like André Trocme did. To be sure, he was engaged in a project which he took to be a moral one—saving particular Jews. But a personal commitment to aid specific persons does not constitute an "ideal," which must be formulated as a general value. Moreover, it was only gradually, toward the end of the war, that Schindler even came to expand his moral horizons to include Jews he did not know (or about whom he was not personally informed). Yet even then this value ('saving Jews from the Nazis', not just saving a particular group of Jews) did not seem to be held by Schindler in the form of a general guiding principle; his own actions continued to be governed more by responding to opportunities to rescue particular Jews he knew of than to a sense of living up to a general principle of saving Jews. (Even if it had functioned as an explicit guide to action might, it is not clear that 'saving Jews from Nazis' is a goal at a sufficient level of value generality to count as an ideal in the relevant sense; it would not, for example, carry Schindler beyond the period, which he and others knew was coming, of the end of the Nazi era. [However, to say all this is not to make a conclusive judgment about how morally worthy it is to be devoted to that less-than-idealist goal compared to being dedicated to an ideal.])

The contrast between Schindler's and André Trocme's lives after the war is instructive in regard to the contrast between responder and idealist. André continued to work for the ideals of non-violence, becoming the European secretary of the Fellowship of Reconciliation, an international organization devoted to non-violence.[30] Schindler, by contrast, led a relatively morally unexceptional life, attempting several unsuccessful commercial ventures but never finding a place for himself. His experience during the war had undermined a comfortable relationship to Germany and to the values of his youth, but had not replaced them in the depths of Schindler's character with a set of higher values—much less ones explicitly articulated as ideals—capable of carrying Schindler into the post-war situation and providing him with some purpose in life. (His case is quite distinct from that of someone who once had ideals but then lost them.) Schindler's moral excellence remained localized to the particular situation of the war.

Magda Trocme, though less so than Schindler, was more of a "responder" than an "idealist." She intentionally shunned her husband André's somewhat grand and sometimes grandiose ideas and ideals (especially their religiously inspired aspect). She responded to people individually and in terms of their particular need. She did not come morally armed with a worked out set of general ideals which she searched for ways to implement. Looking back on the Le Chambon period Magda expressed what, in retrospect, she thought herself to have been like at the time, and how to characterize her involvement in the rescue effort: "I try not to hunt around to find things to do. I do not hunt around to find people to help. But I never close my door, never refuse to help somebody who comes to me and asks for something" (152–53). André

Trocme understood his actions as instantiating his formulated ideals; by contrast Magda understood her actions in terms of helping the particular refugee who presented himself at her door.[31]

Though both responders, Magda differed from Schindler in important ways. Magda had a clearer and more consistent moral self-identity than did Schindler. The traits of character (compassion, caring, courage, understanding of individual needs) which constituted her form of responsiveness were more deeply rooted in her character than were Schindler's morally heroic traits within his. (This is one reason why Magda is a Murdochian paragon as well as a moral hero, while Schindler is only a hero.)

But doesn't Magda's self-characterization ("I never close my door," etc.) represent a kind of 'ideal' of behavior? To this suggestion two things can be said. First, Magda's having given this formulation retrospectively does not mean that the value expressed in it played a role in *guiding* her actions at the time. The later formulation might rather be seen as a kind of in-retrospect summary of what Magda did at the time, rather than a general rule or value which she sought to ensure that she lived up to.

Second, even if we take Magda's self-characterization to reflect how she did think of herself at the time (during the war), the characterization is meant by her precisely to distinguish her own morality from the "morality of ideals" of her husband. In order to function *as* ideals, and as guides to action, ideals (such as André's: 'cherish every human life') must be formulated at a level of abstraction somewhat removed from the concrete particularity of individual situations; moreover, they necessarily speak to only some aspects of the full moral reality of individual situations. Both of these features allow for a gap between an attachment to an ideal, and a full moral response to a situation. Magda perceived this gap in André. She felt that his ideals often threatened to make him lose touch with particular individuals and their perhaps mundane needs, for food, for a coat.[32]

It is not that Magda chose a moral outlook specifically to correct for what she saw as the deficiencies in André's. Rather it seems clear that she was already very much someone who cared about individual persons, who felt a responsibility toward individuals who crossed her path. These dispositions were deep within her character, and for herself she was not particularly drawn to formulating them as general values to guide her, nor did she need to do so. However, an awareness of the potential limitations of André's particular form of moral goodness made Magda more aware of the differences between his mode or moral being and hers. Without the interaction with him, she may never have formulated, even to the extent she did, the self-characterization given retrospectively to Hallie. The following continuation of the quote from Magda cited above is revealing:

> When things happen, not things I plan, but things sent by God or by chance, when people come to my door, I feel responsible. During André's life during the war many many people came, and my life was therefore complicated. (153)

Magda is not a case of a pure responder; but this passage contains hints of what a pure responder's mode in this situation would be: A refugee shows up at her door, and she helps him. But she does not think about what she would do if another refugee shows up. Then another refugee does show up, and she helps her too. But she still does not formulate any general intention, or principle, of helping refugees. Perhaps each time she thinks there will be no more, or perhaps she just does not think one way or the other about it. But she continues to help each refugee who comes across her path.[33]

Magda and André Trocmé were morally complementary. Magda's responder's grounding in the concrete present helped to keep André's ideals more in touch with reality. At the same time this very rootedness in the concrete present can have its own limitations.[34] It is not an accident that it was André's moral vision and long-term perspective, rather than Magda's outlook, which led to the plan of organizing Le Chambon as a haven of refuge. Some moral situations require a degree of distancing from the situation at hand, which the idealist may be in a better position to deal with than the responder. Better than either would be some kind of synthesis—an extremely difficult one to achieve—of the positive features of both the idealist and the responder. But is is nevertheless significant that either moral type by itself can exemplify moral excellence. (And it is also possible for someone who is one to become the other.)

As mentioned earlier, the distinction between idealist and responder cuts across that of saint, or Murdochian exemplar, and hero. André Trocmé is an idealist hero (and, perhaps, a saint as well); Schindler is a responder hero, Magda Trocme a responder saint-hero. And a Murdochian exemplar could be either a responder or an idealist. In some way perhaps the Murdochian paragon has more affinities with the responder than with the idealist—this is certainly so in Murdoch's own account, in which the paragon is understood as "responding to individual reality." However, idealism and Murdochian excellence are not really incompatable either. For one can hold explicit and idealistic values but seek to apply them in only a limited realm. Someone might, for example, hold as a general ideal that one should love one's neighbor, but apply this value only to those with whom one comes in personal contact rather than seeing it as encompassing all of humanity.

It is noteworthy, however, that Ed Corcoran, the Murdochian exemplar, is *not* an idealist in this 'limited realm' sense. His loyalty to his wife, his generous spirit, and his exceptional family love and understanding are not (as I am conceiving him) a reflection or application of general ideals. He is not being portrayed as someone dedicated to the ideal of greater marital fidelity and/or love of neighbor, seeing his own actions as contributing to realizing these ideals. He is, I think, better seen as operating with some purely personal values (of fidelity, etc.) which give moral substance to his life, but which he does not formulate as general and 'objective' values.

CRITIQUE OF WOLF

The intent of my typology of moral exemplars is primarily a constructive one, to begin to map out a psychology of moral excellence; but it can also help to indicate (though I can do so here only briefly) some limitations of some previous influential attempts at a moral psychology of moral excellence. In particular one can see that three characterizations given of the "moral saint" by Susan Wolf, and not challenged by Robert Adams in his partial critique of Wolf, do not apply to all instances of moral exemplars.[35] These characterizations are (1) the moral exemplar as striving to maximize the good; (2) the moral exemplar as striving after moral perfection; (3) the moral exemplar as denigrating the pursuits of others.

We have already seen that the Murdochian paragon cannot be characterized as striving to maximize the good, since, for one thing, she is not characterized in terms of undertaking to realize specific goals, or a 'moral project'. The point can also be seen in relation to the responder (hero or saint). Even if the responder's excellence can be characterized in terms of attention to the needs of particular persons (as Magda's, for example, can be), in seeking the well-being of particular persons the responder does nothing like seek a *maximizing* of the good. As described, Magda's helping particular individuals is not seen by her, even implicitly, as a way of bringing about the most overall good that she can (though perhaps what she does may *be* virtually the most good that she could do).

Though perhaps less obviously so than the responder and the Murdochian paragon, neither does the idealist fit the characterization of 'striving to maximize the good'. He comes *closer* to doing so in that, in contrast to the responder, his way of being is characterized by explicitly striving to realize certain goals which are seen (by him) as good. The idealist-hero (André Trocme for example) does aim to promote what is in fact a great good, and this is an important element in his moral excellence. But this is a far cry from striving to *maximize* good. The idealist's goals are importantly more particular than this. André sees the rescue of refugees as a project at the intersection of his three moral ideals—non-violence, resistance to evil, and cherishing of each individual life—and it is this feature which grounds its hold on him. He does not necessarily see this project as a way to maximize the good.[36]

Nor can moral exemplars be characterized generally as seeking moral perfection. This is especially evident with regard to responders, whose moral excellence is not characterized by the explicit seeking of any distinct set of moral goals; in particular it does not involve taking as a goal a morally characterized state of themselves.

The characterization "striving for moral perfection" might seem better to fit the idealist, who does attempt to guide his actions by explicit moral ideals. However even here Wolf's characterization does not do justice. Striving to implement ideals cannot be identified with striving for perfection. For one thing, if the notion of "perfection" here is meant to imply that every moment of life be thought of as in some way needing to contribute to one's goal (if only as necessary preparation for the effort required, and the like), then, as Adams points out, those whom he might actually regard as saints (e.g., Albert Schweitzer), do not do this; they give some time to purely personal pleasures and pursuits not seen as having moral import whatsoever. And yet we do not see this as detracting from characterizing them as saints;[37] and the same point holds for moral exemplars.

Further, the ideals which the idealist strives for are not necessarily, or typically, seen by himself as exceptionally high, heroic, or perfection-grounding moral standards. To the idealist these standards can and often do seem merely 'right' or necessary, even in a sense ordinary. To André Trocme the ideals of love, non-violence, and

resistance to evil seemed not exceptional or exceptionally demanding ones but necessary and proper concerns in the light of his own experience. The moral exemplar (of
either responder or idealist type) does not typically regard himself *as* a moral exemplar; and in fact there seems an inherent contradiction, or at least a tension, in doing
so, for one is then in danger of the pride, self-aggrandizement, and a sense of superiority, which detract from moral excellence. Hallie's respondents in the village of Le
Chambon, and especially Magda, to whom he spoke while researching his book,
emphasize—and Hallie documents this point throughout the book—that helping the
refugees seemed to them *not* extraordinary or worthy of exceptional praise, but rather
something entirely ordinary. The villagers were greatly perplexed at the notion that
there was anything particularly worthy of note, much less of extraordinary praise, in
sheltering persons whose lives were in danger.[38]

But the Trocmes' own rejection of moral exemplariness as applying to themselves does not detract from the appropriateness of that attribution. Rather it points
to a lack of connection between *regarding* oneself as morally excellent and *being* morally excellent.

I would like, finally, to address the charge that the moral exemplar is self-
righteous and judgmental toward others less morally virtuous. Wolf implies that
because the moral exemplar holds herself to such a high standard of morality, she will
make others feel that they are being judged as wanting, that the exemplar believes that
their less morally impressive pursuits lack value.[39]

But what one may feel in the face of the moral exemplar is a different issue from
whether the moral exemplar is actually judging one negatively. On the former point,
it may well be true that in the presence of a moral exemplar one may come to feel that
one has been caught up in less valuable and significant endeavors than one might be,
or that one has been more self-absorbed and insensitive than one needs to be. And it
may also be true that, because of this, some will steer clear of the exemplars in their
vicinity, in order to avoid having such matters brought to their attention. It is not evident, however, what kind of objection it is to moral exemplariness that we may not
wish to be reminded of our own moral shortcomings and mediocrity. Certainly this
does not render the moral exemplar in some way inherently unattractive or defective,
as Wolf implies.

In any case moral discomfort is not the only effect moral exemplars can have on
others, as we can see by considering the matter of self-righteousness, a genuine charge
of deficiency in the moral exemplar.[40] Here the thought is that the moral exemplar
means to have the effect on others which we acknowledged above that she may in fact
have.

In this regard it is striking that the moral exemplars I have discussed here have
not possessed these deficiencies. André Trocme, in particular, seemed to have quite
an opposite effect on other people. He was able to reveal to them and to encourage
them to develop their own capacities for a stronger moral goodness. He made people
feel that he was indebted to them for whatever they were able to do. A truly morally
excellent person is more likely to have the generosity of spirit and 'love' of others
which is able simultaneously to accept others for what they are, not to make them feel
condemned for how they choose to live, yet also to spur them to their best efforts.[41]

Self-righteousness is a serious moral deficiency, involving a sense of moral superiority to others and often accompanied by contempt; a truly morally excellent person does not possess it.[42]

The thought that someone whose life embodies an exceptionally high moral standard must necessarily think ill of others who *fail* to live up to that standard stems perhaps partly from an overemphasis on moral universality—the Kantian thought that what is right for the agent must be, and must be thought by him to be, right for everyone else. In fact moral exemplars are no more likely, and may even be less likely, to think of their own standards and commitments as setting a standard for, or for assessing, others. That a moral idealist devotes himself to a goal which he regards as not merely personal but as expressing some intrinsic good is a far cry from his thinking that everyone else must or ought to do so as well, and for thinking ill of them for failing to do so.[43]

It may well be that a person lacking in virtue or any pretension to it is less likely than someone of genuine moral standards even to be tempted to apply such standards to others. But this temptation is in any case less likely to arise in someone possessing the virtue of 'acceptance with understanding' than, as suggested above, in the person who is insecure regarding her virtue. Self-righteousness can be found in the morally mediocre as well as in those of somewhat more moral substance.

EMULATING MORAL EXEMPLARS

Inquiring about the appropriate attitude moral exemplars take toward others raises the natural question of the extent to which moral exemplars provide appropriate models of aspiration and emulation for others. There are several questions here. I hope that my descriptions of the moral exemplars discussed in this paper has exhibited them to be appropriate objects of an all-things-considered *admiration;* to do so has been an important part of my task in countering Wolf's suggestion that they might well not be.

This admiration might naturally, though not with conceptual necessity, incline some to wish to be like the moral exemplar. It is important to accept that for most persons this could not be accomplished, no matter how conscientiously one set oneself to become anything like the moral paragons one admires. In this sense moral excellence is not within the scope of the will, of choice; it is a dimension of morality which is not simply 'up to us'.

This may be particularly evident in the case of those exemplars who functioned in what might appropriately be thought extreme circumstances, such as the Nazi terror. Qualities needed for moral excellence in such circumstances may be very different from those needed in more ordinary ones. And those who are excellent in one setting may not easily be so in others. Oskar Schindler's wife Emilie, interviewed after his death, perceptively and poignantly said of Oskar: "He was fortunate, therefore, that in the short fierce era between 1939 and 1945 he had met people who summoned forth his deeper talent" (Keneally, 397).

That moral excellence may often be tied to particular circumstances is, then, a matter of what Bernard Williams and others have called "moral luck" (though Williams does not use the concept in this particular connection). But the specialness of the circumstances in which Schindler and the Trocmes operated should not be overstated either. There is surely enough oppression, horror, injustice, and just plain pain and suffering in our world to render that difference in circumstances at best one of degree (which is not to minimize that degree). Some people experience an urgency about addressing various of these ills of our own world which is comparable to the Trocmes' and Schindler's about saving the lives of Jews; and it is not certain that they are wrong to do so.

In addition to the dependence of some sorts of virtue on circumstances, there are other kinds of moral luck in operation here as well. It is simply not within our power to bring about in ourselves the psychological make-up constituting moral excellence. We cannot get to be courageous, compassionate, principled, kind, loving, or honest—much less some very difficult to achieve combination of these virtues required for excellence—merely by trying to do so, nor by any other method; nor can we similarly rid ourselves of various unworthy desires, sentiments, and dispositions.

What might seem open to all, however, is to adopt certain ideals, and thus to strive directly to be an idealist. This is in a way true and will be considered further in a moment. But while one can *try* to adopt ideals, one cannot ensure success in doing so; sincerely *professing* ideals is not equivalent to adopting them. Moreover (a different point) even if one succeeds in genuinely adopting ideals, one cannot ensure that one comes fully to *live* them, in the way required for moral excellence. Finally, one surely cannot by effort alone, or in any other way, simply bring it about that those ideals become deeply rooted in one's character in the way required for true moral excellence.

I wish to emphasize these limitations on the extent to which everyone, or even everyone who wanted to, could become a moral exemplar, in order to counter views of morality which tie it too closely to the will and to universal accessibility. I also wish to bring out the distance between admiring something and being able to take it as a direct model for one's own action or life.

Yet this is all meant only to clear the way for a realistic picture of what *can* be learned from moral exemplars which *can* affect one's own values and mode of life, and of how emulating them can be a force for one's own moral growth. I have argued only that it is given to very few to *be* moral exemplars. Yet, for one thing, as the example of Schindler shows, we do not always know who those potential moral exemplars are. Robert Adams is no doubt right when he says, "In all probability there could be more Gandhis than there are, and it would be a very good thing if there were."[44]

Moreover, though most of us could not become moral exemplars, we can all learn something from them—something about what is really of value in life. As Philippa Foot says, "It makes good sense to say that most men waste a lot of their lives in pursuit of what is trivial and unimportant."[45] And this formulation accords with Iris Murdoch's characterization of moral excellence in terms of seeing the right relationship and priority between different human values.

While we cannot all be moral exemplars, what we all can be is *better* than we are. For each of us there are surely *some* virtues which we could come to possess in greater degree than we now do, no matter what circumstances we are in. The existence of moral exemplars can help to keep this possibility alive for us, and in some cases to point the way to particular directions we might take in our own moral improvement.

The standard focus of moral theory on choice situations particularly ill-suits what is to be learned from a discussion of moral paragons. The task of moral improvement, of changing our character for the better, cannot be understood if every individual is thought of as faced with an array of options of modes of life and character, among which he or she must choose. Genuine moral change is much more individualized and particular, and much more limited in its possible goals, than that picture suggests.

Returning to Wolf, I have not here disputed that there might be such figures as the Kantian or the utilitarian moral paragon. But it is noteworthy that the types of moral exemplar discussed here, and the individuals I have used to exemplify them, do not correspond to Wolf's portrayal of either of these types. They are not characterized by the continual adoption of an impersonal and universal view on the world, by a striving for maximal good, or for personal moral perfection. So at least many actual moral exemplars are not properly understood in terms of a moral psychology built upon such conceptions of 'the moral'.

Finally, perhaps the very disjunction between the moral exemplars I have discussed and Wolf's conception of the moral saint means that in a sense my argument is irrelevant to hers. Perhaps Wolf's criticisms should be taken to be aimed only at the particular kind of Kantian and utilitarian moral exemplars she describes. Yet clearly Wolf wants in addition to cast some aspersions on the higher reaches of morality in general, and to suggest reasons why we need not be as concerned about morality as some (myself among them) would want us to be. Despite the skeptical eye that some first-rate contemporary philosophers have turned on morality, I myself have never been fully able to shake the conviction that Iris Murdoch is right when she suggests that moral goodness is properly regarded as the central value in a human life, and that the questions, "What is a good man like? How can we make ourselves morally better? *Can* we make ourselves morally better?"[46] should be one of, or even *the,* central preoccupations of moral philosophy. I hope this paper has been a beginning of an answer to them.[47]

Notes

1. Iris Murdoch, *The Sovereignty of Good* (London, 1970).

2. Thomas Nagel, *The View From Nowhere* (New York, 1986); Bernard Williams, *Moral Luck* (Cambridge, 1981) and "A Critique of Utilitarianism" in *Utilitarianism Pro and Con* (Cambridge, 1973); Philippa Foot, "Morality as a System of Hypothetical Imperatives" and "Are Moral Considerations Overriding?" in *Virtues and Vices* (California, 1978), and "Morality and Art" in *Philosophy As It Is,* edited by T. Honderich and M. Burnyeat (New York, 1979).

3. Susan Wolf, "Moral Saints," *Journal of Philosophy* 79 (August 1982). Foot and Williams make some of these points also. Owen Flanagan, "Admirable Immorality and Admirable Imperfection," *Journal of Philosophy* 83 (January 1986) makes the weaker criticism of moral excellence.

4. A significant and impressive step in that direction, though to my mind an unsatisfactory one, is Peter Railton's "Alienation, Consequentialism, and the Demands of Morality," *Philosophy and Public Affairs* 13 (Spring 1984). Some such attempts in a Kantian direction are Marcia Baron, "The Alleged Moral Repugnance of Acting From Duty," *Journal of Philosophy* 81 (April 1984); Barbara Herman, "Integrity and Impartiality," *The Monist* 66 (April 1983); and Adrian Piper, "Moral Theory and Moral Alienation," *Journal of Philosophy* 84 (February 1987).

5. Thomas Keneally, *Schindler's List* (New York, 1983).

6. Protecting one's Jewish workers was itself a remarkable feat during the Nazi era. During the war the use of Jews as labor for the German war effort normally involved literally working them to death, then replacing them by new, healthier ones; for example, at one IG Farben plant in Germany 25,000 of 35,000 workers died. (Keneally, *Schindler's List,* 203).

7. A moving account of one such sheltering—of her own family—is described by Nechama Tec in her memoir *Dry Tears* (New York, 1983). Tec describes and analyzes different moral types of Christian rescue of Jews in *The Light That Pierced the Darkness* (New York, 1985).

8. In her memoir, Tec relates how, at the end of the war, the family which had sheltered her family did not express satisfaction at having been able to help; they were concerned that their neighbors not realize that the family they had been sheltering (i.e., Tec's family) was Jewish. This demoralized Tec's family, and reveals how far the Polish sheltering family's financial motivation in helping them was from a moral concern.

My brief discussion of non-morally heroic rescue masks many important distinctions in the motivations of paid rescuers, some of which Tec discusses in *Light That Pierced the Darkness.* For example, some persons may have initially sheltered Jews for money, which they in fact received, but then developed a concern for those or other Jews which led to engaging in riskier activities than they would have taken on merely for the financial reward.

9. I have no general account of how one discerns 'depth of moral commitment', nor of the degree of such commitment requisite for moral heroism or moral excellence more generally.

10. A defense of part of this broader conception of moral motivation is given in my *Friendship, Altruism, and Morality* (London, 1980) and in "Personal Good and Impersonal Morality: A Critique" (unpublished manuscript).

11. However, willingness to take risks is neither necessary nor sufficient for depth of moral commitment or motivation. It is not necessary because a person may be deeply committed to a moral project which perhaps does not involve great risks, but commitment to which can be shown by the conscientiousness and dedication with which the project is pursued in the face of competing pulls. It is not sufficient, for even the willingness to take some particular risk (in service of a moral project) could itself be a relatively ephemeral element in a given individual's life or character, for example in an individual for whom taking risks had a psychological appeal in its own right.

12. J. O. Urmson, "Saints and Heroes," in *Essays in Moral Philosophy,* edited by A. I. Melden (Washington, 1957).

13. Margaret Rhodes has suggested to me that the troubling element in Schindler's sensuality is that he continued his sensual enjoyments in the face of the material deprivation that the Jews who worked for him suffered (though there is no suggestion that by depriving himself of these pleasures Schindler could have rendered their lives any better). This interesting point raises issues I am unable to pursue here.

14. Some part of the history of the relations between 'morality' and sexuality is discussed by Michel Foucault in *The Use of Pleasure* (New York, 1985).

15. Keneally, *Schindler's List,* 343.

16. On the matter of the sort of personality needed to carry out a morally necessary but complex and long-term deception, it is noteworthy to contrast Schindler with Magda Trocme, a prominent rescuer of Jews and deceiver of Nazis, who will be discussed further below. Magda never became emotionally reconciled to the deceptions—e.g., the making of false ration cards— which she had to practice during the Nazi occupation of France, and clearly kept them to a bare minimum. (See Philip Hallie, *Lest Innocent Blood Be Shed: The Story of the Village of Le Chambon and How Goodness Happened There* [New York, 1979], 126.) Being deceptive, even to Nazis and when necessary to save lives, disturbed Magda Trocme in a way it did not disturb Schindler.

17. Perry London, "The Rescuers: Motivational Hypotheses About Christians Who Saved Jews From the Nazis," in *Altruism and Helping Behavior,* edited by J. Macaulay and L. Berkowitz (New York, 1970).

18. All subsequent page references concerning Magda and André Trocme and Le Chambon will be to this book.

19. Mary Gordon, *Men and Angels* (New York, 1985).

20. Robert Adams, "Saints," *Journal of Philosophy* 81 (July 1984).

21. The argument of this paragraph concerning the degrees of vulnerability and invulnerability of different types of morally excellent characters is influenced by Martha Nussbaum's chapter 11 of *The Fragility of Goodness* (Cambridge, 1986), on character and vulnerability in Aristotle.

22. A recent current of thought, represented for example by Alasdair MacIntyre, *After Virtue* (Notre Dame, Ind., 1982), Robert Bellah et al., *Habits of the Heart* (Berkeley, 1985), Michael Sandel, *Liberalism and the Limits of Justice* (Cambridge, 1982), have argued that we live and are formed in our essential being by wider communities than just our family and friends; so that moral responsibilities toward those wider communities are as important as are the responsibilities of private life.

23. Joseph Butler, Sermon V, section [3], in *Five Sermons* (Indianapolis, 1983), 58. J. S. Mill, Chap. 2 of *Utilitarianism* (Indianapolis, 1979), 19. In the latter passage, Mill is trying to show that utilitarianism does not have the consequence that each individual must take the good of all persons, or all of society, as the goal of his every action.

24. One factor which seems to affect our assessment of persons in light of the 'wider/narrower concern' issue connects with the way in which a given person is, in Michael Sandel's term, "encumbered." (See Sandel, *Liberalism and the Limits of Justice*.) A slightly happier term for the same concept is "implicated," used by Philip Selznick in "The Idea of a Communitarian Morality," *California Law Review* 75 (1987). Consider an individual who is 'encumbered' or 'implicated' as a member of an oppressed group, and whose morally excellent life is devoted to the welfare of that group only, evincing no concern for wider communities. I think we are more willing to regard such a person (for example, Harriet Tubman) as a moral exemplar (provided that they meet the other requirements) despite that limitation than we would someone with a similarly limited scope of moral concern but not so encumbered.

25. This is not to deny the difficulties in drawing a firm distinction between moral and nonmoral excellences; the existence of distinct traditions concerning morality would lead one to expect such difficulties. Certain excellences—for example, perceptiveness, understanding, resourcefulness, even sense of humor—seem to me to strain that distinction.

At the same time I very much want to resist attempts, such as one finds in Aristotelian-influenced writers, to eschew or greatly minimize the importance of the moral–non-moral distinction altogether; see for example Martha Nussbaum, *Fragility of Goodness*, 4–5, 28–30, and Amelie Rorty, *Mind in Action* (Boston, 1988). And I wish to resist the move of those who construe morality as the perspective of the practical "all things considered" (a view vigorously defended by Lawrence Becker in chapter 1 of his *Reciprocity* [London, 1986]). I am aware, however, that I have done little by way of explaining that distinction, though I mean "moral" to have more in common with what Bernard Williams means by "ethical" than what he means by "moral" in his *Ethics and the Limits of Philosophy* (Cambridge, 1985).

26. I would like to mention here the element in Mary Gordon's portrayal of Ed Corcoran which I am leaving out in my own version of "Ed Corcoran." Late in the book Gordon portrays Ed's devotion to his wife as resting on an unconscious regarding of Anne Foster—the woman for whom he has been doing some work and the novel's central character—as a "charade wife, someone doing in another house all the things that were not done in his" (371). It would be fascinating to explore how this unconscious motivation affects our moral assessment of Mary Gordon's Ed Corcoran: Does it, for example, make of his devotion to his wife a sham, and deprive it entirely of moral value? I am assuming, however, that we can imagine an "Ed Corcoran" such as I have described him but without this self-deceptive element in his character (important as that element is for Gordon's fictional personage).

27. John Berger, *A Fortunate Man* (Harmondsworth, 1969).

28. On my penultimate draft of this paper, Owen Flanagan rightly pressed the point that an attribution of moral excellence has, at least in many instances, something to do with an assessment of how a person *would* act in various hypothetical situations. I have not been able to think this important issue through systematically, and am aware of the sketchiness of my few remarks on it here.

29. These points are defended (though without using the term "responder") in chapter 2 of *Friendship, Altruism, and Morality.*

30. At the same time, Hallie documents a sort of moral decline in André after the (probably) accidental death of his son; he became more authoritarian and more self-absorbed (263).

31. The distinction between 'idealist' and 'responder' has some kinship with the distinction between 'justice' and 'care' which Carol Gilligan has developed in her various writings, most famously *In a Different Voice* (Cambridge, 1982). Gilligan sees a gender link here, though not a simple one, with men tending to favor a 'justice', and women a 'care', approach. Such a gendered perspective regarding moral excellence and its modes seems to me a fruitful approach to connect with an appreciation of different types of moral exemplar and their respective moral psychologies.

32. See Hallie, 65, 67, 153.

33. This account is not a fanciful one. Pierre Sauvage's film, "Weapons of the Spirit," a documentary on Le Chambon, involves interviews with several peasants who sheltered refugees during the German occupation (perhaps exemplifying the "virtuous peasant" about whom Iris Murdoch occasionally speaks). Some of their retrospective account accords fairly closely with the description of the "pure responder" given here.

I am grateful to David Wong for pressing me to provide greater clarification than an early draft contained of the contrast between responder and idealist, in regard to the role of guiding principles. I am aware that there is a good deal more to be said on this point, which involves central and much-debated issues in moral theory concerning the adequacy of a principle-based ethic. I have tried to show that a caring responsiveness to particular persons in particular situations constitutes a genuinely alternative form of moral consciousness to one grounded in appeal to principle, in "Particularity and Responsiveness" in *The Emergence of Morality in Young Children,* edited by J. Kagan (Chicago, 1988), and in "Gilligan and Kohlberg: Implications for Moral Theory," *Ethics* (April 1988). On these same issues in connection with Aristotle's emphasis on the concrete particular in deliberation, see Martha Nussbaum, *The Fragility of Goodness,* especially chapter 10, and "The Discernment of Perception: An Aristotelian Conception of Private and Public Rationality," in *Proceedings of the Boston Area Colloquium in Ancient Philosophy* (1985). Nel Nodding's *Caring: A Feminine Approach to Ethics and Moral Education* (Berkeley, 1984) contains some criticisms of a principle-based ethic which accord with some of the pitfalls of 'idealism' mentioned in the paper, though I believe that Noddings tends to underplay the strengths of a principle-based ethic.

34. Keneally relates an incident which illustrates the moral pitfalls of Schindler's form of responder morality in the complex and dangerous situation in which he operated. Schindler responded to his worker/prisoners' hunger by feeding them illicitly; but in the summer of 1943, other worker/prisoners (in other establishments) were so visibly suffering from hunger that the contrast with Schindler's prisoners was "dangerously visible." Schindler thereby risked SS retaliation, though in fact this never materialized.

It is noteworthy, however, that Schindler engaged in this sort of risky activity relatively infrequently. The general middle-term goal of saving Jews (while not, as I have argued, rendering Schindler an idealist) served to temper the pure responder's morality of reacting to each individual situation and person. (I am unsure, however, whether to see this tempering purely as a corrective of a responder morality, or as a possible mode of it.)

35. Adam's critique of Wolf primarily, though not entirely, takes the form of agreeing with Wolf's characterization of the secular moral saint, and accepting the negative assessment of the figure thus characterized, but denying that either those characterizations or those negative assessments apply to what he (Adams) regards as actual, i.e., religious 'saints', such as Gandhi or St. Francis. To a secular moralist such as myself, Adams' criticisms seem to concede too much to Wolf's denigration of a purely moral, non- (or not necessarily) religious excellence. At the same time some of Adams' defense of religious saints can, as I will argue below, be appropriated to defend secular moral saints.

36. Michael Slote has usefully distinguished a "satisficing" from a "maximizing" form of consequentialism (in *Common-Sense Morality and Consequentialism* [London, 1985], chap. 3). Slote's point is, roughly, that sometimes an agent has, from a moral point of view, 'done

enough', and no *further* justification need be given for *not* doing more. While this point supports my argument that moral excellence does not require maximizing the good, my argument is not that moral heroes do enough already, and need not be held to any more demanding standard. For this way of putting the point still sees the 'enough' in the context of some implicit 'maximizing' standard; it is as if the notion of 'enough' involves a distinct rejection of 'maximization'. My point, by contrast, is that the way the good done by the idealist moral hero figures into our assessment of him as excellent is *not* as the thought that it is 'less than the maximum but still enough' (for moral excellence), but only that it is a great good (or prevention of a great evil).

37. Adams, "Saints," 398.

38. See for example Hallie, 20–21 and 154. The same moral outlook of the villagers emerges from Sauvage's film, "Weapons of the Spirit." Hallie partly connects the rejection of the ascription of great moral merit with Magda's (and perhaps the other villagers') Protestantism, in which sainthood and "moral nobility" is eschewed (154). And Sauvage and Hallie also suggest that Le Chambon's geographical isolation kept the villagers from being confronted in a direct day-to-day way with the shameful treatment of Jewish refugees elsewhere in France, a confrontation which might have made their own exceptional behavior more manifest to them.

39. See Wolf, "Moral Saints," 424, 428.

40. It should be said that while Wolf charges that the 'moral saint' will denigrate non-moral pursuits engaged in by others, she does not, as far as I am aware, say explicitly that the moral saint is self-righteous. Nevertheless this is certainly a charge which popular thought associated with moral exemplariness.

41. Adams, responding to Wolf's charge that saints are bland and unappealing, cites the "charisma" that many actual saints had which induced many persons to find them fascinating and to follow them ("Saints," 393). But the quality of generosity of spirit and affirmation and love of others which I am speaking of here cannot be identified with charisma, but is an attitude taken by the moral exemplar explicitly toward others.

42. Self-righteousness is perceptively discussed in Robert Adams's, "Involuntary Sins," *Philosophical Review* 94 (January 1985): 4–6. Marcia Homiak has plausibly maintained (in personal conversation) that self-righteousness quite often stems not from moral excellence but from insecurity and lack of confidence.

43. That holding oneself to a moral standard does not morally or conceptually require holding others to it is argued for in the following: Michael Pritchard, "Self-Regard and the Supererogatory," in *Respect For Persons: Tulane Studies in Philosophy* (1982): 147f., argues that while there is a sense or use of the moral "ought" which does carry universalistic implications, there is another which does not. Gregory Trianosky, in "Supererogation, Wrongdoing, and Vice: On the Autonomy of the Ethics of Virtue," *Journal of Philosophy* 83 (January 1986): 39, argues that "legitimate moral standards or principles can be private at least some of the time." Thomas Hill, Jr., in "Self-Respect Reconsidered" in *Respect For Persons: Tulane Studies in Philosophy* (1982): 132, argues that even a universalistic moral judgment often commits the speaker to no specific judgment about any particular other person, since the speaker may not see "relevant similarities" between himself and any actual others. A. I. Melden, in "Saints and Supererogation," in *Philosophy and Life: Essays on John Wisdom,* edited by Ilham Dilman (The Hague, 1984), argues that saints properly speak of themselves as having "duties" even though they do not regard others as having such duties.

44. Adams, "Saints," 397.

45. Foot, "Virtues and Vices," in *Virtues and Vices,* 6.

46. Murdoch, *Sovereignty of Good,* 52.

47. A small part of this paper is drawn from a short panel presentation at the Institute on the Virtues at the University of San Diego (February 1986). Earlier drafts of this paper were presented at the philosophy departments of Wesleyan University and the College of William and Mary; I thank members of those departments (especially Noel Carroll of Wesleyan) for useful feedback and criticism. I wish to thank David Wong for very useful and perceptive comments on a later draft, and, especially, Margaret Rhodes and Owen Flanagan for marvelously detailed and acute readings of the penultimate draft.

Ethics and the Craft Analogy

JAMES D. WALLACE

Contractarians, Kantians, natural law theorists, and utilitarians—practitioners of the dominant modes of moral philosophy—from time to time discuss such virtues as benevolence, the sense of justice, and trustworthiness. No one doubts that the study of virtues and vices belongs to moral philosophy. A number of philosophers, however, have recommended the study of virtues as an alternative to the dominant modes of moral theorizing. It is the study of virtues conceived as a distinct mode of moral philosophy, different from and in competition with the other modes that people have in mind when they use the term "virtue ethics."

Professor G. E. M. Anscombe described and to a degree recommended such a program in her paper, "Modern Moral Philosophy."[1] Several philosophers have explored the mode.[2] There are, of course, important differences in the views of these individuals, but there are striking similarities, too. These philosophers find unsatisfactory certain epistemological assumptions that underlie much ethical theorizing of the last fifty years. They reject in its several forms non-cognitivism, the view that moral beliefs are not the sort of things that can be either true or false. On the other hand, they do not subscribe to intuitionist cognitivist accounts that rely upon the alleged self-evident truth of fundamental moral beliefs. To explain what makes certain moral beliefs true, they develop and adapt certain ideas they find in Aristotle, ideas in which virtues play a prominent role.

Despite the considerable differences in the accounts offered by these philosophers, a single model plays an important role in their thought. I will call this model the craft analogy. In what follows, I will describe in very general terms the role that the craft analogy plays in these views and discuss some problems that arise in connection with the analogy.

Moral epistemology provides one path to virtue ethics. The route is inviting to a philosophically sophisticated individual who holds the following views. Morality, properly understood, is an absolutely indispensable guide for reasonable and enlightened conduct. Without such a guide and a general recognition of its authority, it is impossible for individuals to live as they should, and it is impossible to sustain the conditions necessary for human social life. Non-cognitivist views, according to which moral beliefs are neither true nor false, despite the heroic efforts of their defenders, cannot in the end avoid the result that adopting one moral belief rather than a contrary one is arbitrary. This result is at odds with the conception of morality as a reliable authoritative guide indispensable for reasonable conduct. Intuitionist theories, on the other hand, according to which basic moral beliefs are known to be true because they proclaim their self-evidence directly to the understanding, are equally unsatisfactory. Such views cannot in the end distinguish between a belief's seeming true and its actually being true. The credentials of moral beliefs as guides for reasonable individuals are irremediably suspect on such a view.

The notion that moral beliefs have such ephemeral contents that either their truth can be grasped only directly by the intellect in an act of intuition or they are incapable of truth at all is incongruous with the idea that these beliefs are indispensable for living intelligently and successfully. That philosophers accept such a notion is symptomatic of serious disorders in their theories. In fact, living is an everyday occurrence that takes place in a complex and demanding world. Living intelligently, presumably, requires knowledge of how to cope with that world, a knowledge grounded in an understanding of the problems encountered in living and how these problems can be solved. The intellectual resources needed to pursue successfully the activity of living are no more ephemeral than the intellectual resources needed to pursue such activities as healing, carpentry, or playing a musical instrument. Here is the craft analogy.

What does one need to know to pursue a craft intelligently and successfully? The question can be answered by considering the point or purpose of the activity and the sorts of difficulties its practitioners encounter. The standard according to which the craft is practiced well or badly can be understood in these terms. That healers need to have certain traits and skills can be shown to be true by considering what healers do, what sorts of problems they face in doing it, and what is known about solving these problems. It is obviously true that there are better and worse ways of practicing crafts, and there is no need to invent extraordinary intellectual acts and faculties for apprehending these truths.

It is plausible to suggest that there are truths about how one should conduct one's life that are known in similar ways. We know that there are better and worse ways of conducting one's life, that certain qualities and capabilities are needed in order to live intelligently and successfully, and that certain ways of proceeding can be shown to be appropriate by reference to standards of acting well or badly—standards that pertain to the conduct of life generally. We could provide an account of how these things are known to be true, if we could develop in a plausible way the idea that living is sufficiently like healing, carpentry, and playing a musical instrument. The craft analogy, of course, played an important role in Aristotle's ethics. He said, for example,

Just as for a flute-player, a sculptor, or any artist, and, in general, for all things that have a function or activity, the good and the 'well' is thought to reside in the function, so it would seem to be for man if he has a function. Have the carpenter, then, and the tanner certain functions or activities and has man none? (*NE* 1097b26–32)[3]

Aristotle maintained that the characteristic function or activity of human beings is activity involving the exercise of certain psychological capacities, specifically intellectual capacities. Such activity comprises the form of living that is peculiar to the human kind. One lives well when one continually performs such activities well, that is, in accordance with the standards appropriate to such activities, that is, in a manner that exhibits human excellences or virtues.

This view suggests two ways of proceeding to develop a more detailed account of better and worse living. One line of inquiry involves expanding the idea of a form of living that is characteristic of the human kind, studying the nature of such activity in an attempt to discover the standards of doing well appropriate to it. Alternatively, an investigator could study specific human excellences in an attempt to develop an account of what sort of activity exhibits those excellences. In either case, the investigator would be developing an account of living sucessfully and intelligently.

In his ethics, Aristotle pursued both of these lines of inquiry. His positive account of living well and doing well for human beings—in *Nicomachean Ethics* 10, for example—is not very plausible to us. His account of the virtues is initially more promising; the Aristotelian world view is less prominent in this discussion. For one who reads this account in search of some concrete data about the standards of living well, however, the result is disappointing. In Aristotle's ethics, moral virtue is defined by reference to the determinations a practically wise man, a *phronimos,* would make. When the account of practical wisdom, *phronesis,* as (roughly) wanting the things a man possessing the virtues would want knowing how to get such things, is placed beside the account of moral virtue as (roughly) the disposition to choose in certain circumstances as a *phronimos* would think one should, it is apparent that the two accounts are circular. After traveling around the circle, one is no wiser about *how* the *phronimos* properly determines what choice should be made, what course of action should be undertaken. Aristotle was aware of this problem. In explaining the difficulty, he used the following analogy: "We should not know what sort of medicines to apply to our body if someone were to say 'all those which the medical art prescribed, and which agree with the practice of those who possess the art.' " *(NE* 6.1138b30–32) This was a serious difficulty for Aristotle, who thought that the point of studying ethics is to learn how to become good and how to help others become good.

For contemporary philosophers who see promise for an ethics based somehow upon the craft analogy, the program Aristotle sketches seems more important than the details of his execution of that program. Contemporary efforts to pursue Aristotle's program, however, encounter difficulty at the same points Aristotle's did. To show that a certain craft is better practiced in one way than another, it is essential to have a clear idea of what the point or purpose of the craft is. In order to pursue the craft analogy in developing a cognitivist account of ethics, we appear to need a clear idea of what the point or purpose of living is. A host of problems threaten to overwhelm us here. Yet, if we abandon the idea that there is something related to living that is analogous to the point or purpose of a craft, we seem to have to give up any hope that the craft analogy will shed light upon what makes beliefs about living well true or false.

There is another way to proceed that promises to circumvent the problem of establishing what the point of living is. We have notions of moral virtues, and our list corresponds, more or less roughly, to the classical virtues. We can undertake to explicate these notions. We know that virtues are exhibited in acting well and living well. Accounts of a representative selection of virtues—accounts that make clear what sorts of choices and actions exhibit those virtues—may reasonably be expected to yield an outline of the general nature of living well. Just as an understanding of the skills and traits possessed by a good physician would shed light on the point of medicine and the standards by which its practice is judged, so the study of human virtues can reasonably be expected to yield accounts of the point of living and the standards for living well or badly. This expresses succinctly the program of "virtue ethics."

In the course of developing accounts of the virtues, however, the circularity that infected Aristotle's views is a serious danger. We describe a certain virtue as a tendency and/or capacity to act in a certain way. What way? What actions exhibit the virtue? It seems impossible to avoid saying that it is acting *as one should* in certain circumstances, with respect to certain considerations or difficulties, that exhibits a certain virtue. So courage is exhibited not just by acting in the face of danger, but (roughly) by acting as one should in the face of danger. More specifically, courage is exhibited by choosing and acting in a dangerous situation in a way that shows that one has given the consideration of danger exactly the weight it *should* be given in the situation. What, though, determines how one should act in the face of danger or how much weight one should give the consideration of danger in a particular circumstance? If the aim of our inquiry is to make clear how such a determination is properly made, so that we see clearly what makes such a determination true or correct, then it will not suffice to say simply that there are standards of correctness here and that there are people especially well qualified to make judgments in accordance with these standards. We must undertake the project of explaining how one properly determines what weight to give a consideration in a particular decision. In other words, we need to produce an account of practical reasoning and of being good at practical reasoning—practical wisdom.

Consider the following remarks by Philippa Foot.

> In the first place the wise man knows the means to certain good ends; and secondly he knows how much particular good ends are worth. Wisdom in its first part is relatively easy to understand. It seems that there are some ends belonging to human life in general rather than to particular skills such as medicine or boat building, ends having to do with such matters as friendship, marriage, the bringing up of children, or the choice of ways of life. . . . The second part of wisdom is much harder to describe, because here we meet with ideas which are curiously elusive, such as the thought that some pursuits are more worthwhile than others, and some matters trivial and some important in human life. . . . But I have never seen, or been able to think out, a true account of this matter, and I believe that a complete account of wisdom, and of certain other virtues and vices, must wait until this gap can be filled.[4]

It can be argued plausibly that certain virtues are perfections of traits necessary for any form of life that would qualify as human. This provides grounds for the judgment that we need such traits and that they are good to have.[5] What makes such judgments true is clear. Alasdair MacIntyre argues plausibly that certain of the goods we seek in a very wide range of "practices" (including crafts) can be obtained only if we possess virtues. This, he maintains, provides only a partial account of what a virtue is.[6]

Such accounts of virtues as these are incomplete, because they do not address the problem of how to determine what weight a consideration should be given in a particular decision. If virtue ethics is to provide an account of morality as a guide for reasonable individuals that makes clear the grounds for the truth of certain ethical beliefs, an account of practical reasoning is necessary. It is not enough merely to say that a virtue involves choosing in a way that shows that one has given considerations the weight they should be given. We must indicate how one determines the weight considerations should be given in a particular decision. Our difficulties in carrying out this project are exacerbated by our tendency to accept certain Aristotelian assumptions.

A number of things conspire to create this problem which defeated Aristotle and plagues his modern followers. A contributor is the notion that life is an activity with a point or function or (if you like) *telos*—as healing or carpentry has a point or function. This, of course, is a particular application of the craft analogy. Another conspirator is a particular view of practical reasoning which I will call the fixed-goal conception of practical reasoning. On this view, the paradigm of sound practical reasoning is choosing an effective means to a clearly defined goal. Assuming that the goal is an appropriate one to pursue, the standard of correctness of choice is, substantially, conduciveness of the action chosen to the realization of the goal. The appropriateness of the goal itself may be determined by showing the conduciveness of its pursuit to still another appropriate goal or by showing that the goal is good for its own sake. This scheme may be complicated in various ways, but the central question with any practical problem will be, which of the alternatives most contributes to the attainment of the appropriate goal? With practical problems concerning the general conduct of one's life, practical reasoning requires that there be an appropriate goal for one's life. The craft analogy—the notion that thinking about how one should conduct one's life is similar in important respects to thinking about how one should heal or make things of wood—suggests that living has a point or function as do healing and carpentry. This reinforces the requirement of the fixed-goal conception of practical reasoning that there be a goal in any reasoning concerning the conduct of life.

On the fixed-goal theory of practical reasoning, in order for us to be able to solve very many of our problems about the conduct of our lives, the conception of the appropriate goal—the point or purpose of living, the effective pursuit of which will be the good life—will have to be in certain respects concrete and detailed. The conception will have to make clear what the components of the good life are, and, if there is more than one component, what the priorities are among them. The relationship of these components to one another—the life's structure—must be clearly articulated. The more vague or unspecific the conception of the goal, the good life, the less useful it will be in solving actual practical problems—that is, the fewer such problems there will be that admit of rational solution.

The fixed-goal view of practical reasoning, when it is applied to questions about the conduct of life in this way, places inordinate demands upon our idea of a good life. How, on this view of practical reasoning, are we to decide how the obvious candidates for important human goods are to be fitted together in the good human life? How are we to choose among the indefinitely many ways we can imagine things being put together? Actual human lives are led in concrete circumstances or contexts that differ from time to time and place to place. These contexts influence enormously how lives are lived; they restrict how lives can be led, what goods can be pursued, what goods can be fitted together. When we attempt to describe the ideal life, in what circumstances do we suppose the life is led? If we cannot supply *any* context at all, how are we to determine how the various desirable elements are to be fitted together? How are we to decide what the life's structure is? If, on the other hand, we describe the ideal life in a determinate context, how can this conception be used in *other* contexts? If proper practical reasoning is a matter exclusively of choosing what most conduces to this goal, what can possibly guide us in adapting the conception of a life led in one set of circumstances to our own quite different circumstances?

I do not mean to deny that it is sometimes useful to use another person's life as a guide for one's own. My point is that on the fixed-goal conception of practical reasoning, there is insufficient provision for the *intelligent* adaptation of a conception of an ideal life described in one set of circumstances to a different set of circumstances, insufficient indication of how the adaptation might proceed more or less reasonably. Thus, the choice to adapt a certain conception to my circumstances in one way rather than another will be to a degree arbitrary. Since the matter of how I adapt the conception will crucially affect what choices I then make to attain this goal, the arbitrariness will infect the subsequent choices as well.

In constructing an account of how choices about the conduct of life are properly made, the fixed-goal theorist is faced with the fact that there are many particular good lives that are importantly different from one another. There will be disagreements among serious people, moreover, about which of the candidates for the status of a good life are genuinely good. Puzzled by how to choose, the theorist may be tempted to look for what all such lives have in common. The description of the goal—the ideal human life—can perhaps mention what is common to all particular good lives, leaving out the differences. The result of this program, however, will be a very abstract and general description of the goal which we are supposed to seek in all reasonable decisions about the conduct of life. This, of course, is hardly the sort of determinate goal that will lead us to solutions of complex practical problems.

For a fixed-goal theorist, the problem of how to demonstrate the appropriateness of a putative life-goal is truly formidable. Either it must be shown that the pursuit of this goal conduces to the attainment of another appropriate goal, or the theorist must fall back upon the claim that the goal described is intrinsically good. It is difficult to see how this use of the fixed-goal theory can in the end escape from some form of question-begging intuitionism about the certification of the appropriateness of "ultimate" goals.

This problem aside, however, the fixed-goal theorist faces a disheartening dilemma. The more specific the description of the goal for all decisions concerning the conduct of life, the more difficult it is to make plausible the claim that every correct choice about the conduct of life must advance *this* particular goal. Aristotle's description of the life of *theoria,* the contemplative life, might be offered as an example of a *relatively* specific goal. It is clearly less specific than a detailed biography of an ideally good person, but it is specific with respect to life's priorities—there is but one. More plausible as a claim about what the best sort of human life is like is the thesis that an active life exhibiting a variety of excellences both of character and intellect is best. There is, of course, evidence in Aristotle's writings that, at least intermittently, he thought of the "good for man" as a complex of activities in accordance with several excellences. There is, however, no indication of how Aristotle thought such a conception of the good for man could be used to resolve conflicts among practical considerations—when, for example, one must choose between loyalty to a friend and loyalty to the *polis.* A goal, described simply as 'a life that combines (somehow) activity in accordance with many excellences' is too unspecific to determine what to do in situations involving conflict problems.

The reader of the *Nicomachean Ethics* is apt to receive the impression that Aristotle wavered between the notion that the ultimate fixed goal of practical reasoning is a life of *theoria* and the view that the fixed goal is the less specific one of a life consisting of a pursuit of many goods, a life that exhibits a variety of intellectual and moral excellences. If indeed Aristotle did waver between these views, it may be that he was impaled upon the horns of the fixed-goal theorist's dilemma. A fixed-goal theory of practical reasoning cannot be worked out in a plausible way. This may explain why Aristotle did not have a developed account of practical reasoning.

The basic weakness of the fixed-goal theory of practical reasoning can be described succinctly in this way. For the idea of a certain life to play the role of the ultimate intrinsic good in a fixed-goal theory, it must be the idea of that which is, in effect, the goal promoted by the *correct* solution of every practical problem of moment—past, present, and future—concerning how human beings should lead their lives. How could anyone have sufficient grounds for the claim that a certain particular conception of the ideal life meets this condition?

The fixed-goal view of practical reasoning must be abandoned. What, though, is to replace it? A consideration of certain of the difficulties that beset the fixed-goal theory suggests that there are many different, more or less independent goals that people pursue, sometimes reasonably. Unfortunately, however, the human condition is such that often—*very* often—in pursuing one good, we must forego another; circumstances force us to sacrifice one good to another. Many of our most difficult practical problems require us to choose one good rather than another. How do we *properly* make such choices? Presumably, we somehow determine which of the conflicting goods is in the circumstances more important or which has the stronger claim upon us. But how is this determined? Philippa Foot complains in the passage quoted above that she can find no satisfactory account of how one properly makes such determinations. If there is no rational way of making such choices, then a great many of the most important choices we make are arbitrary.

Alasdair MacIntyre's claim that we need a modern conception of the human *telos* is based, at least partly, upon his belief that the solution of this problem requires such a conception. He says,

> Unless there is a *telos* which transcends the limited goods of practices by constituting the good of a whole human life, the good of a human life conceived as a unity, it will *both* be the case that a certain subversive arbitrariness will invade the moral life *and* that we shall be unable to specify the context of certain virtues adequately.[7]

In developing this point, however, MacIntyre seems to embrace a version of the fixed-goal theory of practical reasoning. If I understand him correctly, then he is offering an account that suffers from the difficulties of the fixed-goal view. "The good life for man," he says at one point, "is the life spent in seeking the good life for man."[8] It is not clear, however, why a good human life *must* have as its central focus a quest for an understanding of the good life, nor is it clear how aiming at *this* goal will enable one to "order" the other goods, how it will enable one to decide in a particular circumstance whether loyalty to a friend is more important than loyalty to the state, etc.

Giving up the fixed-goal theory of practical reasoning is easier said than done. It can be done, however—and without introducing a "subversive arbitrariness" into our lives—by taking very seriously the craft analogy. In Aristotle's ethics, the craft analogy suggests that living has a point or goal, and this fits neatly with the fixed-goal theory. I propose, however, that the craft analogy be applied in quite a different way. What has a point or purpose, analogous to the way that a craft has a point or purpose, is not living itself; rather it is practical considerations, requirements, and values that have points. How can such a thing as a moral consideration have a point in anything like the way that a craft does? Things that occur in practical reasoning as considerations have reference to learned ways of dealing with certain stituations. There are sorts of practical knowledge that are needed only by some people—people, who because of their circumstances, have special tasks to perform and special problems to solve. The division of labor in a community, for example, brings about such circumstances, and technical practical knowledge is needed. There is, on the other hand, practical knowledge that is needed by every individual in a community in the course of his or her life.

Practical knowledge about the conduct of life generally is fundamentally a hodgepodge, a motley collection of learned ways of dealing with a variety of different problems that arise in our lives. These are ways developed by individuals in real-life situations and, often, modified by countless other individuals in order to adjust the ways to one another and to changing circumstances. Some of these ways were developed to deal with problems connected with the social character of human life— problems we face in living with one another, cooperating with one another, resolving our conflicts with one another, etc. It is the more important of those ways that we tend to classify as "moral." The ways we have developed for dealing with the myriad problems of living together were developed by the use of the same sort of intellectual resources that were employed in the development of agriculture, language, and medicine. It is particular moral considerations, such as the rule of law, respect for human life, and the commitments involved in friendship, that have points or functions analogous to the points or functions of crafts. These considerations refer to shared ways of considerable complexity for coping with certain problems that tend to arise in everyone's life. The ways have a history; they have been modified and adapted to enable them to function in altered circumstances, to solve novel variants of the original problems. In the course of their careers, the purposes and functions of these ways have changed, have evolved, too. Sometimes it is human practical intelligence that is the cause of such changes. What is going on in such cases, however, is not properly described as devising means of attaining a clearly defined goal. Rather, the aim is to resolve an unprecedented difficulty, using ways developed to deal with analogous but crucially different difficulties. In the course of resolving the difficulty, the ways themselves and the understanding of what constitutes a resolution may be significantly modified.[9]

One thing that recommends this contextualist and (in the philosophical sense) pragmatic view of morality and practical reasoning is the account it affords of how certain difficult problems are properly resolved. To determine the relevance of certain considerations and their proper weight in actual moral problems, it is necessary to understand the points of the considerations. The point or points of a consideration will lie in the function, the use of the way that the consideration embodies. The idea that an understanding of the points of moral considerations is indispensable for solving moral problems is plausible because we would not expect to be able intelligently to apply or to resolve conflicts among *any* rules or procedures whose uses and points we do not understand. The task with particular moral problems, on this view, is to determine the applicability of moral considerations and to resolve conflicts among considerations in ways that are intellectually defensible by showing that (1) the solution proposed retains, insofar as possible, the necessary functions of the old ways, (2) the solution addresses the needs of the present situation, and (3) the modifications of our ways implicit in the solution are ones we can live with. In order to develop such solutions, it is necessary to understand the points of the considerations involved, the uses of the ways. David Hume's discussion of the "utility" of private property in Section III of *An Inquiry Concerning the Principles of Morals* is an example of an attempt to explain the points of certain considerations. (It is illuminating to read Hume with the thought in mind that he had not read Bentham, and that it is not necessary to assume that Hume used the term "utility" in the technical sense that Bentham gave it.)

The account sketched above enables us to abandon the fixed-goal conception of practical reasoning, while retaining, in a modified form, the craft analogy. The notion that living itself is like a craft in that it has a certain point or purpose is replaced by the idea that the considerations we consult in practical reasoning have points analogous to the points of crafts. That is, both moral considerations and crafts involve accumulations of practical knowledge developed in response to quite specific problems for specific purposes. This modified version of the craft analogy retains its cognitivist implications for ethics. Beliefs about the correctness of certain solutions to problems about the conduct of life have an epistemological status similar to beliefs about the correctness of solutions to certain problems in medicine and other crafts.

What are the implications of such an account for the program of virtue ethics?

What of the idea that by providing accounts of the classical virtues or some modern counterparts, we can develop an account of living well and the standards by which the conduct of life is properly assessed? The way in which the craft analogy is used in the Aristotelian account lends plausibility to this idea; just as the exercise of the skills and capacities of the good carpenter constitutes the activity of practicing the craft well, so the exercise of the virtues constitutes the activity of living well. The proposed modification in the use of the craft analogy replaces this tidy picture with one that is far more cluttered. It remains true that we need such virtues as courage, honesty, and justice in order to live as we should, but it is equally true that we need such virtues in order to practice crafts successfully—in order to teach as we should, do research as we should, etc. No one, however, infers from the importance of these virtues for the practice of crafts that accounts of the virtues will provide adequate accounts of practicing the crafts well. No one supposes that by studying courage, justice, and honesty we will learn a great deal about the standards by which the practice of a craft is properly evaluated. The virtues, for all their importance, do not contain the particular dispositions—the skills, knowledge, and commitments—that are necessary for practicing a particular craft well. Similarly, accounts of such lists of "moral virtues" as have been offered recently cannot be expected to provide full accounts of the standards by which decisions about the conduct of life generally are properly evaluated. The store of knowledge, skills, and commitments that comprises our resources for dealing with particular moral problems is vast, complex, and specific. Philosophical accounts of the virtues lack the necessary specificity to enable us to draw out of them useful accounts of how difficult concrete practical problems are properly resolved.

I do not conclude from this that the program of virtue ethics should be abandoned. This program, I think, can be adapted to the proposed modification in the use of the craft analogy in ethics. A case can be made for thinking of the very considerations that occur in practical reasoning as having a locus in us in the form of learned dispositions consisting of know-how, skills, concerns, values, and commitments. If moral considerations refer to shared learned ways of dealing with certain practical problems, we can think of the considerations themselves as character traits. So, such practical considerations as the rule of law or respect for human life are thought of as learned ways of acting, character traits. The number of character traits central to ethics will, on this view, far exceed the number of classical virtues. The traits, however, will have points or purposes deriving from the ways that exhibit them. These ways and their points will be far more specific in their application to concrete situations than the corresponding features of the classical virtues. On this conception, the relatively unproblematic phenomenon of adapting a practical skill to an unprecedented situation can provide a model for understanding how certain difficult moral problems might be resolved.[10]

Notes

An earlier version of this paper was presented at a conference on Contemporary Ethical Thought and the History of Moral Philosophy held at Marquette University in October, 1985.

1. *Philosophy* 33, no. 124 (1958): 1–19.
2. See, for example, Philippa Foot, *Virtues and Vices* (Berkeley, 1978); Stuart Hampshire,

Two Theories of Morality (New York, 1977) and *Morality and Conflict* (Oxford, 1983); Alasdair MacIntyre, *After Virtue,* 2nd ed. (Notre Dame, Ind., 1984); and James D. Wallace, *Virtues and Vices* (Ithaca, N.Y., 1978).

3. The reference here is to the *Nicomachean Ethics.* The translation is that of W. D. Ross in volume 9 of *The Works of Aristotle Translated into English* (Oxford, 1915).

4. Foot, *Virtues and Vices,* 5–6.

5. Wallace, *Virtues and Vices,* 10–11.

6. MacIntyre, *After Virtue,* chap. 14.

7. Ibid., 203.

8. Ibid., 219.

9. Compare this with MacIntyre's description of the simultaneous evolution of "practices," the "goods internal to practices," and "standards of excellence" pertaining to practices *(After Virtue,* 187–191). See also John Dewey's account of the evolution of institutions in *Human Nature and Conduct* (New York, 1922), 79–83.

10. This idea is developed in James D. Wallace, *Moral Relevance and Moral Conflict* (Ithaca, N.Y., 1988).

Envy and Jealousy: Emotions and Vices

GABRIELE TAYLOR

I

Envy and jealousy are both emotions and character-traits. The person experiencing emotional envy or jealousy takes a certain view of the situation confronting her. The person who has the relevant character-trait is disposed to see the world in this sort of way and is disposed to experience these emotions. It is possible for her to be aware of such a disposition and to think it unfortunate. In that case she may try to exercise some control over her emotion, with greater or lesser success. Alternatively, she may not so assess herself and leave her disposition unchecked. It is this latter type of person I have in mind when I speak of the envious or jealous person. In the discussion that follows I shall concentrate on the thoughts involved in the respective emotional experience as central to an understanding of the character-trait, and as central to the explanation of why, if at all, envy and jealousy should be regarded as human vices.

As emotions, envy and jealousy are often not clearly distinguished from each other, in either ordinary talk or in philosophical exposition. This is not surprising for there are many similarities: both are hostile and unpleasant emotions, painful for the agent to experience. They often occur together, for one quite naturally leads to the other. In practice it may not be possible for anyone, including the agent herself, to identify with confidence which of the two emotions she is experiencing. Nevertheless, they are distinct emotions, involving different beliefs on the part of the person concerned, at least in the central cases.

In both cases the person experiencing the emotion sees herself as standing in some relation to a valued good, where this good may be some material possession, a social position or position of relative power, a personal quality, or some kind of personal relationship. In each case the relation is seen as unfavorable, for the good in question is thought of as either about to be lost or as not being in one's possession and probably unavailable. The person experiencing jealousy believes or imagines there to be a threat to a valued possession of hers or to something she expects or hopes to possess. The loss would, in her view, leave her worse off than she was before or hoped that she would be. Her first concern is, therefore, the protection of this possession or hoped-for possession. The person feeling envy, on the other hand, thinks of herself as being deprived in comparison with another who is, in the relevant respect, better off than she is. Unlike the jealous person, the envious one cannot be concerned with trying to maintain the *status quo*. On the contrary, she will want to eliminate the discrepancy between herself and the other, she will want in some way to better her position. The initial difference, then, lies in the agent's respective relation to the valued good. From it further differences follow, among them, I shall try to show, a difference in the nature of their respective viciousness. I shall begin with a more detailed investigation of each emotion and go on to an assessment of them as human failings.

II

In ordinary talk we do not sharply distinguish the type of envy where the person concerned focuses on the other as somehow crucially involved in her finding herself in an inferior position from those cases where comparison with another is merely the occasion for realizing her own shortcomings. Here the perception of the other's better position simply serves to direct the person's thoughts to her own deficiencies, and perhaps to the further thought that she should try to improve her position in whatever way is relevant. The other plays no part in her self-assessment except as a possible ideal, and his being better off is not regarded as in any way a threat. So, for instance, in a novel called *Crusoe's Daughter,* the narrator, Polly Flint, envies Robinson Crusoe: "I envied Crusoe his sin, his courage, his ruthlessness in leaving all he had been brought up to respect; his resilience, his wonderful survival after disaster. I envied him his conversion, his penitence, his beautiful self-assurance won through solitude and despair."[1] Polly Flint admires the qualities she sees in Crusoe and wishes she were like him in these respects. But this does not make her an envious sort of person. In her type of envy the comparison with others focuses on their valuable qualities which it would be worth having; there is here no question of competing with the other.

There are two ways of classifying Polly Flint's type of envy: since the focus of attention is the good itself rather than the person possessing the good, it may be labeled 'object-envy'; and since the consequent role of the person possessing the good is that of an ideal or of someone to be admired, it may also be called 'ideal' or 'admiring' envy. Such envy need not be flawless; whether it is or not depends on the sort of good which is its object, and depends also on how domineering the image of the admired person may become in the other's life. But whatever its possible shortcomings may be, this kind of envy lacks those features and defects which characterize the typically envious.

Object-envy is to be contrasted with state-envy: the person concerned is envious not of the good the other has, but is envious of the other's having that good. She sees herself as deprived by comparison. It is the other's comparatively advantageous position (as she sees it) which is the crux of the matter, and is what the envious wishes she could remove. When feeling envy, therefore, her thoughts focus on the supposed comparative advantage of the other, and so on her own disadvantage and deprivation. Given this initial difference between the two types of envy, the role of the possessor of that good is naturally different, too: in state-envy he is seen as a competitor or rival whose success is in some way linked to her own failure. He is, therefore, a thorn in her flesh, rather than an object of admiration.

Envy of this kind is not a comfortable emotion to experience, and the person concerned will want to be free of it. It is no doubt possible to train oneself to be less prone to its onslaught; one may be able, more or less, to reason oneself out of it. But leaving aside such 'external' measures, the subject of the emotion will want her comparative disadvantage to be removed which, given her envious state, leaves her with the alternatives of either wishing to improve her own position *vis-à-vis* that of the other, or of wishing to spoil the other's elevation. The first alternative is usually called 'emulative' envy, the second 'destructive' or 'malicious' envy.

Emulative envy is often thought to be not merely harmless but positively valuable. John Rawls, for example, thinks that the sight of the other's greater good leads us to strive in socially beneficial ways for similar things for ourselves.[2] But it is not clear that what he has here in mind is emulative rather than admiring envy, as I have respectively defined them. Descartes speaks of emulation as a species of courage; it is, he says, "a heat which disposes the soul to undertake things which it hopes to be able on its own account to succeed in, because it sees them succeed with others" *(The Passions of the Soul,* Article CLXXII). Here the person sees the other as an example, not merely in the sense that he is the possessor of these desirable goods, but also in the sense that the fact of his possessing them makes it appear more possible for her to try for similar achievements; it gives her hope. This falls under my heading of 'admiring envy', for the role of the other is still only that of in some way assisting her to get to where she wants to be; she does not envy him his possession of the goods in question. On this interpretation, then, emulative envy does not differ from an admiring envy which may indeed be socially and personally beneficial.

If emulative envy is taken to be a form of state-envy its having beneficial effects is, however, much more questionable. Two different cases may here be distinguished: emulative envy may be 'particular'—the envious person may wish to emulate the other by aiming at acquiring his particular possessions, *his* job, *his* position, *his* wife—or it may be 'general'—she may wish not for these very things but for that sort of thing, that kind of position or kind of treasure. Where such envy is particular, the thought of the other's possession of the good may lead her to effort and achievement which might otherwise not have been hers, and that, perhaps, may count in favor of emulative envy of this sort. Whether what she aims at is better or worse will depend, of course, on the particular object she has in mind. But apart from this, as she is aiming to take over the other's particular possession it follows that in intention at least she must be other-destructive as well as self-improving, for evidently her gain would be the other's loss. In this case, therefore, emulative envy does not seem to be clearly distinguishable from envy which is destructive. It is only if her envy is general, if she aims at removing the painful discrepancy by achieving not the identical but a similar position for herself, that other-destructive thoughts need not form part of her envious state. If so, this kind of emulative envy can be distinguished from destructive envy. It would also differ from admiring envy in that her motive would be different, viz., to improve her position *vis-à-vis* another, rather than to achieve the good for its own sake. Her striving is competitive, and this itself may make at least questionable the claim that this type of envy is overall beneficial.

When feeling destructive envy the other is seen as a target for hostile feelings. As this type of envy is characterized in negative terms, the distinction between particular and general envy is of less importance. The envious person may wish she had precisely what the other has or she may wish merely that she had that sort of thing; either way, she wishes to spoil the other's better position. A further distinction, which cuts across the particular-general one, will help to clarify the nature of the hostility involved: envy may be either 'primitive' or 'sophisticated'. The labels mean what they imply: very young children and some animals may feel envy of the primitive kind. It is, for example, the form of envy discussed by Melanie Klein: the infant, realizing that the source of food and comfort is outside herself, assumes that when she is deprived these riches are enjoyed by the breast itself, and so has the envious impluse to destroy it.³ Typically, the other is seen as possessing that which the child needs for its own comfort, and is seen, therefore, as the source of its own discomfort and so as a suitable focus for hostile and destructive feelings. In primitive envy the other, as the possessor of the good, is seen, rightly or wrongly, as somehow causally responsible for the deficiency in the life of the person envying him: it is because the other has it that it is not available to her. The destruction of the other, therefore, would be a form of retaliation; it may also remove what is between her and the good she needs.

It is sometimes thought to be characteristic of all cases of the destructively envious that the other is seen as the cause of their deprivation.⁴ But this is not altogether plausible. Of course, the thought of the envious may be quite irrational, but on the present suggestion the beliefs involved in envy would be so patently foolish on many occasions that an explanation of the hostility in terms of them is hardly convincing. When what is envied is, for instance, the other's possession of some personal quality, his courage or effectiveness or cleverness, it would usually be inane to think his having such qualities is causally responsible for our lack of them. It is far more likely that the other's possessing such goods is responsible not for our lack of them, but rather for our being seen to lack them. His courage, effectiveness, and cleverness can hardly be the cause of her lacking them, but they may be the cause of showing her and the world that she does lack them. This is the worry of those whose envy is sophisticated. Unlike primitive envy, sophisticated envy requires a consciousness of self, a view of how one wants or does not want to be seen by either oneself or by others. The role of the envied here is not, or is not merely, that of the person responsible for one's own lack of flourishing; it is also that of serving as a reminder that in this or that important respect one's own position is not what one wants it to be.

Sophisticated envy cannot be felt by those who have no conception of themselves and their limitations. It implies concern with self-esteem, and for its degree of intensity will depend on how undermining of her own and other's favorable view of herself the lack of the relevant good is thought to be. Those capable of feeling sophisticated envy may also feel primitive envy, or indeed may feel a mixture of both. The explanation of the thoughts and desires involved in a particular case will vary, naturally, depending on which type is in question. Sometimes reference to sophisticated envy is needed to explain some feature of envy which would otherwise remain obscure. It has been suggested, for instance, that the envious person need not value what the other has, she must think merely that the other values it.[5] This seems implausible where the envy is primitive; unless the sufferer of the emotion wanted the good for herself, her feelings would be unexplained. If the person's envy is sophisticated, however, then it is true that she may not value the other's possession in the sense of sincerely wanting it for herself; possessing it (being effective or powerful or highminded) might make her life far more strenuous than she would like it to be. But this does not alter the fact that she does not want herself and others to believe that she lacks such qualities. She values these goods at least derivatively; they are generally thought to be impressive qualities, and she is sufficiently influenced by that view to want to be able to think of herself as possessing them, or not be forced, at any rate, to have to think of herself as lacking them.

Some thoughts and desires can be explained on only the assumption that the envy in question is sophisticated. This was true of the feature just discussed. It seems to apply also to Aristotle's suggestion that envy is often felt toward those who are 'like' and 'equal' to us *(Rhetoric* 1386b). For this is surely so (where it is so) because the better-offness in some respect of someone like and equal to us brings home with particular force an inferiority of status. Sometimes there are alternative explanations. Hume thought that it is those in our proximity who tend to excite our envy *(Treatise* II.2.8). This may be so because the frequent sight of the other's possession stimulates our desire for it (primitive envy), or because his presence serves as a constant reminder of our inferiority (sophisticated envy). The wish to destroy the other's possession may in the first case be merely spiteful; in the second it would have its own rationale. Similar explanations apply also to a characteristic of envy often pointed out, viz., that the envious do not want the other to have the good in question, even though his not having it is of no advantage to the person herself. Again, this desire may be prompted merely by (primitive) feelings of revenge or spite, while again reference to sophisticated envy will make such an attitude more rational in the given situation: the fulfilment of my intense wish to see you lose your power and effectiveness would be of no advantage to me in the sense that I am unlikely thereby to acquire such valuable properties for myself. From a practical point of view I may even be the loser, for I may have relied on your support. But reference to sophisticated envy can explain the advantage there is for me: at least you would no longer be in a position to underline my feebleness, and so no longer in a position to humiliate me.[6]

'Envy', then, refers to a variety of different though, of course, related phenomena. It is unlikely that any of the types enumerated are ever experienced in their pure form. To experience pure object-envy would require some degree of saintliness, and Polly Flint was no doubt wise to choose as the object of her envy a fictional character. Normally an experience of object-envy is likely to slide into one of state-envy, at least on this or that occasion. But the converse is also true: those who see the other as the successful rival and view him with hostility may at the same time also have feelings of admiration toward him. Similarly, emulative and destructive envy may merge into each other, or primitive into sophisticated. The point of isolating different types of envy is to facilitate the enumeration of those features in virtue of which we think of envy as a vice. From this point of view it is plain that it is state- and not object-envy that deserves attention.

III

There is a use of 'jealous', not the most typical one, which emphasizes one of the features of jealousy as we usually think of it today. Descartes, for example, speaks of a woman being jealous of her honor (*The Passions of the Soul,* Article CLXVIII). The woman greatly values her honor and hence wishes to protect it; if necessary she will defend it in any way she can. It is this 'protective' feature of jealousy which is expressed when we speak of a person as jealously guarding some possession of hers, where 'possession' may refer not merely to personal qualities but also to material goods or to some status- conferring position. The miser will jealously guard his golden ducats; the lucky ones at a time of shortage may jealously guard their food or blankets, the dedicated collector his precious stones. They guard their possession *jealously* because they guard them protectively, as a personal possession which it would be personally damaging for them to lose. They are anxious about these possessions, and so try and anticipate any possible threat. On the face of it the cases of the miser, the hungry, and the collector do not seem to be wholly analogous to that of the woman, for it is strange to speak of them as being jealous *of* their money, food, or stones, as it is not strange to speak of the woman as being jealous of her honor. There will, no doubt, be differences among these cases as the goods in question are related so differently to the persons concerned, but the comparison becomes less strange if we think of them as being jealous not of these particular items, but of their treasure, their comfort, or their well-being. These descriptions characterize the possessions to be protected in terms that show them to be patently desirable, at least in the eyes of some community at some time. Honor is or was such a good, and so is comfort, status, or position, or treasure of any kind. What we are thought to be protectively jealous *of,* it seems, is always something to be regarded as an instance of such a good.

A person may be disposed to be protective of her possessions and so be on the look-out for possible dangers. But the need to jealously guard the valued good arises only on those occasions when its owner believes it to be threatened: someone else wants to take it away in order to enrich himself. The loss of the one would be the gain of the other. There is therefore, in the owner's view, someone responsible for this threat, and whoever is seen as in this manner responsible and likely to profit is thereby a natural target of hostile feelings. Feelings of hostility are consequently a natural (though perhaps not necessary) feature of the state of the person who on some occasion is protectively jealous of a cherished possession.

Both these features, the desire to protect a valued possession and consequent hostility toward anyone (anything) who threatens the person's possession of it, are also present in the case we tend to take as the typical one, that of sexual jealousy, or jealousy concerning a personal relationship. But this case is different and more complex. It is different in that what we are said to be jealous of is not some particular possession seen as the sort of good anyone might like or need to have, but is a particular person. The valued possession is a relationship and hence is inextricably bound up with another person, and it is this relationship which a third person is seen as threatening. This three-term relation introduces an ambiguity: Othello was jealous, but of whom was he jealous, Cassio or Desdemona? It may be possible to explain the ambiguity by reference to a shift in emphasis: what we are now said to be jealous *of* is no longer a good to be protected; rather, we pick out as the 'object' of this type of jealousy that which is the focus of the person's other-directed hostility. The ambiguity can then be accounted for by pointing out that the person feeling jealous will feel hostile toward both the other persons involved, though the hostility will be of a different kind in each case. This is the view Spinoza takes: jealousy, according to him, consists of hatred toward the object of love joined with envy of the rival *(Ethics,* III.xxxv), Othello would then be jealous sometimes of Cassio and sometimes of Desdemona, depending on which type of hostility he is experiencing. But alternatively it might be said that Othello is jealous of Desdemona in the sense that she is the possession to be protected, and jealous of Cassio as the hated rival. This, too, would accommodate the ambiguity as something unavoidable in this complex emotion. It is true that on this account the possession to be protected is picked out by means of a proper name rather than by means of a general description referring to a human good, as seemed to be the case in earlier examples of protective jealousy. But this can perhaps be accounted for by saying that the use of the proper name is merely shorthand for referring to a personal relationship, and a loving personal relationship clearly falls under the heading of 'human good'.

It seems to me that either or any variant of these explanations is possible: we sometimes fasten on the protectiveness and sometimes on the hostility as the crucial feature of jealousy, or on any combination of these. Othello's feelings toward Desdemona during his period of jealousy are not uniform but are sometimes loving and sometimes revengeful, and this is typical of the emotion. The ambiguity as to whom we are jealous of can be explained in alternative ways, either or both of which may apply on a particular occasion.

As in the case of envy it is helpful to encapsulate the point just made in a distinction between 'object'- and 'state'-jealousy. Object-jealousy is protective jealousy: I am jealous of the love or attention of the other I thought I possessed or once possessed and still feel is mine by rights. State-jealousy emphasizes the other-directed hostility: I am jealous of another person threatening to transfer or to take for herself the love or attention I thought or hoped was mine, and should be mine in any case. The most obvious target of hostility here is the third person, so that the most likely hostility involved is the hostility toward a rival. But, as Spinoza points out, the loved object, having shown himself to be unreliable, may equally be the focus of hostility.

The distinction between these two kinds of jealousy will be of help in assessing jealousy as a possible vice, as was the analogous distinction between kinds of envy. But the relation between object- and state-jealousy is different from that between object- and state-envy: a case of state-jealousy is also always a case of object-jealousy (though not vice versa), but this is not so with envy. Here the distinction permitted the elimination of object-envy as a candidate for viciousness, but object-jealousy cannot be dismissed in this way.

Like envy, jealousy is a complex phenomenon whose features cannot be caught by a neat set of necessary and sufficient conditions. For a person to experience jealousy there must be, in her view, a threat to some possession or hoped-for possession she cherishes. She therefore fears that it might be lost. Fear, provoked by the threat of loss, is one of the emotions she experiences. She may fear also those who are responsible for the threat, but it is as or more likely that toward them she feels anger or resentment. The jealous are prone to experiencing all these emotions, to a greater or lesser degree and in different proportions, depending on the particular circumstances and on the individual concerned. But it is conceivable at least that there are cases of jealousy where such hostile feelings are minimal or perhaps even absent altogether, and where jealousy expresses itself in concentrated protectiveness of the possession in question. This may be so because there is in fact no particular rival on the scene. But the concentrated protectiveness implies the agent's fear of the permanent possibility of a rival appearing.

Given the complexity of the phenomenon and the possible range of its manifestations it is safest to give an account of a central case from which various deviations are possible. In the central case of a person being jealous of another there are two crucial features: the person experiencing the emotion wants to hold on to something she believes or hopes she possesses or will possess. She sees that possession or hoped-for possession as threatened by being transferred to somebody else and so be lost to her. She both fears the loss and feels hostile toward those she regards as responsible for the threat. This characterization leaves the type and direction of the hostility unspecified and hence allows for very different sorts of feelings being involved in the jealous state. Envy, as Spinoza says, is likely to be one of these, either of the rival or of the loved object, for both, after all, are seen by the person concerned as better off than she is. So envy is indeed a natural, though not necessary, element in the complex. But the given characterization points to another, conceptual, connection between envy and jealousy: it allows for cases where the distinction between them is so fine that it is not surprising that they are so often not kept apart. The distinction as drawn initially between these emotions centered on the different relation toward a valued good: while (roughly) the jealous have and fear to lose it, the envious lack and want to have it. It is however possible to be jealous in circumstances where one only hopes to gain another's love or special attention and sees that hoped-for good being given to another. Here the subject of jealousy does not even believe that the good is in her possession (or is still in her possession). The only possible and far from clear-cut difference between these two cases is that to the jealous, however hopeless her position may seem to an observer, the good is not yet wholly beyond her reach; there is still hope. The envious, on the other hand, at the time of feeling the emotion, has no hope, she thinks of the good as not available to her. So here, too, the distinction is not altogether tidy: while central cases of jealousy can be clearly distinguished from central cases of envy, there are borderline cases which tend to merge into each other.

Jealousy, like envy, may be either primitive or sophisticated, where again sophisticated jealousy does and primitive jealousy does not require a capacity for self-awareness and self-assessment. To be given love and attention allows the recipient to feel (in some respect and to some degree) cherished and secure. To be in a position which allows such feelings is certainly desirable and a good to be protected, and fearing the transfer to another of love and attention, insofar as this threatens present security and comfort, is a central feature of primitive jealousy. It is likely to be a feature of sophisticated jealousy as well, but here the impact of the threat of loss goes further: being given love and attention implies that the recipient is thought worthy of such goods. Somebody is prepared to spend time and energy on her, or somebody thinks her a worthy object of affection, so she must be of some worth to provoke this response. If so, then the transfer of love and attention is a loss of being valued. She now sees herself as being seen in a less favorable light, as not being worthy of the kind of attention she thought she enjoyed, and this is humiliating and a blow to her self-esteem. Her confidence in herself will therefore be diminished, she will think less of herself. The loss of attention may, then, have implications which go beyond the distress of losing the comfort or pleasure provided by the attention itself. The possibility of losing esteem, of having one's image of oneself disturbed and one's sense of identity undermined, accounts for the often self-directed hostility of the jealous, and accounts for jealousy being potentially a torment.

IV

Envy is regarded as a vice par excellence; it is a deadly sin. Given that it is state- and not object-envy that is here relevant, the reasons for so regarding it seem already patently obvious: the experience of envy of this sort involves other-directed hostile thoughts and destructive impulses, and this by itself may be enough to think it vicious. An exception here seems to be the case of emulative envy isolated earlier, and perhaps this should be excluded from envy's bad reputation. On the other hand, it is unlikely that even this sort of envy can be wholly free of hostile thoughts directed against others, for it is still the other's comparative advantage which is in the person's mind. As the possessor of this advantage the other is a natural object of hostility, particularly so if he is seen as in some way responsible for the plight of the envious. But even if there are cases of hostility-free emulative envy, these would hardly be the ones we should cite as paradigm examples of the emotion; this is not how we tend to think of the envious or of those experiencing emotional envy. Destructive thoughts and desires are a feature of the central case, and it is on this case I shall concentrate.

Envy, then, may be a vice primarily because it involves other-directed hostility and destruction. But there are more, and more interesting, points to be made about the features which contribute to its viciousness. Envy, it is said, spoils the good it covets. If this is what is wrong with envy, or is at least what is partially wrong with it, then we have a shift in emphasis: the destructive and so vicious thoughts now isolated are no longer those directed against the other as the possessor of the good and as the person thereby in some way responsible for our disadvantageous position, but are now said to be directed against the good itself. This indicates a new dimension of the state which would account more fully for its badness than would mere other-directed hostility. If envy spoils the good it covets then the desires of the envious are doomed to failure; they can never achieve the position they hanker after. The situation of the envious would necessarily be a hopeless one. No wonder, then, that it should be thought of as a *deadly* sin, leading to the death of the soul.

The slogan, hinting at an explanation of features of envy which are often associated with it, is therefore likely to make a point. But in what sense, precisely, may it be true of envy that it spoils the good it covets? What is at stake here, of course, is not whether the coveted good is spoilt or likely to be spoilt in actual fact, but whether the thoughts and desires of the envious are destructive of the good in question, so that, were they to be translated into action, the good would be spoilt or destroyed. At first sight the slogan seems mistaken or at least exaggerated. It implies that spoiling the good it covets is an inherent characteristic of envy and hence true of all cases of the type of envy under discussion. But it seems to be true of certain cases only:

a) It is true of those cases of primitive envy where the hostility directed against the supposed source of the deprivation must necessarily affect the good itself, since the good cannot be separated from the source. This is so in the case of the infant in Klein's theory: destructive desires directed against the breast are inevitably also destructive of the flow of milk. But this hardly applies to cases where the good is detachable from the possessor; there it seems that, on the contrary, destroying the other *qua* possessor of the good leaves the good itself intact and so available to the envious.

b) It is true also of cases of either primitive or sophisticated envy where the person feeling the emotion may actually wish for the destruction of the good, rather than see it in the possession of the other. But although spiteful thoughts and wishes of this kind are no doubt a fairly common occurrence in the experience of envy, it seems rash to think that they must be present in every case for it to count as a case of envy.

c) There is a more sophisticated version of the case just mentioned: in *Remembrance of Things Past* Marcel remarks of his great-aunt: "Whenever she saw in others an advantage, however trivial, which she herself lacked, she would persuade herself that it was no advantage at all, but a drawback, and would pity so as not to have to envy them."[7] Proust here points to a quite typical tendency of the envious: the tendency to belittle what the other has. This, too, is a way of spoiling the coveted good.

In all these examples 'the good that is coveted' has been understood in a quite straightforward sense, as being that which the other had and the envier lacked, the toy, the milk, the prestigious position, the mental or physical qualities. There clearly are a range of cases where on this interpretation the slogan is supported; perhaps they are the most typical ones. This does not mean, however, that it is established as a universal truth that envy must involve thoughts and desires of the kind described. But maybe this is too cautious; maybe it can be said of at least all cases of sophisticated envy that they involve spiteful thoughts of precisely this kind. On an occasion when the other's possession of the good is thought to show up one's own lack of it, the wish to destroy that good is surely part of the experience. There is here, however, a confusion about what might be meant by the good to be spoilt. What the envious here want to spoil is the other's possession of the good. If I envy you your courage and think you responsible for showing up my lack of it, then I wish you did not have it, either. But if this is what is meant by the slogan then it is obviously and unexcitingly true: the wish to spoil the other's possession of the good is indeed a universal feature of envy.

Spoiling the good itself is, of course, one way of spoiling the other's possession of it, but it is not the only way; and sometimes the wish to spoil the good itself would hardly be comprehensible.

The notion of sophisticated envy does, however, suggest an alternative interpretation of the slogan. Sophisticated envy is concerned with the person's self-esteem, and it is this which is here the coveted good to be achieved at all cost. This is not to say that envy is *experienced* as a threat or blow to self-esteem. At the time of feeling envy the person perceives the other to be possessing a good which makes his position superior to her own and thereby throws into relief her own inferiority. Sophisticated envy (like primitive envy) is experienced as frustration at not having what she thinks she needs, with consequent anger and resentment directed against the other. In sophisticated envy the good (or kind of good) is thought to be needed not necessarily or not merely for its own sake, it is needed primarily to secure or boost the person's self-esteem. The emotional experience takes place against the background of insecure self-esteem. Her self-esteem must be insecure for her to be feeling as she does: she would not feel as frustrated and hostile toward the other if her view of herself needed no protection from comparison, if there were no fear that painful shortcomings might be revealed. She cannot afford to be reminded by the contrast with the other of what she takes to be her own inferiority.

If this is correct then envy, in its sophisticated form, is a self-protective emotion. It is self-protective in that the thoughts and desires constitutive of it are directed away from the area of vulnerability and toward the other's possession and hence comparative advantage. It is a way of warding off possible feelings of shame and humiliation at one's shortcomings, or at least at their being exposed to oneself and possibly others. The self to be protected is, in the person's own view, a defective self. If this were not so, she would not have the needs revealed in her envy. What it lacks may be something she believes to be itself a requisite for being of worth: money, a certain social position, beauty, personal relationships, etc. Or it may be something which she thinks is needed to give her value in the eyes of others. This would be the case where she values merely derivatively what the other has and she lacks; but in that case she will value in the first sense being well thought of by others. She will require their esteem to be able to esteem herself. Either way, her thoughts and desires when feeling envy are misdirected: her self-esteem is insecure because she thinks of herself as lacking that which would enable her to think well of herself. The rational and straightforward response to this situation would be for her to try and achieve that good, or, where this is not possible, come to terms with herself by finding other grounds for self-esteem. The envy-response runs counter to measures such as these by directing attention away from the supposed defect and focusing on the other's possession. But neither hostility against the other nor any wish to spoil that good can possibly put matters right for the person concerned. On the contrary, by directing her thoughts toward the other's possession of the good and away from her own defect she can disguise from herself what is crucially wrong and save herself from a hostility which is self-directed. But this is a form of self-defense which is quite superficial, for it cannot alter what is essentially wrong with her situation. Not only is the inadequacy of her self-esteem merely ignored rather than mended, but in failing to face the real problem she deprives herself of the chance to repair matters by some form of reassessment of herself and her situation.

The good which the envious desire and yet spoil is a self worthy of esteem. They spoil it at least in this sense, that in thought and desire they pervert their aim by disguising from themselves the insecure foundation of their self-esteem. Envy seems to have a feature which Sartre thought was characteristic of all emotions.[8] It is a case of *mauvais foi:* the envious person aims to change the world by magic; spoiling the other's possession of the good is to magically establish her own worth.

Sophisticated envy is self-defeating; it cannot achieve what it really wants. The position of the envious is even worse if, as is perhaps typically the case, she also in thought and desire spoils the good in its first, straightforward sense, perhaps by belittling what the other has and she lacks. Marcel's great-aunt could maneuver herself into a position where she would pity rather than envy the other, so she could be pleased or proud that she did not have what belonged to the other. But this must be a corrupt and self-deceptive basis for pleasure or pride, given her initial evaluations and her reasons for changing them. She will be confused in her evaluations. In Klein's theory, the infant suffering from serious feelings of envy cannot keep apart successfully love and hate, cannot keep apart the good and the bad object. Similarly, in the case of sophisticated envy the ambivalent attitude toward the good in the case envisaged makes it impossible for the person concerned to be clear on precisely what her self-esteem ought to be based; concerned as she is with her self-esteem she has left herself no means of fostering it.

V

Thought of as vices, envy and jealousy share some obvious characteristics. But there are also important differences, which lead to the conclusion that envy is the more vicious of the two. Envy has emerged as typically involving an interconnected threefold destructiveness: the envious experience hostile feelings toward the possessor of the coveted good; they wish to destroy the other's possession of the good; and their thoughts and desires are destructive of the good itself. Jealousy, too, involves other-directed hostility. But *prima facie* at least such hostility would seem to be on the whole rather more rationally based: the other is seen as the source of a threat to a precious possession, rather than the possessor of a desired good, and if he really is the instigator of such a threat, and has no business to be, then hostile feelings directed against him may conceivably be justified. This thought is supported by the consideration that while the jealous value and therefore want to keep a possession they regard as necessary for their well-being, the concern of the envious is the discrepancy, the relative standing of the other *vis-à-vis* themselves, and what they want primarily is the having-of-the-good-the-other-has, or is the-other-not-having-that-good. They do not value necessarily or mainly the good as such. The jealous may be right in thinking their possession of such worth, and right, therefore, in wanting to protect it; but it is at any rate questionable whether the concern of the envious can ever be justified. And further, since, unlike the envious, the jealous value the good itself, their relevant thoughts and desires are never directly destructive of it. There are here no cases parallel to the ones I enumerated as involving envious thoughts destructive of the good itself. The main desire of the jealous is to keep and protect the good, not to spoil and destroy it.

Envy is aggressive, jealousy is protective. This is so because they are experienced differently: jealousy, unlike envy, is *experienced* as a threat, though the person herself may not always be aware of precisely what it is that is threatened. In the case of sophisticated jealousy it is not merely her security and comfort, but also her self-esteem. The threat to self-esteem may have different sources, some of them more respectable than others: the withdrawal of the other's affection, unique attention, or devotion may itself lead her to doubt her value as a person. But it may not be the loss of these possessions as such which does the damage. The jealous husband may not care particularly for his wife and for what she has to give. Posession of her devotion is of value rather in that it is indicative of his status. Or again, the value of what was his may be thought to lie not in any intrinsic worth, but in the fact of it now apparently being valued by others. In that case, too, the situation is humiliating in revealing the possibility of being unable to hold on to something which has just been shown to be worth keeping. And this would be so, too, where the loss is thought to consist in losing esteem in the eyes of others in consequence of the original loss, for it is humiliating not to be seen by others as one wants to be seen. There is here, at least, a loss of a boost to self-esteem.

Sophisticated jealousy is not a self-protective emotion. It will not, therefore, share those features which made sophisticated envy inherently irrational on the grounds that it involved a misdirection of thought and desire, and was essentially self-deceptive. It follows that, if jealousy is vicious in a manner which is parallel to that of envy, it must be vicious for a different reason; different features must contribute to jealousy being a vice. Having already set aside its other-directed hostility, the relevant feature must be its protectiveness of the possession or supposed or hoped-for possession. While object-envy could be dismissed altogether when considering the viciousness of envy, object-jealousy is on the contrary centrally relevant to the characterization of jealousy as a vice.

We are, in the typical case, jealous of another person. The good to be protected is a personal relationship, a good surely worth having and hence presumably worth protecting. So feeling protective about the relationship seems perfectly rational. However, since the relationship is to another person, retaining that relationship may appear to mean retaining—in some sense—the particular person as well. But this may not be so; being protective of the relationship does not necessarily coincide with being protective of the person. Being protective of the relationship may consist in cherishing it, working at it, being careful not to harm it, rather than in trying to protect it from being transferred to a rival. This possibility may not be at all in the person's mind, and she may believe even that the desired affection or attention may not be harmed by being shared. But a person taking this view of the situation is not a person suffering from jealousy; it is precisely this view of the situation which the jealous cannot take. Their protectiveness of the relation will therefore also be a protectiveness of the person concerned. But being protective of a person in such circumstances is to be possessive of that person, is to wish to prevent him from forming that type of relationship with anyone else. It seems, then, that some degree of possessiveness is built into the typical case of jealousy, and this may make jealousy vicious in a way which is parallel to the viciousness of envy.

Things but not people may be treated properly as possessions, and it is sometimes suggested that what is wrong with jealousy is that it centrally involves treating people as though they were things. This is plainly so in some cases, but since, on the whole, what is valued in a relationship is what only a person can give, the other cannot possibly be seen as merely a thing. Maybe what is wrong is that the jealous are not consistent in their view of the other: while on the one hand they want from him what only a person can give, they on the other regard him as something to be possessed, i.e., as a thing. They may want the best of both worlds. And if it is true, as I claimed, that in the jealous, protectiveness of the relationship entails some possessiveness of the other, then there would be in jealousy (as in envy) an inherent inconsistency. The jealous want the other to be both, a person and a thing to be owned.

Jealousy, since it is experienced as a threat, is not an emotion of self-protection. But, since it is experienced as a threat, it generates a defensive mechanism. Those of a jealous disposition will always be on the their guard against a conceivable threat. This is most clearly seen, of course, in the most serious cases, where it seems that the person's image of herself, her sense of identity, depends on the other person and their relationship. The narrator of *Remembrance of Things Past* is an example which, though of an extreme case, nevertheless highlights certain features of the dispositionally jealous which in a milder form tend to be present in more ordinary cases as well. Marcel's first and obvious move in keeping Albertine to himself is to ensure that she is physically close to him by living in his house. This has at least the negative advantage of having withdrawn her from the world, and so, "if she did not bring me any great joy, was at least withholding joy from others" (vol. 9, pp. 94–95). But this is plainly not enough. To ensure that her whole attention is for him alone Marcel has to have total control not only over her physical movements but also over her thoughts and desires, over that which makes her the person she is. So he is constantly engaged in spying on her, in obsessively interpreting her every word and glance (and indeed lack of glance: "It is hard enough to say 'Why did you stare at the girl who went past?' but a great deal harder to say: 'Why did you not stare at her?' " [p. 112]). He is constantly engaged also in building different theories about what her words and actions can be taken to reveal about her nature. Lying and insincerity are necessary aspects of this enterprise, not only because the other might well object to what he is doing, but mainly because if she knows that she is being constantly watched she will be on her guard and keep to herself her true thoughts and desires.

The good to be protected is, initially, the relationship itself. This clearly is spoilt by Marcel's obsession; even if such watchfulness and deviousness can be tolerated by the other, they cannot yield the kind of relationship needed to give Marcel what he seems to need. Marcel, wanting all of Albertine's attention, is thereby forced to give all his attention to her. This in itself is a perversion of his aim. Moreover, as he himself realizes, his efforts are quite futile: there is no way in which he can get the guarantee that Albertine is his entirely. Treating as a thing to be possessed what is in fact not a thing cannot secure the wanted good. In failing to establish the desired relationship, Marcel also fails to find a stable basis for his self-esteem and sense of identity.

Marcel's jealousy is pathological, and it may be that the characteristics of it do not apply to more 'normal' cases. If the difference is one merely of degree, then these, too, exhibit the faults just enumerated, though in a milder form. But to think of all 'normal' cases of jealousy as being merely less extreme than that of Marcel is probably too sweeping. His thoughts are wholly self-centered, it is his own needs alone that govern them, and govern also the relationship with Albertine he wishes to protect. But not all relationships are like that. I have spoken of being protective of a person, in the sense of not wanting him to give to others the same sort of attention and affection he gives to her, as being 'possessive'. But maybe there is a further distinction to be drawn here: the jealous person's protective thoughts may concentrate primarily on the relationship which she has good reason for thinking worth preserving for both of them, and to the value of which the other is, in her view, temporarily blind. This would involve some degree of protectiveness of the other, for his transfering his affections to a third person would destroy what she believes worth keeping. Alternatively, her thoughts may concentrate primarily on the other, on wanting to keep for herself whatever he has to give, regardless of whether the relationship itself is worth preserving. Maybe it is only the second sort of protectiveness which is properly thought of as possessiveness, maybe being protective of another does not always amount to treating him as a thing. If so, then there may be cases of jealousy which are not inherently self-defeating, and the status of jealousy as a vice would not be analogous to that of envy, for its constitutive thoughts and desires would allow for the possibility of the experience being occasionally justified. This is not to say that jealousy is not a vice: the distinction just drawn between protectiveness and possessiveness is so tenuous that the slide from the one into the other would seem in practice to be almost inevitable. It is in any case true of the dispositionally jealous (as opposed to those who only occasionally suffer from jealousy) that they are possessive, for they will approach any relationship with the desire to keep for themselves whatever the other has to offer.

VI

Since envy and jealousy are vices, neither emotion ought to be felt. But there are (at least) two sorts of objections to this conclusion. The first one is that this is a useless thing to say, at least if we accept that 'ought' implies 'can'. For neither is a feeling we can get rid of. According to the second, very different objection, it is not clear that they ought *never* to be felt, for both, even destructive envy, may sometimes be justified.

I do not know whether feelings of envy and jealousy can be eliminated. But what matters is not whether we, or most of us, will inevitably experience these emotions, but is rather our attitude toward such experiences, and our consequent tendency to indulge or to try to resist them. There is no reason to suppose that we should not be able to at least try and diminish the frequency and severity of their occurrence. But even the possibility of having such an attitude has been questioned. Nozick, for example, thinks that envy cannot be eliminated, on the grounds that self-esteem must be competitively based. We think in terms of our success or failures by comparing ourselves with others, and in this sort of situation the occurrence of envy is inevitable.[9] His contention therefore is that self-esteem is achieved by comparison with others, and in this way only. But this overstates the case. It is very likely true that as a matter of fact people tend to think of their own worth in terms of whether they are more or less successful than their neighbors in achieving what is thought worthwhile. But although more difficult, restricting oneself to pure object-envy is at least a possibility, and it seems unnecessarily pessimistic to think that human nature is such that people cannot acquire a proper sense of their own worth on the basis of having achieved what they believe to be worthwhile for its own sake.

Rawls, although he states initially that a rational person is not subject to envy, later makes an exception, namely: "where envy is a reaction to the loss of self-respect in circumstances where it would be unreasonable to expect someone to feel differently. Society may permit such large discrepancies in primary goods that these differences cause loss of self-esteem. For those suffering this hurt envious feelings are not irrational."[10] Rawls seems here to give a counterexample to my thesis, for if my account is correct then at least the experience of the sophisticated type of envy he has in mind can never be rational. But I think his case shows merely that that envy may be deemed to be rational looked at from one point of view, viz., when certain of the beliefs involved are fully justified and we therefore understand and sympathize with the feeling. This is not incompatible with the account I have given: the beliefs concerning the distribution of the good may be justified, and the person holding them may be perfectly rational in doing so. But envy consists not merely in holding such beliefs. At the time of experiencing emotional envy the other-directed hostile feelings will still be self-protective, and so self-deceptive and self-defeating. While in the throes of the emotion the person concerned still wants to change the situation by magic: the destruction of the other's good is to restore her faith in her own worth, so that on this occasion irrationality in the form of internal inconsistency will remain a feature of envy. Justified beliefs of the sort picked out by Rawls are not sufficient to make the experience rational. It is in this respect, I suggested, that jealousy may differ from envy: depending on what is permissible in treating another as a person, the thoughts and desires of the jealous may on occasion be rational and justified.

In this discussion of envy and jealousy as vices I have concentrated on one central feature: in virtue of their constitutive thoughts and desires both, in different ways, tend to be destructive of the valued good and hence tend to be self-defeating. For this reason envy and jealousy are self-perpetuating and undermining of the person's peace or happiness. There is, of course, much more to be said. Given their respective natures it can be shown how they interrelate with other vices, and why it is that it may seem attractive to be the object of these emotions. It is plain, for instance, that the seriously envious will be incapable of charity, for they will resent and begrudge the other his possession. Insofar as a person is envious, she is also mean and spiteful to some degree. Similar considerations apply to the jealous; their constant anticipation of a possible threat to their possessions will make them suspicious and lacking in trust. In both cases grievances against the other and the need to protect her self-esteem will tend to isolate the person concerned and make impossible the flourishing of any relationship. The concern with self-esteem also points to a connection with pride, since those so preoccupied will try and acquire or hold on to a good they can be proud of. Similarly, those who wish to attract envy or jealousy want to have it confirmed that what is in their possession is worth having. Envy in particular has been linked with pride the sin, for those who are proud, it is thought, will also be envious. This will be true at any rate in a case like that of Satan, where a person's pride or arrogance is such that he takes it to be diminishing of his own worth to see anyone in a position better than (or even equal to) his own; wanting to be supreme he will not tolerate any such advantage in another, and given that such supremacy is unattainable he will never be without feelings of envy.

Notes

1. Jane Gardam, *Crusoe's Daughter* (London, 1985), 174.
2. John Rawls, *A Theory of Justice* (Oxford, 1973), 533.
3. Melanie Klein, *Envy and Gratitude* (London, 1957).
4. Max Scheler, for instance, thinks that envy is due to "a feeling of impotence we experience when another person owns a good we covet. But this tension between desire and nonfulfillment does not lead to envy until it flares into hatred against the owner, until the latter is falsely considered to be the *cause* of our deprivation," *Ressentiment* (New York, 1972), 52 (italics in text).
5. Jerome Neu, "Jealous Thoughts," in *Explaining Emotions,* edited by Amelie Oksenberg Rorty (Berkeley, 1980), 433.
6. Kant, in his lecture "Jealousy and its Offspring—Envy and Grudge," makes a similar point: "To be envious is to desire the failure and unhappiness of another not for the purpose of advancing our own success and happiness but because we might then ourselves be perfect and happy as we are," *Lectures on Ethics* (New York, 1979), 217. The envious may not look for a positive gain but merely hope to remove what interferes with their well-being.
7. Proust, *Remembrance of Things Past* (London, 1966), vol. 1, 27. Page references to this work in section 5 are to this edition.
8. Sartre, *Sketch for a Theory of the Emotions,* section III.
9. Robert Nozick, *Anarchy, State and Utopia* (Oxford, 1974), 243. Hume puts forward a similar view: "So little are men govern'd by reason in their sentiments and opinions, that they always judge more of objects by comparison than from their intrinsic worth and value" *(Treatise* II.2.8). Kant naturally disagrees: "There are two methods by which men arrive at an opinion of their worth: by comparing themselves with the Idea of perfection and by comparing themselves with others." The latter, disasterous method is, he thinks, largely instilled by upbringing: "To ask our children to model themselves on others is to adopt a faulty method of upbringing, and as time goes on the fault will strike its roots deep" ("Jealousy and its Offspring," 216–218).
10. Rawls, *Theory of Justice,* 534.

MIDWEST STUDIES IN PHILOSOPHY, XIII (1988)

A Man by Nothing Is So Well Betrayed as by His Manners? Politeness as a Virtue[1]

FELICIA ACKERMAN

Politeness and rudeness are important dimensions in social life and in day-to-day evaluations of people's behavior and character. But these concepts have received little philosophical attention. This paper aims at remedying that lack by explicating the concept of politeness and discussing the status of politeness as a virtue and its relation to other virtues.

I

Politeness is one of a family of concepts whose members include such notions as civility, good manners, courtesy, and etiquette, along with their opposites of rudeness, incivility, bad manners, and discourtesy. Within each group are concepts that have subtle differences of nuance. This paper concentrates on politeness/good manners as the central notion and uses the terms 'politeness' and 'good manners' interchangeably.

For attempts at general characterizations of good manners, it seems natural to consult etiquette books. As a sample, consider *Drebett's Etiquette and Modern Manners,* which describes good manners as follows:

> The object [of manners] is to put everybody at ease, whatever their [*sic*] age or rank.[2]

> Good manners mean showing consideration for others—a sensibility that is innate in some people and has to be carefully cultivated in others.

> Whatever its sources, however, its purpose is to enable people to come together with ease, stay together for a time without friction or discord, and leave one another in the same fashion. This is the role of custom and of courtesy: the first

stimulates personal confidence and reduces misunderstandings, the latter reassures us that our associates mean to be friendly.[3]

This account has a number of strengths. It recognizes that manners inherently involve some notion of consideration for others and of helping social encounters flow smoothly. It also recognizes that manners have both a conventional side (as illustrated by the fact that handshaking is a customary greeting in American but not in Indian society), which seems to be what *Drebett's* means by 'custom', and a non-conventional side, which seems to be what *Drebett's* means by 'courtesy' and which sets down limits on the aims and functions a rule can have in order to count as a rule of good manners at all. Thus, regardless of which society one is considering, a system of rules for eating will not count as a system of table manners unless it has certain ends (preventing sudden death from choking or food poisoning would not qualify, for example), but how these appropriate ends are to be implemented will, of course, vary from society to society.

The term 'custom' is actually a bit misleading here. What counts as polite behavior in a given society is less a matter of how people in that society customarily behave than of how whatever authorities the society recognizes on the subject of manners say good manners require people to behave. (Note the parallel here with rules of correct usage of a language. Whether 'ain't' counts as correct English is not a matter of whether English speakers customarily use it, but of whether it would be sanctioned by the sources English speakers recognize as authorities on correct usage.)

An important weakness of *Drebett's* account is that the purpose specified for good manners is too broad. Rules of good manners do not aim to prevent just any kind of discord; for example, they do not aim to prevent political discord in Congress. Similarly, they do not always aim to enable people to "come together with ease"; for example, they may aim to make it difficult to approach the Queen. *Drebett's* itself notes elsewhere that rules of good manners may be designed partly to exclude and confuse *"arrivistes."*[4] Moreover, good manners can often be used on specific occasions to make one's enemies feel guilty, inferior, or otherwise uncomfortable, a practice often advocated by etiquette writer Judith Martin (a.k.a. Miss Manners), who delights in recommending "faultlessly polite and cheerful ways to drive others into the madhouse."[5]

Social scientists have suggested somewhat more sophisticated accounts. Thus, Goffman characterizes ceremonial rules (as opposed to substantial rules) as follows:

A ceremonial rule is one which guides conduct in matters felt to have secondary or even no significance in their own right, having their primary importance—officially, anyway—as a conventionalized means of communication by which the individual expresses his character or conveys his appreciation of other participants in the situation. . . . in our society, the code which governs ceremonial rules and ceremonial expressions is incorporated into what we call etiquette.[6]

This overlooks the rules for conventional expressions of aspects of one's character whose violation would not constitute a breach of manners or etiquette. For example, it is conventional (at least on college campuses) to wear buttons with slogans expressing one's political (or other) views, but it is not automatically a breach of manners or etiquette to wear a button proclaiming views one opposes instead. Similarly, during an election campaign, it is conventional to wear a button bearing the name of one's favored candidate, but it is not automatically a breach of manners or etiquette to attempt to mislead by wearing a button for a candidate one opposes. Also, there are rules of good manners or etiquette that originally had (and sometimes still have) important "substantial" purposes beyond the ceremonial ones Goffman allows. The rule about not talking with one's mouth full has an aesthetic purpose. Rules of manners or etiquette regarding asking permission to smoke in social gatherings seem as much concerned with people's physical comfort as with their sensibilities. But there are limits. It may be impolite to smoke and make a mildly allergic person cough or to smell up a room with a cigar, but where the expected physical consequences are drastic enough (for example, in a case where one knows someone would drop dead instantly upon being exposed to one's cigar smoke), speaking of rudeness and politeness seems ludicrous.[7]

How might an improved account go? The following conditions seem relevant to whether a rule is a rule for polite behavior.

1. The rule concerns social behavior, i.e., behavior between people or between people and other sentient beings normally capable of grasping rules of the system.[8]
2. The rule is extra-legal and is not enforced by legal sanctions.
3. The rule is part of a system of rules (or may be the whole system as a limiting case) having the original purpose and/or current function for the intended beneficiaries of making social life orderly, predictable, comfortable, and pleasant, over and above considerations of survival, health, safety, economy, religious edicts, or playing a game,[9] and doing this by such means as:
   a. making social life aesthetically appealing and avoiding situations perceived as aesthetically repellent;
   b. minimizing embarrassment, hurt feelings, and unpleasant surprises;
   c. showing consideration for others, respecting and defining their social privacy and autonomy;
   d. providing the security of conventional forms and rituals;
   e. reflecting distinctions of rank and privilege considered important.
4. It is socially sanctioned to take a violation of the rule by other people in situations involving oneself as an affront to oneself.

Note that rules of polite behavior help define as well as reflect what counts as aesthetically repellent, embarrassing, intrusive, etc. I suggest that being a rule of polite behavior is a concept that has what Alston calls combination-vagueness;[10] i.e., in order for something to fall under the concept, "enough" of a series of conditions must be satisfied where it is unclear in principle how many are enough, and they may be unequally weighted. Thus, the rules relating to American eating habits that concern which utensils to use, when and who is served in what order, as well as such matters as chewing with closed mouth, not pressing others to violate their diets, or grabbing food from other's plates, etc., are clearly rules of good manners. Laws against murder and rules for playing solitaire clearly are not.

Matters can be less clear when only some of the conditions are satisfied. Conditions 1, 3b, 3c, 3e, and 4 seem particularly important, the others less so. For example, rules of polite behavior in medieval Japan violated condition 2. They were enforced by law,[11] as are contemporary rules against loud night parties in some cities (which does not seem to keep annoying one's neighbors by having such parties from being rude). But the reason rules of grammar or rules for playing a musical instrument, unlike rules restricting the use of obscene language, do not count as rules of polite behavior seems to lie in conditions 3b, 3c, and 4. Rules of grammar or musical performance do not seem rooted in consideration for the feelings of others, and it is not socially sanctioned to take violation by others of these rules in social interaction with oneself as an affront. There is some social sanction, however, for feeling affronted by one's dinner companion's poor table manners, although the sanction for this decreases as the manners in question become more esoteric (using the wrong fish fork, for example). Note that condition 1 does not commit us to Martin's extreme view of the social nature of manners, that "In manners, as distinct from morals, . . . the only [act that counts] is one that has been witnessed [by someone else]."[12] Such a view seems excessive, as it precludes attributing rudeness to someone who says to his comatose grandfather in no one else's hearing, "Hurry up and croak, you old idiot, so I can inherit your money."

Some of the most interesting problems in characterizing rules as rules of polite behavior have to do with the qualification in condition 3 that mentions the intended beneficiaries of the rules. This, along with condition 3e, allows for the possibility that a system of manners may not only be hierarchical but may not benefit or even be intended to benefit all the categories of people to which it applies. Several cases can be distinguished here. First are such cases as the rules of manners for showing "respect" for women or old people. While it can, of course, be argued that this sort of respect is actually a form of condescension whose function is to reinforce the subordinate role of its recipients, as long as there is an official rationale that these rules benefit and show respect for the recipients, the rules clearly count as rules for good manners, although not necessarily desirable rules. But what about such cases as the practice that a lord is to walk through the door ahead of a commoner, or the elaborate "Jim Crow" set of rules of social segregation in the pre–1960s American South? "Jim Crow" rules had components that were legally enforced (such as blacks having to sit in the back of busses) and components that were not (such as blacks not entering the homes of whites through the front door or being entertained as guests in the living room). Limiting consideration to the cases that did not involve legal sanctions, we can distinguish three sorts of cases. The first would involve a rationale (however preposterous) that the rules in some sense benefited subordinates as well as superiors, for example, by making for a more orderly society[13] or one where people would not be embarrassed by being strained beyond their "true capacities." This still seems to count as a system of politeness, and one where there are politeness-obligations from the members of the superior class to those of the subordinate class, as well as vice versa. An even more debased case would involve no claim that the rules benefit the commoners or blacks, but would claim that members of the subordinate class are natural inferiors who accordingly owe deference to their natural superiors. At most, this seems to be a one-way system of politeness, where members of the subordinate class have politeness-obligations to members of the superior class, but not vice versa. A final case involves inegalitarian rules with no rationale at all beyond the power of the superior class to enforce them. It seems doubtful that this would count as a system of politeness at all, in which case condition 3 should be amended to require that an appropriate rationale (of one of the sorts mentioned above) for the social distinctions in question be part of the system.

My account, like *Drebett's,* allows for both conventional and non-conventional sides of politeness. There are actually three levels here. At the most general level are my conditions 1–4 that can be used cross-culturally to decide whether a given rule is to count as a rule of politeness at all. Second is the room for cross-cultural variations in the specifics of the aims and functions in condition 3. For example, societies may differ as to what distinctions of rank and privilege are to be respected. Finally, there are the conventional expressions of polite social gestures, such as my earlier example that a handshake is a common greeting in the United States but not in India (even if the two societies have similar cultural values about the importance of greeting a stranger with friendliness and respect).

These distinctions allow for the possibility of some polite behavior even from a person who does not know the conventions of a society he is visiting: he can at least stay off any topic that he has reason to believe his listener will find embarrassing or unpleasant and that there is no overriding need to discuss. Someone who is largely ignorant of the conventions of another society may still happen to know of a topic some particular person in that society would find embarrassing or unpleasant.

These distinctions also point to a way there can be a split between what one might call the letter and the spirit of good manners, as in the popular anecdote about a host who drinks the water in his fingerbowl to set at ease his guest who has made a similar move out of ignorance. Another, more interesting split of this sort involves flaunting one's pleasantness, professed interest, and considerateness as a means of making another person uncomfortable. As I have mentioned, Martin gives cases where one can (and on her view should) use politeness in this way, for example, by frustrating unsolicited advice-givers by repeatedly requesting ever-more-detailed suggestions, listening quietly, and then ignoring the advice ("one of Miss Manners' favorite faultlessly polite and cheerful ways to drive others into the madhouse")[14] or by making someone who did not invite one to her birthday party "feel terrible and remorseful—and all by behaving like a perfect lady!"[15] (in this case by telling her one hopes she had a wonderful birthday and inviting her to one's own birthday party). Is this genuinely polite behavior? Consider another case. Normally, greeting one's colleagues is polite, but suppose someone knows one of his colleagues would resent being subjected to his greeting, perhaps because she knows he was instrumental in denying her tenure. It seems clear that it would be kinder for him not to greet her, but would it also be more polite? In both cases, the answer seems to hinge on what, if anything, the society's rules of politeness have to say about what to do when the usual forms of politeness appear to defeat some of their own ends. Martin seems right that our society's concept of politeness allows unkindness in the sorts of cases she presents. For my question about the case involving the colleagues, the answer seems less clear.

II

Is politeness a virtue? If so, how is it related to other virtues? It may seem that if politeness is a virtue, it differs from the usual cases of moral virtues in a way illustrated by Philippa Foot's remark that "moral judgment concerns itself with a man's reasons for acting as well as with what he does. Law and etiquette require only that certain things are done or left undone, but no one is counted as charitable if he gives alms 'for the praise of men', and one who is honest only because it pays him to be honest does not have the virtue of honesty."[16] This is certainly oversimplified for the case of law, which takes into account someone's intentions as well as what he does. It may be oversimplified for politeness as well. A person's actions may count as polite provided they accord with society's rules of polite behavior, but it seems at least questionable whether habitually acting politely is enough to make him count as a polite person. Suppose he aims at being rude but inevitably ends up doing what counts as polite through misinformation about his society's conventions. Is he a polite person? "In a sense, yes; in a sense, no?" Someone who follows the conventions of politeness "for the praise of men," on the other hand, clearly does count as a polite person. As long as he habitually acts with deliberate politeness, ulterior motives seem irrelevant to the question of whether he is a polite person. Thus, it is politeness that is not ulteriorly motivated whose status as a virtue should be examined. I will call this "intrinsic politeness."

Precisely what is the connection between intrinsic politeness and morality? Eugene Valberg has pointed out that "it is obvious that statements of etiquette are not in and of themselves moral statements."[17] But, of course, there can still be moral grounds for obeying the rules of polite behavior, insofar as there are moral grounds for such ends as those in conditions 3a–e and for avoiding actions that will give other people social sanction for feeling affronted (condition 4). The diversity of these ends shows some of the complexity of this issue. For example, it is obvious that both moral defenses and moral objections can be made concerning the distinctions of rank and privilege embodied in a given system of manners. What is less obvious is that these distinctions may involve priorities that are a matter of gradations less standard than distinctions of age, gender, social class, or social caste. Martin, for example, is a staunch believer that good manners require unhappy people, even those who "have had a genuine tragedy in their lives,"[18] to put on a happy social face in order to avoid blighting the day of anyone who might be better off—a position that might be criticized as the equivalent of taxing the poor to support the rich. A related objection can be raised to the stricture that requires the newly bereaved to pen handwritten replies to (possibly hundreds of) sympathy notes. But it might also be claimed that the pressure to maintain conventional forms and rituals is diverting and beneficial for the sufferer.

To the extent that intrinsic politeness is a virtue, it is presumably so because either the distinctions embodied in condition 3e, the forms of consideration embodied in 3a–c, the security embodied in 3d, or the avoidance of making people feel affronted (condition 4) are things that are intrinsically good. Thus, it seems doubtful that there is much virtue in forms of intrinsic politeness that involve obeying the letter of conventionally polite forms that defeat the spirit of politeness in other conditions, except insofar as there is some virtue in upholding the system of rules itself (for example, to discourage defections by others or to provide the security of convention, as indicated in condition 3d, which cannot be defeated when the letter of conventionally polite forms is followed).

Common sense suggests that insofar as it serves the aims of conditions 3a–d, intrinsic politeness is a virtue, but not one of the most important ones.[19] It seems ludicrous, for example, to attach weight to whether someone who successively and painlessly murdered six wives in their sleep was an intrinsically polite person (let alone whether he was polite to his wives!). But apparently not everyone finds this sort of consideration ludicrous. Newspaper stories from the 1950s and 1960s frequently quoted neighbors of a newly discovered ex-Nazi torturer as objecting to his extradition or prosecution on the grounds that he had rehabilitated himself as a decent person living a decent life, as witnessed by his good manners, neat appearance, and well-tended lawn.

The limited importance of intrinsic politeness as a virtue leads to moral dangers in giving it undue weight. One way this can happen is by giving someone's manners undue weight in judging him as a person. Even Martin grants that "there is a ridiculous emphasis on the superficial [in the fact that] people will be judged more on their manners . . . than on their character,"[20] and quotes Somerset Maugham's remark that "few can suffer manners different from their own without distaste. It is seldom that a man is shocked by the thought that someone has seduced another's wife, and it may be that he preserves his equanimity when he knows that another has cheated at cards or forged a check . . . but it is hard for him to make a bosom friend of one who drops his aitches and almost impossible if he scoops up gravy with his knife."[21]

Even adherence to the spirit of politeness can be overrated in judging a person. For example, someone may be overvalued for his good manners, when his intrinsic desire to maintain pleasant surfaces and avoid embarrassing others keeps him from speaking out against injustice. Similarly, politeness can be overvalued in making one's own decisions about how to behave. Another virtue that can conflict with intrinsic politeness is honesty, although it is often unclear how this conflict should be resolved. Martin holds that "Hypocrisy is not generally a social sin, but a virtue"[22] in explaining why one should answer someone's question about the merit of her granddaughter's unmeritorious performance with insincere praise. But a natural objection to this sort of tact is that once it becomes a social practice, it undermines trust about the relevant situation. If politeness requires an affirmative answer to 'Did you like my flute solo?' an affirmative answer will not be a reliable guide to the speaker's opinion. This problem is inherent in the nature of tact as a social practice, rather than being an avoidable result of taking polite conventions too literally, as in the sort of person who gives a literal answer to 'Hello. How are you?' 'How are you?' (as opposed to 'Tell me how you've been; I really want to know') is not intended to be taken literally, but tactful praise is intended not only to be polite, but to be believed. That is what makes it reassuring. And tact also requires a polite lie in response to, 'Tell me, what did you *really* think of my flute solo? I really want to know.' It might also be argued that it is condescending to assume someone "really" wants or needs reassurance when he appears to be asking for an opinion.

Any virtue (other than loyalty itself) seems able to conflict with loyalty, since its requirements may conflict with the interests or desires of someone to whom one is or should be loyal. But politeness, with its usual stress on widespread impersonal a-greeability, provides an especially fertile field for such conflicts. Suppose a man's wife wants him to "cut" (i.e., snub) someone who has done her a serious wrong. The spirit of politeness requires that the husband greet this person pleasantly (and even the let-ter of politeness may afford no means for a snub in this situation), but the wife may reasonably see such politeness as a breach of loyalty—and, of course, it may be a breach of loyalty even if she is not there to witness it. Politeness can also conflict with loyalty when there is no prior act of wrongdoing to be given its due (?) by a snub. Con-sider the following case.[23] A woman is emotionally devastated by the unexpected dis-covery that she is going blind and a few hours later is impetuously rude to a waitress in a restaurant. Her lover is far more upset by her rudeness than by her fear of im-pending blindness and in her presence apologizes to the waitress for this rudeness—a move which the first woman considers a betrayal. 'A man by nothing is so well be-trayed as by his manners' here can have, not its original import that one can betray his boorishness and crudeness by his bad manners, but the import that one can also be-tray his superficiality and small-mindedness by his overemphasis on good manners where their display is incompatible with deeper values.[24]

Notes

1. "The gentle mind by gentle deeds is known / For a man by nothing is so well bewrayed / As by his manners." (Edmund Spenser, *The Faerie Queene,* Book VI, Canto 3, Stanza 1.)

2. *Drebett's Etiquette and Modern Manners,* edited by Elsie Burch Donald (London, 1982), 7.

3. Ibid., 10.

4. Ibid., 9. See also Judith Martin, *Miss Manners' Guide to Excruciatingly Correct Behavior* (New York, 1982), 7, and Judith Martin, *Miss Manners' Guide to Rearing Perfect Children* (New York, 1984), 327–28.

5. Ibid., 288. See also ibid., xviii and 178, and Martin, *Guide to Excruciatingly Correct Be-havior,* 7, 195, and 215, as well as Peg Bracken, *I Try to Behave Myself: Peg Bracken's Etiquette Book* (New York, 1963), 72.

6. Erving Goffman, "Deference and Demeanor," in Erving Goffman, *Interaction Ritual* (Garden City, N.Y., 1967), 54–55.

7. Thus, see Bracken's facetious remark about "Good Manners for the Smoker": "He mustn't smoke where there are NO SMOKING signs, for these usually mean business. It is bad form to explode a planeload of people or to blow a hospital sky-high." Bracken, *I Try to Behave Myself,* 41.

8. Thus, Martin seems right in saying that "the whole concept of proper and improper be-havior does not apply between people and machines" (Martin, *Guide to Excruciatingly Correct Behavior,* 202) and that it is ludicrous to speak of politeness toward one's dog (Ibid., 191). But simply someone's status as a human being seems adequate to make him a suitable object of po-lite behavior even if his particular cognitive capacities are not up to understanding or reciproca-tion. (For example, see Martin, *Guide to Rearing Perfect Children,* 336–37, on polite behavior toward "senile" people.)

9. The qualifier here reflects the insight behind Goffman's view about the limitations on

the "substantial" function of ceremonial rules of etiquette, although my above counterexamples show that his view is too strong.

10. See William P. Alston, *Philosophy of Language* (Englewood Cliffs, N.J., 1964), 87 ff.

11. See Myra Waldo, *Myra Waldo's Travel Guide: Orient and Asia* (New York, 1965), 53–54.

12. Martin, *Guide to Excruciatingly Correct Behavior,* 249.

13. "When Dr. Johnson declared that it makes things much simpler to know that a lord goes through a door ahead of a commoner, he was no more striking a blow against individualism than against equality: he was only interested in saving everybody time." Louis Kronenberger, quoted in Bracken, *I Try to Behave Myself,* 17. The obvious objections to this rationale (why not have the commoner or the taller man go first?), like the obvious objections to racist claims that segregation benefited blacks, need not concern us here.

14. Martin, *Guide to Rearing Perfect Children,* 288.

15. Ibid., 178.

16. Philippa Foot, "Morality as a System of Hypothetical Imperatives," *Philosophical Review* 83 (1972): 312–13.

17. Eugene Valberg, "Phillipa Foot on Etiquette and Morality," *Southern Journal of Philosophy* 15 (1977): 388.

18. Martin, *Guide to Excrutiatingly Correct Behavior,* 243. See also ibid., 678–79, and Martin, *Guide to Rearing Perfect Children,* 319–20. A similar rule is supported by Emily Post. See *Emily Post's Etiquette: The Blue Book of Social Usage,* revised by Elizabeth L. Post (New York, 1965), 41.

19. "Think of situations like 'I *know* Emily Post wouldn't approve, but etiquette hasn't got anything to do with this. This is *serious*,' " Lawrence Becker, "The Finality of Moral Judgments: A Reply to Mrs. Foot," *Philosophical Review* 82 (1973): 369. (Italics in original.) Even using the less trivial-sounding terms 'good manners' or 'courtesy' does not militate against the view that "For all practical purposes, we may ignore considerations of [good manners] in life-or-death situations." (Ibid.)

20. Martin, *Guide to Rearing Perfect Children,* 186.

21. Ibid., 185–86, quoted from Somerset Maugham, *The Narrow Corner.*

22. Ibid., 85. Compare Ze'ev Chafets' affectionate description of manners in Israel: "Excessive displays of . . . good manners are considered suspect, manifestations of superficiality or worse. If you are in a good mood, you show it; if your feet hurt, you show it, too." Ze'ev Chafets, *Heroes, Hustlers, Hard Hats, and Holy Men: Inside the New Israel* (New York, 1980), 201.

23. See Felicia Ackerman, "A Man by Nothing is So Well Betrayed as by His Manners," *Mid-American Review* 6 (1986): 1–12.

24. I am deeply grateful to Marilyn McCord Adams, Katrina Avery, Sara Ann Ketchum, and James Van Cleve for graciously discussing various issues in this paper with me.

Remorse and Agent-Regret

MARCIA BARON

1

This essay issues from my fascination with Williams's essay, "Moral Luck," particularly with the notion of agent-regret, and from a belief that the notion, which remains sketchy in Williams's work, deserves further development and scrutiny.[1] My interest in agent-regret stems from two concerns.[2] The first has to do with the ethics of duty-ethics of virtue debate; the second with questions about collective responsibility.

One of the chief disagreements between defenders of ethics of duty (ED) and proponents of ethics of virtue (EV) is that the former hold, while the latter deny, that a moral agent who lacks a sense of duty is, as a moral agent, deficient.[3] The disagreement can be put this way (despite the fact that different things are meant by "a sense of duty"): ED proponents hold that a moral agent is deficient if she never judges that she morally ought to do x; EV proponents, questioning the importance to moral conduct of thoughts that one morally *ought* to do x, and believing that one can be perfectly moral—in one's motives as well as in what one effects—without having such thoughts, deny that a moral agent needs to have and be guided by thoughts about what she or he morally ought to do.[4]

One way to test our ideas on this issue, though by no means the only way,[5] is to change the topic slightly and ask: Would a moral agent who never felt and never was disposed to feel remorse (or guilt) be ipso facto deficient? The connection is this. Remorse, I take it,[6] involves a judgment on the agent's part that she acted wrongly and should and could have acted differently. Moreover, the judgment is action-guiding; it does not leave the agent cold. It has motivational force.[7] Now, if someone could be perfectly good as a moral agent without ever feeling remorse or being disposed to feel it, that would be a strong indication that a perfectly good moral agent need not ever judge that she morally ought to have acted in such-and-such a way. (Whether it would be decisive depends on how it is defended, i.e., on whether the defense focuses on the cognitive component of remorse or only on the affective component.) What bearing would it have on the thesis that such a moral agent need not ever judge that she morally ought *to act* in such-and-such a way? It does not tell directly in favor of that thesis, but indirectly it does; for while it is not inconceivable that someone might make first-person "moral ought" judgments in the present tense but never in the past tense, it would be odd. It would be strange since our thoughts about *how we should have acted* are one of the main sources of ideas as to *how we should act*. So, if remorse or the disposition to feel it is not a crucial part of the character of a perfectly good moral agent, that tells in favor of ethics of virtue. For the same reasons, if the disposition to feel remorse is a crucial part of such an agent's character, that tells in favor of ethics of duty. In neither case is the consideration decisive, but the connection between the two questions (about remorse and about 'moral ought' judgments) is significant, and an answer one way or the other on the question of remorse is highly relevant to the ED-EV debate.

Bernard Williams's notion of agent-regret lends support to the EV thesis, for, as we will see, it lends plausibility to the thought that a disposition to feel remorse might not be an important part of the character of a perfectly good moral agent.[8] I will argue that the disposition to feel remorse remains an important part of the agent's character. Its importance is not displaced by that of a disposition to feel agent-regret.

The second motivation for this paper has a moderating effect on the first because it pulls in the opposite direction, away from what Williams likes to call "the morality system." This second motivation is a hope that (although Williams does not claim this) the notion of agent-regret may help us understand what are often thought of as irrational, senseless, "overextended" or neurotic feelings of—vaguely—guilt, and to see them as altogether appropriate. What I will suggest—and I will do no more than that—is that while remorse does retain its importance even once we recognize the significance of agent-regret, the notion of agent-regret helps us to avoid accepting too narrow a notion of responsibility, or more accurately, too tidy a division between those things that are our responsibilities and those that are no concerns ours.

I will not couch the discussion of the paper in terms of the ED-EV debate, and will return only at the end of the paper to the second topic that motivates my discussion. My focus will be on understanding agent-regret, and considering whether its importance displaces that of remorse.

2

What attitude and emotion would it be appropriate to have in the following circumstances? While driving—sober, alert, within the speed limit, and in your well-maintained automobile—you hit a small child, causing him serious injury as well as considerable pain. He darted in front of your car; you could not avoid hitting him. I take it as obvious that you should feel something, and some form of pain. I take it as obvious, furthermore, that the pain should not take the form of mere annoyance that now you will have to stop and thus be late for an appointment, or worry that the accident will damage your reputation in some way (for will others be convinced that you could not have avoided hitting him?). What should you feel, besides general upset and deep concern for the child? Guilt and remorse would be out of place, since it is not as if you did something wrong, something you should not have done. Or rather—since someone might say "Of course you did! You hit Joey!"—it is not as if you did something for which you can rightly be blamed, or even something which you could and should have avoided doing.[9] Yet what you feel, should, as Williams emphasizes, have a special character in virtue of the fact that you were the driver and not someone who saw the accident from her living room window (and like you, did not know the child). As Williams writes,

> The lorry driver who, through no fault of his, runs over a child, will feel differently from any spectator, even a spectator next to him in the cab, except perhaps to the extent that the spectator takes on the thought that he himself might have prevented it, an agent's thought. Doubtless, and rightly, people will try, in comforting him, to move the driver from this state of feeling, move him indeed from where he is to something more like the place of a spectator, but it is important that this is seen as something that should need to be done, and indeed some doubt would be felt about a driver who too blandly or readily moved to that position. We feel sorry for the driver, but that sentiment co-exists with, indeed presupposes, that there is something special about his relation to this happening, something which cannot merely be eliminated by the consideration that it was not his fault. (*ML,* 28)

The pain that the driver feels about what happened is not just pain about *that.* He was centrally involved in what happened; indeed, he was the agent. That *he was the agent,* even though what he did was unintentional and even unforeseeable, is ineliminably a part of what he feels.

Williams labels the driver's sentiments those of "agent-regret." With some reservations, I will follow suit. (I have qualms not about "agent" but about "regret." It seems out of place—especially given the example—because it is so mild. The spectator who sees the accident does not simply *regret* that it has occurred; she feels more than regret, perhaps grief and horror.) Piecing together assorted remarks in Williams's writings, I want to reconstruct what agent-regret is, how it resembles and how it differs from its nearest relatives, remorse and ordinary regret. I will then assess its significance, comparing this significance with that of remorse.

3

3.1

Let us first consider what distinguishes agent-regret from regret in general, of which agent-regret is a species. (I will use 'regret' to refer to regret in general.) Regret can be felt toward states-of-affairs or toward one's own actions (*ML,* 27). Its constitutive thought, Williams says, is "something like 'how much better if it had been otherwise'." Agent-regret is regret which one feels *qua* agent.[10] It can be felt only toward one's own past actions, or, Williams adds, "at most, actions in which he regards himself as a participant" (*ML,* 27).

Agent-regret thus differs from regret in what it can take as its object: it must be something that the agent did or something in which (as he sees it) he participated. It differs also in how it is felt; more precisely, in what it is that pains the agent. With agent-regret, one feels pained at what one has done, not (just) at what has transpired. If I accidentally mow the flowers that my child has lovingly nurtured, my thought is not likely to be just "What a shame!" or "How awful that that happened!" but rather "What have I done?!" I am not upset merely at the fact that the flowers are no longer growing or that they were mowed, but also, and primarily, at the fact that I destroyed them (albeit unintentionally).

I detect a further difference, though Williams does not note it: agent-regret has an ethical dimension which plain regret lacks. Agent-regret is felt toward the sorts of things which, if done deliberately, would properly occasion guilt. If (say, in a mood of anger) I intentionally mow down the flowers my child has nurtured, guilt or remorse would be in order; if I do it accidentally, I feel agent-regret;[11] if the neighbor I hire to mow the grass accidentally mows the flowers despite my warning not to, I am sad, but not remorseful or agent-regretful.

Contrast this case with one in which I failed to buy a particular pair of shoes for myself before they became unavailable. Clearly I can regret this, but can we imagine this regret to be agent-regret? I could feel agent-regret toward a "wider" action of which this is a part—imagine that a friend urged me to buy the shoes, and was very hurt that I did not follow his advice. But agent-regret simply toward my failure to buy myself a pair of shoes that I liked does not seem possible. What I failed to do was too trivial and too remote from ethical concerns. The guilt test helps to bring this out—if I had deliberately decided not to buy the shoes, knowing it was the last pair, certainly this would not be an occasion for guilt.

Without looking at each case contextually, there is no straightforward way to spell out which occasions call for agent-regret and which call only for plain regret. Some cases are clear: I cannot have agent-regret toward something that simply transpired, without my participation; but other cases are not clear. Importance is what most matters here, especially ethical importance; though degree of participation may also enter in. In general we can distinguish three types of cases: (1) actions and states-of-affairs toward which one may experience plain regret but not (without a special story) agent-regret; (2) actions toward which one may experience either; and (3) actions toward which we expect the agent to feel agent-regret. I have already discussed the first. In the second, the reason the agent may experience either is that there is room for disagreement both as to the importance of the action (e.g., having said something mildly hurtful) and also as to the degree to which it was the agent's doing (even if not deliberate doing) as opposed to external circumstances. (Here imagine regret at not having visited someone. This could, depending on how we fill in the details, take the form of regret, agent-regret, *or* remorse.) With respect to certain situations, we expect people to feel agent-regret, and not mere regret. The example of the lorry driver fits into the third category.

3.2

I have been focusing on agent-regret occasioned in a particular way, but careful scrutiny of Williams's examples reveals that there are two types of occasions for agent-regret—two types of instances, that is, in which we would think less of someone who felt no agent-regret, but only the regret of a spectator. There is on the one hand the case of the lorry-driver, someone who caused something bad to happen but not because of any negligence, recklessness, or malice on his part. A different sort of case from that of the lorry-driver is one in which the bad thing that one caused is more closely connected to a choice that one made: one chose (knowingly) the lesser of two evils. As both really were evils, it is quite appropriate to feel agent-regret about what one did, even while believing, reasonably and even correctly, that one could have done no better in the circumstances. In an essay written before he coined the term "agent-regret," Williams gives as an example that of Agamemnon, who killed his daughter Iphigenia, believing it to be required by his responsibilities as a commander, by considerations of honor, etc.[12] If we set aside our doubts as to whether he was right to kill her we can see the point of the illustration. The fact, if it is a fact, that he made the correct choice in no way shows it to be irrational for him to suffer intense agent-regret for what he did—and it is important that this is pain over what *he did,* not just pain about the loss of his daughter.[13] This case differs from that of the lorry-driver, since it involves deliberative choice in circumstances in which one was aware of what each choice would mean; in the case of the lorry-driver, luck plays a rather larger role, and agency a smaller one. To be more precise, agency is involved, but in the form of acts whose aim was something quite different from the actual consequences. Moreover, the actual consequence was not only unintended, but unanticipated (although known to be a possibility, the sort of thing that occasionally does happen as a result of such actions).

Since most of us are inclined to think that Agamemnon made the wrong choice, it is easy to get confused in thinking about the above example and to miss the point. To make sure that the point is clear, let us consider a different example, one where it is easier for us to believe that the agent did choose the lesser of two evils. Consider someone who decides that she really has to end her unhappy marriage, even though doing so is likely to cause, in the immediate future, more intense suffering than is continuing the relationship. She decides to end it against the wishes of her husband, who although not very happy in the marriage either, clings to it or to her (it may not be clear which it is). Aware of what a dissolution of the marriage is likely to mean for both of them (as well as for others), she is also convinced (correctly, we have to imagine) that given the emptiness and lovelessness of the marriage, they are both languishing, and in some sense wasting their lives. The pain of the break-up she judges to be less bad than remaining in the marriage. The point to make here is that we expect such a person *to be pained* at what she is doing, despite the fact that she believes that she is doing what she ought to do, doing what is best in the circumstances. We might say to her "Don't feel bad; you're doing the best thing possible," but it is as it was with the lorry-driver: if she cheered up without a trace of sadness and later told us that our remark had made all the difference, that she realized that we were right, she had no reason to feel any concern about her husband's depression since after all it was the right decision, and so on, we would be disconcerted. We expect sorrow on the part of a person making such a choice, although of course we are not surprised when, as often happens, she does not exhibit her sadness in our presence. We understand if the main sentiment is relief or an eagerness to get a "fresh start"; and we realize that she may need to "steel" herself so as not to dwell on the pain the dissolution causes and so as to weaken (or perhaps reconstruct) her emotional bond to her soon-to-be ex-spouse. But none of that changes the point: we expect sorrow, a sorrow different from that of a sibling, friend, or other "outsider," a sorrow which reflects the fact that her role is that of an agent.

Hence the point of seeing this sorrow as agent-regret. But there are differences between the two types of agent-regret. I have already noted one (that luck plays a larger role in the first type of agent-regret than in the second, and agency plays a larger role in the second). There are others. As Williams explains, agent-regret in the first case involves a wish on the agent's part that he had acted otherwise: "He deeply wishes that he had made that change which, had he known it, was in his power and which would have altered the outcome" (*ML,* 31). But in a case where one chooses the lesser of two evils, one does not regret, all things considered, what one did. Regret of any sort "necessarily involves a wish that things had been otherwise, for instance that one had not had to act as one did. But it does not necessarily involve the wish, all things taken together, that one had acted otherwise" (31). It does involve that wish in the case of the driver who might have spent the evening at home. But the wish is not involved if one judges that one made the right choice—e.g., to lay off a particular employee—but feels terrible about the suffering the choice causes to the employee, and wishes that she had not had to lay anyone off.[14]

To sum up: there are two types of agent-regret. One, typified by the case of the lorry driver, is regret over something that happened through a combination of bad luck and the fact that you were in the wrong place at the relevant time. In that case you feel regret at what you did, while not believing either that you could have *foreseen* the situation, or that, once in the situation, you could and should have acted differently. We imagine here that the driver *could not* have swerved out of the way to avoid hitting the child, because it just happened too fast. He regrets having gone out that night, but of course could not have foreseen the calamity. The other kind of case of agent-regret is typified by the person deciding to end her marriage in the circumstances described, by the boss who had to fire one of her employees, and by Agamemnon. They *chose* the deed toward which they now feel agent-regret, but they have agent-regret without wishing that they had acted differently or believing that they should have acted differently. Still, they are pained at what they did and wish that they had not *had* to act as they did.[15]

4

Williams's intriguing discussion of cases such as these makes it plain that our notions of remorse and simple regret—the regret of the spectator—do not capture the complexity of our experience. In that respect the significance of agent-regret is plain. Recall the lorry driver. If the driver is not at fault, remorse would not be an appropriate response. Neither would plain regret (even if attended by grief and horror), no matter how deeply felt. For he would then be feeling a pain no different qualitatively from what one would feel if one witnessed the calamity and was uninvolved. Beyond sheer horror, the pain that the driver can be expected to feel is agent-regret.

Important though it is to point out that there is this phenomenon, which he labels agent-regret, and that our classifications in moral psychology and in everyday life need to be adjusted accordingly, Williams means to do more. It is clear that he thinks that his discovery has a further significance. What might it be? To put the question differently: What reforms does Williams believe are in order?

The first reform is contained in what we have already said: we should recognize that if I chose the lesser of two evils, the fact that I made the right choice, did the best I could in those circumstances, by no means renders a feeling of pain about what I did inappropriate. Indeed, a "fully admirable moral agent,"[16] would have such reactions (depending on what the evils were[17]). Putting the matter in terms of conflicting *oughts* (or obligations), Williams points out that the *ought* that was overridden does *not go away*.[18] Hence the appropriateness (depending on the content of the overridden obligation) of agent-regret about what one had to do, or had to neglect—even though one is convinced that one had to, even morally had to, do it.

Outside of philosophy (and away from popular self-help manuals), we are already fairly, albeit insufficiently, aware of this, though propriety and considerateness often bar us from giving voice to our recognition of that lingering 'ought'. But moral philosophers, on Williams's view, really need to reform. Indeed, he writes in "Ethical Consistency," it "seems to me a fundamental criticism of many ethical theories that their accounts of moral conflict and its resolution do not do justice to the facts of regret and related considerations: basically because they eliminate from the scene the *ought* that is not acted upon" (*ML*, 175).[19] To reform, moral philosophers need to recognize that the overridden 'ought' remains an 'ought', and that pain over the failure to meet the obligation (and in particular, over any suffering caused by the failure to do so) is appropriate.

But this is not all, Williams thinks; more reform is needed. Indeed, at least some of the moral philosophers Williams has in mind *do* recognize the appropriateness of pain about the 'ought' that lingers. In particular, W. D. Ross explicitly allows it:

> When we think ourselves justified in breaking, and indeed morally obliged to break, a promise in order to relieve someone's distress, we do not for a moment cease to recognize a *prima facie* duty to keep our promise, and this leads us to feel, not indeed shame or repentance, but certainly compunction, for behaving as we do.[20]

Although he does not cite this passage from Ross's *The Right and the Good*, Williams seems to have it in mind when, speaking in *Ethics and the Limits of Philosophy* of the situation in which I fulfill the overriding obligation, he describes "morality's" view of the conflicting, and now overridden, obligation as follows:

> It is conceded that I may reasonably feel bad about it, but this feeling is distinguished by the morality system from remorse or self-reproach, for instance under the title "regret," which is not a moral feeling. This reclassification is important, and very characteristic of what happens when the ethical is contracted to the moral. To say that your feelings about something done involuntarily, or as the lesser of two evils, are to be understood as regret, a nonmoral feeling, implies that you should feel toward those actions as you feel toward things that merely happen, or toward the actions of others. The thought *I did it*

has no special significance; what is significant is whether I voluntarily did what I ought to have done.[21]

Ross says "compunction," not "regret," and one may question whether Williams really is, on this matter, in disagreement with him. This is a side issue, however, our aim here being to understand what reforms Williams thinks are in order once it is recognized that there is such a thing as agent-regret. Williams's concern is with how "the morality system" regards the agent's pain about having had to commit some evil, because the alternatives were more evil: Does it regard the pain as nonmoral, and as sharply different from "moral" responses such as remorse? To appreciate the concern we need to try to see what he means by "the morality system."

In the morality system, "the ethical is contracted to the moral" (*ELP*, 177). While the meaning of this claim is not entirely clear, I take him to be saying that the proponents of the morality system (or those who, less self-consciously, simply accept its parameters) try to understand the complexities of ethical experience in terms of what Williams thinks of as standard "moral" notions: obligation, guilt, blame, and responsibility. In doing so they distort; an example of how they/we distort is offered in the above quote.

The broader reform that Williams thinks is in order appears to be this. Rather than put the emphasis on whether I voluntarily did what I ought to have done, we (moral philosophers but presumably others, as well) should shift our attention to the bare fact that we did (or did not do) such-and-such.[22] Williams's proposal seems to be to downplay "moral" concepts and feelings, and to see if we cannot capture what the morality system tries to capture with these moral concepts with "ethical" concepts instead. Perhaps we are wrong to assume, as we do insofar as we subscribe to the morality system, that someone who was not disposed ever to feel remorse or guilt is not a fully admirable moral agent. This assumption, Williams hints, is based on too limited a vision, on a tacit assumption that the only ethical concepts are moral ones. Suppose someone was not disposed to feel remorse or guilt, but was disposed to feel agent-regret? The grip of the morality system has prevented us from recognizing agent-regret, and thus has kept us from considering this possibility. "Remorse or self-reproach or guilt" is, he says, "the characteristic first-personal reaction within the system, and if an agent never felt such sentiments, he would not belong to the morality system or be a full moral agent in its terms" (*ELP*, 177).

It is this question that I wish to address: Could someone be a fully admirable moral agent who was disposed to have agent-regret, but not—not ever—remorse? While I agree with many of Williams's other claims—that we need to recognize that someone who was never disposed to feel agent-regret would not be a fully admirable moral agent, and the related point that moral conflicts often, even when ideally resolved, leave a residue (an overridden 'ought' which, though "correctly" overridden, does not vanish)—I believe that the question just posed should be answered in the negative. I will argue that remorse retains an importance of its own (and indirectly that "moral" concepts in general do) and that it would be a mistake to collapse the distinction between remorse and agent-regret, or to hold that a fully admirable moral agent need not be disposed to experience remorse, as long as she is disposed to experience agent-regret.

So, having explained what Williams seems to take the importance of agent-regret and of his discussion of it to be, I turn now to remorse. I first explain what I understand remorse to be, and then argue that agent-regret is no substitute for remorse, just as remorse is no substitute for agent-regret. Two clarifications: (1) My characterization of remorse is not intended either as an alternative to his, or as a straightforward development of his remarks about remorse; I believe it to be in keeping with what he says remorse is, but since he says very little about it, I cannot be certain that he would agree with my account. (2) Since only one type of agent-regret could plausibly be thought to substitute for remorse, my argument that agent-regret is no substitute refers to that type, viz., agent-regret of the sort experienced by the lorry-driver, not agent-regret prompted by a realization that while one chose the lesser of two evils, it *was* an evil.

5

Remorse, I have already suggested, differs from agent-regret (and all regret) in its dependence on the agent's belief that she acted wrongly and should have acted differently. Recall the unlucky driver. In experiencing agent-regret, he may think such thoughts as "Oh my God, if I had just left home a little later, or stayed in and watched the television show that I usually watch. . . . " 'If only' locutions, so appropriate to agent-regret, are singularly inappropriate to remorse. Suppose the driver hit and killed a child who was riding a bicycle in the middle of the street. Annoyed at the child's behavior, the driver aimed to "show that kid who's boss," that is, frighten him and force him to move closer to the curb by refusing to slow down. "If only I had slowed down," no matter how anguished, would not express remorse without some added feature which reflected a horror not only at *what happened through him,* but at *his conduct* (and in this instance, perhaps his character, as well). And more than this: for suppose that the 'If only . . . ' expression makes reference to the agent's character. If he thinks "If only I weren't so rash," then he recognizes the connection between his character and the catastrophe;[23] but he waves it aside, as if to say, "It's not my fault; I can't help being the way I am." Remorse involves not just a judgment that it would have been much better if one had acted otherwise, and not just (in addition to this judgment) recognition of the connection between his character and the catastrophe. It involves a judgment that one could have acted otherwise and, more important, that one *should* have.[24]

When one feels remorse, one sees the conduct in question not only as one's own, and as something that could have gone differently; one sees it as something over which one had (some) control, and for which one is responsible.[25] The connection between remorse and agent-regret is analogous to that between agent-regret and regret in general: the domains of the subject-matter intersect, but the character and expression of the feelings differ even when the object is the same. This comparison helps us to see regret, agent-regret, and remorse as lying on a slide, where the second is a form of the first, and the third a form of the second. The move from regret to agent-regret to remorse involves no discarding of notions, but only the addition of layers. One goes from "If only it had been otherwise" (general regret) to "And it happened through me" (agent-regret) to "And I could have averted it"—and if at this stage the 'could' implicitly involves a 'should', we reach remorse.[26]

There is a second respect in which regret, agent-regret, and remorse lie on a slide: one might experience something between plain regret and agent-regret, or between agent-regret and remorse. It would not be at all odd for someone in a position like that of the lorry driver to search the situation for signs that he acted wrongly, and as long as he suspects that he acted wrongly, he may feel a mix of remorse and agent-regret. Or, like Sophie in William Styron's *Sophie's Choice*[27] one might recognize one's part in a ghastly, hideous project and, unsure as to whether one perhaps could and should have avoided contributing to it, or have done something to weaken it, one might feel something which wavers between remorse and agent-regret. Insofar as Sophie compares herself to friends who worked in the Resistance, the anguish she feels is remorse;[28] if in other moments she manages to convince herself that self-reproach is not warranted, and feels that her part (e.g., as secretary to Rudolph Höss while imprisoned in a concentration camp) was unavoidable, the pain may persist, but now as agent-regret rather than remorse.[29]

Someone might object that what I am calling remorse is really guilt. Perhaps so; I do not have strong views on the terminological and taxonomical question of what we should call 'remorse' and what falls under the heading of 'guilt'. My hunch is that guilt, unlike remorse, does not necessarily involve a judgment that, all things considered, one acted wrongly and should have acted otherwise. Guilt can be more general and all-encompassing than remorse; remorse is relatively specific, focused on some particular action or form of conduct, usually to some particular time-slice.[30] My concern, however, is not to press that view, but rather to show that agent-regret cannot substitute for an attitude or emotion which involves, in addition to pain at what one did, a judgment that one acted wrongly and should have acted differently. (More precisely, it is the readiness to experience or "try on" that attitude that is important.) Whether this *is* remorse is of relatively minor interest to me. Were my paper to be rewritten so as to label it 'guilt' rather than 'remorse', I would regard it as in substance almost the same paper.[31]

6

Having indicated how, as I see it, remorse differs from agent-regret, I turn now to the question of just what moral significance remorse has. My remarks are directed toward explaining why a capacity for and readiness to feel remorse are important alongside a capacity for and readiness to feel agent-regret. They do not constitute an argument so much as an attempt to make vivid something which I think becomes evident on reflection.

We can best appreciate the value of remorse by imagining someone who was capable of agent-regret, but not of remorse.[32] Imagine further that this person feels agent-regret when something unfortunate issues (in part) from his own actions. He feels agent-regret if he accidentally mows the flowers that his son planted, or if his caustic wit gets out of hand, injuring a colleague's already wounded self-esteem, or if he picks a fight with a friend, or if he causes someone's death. Of course he does not feel agent-regret to the same degree with respect to each instance, but the tone of the feeling is roughly the same: in each case he feels very bad, and part of what he feels is the awareness of his part in what happened. He does not regard the situation externally; in Williams's terminology, he does not relegate the cost to "the insurance fund." He accepts (and very much feels) the fact that what happened happened in part through him.

But this person cannot discriminate between situations in which he could and should have acted differently, and situations in which he could not have prevented the calamity—or could not have been expected to foresee it and to guard against it. Consider the lorry case again. Just as we would be perturbed if the lorry driver felt plain regret rather than agent-regret in the situation that Williams describes, we would be very bothered if the man had been driving recklessly, realizes this, and yet feels no remorse. If he was driving recklessly, agent-regret, no matter how intense or how deeply felt, would be an inappropriate response. We expect him to feel pain not only at having been part of the causal mechanism which brought on this disaster, but also at having causally contributed to it needlessly, avoidably, and through his own recklessness (or, in other instances, through malice, inconsiderateness, etc.). It seems clear, then, that someone whose affective responses do not discriminate between, on the one hand, situations in which he did the best possible under the circumstances (or could not have foreseen the consequences and had no reason to think he should act differently) and, on the other, those in which he could and should have acted differently, is morally deficient.

The problem with such a person can be summed up in this way: Despite what Williams's term would seem to suggest, the person who feels only agent-regret does not, with respect to the situation at hand, really see himself as an agent. Instead he views himself, in this instance, primarily as a link in a causal chain. He feels (perhaps very deeply) his causal agency and identifies vividly with it. He does not regard his actions externally. Nonetheless, his experience is that of a thing that causes, not of a thing that also chooses (and chose carelessly). He does not accept moral responsibility, though he does accept causal responsibility. Without claiming to capture Sartre's notion of bad faith, we might say that the person capable of agent-regret but not of remorse is in one (highly attenuated) sense free of bad faith and in another (with respect to certain situations) guilty of it. He does not try to pass the buck or to say 'It wasn't me'; he does not point the finger at fate, circumstances, or another person. In this sense, he owns up to his actions. Yet at the same time he hides from his own agency; he refuses to recognize that he did not have to act as he did. He refuses to accept full responsibility for himself *qua* agent, and in this sense he exhibits bad faith.

7

I have been attempting to show that certain situations call for remorse, not merely agent-regret, and that we would judge someone who felt only agent-regret in such situations to be morally deficient. Perhaps this will become clearer if we examine an autobiographical sketch. It will help if we isolate three types of character deficiencies, corresponding to regret, agent-regret, and remorse; then we can ask which of these three defects explains (or explain) what makes the autobiographer's attitude toward the episode he describes so disturbing. The three deficiencies are as follows: first, indicating a lack of any sort of regret is the defect of *callousness,* especially a dearth of pain in response to another person's suffering; second, reflecting a lack of agent-regret: very little awareness that the pain came about in part because of *what one did.* A third defect, this one signifying a lack of remorse, is: no proneness to consider whether one could and should have acted differently—or, if one considers it, a negative answer issues with peculiar speed and confidence. With these deficiencies in mind, we may examine a passage from Bertrand Russell's autobiography. Assuming that we find his attitude disturbing (and it is his attitude as exhibited in the passage that interests me, not his past conduct), we can ask what it is about it that is disturbing. I will argue that part of the problem is his apparent lack of remorse. Russell recounts:

> I only saw the girl a few times in Oxford, but I found her very interesting and wished to know her better. When I was coming to Chicago, she wrote and invited me to stay at her parents' house. . . . I spent two nights under her parents' roof, and the second I spent with her. . . . She was very delightful, not beautiful in the conventional sense, but passionate, poetic, and strange. Her youth had been lonely and unhappy, and it seemed that I could give her what she wanted. We agreed that she should come to England as soon as possible and that we would live together openly, perhaps marrying later on if a divorce [his] could be obtained. Immediately after this I returned to England. . . . [Brief discussion of the progress of his affair with another woman:] Ottoline could still, when she chose, be a lover so delightful that to leave her seemed impossible. . . . We took to going to Burnham Beeches every Tuesday for the day. The last of these expeditions was on the day on which Austria declared war on Serbia. Ottoline was at her best. Meanwhile the girl in Chicago had induced her father, who remained in ignorance, to take her to Europe. . . . When she arrived [five-nine weeks later] I could think of nothing but the war, and as I had determined to come out publicly against it, I did not wish to complicate my position with a private scandal, which would have made anything that I might say of no account. I felt it therefore impossible to carry out what we had planned. She stayed in England and I had relations with her from time to time, but the shock of the war killed my passion for her, and I broke her heart. Ultimately she fell a victim to a rare disease, which first paralyzed her, and then made her insane. . . . Before insanity attacked her, she had a rare and remarkable mind, and a disposition as lovable as it was unusual. If the war had not intervened, the plan which we formed in Chicago might have brought great happiness to us both. I feel still the sorrow of this tragedy.[33]

In discussing this passage my concern is not, of course, with Russell himself. My aim is not to judge his character or conduct, or even to understand the latter in the context of his life. Therefore I will look at the passage as it stands, without appealing to other portions of his autobiography, his essays, biographies of him, and the like, and without worrying about whether what I say is true of the real Bertrand Russell. I will use the name 'Russell', but we should think of it as referring to a (perhaps) some-what fictionalized Bertrand Russell.

What strikes us about Russell's reflections on this sad chapter of his life is not primarily callousness. He does exhibit a strain of callousness, or at least self-centeredness and selfishness, when he completes the second to the last sentence in the passage cited by alluding sadly to the happiness that the two of them might have had. As if this was the grave loss! It is as if what happened was comparable to, say, her hav-ing decided not to make the trip to England, recognizing that he was unreliable. But in light of everything else that he says, I do not think this is strong evidence of callous-ness. To the extent that we suspect that he is *not* deeply pained at what happened, it is, I believe, because we find it difficult otherwise to understand his apparent lack of agent-regret and remorse. Let us set callousness to one side, then, and examine his ap-parent lack of agent-regret and remorse.

I want to claim that part—indeed a large part—of what bothers us about Rus-sell's narration is the absence of any hint of remorse. It is this that is at issue, however, for it might be argued that insufficient agent-regret is the explanation. I will try to show that this explanation is inadequate, and in so doing, to bring out more sharply the significance of remorse.

We do see a dearth of agent-regret in Russell's description, particularly in the sentence I just alluded to: "If the war had not intervened, the plan which we formed in Chicago might have brought great happiness to us both." Yet there are also strong hints of agent-regret in the repeated first-person presentation of painful matters: "I could think of nothing but the war . . . I did not wish . . . I felt it therefore impossi-ble . . . " rather than a distant, impersonal report, e.g., 'When she arrived it was im-possible to carry out the plan.' "I broke her heart" might also express agent-regret (though the trite phrase does ring rather hollow). Thus, lack of agent-regret cannot be what principally bothers us, though too little agent-regret *could* be the problem.

This last explanation may seem quite attractive as we contemplate the explana-tion which centers on remorse. For, someone might argue, "Fine, I grant that he ex-hibits no remorse at all. But why suppose that he *should* be remorseful? To say that he should entails, on your view, saying that he should have acted differently. But what should he have done differently? Should he have lived with her as they had planned, running the risk he cited? That is by no means clear. Was he wrong to encourage her to move to England and live with him? More likely, but we do not know enough to say. Perhaps she pushed for it as much as he did; perhaps he had every reason to think that it would work out, etc. Shouldn't he have written to tell her that he could not risk a personal scandal at this time? Probably, but again we do not have much to go on; for all we know, he did write her something of this nature. So why fault him for re-morselessness?"

The objection is well taken, but it does not go very far. It does not give us any reason to think that insufficient agent-regret is the main problem in Russell's attitude. For while we cannot fault Russell for failing to be remorseful, surely we are right to think that he should have *questioned* his past conduct, asking the sorts of questions which my imaginary critic just raised.[34] He exhibits no *readiness to be remorseful,* no willingness to subject his conduct to moral scrutiny. It is this that is objectionable, and if I am right to say that this is what bothers us, then his case exhibits the importance that we attach to remorse.

Someone might still urge that his story would not disturb us if he only seemed more prone to agent-regret. Would that suffice? To determine this, let us reconstruct the case so that it expresses agent-regret. Imagine that he wrote, "If I had not been so impetuous . . . " or "If I had never stayed at her parents' house, she might have had a better life." This would certainly make things better. But it still is not enough, unless implicit in these thoughts is a judgment that he acted badly, and an acceptance of moral—not merely causal—responsibility. We rightly expect from someone reflecting back on his life a readiness to feel both agent-regret and remorse, and indeed a willingness to move from the safer, less exacting agent-regret to remorse.[35]

8

In this section, I consider some possible objections. The first is primarily an objection to seeing as much value in remorse as I do, but to a lesser extent it applies to agent-regret. A critic might observe that there is, after all, something moralistic about encouraging ourselves to be remorseful—and something masochistic, too—and ask, "What is the point of nourishing this backward-looking self-critical attitude? Remorse may be suitable for Dostoevsky's Underground Man, but surely not for a healthy human being. It serves no purpose other than to breed self-hatred."

Presented this way, the objection is not difficult to meet. Remorse need not be fruitless (or productive only of self-hatred), for fairly obvious reasons. Remorse is useful in that it leads naturally to thoughts about how I should act differently (in a sense of 'should' that implies 'can or probably can'). Indeed, it is difficult to imagine that we could learn from our mistakes unless we recognized them as such.[36] Although initially backward-looking, remorse often yields in constructive thoughts; and its affective component gives these constructive thoughts some motivational force. (The criticism could be recast to take agent-regret rather than remorse as its target, for while agent-regret is not moralistic, nor *as* self-lacerating as remorse, it might be thought to be pointlessly self-critical. The response in defense of remorse fits agent-regret poorly, since agent-regret does not involve quite the same acceptance of responsibility that remorse generally does, and for this reason is much less likely than remorse to issue in resolutions of self-improvement. However, agent-regret has a positive contribution to make as well. This will emerge shortly.)

While this deflects one aspect of the objection to the position that a perfectly admirable moral agent would be disposed to experience remorse, it certainly does not put an end to the matter. The objection can be developed to point out that nourishing a disposition to be remorseful does have its risks, and these need to be addressed. If we are to encourage in ourselves (and perhaps in others, as part of moral education) a disposition to remorse, we had better consider the risks.

The first risk is that remorse about what one did—specifically, a vivid awareness of the wrongness of what one did and its avoidability—might leave one "paralyzed," fearful of making any significant choices.[37] Rather than resolve, chin up, to reform in this respect or that, one may try (futile though it is) to flee the responsibilities of agency. Remorse may thus bring on despair, deepen one's conviction that he cannot do anything right, and thus be morally (and otherwise) debilitating. In a slightly different form, this risk may afflict agent-regret. The lorry-driver may be fearful of driving, perhaps even be a nervous driver for years after his accident. The risk associated with remorse is in a sense more interesting, because it involves a sense of horror of one's own agency—not of one's capacity to cause harm through no fault of one's own—too acute an appreciation, one might say, of the responsibilities of agency.

The second risk pertains only to remorse, not to agent-regret. The danger is this: One may wallow in the feeling of remorse, as if by doing so one makes up for what one did, or, alternatively, comes to be excused. There are various forms (including combinations of same) which the phenomenon may take. One accuses oneself so vigorously that the response of others—and swiftly, his own response—is sympathy or compassion. ("Don't feel so bad!")[38] Here it can be either that what he did is intentionally overlooked ("Don't beat him when he's down") or that he is seen, and sees himself, as doing penance. Remorse may seem to the agent to be self-purification: he has done penance and emerged with a clean slate; responsibility is washed away.[39] Another aspect that this phenomenon may have resembles that described in the previous paragraph: acutely aware of the wrongness of his conduct, the agent may conclude, "I'm hopeless; there's nothing I can do to change." In this deviant form, remorse is fatalistic, not at all an impetus to self-improvement.

What is striking is that while the agent's remorse initially has the characteristic acute sense of responsibility—"I did it; it was wrong of me; I could have acted differently and should have"—through soaking in remorse he ends up fleeing from acceptance of responsibility. Acceptance of responsibility entails a recognition that one's character is one's own, and one's to shape and improve; it will not do to appeal to the badness of one's character as a justification for not trying to do better.[40]

The objections raise interesting questions, and I will unfortunately not be able to do justice to them. They call for two sorts of answers: first, pragmatic answers, to explain how (if at all) we can cultivate the disposition to be remorseful without at the same time cultivating disabling fears, a disposition to despair and so on; this question I will not even attempt to answer. But the objections raise another type of question, as well: Don't we, in encouraging a disposition to remorse, encourage people to have an exaggerated sense of control, an inflated conception of agency? The question here pertains less to pragmatic concerns than to theoretical ones; it concerns us primarily as moral philosophers, not as educators or practitioners. The worry is that there is a sort of deceit in taking the position I have been defending, for it asks people to regard themselves as more responsible, more in control than they really are. It exaggerates the extent to which we are agents. The worry is suggested by Williams's remarks about our attachment to the morality system in *Ethics and the Limits of Philosophy,* but also by an elusive passage in "Moral Luck." He writes in that essay,

One's history as an agent is a web in which anything that is the product of the will is surrounded and held up and partly formed by things that are not, in such a way that reflection can go only in one of two directions: either in the direction of saying that responsible agency is a fairly superficial concept, which has a limited use in harmonizing what happens, or else that it is not a superficial concept, but that it cannot ultimately be purified—if one attaches importance to the sense of what one is in terms of what one has done and what in the world one is responsible for, one must accept much that makes its claim on that sense solely in virtue of its being actual. (*ML,* 30–31)

One might argue that the position concerning remorse that I have been defending fails to admit the extent to which luck has to be part of the explanation of what "we did," and exaggerates the importance of agency (i.e., of agency purified of luck). I believe that the objection is a significant one, and would be quite serious were it not for the fact that I recognize the importance of agent-regret along with remorse. That is, an agent who was disposed to feel remorse but not agent-regret would be faulty *and* a moral theory which held a disposition to remorse but not a disposition to agent-regret to be part of good character would err in the way the objection suggests: it would presuppose too "purified" and too robust a concept of agency. Remorse and agent-regret mutually temper one another. An analogous point holds within moral theory: a moral theory which recognizes the importance of one but not the other is likely to have a skewed picture of moral agency. If it recognizes the importance of agent-regret but not of remorse, it does not fully appreciate the difference between causal responsibility and moral responsibility, and between being a (contributing) cause and being an agent; if it recognizes the importance of remorse but not of agent-regret it errs in the way described in the first part of this paragraph.

What I want to do in the remaining pages of this essay is revisit the question of agent-regret's significance, looking now not at its significance in isolation from remorse, but rather at its role in moderating remorse. I will focus my remarks on character and character-flaws, rather than on moral theory and flawed conceptions of agency within moral theory, but the discussion could be transposed to make the analogous points about moral theory. I believe that the dangers described above in connection with the disposition to feel remorse are lessened if the agent is disposed to feel agent-regret, and that a related danger, that of too individualistic a conception of responsibility, is also mitigated by a disposition to have agent-regret. I will address the latter, and will do so by suggesting that agent-regret may be helpful on an issue Williams does not mention: that of collective responsibility. Specifically, it may shed light on the question of whether it is ever appropriate to feel a sense of responsibility for something that went wrong, if one could not have prevented it and thus cannot be held responsible for its having gone wrong. If I can show, through this discussion, that agent-regret helps to widen our conception of responsibility, it will be apparent how it tempers remorse.

9

Most of us know—some of us *are*—U.S. citizens who (perhaps for want of a better word) speak of the *guilt* they feel for the United States' role in the Vietnam War.[41] A common reaction is to be dismissive ("Guilty!? What is this?? You think you're General Westmoreland or something? You weren't responsible! What could you have done?"). While this reaction is occasionally like the reassurances offered to the lorry-driver—reassurances whose success, if complete and immediate, would disconcert the reassurer—often it is more deeply genuine. Indeed, people who profess "guilt" about their country's recent wrongs (or profound sadness at the news that their government has just invaded a tiny Caribbean country, sadness different from that felt upon learning that France, a country not "theirs," bombed a Greenpeace ship) are, at least in the United States, treated as a little peculiar. The thought seems to be that unless one is "directly" responsible (whatever that means), nothing but the pain of a spectator ("regret" in Williams's terminology) is appropriate. (Nothing, that is, except for shame—but to that shortly.)

It seems to me that something more is often appropriate. My disagreement with those who think that such sentiments as those noted above are baseless has to do with responsibility, i.e., under what conditions it is appropriate to feel some sense of responsibility for what happened. They think that a sense of responsibility is in order only insofar as the person in question is to blame, i.e., could have acted differently and should have. I think that the degree to which one was a participant in the objectionable scheme or course of action is also relevant, where being a participant need not mean that one could have altered the course of action or prevented the calamity, or even that one's contribution to the scheme was a considerable one.

Various considerations bear on whether one counts as a participant, but before enumerating them, let us return to the notion of agent-regret. Does it have anything to do with the disagreement about responsibility just noted? It would seem not to. In developing the notion of agent-regret, Williams stresses that whether or not an action was under one's control is not all that matters; the fact that one did it itself serves as a basis for feeling pained at what one did, viewing it *as* something that one did. Developed in this way agent-regret would not seem to be pertinent to cases where an ordinary U.S. citizen feels guilty about her country's role in the Vietnam War. But there is another aspect of agent-regret which we have not yet explored. Agent-regret, Williams said, is regret that one feels toward one's own past actions or "at most, actions in which he regards himself as a participant" (*ML*, 27). Now, his words "at most" may signify that he is not sure that he wants to allow that one can feel agent-regret toward actions in which he regards himself as a participant, so he may not be happy with my attempt to develop this aspect (or possible aspect) of agent-regret, but I will proceed without worrying about that.

If we understand agent-regret broadly, as suggested by the quote, the notion of agent-regret may help us to make sense of the vague sense of responsibility felt in cases where one does not believe one could or should have acted differently, and where one's own actions had very little to do with the atrocities or whatever it is to which one feels, in some vague way, linked. It helps by suggesting that one may feel a special pain *as a participant.* This is not to say that the pain "feels the same" as other types of agent-regret; the lorry-driver's agent-regret is quite different, and is experienced as such; Agamemnon's agent-regret is different still. One might argue that they are so different that they should not all be classified under 'agent-regret'; that is an interesting question, but one that I will not pursue. Instead, I want to focus on the notion of participation and suggest the following: (1) Much of our reluctance to take seriously the notion of collective responsibility stems from seeing too many instances in which a person is wrongly regarded as a participant in some objectionable activity and accordingly held responsible. Our resistance to the notion of collective responsibility may be due less to what we usually suppose—that collective responsibility is either a dangerous, ugly concept that upholds "guilt-by-association," or else is really individual responsibility in disguise—than to disagreement about what it is to be a participant. (2) A related reason for resisting the notion is this: We may agree that such-and-such constitutes being a participant, at least in an attenuated sense of 'participant', but firmly believe that being a participant in that sense or in that way is *not* something for which a person should be held punishable by the State or even in some less dramatic way held publically responsible. If, however, we distinguish grounds for *feeling a sense of responsibility* for some act from grounds for holding someone responsible, i.e., answerable to others, we may be able to make sense of what are common feelings of—as it is loosely called—guilt, and see them as (if not exaggerated) appropriate.[42]

Now, just what it is to be a participant is a complicated matter which I cannot adequately deal with here; it is, furthermore, shaped by the particular context—what it is that one is arguably participating in, and in what circumstances. If, for example, one is a citizen of a democratic country, the case that one is in no way a participant in the policies of one's government is (though certainly not impossible) harder to make out than it is if one is a citizen of a nation ruled by a dictator. Here I will limit myself to mentioning one basis for believing oneself to be a participant, a basis that is often overlooked.

In an unpublished manuscript, Onora O'Neill speaks of "shared intentions," giving as examples building a bridge and playing a game of football. ("Some people are building a bridge. An enquirer asks . . . 'What are you doing?' and is answered 'We're building a bridge'; nobody claims 'I'm building a bridge'; individual intentions are not absent, for one may intend to saw planks and another to build up the banks of the stream; but all recognize as a central intention the shared intention to build the bridge."[43]) The shared intention is needed to coordinate and give a point to the individual intentions. If I have good reason to believe that I share (or shared) an underlying intention—e.g., to ignore whatever suffering our endeavor, as Americans, to live sumptuously inflicts on the extremely poor in Third World countries—which underlies and gives point to many of the worst aspects of U.S. foreign policy, that provides a reason for seeing myself as a "participant." It provides some basis for the feeling of sadness tinged by a sense of responsibility that I have when I meet a Chilean who has been living in exile since the U.S.-backed overthrow of Allende.

A similar explanation helps to make sense of Sophie's acute sense of guilt in *Sophie's Choice*. Sophie has much to be ashamed of: (1) her Nazi father, who zealously advocated the extermination of the Jews; (2) the fact that, ever obedient to him, she typed and helped to distribute his pamphlet, *Poland's Jewish Problem* (though she does have the consolation of knowing that she was repelled by its contents); (3) her service as Rudolph Höss's secretary while imprisoned in Auschwitz-Birkenau; and (4) her refusal to take an active role in the Resistance. In addition there is the terrible "choice" she made between her children (see note 30); while there is no ground for believing that she should have acted differently (except perhaps the thought that an immediate death would have been less of an evil than the slow death presumably suffered by Jan, the child spared from the gas chambers), it is understandable that she has a sense of having participated in her daughter's death. No doubt part of what made the proposal so amusing for the SS guard is that it forced Sophie to be a participant of sorts.

But the intensity of Sophie's guilt goes way beyond what (given the circumstances in which she aided her father and Höss) these facts warrant. She has reason to feel some shame, comparing herself to friends in the Resistance, but her self-accusations go beyond this. She feels tainted, a "filthy" *collaboratrice.* [44] Why? What explains her acute sense of guilt? One might shrug and say, "It's pathological." While it is pathological in its expression, I think that something more can be said to explain it.

The comforting thought that she was, if an accomplice, invariably an unwitting one; that if she participated, it was entirely against her will, is not one that Sophie can latch onto. While she did not share her father's fervent anti-Semitism and was sickened by the realization that Jews really were being rounded up for extermination, there is something apathetic about her reactions to the Holocaust, and this apathy binds her to the many apathetic people whose unwillingness to risk their lives and those of their loved ones (and worse yet, unwillingness to take even tiny risks, or to pass up an opportunity for job advancement) helped to make the Holocaust possible.[45] 'Apathetic' is not quite the right word here; the problem is primarily that her concern is almost entirely for her children and herself. Sophie recounts:

> And yet when I'd walk past the ghetto at a distance I would stop and really be *entranced* by certain sights, by seeing them rounding up the Jews. And I knew then the reason for this fascination, and it stunned me. . . . It was just that . . . as long as the Germans could use up all this incredible energy destroying the Jews . . . I was safe.[46]

None of this is to say that she is evil, or that guilt rather than self-pity is what she *ought* to be feeling after the war; what I am trying to show is that her guilt makes a great deal more sense if we see that certain attitudes and "maxims"—in particular, the maxim of doing whatever she must to save herself and her children, no matter what the cost to others—renders her a participant. Not a Höss, to be sure; the group with whom she was united by "shared intentions" is not a particularly wicked one; but it is also not an especially admirable one, and more importantly, it is not, as a group, benign. While she does not have reason to see herself as wicked, she correctly recognizes that she was part of the fabric without which the mass extermination could not have been anywhere near as widespread. Hence the feeling that she was a collaborator. As she reports, while she lacked the courage to provide the Resistance with information gleaned while working for Höss, if "Höss had give me a knife or a gun and told me to go kill somebody, a Jew, a Pole, it don't matter, I would have done it without thinking, with joy even, if it mean seeing my little boy for only a single minute."[47]

Contrast these examples of seeing oneself as a participant to instances in which one feels that simply because one is a German, one is stained—one shares in the collective guilt. We rightly reject such a claim, because here there is no reason to believe that one participated. *Shame* is appropriate, but that is because shame need involve only a sense of association, none at all of responsibility. Likewise if the only basis for her sense of being tainted were the fact that her father was a Fascist: it would make sense to feel ashamed of him, but not to feel tainted (unless, of course, she detected traces of his despicable attitudes in herself).[48]

My suggestions concerning the relevance of agent-regret to the thought that a sense of collective responsibility is sometimes appropriate, even when one could not have prevented or significantly slowed whatever it is for which one feels some sense of responsibility, have had to be very sketchy.[49] But if they have any merit they indicate how the notion of agent-regret may help us to avoid too narrow a conception of responsibility. They add to Williams's points—that too exclusive a focus on remorse keeps us from seeing that the regret of an agent is in order even when one did the best anyone could in those circumstances—by drawing attention to the possibility that we are right to feel vaguely, indirectly and collectively responsible for happenings for which we are not (even causally) to blame as individuals. Agent-regret may help us not only to see the things that Williams brought out, but may also help to keep us from thinking that only a very narrow, very individual notion of responsibility makes sense.

I said earlier that agent-regret and remorse temper each other; I hope it is now apparent why that is so. Both contribute to shaping our conception of responsibility, and to focusing our attention on different aspects of our character and conduct.[50]

Notes

1. "Moral Luck" appears as chap. 2 in Williams's *Moral Luck* (Cambridge, 1982). References to this work will be given parenthetically in the text of the paper, preceded by *ML*.

2. These are the two that I can locate; but I suspect that agent-regret is important for other reasons, as well, reasons that I have not yet pinpointed.

3. I argue that it is the chief disagreement in my "The Ethics of Duty/Ethics of Virtue Debate and its Relevance to Educational Theory," *Educational Theory* 35, no. 2 (1985): 135–49. For other discussions of the debate, see the following pieces by William K. Frankena: "Prichard and the Ethics of Virtue: Notes on a Footnote," *Monist* 54 (1970): 1–17; "The Ethics of Love Conceived as an Ethics of Virtue," *Journal of Religious Ethics* 1 (1973): 21–36; and "Beneficence in an Ethics of Virtue" in *Beneficence and Health Care,* edited by Earl E. Shelp (Dordrecht, 1982), 63–81; and Robert Louden, "Kant's Virtue Ethics," *Philosophy* 61 (1986): 473–89, especially 474–76.

4. Is it crucial to the disagreement that the thoughts be couched in terms of 'ought'? No. I explain this in "The Ethics of Duty/Ethics of Virtue Debate." This is, to be sure, a controversial view; Louden and, in some of his pieces, Frankena, seem to disagree.

5. I explore other ways in my "De-Kantianizing the Perfectly Moral Person," *Journal of Value Inquiry* 17 (1982): 281–93 and "Varieties of Ethics of Virtue," *American Philosophical Quarterly* 22, no. 1 (1985): 47–53.

6. Some might say that this is guilt, not remorse; see the end of section 5 for a brief discussion of that question.

7. I add this for readers who are externalists, or undecided. (Since I am an internalist, the two sentences beginning with "Moreover" strike me as superfluous.) For an explanation of the distinction between externalism and internalism, see W. D. Falk, " 'Ought' and Motivation" in *Proceedings of the Aristotelian Society* 48 (1947–48): 429–510; reprinted in *Readings in Ethical Theory,* edited by Wilfrid Sellars and John Hospers (New York, 1952) and in W. D. Falk, *Ought,*

Reasons and Morality: The Collected Papers of W. D. Falk (Ithaca, N.Y., 1986), chap. 1. Falk, an internalist, coined the terms. Subsequent discussions include W. K. Frankena, "Obligation and Motivation in Recent Moral Philosophy" in *Essays in Moral Philosophy,* edited by A. Melden (Seattle, 1958) and Stephen Darwall, *Impartial Reason* (Ithaca, N.Y., 1983), chap. 5.

8. I am indebted to Gerald Postema for having pointed this out to me several years ago.

9. Contrast Gabrielle Taylor, *Pride, Shame, and Guilt: Emotions of Self-Assessment* (Oxford, 1985). Taylor writes in connection with just such an example: "I have done a terrible thing, and my seeing it as such is enough for me to suffer from guilt. . . . Causal responsibility is . . . sufficient for guilt, and . . . is also necessary" (91).

10. But see section 5, below.

11. Like most examples, this one is oversimplified. If the flowers are easy to avoid, the lawnmower in good-working order, and so on, the fact that I mowed the flowers accidentally may betoken a lack of concern for my child's flowers (or feelings). If it does, something more than agent-regret would be in order—perhaps self-scrutiny, and remorse about what I did.

12. Williams, "Ethical Consistency," *Problems of the Self* (New York, 1973), 173. Hereafter abbreviated as EC.

13. Or, Williams qualifies, if it *is* something we want to call irrational, we do not "intend 'irrational' pejoratively: we must rather admit that an admirable moral agent is one who on occasion is irrational" (EC, 175).

14. The example is from Amelie Rorty's "Agent Regret" in *Explaining Emotions,* edited by A. O. Rorty (Berkeley, 1980).

15. Williams's examples of Anna Karenina and Gauguin might be thought of as forming a third type of case, but I view them as instances of the second type. In choosing to abandon his family and go to the South Sea Islands, Gauguin (as Williams depicts him) was regarding that as a lesser evil than the option of remaining where he was, and where, he believed, his art would only stagnate, his talents never bear real fruit. If their projects succeeded (as his did and hers did not), they would nonetheless feel agent-regret—pain about the toll that their choices took on people (who had been) dependent on them; if their projects failed, they would feel agent-regret, but without even having a standpoint from which to judge that their decision was justified (even if the standpoint is not one which was open to those whom (Williams acknowledges) they had wronged.

16. The phrase in quotes is one that Williams uses in "Ethical Consistency."

17. If the lesser evil is either decidedly minor, or middling but drastically outweighed by the greater evil, the fully admirable moral agent would probably not feel agent-regret. (Imagine that the agent misses an appointment with a student in order to take a colleague who is having a miscarriage to the hospital.)

18. Cf. Stuart Hampshire, *Morality and Conflict* (Cambridge, Mass., 1983).

19. Williams does not name the philosophers he has in mind in this passage, but a few pages earlier he cites Hare and Ross as ethical theorists who have thought that to hold (e.g.) "that I ought to do *a* and that I ought to do *b*", yet that "I cannot do both *a* and *b* . . . would involve some sort of logical inconsistency" (171).

20. Sir David Ross, *The Right and the Good* (London, 1930), 28. Thanks go to Dick Brandt for drawing my attention to this passage.

21. *Ethics and the Limits of Philosophy* (Cambridge, Mass., 1985), 177. Hereafter abbreviated as *ELP.*

22. The morality system, Williams writes at *ELP,* 177, "turns our attention away from an important dimension of ethical experience, which lies in the distinction simply between what one has done and what one has not done."

23. This depends on the tone of the thought, i.e., how it would sound if spoken. Imagine the thought, "If only I weren't so rash," said with a sigh, a tone of regret and resignation.

24. I should clarify that regret sometimes involves that thought as well. For instance, I may regret having been abrupt to someone. I believe that I should not have been abrupt and that I could have done otherwise; still, I am not remorseful. The reason is that it is (in this instance) not a serious matter. So we can and do sometimes regret those things which if more serious, would occasion remorse in us.

25. For a different view of remorse, see D. Z. Phillips and H. S. Price, "Remorse Without Repudiation," *Analysis* 28, no. 1 (1967): 18–20. Their characterization fits my understanding of guilt.

26. Williams speaks as if the difference between remorse and agent-regret is that the former applies strictly to the voluntary, while the latter can apply to either; but I do not think that this is the whole of it. In feeling remorse I do not merely judge that I could have acted differently (Gauguin and Anna Karenina, if they are honest, make that judgment), but that I *should* have.

27. William Styron, *Sophie's Choice* (New York, 1980).

28. And along with it, self-hatred: "Why don't I tell the truth about myself? Why don't I write it in a book that I was a terrible coward, that I was a filthy *collaboratrice,* that I done everything that was bad just to save myself?" Ibid., 554.

29. In a case where agent-regret and remorse are mixed, whether one's sentiment tends more to remorse or to agent-regret will depend on other factors besides (believed) avoidability. The remorse will be more predominant if I have acted in a way which I could not fail to know was very likely to cause harm of the proportion that it in fact ends up causing as, for instance, when I rebuke a child relentlessly, leaving him hurt and troubled as a result; or, in a fit of anger, smash a vase which someone dear to me loves. *Caeteris paribus,* negligence gives less cause for remorse than malice or rage, and provocation also alters the case.

30. There are at least two reasons why guilt does not require a judgment that one has acted wrongly. First, one may feel guilt over something one has done which one regards as the lesser of two evils. While this may occasion only agent-regret, if what one had to do was terrible enough, it may occasion guilt. Sophie's choice illustrates the point. Forced either to see both of her children sent to the gas chamber or to choose which of the children will die and which one will be spared, she chooses. Not surprisingly, she suffers intense guilt over this. Second, guilt may be felt toward a benefit one has reaped through a wrong commited by others on one's behalf, or through a wrong, perhaps a social injustice, perpetrated or at least upheld by someone to whom one feels relevantly related. I am indebted on both these points to Greg Kavka's unpublished manuscript, "Wrongdoing and Guilt," from which I have learned a great deal.

31. For a discussion of the differences between remorse, guilt, and shame, see chap. 4 of G. Taylor, *Pride, Shame and Guilt.*

32. To iterate and expand on something indicated earlier (at the close of section 3): because of the type of situation we are discussing, viz., one which calls for remorse but which in fact occasions only agent-regret, it is only the first type of agent-regret (that exemplified by the lorry-driver case, as opposed to that of Agamemnon) that is relevant to this discussion. Although one could feel agent-regret of the second type with respect to circumstances that call for remorse—if one wrongly thought that he had chosen the lesser of two evils when, in fact, he had chosen the greater of two evils, or where there actually was (and he should have known there to be) a third option which he should have taken—this is not pertinent to our discussion. Clearly if the issue is whether the importance of agent-regret displaces that of remorse, what we need to consider seriously is whether it suffices that a person think, in situations where she has done something dreadful, just the thoughts expressive of agent-regret ("How terrible! What have I done?"), and not also thoughts that she *should not* have done what she did (and that she could have avoided doing so). The relevant remorse–agent-regret contrast thus concerns the first type of agent-regret, where the agent regrets having done what she did, but does not believe that she could have done otherwise.

33. Bertrand Russell, *The Autobiography of Bertrand Russell* (London, 1975), 221–22.

34. All the more so given that he seems clearly *not* to view her disease as unconnected to his treatment of her. "If the war had not intervened, the plan . . . might have brought great happiness to us both" makes no sense unless we suppose that Russell believes that if the war had not taken place, she would have been free of her disease; and unless he thinks that the war itself (or some ramification of it other than its effect on him) led to her illness, he must believe that the deep unhappiness that he caused her is part of the explanation of her severe illness.

35. It is different, of course, if the agent is very near death; it would be harsh indeed to expect moral self-scrutiny on the death-bed.

36. This is not to say that remorse rather than, say, guilt, is needed for self-improvement.

What is crucial is the disposition to reflect on one's past conduct and subject it to moral scrutiny, together with a genuine concern to make amends and do better in the future. The concern is likely to proceed from pain in the form of remorse or perhaps guilt over the wrongness of one's conduct.

37. I am indebted to Larry May for this point.

38. In *The Passions* (Garden City, New York, 1977), Robert Solomon cites this as the "strategy" of remorse. He writes (p. 349), "As a sense of particular guilt, it succeeds in warding off censure and punishment from other people by first inflicting it upon oneself. ('He's suffered enough from his own remorse.') He regards remorse as an "extremely self-indulgent emotion," but says the same about guilt (321).

39. Kant writes in *Anthropology,* translated by Victor Lyle Dowdell (Carbondale, Ill., 1977): "The penitence of a self-tormentor, who should quickly apply his disposition toward finding a better way of life, is simply a lost labor. And it has, in addition, the bad consequence that he regards his guilt as thereby erased (simply through remorse) so that he does not have to subject himself to striving for the better."

40. A different objection might assert that so to prize remorse invites excessive criticism and moral scrutiny of others. It is important to recognize, however, that self-criticism may well be in order when criticism of others is not. From the fact that it would be wrong for anyone other than *S* to question *S*'s conduct in a particular instance there is no reason to conclude, even tentatively, that *S* should not (morally need not) question her own conduct. This point is made by Peter Winch in "Moral Integrity," a discussion which in other ways, as well, is relevant to the notion of agent-regret. (Winch, *Ethics and Action* [London, 1972], 171–94, especially 184–85.) Still, the critic might be unconvinced, suspicious that in nourishing a disposition to remorse one very likely will be nourishing a disposition to subject the conduct of others to moral scrutiny. This question calls for an answer to the question of how (if at all) we can cultivate the one without cultivating the other, an answer which I will not attempt to provide.

41. Not surprisingly, we more often hear it said (in the U.S.) that Germans, at least those born before 1920 or so, ought to feel a sense of responsibility for the Holocaust.

42. To those who see all morality as positive social morality, this distinction will no doubt seem odd (to put it mildly). But I think that unless one sees morality in this way, it is not only a plausible but a very important distinction. (Cf. note 40.)

43. Onora O'Neill, "The Limits of Intentional Ethics," 18.

44. *Sophie's Choice,* 554.

45. See on this subject C. P. Taylor's play, *Good* (London, 1982), 40.

46. *Sophie's Choice,* 569. Many other passages could be cited. E.g., Sophie imagines saying to her friend in the Resistance, "The one and only thing which might lure me into your world would be that radio. Would be to listen to London. But not to war news . . . No, quite simply I think I would risk my life as you do and also give an arm or a hand to listen just once again to Sir Thomas Beecham conducting *Cosi fan tutte"* (454).

47. Ibid., 350. Relevant too is the fact that she repeatedly appeals to her pro-Nazi credentials to improve her situation. While this is not a basis for remorse—surely it is justifiable to appeal to any consideration, at least if it will not do damage to others, to try to get oneself out of a death camp—appeal to her father's deeds and her aid to him does make it more difficult for her to divorce herself from him and from their collaboration on the pamphlet.

48. For another discussion of Sophie's sense of guilt, see Patricia Greenspan, "Moral Dilemmas and Guilt," in *Philosophical Studies* 43 (1983): 117–25.

49. For some intriguing discussions of collective responsibility, see the essays in *Individual and Collective Responsibility: The Massacre at My Lai,* edited by Peter French (Cambridge, Mass., 1972).

50. Early versions of this paper were completed during my tenure as a fellow of the American Council of Learned Studies. I gratefully acknowledge the foundation's support for my work. I would also like to thank Richard Brandt, Robert Ennis, Gregory Kavka, Larry May, Robert McKim, Daniel Nathan, and Onora O'Neill for helpful written comments on earlier drafts of this paper. I presented a version of this paper at Kalamazoo College in April 1987; discussion there helped to shape the final version.

MIDWEST STUDIES IN PHILOSOPHY, XIII (1988)

Shame and Moral Progress

JOHN KEKES

I

The most illuminating accounts of shame I know of are Gabrielle Taylor's[1] and Arnold Isenberg's.[2] They agree on many points, but they conspicuously differ in their assessments of shame. Taylor thinks that "genuine shame is always justified,"[3] while Isenberg concludes that "it is as unreasonable to tolerate the sear of shame upon the spirit as it is to permit a wound to fester in the body."[4] This disagreement is not new. Plato regards shame as one of the important safeguards of morality,[5] but Aristotle argues that "if shamelessness—not to be ashamed of base actions—is bad, that does not make it good to be ashamed of doing such actions."[6]

We can sympathize with both lines of thought leading to these incompatible attitudes to shame. Shame is caused by the realization that we have fallen short of some standard we regard as important. Those who are incapable of this emotion cannot be seriously committed to any standard, so they are apt to lack moral restraint. Shame is a sign that we have made a serious commitment, and it is also an impetus for honoring it, since violating the commitment painfully lowers our opinion of ourselves. The doubts about shame are occasioned by this self-denigrating aspect of it. Shame does not merely alert us to our shortcomings, it makes us feel deficient on account of them. This feeling of deficiency, coming from such an unimpeachable source, is likely to be self-destructive. It tends to undermine our confidence, verve, and courage to navigate life's treacherous waters. Thus shame threatens to diminish our most important resource. It jeopardizes the possibility of improvement by weakening the only agency capable of effecting it.

I shall argue in this paper that doubts about shame are justified. But this is not because it is mistaken to regard shame as an index to the seriousness we feel about standards. Shame is such an index. It is rather that whatever value there is in shame can be achieved in less self-destructive ways. The movement away from shame to-

ward other responses to the realization of our deficiencies is, I shall argue, moral progress. By this, I hope not only to contribute to the enlargement of our moral
possibilities, but also to show how moral progress may occur.

II

Shame is not amenable to a precise definition. It shades into embarrassment, humiliation, chagrin, guilt, dishonor, regret, remorse, prudishness, disgrace, etc. To attempt
to list necessary and sufficient conditions for shame is arbitrarily to simplify a naturally complex experience.[7] Another sign of the imprecision and complexity of shame
is that it has many antonyms referring to feelings incompatible with it: pride, honor,
self-respect, propriety, modesty, and self-esteem are some. These feelings are incompatible with different aspects of shame, and it is these aspects which are responsible
for the complexity and imprecision of it. However, my argument requires a way of
identifying and analyzing many, but not all, cases of shame. It will be sufficient for my
purposes to have made out a case for many generally recognized instances of it. This
qualification should be understood to hold throughout the paper.

One fundamental characteristic of shame is that it is a self-directed feeling: the
subject who has it and the object toward which it is directed are one and the same. It
is a bad, unpleasant, painful, disturbing feeling, for it involves regarding ourselves in
an unfavorable light. We do so, when feeling ashamed, because we recognize that
there is some standard of which we have fallen short. Is is essential that we ourselves
should accept the standard, otherwise we would not feel badly about falling short of
it. From the fact that some action or characteristic is regarded as shameful by others,
it does not follow that we shall feel ashamed for having or doing it, since we may be
indifferent or hostile to the prevailing opinion. Of course, few people are so totally at
odds with their society as to be utterly indifferent to the opinions of others. Usually,
we feel shame about something which others also regard as shameful. This is the emotive aspect of shame, and I shall now turn to its cognitive aspect.

Shame is a self-conscious feeling. We are not merely the subjects and objects of
it, we are also aware of ourselves *as* objects when we feel ashamed. The experience involves seeing ourselves as having failed in some respect. The form which self-
consciousness takes is that of comparison between some aspect of ourselves and what
we think that aspect ought to be. If we do not think that we have fallen short, we
would have no occasion for feeling ashamed. But to recognize a failure in ourselves
requires the comparison between some aspect of our present selves and the standard
which a better self would have more closely approximated than we have done.

One requirement of this self-conscious comparison is detachment. We view a
characteristic or action of our own as others would see it, of often as others do see it,
and we accept their actual or hypothetical assessment. But we accept it because we accept the standard by which our characteristic or action is adversely judged. Of course,
we may have acquired the standard by internalizing a publicly accepted one. The important point is not the origin of the standard, but that it is now ours.

I say that this point is important because the failure to recognize it permeates the literature on shame. Rawls, for instance, holds that "shame implies an especially intimate connection . . . with those upon whom we depend to confirm the sense of our own worth,"[8] and part of the explanation of shame is that a person "has been found unworthy of his associates upon whom he depends to confirm his sense of his own worth."[9] The general mistake this view exemplifies is the supposition that in order to feel ashamed an audience is necessary.[10] It is supposed that, following anthropologists, we can distinguish between shame-cultures and guilt-cultures. In the former, sanctions are largely external and they are imposed by the community, while in the latter sanctions are mainly internal and they are imposed by individuals on themselves. Shame, then, is said to be the dominant form of external sanction, and guilt is the paradigmatic internal sanction.

But this view cannot account for two distinct types of experiences. One is that we often feel shame when no one is present to observe us. So audience cannot be necessary. It is no use to postulate an imagined audience in whose hypothetical eyes our unobserved selves must feel shame. For we often feel shame for things that outsiders would not regard as shameful, such as not achieving our personal best when we want to or falling short of some higher than accepted standard we have set for ourselves. Second, although we may acquire many of our standards by internalizing public ones, not all of our standards are like this. For if they were, we could not come to reject prevailing public standards in the name of standards we regard as higher. And, of course, we can feel ashamed for having fallen short of these higher standards, although there may be no one who shares them with us.

Taylor's observation on this point seems to me to be absolutely right: "There is, then, this point to the metaphors of an audience and being seen: they reflect the structural features of the agent's becoming aware of the discrepancy between her assumptions about her state or action and a possible detached observer-description of this state or action, and of her further being aware that she ought not to be in a position where she could be so seen. . . . For in particular cases of shame an actual or imagined observer may or may not be required . . . whether or not there is, or is imagined to be, such an observer is a contingent matter."[11]

What is essential to shame is to detach ourselves from what we are, have, or do to the extent that we can view it as falling short of some standard. This standard, however, need not be public. I am quite willing to acknowledge that it often is public, that purely private shame is a rare experience, and that there are not many reformers of public standards who come to feel shame for having fallen short of yet to be instituted standards. I want to insist only on the possibility of private shame, because moral progress is connected with it.

Shame is felt, then, when we make a detached comparison between some aspect of ourselves and a standard we want to live up to, and the result is that we find ourselves wanting. It often happens that reflection on ourselves yields a conclusion only gradually. If we wonder whether we are oversensitive, stupid, rigid, or tactless, we may need to gather evidence, think through putative confirming or disconfirming instances, compare ourselves to others who clearly lack or exemplify the trait, and ponder what we find. It is otherwise with shame. Shame assails us, it is a sudden realization, a shock, a discovery. This dramatic aspect of shame, as Taylor aptly calls it, occurs because shame disrupts our previous equanimity. Calm prevails up to the occurrence of shame either because we have not engaged in self-conscious examination or because the result of the examination has been to subsume the relevant characteristic or action under a neutral or complimentary description. If we assess ourselves at all, we may say privately that we are cautious, or just, or clever, and then something happens, the veil is lifted, and we realize that, in fact, we have been cowardly, or cruel, or dishonest. Self-deception, lethargy, and stupidity have great scope here. But the point that concerns us is that when shame occurs, we suddenly see some aspect of ourselves in a new and unfavorable light. We see what has been there, but we see it for the first time or we see it differently from the way we used to. Shame involves interpretation, which is often reinterpretation, and what produces it is some episode, some criticism, some comparison which we encounter and whose significance forces itself on us, such as Adam and Eve discovering that they were naked.

I shall now leave the cognitive aspect of shame and consider its moral aspect. I think that shame is a moral feeling, thus I am committed to rejecting the distinction often made between natural and moral shame.[12] According to the distinction, we may experience natural but not moral shame because we are ugly, stupid, deformed, or have the wrong accent. These may detract from our self-respect, but they do not violate moral standards. They are misfortunes, but they are not blameworthy. Or people may invade our privacy, observe our intimate frolics or rituals, and make us feel ashamed by their violation of our dignity, even though we had done nothing morally censurable. Moral shame, by contrast, is supposedly caused by the realization that we are in some respect morally deficient. Acting in a cowardly way, betraying a friend, being caught in a lie, carelessly hurting someone we love are such morally blameworthy experiences. Thus both natural and moral shame depend on injury to our self-respect, but one is and the other is not a moral injury.

But if we take a sufficiently broad view of morality to accommodate a wide enough range of moral experiences, this distinction becomes untenable. The distinction rests on the assumption that morality and the domain of choice coincide. Since the objects of natural shame are not chosen, natural shame is placed outside of morality. However, the domain of morality is wider than the sphere of choice. Morality is concerned with living good lives and there are many constituents of good lives about which we often have no choice. A secure society which is hospitable to our endeavors, the possession of native endowments which could be developed, the absence of paralyzing personal or social handicaps are as necessary for living good lives as are morally praiseworthy choices. If we commit ourselves to living a certain kind of life, and we find that we have failed, our self-respect may suffer and we may come to feel shame. What matters to shame is not so much that we made blameworthy choices, but that we suffer loss of self-respect. The two often coincide, but they need not. As Rawls himself recognizes, although inconsistently it seems to me, "we should say that given our plan of life, we tend to be ashamed of those defects in our person and failures in our actions that indicate a loss or absence of excellences essential to carrying out our more important associative aims."[13] But the defects and failures may exist independently of our choices.

It is essential to living a good life that we should, at the very least, not feel bad about ourselves. Our self-respect depends on the sense that we are living up to our standards. Shame may occur when we realize that we have fallen short of these standards. Thus shame is an experience of failure, but it may or may not be culpable failure. Shame is not guilt; it is not the verdict of a private court, as guilt may be the verdict of a public one.

Furthermore, whether we feel ashamed depends on our standards and not on whether the failure to live up to them was due to innate or acquired, voluntary or involuntary, accidental or cultivated causes. There is a kind of relentless absolutism about shame. It understands only success and failure; the language of motive, intention, effort, the consideration of causes, obstacles, and odds are foreign to it. If we feel shame, appeal to these extenuating factors rarely brings relief. Shame painfully brings home to us the brute fact that we have committed ourselves to be a certain way and we did not live up to the commitment. Since the reason behind the commitment was that being that way was a good way of being, having failed, we feel bad about the way we are. Shame is this primitive, inexorable feeling. Like grief or unrequited love, it is contingent on an unarguable fact. And shame is a moral feeling, because the fact in its case is that we find some aspect of our lives bad.

Shame varies in intensity; it is proportionate to the centrality of the unfulfilled commitment to our conception of a good life. The more important a commitment is, the more shameful is its violation. But all the commitments whose violations are shameful are constituents of what we think of as good lives. So the occurrence of shame is always significant. It is true that we often speak of shame casually, in connection with peccadillos. In these cases, shame is used to mean embarrassment. It does not matter much whether we distinguish between serious and trivial shame, or whether we reserve shame for the serious feeling and use a synonym, like embarrassment, for the lighter one. My preference is for the latter usage, and so I shall regard even less intense experiences of shame as significant. It should be remembered, however, that my intention is not to give a complete account of shame, but to identify and analyze those numerous instances of it which bear on moral progress.

To sum up this description: in its emotive aspect, shame is a painful self-directed feeling; in its cognitive aspect, it is a self-conscious detached comparison yielding the conclusion that we are in some way deficient, because we have fallen short of some standard we regard as important; and in its moral aspect, we feel the importance of the standard we violated, because our conception of a good life requires that we should have lived up to it. Thus in feeling shame, we feel the loss of self-respect.

III

Let us approach the connection between shame and moral progress by reflecting on one of the remarkable stories Herodotus tells.[14] It concerns Candaules King of Lydia, his wife the Queen, and Gyges the King's friend and advisor. The King was so besotted by his wife's charms that he could not keep his great good fortune to himself. He bragged to Gyges about his marital bliss and bullied him to hide in their bedroom so that Gyges could have direct evidence of the Queen's superior graces. Gyges was horrified at the King's plan: "What an improper suggestion!" he said. But the King persisted, " 'Off with her skirt, off with her shame'—you know what they say about women." Gyges pleaded, "Do not ask me to behave like a criminal." Kings, however, have a way of prevailing, and Gyges finally did as he was told, and hid in the bedroom. "Unluckily, the queen saw him. At once she realized what her husband had done. But she did not betray the shame she felt by screaming, or even let it appear that she had noticed anything. Instead she silently resolved to have her revenge. For with the Lydians . . . it is thought highly indecent even for a man to be seen naked." Next day, the Queen summoned Gyges and said to him, "There are two courses open to you, and you may take your choice between them. Kill Candaules and seize the throne, with me as your wife; or die yourself on the spot, so that never again may your blind obedience to the King tempt you to see what you have no right to see. One of you must die: either my husband, the author of this wicked plot; or you, who have outraged propriety by seeing me naked." Gyges chose to live. The next night he hid, once again, in the bedroom, but this time at the Queen's pleasure, and killed Candaules. He succeeded him, married the Queen, and reigned for thirty-eight years.

The story could be told from the point of view of each character, and in each version shame would figure significantly.[15] King Candaules was shameless; Gyges had a proper sense of shame, but he was not strong enough to act on it; and the Queen, whose strength matched her charms, was moved by shame. I shall concentrate on her perspective. The Queen's reaction was like a volcanic eruption: majestic, inexorable, and indifferent to morality. Once the lava of her passion cooled, quiet descended and life resumed. But why the eruption? If we understand the emotional context from which her reaction follows, we shall have a better grip on both shame and moral progress.

Our first response to the Queen's role may be that arranging the murder of her husband was a disproportionately violent reaction to his vulgar sophomoric plot. Certainly, she was badly used, but not so badly as to call for blood. The inadequacy of this first response comes from too simple a view of shame. Lydians are touchy about being seen naked; she was so seen, she was ashamed, she should be resentful of her husband, but let that be the end of it. Behind this line of thought lies the view that the standards violated in shame are standards of propriety, decency, seemliness. Call this view of shame *propriety-shame*. This is what we feel when our privacy is invaded. It is rightly thought that while propriety matters, it is hardly a serious moral concern. It belongs to a class of minor graces of which cheerfulness, politeness, and tact are other members. Good and evil are considerations too weighty for this context to support. But shame is not always a negligible reaction, and that shows that there is more to it than propriety-shame.

The Queen's reaction will seem less excessive if we recognize that Lydian standards of propriety became her moral standards. She was not a superficial person who cared a lot about appearances; rather, how she appeared was for her a question of honor, and thus of morality. Her morality dictated that how she was and how she appeared to others should not be distinguishable. Her honor, dignity, status, and self-respect all demanded that she should ring true all the way through. This does not mean that she conflated the public and private spheres. On the contrary, her honor was inseparably connected with maintaining their distinctness. In her view, there were activities proper to each sphere, and morality consisted in playing the appropriate role and performing the appropriate actions in these different contexts. The language of play, role, and performance, however, should not lead us to suspect her of hypocrisy or insincerity. She was what it was her role to be. So her husband's plot was not a superficial offense against standards of propriety, but a very serious offense resulting in her dishonor. Her husband caused her to see herself diminished in her own eyes. Her experience was *honor-shame,* a feeling much deeper and morally more significant than propriety-shame.

But this is not all. She did not merely feel ashamed, because she was dishonored. She realized that her husband causing her dishonor revealed that he did not respect her, did not see how crucial and important her honor was to her conception of a good life. Thus her shame, honor-shame, and the resulting resentment at her husband for having caused it and for not understanding what he was doing in causing it—remember his "off with her skirt, off with her shame"—conspired to produce her revenge. We may still have moral objections to it, but it no longer seems psychologically perverse. Especially not if we realize that the Queen is made of a heroic mold familiar to us from the literature of ancient Greece. Achilles, Oedipus, and Medea came from the same mold. Each was dishonored, each felt the burn of honor-shame, and each reacted by rage. Its expression in dramatic action did not remove the dishonor, but it made the shame easier to bear by dissipating their pent-up emotions.

Now contrast this with Nietzsche's portrayal of Mirabeau, "who had no memory for insults and vile actions done to him and was unable to forgive simply because he—forgot. Such a man shakes off with a *single* shrug many vermin that eat deep into others. . . . [T]hat is the sign of strong, full natures in whom there is an excess of the power to form, to mold, to recuperate and to forget."[16] The trouble with the Queen was that she lacked a morally accredited way of purging herself of the vermin in her soul. Her inability, however, was not her fault; it was a consequence of her moral tradition, which came as close as any to being a shame-culture.[17]

In her moral tradition, morality took the form of the internalization of public standards. Well-trained moral agents, in such contexts, do not and cannot make a distinction between public and private standards, for the two are the same. This, of course, does not mean that the distinction between private and public spheres also disappears. They remain separate; the bedroom is private. What happens, however, is that the *standards* by which conduct is judged in these spheres are neither public nor private, but both, because the public is made private. In such a tradition, therefore, the distinction between social morality, where public standards prevail, and personal morality, where private standards are appealed to, disappears. Or, since no tradition is perfectly homogeneous, in the Lydian tradition the existence of a distinction between social and personal morality was a sign of moral failure. The extent to which the distinction existed was the same as the extent of the failure to live up to the ideal of having internalized public standards.

The consequence of having such a morality is an impoverishment of moral life; there are important possibilities foreclosed by it. It becomes impossible, or a sign of failure, to mount a moral protest against the prevailing standards. For if all standards are or ought to be internalized public ones, then individuals cannot have a moral justification for criticizing the prevailing standards. Such criticism would have to appeal to some standards, but there are none to which appeal is possible. Hence individuals must see their own moral dissatisfaction as moral failure, and shame is symptomatic of the perception of this failure. But there is nowhere for shame to go. Like a vermin it eats deeper and deeper into the soul. The moral reform which would remove the failure is the very thing that is inexpressible in justifiable terms in that morality. So the self-destructive feeling just sits there and suddenly explodes in some spectacular action, like the Queen's revenge, for example—after which, the feeling spent, she settled into married life with Gyges.

Another way moral life was impoverished in this moral tradition was that no room had been left in it for a certain kind of excuse for failure. It made no difference to the Queen's feeling of honor-shame that she had not in any way contributed to her dishonor. No matter how loyal, modest, and honorable was the Queen, what really counted was that, given the standards, in that particular instance she failed: she was seen naked. Desert, motive, intention, effort were irrelevant to failure in that moral tradition. What counted was achievement, and it was measured by living up to the standard. When people fell short of the standard, and, being well-trained moral agents, felt ashamed, they could not articulate, could not give moral weight to the fact that they were the victims of circumstances and not the agents who brought about their own failure. Once again, therefore, frustration and bitterness pervaded their emotional lives, and there was no morally acceptable way of coping with them.[18]

Nietzsche's Mirabeau, however, had such a way available to him. He could shrug off the insults which would have moved the Queen to seek blood because his moral tradition allowed him to distinguish between social and personal morality. It was possible for Mirabeau to maintain a moral sphere where what counted was his own conception of a good life, his own standards of excellence, his own judgment of success and failure. He could juxtapose this private sphere with the public one, and say to himself, and to others, that on some occasions it is the private sphere, with one's own standards and judgments, that matters. Thus he could dismiss other people's imputation of failure to him, because he had a ground for overriding the standards to which his critics appealed. Mirabeau's moral tradition enabled him to associate his self-respect partly with this private sphere, while the Queen's moral tradition had no scope for this moral possibility.

Now, this moral possibility is of having a private conception of a good life which is different from the private conceptions of others. It is a possibility which allows for pluralism, individual differences, experiments in living. What her moral tradition denied to the Queen was not a conception of a good life, not the distinction between the private and the public, not connecting a good life to these standards, what was denied to her was the possibility of differing from others in her moral tradition with respect to her standards and, consequently, her conception of a good life. In her moral tradition, the moral ideal was the internalization of social morality whose standards were public and the same for everyone. It was this moral ideal which made it impossible for her to criticize her own moral tradition, because she did not have available a distinct private and yet moral standpoint in terms of which she could disagree with her social morality. And it was for the same reason that she was locked into honor-shame, although the failure she, and others, attributed to herself was not her fault.

Of course, this is not to say that Mirabeau, in his different tradition, was immune to shame. On the contrary, he was just as liable to it as the Queen was. However, it was neither propriety-shame nor honor-shame, but, what I shall call, *worth-shame* that could befall him, were he to fail. His self-respect partly depended on living up to his private standards, which were his own in the double sense of deeply caring about them and their being definitive of his conception of a good life. This is why his estimate of his own worth was connected with them, and this is why shame, worth-shame, could follow from his violation of them. In possession of a personal morality, Mirabeau could reasonably criticize his social morality, because he had an independent moral perspective. He could reasonably reject the criticisms of others on the ground that they judged him by inappropriate public standards; and he could reasonably excuse his own failure to live up to his private standards if he could truthfully claim that he did what he could to avoid failure. Worth-shame would be appropriate for Mirabeau only if these defenses failed.

The availability of the distinction between personal and social morality is not an unmixed blessing. A personal morality could be just as deficient as a social morality. Furthermore, the distinction not only makes possible the moral criticism of a society by its individual members, but it also introduces the possibility of conflict between individuals and their society, and, through such conflict, alienation. Nevertheless, having the distinction is morally better than not having it, because without it individuals are at the mercy of their moral tradition, while with it, they can articulate their moral dissatisfactions and possibly remedy them. Of course, we should not suppose that such criticism is always justified, or that when personal morality conflicts with social morality, the former should always prevail. How to balance the claims of personal and social morality is one great question that comes with distinguishing them. But having to answer the question is not too large a price to pay for freeing us from moral rigidity.

I can now state my first claim regarding moral progress. The movement of individuals from liability to propriety-shame, to honor-shame, to worth-shame is one kind of moral progress. It is progress, first, because it moves from a superficial toward a deeper attitude to moral standards. Propriety-shame is caused when standards set by appearances count against us; we are seen naked, when nudity is improper. Honor-shame is consequent on having made standards of appearance definitive of our honor, and it is caused when we fail to conform to these standards; our privacy is invaded, when honor depends on the separation of the private and the public. Worth-shame is independent of appearances, it is caused by a culpable failure to live up to private standards; we allow our privacy to be invaded when our sense of worth depends on protecting it, regardless of prevailing public standards. In propriety-shame, we care about appearances; in honor-shame, we care about appearing as we are; in worth-shame, we care about being in a certain way and do not care about appearances. The progress is from caring about how we seem to caring about how we are.

Second, the progress is in the direction of greater self-direction. People whose chief moral concern is with appearances are at the mercy of public opinion and depend on it for their choices and judgments; people moved primarily by honor subordinate their choices and judgments to public opinion, but they have made it their own opinion; while people whose moral standards include both public and private ones can criticize and correct their choices and judgments in both social and personal morality. Thus greater self-direction brings decreased dependence on others, greater scope for moral criticism, and consequently, a better chance of moral improvement.

Third, the prospects of a good life depend both on what moral agents do and what happens to them. In both, fortuitous circumstances play a considerable role. The more we concentrate our moral resources and attention on what is in our control, the less scope we leave to chance. And since our control over the private sphere is always greater than our control over the public one, a moral attitude which concentrates on the private is more likely to lead to a good life than others. Since the change from propriety-shame to worth-shame is toward greater emphasis on the private, it constitutes progress toward increasing the area in our lives we can control, and thus our chances of living good lives.

In claiming that progress is possible through greater depth, self-direction, and control, I do not mean to suggest that we cannot go wrong. It may happen, for instance, that we progress toward defective standards. Good lives depend on many things: one is having the right attitude to our standards, another is having the right standards. Both are necessary, neither is sufficient.

My first claim is about the moral progress of individuals, the next one is about the moral progress of entire moral traditions. A moral tradition improves as it becomes more hospitable to the moral progress of its members. And since individuals progress by moving from propriety-shame to worth-shame, so the moral tradition progresses by encouraging this process. This involves encouraging individuals to develop private moral standards, alongside the public ones.

IV

My third claim about moral progress is that the reasons for regarding the change through the three forms of shame as moral improvement are also reasons for moving away from all forms of shame toward other responses to moral failure. And, as before, these reasons are reasons first for individuals and then, by implication, also for moral traditions.

There was a time when the prevailing wisdom in one dominant school of medicine was to respond to illness by administering various poisons as antidotes to patients; it was thought that judiciously selected poisons would counteract the poisons which caused the illness, and thus cure it.[19] There actually were some illnesses which responded well to this treatment, but it was found that on the whole the treatment considerably weakened patients and left a residue of poisons with which the patient, in a weakened state, had to contend. My doubts about shame are analogous: it weakens moral agents and it leaves a residue which adds a burden to the deficiency with which they already have to contend.

To begin with the obvious: shame is a bad feeling. It is not just painful, but the pain it makes us feel is on account of our own deficiencies. It diminishes our self-respect, and it does so in important ways, because the deficiencies which occasion it are obstacles in the way of living what we regard as good lives. Thus shame is a kind of moral double jeopardy. Not only are we saddled with deficiencies, but we have shame to pillory us for them.[20]

It will be said against this that while shame may be painful, it is a morally necessary pain. "If someone has self-respect then under certain specifiable conditions he will be feeling shame. A person has no self-respect if he regards no circumstances as shame-producing. Loss of self-respect and loss of the capacity for shame go hand in hand. The close connection between these two makes it clear why shame is often thought to be valuable. It is, firstly, that a sense of value is necessary for self-respect and so for shame, so that whatever else may be wrong about the person feeling shame he will at least have retained a sense of value. And secondly, it is a sense of value which protects the self from what in the agent's own eyes is corruption and ultimately extinction."[21]

There are several reasons for doubting these claims. First, let us agree that shamelessness is bad and self-respect is good. But shame is not the only possible reaction to our violation of moral commitments. Anger at ourselves, resolution to improve, the desire to make amends, a quest for understanding why we did what we regarded as wrong are some others. Because we may not feel shame at our own recognized moral failure does not mean that we are bound to lack self-respect. We may sustain our self-respect in other ways.

Second, the protection against corruption and the extinction of the self which shame allegedly provides may be forward or backward looking. If it is forward looking, it is supposed to protect us from doing wrong in the future. But it cannot be shame which thus protects us, since, *ex hypothesi,* the wrong is in the future, so we have nothing yet to be ashamed about. The best that can be said is that the protection is provided by *fear* of shame, not by shame itself. However, why should fear be necessary at all, and if there is fear, why should it be of shame? We can be deterred from future wrongdoing by our self-respect itself, by understanding the consequences of our contemplated wrong actions on others, or by pride, honor, vanity, kindness, etc. And if we have fear as deterrent, then fear of punishment, loss of love, respect, or status may serve just as well as fear of shame.

On the other hand, if the alleged protection provided by shame is backward looking, concerning a wrong we have already done, then I fail to see how it can protect the self from "corruption and ultimately extinction." For such corruption as there is has already set in due to the wrong we have done. We recognize it, but, as we have seen, there is no reason to suppose that unless the recognition takes the form of shame, we shall be incapable of limiting or removing the corruption. Not to recognize our corruption is worse than to recognize it, but its recognition may produce many morally acceptable reactions of which shame, at best, is only one. Remember Aristotle: "If shamelessness is bad . . . that does not make it good to be ashamed."

As to the danger of the extinction of the self, it seems to me that shame makes it more, rather than less, likely to happen. Recall how Mirabeau's capacity for shame was an improvement over the Queen's. The trouble with honor-shame was that it had no outlet, for there was no way to undo the dishonor, not even if it was undeserved. When a likely target appeared in the form of people who did deserve some enmity, the subjects of honor-shame reacted to their hapless victims with disproportionately excessive rage, and thereby purged themselves of the large residue of emotion which was poisoning them. Mirabeau, we have said, was in a better position, because his shame was worth-shame; it was not the result of internalized public opinion, but the consequence of his private standards. He could handle shame better than the Queen, because he could spurn public opinion in the name of private standards, which gave him grounds for refusing to accept what others regarded as shameful. Nevertheless, while this is an improvement, in other respects he was as badly off as the subjects of honor-shame.

Both Mirabeau and the Queen were the objects of their shame. Their experiences were of personal failure. They had been counted, and they had been found, in their own eyes, wanting. The causes of their shame were different, but the experience of personal shortcoming, their diminished self-respect, the weakening and undermining of their selves were the same, and it is the same for all the experiences of shame I have discussed. Thus the more ashamed we are, the closer we come to the extinction of ourselves. Taylor says that shame is a bulwark protecting the self from extinction, because it shows that the agents have retained a sense of values. However, since the use to which the retained values are put is self-condemnation, they are not the bulwark, but the enemy against which a bulwark is needed. If moral life is to go well, there must be a robust self capable of engaging in it. It must be able to make more or less detached choices and judgments, it must be able to withstand adversity, it must have strength, confidence, and integrity. Shame undermines all this, weakens the self, and that is why moral progress consists not merely in developing from propriety-shame, through honor-shame, to worth-shame, and thereby growing in independence and self-direction, but also in developing from worth-shame to less destructive forms of moral response to the recognition of our moral failures.

This is not seen by many writers on shame. Morris, for instance, thinks that "feeling shame because of what we have done, we actually see ourselves as shameful persons and the steps that are appropriate to relieve shame are becoming a person that is not shameful. Shame leads to creativity."[22] But why should it lead to creativity, rather than to self-loathing? How could we take the appropriate steps to relieve shame when it is the nature of the experience to tend to make us doubt, suspect, and denigrate the only agency capable of taking those steps? Where do the energy, the confidence, the moral aspiration come from when it is the likely consequence of shame to sap them? The trend of moral economy is that the more intensely we feel shame, the less capable we are likely to be of the moral creativity required for reform.

My reason for the claim that moral progress leads us away from shame toward other moral responses is that shame undermines self-direction, reduces the chances of moral reform, and weakens our selves. Correspondingly, a moral tradition which makes available moral possibilities other than shame is better than one which does not.

V

I need to say something now about the moral possibilities whose realization constitutes moral progress over the cultivation of shame. I have already mentioned several such possibilities, but I want to concentrate on one. In feeling shame, we respond to our moral failure by dwelling on the deficiency which produced it. The alternative I have in mind is to respond to moral failure by dwelling on the attraction of the goal we have failed to reach. The goal is to live a good life. My suggestion is that the moral enterprise is far more likely to be carried on if instead of flagellating ourselves with the stick of shame, we concentrate on the attraction of the carrot which our conception of a good life represents. It is better to respond to failure by reminding ourselves of what we want to achieve and why than by concentrating on our faults. What makes it better are the attraction of the goal, the fact that our moral energy is limited, and that it is a wiser use of our limited energy to motivate such capacities as we have than to focus on the shortcomings from which we suffer.

It will be objected that I assume that our feelings of shame are voluntary, but this is not so. Nobody wants to feel shame, we are assailed by it. Shame happens to us; it is an experience we can produce or prevent only in the sense of producing or preventing the state of affairs to which shame is the appropriate response. If we have self-respect and know that we have failed morally, shame will come to us. The objection to my suggestion that another feeling would be better than shame is that we cannot have direct control over our feelings of shame.

My reply is that while it is true that we cannot have direct control over shame, we can have indirect control over it. We cannot make feeling shame dependent on a decision to have it or not have it. But once we have it, we can decide to cultivate or to minimize it, to strengthen or to weaken it, to attribute greater or lesser importance to it. What makes this possible is that in addition to the emotive aspect of shame, which is beyond our direct control, shame also has a cognitive and a moral aspect, and these we can control.

The cognitive aspect of shame involves a self-conscious detached comparison between the deficiency responsible for our failure and the standard of which we have fallen short. The moral aspect of shame is the identification of the standard as an essential component of our conception of a good life and the acceptance of the standard for the evaluation of our own character and conduct. It is a necessary condition of the experience of shame that the comparison be made, and, initially, we cannot help making it, for we find the discrepancy between how we are and how we ought to be flagrant and forced on us. But once made and accepted, it need not be made again; we can direct our attention away from it toward other objects; we can refuse to concentrate on the feeling, relegate it into the background, and deliberately hold some other object in the focus of our attention. Shame, however, is an insistent feeling, so the object upon which we focus in preference to it must have sufficient force to counteract the pressure of shame to reclaim center stage. My suggestion is that this object should be our conception of a good life. It is bound to have sufficient force to counteract shame, for the intensity of our shame depends on how much we mind having fallen short of the conception. Thus, the stronger our shame is, the more attractive we must find the goal of which we are ashamed to have fallen short. And if the goal is not very attractive, then we could not mind all that much the failure to achieve it. So we can always derive from shame the clue to a better, less destructive response.

Of course, the assertion of control by the cognitive and moral aspects of shame over its emotive aspect requires effort, often great effort. Whether the effort is made depends on many things, but one of the most important among them is the moral education of the agent. We can be trained to regard shame as the emotion of self-respect, as Taylor proposes, and then we shall want to hang on to it as our last moral straw, rather than make an effort to minimize it, as I am suggesting. Or we can learn to shun shame as the emotion of failure which further exacerbates the moral difficulty in which we find ourselves, and in that case we shall make an effort to demote it to a lesser rank. I have been arguing that the latter course is better, that a moral tradition educating its young to lessen their vulnerability to shame constitutes moral progress over a tradition which aims to inculcate in them a receptivity to shame.

VI

If my arguments are sound, they lead to the undesirability of regarding shame as an important moral force. But they have another implication as well. I tried to illustrate how moral progress is possible by concentrating on shame. If moral progress *is* possible, if one moral tradition can be morally better than another, then, to that extent, the claim that morality is objective has been substantiated. At least in regard to shame, we can reasonably compare and evaluate different moral traditions. It seems to me that the best hope of establishing the objectivity of morality in general is not by meta-ethical arguments, but by treating very many substantive moral phenomena as I have endeavored to treat shame.[23]

Notes

1. G. Taylor, *Pride, Shame and Guilt* (Oxford, 1985), especially chap. 3.
2. A. Isenberg, "Natural Pride and Natural Shame," *Explaining Emotions,* edited by A. Rorty (Berkeley, 1980), 355–83.
3. Taylor, *Pride, Shame and Guilt,* 3.
4. Isenberg, "Natural Pride and Natural Shame," 369.
5. See *Republic* 465a and *Laws* 671c.
6. *Nicomachean Ethics* 1128b31–34. For an illuminating comparison of Plato and Aristotle on this point, see M. C. Nussbaum, "Shame, Separateness, and Political Unity: Aristotle's Criticism of Plato," in *Essays on Aristotle's Ethics,* edited by A. Rorty (Berkeley, 1980), 395–435.
7. An example of this is the title essay by A. Heller, *The Power of Shame* (London, 1985).
8. J. Rawls, *A Theory of Justice* (Cambridge, Mass., 1971), 443.
9. Ibid., 445.
10. See, e.g., J-P. Sartre, *Being and Nothingness,* Part III, Chapter One, Section IV, translated by H. E. Barnes (New York, 1956) and A. C. Danto's discussion in *Jean-Paul Sartre* (New York, 1975), chap. 4; also H. Morris, *Guilt and Innocence* (Berkeley, 1976), 59–63.
11. Taylor, *Pride, Shame and Guilt,* 66. See also A. O'Hear, "Guilt and Shame as Moral Concepts," *Proceedings of the Aristotelian Society* 77 (1976–7): 73–86.
12. See e.g., Rawls, *Theory of Justice,* 444–46.
13. Ibid., 444.
14. Herodotus, *The Histories,* i.8–12, translated by A. De Selincourt (Harmondsworth, 1954), 16–18.
15. E. Heller in "Man Ashamed" traces the many literary and dramatic treatments of this story; see *In the Age of Prose* (Cambridge, 1984), 215–32.
16. F. Nietzsche, *On the Genealogy of Morals,* First Essay, Section 10, translated by W. Kaufmann (New York, 1966), 475. I have rearranged the order of the quoted sentences.
17. For a superb discussion of this point, see E. R. Dodds, *The Greeks and the Irrational,* chaps. 1–2 (Berkeley, 1971).

18. In a series of interesting studies, J. B. White in *When Words Lose Their Meaning* (Chicago, 1984) describes several moral traditions thus handicapped.

19. For a fascinating account, see H. Trevor-Roper, "The Paracelsian Movement," *Renaissance Essays* (London, 1985).

20. Isenberg is excellent on this point.

21. Taylor, *Pride, Shame and Guilt,* 80–81.

22. Morris, *Guilt and Innocence,* 62.

23. I am grateful to James Kellenberger and Lynne McFall for their comments on this paper.

MIDWEST STUDIES IN PHILOSOPHY, XIII (1988)

Common Projects and Moral Virtue

ROBERT MERRIHEW ADAMS

I

We speak of someone being a "good colleague" in a philosophy department, in a sense that has little to do with philosophical, pedagogical, or administrative talent, and much to do with motives and traits of character. A good colleague in this sense is considerate of students and co-workers, sensitive to their needs and concerns, conscientious in carrying out responsibilities to them, and cares about them as individuals. These qualities are forms of benevolence and conscientiousness, and it is obvious that they are morally virtuous. There are other qualities of a good colleague, however, which do not seem to be forms of benevolence and conscientiousness. A good philosophical colleague cares about philosophy for its own sake. She wants to do it well herself, and she wants other people, specifically including her students and colleagues, to do it well. She wants them to do it well, not only for their sake, but also for philosophy's sake. And she cares about her department for its own sake, in a way that is not simply reducible to caring about the welfare of the individuals involved in it. She wants it to be the best philosophy department it can be. If she has been devoted to this goal for many years, has labored effectively to build and improve the department and strengthen its position in the university and in the discipline, and has shown a consistent loyalty to this project, and a willingness to make personal sacrifices for it, her colleagues owe her a great debt of gratitude. Members of other (to some extent competing) departments do not owe her the same debt of gratitude, but they ought certainly to admire her for being such a good colleague. I think this is *moral* admiration, not only insofar as it is admiration for her benevolence and conscientiousness, but also insofar as it is admiration for her devotion to the project of making a certain philosophy department the best it can be.

Similar judgments can be made on the side of deficiency. Suppose that after fifteen years as a member of the UCLA philosophy department, having been generally well-treated by my colleagues and the university, I were conscientious and benevolent toward my students and colleagues as individuals, but cared not at all about the department's collective aspiration to be an exceptionally good philosophy department. This lack would appropriately elicit some anger from my colleagues, and disapproval from others. And I think the disapproval would have a strongly moral flavor.

Being a good or bad philosophical colleague is not an isolated case. Someone who plays on a serious athletic team without caring about winning, or in an orchestra without caring about the musical quality of the performance, is apt to be perceived as "letting the side down." This is a morally tinged criticism, and it applies even if the offender is attentive to the interests of her associates as individuals. (What would be more likely to blunt the criticism would be the discovery that she was distracted with some personal grief or worry.) Conversely, one who "puts her heart into" the game or the music is perceived as exhibiting a moral or quasi-moral virtue. Similar considerations apply to most situations in which one cooperates with other people to make a product or perform a service. One is expected to care about the product or the service in a way that is not easily or obviously reducible to caring about the welfare of the individuals affected.

At work and at play we are involved in a great variety of common projects, projects that we share with other people. They make up an enormous part of the fabric of our lives. And in most cases the project will go better if participants care about it for its own sake. A capacity for investing emotionally in common projects is a quality much to be desired in an associate in almost any area of life. I think it is largely because they are believed to contribute to the development of that capacity that team sports are widely regarded as useful for moral education.

It may be suggested that the sort of devotion or caring or commitment of which I am speaking enters the purview of morality as a kind of *loyalty*. I have no objection to the use of that term; but if what I am speaking of is a loyalty, it is a loyalty to a project as such, rather than to a group of people as such. If I join a choir, I ought to care about the quality of its singing; but there is no reason why I should be committed to the group in such a way as to want it to continue to exist as a group, and want to belong to it myself, if it ceased to be a choir. Perhaps it will be said that the loyalty one ought to have as a choir member is to the choir as an institution, though not to a group of individuals as such. Again I need not disagree; for I count institutions, or their development, maintenance, and flourishing, as common projects. I am thus focusing on the common projects of groups of people that are associated for a specific purpose, or for a limited range of purposes. Such associations play a dominant role in our pluralistic, technological society. Their projects are a good starting point for our reflections, though the discussion will be extended, before the end of this paper, to projects characteristic of associations, such as family and friendship, that are not for special purposes but for a more comprehensive sharing of life.

I am arguing that caring about a common project for its own sake is morally virtuous, at least in some cases. Of course devotion to a common project is not always virtuous. Devotion to an evil project is not virtuous, and the most horrendously evil projects are usually common projects of groups. And even devotion to a good project can be a morally ugly thing if it is too ruthless, or is not seasoned with a lively concern for the rights and welfare of other people.

The theme of this paper, then, is that caring, in an appropriate way (not too ruthlessly, for instance), about good common projects for their own sake is morally virtuous. I will develop one possible rationale for this view in sections II and III, and will then suggest in section IV that these considerations may help to explain how caring for their own sake about personal relationships and about one's good could be morally virtuous.

II

For present purposes we can grant that moral virtue has to do in some way with human good, and perhaps even specifically with the good of other people. The first step toward understanding how caring about common projects for their own sake can be morally virtuous is to see the relation of common projects to human good. In much of ethical theory there is an emphasis on aspects of human good that can be thought of in terms of *commodities,* an emphasis that is rooted in what we may call "the economic model" of beneficence. Being good to people is widely understood in terms of conferring benefits on them, and that in turn is conceived on the model of giving them money. This is obviously true of utilitarian theory, in which the concept of utility is supposed to structure the measurement and distribution of benefits in general as money structures more narrowly economic transactions; but I think the influence of the economic model extends far beyond utilitarianism. It captures what is most important in some contexts. Commodities provide an indispensable physical basis for human good, and economic issues are among the most important topics of public morality.

In other contexts, however, the economic model of beneficence is very misleading. Human good is not itself a commodity. A person's life does not consist in abundance of possessions.[1] And in order to be humanly good to one's associates it is often not enough to be a benefactor on the economic model.

A famous argument of Butler's is relevant here. "Happiness," he says, "consists in the gratification of particular passions, which supposes the having of them."[2] By 'particular passions' he means, roughly, first-order desires or interests, in which one cares about something besides the satisfaction of other desires or interests of one's own. Butler argues that one must have such desires or interests in order to be happy, because happiness consists in having them satisfied, and having them satisfied presupposes that one has them.

Aristotle thought that human good or happiness consists, not in the satisfaction of desire, but in activity of a certain sort.[3] This activity must fulfill an interest that one has, however, if it is to make its contribution to one's good. One must value the activity for its own sake, or else see it as a way of achieving something else that one desires. Since there is a vicious regress in the idea that one might have interests but be interested in nothing besides the satisfaction of other interests that one has, Aristotle could agree with Butler that one must have first-order desires or interests in order to be happy.

Without committing ourselves here to any theory of what happiness or human good *consists in,* we can agree with Aristotle that it is found largely in good activity, and with Butler that it requires first-order desires or interests. In the terminology of the present paper, the happy person, the person whose good is realized to any very satisfactory extent, must have projects, must engage in activities that derive their point or meaning from first-order desires or interests. For this reason, and because it is clear that an excessive preoccupation with our own good as such is apt to prevent us from developing the more "particular" interests that would be most likely to engage us in fulfilling activity, we can also agree with Butler that "that character we call selfish is not the most promising for happiness."[4]

I have no *a priori* argument to show that a happy person must care about some activities for their own sake. One can imagine people who engaged in no activities except in order to satisfy their physical needs, and who found their activities meaningful and satisfying only because of their orientation toward their physical needs. But such a life would barely be recognizable as human. We surely would not desire it. Even in a subsistence economy, people typically develop activities of play, conversation, ritual, and art that are carried on largely, if not solely, for their own sake. And even in economically necessary activities, such as farming and cooking, people learn to find satisfaction in the activity itself, and the *way* in which it is done becomes something they care about for its own sake. It is clear, at a minimum, that such interest in activities for their own sake is in fact a major contributor to human good or happiness, and the disappearance of such interest would be a loss for which there could be no adequate compensation in any human life that is likely to exist in this world.

This much about the importance of projects and the interest we have in them for their own sake would be accepted by most moralists, I think. Many writers in ethics have made use of it, John Rawls being an obvious example. What is less often emphasized in moral philosophy is the extent to which these projects are common projects.

Conversations essentially require the participation of more than one person. So do concerts and dances and most games and rituals. Political activity is by its very nature situated in the context of some common project of social organization; the only possible exceptions would be acts of rebellion so isolated and so alienated as to be at most marginally political. Science and philosophy could to some extent be carried on in isolation, but we would not get very far with them as purely private projects. Some forms of work could in principle be solitary, others could not, but almost all work is in fact done in the context of some common project.

Except for the most rudimentary activities of satisfying physical needs, moreover, all our activities depend on abilities and interests that are acquired only through participation in shared projects. Education is an induction into common projects. Educationally the most fundamental of common projects is conversation. Almost all distinctively human activities depend in one way or another on language, and language is acquired by children in conversation with their elders—mainly, I suspect, in conversations that are ends in themselves for both the child and the elders. As we acquire language, so also we acquire a culture, anthropologically speaking. We are inducted into a culture as we grow up. And a culture depends for its existence on common projects which very largely determine what activities will make sense to people who participate in the culture.

Thus human good is found very largely in activities whose point and value depend on the participation of other people in a common project. The value of the activities depends also on other people's caring about common projects. Common projects are not mindless biological processes like digestion and metabolism. They exist only because people care about them. And if too many of the participants do not care enough about them, the activities connected with them are apt to lose value for all the participants.

This helps to explain why one must be more than an economic benefactor if one is to be humanly good to one's associates. The benefits conferred in the economic model are commodities, or at any rate benefits to which the motives of the benefactor are external. Even if they are in fact conferred out of benevolence, they would be the same benefits if the benefactor's motive were more mercenary. Benefits of this sort are vitally important, but a very full realization of human good also requires benefits of another kind. In particular, as I have been arguing, it requires the opportunity to participate actively in common projects that engage the interest, in some cases even the enthusiasm or devotion, of other people. That opportunity is a great benefit that other people give us by their interested participation in the common project. It is a benefit to which their motivation, their interest in the project, is essential and not external. And as that interest in the project is distinct from a benevolent interest in the good of the recipient, this benefit is one that cannot be given solely out of such benevolence.

A lively interest in common projects for their own sakes is therefore a normal part of being humanly good to one's associates. It is a normal part of being a good colleague, a good teammate, a good citizen, a good mentor, a good friend, a good spouse, a good parent, child, or sibling. And being a good exemplar of these relational kinds is a moral achievement. It is morally virtuous. Being a colleague, friend, or parent, but not a good one, on the other hand, is a moral shortcoming, or in extreme cases a moral failure. Not caring appropriately about common projects can constitute such a shortcoming or failure.

Being good to one's associates in these ways is far from the whole of moral virtue. A general benevolent interest in the welfare of other people, including people with whom one has little or no association, and a conscientious regard for their rights, are even more important morally. But an exclusively benevolent or conscientious motivation that was totally focused on human welfare and rights as such might keep one from being as good a friend or colleague, and in general as good an associate, as one should be, if it kept one from caring about common projects for their own sakes when the projects are not explicitly aimed at welfare or justice as such. Butler's claim that "that character we call selfish is not the most promising for happiness" is closely preceded by the statement that "over-fondness for a child is not generally thought to be for its advantage."[5] If these words contain a suggestion that "too much love" might be bad for a child, I would not wish to endorse it. But if the suggstion is that an exclusively benevolent (or even an exclusively benevolent and conscientious) motivation is not the most promising for being good to a child in the way that a parent should be, I would agree. A parent who shares with a child an activity that he himself enjoys gives the child more than if he engaged in the activity only for the child's good. Similarly a teacher who cares about both her subject and her students, for their own sakes, gives the students more than a teacher who cares about only one or the other.

III

The claims I have made thus far about moral virtue have been plausible (I hope), but also rather dogmatic. I have no intention of developing here a full-fledged theory of the nature of virtue, and I doubt that I will be able entirely to dispel the air of dogmatism. But certain things at least should be said about reasons for which, and the extent to which, caring appropriately about good common projects may be said to be morally virtuous and being willing and able to invest emotionally and motivationally such projects may be regarded as a moral virtue.

Few would disagree with Philippa Foot's statement that "virtues are in general beneficial characteristics, and indeed ones that a human being needs to have, for his own sake and that of his fellows."[6] In the previous section I argued, in effect, that a willingness and ability to invest one's concern in good common projects satisfies this condition. But it is clearly only a necessary and not a sufficient condition for being a moral virtue, as Foot points out.

A similar necessary condition is suggested by James Wallace, who classifies virtues as human excellences and says that "human excellences will be tendencies and capacities for living well the sort of life that is characteristic of human beings."[7] The sort of life that is characteristic of human beings, Wallace emphasizes, is a social life. The aspect of social life that he singles out for special mention is that it is "informed by convention." Conventions (most pervasively and crucially, linguistic conventions) are indeed characteristic of human life, and Wallace is right to insist on the moral importance of this fact. But common projects are no less characteristic of human life, and a willingness to invest in good ones is no less important for social life. This disposition therefore satisfies Wallace's initial necessary condition for being a virtue.

Both Foot and Wallace are concerned to distinguish virtues from other human excellences, such as strength and skill. Foot suggests that this may be accomplished by saying that "virtues belong to the will," though " 'will' must here be understood in its widest sense, to cover what is wished for as well as what is sought," and 'belong' must also be construed fairly broadly, as she makes clear.[8] This presents us with another plausible necessary condition for being a virtue, and another condition that is plainly satisfied by the disposition that interests us, for caring about a common project certainly belongs to the will, in the indicated broad sense.

Another point on which Foot and Wallace agree is that virtues must be useful and important for the living well of human life *in general*. One reason why the love of philosophy, for example, is not a virtue is that many (perhaps most) human beings can live well enough without it, though it is important equipment for a philosopher. A willingness and ability to invest one's concern in good common projects qualifies as a virtue on this count too, because one needs it to do well in almost any human relationship.

The points I have mentioned thus far, however, do not suffice to distinguish moral virtues from all other human excellences. I take it that curiosity and a taste for physical exercise are not moral virtues; but why not? Both belong to the will, in the broad sense. They are interests in certain goods (knowledge, and activity suited to one's physical capacities). And both are useful in almost any sort of human life. Perhaps it is relevant here that while curiosity is important for a great variety of human concerns, and not just for a particular specialized pursuit like philosophy, it may not be important for *everybody* to be curious, so long as enough people are. But a moderate taste for exercise would enhance almost anyone's prospects for health, and it would probably be advantageous to almost any human community if all its members had such a taste—and still it is not a moral virtue.

Need I concern myself with this, since I am not proposing a comprehensive theory of the nature of virtue? We may reasonably believe that honesty is a moral virtue and a taste for exercise is not, even if we cannot explain why. It is incumbent on me, however, to be concerned about the possibility of explanations that would suggest or imply that devotion to good common projects for their own sake is not a moral virtue. One such explanation would focus on the fact that a regard for the rights and interests of other people is not involved in a taste for exercise as it is in honesty. The only concerns or interests or desires that are morally virtuous, it might be suggested, are those that are conscientious or benevolent, having the rights or welfare of others as their object—to which caring appropriately about one's own moral virtue might perhaps be added as a second order moral virtue. This suggestion is in tune with some ethical theories, and is not incompatible with regarding courage and self-control as moral virtues, since what is virtuous in them is not a particular sort of interest or desire, but a capacity for dealing with one's actual and potential fears and desires in such a way as not to be hindered from virtuous disposition and action.[9] Nonetheless I think it expresses too narrow a conception of moral virtue. It is inconsistent with the main thesis of this paper, since caring about a common project for its own sake is different, in most cases, from caring about the rights or welfare of affected persons. In order to defend my thesis against this suggestion, it would be advantageous to be able to indicate a difference between devotion to good common projects and a taste for exercise which might be a reason why the former is a moral virtue and the latter is not.

This can be done, and it can be done in a way that accommodates the widely held view that morality has to do with how one relates to other persons.[10] For though an interest in a good common project is not an interest in the good of other persons as such, it is an interest in something of a sort in which much of their good is found—and found not by accident, but by virtue of deeply rooted characteristics of human life. As I argued in section II, the capacity for caring about good common projects is therefore essential equipment for being a good colleague, a good friend, a good family member, and in general for being humanly good to other people in most sorts of human relationships. None of this is true of curiosity or a taste for exercise. Caring about projects in which much of the good of other people is to be found, and caring about such projects in a way that is necessary if one is to be a good person to be associated with, is plausibly regarded as morally virtuous even if it is not the good of other people as such that one cares about.

This would not be plausible, I think, without the proviso that the projects one cares about are good. That is not to say that a common project must be noble or exalted if moral virtue is to be manifest in devotion to it. Putting one's heart into a pick-up basketball game, and caring with some enthusiasm about the success of the team one happens to be on, can be an expression of the virtue I am talking about.[11] But, other things being equal, devotion to a nobler project is more meritorious.

Indeed consuming devotion to a relatively trivial project is not virtuous at all. And one's interest even in a project greatly good can be excessive to the point of vice. This is an important point, for it is a dangerous truth that I am defending here. Precisely because of the moral aspect of devotion to common projects, some of the most appallingly seductive temptations to idolatry are found in them—not least in those projects that go under the name of patriotism.

There is doubtless much more to be said about the conditions under which, and the extent to which, devotion to a common project is morally virtuous, and the absence of such devotion a moral shortcoming. I make no claim to be saying here all there is to be said about this subject, but I will mention one further point, by way of example. There seems to be less reason to regard not caring about a project as a moral fault if one has not been treated well by the people with whom one shares the project. The reason for this, I suspect, is that what is virtuous here is not just caring about certain kinds of projects, but developing a concern for them as a part of one's forming a social union with other people; and it is less of a fault (if a fault at all) to fail to form social bonds with people by whom one has been ill-treated.

IV

It is my hope that the line of thought developed here may help us to recognize more adequately in our ethical theories the moral value of some important types of motivation. Two types in particular will be discussed to conclude this essay. In both cases I will be arguing for the moral worth of motives that are not forms of conscientiousness or benevolence.

(A) *Friendship*. Moral virtue is shown in being a good friend, as well as in less intimate relationships. This can be understood partly on the basis of the fact that a good friend is conscientious, committed to do his duty to his friend, and benevolent, wanting his friend to flourish. The importance of conscientiousness and benevolence in ethical theory (and in popular moral thinking) may tempt us to think they are all that is morally virtuous in the good friend. Even such an eloquent apostle of the moral value of friendship as Lawrence Blum appeals only to the benevolent aspect of friendship in arguing for its moral worth.[12]

But conscientiousness and benevolence are not all that is involved in being a good friend, as Blum would surely agree.[13] Another characteristic of a good friend is that she values the friendship for its own sake; she is glad to be this particular person's friend, and she wants very much to continue and enhance the relationship. Why shouldn't this aspect of being a good friend also be regarded as virtuous in its own right? I think in fact it is. My reasoning about common projects supports this view.

A friendship is, in a broad sense, a project shared by the friends; and as such it is a particularly important type of common project. Few of us would want to be without friendships, and having good friends is generally acknowledged to be important to human happiness. The value of a friendship, moreover, depends very much on both

parties caring about the common project (their relationship) for its own sake. An os-
tensible friend who does not value the relationship in this way is apt to be perceived
as spoiling the common project—"letting the side down," so to speak. It may even be
doubted whether a friendship really exists unless both parties care about the relationship for its own sake, no matter how great their benevolence and conscientiousness
toward each other. What is usually understood (and desired) as "the gift of friendship" is therefore one of those goods that no one can give you solely out of a desire to
benefit you.

For reasons such as these, the disposition to prize a friendship for its own sake
is not only an instance of the (virtuous) general disposition to invest oneself in a common project. It is itself a trait that is important for living well the kind of life that is
characteristic of human beings, and a quality that is important for being humanly
good to another person in a type of relationship that virtually everyone has reason to
want. These considerations support the view that it is a virtue.

(B) *Caring about one's own good.*[14] It may seem strange to speak of concern for
one's own good as a moral virtue. One reason for this is that persons are rarely
thought to be remarkable for this quality unless it is carried to that excess which is
known as selfishness, which is obviously a vice rather than a virtue. To care about
one's own good to (at least) an appropriate degree seems so normal and natural that
no one gets much credit for it. Certainly it is possible, however, to care too little, or
have too little respect, for one's own good. I believe that it is (or can be) a moral shortcoming, and that an appropriate regard for one's own good is at least a part of moral
virtue, even if it rarely deserves to be singled out for special praise. Perhaps we can
think of it, on the Aristotelian pattern, as a mean between the opposing vices of
selfishness (excess) and self-neglect (deficiency), though I suspect that these traits are
in fact distinguished by something more subtle than quantitative differences in intensity of self-interestedness.

More than one rationale can be given for regarding an appropriate form and degree of this concern as virtuous. One might think it morally virtuous simply because
a human individual can hardly flourish without it. On the other hand, that might
seem an inadequate reason to those who believe that morality is a matter of how one
relates to other persons. I will not try to adjudicate that dispute here. I will only point
out that there is an alternative rationale according to which the moral value of an appropriate concern for one's own good has roots in one's relations with other people—
namely, insofar as one's own good is a common project that one shares with others.

This may at first seem a far-fetched idea, but I believe discussion of objections
to it will reveal its merits. The most obvious objection is that it is unrealistic to think
of caring about one's own good as caring about a common project—that one's own
good is one's own project, and caring about it is an instinctive, individual phenomenon, rather than a social one. This objection is mistaken, however. No doubt human
beings are instinctively or innately self-centered in various ways. But we are not innately concerned for our own good. For concern for one's own good presupposes a
concept of one's own good; and that is not innate. Virtually all of us acquired it from
people who not only had the concept of our good before we did, but also cared about
our good before we could even conceive of it. It is a basic feature of human life that

children have to be *taught* to take care of themselves; that is and has to be a very large part of all early childhood education. In learning to take care of himself the child begins to conceive of and care about his own good. This process can be thought of as an initiation into a project that the child shares with his parents and teachers, or with whoever is nurturing and teaching him—a project of caring for his good.

"This is very well for children," the objector may reply, "but it is part of maturity that a person's good ceases to be a common project and becomes his own individual affair." Not so, I think. In any normal or desirable human situation adults too pursue their good in the context of relationships in which the good of each person is an object of common concern and cooperative effort. This is a feature of family life and friendship. At a less intimate level it is also a feature of educational and medical institutions in which adults are involved, and of whole communities insofar as they take some responsibility for the welfare of their members. Most people find an important part of their own good in caring for the good of others; and it is therefore an important way of being humanly good to other people to share with them the project of promoting one's own good.

The project of promoting my good, however, is one for which my interested participation is crucial. There are many ways in which my good will not be effectively promoted or even protected unless I care about it and pursue it. To be sure, it is also a familiar and important truth that there are ways in which my good will not be advanced by my being too concerned about it; caring more about other things than about oneself is good for one. But if I do not care for my health, avoid bad habits, and take an interest in my education, there is not a lot that my friends can do to rectify these deficiencies. This is a frequent source of anxiety and frustration to people who care about other people. Such facts help to make it intelligible that people who neglect their education or their health, harming (directly) no one but themselves, are sometimes spoken of as "irresponsible." Since people do find much of their good in participating in advancing the good of others, caring appropriately about one's own good is apt to be important to the good of others as well as to one's own.[15] That is a reason for thinking such a concern virtuous.

The idea of an individual's good being a common project may raise in some minds the specter of an objectionable paternalism. There are errors to be avoided on both sides here. On the one hand, it would not be a morally good thing to say (in any desirable human situation) that whether I am happy or miserable is nobody's business but my own. That would be an affront to any relationship or community of mutual love or benevolence. On the other hand, it would be a dangerous mistake not to see that even if my flourishing is a common project, it is one that is related to my will and commitments in a way in which it cannot and should not be related to anyone else's. For the goal of the project is that I should live a good life; and on any attractive conception of a good life, that presupposes that *I* live my life, making choices, developing interests and tastes and convictions of my own. The concrete form that the project of my flourishing is to take must therefore be determined very largely by my will.

The advancement of *my good* is a different project from my being or becoming a good philosopher, or financially secure, or an accomplished pianist. The latter are projects that people who care about me could share with me, and their sharing them would be fine if my adoption of them is not the result of manipulation or pressure. But not embracing such projects need not be a moral shortcoming in me, even if they are espoused by well-meaning friends. That I should care in an appropriate and general way about my own good as such (and thus value my own life as a project) is important for my fruitful participation in any decently benevolent human community. That I should agree with my friends about which of the careers that are open to me would be best for me is not similarly important for my participation in any but an oppressive society. To be seriously mistaken about what would be good for oneself may in some cases be a moral fault; but if so, the fact is not explained by anything that has been said in this essay.

Notes

1. Luke 12:15.

2. Joseph Butler, *Butler's Fifteen Sermons Preached at the Rolls Chapel* and *A Dissertation of the Nature of Virtue,* edited by T. A. Roberts (London, 1970), 102.

3. Aristotle, *Nicomachean Ethics,* 1.7. 1097a22–1098b20.

4. Butler, *Fifteen Sermons,* 102.

5. Ibid.

6. Philippa Foot, *Virtues and Vices and Other Essays in Moral Philosophy* (Berkeley, 1978), 3.

7. James D. Wallace, *Virtues and Vices* (Ithaca, N.Y., 1978), 37.

8. Foot, *Virtues and Vices,* 4–7.

9. See Wallace, *Virtues and Vices,* 160f. Wallace's statements are compatible with the suggestion I am mentioning here, though I don't think they commit him to it.

10. I do not mean to commit myself to this exclusively social view of morality—only to show that the view I am defending is not inconsistent with it.

11. Games illustrate another point that deserves to be noted here. The goal of a good project need not be intrinsically valuable. Games are often good projects even though the goal of the project (winning) is highly artificial and has neither value nor sense apart from people's commitment to the project.

12. Lawrence Blum, *Friendship, Altruism and Morality* (London, 1980), chap. 4. See, e.g., 67f: "[O]ther things being equal, acts of friendship are morally good insofar as they involve acting from regard for another person for his own sake. . . . [T]he deeper and stronger the concern for the friend . . . the greater the degree of moral worth (again, other things being equal)."

13. Cf. Blum, *Friendship,* 82, where he expresses a desire to avoid "an overmoralized view of friendship" that "sees the concern for the friend's good as the central element in friendship, downplaying or neglecting the liking of the friend, the desire to be with him, the enjoyment of shared activities, etc."

14. In what I have to say about this subject I am much indebted to discussions with Lisa Halko.

15. Even someone who did not value her own good could try to be considerate of other people's interest in her good. But I think this is not likely to be a very satisfactory substitute.

On the Advantages of Cooperativeness
FRED FELDMAN

1.

I stand over my newborn baby's crib, filled with paternal love as I look down at him. I want his life to go, for him, as well as possible. Indeed, at this moment, my concern for his welfare blots out all other interests. The only thing I want is that his welfare be maximized. Accordingly, I express a hope: 'I hope that, on all occasions of choice, you will choose from among your alternatives one that in fact maximizes your welfare. If you consistently do this, you will be making the greatest possible contribution to your own welfare, and your life will go, for you, as well as you can possibly make it go'.

Some philosophical friends, having overheard my expression of hope, call me aside. They remind me that my son may someday find himself in a prisoner's dilemma. They go on to remind me that, in prisoner's dilemmas, straightforward maximizers are unable to achieve optimal outcomes. They urge me to reconsider my hopes for my son. One of them suggests an alternative: 'Why don't you hope instead that your son becomes a straightforward maximizer in all situations except prisoner's dilemmas, and that in prisoner's dilemmas he be resolutely cooperative (provided that others are cooperative too). In this way he will gain all the benefits of straightforward maximization, plus the chance of a bonus in the form of extra benefits that can only be achieved by being cooperative in prisoner's dilemmas. If he thus becomes a partially cooperative maximizer, his life cannot go any worse than it would if he were a straightforward maximizer, and may very well go a bit better for him'.

In the present paper, I assess the cogency of my friends' suggestion. Obviously, however, before the suggestion can be assessed, the terms in which it is formulated must be clarified, and its rationale explained. Since I characterize straightforward maximization in a slightly unorthodox way, it will be necessary at the outset to explain my characterization of this central concept. Subsequently, I give an account of prisoner's dilemmas, and I present more detailed accounts and evaluations of several versions of my friends' reasoning. My conclusion is that my friends are wrong. There no advantage to being cooperative.

2. STRAIGHTFORWARD MAXIMIZATION

Standard accounts of straightforward maximization generally begin with the assumption that at each moment of choice, an agent faces a bunch of "alternatives." Each of the alternatives is, in an important sense, "possible" for the agent at the time. They are also "incompatible" in the sense that it would not be possible for the agent to perform any two of them together. Furthermore, the whole set of actions is "exhaustive"—the agent will have to perform at least one of them. Finally, it is generally assumed that all the members of a set of alternatives are "timewise identical"—the time at which any one of the set would be performed, if it were chosen, is the same as the time at which any other would be performed, if it were chosen.[1]

Furthermore, on the standard account, it is generally assumed that for each alternative, there is an outcome. The outcome is what would happen if the alternative were performed. Each outcome has a value for the agent. On one approach, the value of the outcome is an objective measure of how good or bad that outcome would be for the agent. We can then say that the "utility-for-the-agent" of an action is equal to the net value for him of the outcome that would result if the action were performed.

The policy of straightforward maximization is typically taken to be the policy that enjoins an agent to perform an action if and only if no alternative has a higher utility-for-him.

I think there are fairly serious problems with this formulation of the doctrine of straightforward maximization.[2] One problem concerns complex courses of action. I believe it can happen that some course of action maximizes utility for some agent, even though some component of that course of action does not maximize utility for that agent. When this happens, the standard formulation of the policy of straightforward maximization generates incoherent mandates. The agent must perform the course of action (it has higher utility-for-him than any alternative), but he must not perform some component of the course of action (since the component has lower utility-for-him than some alternative).

In light of this difficulty with traditional formulations of the policy of straightforward maximization, I prefer to formulate things in a slightly different way.[3] Instead of starting with the concept of alternative actions, I prefer to think that, at each moment of choice, there are several possible worlds "accessible" to the agent. Roughly, we may say that a possible world is accessible to an agent at a time iff there is some maximal course of action open to him at the time, such that if he were to perform all the actions in that course of action, then that world would occur, or "be actual." I indicate that a world, w, is accessible to an agent, s, at a time, t, by 'As,t,w'.

When we say that some action is "possible" for an agent, we mean that there is still accessible to him some world in which he does that action. A world may be accessible to an agent at a time, but, once the agent behaves in some way other than the way he behaves in that world, it is no longer accessible. It has been "bypassed." Thus, we must be careful, when speaking of what an agent can do, to take note of the time at which the action is possible for him, for an action that I would perform next week might be possible for me now, but might cease to be possible tommorrow. Obviously, we must also take note of the time at which the action would be performed, for clearly that time may be quite different from the time at which it is possible.

Instead of judging actions by appeal to the values of their outcomes, I prefer to judge them by appeal to the values of the accessible possible worlds in which they are performed. Since we are attempting here to give an account of straightforward maximization of the agent's own welfare, it makes the most sense to evaluate worlds by appeal to the welfare-level of the agent in the world. In other words, in order to determine the value of a world for a person, we consider how well the person fares in the world. For present purposes, it will be easiest to assume that this is an objective measure of the extent to which the person enjoys goods and suffers evils in the world. It is not a subjective measure of the actual (or any counterfactual) ranking of the world in the agent's preference ordering. I represent the value of a world, w, for a person, s, as '$V(s,w)$'.

As I see it, a straightforward maximizer is a person who always behaves as he does in the best-for-him of the accessible-to-him worlds. We may (somewhat unrealistically) view the straightforward maximizer as a person who, at every moment of decision, first determines which possible worlds are accessible; then determines which of these are the best-for-him; and then sets out to behave as he does in those worlds.

All this talk of "determining," "considering," and "evaluating" should not be taken too seriously. As I see it, good luck plays a big role in straightforward maximization. A person may want to follow the policy of straightforward maximization, but, due to poor information about what is accessible or what it is worth to him, he may fall short of the mark. Real life people can at best hope to approximate the fully successful, perfectly informed straightforward maximizer.

More precisely, then, my conception of straightforward maximization can be explained as follows:

B: a possible world, w, is a *best* for s at $t = df.$ As,t,w & $\sim$ (Ew') [As,t,w' & V(s,w') > V(s,w)]

SM: as of t, s is to do a iff $(w)(w$ is a best for s at $t \rightarrow s$ does a in $w)$

Intuitively, the idea is this: the *bests* for s at t are the best-for-s worlds accessible to s at t. SM requires s to do a as of a time iff s does a in all of his bests as of that time. A related principle would permit s to do a iff s does a in some current best; and another would forbid s to do a iff he does not do a in any current best.[4]

This account of straightforward maximization, unlike the standard account, permits a person sometimes to perform actions that fail to maximize utility-for-him. This happens, for example, when a person's best total course of action contains some components that are less good for him than some of their time-identical alternatives. On my formulation, the policy of straightforward maximization requires these components (because they are performed in the best-for-the-agent accessible world) even though, if compared to their time-identical alternatives, they do not seem so valuable.

3. PRISONER'S DILEMMAS

Suppose my son conspires with a partner to embezzle money from the bank where they work. Suppose they are caught, but the DA lacks sufficient evidence to convict them. My son and his partner are in separate cells. The DA comes to my son and offers him a deal designed to make him want to confess. He shows him this matrix:

FIGURE ONE

		THE PARTNER	
		Silence	Confession
MY SON	Silence	1,1	10,0
	Confession	0,10	9,9

He explains as follows: 'Each box indicates the outcome of a pair of actions, one by you and one by your partner. The numbers in the boxes indicate years in prison, with your sentence on the left, and your partner's sentence on the right. So the upper right box indicates what will happen if you are silent and your partner confesses. In that case, you will get ten years, and he will go free today.' He goes on to explain that the policy of straightforward maximization requires my son to confess. He puts it this way. 'Since you want to get out as soon as possible, it's reasonable for you to confess. If your partner is silent, confession will get you out today rather than in a year. If your partner confesses, confession will get you out in nine years rather than ten. So, no matter what your partner does, you're better off confessing.' He then leaves, telling my son that he (and the stenographer) will be back in one hour to receive his confession.

He shows the same matrix to my son's partner, and explains it to him in the same way.

It is not entirely clear what further conditions must be satisfied for this case to count as a prisoner's dilemma. Some, for example, have imposed complex epistemic conditions. Others have insisted on the isolation of the players. Still others have insisted that each player must be a straightforward maximizer. I think the case is interesting and puzzling even in the absence of some of these conditions. Let us add a minimal set of further conditions.

(i) If either player can make the other choose to remain silent, the case loses considerable interest. Suppose, for example, that my son can somehow force his partner to remain silent. Then, given natural assumptions, my son's best choice is to confess and make his partner remain silent. Then my son goes free today. In order to avoid this, we stipulate that the actions of the agents are *independent,* in the following sense: No matter what choice either makes, he would still make that choice no matter what choice the other makes.

(ii) If either player stands to receive payoffs in addition to the ones listed in the matrix, the game may become uninteresting. For example, suppose my son's partner is vengeful and has an elephantine memory. If my son rats on him while the partner remains silent, the partner's anger will smolder for ten long years. When he gets out, he will search for my son, find him, and eventually murder him. In this case, the payoff '0,10' in the lower left box is surely misleading.

To deal with this problem, let us further stipulate that there are *no hidden pay-offs*. Neither player will gain or lose anything as a result of any choice of actions beyond what is listed in the payoff matrix. So we assume, in the present case, that the only relevant evil is directly proportional to time in prison, and that the numbers in the boxes accurately indicate the amount of time each player will spend in prison in each outcome.

Some philosophers who have discussed this topic have suggested that we must also stipulate that the players do not have "nontraditional values."[5] This stipulation is meant to rule out cases in which the players value cooperativeness, or mimicry, or self-sacrifice. Presumably, it is feared that if we permit the players to value such things, then the full force of the dilemma will be blunted.

Upon reflection, however, it seems to me that there is no need to add this stipulation. If the numbers in the boxes accurately reflect the total payoffs, the policy of straightforward maximization will require the prisoners to choose in certain ways, regardless of their values. If players have nontraditional values, the dilemma may fail to bother them—they may "escape" it. However, what makes the dilemma interesting (as I see it) is what it shows about straightforward maximization. SM seems to prohibit a sort of advantageous cooperation. Surely we can consider the interesting implications of SM on this sort of case even while recognizing that certain individuals, with certain values, would be able to achieve a cooperative outcome in similar circumstances.

(iii) Finally, it is important to stipulate that there are *no unlisted choices*. The game would surely be of considerably diminished interest if, for example, one of the players had, as an unlisted third choice, the option of escaping from prison, or bribing the DA, or making an even better deal for more information about some previously unmentioned third conspirator. In any such case, SM might require the player to do this other thing, which is not even mentioned in the matrix.

Shall we add some further epistemic stipulation? For example, shall we add that each player knows that each is a maximizer, or that each knows that each knows that each is a maximizer?[6]

It seems to me that there is no need, at this point, to add any such epistemic stipulation. As I see it, in the example cited, with the stipulations I have mentioned, SM requires each to confess—and the policy requires this of each regardless of the behavior of the other, and regardless of either's knowledge of the behavior of the other. Whether or not my son knows what his partner is going to do, my son will still do best for himself by confessing. Since the case is just as interesting (and far more realistic) without the epistemic stipulations, I prefer to leave them out.

I think it would be consistent with current usage to say that, in the example cited, my son and his partner are in a prisoner's dilemma.[7] The values of the outcomes for each player are determined in part by the actions of the other; neither can affect the choice of the other; if each does what the policy of straightforward maximization requires him to do, each will get an outcome with less value-for-him than the outcome he would have gotten if each had done something that the policy prohibits.

4. AN ARGUMENT FOR COOPERATIVENESS

Suppose my son and his partner are straightforward maximizers in the sense suggested by SM. After talking with the DA, each of them confesses. Each of them gets a nine-year sentence. Suppose they have adjoining cells. They might discuss their misfortune. I can imagine one of them saying, 'We were stupid to be straightforward maximizers. Each of us could have remained silent. If we both had remained silent, we would be out of here in just one year instead of nine. Each of us would have been better off by eight years. The policy of straightforward maximization is an unsatisfactory policy—those who follow it are sometimes worse off, even in its own terms, than those who cooperate.'

Given plenty of time to reflect on their policies, my son and his partner might resolve to cease being straightforward maximizers. They might decide to adopt a more complex policy. This new policy coincides with SM in all cases except prisoner's dilemmas. The new policy requires doing what we may call "the cooperative thing" in prisoner's dilemmas. In a prisoner's dilemma, there is an outcome that (a) is "optimal" in the sense that no other outcome offers any player a better payoff unless it also offers someone a worse payoff; but which (b) is not in equilibrium—each player would get a better payoff by defecting, provided that the other did not defect. We can call this the cooperative outcome.[8] In figure 1, this outcome appears in the upper left box. We say that a player "does the cooperative thing" provided that he does the act he must do in order to generate the cooperative outcome. In the example, doing the cooperative thing is equivalent to keeping silent. Notice that the payoff each player gets when each does the cooperative thing is better than the payoff he would get if each acted in accordance with SM.

Let us call this "the policy of resolute cooperativeness":

RC: When not in a prisoner's dilemma, do what SM recommends; when in a prisoner's dilemma, do the cooperative thing.

A number of philosophers have suggested that a policy such as RC is in fact superior to SM, even when evaluated strictly in terms of self-interest.[9] In other words, these philosophers have suggested that if a person wants to maximize his payoffs, and may fall into prisoner's dilemmas, he ought to adopt something like RC rather than SM. If this is right, then, as I look over my infant son in his crib, I should hope that he adopts something like RC rather than SM. I should hope that he becomes resolutely cooperative, not because it is morally better to be cooperative, but because it is better in terms of self-interest to be cooperative. It will be advantageous for him to be cooperative in prisoner's dilemmas.

The reasoning behind this conclusion may be this: in all cases that are not prisoner's dilemmas, RC requires just what SM requires, so in these cases people will do just as well with RC as they would have done with SM. In prisoner's dilemmas, RC requires people to act in the cooperative way. But, if they act in the cooperative way in prisoner's dilemmas, each will be better off than he would have been if each had acted in accordance with SM. Thus, on balance, people may be better off acting in accordance with RC, but they cannot be worse off.

It seems to me that this line of reasoning is defective. It is certainly true that each party to a prisoner's dilemma does better when both act in accord with RC than he does when both act in accord with SM. But in genuine prisoner's dilemmas, neither player can make the other adopt a new policy, or choose a certain act. So the comparison seems irrelevant. What matters is whether an individual will do better if he acts in accord with RC than he does if he acts in accord with SM. I think he does not. To make things simple, let us suppose my son is going to face exactly one prisoner's dilemma sometime in the future. Let us also suppose that the matrix in figure 1 accurately reflects the payoffs.

It seems to me that there are two main cases to consider. First, let us see what happens if my son's partner acts in accord with SM. In this case, my son's partner will confess. If my son acts in accord with RC, he will do the cooperative thing. In other words, he will keep silent. The result will be that my son will get ten years. On the other hand, if he acts on SM, he will confess and get only nine. So in this case, the adoption of RC seems to be counterproductive. If my son adopts RC instead of SM, he will be worse off by one year.

Second, let us consider the case in which my son's partner acts on RC. In this case, my son's partner will keep silent. If my son also acts on RC, he too will keep silent, and will go free after only one year in prison. On the other hand, if my son acts on SM, he will confess, and he will avoid prison altogether. So in this second case—the case in which the partner acts on SM—acting on RC by my son seems counterproductive. If my son acts on RC instead of SM, he is sure to be worse off by one year no matter what his partner does.

These results can be displayed graphically in another matrix. In figure 2, numbers in the boxes indicate the number of years my son will spend in prison on various combinations of policy choices by his partner and himself.

FIGURE TWO

		His Partner	
		SM	RC
My Son	SM	9	0
	RC	10	1

The implication is clear: if my son acts on RC rather than SM, he is sure to be worse off by one year no matter what his partner does. Clearly, then, I ought not to hope that my son acts on the policy of resolute cooperativeness. It appears that, if I want him to do the most advantageous thing, I ought to hope that he sticks with SM. There is no advantage to being cooperative (in the sense suggested by RC.)

5. A MORE COMPLEX COOPERATIVE POLICY

The central defect of the policy of resolute cooperativeness seems to be its utter insensitivity to the behavior of fellow players. If my son is resolutely cooperative, then my son (a) leaves himself open to exploitation if his partner acts on SM, and (b) fails to take advantage of opportunities if his partner acts on RC. A more sensible policy, it may appear, is one that recommends cooperativeness only when others are prepared to be cooperative. Let us investigate this idea.

A restricted form of resolute cooperativeness would coincide with SM for all cases that are not prisoner's dilemmas. It would discriminate between two sorts of prisoner's dilemmas. Some prisoner's dilemmas involve partners who are straightforward maximizers. There is no point in being cooperative with these people. If you are resolutely cooperative, they will only exploit you. So RRC recommends straightforward maximization in these cases. However, if a prisoner's dilemma involves a partner who is cooperative, then RRC recommends doing the cooperative thing, too. So the policy is this:

> RRC: If in a prisoner's dilemma with a person who will do the cooperative
> thing if you do, do the cooperative thing. Otherwise, act in accord with
> SM.

Since RRC coincides with SM in cases that are not prisoner's dilemmas, as well as in prisoner's dilemmas involving uncooperative partners, there is no point in comparing their payoffs for such cases. The payoffs are the same. The policies differ only with respect to prisoner's dilemmas involving partners who will do the cooperative thing if you do. It may be thought that RRC generates better results in this narrow class of cases, and so is to be preferred overall to SM.

Once again, however, I think there is an error in this reasoning. A certain narrow class of prisoner's dilemma-like situations is relevant here. Turning again to my infant son, we can characterize this class as the class in which his partner will do the cooperative thing if my son does. However, it seems to me that this class naturally breaks down into two subclasses. The first of these is the class consisting of those cases in which my son's partner will do the cooperative thing if *but only if* my son does the cooperative thing.[10] The other class consists of cases in which my son's partner will do the cooperative thing *whether or not* my son does the cooperative thing. Let us consider the cases.

Suppose again that my son is facing the prisoner's dilemma-like situation suggested by the matrix in figure 1. Suppose his partner will do the cooperative thing if and only if my son does the cooperative thing. If my son keeps silent, his partner will keep silent as well. Each will get one year in prison. If my son confesses, his partner will confess as well. Each will get nine years in prison. If my son acts in accord with RRC, he will keep silent and suffer just one year's imprisonment. This seems to show that following RRC yields beneficial outcomes in certain cases. But what does following SM yield in this case?

In the case we are currently considering, my son's partner has an important disposition. He will be cooperative if and only if my son is cooperative. So my son has his choice: he can be cooperative or he can be uncooperative. Being cooperative is equivalent to being silent. In this case, the partner will also be silent, and my son will get one year in prison. On the other hand, my son can be uncooperative. Being uncooperative is equivalent to confessing. In this case, the partner will also confess, and my son will get nine years. Clearly, given the dispositions of his partner, the policy of straightforward maximization instructs my son to be silent and take the year in prison. The results of following SM are the same as the result of following RRC.[11]

Suppose, to consider the second sort of case, that my son's partner will do the cooperative thing no matter what my son does. In this case, if my son follows RRC, he will do the cooperative thing too. Each will get one year in prison. On the other hand, if my son follows SM, he will take advantage of his partner's cooperativeness. He will confess while his partner remains silent. In this case, my son will avoid prison altogether, while his partner gets ten years. Clearly, then, in this sort of case following SM is more advantageous for my son than is following RRC.

This comparison is a bit complicated. A chart may make things a bit clearer. Once again, the numbers indicate my son's prison sentence under various combinations of actions and dispositions by himself and his partner. "Coop whether or not" indicates that the partner will do the cooperative thing whether or not my son does. "Coop only if" indicates that the partner will do the cooperative thing only if my son does it too.

FIGURE THREE

		His Partner	
		Coop whether or not	Coop only if
My Son	SM	0	1
	RRC	1	1

Thus it would appear that, if my son's welfare is my only interest, I would do better to hope that he becomes a straightforward maximizer, rather than a restricted resolute cooperator. In the only sort of case in which the two policies yield different results, SM yields better results for my son.

6. A STILL MORE COMPLEX COOPERATIVE POLICY

It is reasonable to suppose that my son will come to have the concept of an agreement. He will understand the practice of entering into, and being committed by, "undertakings." Let us make use of this idea to formulate a still more complex policy of limited cooperativeness.

Suppose my son and his partner find themselves in the situation illustrated by the matrix in figure 1. Suppose this time however that the DA gives them a few minutes to discuss their situation before making their choices. My son might say this to his partner: 'If each of us confesses, each of us will spend nine years in prison. That will be bad. On the other hand, if each of us remains silent, each of us will spend just one year in prison. That will be much less bad. I realize that, if we both remain silent, each of us will be forgoing the opportunity to exploit the other. But for my part I am willing to forgo that opportunity if you commit yourself to forgoing it as well. What do you say? Shall we agree to keep silent? I will commit myself to remaining silent if you will commit yourself too.'

My son's imagined remarks suggest a policy of agreed cooperation where possible, and straightforward maximization everywhere else.[12] Let us attempt to formulate this policy clearly.

The policy is based on the idea that some dilemma-like situations may permit pre-choice discussion.[13] In some of these cases, the pre-choice discussion may contain a mutual giving of conditional undertakings. Each player commits himself to doing the cooperative thing provided that the other commits himself similarly. Consider cases in which, if each player acts in accordance with such a commitment, and actually does the cooperative thing, each will be better off than he would have been if each had failed to discuss agreements and had acted in accordance with SM. We can say that such agreements are agreements to do the "advantageously cooperative thing."

"Agreement Constrained Cooperation" or "ACC" is the policy of making and then acting in accord with agreements to do the advantageously cooperative thing when such agreements are possible, and acting in accord with SM otherwise. It might be thought that a person would do at least as well, and perhaps better, if he adopted and consistently acted on ACC, than he would if he acted on SM. Perhaps this is the idea behind the notion that cooperation is sometimes advantageous.[14]

It seems to me, however, that the advantages of ACC are purely illusory. Once again, the difficulty can be seen if we reflect more carefully on the dispositions of the second parties in the dilemma-like situations. Consider my son and his partner. Suppose their situation is as before, except that they have an opportunity to engage in mutual undertakings to cooperate.

Either my son's partner is disposed to abide by his commitment to cooperate, or he is not. Let us consider first the case in which he is not. If he commits himself to do the advantageously cooperative thing, he will then violate the commitment, and do the selfish thing. If my son is guided by ACC, my son will make and then act in accordance with his commitment. He will keep silent. His partner will violate his commitment. As a result, my son will spend ten years in prison. If he had either ignored the opportunity for making commitments, or had (like his partner) made and then violated the commitment, he would have been out in nine. In this case, there is no advantage to cooperativeness. Entering into and then abiding by commitments of this sort merely offers your unscrupulous partner a fine opportunity for exploitation.

Consider now the second case, in which my son's partner will abide by his commitment to cooperate. Here, if my son is guided by ACC, he will make and abide by a commitment to keep silent. He and his partner will be out in one year. Clearly, however, it would be more advantageous for my son to make the commitment and then violate it—for then he would avoid prison altogether. So in this case, there is no advantage to cooperativeness. Entering into and then abiding by commitments of this sort merely prevents you from taking advantage of a fine opportunity for exploitation. On balance, ACC seems to offer no advantage in either case.

Perhaps a modification to ACC will generate more interesting results. Consider the policy of entering into and abiding by commitments to do the advantageously cooperative thing. Although it is hard to visualize any practical way of implementing this change, it might seem a good idea to change the policy by requiring one to abide by such commitments when and only when one's partner also abides. In this way, one assures himself that he will not be exploited. (Of course, one also gives up the opportunity to exploit one's partner—maybe this is a price worth paying.)

ACC': Enter into agreements to do the advantageously cooperative thing whenever possible; abide by such agreements when and only when your partner abides; otherwise act in accord with SM.

It may appear that my son's life might go slightly better for him if he were to adopt ACC' rather than SM. The reasoning might be this: In almost all circumstances, action in accord with ACC' will be indiscernible from action in accord with SM. In some cases, however, ACC' may yield an advantage. If my son should happen to be in a prisoner's dilemma-like situation, and if his partner should happen to be willing to engage in preliminary discussion, and if the partner should happen to agree to do the cooperative thing, and if the partner will indeed abide by his commitment only if my son also abides by his commitment, then my son will be able to get out of prison in just one year. This, clearly, is better than rotting in prison for nine or ten years. Hence, there is an advantage to being cooperative (in the sense indicated by ACC').

The preceding bit of reasoning is not cogent. It does not seem to me that my son's life could be in any way improved by the adoption of ACC'. Once again, the problem can be seen most easily if we distinguish some cases concerning his partner's dispositions. His partner might be disposed to make advantageously cooperative commitments. He might also be disposed to abide by these commitments once made regardless of my son's dispositions. In this case, my son would do better to be guided by SM. For if he were guided by SM, he could enter into and then violate an advantageously cooperative agreement with his partner. He could avoid prison altogether, rather than languish for even a year.

Suppose the partner is disposed to make such agreements, but to abide by them when and only when my son abides, too. In other words, suppose my son's partner is disposed to act in accordance with ACC'. Then my son will not be able to induce his partner into an agreement, and then violate it. In this case, it seems that it makes no difference whether my son is guided by SM or by ACC'. In either case, his best choice is to enter into an agreement to keep silent, and then to keep silent. This may need a bit of explaining.

We are imagining that my son and his partner face the matrix illustrated in figure 1. They have the opportunity to engage in preliminary negotiations. The partner, having adopted ACC', is prepared to negotiate. If my son fails to take the opportunity, each will in effect be guided by SM. Each will keep silent. Each will spend nine years in prison. My son is better off negotiating. Suppose they exchange mutual undertakings to keep silent. My son's partner will abide by this agreement if and only if my son does. Hence, my son cannot exploit his partner's commitment. No world is accessible to my son in which he confesses but his partner is silent. If my son confesses, so will his partner. Thus, the payoff for my son for confession is nine years in prison. On the other hand, if my son is silent, his partner will abide by his commitment and will also be silent. The payoff will then be one year for each. Thus, if my son's partner is guided by ACC', the best world accessible to my son is one in which he enters into and abides by an agreement to keep silent. SM recommends just this course. Clearly, ACC' cannot offer any better payoff. Thus, no matter what the partner's dispositions, there is no advantage to being cooperative.

It is perhaps interesting to notice that this last class is not very prisoner's dilemma-like. Each party seems to have a previously unmentioned third choice: he can offer to engage in pre-action discussion with the possibility of entering a mutually advantageous compact. No mention of this appears in the matrix. Second, in the final case it is stipulated that the partner will abide by his commitment if and only if my son abides by his. This stipulation violates the independence condition. It is not the case that the partner will act as he in fact acts no matter what my son does. The partner's choice will be, in some sense, "determined" by my son's choice.

7. TRANSPARENCY

Some commentators have suggested that cooperativeness is especially advantageous in the case of "transparent" individuals—individuals whose policies cannot be hidden from those with whom they interact.[15] It might be thought that if my son were permanently transparent, then his life would go better for him if he were guided by some cooperative policy rather than by SM. Let us consider this idea.

Assume that my son will be irrevocably transparent. Assume also that, once in his life, he will face a dilemma-like situation relevantly like the one suggested by the matrix in figure 1. Assume that there will be time for negotiation between my son and his partner before either confessing or not. Finally, assume that his partner in this situation will be reasonably perceptive and intelligent. He will be able to discern my son's (transparently obvious) policy, whatever it may be, and he will be able to figure out how my son is going to act.

In these circumstances, my son will not be able to fake cooperativeness, enter into, and then advantageously violate an agreement to do the cooperative thing. For, if he attempts to do any such thing, his partner will realize immediately that my son is planning to exploit his (the partner's) cooperativeness. The partner will either refuse to enter into the agreement, or else will enter the agreement with no intention of abiding. "Straightforward maximizers are disposed to take advantage of their fellows should the opportunity arise; knowing this, their fellows would prevent such opportunities arising."[16] No such difficulty arises for one who has genuinely accepted a policy of cooperativeness. Assuming transparency, then, it seems to follow that "because they differ in their dispositions, straightforward and constrained maximizers differ also in their opportunities, to the benefit of the latter."[17]

Gauthier's argument seems to be this: If my son is transparent and guided by SM, his partner will realize that my son is disposed to take advantage of cooperative partners. My son's partner is no fool. He will refuse to be snookered. So my son will be unable to enjoy the benefits of mutually advantageous cooperation in this dilemma-like situation. His best outcome in the situation we have been discussing will be nine years in prison. On the other hand, if he is transparent and guided by a cooperative policy such as ACC, he may be acceptable as a party to an agreement to keep silent. In this case, his best outcome will be one year in prison. Hence, there is a certain sort of case in which cooperativeness has its advantages.

I believe that Gauthier is at least partially right here. In the case described, if my son's behavior is guided by something like ACC, he may be able to reap the benefits of cooperation. He may be able to get out of prison in just one year. However, the fundamental question here is the question whether the cooperative policy is superior in this case to the policy of straightforward maximization. We must consider what would happen in this very case if my son's behavior were guided by SM. Will my son inevitably do worse for himself if his behavior is in accord with SM, or will he perhaps do just as well (or even better) for himself as he would if it is in accord with some cooperative policy? Let us look more closely into this central question.

Let us imagine that the situation is as described above. My son is transparent; his partner is sufficiently perceptive and intelligent—he will correctly identify my son's policy and its implications; they face the matrix in figure 1. The partner is willing to cooperate, but he is not willing to be snookered. Let us first recall what will happen if my son is guided by a suitable cooperative policy. The partner will recognize that my son is disposed to be cooperative in this sort of situation. The partner will agree to enter into negotiation. They will agree to keep silent. My son will keep silent. Since the partner is also guided by some cooperative policy, he will keep silent, too. This will generate an outcome in which each player spends one year in prison.

In order to generate the other half of the comparison, let us now suppose my son's behavior is guided by SM. In this case, he does what he does in the best-for-him of the accessible-to-him possible worlds. What worlds are accessible to my son? How well does he fare in them? The answers to these questions depend in part upon the dispositions of the partner. Let us consider some possibilities.

Let us first suppose that the partner is disposed to abide by an agreement, should one be made. In this case, every world accessible to my son has these features: he is transparent; his partner is perceptive and intelligent; they face the matrix in figure 1; the partner would abide by an agreement to keep silent, should such an agreement be made. In these circumstances, my son cannot exploit his partner's cooperativeness. No world is accessible to my son in which he enters into an agreement, and then violates it. His own transparency prohibits that. For an agreement between them to occur, my son must first convince his partner that he would abide by an agreement to keep silent, should such an agreement be made. Since he is transparent, my son can convince his partner only if he in fact would abide by such an agreement. Assuming that my son is able to make himself trustworthy, it is clear that the best-for-him accessible worlds are ones in which he in fact is trustworthy. In such worlds, the partner recognizes my son's trustworthiness, is willing to enter into an agreement, and does so. Furthermore, we have assumed that the partner is disposed to abide by the agreement. In these good-for-my-son worlds, then, my son does not violate the agreement (in order to get any agreement, he had to be genuinely trustworthy in the first place—he could not fake it). Payoff for my son: one year in prison.

These reflections show, I think, that it is wrong to suppose that people whose behavior is guided by SM will not be able to enjoy the benefits of cooperation. If there is a world accessible to my son in which he cooperates with his partner, and my son fares better in this world than he does in any in which he fails to so cooperate, then SM directs my son to behave as he does in this cooperative world. (If no such world is accessible to my son, then there is little point in discussing the relative merits of SM and some cooperative policy. *Ex hypothesi,* my son cannot adopt the cooperative policy.)

Now suppose the partner is disposed to violate an agreement, should one be made. All worlds accessible to my son are ones in which he is transparent; his partner is intelligent, perceptive, and treacherous; they face the matrix in figure 1. The best-for-my-son of these worlds are ones in which my son confesses. It does not matter whether he tries to fake cooperativeness, or whether he enters (pointlessly) into an agreement. Given the partner's treachery, silence on my son's part will generate ten years in prison. Thus, if the partner is treacherous, SM yields a payoff for my son of nine years in prison. A policy of cooperativeness might have yielded ten years in prison.

The conclusion is clear. If it is best for my son to act in accord with some policy of cooperativeness, then SM directs him to do so. On the other hand, if commitment to such a policy is pointless or self-destructive, SM does not direct him to be committed to it or to abide by it. So if my son's behavior is ultimately guided by SM, he is sure to do at least as well, and may do better than he would have done if his behavior were ultimately guided by some cooperative policy.

What moral shall we draw from all this? I think it is this resounding triviality: You cannot do better for yourself than you would do if you were to do the best you can for yourself. No policy of cooperativeness can possibly offer my son a life better than the one he would get if he consistently acted in accord with the policy of acting as he does in the best-for-him of the accessible-to-him worlds.[18]

Notes

1. This conception of alternatives is widely used in the literature on utilitarianism. I believe that Lars Bergstrom was the first to formulate it clearly. See Bergstrom (1966) as well as Bergstrom (1971, 237–52).

2. I have attempted to explain versions of several of these problems as they apply to standard formulations of act utilitarianism. See chapter 1 of Feldman (1986). As I see it, the arguments there discussed apply, with appropriate modifications, to the doctrine of straightforward maximization here under consideration.

3. This formulation of the doctrine of straightforward maximization is relevantly like my formulation of the doctrine of "prudential obligation." See Feldman (1986).

4. Compare the definition "PO" on page 107 of Feldman (1986).

5. See, for example, Braybrooke (1976) and Sobel (1976).

6. See, for example, Jordan Howard Sobel's discussion of "hyperrational maximizers" in Sobel (1976). Sobel describes hyperrational maximizers as "unerring maximizers who know they are unerring, know the utility structures of their situations, know that they know these things, and so on." In Campbell (1985, 5), under the title "What is the Prisoner's Dilemma?"

Richmond Campbell says: "Third—this is a key assumption for the discussion to follow—you know (from the prosecutor and witnesses present) that the other prisoner faces the very same dilemma. Your situations are exactly symmetrical, with respect to information and desires. Finally, each of you knows that you both know all of this; your awareness of your separate dilemmas is fully mutual."

7. One of the clearest discussions of the concept of the prisoner's dilemma can be found in Richmond Campbell's excellent introduction in Campbell (1985). As should be clear from note 6 above, Campbell's account of the essential components of the dilemma are slightly different from mine. He includes epistemic considerations. I exclude them.

8. I write here as if there would have to be exactly one cooperative outcome in each dilemma. Strictly, this seems wrong. For present purposes, it may be viewed as a simplifying assumption.

9. In Held (1977), Virginia Held seems to defend something very like RC, but with different terminology. She advocates "reasonableness" rather than "rationality." On page 737, she says:

> This concept of the reasonable would recommend the development of cooperative strategies in repeated prisoner's-dilemma situations at least up to the point that as much could be gained by cooperation as by competition. And this conception of the reasonable would recommend that even in one-shot situations, where one party cannot estimate the probabilities concerning the other's choice of policies, it is reasonable to take a chance on a cooperative approach, if to do so jointly will be better for both than a joint choice based on pure self-interest.

10. Since the partner's action is in this way determined by my son's action, this example violates the independence condition and is not (in my sense) a prisoner's dilemma.

11. I think it is interesting to note that in this sort of non-prisoner's dilemma, SM requires my son to be silent—in effect, to do what he would do if he were cooperative. Given the stipulated dispositions of the partner, it seems that my son has two main choices: (i) he can be silent, and (ii) he can confess. If he is silent, the partner will be silent, too, and in effect my son will realize the upper left box of the matrix in figure 1. If he confesses, the partner will also confess, and my son will realize the lower right box of the matrix in figure 1. Since the prison terms for my son of the two outcomes are, respectively, one year and nine, SM dictates the first choice. He must keep silent. However, it would be most misleading to suggest that there is something "cooperative" about my son's silence in this situation. He would just be looking out for number one.

12. This policy is intended to be equivalent to the policy of "Agreement-Constrained Maximization" discussed by David Gauthier in Gauthier (1975, 428) and elsewhere. After explaining that a person engages in "agreed optimization" if he enters into and abides by "agreements intended to secure optimal outcomes, when maximizing actions performed in the absence of agreement would lead to non-optimal outcomes," he goes on to say, "And by constrained maximization, I shall mean that policy, or any policy, which requires individual utility-maximization in the state of nature, and agreed optimization in society."

13. Once again, I think it is important to recognize that any such situation is significantly different from our paradigm prisoner's dilemma. For one thing, there are more alternatives available: one can enter into an agreement and then keep it; one can enter into the agreement and then violate it; one can refuse to enter into any agreement and then keep silent; one can refuse to enter into any agreement and then confess. Thus, instead of the standard 2 x 2 matrix, we need a 4 x 4 matrix. Furthermore, if the partner is disposed to abide by agreements, then his action is at least partially determined by my son's action. In this case, the independence condition is again violated.

14. This certainly seems to have been Gauthier's view in Gauthier (1975, 429). He there argues that the policy of constrained maximization is superior to the policy of straightforward maximization:

If we compare the effects of holding the condition of straightforward maximization with the effects of holding the condition of constrained maximization, we find that in all those situations in which individual utility-maximization leads to an optimal outcome, the expected utility of each is the same, but in those situations in which individual utility-maximization does not lead to an optimal outcome, the expected utility of straightforward maximization is less. In these latter situations, a constrained maximizer, but not a straightforward maximizer, can enter rationally into an agreement to act to bring about an optimal outcome which affords each party to the agreement a utility greater than he would attain acting independently.

15. See, for example, Gauthier (1986, 173–74).

16. Ibid., 173.

17. Ibid.

18. Throughout the time I have been working on this paper, I have benefited enormously from the critical comments of students who attended meetings of Philosophy 760 during the fall of 1986. None was more helpful than Ishtiyaque Haji. I am also very grateful to Ned McClennen and David Gauthier, each of whom read a draft of the paper and provided useful critical comments. I am especially indebeted to McClennan, who pointed out a serious error of attribution in the draft. I am also grateful to Derek Parfit, whose prodigiously rich and informative *Reasons and Persons* provided insight and motivation.

References

Bergstrom, Lars. 1966. *The Alternatives and Consequences of Actions.* Stockholm.

———. 1971. "Utilitarianism and Alternative Actions." *Nous* 5: 237–52.

Braybrooke, David. 1976. "The Insoluble Problem of the Social Contract." *Dialogue* 15: 3–37. Reprinted in Campbell and Sowden (1985, 277–306).

Campbell, Richmond. 1985. "Background for the Uninitiated." In Campbell and Sowden (1985, 3–41).

Campbell, Richmond, and Lanning Sowden, editors. 1985. *Paradoxes of Rationality and Cooperation: Prisoner's Dilemma and Newcomb's Problem.* Vancouver, British Columbia.

Feldman, Fred. 1986. *Doing the Best We Can: An Essay in Informal Deontic Logic.* Dordrecht.

Gauthier, David. 1975. "Reason and Maximization." *Canadian Journal of Philosophy* 4: 411–33.

———. 1986. *Morals by Agreement.* Oxford.

Held, Virginia. 1985. "Rationality and Reasonable Cooperation." *Social Research* 44: 709–44.

McClennen, Edward. 1985. "Prisoner's Dilemma and Resolute Choice." In Campbell and Sowden (1985, 94–104).

———. Forthcoming. "Constrained Maximization and Resolute Choice." *Social Philosophy and Policy.*

Parfit, Derek. 1984. *Reasons and Persons.* Oxford.

Sobel, Jordan Howard. 1976. "Utility Maximizers in Iterated Prisoner's Dilemmas." *Dialogue* 15: 38–53. Reprinted in Campbell and Sowden (1985, 306–19).

On Flourishing and Finding
One's Identity in Community

DAVID B. WONG

1. INTRODUCTION

The revival of interest in the notions of virtue and character has meant a renewed willingness to think about the relation between philosophical anthropology and ethics. More attention is being given to the ways that *human* nature, and not merely the nature of all rational beings, has important implications for the kind of ethic we ought to have. The return to philosophical anthropology, in turn, has meant renewed attention to the theme that human beings have a social nature. I want to address one line of thought that embodies this theme. The line is that our flourishing as *social* beings requires that we have certain sorts of relationships with others. The character of these relationships with others is partly defined and partly sustained by duties we have to them. Therefore, the reason for performing some of our most important duties is our social nature and our own flourishing.

    This communitarian and neo-Aristotelian line of thought is usually coupled with a criticism of liberal ethical theory. By "liberal theory," I mean one that contains three claims: first, that there is a significant plurality of conceptions of the good life that are equally valid, or at least, there is a significant plurality of ones that rational and informed people accept; second, that principles of right action and of justice should be neutral with respect to this significant plurality insofar as their justification does not depend on accepting any one conception of the good life; third, that a necessary feature of a right and just social order is that it respect the autonomy of all its citizens, where autonomy includes the freedom to choose among competing conceptions of the good life and to act on the conception one chooses so long as one conforms to the principles of right and justice. The criticism is that liberal theory, with its toleration of competing conceptions of the good life, its separation of the right from the good, and its emphasis on autonomy, cannot recognize the way that our social nature determines what can be a good life for us and the way that the social content of a good life for human beings grounds some of our most important duties to others.[1]

I believe there is something to this line of thought and the accompanying criticism of liberal theory. But it will not persuade until we clarify the content of the claim that human beings have a social nature and the way that the claim leads to a social conception of flourishing which in turn provides reasons for our duties to others. The claim could mean a number of things, and it is unclear how any of these meanings provides a persuasive argument for duties. In this paper I intend to develop a plausible interpretation of the claim and of its ethical implications.[2]

2. WHAT DOES IT MEAN TO HAVE A SOCIAL NATURE?

It might mean, for example, that human beings have an innate tendency to communicate and interact with other humans. This possible meaning would have to be developed and qualified in various ways: the necessary forms of communication and interaction spelled out, the conditions for activation of the tendency identified. It should be apparent, however, that such a claim, once developed and qualified, would have to be extremely general to cover the variety of human interaction, from life in a commune to Wall Street. It might be argued that any viable conception of the good life for human beings must take into account the tendency to sociability, but the variety of human interaction would make this a very weak constraint, one that would have no straightforward nor easily discerned implications for the question of how we ground our duties to others. That is, our innate tendencies may underdetermine any truly interesting claim that we would want to make about the sorts of relationships necessary for flourishing. Another problem is the connection between innate tendencies and flourishing. It does not seem true that any innate tendency to seek a certain sort of relationship would show that satisfaction of the tendency is a component of our flourishing. If we were innately aggressive creatures, as some believe, would that mean that our flourishing required successful aggression against others?

Another possible meaning for the claim that we have a social nature is suggested by the observation that our characters are "social products." That is, the complexes of traits, habits, cognitive and behavioral dispositions, and ends, needs and desires that make up our characters are the results of our interactions with particular others and, more generally, of the communities and cultural traditions to which we belong. But here again, it is unclear that some conception of the good life or some restricted range of conceptions is better supported by this claim. Perhaps this claim grounds our duties to others without determining specific notions of flourishing. The thought may be that we should be grateful to those who have shaped us, that we should repay them in some way. But it remains to be shown why gratitude is the required response to the simple fact that others have shaped us. It is most natural to speak of our owing a debt of gratitude when we have received benefits. And while particular others and even the culture of a community may shape our characters in beneficial ways, not all shaping is beneficial. A related objection is that being grateful for whatever way in which we have been shaped by others is to abdicate our responsibility to critically evaluate the norms of these others and of the culture around us. I once heard the son of a Nazi official remark on the ways in which he had come to realize that he is like his father, but his remark was made with regret, not gratitude.

Still another possible meaning for the claim that we have a social nature is that we are at least partly "constituted" by our relations to others. It sometimes is said in criticism of liberal ethical theory that it is "atomistic" and that it neglects the fact that our "identities" are "defined" by the communities of which we are a part. The language of constitution and definition implies something stronger than the causal claim that our characters are social products. And there does seem to be something plausible about this claim when we reflect on the fact that people do say it is part of their identities to be fathers, to be Jews or Chinese, or to be Southerners, for example.

But it is unclear what kind of identity is at stake in this claim. One possible meaning is that my metaphysical identity as the particular person I am is partly defined by my relations to others. That is, the relevant sense of 'identity' is the one that is the usual topic of contemporary metaphysics, concerning the properties that allow us to reidentify people at different times in their lives as the same individuals. The claim about identity would then mean that the relevant identificatory properties include the relational properties of being a member of certain groups, or having some role in relation to certain others. Construed in this way, the claim is quite controversial and cannot be taken for granted. Furthermore, it is again unclear what follows from such a claim concerning my duties to those others who "enter into my identity." It might be suggested that being a father is to have certain duties toward one's children, and that in general, having a social role means having certain duties. But then the claim amounts to the assertion that the properties that make me who I am include the properties of having certain duties toward others, and this looks like the conclusion of an argument, not a premise to which we can readily assent.

Sometimes the word 'identity' is used in a non-metaphysical sense to embrace an individual's ways of understanding and interpreting the world, her characteristic ways of behaving and relating to other people, her views as to what is most important and valuable in life, and what are in fact her most important ends and desires. In this case, the meaning of 'identity' is unproblematic, even if quite diffuse and vague. But the problem remains in explaining what it means for an identity to be *defined* or *constituted* by one's relations to others. It is plausible to say that identity in this sense is fundamentally *shaped* by others, not just particular others but the cultural traditions of our communities. But the language of shaping recalls the causal-origin claim discussed above, along with its problems. Still another problem is that our duties to others do not seem to flow straightforwardly from whatever identifications we make. The son of the Nazi official I mentioned above felt contemporary German culture still contained tendencies that had helped to cause the Holocaust, and he may have felt that he shared with his father certain of those tendencies. He may even have felt his *identity* included them. But he certainly would not have believed that duties flowed from such an identification, unless they were duties to prevent any further terrible consequences of it in himself and in others.

Another possibility for understanding the claim that we have a social nature is the claim that one of our most important *needs* is to have certain sorts of relationships with others. The advantage of this possible meaning is that it seems well-connected to the claim that our flourishing must be social in nature. To make the claim under this possible meaning does seem to affirm the social nature of flourishing. The disadvantage of this possible meaning is that it may be *too* closely connected to the claim about flourishing. The relevant sense of "important need" seems to denote some objective requirement for human welfare. It in fact seems to have entered into a definitional circle with 'flourishing'. One flourishes when one's important needs as a human being are fully met, and important needs are the various conditions that must be fulfilled for flourishing to obtain. If there is a circle here, the claim about need provides no independent support for the claim that our flourishing requires certain sorts of relationships with others.

Without further explanation, the claim about flourishing cannot be accepted straight off, as if it were self-evident or verifiable upon a bit of reflection. And whatever the further explanation will be like, it must include a specification of the sort of relationships we need. Here the task is to steer a course between making the required relationships so general that nothing much of significance has been shown, and making the required relationships so specific that the notion of flourishing seems unreasonably monistic. The latter possibility is a general danger for advocates of the communitarian and neo-Aristotelian line of thought. Many of us, in modern Western democracies at least, are liberals in the sense that we accept as valid a fairly broad range of conceptions. Liberalism, in this sense, is not just another philosophical theory but is deeply rooted in a culture that embraces many different cultural strands. "That is part of the problem," it may be replied. But the counterreply is to ask for a practical and morally acceptable alternative to theories of right and of justice that attempt to occupy a neutral ground with respect to competing conceptions of the good life.

Despite these difficulties, I believe there is a way in which our social nature provides grounds for our duties to others, though it does so in a manner that is more indirect, complex, and qualified than the ways sketched above. This way, moreoever, allows for a significant pluralism in conceptions of flourishing. My strategy will be to interpret the social-nature claim as meaning that the necessary conditions for effective agency include the having of certain sorts of relationships with others. By effective agency, I mean, roughly, the set of abilities that allow us to formulate reasonably clear priorities among our ends, and to plan and perform actions that have a reasonable chance of realizing our ends, given all the conditions beyond our control. I will argue that the relationships necessary for effective agency are partly defined and sustained by the duties we have toward others. Since effective agency is a necessary condition of all forms of flourishing, we have a ground for some of our most important duties.

My line of reasoning will incorporate some of the claims discussed above. I will make use of the conception of character as inherently social in origin, since the argument will be that the formation of a character with a significant degree of effective agency requires certain sorts of relationships with others. I also will explain how the required sorts of relationships lead effective agents to define their identities in relation to others, and I will specify a sense in which identities can be so defined that is not metaphysically controversial, nor does it reduce to the causal-origin claim. I will be using the idea that we need to have certain relationships to others, in the sense that the relationships are necessary for effective agency. While this amounts to the claim that we will not flourish unless we have the relationships, I do not think I am making a particularly controversial claim about what our flourishing requires. Regardless of what else it requires, we can agree that it requires effective agency. And so I will be using the idea that the ground of some of our most important duties to others is connected to the notion of flourishing, but in such a way that is not undermined by a reasonable pluralism. Since effective agency is *only* a necessary condition of flourishing, it does not fully determine the content of all valid conceptions. When I have fleshed out this strategy, I will be in a position to discuss the issue of whether liberal theory undercuts or ignores the way our social nature grounds our duties to others.

3. EFFECTIVE AGENCY AND PRACTICAL IDENTITY

I begin by connecting the notion of effective agency with the notion of identity. My aim is to show that the development of effective agency is bound up with the formation of a certain sort of identity for ourselves, but to accomplish that aim I must clarify the relevant sense of 'identity'. Let me start with the very broad kind of identity mentioned above, which covers the characteristic set of ways that a person has for interpreting and behaving in the world, her views as to what is important, and her actual ends and desires. I want to focus on one facet of this kind of identity that seems connected with effective or ineffective agency. When someone is going through an "identity crisis," she expresses confusion, uncertainty, and disorientation. Her confusion about who she is involves confusion as to what she stands for and how to act toward those around her. She may be unclear about what is important to her, or on what her most important ends and desires are. Another possibility is that she may be unable to connect her actions (her job, her family life, her presence in school) with what she *believes* is important to her. And when someone "finds her identity," she achieves greater clarity and certainty about what she does stand for and how she is to act toward others. She knows better what is important to her and what her most important ends and desires are. Or she may have a better sense of the connection between what she is actually doing with her life and what is important to her. Or she may change what she is doing with her life so that it is more congruent with her sense of what is important.

My suggestion is that one facet of the broad kind of identity is constituted by those features of a person's character that fix her practical orientation toward the world.[3] Let me call this set of features her "practical identity." What goes into practical identity? A person's sense of what is important will be based on the kind of evaluations she makes. That is why I think there is something right about a definition of 'identity' that Charles Taylor has given, which refers to the reflective evaluation of desires.

Offering a definition of 'identity' as the term appears in "finding one's identity" or "going through an identity crisis," Taylor claims that "identity is defined by our fundamental evaluations," ones that form "the indispensable horizon or foundation out of which we reflect and evaluate as persons."[4] Taylor means "strong evaluation" in the above definition, which is a qualitative evaluation of our desires as, for example, base or noble, fragmented or integrated, honorable or dishonorable. To have an identity, according to him, is to have a conception of where we stand evaluatively and to assess our possible motivations accordingly.

A possible objection against this definition of identity, though, is that it depends on a controversial foundationalism with respect to evaluations. Perhaps there are no fundamental evaluations but a "web" of evaluations; and it would be implausible to define identity as an entire system of such beliefs. Let us then eschew talk of absolutely foundational evaluations. But even non-foundationalists talk about beliefs that are firmer than others, ones that will be among the last to go when revision is forced upon us, ones that support many others, such that their rejection will require rejection of many others. We need only equate identity with the firmest of evaluative beliefs. This allows for change in identity when the need for revision finally touches the firmest ones, while it keeps identity constant through most changes in evaluative belief.

I take more seriously another criticism of the Taylor definition: its narrowness as a definition of practical identity. It is not clear whether Taylor means to include judgments as to the justness or fairness or rightness of a desire when he writes about qualitative evaluations, but the firmest of such normative beliefs should be constituents of the kind of identity that determines practical orientation. And surely our primary desires and goals go into our practical identities. To form a conception of what one wants most of all and what one is out to achieve is part of the project of finding a practical self. What is a primary desire or goal, though? We form a conception of which goals and desires are primary for us by assigning priorities to some of them, and by determining which desires and goals are such that their satisfaction or achievement would affect many areas of our lives. Amélie Rorty has pointed out to me, however, that a desire or goal may be primary without our being *aware* that it is. It may be appropriate, then, to speak of our having second-order desires and goals that we may not have consciously formulated and that define our priorities, and to allow for the possibility that we do not have adequate awareness of which first-order desires and goals affect many areas of our lives. The task of "finding ourselves" would involve conscious formulation and greater awareness.

Rorty has also suggested to me that desires and goals which are part of our practical identities are ones that can directly motivate behavior independently of reinforcement by other elements in our motivational systems, and that a perceived threat to such desires and goals directly mobilizes defensive strategies aimed at their preservation. I take it that a threat could be posed by a person or thing that makes more unlikely the satisfaction of the desires and goals, or by a person or thing that would undermine their importance, legitimacy, or rationality. Defensive strategies would be aimed at blocking their threatened frustration or defending their importance, legitimacy, or rationality. Let us roughly characterize primary desires and goals, then, as the ones that have high priority, that have relatively pervasive effects on our lives, that are directly motivating, and that can directly motivate defensive strategies for their preservation. The desire for relationships of affection and intimacy would score highly on all these measures for most people, I believe.

Finally, another possible constituent of practical identity is the character trait. To think of oneself as typically friendly or empathetic or shy or ambitious can be part of gaining a sense of one's practical identity. Not all our traits go into our practical identities, however. Can we define primary traits? A trait is a nexus of perceptual dispositions to pick out certain features of a situation as salient and as reasons to act; it involves the display of behavioral patterns, and of motivations for acting in those patterns. Take the trait of friendliness. It involves the perceptual disposition to see a business transaction, for example, as an opportunity to make friends, the behavioral pattern of displaying interest in people beyond that required to complete a business transaction, and the desire to interact with others who have mutual interests. Now a trait may be primary in the following ways: it involves acting out of primary desires and goals; its associated perceptual dispositions and behavioral patterns manifest themselves in many areas of our lives, or at least in those projects and relationships that are important as defined by our firmest normative beliefs and primary desires and goals; and threats to the trait (in the form of denials that it in fact belongs to us or of denials of their importance, legitimacy, or rationality) will directly lead to defensive strategies.

What is the point of grouping primary character traits with desires, goals, and normative beliefs? Insofar as traits involve our characteristic ways of behaving in the world, and the perceptual dispositions that set up our decisions to act, we certainly can see them as helping to fix our practical orientation toward the world. Furthermore, gaining a sense of what our characteristic perceptual dispositions and behavioral patterns are is important for planning our future actions.

The fact that we can take different attitudes toward our traits suggests still another way that an evaluatively charged conception of traits becomes a part of identity as a practical orientation toward the world. To possess traits is to be disposed to have certain kinds of practical orientation toward the world, or at least fragments of such orientation. To take positive or negative attitudes toward one's traits is to engage in evaluation of the ways one is disposed to act when one is acting from one's traits. To approve of one's traits is to have a kind of second-order practical orientation and so to reinforce their influence on one's action. Such reinforcement occurs when a woman who is in a dangerous and tricky situation will remind herself that she has proven herself in past situations of the same kind. To disapprove of some of one's traits, on the other hand, may have the effect of weakening their influence, if other elements of one's motivational system can be brought to bear in counteracting it.

In summary, let me say that practical identity just is the set of attributes of the self that provides an individual with a practical orientation. This orientation is a kind of constant frame that fixes the parameters of practical deliberation. It is the set of motivational factors—firmest normative beliefs, primary desires, goals, and traits—that we hold constant in the course of practical deliberation, or at least relatively constant, since we are staying away from absolute foundations. These factors have the best chance of staying constant while other factors in our motivational systems come and go, as we rethink our desires and goals and stop having them, as we reevaluate some of our traits and modify them. Everything would be "up for grabs" without a sense of some constancy in possible motivational factors. Being able to change *too* much about ourselves threatens our capacity for effective choice. I take it that an "identity crisis" can stem from a lack of this sense of constancy. That is why Erik Erikson holds that the key problem of identity involves the capacity to sustain sameness and continuity in the face of change.[5]

A major advantage of the definition of practical identity just given is that it enables us to give a plausible sense to the observation that many people conceive their identities to include various groups and communities of which they are members. In some groups and institutions, there are established social roles that carry with them duties, privileges, powers, and rights. Roles such as those of father and husband are examples. Such a role also may carry an ideal of the motivations and traits that are to be had by a person who performs it well. A father has a primary desire to promote the welfare of his child, according to an ideal many people have. A good teacher may be conceived as having the primary trait of being an attentive listener. To say that the identities of persons includes their social roles is to say that their firmest normative beliefs include ones that spell out the duties, privileges, powers, and rights of their roles; it may also be to say that their primary desires, goals, and traits include the ones that are parts of the ideals associated with the roles.

Groups and communities may be distinguished by the fact that all or at least many of their members share primary normative beliefs, desires, goals, and perhaps even traits. To say that it is part of one's identity to be a member of such a group or community may be to confirm that one shares the relevant beliefs, desires, goals, or traits. I submit that this is a meaningful sense for the claim that it is part of one's identity to be a Jew or Chinese or a Southerner.[6]

It should be apparent now why I think that finding a practical identity is intimately connected with the question of effective agency. If a practical identity just *is* the relatively constant frame of motivational factors that provides us with a practical orientation toward the world, we need to have one in order to be effective agents. But not only do we need a practical identity, we need one with certain properties.

A practical identity that carries along with it an adequate degree of effective agency (I will call such an identity an "effective identity" from now on) must have the trait of being able to determine what social norms require. Why? Return to the weak claim that was first considered as a possible meaning that human beings have a social nature: that we are innately inclined to communicate and interact with others. Nothing very interesting follows from that claim alone, I argued. But if we set that claim in the context of looking for necessary conditions of an effective identity, we can conclude that a person's practical identity must include some minimal degree of knowledge about what is required by the norms of the society in which she finds herself. This would be true even if she had no consistent intention to conform to the norms and instead intended to manipulate and work around them to achieve her ends.

An effective identity also possesses a reasonable degree of congruence among its component desires, goals, character traits, and normative beliefs. I use the word 'congruence' to include not only the strict logical relation of consistency that can hold among normative beliefs, but also a looser and more intuitively conceived relation that can obtain between, say, desires and normative beliefs. If I had the normative belief that I should be a caring person who helps people in great need, but had no desires to help in the relevant situations, my practical identity would lack congruence in this sense. Similarly, a character trait may not be congruent with a normative belief if its exercise regularly prevents me from conforming to the belief. Stinginess, both with respect to money and time spent in helping others, would be incongruent with the normative belief that one should be generous to others. I say that a "reasonable" degree of coherence is required because we come to desire and become committed to a great many different kinds of things, and the result is an avoidable degree of tension and conflict among the motivational factors surrounding those desires and commitments. The matter of judging whether our practical identities possess a reasonable degree of congruence is necessarily inexact, and it must allow for a healthy richness of commitment.

Another property of an effective identity is that it contains the particular trait of self-esteem which involves a belief in one's own worthiness and in the merit of one's primary goals and desires, and also a confidence in one's ability to satisfy the goals and desires if given a reasonable opportunity to do so. As John Rawls has emphasized in *A Theory of Justice,* we will be unable to realize our ends, whatever they are, unless we accept ourselves as worthy of having our ends satisfied, and have confidence in our abilities to achieve them. Self-esteem can be seen to depend, at least in part, on some possible properties of identities already mentioned. It would be undermined in us if we saw serious incongruence between our normative beliefs on the one hand, and our primary goals, desires, and traits on the other. It would be bolstered by positive, self-accepting attitude toward our own traits, as opposed to wishing we were different.

4. RELATIONSHIPS AND THE FORMATION OF EFFECTIVE IDENTITY

If we look more closely at what is involved in producing practical identities with adequate knowledge of social norms, reasonable congruence, and self-esteem, we can begin to see the necessity of certain sorts of relationship with others.

To have a practical identity at all, we take from others who raise us. The child's tendency to imitate others is well known, but the tendency seems to go way beyond outward imitation of behavior. The neo-Freudian Melanie Klein has written of the way in which the child comes to internalize or incorporate the other who is caring for her. Richard Wollheim, drawing from her work, outlines a crucial stage of incorporation that he calls "identification." This is an imaginative activity whereby the child imagines another "centrally." The activity is analogous to an audience empathizing with the character of a play. As the audience represents the thoughts, feelings, and experiences of a character as though they were its own, so does one who centrally imagines another. A child imagines what a parent would do if faced with a certain kind of situation. She imagines what the parent would think, feel, and experience in that situation, and she imagines these as if they were her own. Now the internal life of a child who centrally imagines is altered, for she finds herself in the condition in which thinking, feeling, and experiencing those things would have left her. Her internal life is to some extent fashioned after the imagined internal life of the other. In this way, a child's emotional range is enlarged; she acquires new objects of care. She acquires her first set of ideals.[7]

Perhaps the details of this story are not quite right, but it is a way of explaining how others have a deep effect on the formation of our characters, and in such a way as to shape many of the fundamental attitudes we carry into our relationships with others and into the projects of achieving our most important ends.[8] But this is only the beginning of the story of how others affect our practical identities, for they can help or hinder us in the acquisition of those properties necessary for effective agency.

Consider the path to knowledge of social norms. The sorts of rules we find in most social institutions and practices cannot be codified very specifically. Their application is a matter of context-dependent judgment. Parents have the common experience of having to correct a child's too-literal application of some elementary social norm, and they know that explicit explanation of why their child's application is too literal can only go so far. Consider the task of teaching a child the line between acceptable friendliness to strangers and being overly familiar. Sometimes the best way to teach the content of a general norm is to give examples of what is to be done in this or that situation, or to point out when the child has got it right or wrong in a particular situation, until she knows how to go on in the right way, where the right way cannot be spelled out except in a very general and deliberately vague fashion. The child learns to know *how* to go on in the right way, without an explicit and specific knowing *that,* to use Ryle's distinction.

To have a minimally adequate knowledge of social norms, then, requires that we enter into a learning relationship with others, in which the "right way" is shown throughout various situations over an extended period of our lives. Learning how to go on in the right way is acquiring judgment. The relationship in which judgment is cultivated must be regular and extend to many domains of our lives, given the extensive scope of social norms. This learning, as all learning does, presupposes a certain degree of trust between learner and teacher. The learner must believe that the teacher intends to and is in fact cultivating the relevant abilities, by and large.

Now consider reasonable congruence. We are not simply given practical identities with such a property. We must form our important commitments with an eye to their possible congruence with our traits, and to the extent that we can alter or develop our own traits, we should alter or develop them with an eye to their possible congruence with our ends. An effective identity, therefore, requires the ability to judge the congruence between our commitments and our character traits, and therefore requires a substantial degree of self knowledge. Others play an essential role in the acquisition of this knowledge. This is not just because it can be difficult by ourselves to judge what we are, as opposed to what we would wish to be, but also because we are liable to blame others and the world for our failures, rather than to look for some conflict between what we want to achieve and what our traits enable us to achieve. We need the perspective of others to correct for self-deception and lack of self-perspective. And getting such help and being able to use it again presupposes a substantial degree of trust. We must believe that others are giving objective information about ourselves. What is more, we sometimes are unable to accept negative information unless we believe that the one who is giving it to us is also one who thinks well of us, overall, and wishes us well.

Consider the question of acquiring self-confidence and self-esteem. Recent offshoots of psychoanalytic theory, "object-relations" and "self-psychology" theories in particular, have located the sources of healthy self-assessment in the interaction of the individual with others, especially in early life. This is a shift from the time when the sources were located in the purely internal dynamics of the individual's drives (as much of Freud's early work does), and surely something like the former view must be correct.

The "self-psychologist" Heinz Kohut emphasizes the need of the child for "mirroring," a process that involves expressing pleasure in the child's developing abilities and acceptance of the child's ambitions. Parents may fail to adequately mirror a child because of their own defects in self-confidence. Kohut gives the example of a girl who comes home from school eager to tell her mother of her great successes, but the mother, instead of listening with pride, talks about her own successes. This child may become a "mirror-hungry" personality, which is sometimes manifested in the demand for exclusive attention and reassuring praise from others to counteract the internal sense of worthlessness. Much of her psychic energies will be taken up by the attempt to compensate for the inadequate mirroring of her childhood. Kohut also stresses the need for parents to curb a child's grandiose ambitions and self-image at the appropriate moments.[9] To fail in this is to expose the child to a collapse of self-esteem when she inevitably fails to live up to her grandiose self-image. Here again, we must note that the mirroring relation requires trust. The child must be ready to receive correction from the parents when they point out some incongruence between her ambitions and her traits, and to do that, she must trust in their motives and their judgment.

We have arrived at a picture in which the individual develops in relationship to others not only a practical identity but the properties of an identity that are necessary for effective agency. These relationships involve trust.[10] Where do we find these others who can be trusted? Clearly, there must be others who are firmly committed to providing the required nurturing, and who will persevere despite the many frustrations and setbacks that inevitably accompany such nurturing.[11] And just as clearly, one cannot reasonably expect human beings to make such commitments without some reciprocation from those they nurture.

That is why duties of care by parents and duties of gratitude and obedience by children define and sustain relationships that help to form effective identities. Fortunately, there are deep satisfactions obtained from nurturing, and deep tendencies to reciprocate, even if these tendencies can be and are overridden. So duties of care and of reciprocation through gratitude and obedience find some hospitable soil in our natures. But the frustrations and contrary tendencies make it necessary for these duties to be affirmed within our communities in such ways that we are motivated to focus on the satisfactions and the urge to reciprocate. Only then do most people have a reasonable chance of receiving consistent and reliable help in the task of achieving effective identities.

So far, I have asserted a *causal* connection between the formation of effective identities and certain sorts of relationships. But recognition of the causal relation leads to the conclusion that effective identities include within their *content* some of these relationships. I gave above a sense in which one's practical identity could include within its content the relational property of being a parent: one's primary normative beliefs could include the duties associated with the social role of parenting, and one's primary ends, desires, and traits could include those required by the ideal of a parent. Now the task of nurturing an effective identity in one's child would seem to require the degree of commitment that implies that one's practical identity includes the role of parent. Furthermore, the sort of commitment to reciprocate that is required to sustain the relationship implies the child's practical identity includes the role of son or daughter. If we have the sort of parent-child relationship that is likely to lead to an effective identity for the child, parents and child will identify with their roles.

We have arrived at the conclusion that the nurturing of an effective identity in an individual requires relationships with others that are partly defined and sustained by reciprocal duties. These relationships require of the participants a degree of commitment that is reflected in the content of their practical identities. We have grounded certain duties to others in the requirements for effective agency. In particular, a person has duties toward those who are helping him realize conditions for his effective agency, which are in turn necessary conditions for his flourishing. We may expect some variation in the specific content of those duties as we cross cultures, but the range of variation is constrained by the condition that performance of these duties be such that it contributes to the sustaining of the relationship. We would expect these duties to reflect a concern for the welfare of those nurturing the individual. There would be duties to trust, at least those who have given the individual reason to trust through their actions toward him in the past. Think of how wounded we feel when a friend or child distrusts us, when we think there is no reason for it. And duties of obedience from children involve their having to trust in the judgment of parents who require them to do certain things.

I am not arguing that the duties flowing from our identifications are valid ones, simply by virtue of their connection with our identifications. I am arguing that if the particular identifications we have are not morally acceptable, it is *morally* necessary to find some that are, because effective *moral* agency involves effective *agency*. I define moral agency as the ability to formulate reasonably clear priorities among one's moral ends, and to plan and carry out courses of action that have a reasonable chance of realizing those ends. Having a viable morality requires that there be the sorts of relationships that promote identifications, and that these identifications involve the bonds of trust and reciprocal care which promote effective agency.

The sort of argument I have just given would seem to require that there be relationships of such a type within the family, or more generally, to small groups that have taken on the task of raising children.[12] That is because the nurturing received in childhood shapes in major and permanent ways those properties of our practical identities relevant to effective agency. It is not surprising that we in the contemporary West, with a culture so penetrated by the language and explanations of psychology, should be ready to recognize the profound effects of child-rearing. Many of us do not adequately recognize, however, that effective identities need sustenance and further development as the individual achieves maturity and moves into the wider network of her society's institutions and practices. It is somewhat surprising that we, with our heavily psychologized culture, do not recognize the extent to which this is true. The reason for the lack of recognition may have something to do with a popular belief associated with the ideal of the autonomous individual: the belief that a good upbringing results in an independent person who is more or less fully equipped with the traits that will allow her to fulfill her own conception of flourishing.

But if we go back to the properties of effective identities, we will see how difficult it is to sustain such a belief. Surely the most ideal parenting does not ensure knowledge of norms that is necessary for acting effectively within institutions and practices beyond the family. And congruence between traits and ends is not achieved once and for all within the family. This is not just because our ends change, and not just because different relationships may require different skills and abilities. We sometimes talk of character traits as if they were properties that "stick" to us as we move from context to context. Yet many of our traits must be described with implicit reference to situations that elicit or suppress the relevant behavior.

A person we characterize as generally friendly may not be so when he is taken from his familiar community and placed in a new social context. And it is not unusual to encounter persons who manifest certain traits to family and close friends, such as warmth and generosity, but who manifest very different ones to those with whom they work. It should not be surprising, after all, that many of our traits are context dependent. We are relatively complex beings who have created for ourselves complicated social worlds. Now the context-dependence of traits suggests that qualities such as patience, thoroughness, and decisiveness, which may promote effective agency for a person and which may have been cultivated within the family, cannot be assumed to transfer to social domains outside the family. If these qualities are needed for effective agency in the other domains, they may need to be developed through further interaction with others.

Let us also note Amélie Rorty's observation[13] that the specific form our actions take is determined through interactive process with others. Many of those actions that flow from settled character traits are also actions that are elicited by the people with whom we interact, because our characters are configurations of traits. Different ones can be elicited by different people and by different interactive processes. It is often the case, therefore, that getting the best out of ourselves means getting the right company. Rorty's observation suggests to me another, more fundamental sense in which we depend on others to get the best from ourselves. An important reason for the context-dependence of our character traits is that different people, and the nature of our relationships to them, make different contexts. That is why we can be startled when we discuss with others the character of some common acquaintance. We sometimes find ourselves wondering whether we are talking about the same person. The characters of others penetrate and shape our own traits, at least to a significant extent, and that means that the traits needed for effective agency will be penetrated by others.

As to self-esteem, it is probably true, as many psychologists stress, that appropriate nurturing will provide a child a base of self-regard that she will carry throughout her life. Yet it is very unusual to encounter a person to whom the opinions of her peers made no difference at all. More importantly, such a person would have an unhealthy self-regard, for her indifference to the opinions of others would indicate a lack of awareness of her own fallibility in determining her strengths and weaknesses.

All these observations reinforce the conclusion that the qualities needed for effective agency require continual sustenance and development as we move through adulthood. We would expect the *nature* of the relationships that could provide such sustenance and development to be different from that of a child to his parents, but trust is required here too. To learn from others, to receive their correction and support, we must trust them, even if our trust is much more qualified and limited than the sort that ideally obtains between parent and child. So there must be others outside the family who, for whatever reason, are committed to providing us what we need. Individuals vary in having the opportunity and ability to find those who can help. Undoubtedly some of the variation is rooted in the simple luck of circumstances and innate temperament, but also in differences in the ways people are raised within their families. Some are well prepared to learn from and engage in fruitful interaction with others; others may be crippled in just these respects.

It is arguable that there will be greater opportunities for more people if there are associations other than the family, and smaller than the state, that bind individuals together in pursuit of a common end. In such "intermediate" associations, which are small enough to allow significant face-to-face interaction among their members, and which include informal social groups, churches, business associations, trade unions, universities, benevolent societies, cooperatives, and mutual aid groups, there will be greater opportunity for the formation of ties in which each comes to care about the other's effective agency, since members are in pursuit of a common end. A common function of such associations, furthermore, is the communication of social norms, and these norms often pertain to institutions and practices far removed from the family. And finally, if we keep in mind the context-dependence of character traits, we can note that the members of such associations are able to help each other with the development of the traits necessary for effective agency, as those traits need to take form relative to certain kinds of social contexts. Consider a graduate student trying to find a teaching style suited to his particular strengths, and receiving help from professors and his fellow students.

5. ASSOCIATIONS AND LIBERAL THEORY

The role of such associations in the promotion of effective agency leads to a criticism of liberal ethical theory: its characteristic lack of attention to such associations and to the whole complex of issues and problems that the promotion of such associations implies. To illustrate the way this criticism could be made out, I want to discuss the liberal theory that takes as much account of these associations as any liberal theory does. The idea is to take the best existing case of the liberal treatment on the subject, and to show that there is a serious failure even here. In that part of *A Theory of Justice* concerning moral development in the ideally just society, John Rawls outlines three stages. The first stage imbues the individual with the "morality of authority," which essentially is the morality learned in a family in which the parents love and care for the child and affirm her sense of worth. The child reciprocates in love and trust. The second stage imbues the individual with the "morality of association." The individual becomes aware of herself as a member of a group, and conceives of the moral norms that apply to her as stemming from the role she plays in the group. The third stage brings the "morality of principles," in which the individual comes to understand the most general and fundamental principles (including the two principles of justice) governing her society, and in which she comes to understand the reasons for these principles. Through his sequencing of the stages, Rawls certainly recognizes the necessity of at least some of the processes of nurturing and growth that I have described above.[14]

One problem with his treatment, however, is that he seems to assume that the necessary associations will exist in a society that satisfies his two principles of justice. Yet if we look at the way Rawls himself describes the major political and economic institutions of the just society, there seems to be nothing to ensure that there will be associations able to perform the functions described above. Nor does Rawls address those social critics who see the forces that make for modern liberal democracies to be the forces *undermining* intermediate associations. These critics see that increasing homogeneity and interdependence of modern democracies as reinforcing the ideology of equality regardless of social station, and simultaneously as undermining the vitality and autonomy of intermediate associations. There are also forces such as the increased tendency to treat all social relations as contractual ones, which, the critics say, undermines the sort of commitment and trust that should obtain within families and secondary associations. As a result, there are fewer such associations with which people can identify. Under my conception of practical identity, that observation translates into the claim that the normative beliefs associated with roles in intermediate associations are not among the primary beliefs in the practical identities of an increasing number of people, and that the character ideals associated with social roles are not ideals that these people most want and tend to realize.

Now this trend seems to undermine the sort of role morality that characterizes Rawls' second stage, and which he sees to be a necessary condition of advancing to the third stage. Rawls is right in characterizing that second stage as necessary. It is necessary for effective agency, which is necessary for effective moral agency. To the extent that a theory of justice must be concerned with effective moral agency, it must be concerned with the ability of people to identify with groups that nurture and sustain effective agency in them.

What we need is a concern for the conditions of effective agency that is wider in focus than the very genuine concern that Rawls shows. His two principles of justice primarily concern the distribution of goods such as liberties, wealth, and income. These goods surely are relevant to effective agency. But there is the question of the way that the nature and content of relationships between people affects the nurturance and sustenance of effective agency. This question relates to the question of distribution in complex ways, but does not reduce to the question of distribution. Communitarian criticism of Rawls is sound to the extent that it strikes at Rawls' silence on the question of whether we are losing the social structures whose effect on agency is not reducible to distributional matters. It is true that Rawls talks about self-esteem, but mainly in connection with the question of how distribution of the other goods affect it.

Liberal theorists may reply that I am confusedly accusing Rawls of *endorsing* the alleged effects of increasing homogeneity and the contractualization of all relations. I am not accusing him of this, but of failing to address forces which may, as a matter of fact, have consequences that bear on the viability of his theory of justice. The ideal of a just society requires effective moral agents. And to the extent that a theory is egalitarian in thrust, as Rawls' is, it requires widespread effective moral agency. In this respect, Rawls has more reason than other theories, even some communitarian theories, to be worried about the undermining of associations that nurture and sustain effective agency.

My point, then, is that liberal theorists are guilty not so much of holding some "atomistic" model of the person that *contradicts* any of the ways we depend on others for our effective agency, as they are of not fully attending to these ways and how they may or may not be realized. This results in problems other than the one just described above. Take Rawls again, and assume that we do have the intermediate associations necessary for promotion of the role morality in the second stage. Rawls characterizes the transition to the third stage in the following terms: in the second stage, we develop ties of trust and loyalty with other members of the associations to which we belong; as we come to understand how the two principles affirm everyone's worth and work to everyone's advantage, we come to realize how they benefit the people with whom we have ties; we develop an attachment to the principles themselves.

This makes the transition to the third stage sound unproblematic and natural, but we should remind ourselves of the times when our loyalties to particular others conflict with our sense of what constitutes impartial and fair treatment of all.[15] The role morality of associations is not so easily subsumed under principles that are generated from choice under the veil of ignorance. When role morality penetrates our practical identities, it binds us because of our tendency to reciprocate the care and trust that *particular* people have shown to us. Yet the two principles are founded on the idea that we owe people certain things regardless of the special relationships we have. There need not always be a conflict between special loyalties and the ideal of impartiality, but there are enough occasions of conflict so that the commitment to impartial fairness cannot be seen as an unproblematic extension of the commitments underlying the special loyalties. We furthermore cannot assume that when there is conflict, the principles of justice take precedence, not if our bonds to particular others help to promote and sustain effective moral agency. I do not mean to suggest that the conflicts are unmanageable, but they are an important feature of the moral landscape for human beings.

Nothing I have said so far offers a solution to the problems I have raised for liberal theory. The time of vital and relatively autonomous associations was also a time when hierarchy and privilege were acceptable to a much greater degree than they are now. If these associations provided the opportunities for nurturing and sustaining effective agency in their members, it is also true that some of them had the effect of restricting the life prospects of their members by confining them to certain social roles. Others may not have had this effect on their members, but were so powerful that they restricted the life prospects of members of other associations. But addressing the problems of a communitarian perspective requires that we recognize its great positive power over us. It is no accident that the reaction against modern liberal theories has taken a neo-Aristotelian and communitarian turn. It is an indication of the nature of what is lacking in these theories.

Perhaps the beginning of a solution lies in recognizing that the problems I have raised do not call for realization of a vision of a social and political order organized around a single vision of flourishing. We do not have to realize such a vision to address the problem of the increasing pressure on the family to perform the functions of nurturing and sustenance that intermediate associations in the past helped to perform. Federal support of day-care programs is a way of addressing this pressure. It also is in important respects consistent with the kind of liberal egalitarianism that many of us who are sympathetic with communitarianism would be unwilling to give up. For it is now true that of those who need day-care, only the effective agents with the material means are likely to find a satisfactory solution.

Turning our attention to the social conditions of effective agency also requires more sophisticated attention to the way that egalitarian values are implemented in family and divorce law. Philip Selznick, drawing from Lenore Weitzman's study of the recent abandonment of the fault principle for divorce, acknowledges that the change to a more neutral breakdown principle reflected and reinforced the movement for feminine equality and independence. The idea of marriage as a contract between equals was translated into equal sharing in the allocation of marital assets. But this sort of equality, Selznick points out, often runs counter to the social reality of the economic vulnerability of women, the needs of children, and the opportunities of ex-husbands and fathers to avoid responsibility. The result, he concludes, was a retreat from the idea that our law should have special concern for institutions with the historic function of making males responsible for their families, and for creating units within which obligations stem not just from a contract, but from "identity and relatedness."[16] It is sometimes admitted by liberals that they cannot, after all, be completely neutral toward competing conceptions of flourishing, because their own principles reflect the priority placed on autonomy. But if autonomy is to be combined with effective agency, that neutrality must be compromised further, in light of the ways in which our human nature is indeed a social nature.

Notes

1. I believe this line of thought can be found, at least as one strand, in the work of the following authors: Alasdair MacIntyre, *After Virtue* (Notre Dame, Ind., 1984), and "Is Patriotism a Virtue?" *Lindley Lecture,* University of Kansas, 1984; Charles Taylor, *Hegel* (Cambridge, 1975), and "The Nature and Scope of Distributive Justice," in *Justice and Equality Here and Now,* edited by Frank S. Lucash (Ithaca, N.Y., 1986); Michael Sandel; *Liberalism and the Limits of Justice* (Cambridge, 1982); Robert Bellah, Richard Madsen, William M. Sullivan, Ann Swidler, and Steven M. Tipton, *Habits of the Heart* (Berkeley, 1985); and Philip Selznick, "The Idea of a Communitarian Morality," *California Law Review* 75 (1987): 301–19.

2. Work on this paper was supported by the American Council of Learned Societies. I gratefully acknowledge its support. I also must acknowledge the great benefit I have received from discussion with Amélie Rorty, Lawrence Blum, and Laura Weisberg on various topics that are treated in this paper.

3. I first presented this concept of identity in another paper, "Anthropology and the Iden-

tity of a Person," given at the Eastern Meeting of the American Philosophical Association in December 1985. I owe a great deal to Amélie Rorty, Laura Weisberg, Lawrence Blum, Eli Hirsch, and Sissela Bok, who helped me sharpen my conception of identity.

4. "What is Human Agency?" in *The Self: Psychological and Philosophical Issues*, edited by Theodore Mischel (Oxford, 1977), 124–25.

5. *Insight and Responsibility* (New York, 1964), 95–96.

6. There may be other senses in which it can be part of one's identity to be a member of a group. Going back to the broad kind of identity that includes ways of interpreting and experiencing the world, we can say that some groups have a common identity when they share some of these ways. For example, Laurence Thomas has pointed out to me in correspondence that blacks may have a common identity based on their experience of oppression.

7. See "The Good Self and the Bad Self," by Richard Wollheim in *Rationalism, Empiricism, and Idealism*, edited by Anthony Kenny (Oxford, 1986), 151–76. See also his *The Thread of Life* (Cambridge, Mass., 1984), 78–82, 123–25.

8. For an interpretation of Aristotle's view of the importance of modelling, see Martha Nussbaum's *The Fragility of Goodness: Luck and Ethics in Greek Tragedy and Philosophy* (Cambridge, 1986), 363. For an interpretation of Confucius' view, see my "Universalism versus Love with Distinctions: an Ancient Debate Revived," forthcoming in the *Journal of Chinese Philosophy*.

9. See Heinz Kohut and Ernest Wolf, "Disorders of the Self and Their Treatment: An Outline," *International Journal of Psycho-Analysis* 59 (1978): 403–25, for an introduction to Kohut's theory.

10. In emphasizing the importance of trust in relationships that nurture effective identities, I take myself to be confirming Annette Baier's claim that trust is a central but neglected concept for ethical theory. See her "What Do Women Want in a Moral Theory?" *Noûs* 19 (1985): 53–63.

11. Alasdair MacIntyre, in "Is Patriotism a Virtue?" points out the necessity for such a commitment for the nurturing of moral virtue, and reading his article set me on the line of thought that culminates here.

12. I think the Chinese philosophy of Confucianism, more than any other, has recognized and articulated the value of the family. See my "Universalism versus Love with Distinctions: an Ancient Debate Revived."

13. In "Virtues and Their Vicissitudes," in this volume.

14. *A Theory of Justice* (Cambridge, Mass., 1972), 462–79.

15. On this kind of conflict, see Alasdair MacIntyre, "Is Patriotism a Virtue?" For the way this conflict is played out in ancient Chinese philosophy, see my "Universalism versus Love with Distinctions: an Ancient Debate Revived."

16. Selznick, "The Idea of a Communitarian Morality," 307–8.

Virtue, Religion, and Civic Culture

RICHARD J. REGAN, S.J.

As the sun prepares to set on the twentieth century, Westerners can rejoice above all else in the triumph of the democratic liberal ideal. The ideal of freedom for persons and societies is properly human, and Westerners rightly rejoice in its institutional realization. The triumph came at the high price of many revolutions and two world wars, and liberal democracies continue to live under the twin threats of militant Communism and potential Fascisms. But Westerners have free institutions, and they overwhelmingly support and defend those institutions.

The Western world seems safe enough for democratic liberalism. But one may ask whether or not a democratic liberalism without moral moorings is safe enough for the Western world. Freedom, by itself, is no guarantee that persons and societies will act wisely, and Westerners have tended to divorce the exercise of freedom from the goal of proper human development, subjective will from objective reason. As a result, liberal societies have become indifferent to moral virtue as the foundation of private and public well-being.

The indifference of liberal societies to moral virtue manifests itself at two levels. On the private or personal level, individuals in liberal societies tend to be indifferent or hostile to moderation of appetites beyond what is necessary to allow others the freedom to satisfy theirs; Western liberal societies have spawned appetitive individuals. On the second level, the public or social level, individuals tend to be indifferent or hostile to the material needs of their disadvantaged fellow citizens for proper human development; Western liberal societies have spawned possessive individuals. Not everybody in liberal societies, of course, is selfishly indulgent or without sensitivity to the material needs of others, but the pattern is widespread enough to cause reflective citizens concern.

Marxists claim that liberal democracies lack moral direction, and that the defect is structural. The alternative they propose is a society in which members work consciously and exclusively for communal production and share equally in the product according to their needs. However laudable the goals of human solidarity and economic justice, the price of achieving them the Marxist way is very high; Marxism requires individuals to subordinate themselves totally to the community. The Marxist ideal cannot be realized without a complete reconstruction of human consciousness about self and society. This will necessarily entail restrictions on freedom of political, artistic, and religious expression. Anticommunist ideas and ideals must be eradicated, and those with such ideas and ideals must be restrained from propagating them or acting according to them. Communism itself cannot be open to debate. Those in the Third World who think that it is possible to achieve the Marxist ideal without a police state are romantic, and those in the First World who think that periodic liberalizations of Marxist regimes presage democracy in the Western sense are naive.

But an individualism without communal moral goals and a collectivism without personal freedom for individuals are not the only ways in which humans may choose to organize their society. An alternative way is available, and it is to be found in the origins of Western political thought.

THE TRADITION OF REASON

In Athens of the fifth century B.C., Socrates confronted a situation very similar to and almost identical with the one Western society faces today. The Sophists of fifth-century Athens, like many post-Enlightenment liberals of the twentieth-century West, made achievement of each individual's aspirations the measure of all things without regard for the relation of those aspirations to the properly human development of the individual in community with others. Socrates, followed by Plato and Aristotle in the fourth century B.C., opposed the subjectivism and privatism of the Sophists, and the three suggested principles relevant today to serve as the basis for a civic culture conducive to personal and communal virtue.

Socrates' point of departure was knowledge of one's self. Humans know themselves as the source of their conscious activity, and they know that their conscious activity is rational. This rational activity involves more than the ability to reason from premises to conclusions; it embraces as well and primarily insight and understanding, albeit limited insight and understanding, of the basic structure of the human person and the world humans live in. Accompanying the capacity of the human intellect to understand, and reason about, self and world is the capacity of the human will to choose how to act with respect to self and world. Humans can decide for themselves whether or not they will act in accord with the structure and purpose of their human personality. If they choose to do so, they will be fulfilled as human persons; if they do not choose to do so, they will not.

Rationality is the distinctive characteristic of the human person. By the activities of reason itself, humans develop themselves intellectually and culturally; by activities in accord with right reason, they develop themselves morally. Humans cannot develop themselves intellectually, culturally, and morally without cooperative association with other humans, and human society should be so organized as to foster this development for all its members.[1] Citizens, in turn, should contribute to the common goal by developing themselves in a properly human way and by producing the material goods prerequisite for properly human development.

I submit that the principles briefly sketched here, undoubtedly in need of refinement and elaboration, could and should serve as the nucleus of a public philosophy for the West. They derive from the origins of Western civilization; they appeal to reason rather than to any article of religious faith; they should prove acceptable to reflective and responsible citizens.

The tradition which makes reason in its full range central to human purposes and social intercourse is not without its critics. Some would challenge the capacity of the human mind to grasp the essence of things or even the reality of one's own self. Some would deny intrinsic purposes to humans and nonhumans. Some would deny that humans have the psychological freedom to choose. Some view moral judgments only as emotional preferences or products of cultural conditioning. Can proponents of the tradition of reason respond adequately to these criticisms?

Advocates of the tradition of reason can and should attempt to respond on strictly philosophical grounds. But advocates and critics alike should keep foremost in mind the purpose and primary function of a public philosophy. A public philosophy is not simply a set of speculative principles for scholars and academics to debate. Rather, the purpose and primary function of a public philosophy is to provide a set of practical principles for the communal human enterprise.[2] The vitality of a public philosophy does not depend so much on the quality of the arguments that support it as on the quality of life that it supports. The central question to be asked about the tradition of reason, therefore, is whether or not it promotes a desirable and achievable quality of human life.

The West cannot opt out of choosing a public philosophy; all human societies have one, at least implicitly. A public philosophy identified with a specific religious creed or based on an authoritarian ideology, of course, would be inconsistent with democratic pluralism, and so the West cannot choose such public philosophies if it wishes to remain democratic and pluralist. This leaves a choice between a public philosophy based on the structure of the human person and the human community and one based solely on individual whim and majoritarian will. If the West rejects the former, it will effectively have chosen the latter.

Many critics fear that a normative public philosophy with its roots in the rational structure of the human person and community would entail ideological absolutism. Quite the opposite should be the case. Precisely because the tradition of reason is of reason, it should be open to all reasoned arguments, including those which challenge the tradition itself. Nor should a normative public philosophy based on reason entail political absolutism. To the contrary, a public philosophy rooted in the rational structure of the human person and community should support the maximum freedom of human persons for their *self*-development.

LEGAL COERCION AND THE TRADITION OF REASON

It cannot, unfortunately, be gainsaid that there have been authoritarian strains in the tradition of reason. Plato had his guardians, and Aristotle his project of comprehensive laws to make Athenians good. But the tradition of reason is not frozen in a time-capsule from fifth-century B.C. Greece. Medieval thinkers like Aquinas inched the tradition in the direction of limited and constitutional government.[3] Enlightenment philosophers, however much they exalted individuals at the expense of the social bonds which unite them, prodded the tradition to articulate explicitly that human freedom and equality are constitutive parts of the common good.[4] It was thus by the exercise of reason itself in the course of history that thinkers in the tradition came to understand and recognize more fully the political implications of human personhood.

In modern times, philosophers in the tradition of reason like Jacques Maritain articulated what is called the principle of subsidiarity: the state should do for its citizens only what citizens and voluntary associations of citizens are unable or failing to do for themselves.[5] Against those who would have the state organize every facet of human society (or permit it to do so), they argued that other units beside the state promote, and should be allowed to promote, the common good according to their own structures. On the other hand, against those who would limit the state to peace-keeping functions in human society, they argued that the state is specifically charged with the task of promoting the common good, that it is hierarchically supreme over other social groups, and that it is responsible for ordering the activities of the latter to the common good. In other words, the state and the machinery of state exist to supplement and foster, not to supplant or hinder, the self-development of citizens through individual effort and voluntary association with others.

The principle of subsidiarity assigns only a limited role to the state in the development of a civic culture conducive to moral virtue. The state is only one of many units of organized society concerned with virtue, albeit the hierarchically supreme unit. Other units of society—familial, educational, religious, fraternal—have their proper roles to play, and the state should encourage them to do so. When voluntary associations of citizens prove inadequate or fail to protect the common good, of course, the state may be required to use its coercive power to secure that good. But legal coercion in a rightly ordered society should be the last, not the first, means of promoting virtue.

While the subject of legislation concerning public morals is undoubtedly difficult and complex, extreme positions should be rejected at the outset. One extreme position would deny to the state any legitimate power to regulate public morals. That position either ignores or cannot adequately explain the fact that every organized society proscribes certain behavior altogether and regulates other behavior extensively; criminal laws proscribe murder, theft, fraud, and the like, and criminal laws regulate the sale and consumption of alcohol, drugs, and the like. Only a Marxist or a Millennist could conceive the possibility of human society without a criminal code. Laws are and will be necessary to protect the person and possessions of citizens from deprivation by other citizens. Laws are and will be necessary to deter and punish behavior which would corrupt the morals of the young or take unfair advantage of the mentally deficient. Laws are and will be necessary to restrict activities which, though not immediately affecting the person and property of others, threaten harm to others when practiced widely (e.g., use of alcohol and drugs). It may even be the case that certain behavior poses a specifically moral danger to the community, even without actual or potential physical harm to citizens, and so warrants restrictive legislation.

At the opposite end of the spectrum, another extreme position would defend the legitimacy of legal coercion to secure any moral good. That position ignores the social and political costs of using legal coercion to achieve moral objectives. Legislators need to weigh whether or not enforcement of public morals will do more harm to society than good. Can the law be effectively enforced without recourse to draconian methods? Will the law have undesirable social by-products? Will the law affect freedom of expression to the detriment of art, science, or the democratic political process? Would the legislation be broadly acceptable to citizens of different religious and ethical persuasions?

With extreme positions rejected, I suggest that legislation to enforce public morals, as a matter of prudence, should satisfy two principal conditions. First, such legislation should concern activities which cause serious harm to citizens and the community. Second, the legislation should enjoy broad support from citizens of different religious and ethical persuasions. The two are interrelated: legislation prohibiting or regulating activities causing serious harm to citizens and the community are likely to enjoy broad support, and legislation enjoying broad support is likely to involve activities which cause serious harm to citizens and the community. But that will not always be the case, since some citizens may think that certain activities cause serious harm while others may think that they do not. In my opinion, the pluralist character of Western democracy requires that the second condition be satisfied as much as the first.[6]

Abortion is currently a controversial area involving public morals. Critics of abortion base their case on the status of the fetus; they argue that the fetus, as a living human organism, is worthy of legal protection. If one accepts the critics' premise, abortion surely involves serious harm to the community. But legislation generally prohibiting abortion will not be prudent public policy unless there is a broad consensus to support it. Since such a consensus does not exist in most Western societies, it would be unwise to enact generally prohibitive legislation even if opponents of abortion had the political power to do so. Critics need first to develop a broadly based consensus that abortion is generally wrong.

(What I say above about the imprudence of generally prohibitive legislation against abortion in the absence of a broad consensus to support it does not apply to efforts to overturn *Roe v. Wade*.[7] That decision denied altogether the right of popularly elected representatives, whatever the consensus, to prohibit or regulate abortion during the first two trimesters of pregnancy for the purpose of protecting the life of the fetus. To do no more than overturn *Roe v. Wade* would simply return the abortion question to state legislatures. Popularly elected lawmakers would then be free to regulate abortion in the interest of the fetus throughout pregnancy, although they would be unwise to prohibit abortion generally without a broad consensus to support such legislation.)

Another area of public morals which has stirred debate, and is likely to stir still more, concerns the practices of artificial insemination and surrogate motherhood. The practices raise many moral issues. Under what conditions, if any, is experimentation on artificially conceived embryos morally right or desirable? Is it morally right or desirable to discard artificially conceived embryos deemed surplus or defective? Is commercial surrogate motherhood morally right or desirable? Is noncommercial surrogate motherhood morally right or desirable? Is artificial insemination of a woman by a donor other than her husband morally right or desirable? Is any manner of artificial insemination *in vitro,* even by a donor-husband, morally right or desirable? These practices raise moral questions for individuals, and some of them may call for a community response.

According to the criteria suggested above, citizens and lawmakers should weigh both the seriousness of potential harm to citizens and community from the practices and the degree of consensus about placing legal restrictions on them. How serious one views the harmful effects of some practices (e.g., discarding embryos, experimenting on embryos without regard for their individual well-being) will mirror one's views on abortion. How serious one views the harmful effects of other practices (e.g., surrogate motherhood, artificial insemination by a donor other than the husband) may be assessed without respect to one's position on abortion. The relatively minor harm, if any, by still other practices (e.g., artificial insemination *in vitro* by a donor-husband outside normal intercourse) can be admitted by those morally opposed to the practices. In any case, legislation restrictive of the practices should enjoy the support of a broad consensus, and such a consensus will only be possible after full and open-minded debate.

RELIGION AND THE TRADITION OF REASON

Misunderstandings about the relation of the tradition of reason to religion are responsible for two pervasive but contrary fears. On the one hand, some Protestant Christians fear that the tradition so elevates human endeavor and natural reason as to demean or deny divine initiative and the necessity of supernatural faith. On the other, some secular humanists fear that the tradition is merely a rationalization of specifically Christian (especially Roman Catholic) beliefs and mores. A better understanding of the tradition would dispel those fears, at least theoretically. To apprehensive Protestant Christians, defenders of the tradition can point out that the tradition makes very modest claims for the capacity of human reason to recognize specific moral mandates and of human will to carry out the mandates if recognized. To apprehensive secular humanists, defenders of the tradition can, in like manner, point out that the tradition makes very modest claims for specific moral norms and no appeal at all to religious inspiration or ecclesiastical imprimatur.

The tradition of reason, to be true to itself, must be open to the role of religion in human society. This is so, first of all, because all religions purport to teach ultimate truths, and most religions profess belief in a transcendent God with purposeful designs for humans. Because human reason is ordered to truth, the tradition of reason is open to the possibility of truths beyond the capacity of reason itself to discover. And from the political perspective, humans should be free to seek religious as much as any other truth and to live according to its prescriptions. In the tradition of reason, freedom of human persons is essential to the right ordering of society.

Philosophers like Hobbes and Locke, however "enlightened" their personal views on the subject, accorded religious beliefs and institutions a place in organized society. They disagreed about the role of government in matters of religion: Hobbes, to preserve peace in the commonwealth, would have the sovereign determine religious orthodoxy and prescribe religious observance; Locke, to achieve the same objective, would have the legislative power permit general, albeit not universal, religious freedom. But both recognized the potential contribution that religion could make to the commonwealth: Hobbes explicitly relied on an officially sanctioned religion to be a sort of moral glue to help restrain the anarchic impulses of naturally "brutish" humans;[8] Locke too seems to have expected that religion, both established and tolerated, would help restrain "degenerate" humans.[9] The promise of heavenly bliss to those who keep the Ten Commandments and the threat of hellfire for those who do not would help to induce the masses of unenlightened citizens to be law-abiding and civil.

The tradition of reason, of course, cannot accept the Erastian position of Hobbes. The purpose of government is to protect and promote the common good of intellectual, cultural, and moral self-development, and governments are altogether without competence to determine religious orthodoxy or practice. (Nor, for that matter, can any religion claiming supernatural inspiration accept the Erastian position. Supernatural religions claim that the truths they preach about God and humans have been revealed by him, and that the observances required are by his authority.) But the tradition of reason can recognize the practicality of the argument that religion offers a potential bulwark for civic virtue. This is as much or more true in the twentieth, as in the seventeenth or eighteenth century. It takes no great intellectual acumen to perceive that self-indulgence and narrow self-interest are threats to Western civilization, and that Judaeo-Christian and other religions make demands on individuals to curb their self-indulgence and to transcend their self-interest. In particular, Western religious leaders today are exhorting their faithful and citizens generally to fulfill moral responsibilities for national and international justice.

Political thinkers from Plato and Aristotle to Marx and Lenin recognized that the mass of humanity is neither very wise nor consistently virtuous. They realized quite well that this facet of the human condition poses a central problem for constructing and maintaining a rightly ordered society, however the right ordering of that society is conceived. Aristotle sought a solution in laws of Athens which would foster character-formation, and Marx sought a solution in a dictatorship of the party elite which would reconstruct the consciousness of the masses. A liberal democracy, however, must rely principally on voluntary associations. While the family is the primary association responsible for the moral education of citizens, religion too has an important role to play. From the viewpoint of enlightened self-interest as well as that of proper moral development of citizens, liberal democracies would be well advised to encourage citizens to exercise their freedom in response to religious commitment.

Despite the fact that the tradition of reason makes no appeal to religious inspiration, and that the origins of the tradition were in pagan Athens, there seems to be a historical linkage between the way the tradition evolved over the centuries and the Judaeo-Christian heritage. For all the glory that was the Greece of Socrates, Plato, and Aristotle, Westerners have come to recognize better than they the fundamental dignity of each human person. Because of that dignity, human society should be so organized as to maximize the freedom of all to develop themselves as persons and to treat all as equals without regard to ethnicity, ancestry, or sex. The great philosophers of ancient Greece could not transcend their own culture in very important respects: they accepted as natural the superiority of Greeks over non-Greeks, of some Greeks over other Greeks, and of men over women. Judaeo-Christian biblical ideals about the dignity of the human person were introduced to Western minds with the Christianization of Europe. However unspecific those ideals, and however much their full implications were unperceived for so long, they seem to have acted as a leaven in the evolution of Western thought and institutions toward freedom and equality. To determine the precise influence of ideas on history is always chancy, but the coincidence that politically institutionalized freedom and equality originated in a West which professed Judaeo-Christian ethical ideals suggests some linkage between the two. In any case, it seems clear that totalitarian regimes like Nazi Germany and Soviet Russia cannot tolerate unrestricted practice of the Jewish and Christian religions in large part because they recognize the incompatibility between the ethical ideals of those religions and their own.

There is another, darker side to religion, as practiced by partisans past and present, which undermines rather than supports a rightly ordered society. Those who are religiously committed may not only reject the differing beliefs of others but also seek to persecute others who hold differing beliefs; a good part of the history of the West has been a history of religious intolerance and persecution. The tradition of reason requires, and the West today accepts, the principle of religious freedom: all persons and sects are entitled, as a matter of moral and juridical right, to freedom of religious exercise. This right, like all rights, is subject to the requirements of a just order in society.[10] When, therefore, religious practices incite violence, conflict with the rights of others, or threaten the moral well-being of the community, the state may justly restrict the practices. (Some practices of present-day religious cults raise serious questions in this regard.[11]) Nor does the principle of religious freedom mean that individuals who disobey the laws of society should be immune from punishment simply because the individuals act out of religious motives. A democratic society should indeed attempt to accommodate individuals so as not to coerce them to act against their religious conscience (e.g., those with conscientious objections to participation in war), but a democratic society cannot accommodate individuals so as to permit them to act in every way they believe to be religious duties (e.g., those whose conscience impels them to burn abortion clinics or obstruct war-related facilities).[12]

CONCLUSION

I have argued in this article:

(1) that the tradition of reason should constitute the public philosophy underlying the civic culture of Western democracies;

(2) that the state should play a limited—and only a limited—role in coercing moral behavior;

(3) that freedom of religious belief and exercise is part of the tradition of reason, and that religious commitment, for the most part, contributes to the formation of virtuous citizens.

I have not considered the role that voluntary associations other than religious have to play in forming virtuous citizens. Families and schools are the foremost of such associations, and I shall close by making a few, very brief comments about public policies related to their contribution to the virtue of citizens.

The state can and should directly regulate family life in only limited ways, e.g., to safeguard the physical and mental well-being of children. The state also can and should indirectly promote family welfare by supporting counseling services and financially assisting poor families. (Citizens should be asking themselves whether or not Western societies are doing enough today to insure that those least well-off have the means to develop themselves and their children in a properly human way.) Religion also contributes to healthy human life. As religion generally supports the development of morally responsible citizens, so religion specifically supports the development of morally responsible families.

The state's role in the schools is much larger than its role in family life. This is so because the state itself owns and manages the principal school system. Since Western societies are pluralist societies, can public schools teach moral values in ways which are acceptable to citizens of diverse ethical convictions? They already do so, and they might do more. First, schools teach moral values by the quest for truth which is at the heart of the educative process and by the codes of conduct they require. Second, schools teach moral values—with or without formal courses—by the civic culture they transmit. Third, courses in humanistic subjects like history and literature touch on moral themes and values. Fourth, school administrators may be able to devise value-oriented courses on personal and community responsibility which will be acceptable to the religiously committed and secular humanist alike. Fifth, secondary school administrators may be able to accommodate religiously motivated students who wish, on their own initiative, to meet together for extracurricular activity or study.

As these cursory comments on the institutions of family and schools show, there is no magic touchstone for translating public philosophy into public policy. The effort, however, is both necessary and proper if we wish to achieve a rightly ordered society.

Notes

1. In the tradition of reason, the good of the community is ordered to the integral development of individual human persons and not the other way around. This theme is well developed by Jacques Maritain, "The Person and Society," in *The Person and the Common Good* (Notre Dame, Ind., 1966), 47–89. I summarize the theme in *The Moral Dimensions of Politics* (New York, 1986), 67–69.

2. See Walter Lippman, *The Public Philosophy* (Boston, 1955); Sir Ernest Barker, *Traditions of Civility* (Cambridge, 1948); John C. Murray, S.J., *We Hold These Truths* (New York, 1960).

3. Thomas Aquinas, *Summa Theologica,* I–II q. 90, a. 3; I–II q. 97, a. 3, *ad* 3; I–II q. 105, a. 1.

4. Maritain, "The Person and Society."

5. Maritain, *Man and the State* (Chicago, 1951), 9–19. I summarize his development in *Moral Dimensions,* 40–42, 93–94.

6. For a fuller development, see *Moral Dimensions,* 92–106.

7. *Roe v. Wade,* 410 U.S. 113, 93 S.Ct. 705, 35 L.Ed.2d 147 (1973).

8. Thomas Hobbes, *Leviathan,* edited by Michael Oakeshott (New York, 1962). Hobbes's sovereign determines what doctrines are fit to be taught (chap. 19, p. 137), and he establishes a church subservient to him (chap. 39, p. 340). Hobbes's principal concern was to prevent religion from becoming a source of dissension in the commonwealth. But since Hobbes held that humans are naturally brutish (chap. 13, p. 100), the sovereign is clearly well advised to use the established religion to bolster the regime by preaching obedience and self-restraint.

9. Locke sharply distinguishes the business of government from that of religion. "Letter concerning Toleration," *The Works of John Locke,* 12th ed., vol. 5 (London, 1824), 9. But Locke holds the law of nature insufficient to secure for individuals their lives, liberties, and properties because of the "corruption and viciousness of degenerate men." *Second Treatise of Government,* edited by C. B. Macpherson (Indianapolis, 1980), chap. 9, no. 128, p. 67. The threat to individuals from "degenerate men" persists after the formation of civil society, and the moral preachments of religion will help the civil power to meet it.

10. Cf. "The Declaration of Religious Freedom," *The Documents of Vatican II,* edited by Walter M. Abbott, S.J. (New York, 1966), pp. 685–87. For a survey of legal conflicts between religion and government in the United States up to 1971, see my *Private Conscience and Public Law: The American Experience* (New York, 1972).

11. See my "Regulating Cult Activities: The Limits of Religious Freedom," *Thought* 61 (1968): 185–96.

12. Cf. *Private Conscience,* chap. 1, 1–20; *Moral Dimensions,* 83–86.

MIDWEST STUDIES IN PHILOSOPHY, XIII (1988)

Civic Virtue, Corruption, and the Structure of Moral Theories

MICHAEL DAVIS

"In any country, if a high official does something for you, you show him gratitude with gifts. It is only natural, no?"
—the mother of Marcos supporter Roque Ablan, Jr.[1]

Moral theory has certainly benefited from revived interest in the virtues. We have been reminded of virtues long forgotten, been made to appreciate their part in the moral life, and even come to recognize a place for considerations of virtue in determining what acts are right. We have relearned that morality will resemble a monastery, brothel, or chimera if moral theory does not reserve a prominent place for the virtues.

I have no quarrel with any of this. My subject is not the virtues as such but a proposition associated with much recent work on the virtues (though logically independent of most of it). The proposition might be stated this way: *The virtues are more fundamental to understanding what makes an act morally right or wrong than are rules* (whether "rule" is understood as a linguistic entity or social practice).[2] My subject is, in short, the abstract question of how best to organize a moral theory.

To compensate for this abstractness, I devote the body of the paper to a fairly concrete question: What can "virtue theory" tell us about how public officials should act that "rule theory" cannot? I conclude that what virtue theory can tell us is more or less equivalent to what rule theory can tell us and that this conclusion does not seem to be a mere artifact of the concrete question with which I began. I then briefly consider what advantages virtue theory might have over rule theory even if the two are more or less equivalent descriptions of moral practice. My conclusion here is similar. Virtue theory has no clear advantage over rule theory. The virtues seem no more fundamental to morality than do rules.

My reasons for focusing discussion on how public officials should act rather than on a more traditional question of private morality is in part autobiographical. I came to my present view about virtue theory while trying to find a way to understand the peculiar ethical problems of public officials.

My reasons for this focus are, however, not entirely autobiographical. A focus on the virtues of public officials has the advantage of novelty. It also has the advantage of encouraging explicitness about the social character of morality, the contribution morality makes to creating a framework of cooperation. Since others have argued for much the same conclusion about virtue theory as I shall argue for, but without much worrying virtue theorists, perhaps this is the time to refocus the argument.

I. SOME PRELIMINARIES

"Virtue theories" are generally thought to have a structure quite different from "rule theories." A virtue theory begins with a description of virtues (showing in what way they are required by reason, necessary for happiness, or the like). Moral rules, duties, and/or other requirements are then derived by considering how to realize the virtues in practice. Rules serve the virtues.[3] A rule theory, in contrast, begins with a set of rules (including some proof that they are required by reason, necessary for happiness, or the like).[4] Virtues are then introduced, if introduced at all, as dispositions to follow certain rules. The virtues serve the rules.

Rule theories can be divided into utilitarian and deontic. In a utilitarian theory, doing as required is, as in virtue theory, a means to a state of affairs that can be defined without reference to the means of attaining it (but, unlike virtue theory, also without reference to any virtue). The state of affairs in question might, for example, be simply the most pleasant or the one satisfying the most preferences. Rules serve (nonmoral) goodness. In a deontic theory, on the other hand, doing as required is good in itself. The moral status of any state of affairs cannot be known without some account of how it came to be. Was it achieved by following the rules or by violating them? So, for example, while the pain a theft causes is bad, the pain imposed as part of a just punishment is good (not good as a means merely but good whatever follows from it). Deontic theories are (in this respect at least) not teleological.

This is caricature, of course. But it will do if (as I suppose) it picks out the big differences between the three classes of moral theory. If we are more or less agreed on the differences, then comparing virtue theory with deontological theory will seem preferable to comparing virtue theory with utilitarian theory. Utilitarian theory is more or less a mean between virtue theory and deontological theory. We are likely to learn more if we compare the extremes.

Near the end of this paper, I shall need to illustrate a few points by referring to a representative deontological or virtue theory. I shall treat Gauthier's *Morals By Agreement*[5] as the representative deontological theory and Becker's *Reciprocity* as the representative virtue theory. I shall use Gauthier for this purpose rather than the more conventional Kant or Rawls to bypass the jungle of interpretation that has grown up around them. I shall use Becker rather than the more conventional Aristotle or MacIntyre because Becker's work seems to me a significant advance on theirs. Much that is ambiguous, unargued, or merely hinted in their work is clearly stated and defended in his.

II. THREE VIRTUES AND SOME
PUBLIC OFFICIALS I HAVE KNOWN

Though my concern is ultimately theoretical, I think the place to begin is with the practical problem with which I myself began. In the fall of 1986, I was asked to prepare a program on ethics for the heads of the forty-two departments of the City of Chicago (and other members of the Mayor's cabinet). Because the conjunction of "ethics" and "City of Chicago" seems to strike many people as at best incongruous, I should explain that the mayor at that time, Harold Washington, was (by Chicago standards at least) a reformer. In the nine months before I was brought in, he had issued a code of conduct for the executive branch ("the Mayor's Ethics Order"), established a small Department of Ethics (including a Board of Ethics with enforcement powers), and instructed the Department to make the code a practical guide for his administration. A few months after I was brought in, he managed to win from City Council an ordinance extending the Executive Order to Council and to anyone doing business with the City. With that, Chicago became a pioneer in "municipal ethics."

I must admit to having known little of this, or of much else about Chicago's government, when I agreed to do the program. I therefore began by reading all the relevant documents and interviewing department heads. (I eventually interviewed about half of the department heads, as well as a few of their subordinates.) I interviewed them in part to collect problems suitable for use in the program. But, in part too, I did it to get some idea of what my audience needed. The interviews taught me much.

The public officials I interviewed were generally better educated than I expected, more thoughtful, more sensitive to ethical problems, and more concerned to do the right thing. Their world lacked the evil undertow one might expect from reading Walzer's discussion of political action.[6] Their world also lacked the jet-set dilemmas of the usual political ethics text.[7] The problems I collected were, however difficult in their own way, surprisingly pedestrian.

Though the public officials I interviewed seemed on average at least as virtuous as the average college teacher, they still needed a philosopher's help. The code of conduct was thirty pages of legal prose, followed by ten more pages of amendments, some only a few weeks old (with more expected). Many terms had technical definitions. Many provisions were also poorly drafted, a rat's nest of subordinate clauses. Reading the code left a blur rather than a clear impression. The administrators wanted a checklist so that they would be alert to problems and some way to think about the problems so that they would know whether to resolve them immediately or direct them to a staff lawyer or the Board of Ethics for a recommendation. They wanted to understand a code they knew they could neither learn by heart nor leave to the lawyers.

One plausible way to think of these administrators is as people lacking (what we might call) "civic virtue." They did not have the disposition an experienced and judicious administrator in a well-ordered city would have developed in the normal course of things. They possessed (we might say) only the virtues of a private citizen (and perhaps some of the corrupt tendencies long experience with the City of Chicago could produce). So, for example, if one of them wondered whether he should accept a $30 Christmas present from a developer doing business with his office, this was only because he was not as virtuous as he should have been. A virtuous administrator would simply refuse such a gift.

If we think of these administrators in this way, it will seem that I had been called in to teach them civic virtue. Though I did *not* in fact think of what I was doing in this way, I proceeded much as I would have if I had. After studying the code of conduct, I drew up a set of rules corresponding to (what we are calling) civic virtue:[8]

RULE ONE: *Always act as a faithful trustee of the City.* In particular,

1. Don't accept for yourself or for your family, friends, or party anything of value for what it is your job *not* to do. (No bribes.)
2. Don't accept for yourself or for your family, friends, or party anything of value to do what it is your job to do anyway. (No "grease" payments.)
3. Don't use your position in government to hire, promote, or otherwise benefit any person except as justified by the good of the City and then only in accordance with legally established procedures. (No favoritism.)
4. Use City property only as justified by the good of the City and then only in accordance with legally established procedures. (No abuse of privilege.)

RULE TWO: *Don't do anything that might reasonably be mistaken for a violation of Rule One.* In particular,

1. Avoid making an official decision in which you, either directly or through family, friends, or party, have a stake any other citizen in your office would not also have. (No conflict of interest.)
2. Avoid any *special* gift or service from anyone whom your office gives you the power to benefit or harm. A gift or service is special if it comes to you at least in part because you hold office. (No conflict of interest, again.)
3. Err on the side of caution when resolving doubts about what might reasonably be mistaken for a violation of Rule One. (No appearance of conflict of interest.) In particular,
   a. Don't hire, supervise, or otherwise put yourself in a position to use your office to benefit a relative, even though you care no more about him than about a perfect stranger.
   b. Don't leave office to take a job with a business which you benefited while in office.
   c. Don't put yourself in a position to benefit a business for which you worked before taking office, even if you have no reason to treat it better than you would any other.
   d. Avoid non-official contact with anyone whom your office gives you the power to benefit or harm.
   e. Don't accept anonymous gifts.

RULE THREE: *Disclose enough information about yourself so that any citizen with a reasonable doubt about your official conduct could determine that you have acted as you should.*

These rules proved useful. They provided the administrators with a reasonably clear picture of the underlying structure of the code of conduct, the ideal toward which it seems oriented. An administrator could use the rules as a checklist to identify decisions with the potential for ethical trouble. Whatever the rules allowed was probably proper.

The rules had another advantage. Using them need not remain conscious for long. They formed a sufficiently coherent whole to assure that use would quickly make them part of the unconscious machinery of decision. Use could give the administrators using them the virtue they now lacked.

I nevertheless found the rules to be a poor statement of civic virtue. Or rather, I found them so *supposing* (as we have been) that "civic virtue" refers to *the* special disposition even an honest and competent city official could fail to have. Those rules left too much of the code of conduct unexplained. For example, the code in fact *permitted* gifts "under $50" so long as they were not given with the intent to influence (while forbidding all other gifts).

As I read and reread the code, I began to see that "civic virtue" must name a set of competing virtues (or a virtue with several competing elements). The rules I initially thought to state civic virtue might be better thought to state (what we may call) "the virtue of impartial administration." Among the other virtues included in civic virtue, I identified two as particularly important, (what we may call) the virtues of *efficiency* and *democracy*. I eventually formulated these two virtues in this way:

EFFICIENCY: *Give preference to providing important city services at reasonable cost when, all else equal, providing such services is inconsistent with the impartial administration of city business.* In particular,

1. Don't adopt procedures that discourage too many people from entering government.
2. Don't adopt procedures too complicated or expensive.
3. Don't adopt procedures that alienate too many city employees.

DEMOCRACY[9]: *Don't adopt practices clearly at odds with how most citizens want city business to be transacted.* In particular,

1. Don't so burden city employees with procedural safeguards that they lose touch with the ordinary citizen.
2. Don't make the procedures of communication with city government so complicated, expensive, or otherwise forbidding that most citizens will try to get around them or conclude it is time for a new government.

The virtues of impartial administration, efficiency, and democracy, though competing, are not all of one type. The rules of impartial administration seem to be addressed to administrators as such, while those of efficiency and democracy seem addressed as much to those regulating the administrators as to the administrators themselves. In this respect at least, impartial administration seems to be a virtue different from the other two. In another respect, however, democracy seems the different one. Impartial administration is a virtue of an administrator as such. All else equal, it would be a virtue anywhere. The same would be true of efficiency. But the virtue of democracy might well seem more like moral weakness or opportunism in a city the government of which was *not* supposed to be a democracy. Think, for example, of what might count as a virtue in one of Stalin's municipal officials.

Administrators in Chicago seem to work at the intersection of virtues it is not easy to reconcile fully. So, for example, the virtue of impartial administration demands that administrators refuse all gifts to avoid even the appearance of impropriety. But an administrator who refuses a small Christmas gift from a developer, a token of appreciation for some special effort, or the traditional gift upon the closing of a major deal risks alienating those with whom he does business, not because he will seem incorruptible but because he will distance himself from those social exchanges by which we recognize our essential equality with one another. He will fail to exhibit his participation in (what we might call) "civic friendship." He will (in that respect at least) be undemocratic.

III. VIRTUES, COORDINATION PROBLEMS, AND RULES

If impartial administration is a virtue of an administrator as such (as it seems to be), then a public official can be "too democratic." But if participating in civic friendship is a virtue of administrators in a democracy (as it seems to be), then an administrator can also be "too much the administrator" (or, in other words, a "bureaucrat"). Much the same would be true of the relation the virtue of efficiency has to the other two virtues (except that, all else equal, efficiency preempts impartial administration). From the perspective of each virtue (at least prima facie), the other virtues are (in part) prescriptions for excess or deficiency.

There are at least three possible responses to this common observation that virtues can conflict. One is that a special virtue, judgment, can harmonize other virtues *case by case.* Virtues conflict prima facie but not all things considered. A second response is that virtues do not conflict even prima facie. When two virtues seem to conflict, at least one must have been misunderstood. The virtue is not what it seemed to be. We need to reformulate at least one of the virtues. If we think of the first response as a sort of intuitionism not unlike Ross's (the virtues having the certainty of Ross's prima facie duties), we might think of the second as an intuitionism more like Rawls's reflective equilibrium (any formulation of a virtue being as corrigible as Rawls's principles of justice are).

If this seems a fair analogy, then we must consider a third possible response to the problem of conflict between virtues, one differing radically from the other two. Unlike the second response, this one admits that the virtues can conflict, even when accurately formulated; but unlike the first, this one denies that mere judgment can always resolve the conflict. Sometimes the only way to resolve a conflict is to adopt a social rule. The cause of conflict among the virtues of individuals (according to this third response) is social arrangements, not the virtues themselves. The virtues of individuals conflict only because (and only while) society is deficient in some virtue.[10]

Of these three responses, the third seems to provide the best analysis of the conflict of virtues described in the last section. The conflict between impartial administration and democracy is not just a prima facie conflict, as the first response would have us believe. Even a judicious administrator might not be able to resolve it fully. If other administrators accept gifts while he does not, any compromise will fail to satisfy at least one of the virtues. If, for example, he asks that a gift be given to charity instead of to him, or indicates that he will pass it on to the City, he will distance himself from the giver more than other administrators do (and so, more than an ordinary citizen would like). He will, in that respect, be undemocratic.

The conflict between impartial administration and democracy is also not a function of my failure to formulate the virtues properly. While I could, I think, draft rules that would avoid all (or at least most) conflict between the two virtues, the draft would have much the same complexity as the code of conduct. The resemblance would not be accidental. The code is complex, in part at least, because its drafters tried to combine as much as possible impartial administration with democracy. The compromise, though apparently workable, does not seem to be workable *except as a set of rules.* Administrators will never be able to rely "on the seat of the pants" to decide whether conduct is permissible under the code. They will forever have to refer to the letter of the code.

I am not here claiming that someone could not actually learn the code, or that someone could not actually develop a disposition to follow it to the letter. I am willing to admit that someone who devoted himself wholly to following the code might eventually internalize it all. What I wish to deny is, first, that an *ordinary* administrator *could* internalize the code and, second, that *any* administrator *should* try. The normal press of business and the code's continual amendment seem to me to make such internalization unreasonable. Everyone will, on the whole, be better off if administrators devote their limited time to other matters. Even under the best conditions reasonably to be expected, a disposition to follow the code as such is impractical (if not humanly impossible). The code itself corresponds to no virtue.

The code nonetheless provides a general solution to our problem of conflict between virtues. An administrator operating under the code need not choose between impartial administration and democracy. The code provides that he can properly accept a gift worth no more than $50 if evidently given with no intention to affect his decision. Because the code so provides, accepting such a small gift cannot reasonably be mistaken for a violation of Rule One. Its acceptance is consistent with the virtue of impartial administration. And because the code expressly forbids accepting gifts above $50, the virtue of democracy cannot require an administrator to accept a larger gift. "The people" have defined the limit of civic friendship. The virtue of democracy cannot require an administrator to exceed the limit the people themselves have set. The administrator may now refuse gifts worth more than $50 without being undemocratic.

The third response thus analyzes the conflict between virtues as creating a problem of social coordination to which a code of conduct is the solution. Each administrator, acting separately, must choose between being too democratic and being too much the impartial administrator. No matter which he chooses, he will be less than virtuous. He has a humble form of Walzer's problem of dirty hands. But, unlike the problems Walzer discusses, this one can easily be resolved. By expressly allowing as part of unobjectionable appearance what democracy seems to require, the code of conduct permits each administrator to be both democratic enough and impartial enough. The code coordinates the conduct of administrators so that neither impartial administration nor democracy requires them to do what the other virtue condemns.

This solution to the problem of conflicting virtues does not require any new virtue in administrators. Nor does it require that any virtue be reformulated or that the dispositions of any administrator be changed. On the contrary, this solution helps us to see why we should be happy that administrators have exactly the virtues that, absent the appropriate code, would generate a problem of dirty hands. An administrator with those virtues will be uncomfortable taking small gifts even when the code of conduct expressly permits. He will take them for the sake of civic friendship (that is, out of a sense of duty). Uncomfortable taking even permitted gifts, he will be alert to gifts he should not take. Leaving administrators as they are thus assures that they will be on guard where guards are most needed.

Though not requiring any change in the administrators, our solution will, it seems, still change society, that is, the City of Chicago. Because the code defines the limit of civic friendship, individuals will have less reason to go beyond the limit when giving gifts to City administrators. They will have less reason to worry that others will give more, or that their failure to give more will be misunderstood. They will also have less reason for concern that what they are doing is corrupt or corrupting. Introducing the code of conduct should enhance the impartial administration, efficiency, and democracy the City already has to a signficant degree. In this respect, the city will be better ordered and so more virtuous.

Though the City will be more virtuous, it will not have a *new* virtue defined by following the code. The code of conduct can no more become a virtue of society than it can become a virtue of any particular administrator. The code is, of course, a social practice and, indeed, a social practice likely to make people more virtuous. But because it is a social practice heavily dependent on the *conscious rule-following* of individual administrators, contractors, and the like, it cannot become more than a social practice. It cannot become a social disposition sufficiently fixed and unconscious to be called a virtue.

IV. MORALITY, ETHICS, AND LAW

The rules we have been discussing are, of course, laws, not basic moral rules like "Don't kill" or "Keep your promises." So, this whole discussion may seem out of place in a paper that claims to be about how to organize a moral theory. Is the relation between virtue and Chicago's code of conduct anything more than a poor analogue of the relation between virtue and morality?

This is, I think, a question more likely to come from a fellow rule theorist than from the virtue theorist against whom my argument is directed. It is, nonetheless, a question that should be answered before we begin using our "analogue." My answer has two parts, the first appeals to ordinary usage, the second to moral theory.

Chicago's code of conduct is (like similar legislation elsewhere) generally described as "ethics legislation." (The official name of the legislation in which the code is now embedded is "Governmental Ethics Ordinance." Those violating the code are not simply described as engaging in illegal conduct. They are explicitly said to have behaved unethically. The administrators I interviewed were concerned about the code in a way they were not concerned about other City ordinances. They regarded following the code as something they were bound in conscience to do. Any moral theory that cannot find a place for such phenomena is, all else equal, substantially less satisfactory than one that can. The ethical seems to be part of the moral.

Virtue theorists generally have no trouble finding a place for such phenomena in morality. For virtue theorists, Chicago's code of conduct is part of morality because, like the basic moral rules, it is derived by considering what is necessary for a virtuous life. If virtue theorists have a problem, it is in distinguishing the code of conduct from ordinary legislation. Virtue theorists have a tendency to see all laws—and, indeed, even the basic moral rules—as justified by their relation to the virtuous life. For virtue theorists, Chicago's code of conduct differs from other moral rules, if at all, only in being more local and from other laws, if at all, only in being more closely connected to the virtues.

For rule theorists, however, understanding what Chicago's code of conduct has to do with morality is more difficult. Moral rules are (they hold) not local rules. At a minimum, they must cover an entire society. And, for many rule theorists, the moral rules must cover much more, that is to say, all rational persons. Chicago's code of conduct plainly cannot be part of morality if morality consists entirely of such general rules. The code is a "special morality" applying only to a part of the society (that is, to City administrators, other City employees, aldermen, and persons doing business with the City). It is, it seems, in the same category as the rules of particular religions ("religious ethics"), of particular occupations ("professional ethics"), and of particular "movements" ("marxist ethics").

Though rule theorists often talk as if morality consists only of general rules, they cannot mean what they say. At least two of the general moral rules—"Keep your promises" and "Don't cheat"—provide a way to make special moral rules.[11] So, for example, if I promise to obey the rules of a club (and the rules do not require anything morally wrong), the rules will thereafter be as morally binding *on me* as any general moral rule is even if, before I promised, the rules were morally indifferent. I cannot violate the club's rules without breaking a promise. Similarly, if I participate in a voluntary practice the rules of which require participants to do certain things not themselves morally wrong, and the benefits of which depend in part at least on the rules being generally observed, the rules of the practice are as morally binding on me (while I participate) as any general moral rule is. I cannot violate a rule of the practice without cheating.

We have already observed that Chicago's code of conduct can be understood as the solution to a problem of social coordination. We can now explain why (according to rule theory) the code is *morally* binding on City administrators. Without the code, administrators would sometimes face certain problems they would rather not face (a problem of dirty hands). The code protects them from those problems. But it does so only while administrators generally act as the code requires. If administrators did not generally obey the code, individual administrators would soon be in much the same situation they were in before the code was adopted. For example, as soon as a developer heard that some administrators were accepting gifts above $50, she would have good reason to expect the administrator with whom she was dealing to do the same. If he refused, she would have reason to feel snubbed. He would be putting more distance between himself and her than is necessary. To avoid offending her, he would have to accept her gift. He would be in exactly the situation he would have been in before the code was adopted. Because to be a City administrator is to participate in a voluntary practice in part defined by the code of conduct, because the benefits administrators receive from that code depend in large part on the code being generally obeyed, and because the code does not require anything morally wrong, an administrator who does not do as the code requires is doing something morally wrong. He is cheating.[12]

Let us reserve the term "ethics" for all those "special moralities" violation of the rules of which would constitute cheating. Chicago's code of conduct is, then, a code of ethics. The code may, however, still seem a poor analogue of general moral rules. The moral authority of ethical rules is, it seems, derived from a basic moral rule ("Don't cheat"). The code therefore has a source of authority different from the one the basic moral rules have. A basic moral rule does not derive its authority from another basic moral rule. A basic moral rule derives its authority from. . . .

The preceding sentence has no interesting end about which all rule theorists would agree. But, for an important class of rule theorists of which Gauthier is one, the proper end of that sentence would explain why the moral authority of ethical rules is not a mere analogue of the authority of the basic moral rules but, instead, an instance of it. For these rule theorists, every basic moral rule is (like Chicago's code of conduct) the solution of a coordination problem. Its moral authority is a function of that fact. So, for example, Gauthier might explain the moral authority of the rule "Keep your promises" by pointing out that it is something each rational bargainer would agree to because each would be better off, all things considered, if each kept his promises while the others did the same. Each would, of course, be even better off if he could ignore his promises while the others kept theirs. Each would, in other words, be better off if he cheated while the others did not. But, if each thought that way, each would cheat and everyone would be worse off than if everyone kept his promises as the rule required.[13] This, of course, is exactly the argument we gave for the moral authority of Chicago's code of conduct.

I conclude that the code does not differ from other moral rules in any way important here.

V. VIRTUE THEORY AND RULE THEORY COMPARED

So far, I think, virtue theorists and rule theorists need not disagree. But we must now consider two questions about which disagreement seems more likely. The first is *whether the foregoing analysis could be recast giving rules rather than virtues the fundamental role.* The second question is, if the analysis can be so recast, *which version of the analysis, the virtue version or the rule version, is the better.* This second question would bring us (at last) to the real subject of this paper, the claim that virtues are more fundamental to understanding morality than are rules. If a rule version of the analysis is possible, and if it is not worse than the virtue version, then, for "political morality" at least, virtues cannot be more fundamental than rules.

Recasting the foregoing analysis in terms of rules rather than virtues is, I think, trivial. The rules are already there in the code of conduct. We need only think of ourselves as first considering what rules, all things considered, should govern administrators in the City of Chicago. Among the things to consider would, of course, be how easy it would be for people to learn the rules in question. But also among the things to consider would be whether social arrangements might make it possible to get people to act in accordance with the rules even if they cannot be learned. The connection between particular rules and the virtues need not be considered. The question of what can be learned is, though closely related, not quite the same as that of what can be a virtue. We may then simply think of the rules as the product of a negotiation of the sort Gauthier describes.

Having thus derived rules of conduct, we might, of course, want to ask what dispositions of people, including those of administrators, would most help make the rules a social practice. That we could want to ask such a question may seem an embarrassment to the project of converting a virtue analysis into a rule analysis. There is no embarrassment. The structure of a rule theory must (by definition) be different from that of a virtue theory, but a difference in structure is consistent with both types of theory having exactly the same elements. Converting a virtue analysis into a rule analysis means giving pride of place to rules rather than to virtues, nothing more. Once we have done that, we need not be embarrassed if we must, for example, argue from the rules to a need to cultivate certain virtues because they serve the rule (or, indeed, from such a derived virtue to the need for certain secondary rules).

So, the answer to our first question is yes. Our analysis of civic virtue can be converted into an analysis giving rules rather than virtues the fundamental role. That brings us to the question whether the virtue analysis is in any way better than the rule analysis. Since the one analysis can be converted into the other, the question is, I think, best approached by comparing the relative merits of the *theories* yielding the two analyses. There are, it seems, at least four ways in which virtue theory might be better than rule theory: (1) virtue theory might be simpler, (2) it might provide a better approach to moral education, (3) it might fit practice better, and (4) it might fit our presystematic intuitions better. Let us take these in order.

1. *Simplicity.* Judging the relative simplicity of theories is never a simple matter. Simplicity is in part a function of one's experience. All else equal, the familiar seems simpler than the strange. Simplicity is also a function of one's theoretical agenda. A theory that eliminates entities considered troubling seems simpler than one that eliminates the same number of unobjectionable entities. And so on. To these complexities, a comparison of complex theories is likely to add problems of weighing generally conceded gains in simplicity in one respect against generally conceded losses in other respects. When, as here, the comparison is between two *types* of theory, each ranging from relatively simple to quite complex, the difficulties of comparison are multiplied.

Still, I do think it possible to see why virtue theory as such is not likely to be simpler (or more complex) than rule theory. (Consider: Imagining a virtue theory without rules is as easy as imagining a rule theory without virtues. What is interesting about these imagined extremes is that their simplicity seems to be paid for by loss of plausibility. So, for example, a virtue theory without rules ("Be virtuous and do what you like") assumes that the virtues include a solution to every coordination problem (much, perhaps, as the instincts of bees do). The assumption is implausible without an argument powerful enough to explain away the obvious importance we assign to rules, not simply as machines for organizing the world, but as claims upon our conscience.

If, instead of imagining such extremes, we look at actual moral theories, what we seem to find is that virtue theories always make some place for rules and that rule theories always do the same for virtues. Becker, for example, clearly recognizes an important place for moral rules in his theory. Some of the virtues are defined in part at least as disposition to act in accordance with certain rules. These he calls "deontological virtues."[14] He also recognizes that some rules may be justified even if they are not good for any virtue.[15]

Though Gauthier's primary concern is much more abstract than Becker's, he can no more do without virtues than Becker can do without rules. Gauthier's derivation of moral rules begins by assuming that his bargainers have the (nonmoral) virtue of rationality. The moral rules are what it would be rational for his bargainers to agree to. Having thus derived the moral rules, he must explain what motivation his bargainers could have to do as they agreed. Gauthier's explanation assumes that his bargainers have the disposition of "translucency," that is, the *moral* virtue of tending to be as trustworthy as one seems.[16] Virtues have as prominent a role in Gauthier's rule theory as rules have in Becker's virtue theory.

2. *Moral Education.* One advantage virtue theory may seem to have over rule theory is a closer connection with the theory of moral education. If even Gauthier must assume some virtues in his rational bargainers in order to make morality more than an empty bargain, is not rule theory dependent on virtue theory in a way virtue theory is not dependent on rule theory? Though this question probably deserves a book to do it justice, I think the short answer is simply no.

Most virtues are developed by practice, even such nonmoral virtues as fluency in one's native language or such moral virtues as kindness, trustworthiness, and friendship. Part of teaching virtues is teaching rules to follow until the virtues are learned. So, any plausible virtue theory of moral education should, it seems, begin (in part at least) with teaching rules rather than with teaching virtues as such. The rules need not, of course, be moral rules. For example, the rules on my checklist did not in fact correspond to what conduct should be, all things considered. They were aids to developing a certain moral virtue. They are not themselves moral rules. But, for many of the moral virtues (Becker's deontological virtues), it is hard to imagine their being taught without the corresponding moral rules.[17] For example, citing "Don't kill" is so much a part of virtuous deliberation concerning whether one should kill, that someone for whom the rule had no authority would, it seems, be deficient in the virtue corresponding to that rule. Here too virtues seem to be no more fundamental than do rules.

3. *Practice.* Evaluating theories according to their fit with practice has many of the same problems as evaluating their relative simplicity. Few, if any, theories fit all aspects of practice equally well. Deciding whether virtue theory fits practice better

than rule theory will depend on which aspects of practice it seems more important for a theory to fit. For example, does a theory providing a good analysis of friendship but a lame analysis of obligation to obey the law fit practice better or worse than one doing the reverse?

These observations suggest caution. I shall therefore offer an example in which rule theory as such seems superior to virtue theory as such. The example is *not* supposed to prove, or even to suggest, that rule theory *generally* fits practice better than virtue theory. Its purpose is simply to suggest the difficulties in the way of proving that *virtue* theory generally fits practice better than rule theory does.

Consider the practice we have been discussing all along. Why was I concerned that the administrators I interviewed lacked the virtue of impartial administration? The answer is not that the virtue is good in itself, that it is necessary for human flourishing, or anything like that (though I may well be willing to admit such things). I was concerned that they lacked the virtue because of its connection with their ability to use the code of conduct. In practice, I gave the code priority over the virtues.

I do not believe this priority is peculiar to my example. Our interest in morality is not primarily intellectual. Morality is about how people should act. The virtues are not, it seems to me, clearly more important to action than rules are. Sometimes, of course, we want people to express their virtues, not follow rules. For example, we prefer the spontaneous gift of a friend to the same gift given from deliberation concerning the duties of friendship. Sometimes, however, the reverse is true. For example, we value more another's conscious acknowledgment of our right when he is obviously tempted to violate it than we do the off-hand acknowledgment of one too virtuous to be tempted. So, overall, it is far from clear that virtue theory fits practice better than rule theory does.

4. *Intuitions.* To the degree that our intuitions are indistinguishable from practice, we have, I think, already said enough about intuition. There is, however, a sort of intuition we have about the *general* fit of theory to practice, a question of overall balance. And here, I think, virtue theory is, if anything, at a disadvantage. The achievements of virtue theory so far seem to concern such personal virtues as friendship, trustworthiness, and the like; the achievements of rule theory, such pillars of social life as the basic moral rules, punishment, and social justice. My impression is that most people today would consider the achievements of rule theory more important.

MacIntyre's criticism of contemporary moral theory, that is, rule theory, clearly recognizes that rule theory, not virtue theory, fits the modern temperament better than virtue theory does. Indeed, part of his project is to explain rule theory's intuitive appeal to the modern mind in a way that will prevent that appeal being used against virtue theory.[18] Since MacIntyre seems to have persuaded few among those not converted to virtue theory before he published *After Virtue,* the intuitive appeal of rule theory seems far more certain than the reasons he gives for not using that appeal against virtue theory.[19]

VI. CONCLUSION

I undertook to argue that virtues are not more fundamental to morality than are rules. I have, I think, done that. I should, however, point out how easy my undertaking was.

I undertook to defend a type of theory that has had wide appeal over many centuries against an equally ancient type of theory. The enduring appeal of the type I defended makes it unlikely that its ancient competitor could have any decisive advantage over it. If virtue theory had such an advantage, someone should have discovered it long ago. The reverse is, of course, also true. That virtue theory also has had an enduring appeal, even in centuries when rule theory has dominated, makes it unlikely that rule theory has any decisive advantage over it. The emphasis of each seems to make up for something lacking in the other.

So, my conclusion should not surprise. Those who find virtue theory more to their liking (as I do not), need either to provide some argument for the clear superiority of their way of doing things or to admit a permanent rivalry between virtue theory and rule theory not unlike that between political parties in a democracy. One or the other may for a time win over the vast majority of the "moral electorate." The loser may then borrow many "planks" from the winner's "platform" and, in time, become the winner. But, win or lose, the two parties will remain distinct. The platform of each, though resembling the other's in many details, will have a structure all its own.

Notes

I should like to thank Robert Ladenson for many helpful comments on the first draft of this paper.

1. *New York Review of Books,* Nov. 6, 1986, p.20.

2. See, for example, Alasdair MacIntyre, *After Virtue,* 2nd. ed. (Notre Dame, Ind., 1984), 150: "Hence perhaps the most obvious and astonishing absence from Aristotle's thought for any modern reader: There is relatively little mention of rules anywhere in the *Ethics.* Moreover, Aristotle takes that part of morality which is obedience to rules to be obedience to laws enacted by the city-state—if and when the city-state enacts as it ought."

3. For a detailed example of how a virtue theorist might derive specific moral rules from specific virtues, see Lawrence C. Becker, *Reciprocity* (London, 1986), 170–72.

4. This is true even of act-utilitarianism. Act-utilitarianism simply begins with a single rule like: "Maximize expected utility." Virtues are to be supported (if they are) only when (and only insofar as) doing so maximizes expected utility. I leave open the question whether some forms of utilitarianism might be forms of virtue theory rather than rule theory. Think, for example, of the peculiar utilitarianism found in Richard Brandt's *A Theory of the Good and the Right* (Oxford, 1979). For Brandt, moral rules are simply dispositions it is rational to have. For a related point, see Michael Davis, "Realistic Utilitarianism and the Social Conditions of Cognitive Psychotherapy," *Social Theory and Practice* (1987): 1–23, esp. 17–18.

5. David Gauthier, *Morals By Agreement* (Oxford, 1986).

6. Michael Walzer, "Political Action: The Problem of Dirty Hands," *Philosophy and Public Affairs* 2 (1973): 160–80.

7. See, for example, Amy Gutmann and Dennis Thompson, *Ethics and Politics* (Chicago, 1984).

8. I am not, I believe, here confusing rule theory with virtue theory. Any virtue may be characterized by a set of rules— *provided* the rules are understood to state a disposition (that is, a character trait) desirable for its own sake, for human happiness, or the like rather than desirable merely because it tends to support obedience to some other rule (whether understood as a linguistic entity or social practice). Note, for example, how Becker describes the virtue of reciprocity, 74.

9. I must admit to some unhappiness with this term. "Democracy," as used here, does not refer to a decision procedure ("majority rule") or to a certain conception of society ("equality") so much as to a certain compatibility with the surrounding society. In a traditional caste society, for example, this rule might well have clearly undemocratic consequences. I am nevertheless

sticking with "democracy" because (a) I haven't hit on a better term and (b) this one seems right in a context like Chicago where virtually everyone is a democrat and, indeed, a Democrat).

10. These are, of course, not the only responses possible (though they are, I think, the only ones we need consider here). Becker provides a (principled) example of what else is possible. Because he thinks moral judgments are simply all-things-considered judgments, he necessarily takes the rules defining any virtue as stating only what one should do, all else equal. Conflict with another virtue would, of course, make all else less than equal as would any serious practical problem *(Reciprocity,* 164). Becker's full response seems to be a variation of our third.

11. Since Gauthier does not actually derive any moral rules, I am drawing on Bernard Gert's useful list, *The Moral Rules* (New York, 1970), 104–106, 107–109. While I do not so indicate, all Gert's rules have exceptions. Though Gauthier does not derive any moral rules, his list of what he might derive seems close enough to Gert's. See, for example, *Morals By Agreement,* 156.

12. For more on this way of connecting morality and ethics, see Michael Davis, "The Moral Authority of a Professional Code," in *NOMOS XXIX: Authority Revisited,* edited by Pennock and Chapman (New York, 1987), 302–37.

13. Gauthier, *Morals By Agreement,* 113–56.

14. Becker, *Reciprocity,* 68–69.

15. Compare, *Reciprocity,* 164–65: "while the rules of a given social structure might well be bad for virtue, we still might have overriding reasons, all things considered, for adopting them." Since, for Becker, moral reasons are simply all-things-considered reasons, the rules in question, though bad for virtue, are still morally required. This seems to be one place where Becker breaks decisively with most virtue theory.

16. Gauthier, *Morals By Agreement,* 174–79.

17. Becker, *Reciprocity,* 371–72 ("conscientiousness").

18. "The hypothesis which I wish to advance is that in the actual world which we inhabit the language of morality is in the same state of grave disorder as the language of natural science in the imaginary world which I described. What we possess, if this view is true, are the fragments of a conceptual scheme, parts of which now lack those contexts from which their significance derived. . . . We have—very largely, if not entirely—lost our comprehension, both theoretical and practical, [of] morality" *(After Virtue,* 2). My final criticism of virtue theory is not as fair as it may seem from this quotation. Some virtue theorists, for example, Becker, seem at home in this century.

19. I do, however, think MacIntyre has put his finger on an unfortunate tendency of much of this century's moral thinking. I will offer one example of my own. Statutes forbidding political bribery, extortion, grease payments, and the like often require that the prohibited act be done not only intentionally but "corruptly" (or "with corrupt intent"). The requirement has caused surprising confusion. The majority view among legal theorists seems to be that "corruptly" is redundant. Those arguing otherwise have had considerable trouble offering an alternative. None seems to have thought to identify the appropriate virtue (or virtues) of a public official and then interpret "corruptly" as indicating inconsistency with that virtue (or those virtues). Why has no one thought of it? It is hard to give any other answer than MacIntyre's. The vocabulary of virtue seems to be dead for many who should know better. For a good summary of the literature on corrupt intention, see Daniel H. Lowenstein, "Political Bribery and the Intermediate Theory of Politics," *UCLA Law Review* 32 (1985): 784–851.

Moral Motivation: Kantians versus Humeans (and Evolution)

LAURENCE THOMAS

> Moral judgements are, I say, hypothetical impera-
> tives in the sense that they give reasons for acting
> only in conjunction with interests and desires. We
> cannot change that, though we could keep up the pre-
> tence that it is otherwise.
> —Philippa Foot, "A Reply to Professor Frankena"

Neo-Kantians are contemporary ethicists who are primarily concerned to defend Kant's account of moral motivation and are to be distinguished from those who are primarily concerned to defend Kant's account of the right, including duties to the self. The former are essentially concerned to show that the motivation to act in accordance with the requirements of an altruistic (other-regarding) morality can be explained without any reference to desire whatsoever, but in terms of reason alone. Neo-Kantians tell us that it is possible for a person to have a reason to perform an action required by altruistic morality, and for that reason to be efficacious, in and of itself, in motivating the individual to act, where the desires of the person do not at all figure into the explanation of the behavior in question. As we shall see in section 1.1, where I discuss Darwall (1983), neo-Kantians are not talking about mere logical possibility. They insist that in precisely this way people can actually be moved to do what is morally right. Humeans, obviously, will hear none of this, insisting that desires, and only desires, motivate a person to act. If a person does what is morally right, that is because in the end, after all is said and done, that is what the person desires to do.[1] As I hope to show, I believe that a Humean conception of the motivational structure of persons is quite compatible with persons acting in accordance with the requirements of an altruistic (other-regarding) morality.

Obviously, if neo-Kantians are right, then when it comes to acting in accordance with the requirements of an altruistic morality it matters little whether an account of human nature yields a picture of human beings as being essentially self-interested (egoistic) or altruistic in their desires, since we are told that reason can motivate independently of what the desires of persons actually are. By contrast, if

Humeans are right then it matters dearly. As far as I can see, the convictions of neo-Kantians concerning motivation are tied not so much to a demonstration of the truth of the view which they advocate nor an abhorrence of what they take to follow from the Humean position, namely that individuals are simply at the mercy of their desires when it comes to doing what is morally right, but rather a concern to show that individuals who are basically self-interested (egoistic) in nature can be moved to act in accordance with the requirements of an altruistic (other-regarding) morality. I shall say more on this in section 1.1. Suffice it to say for now that strictly speaking, it does not follow from a Humean conception of our motivational structure that human beings are either essentially self-interested or altruistic in nature; though, to be sure, the Humean conception is compatible with either view of human nature. As we shall see in our discussion of Darwall, a Humean conception of our motivational structure is usually combined with a Hobbesean (self-interested) conception of the content of our desires.

In the main, I believe that there are two reasons why the neo-Kantian position has been found so attractive. The most commonly put forth reason is the one that I have already alluded to, namely that it has the virtue of showing that persons who are self-interested in nature can be nonetheless moved to follow the demands of an other-regarding morality. The other reason, which is rarely discussed explicitly but seems to be a deep background assumption, is that being equally objective the True and the Good are both parallel with respect to rational assent—that is, believing a proposition to be true and accepting it as such. One should assent at least to the point where one is moved by it, and so one's actions and reasoning are guided by it. Thus understood, assenting carries in its wake a significant measure of motivational force independently of the desires of persons. For example, on the assumption that '2 + 2 = 4' is objectively true, then presumably, to be rational just is to assent to that and to reason that one has four items of the same kind when, being aware that one already has two items of a certain kind, one is given two more. Similarly, following Susan Wolf,[2] if 'Needlessly killing innocent people is wrong' is objectively good, then to be rational just is to assent to that and, at the very least, to refrain from doing so. The two reasons are related because the second is the explanation for the first; for if as a matter of conceptual truth to be rational is to assent to the True and the Good, then so assenting would not in any way seem to be contingent upon our desires. (I do not attempt to say how the True and the Good are distinguishable from one another. It suffices for our purposes that propositions of ethics and aesthetics are generally regarded as paradigmatically falling under the Good and propositions of mathematics and logic and propositions expressing contingent truths which are purely descriptive are regarded as paradigmatically falling under the True.)

Although the view that the True and the Good are parallel with respect to rational assent is certainly a very captivating one, I believe that in the end it must be rejected as unsound, as I shall argue in the section which follows. A Humean conception of our motivational structure is defended in section 2. Drawing upon evolution, I believe that an account of human nature can be shown to yield a picture of human beings as being more altruistic than self-interested than perhaps one is inclined to suppose.

1. KANTIAN MOTIVATION

1.1 Motivation without desire

Negative demonstrations are hard to come by; I do not have one to show that the neo-Kantian conception of motivation must be rejected as indefensible. But a very good reason for considering an alternative to this conception is that no defense of this view has survived careful scrutiny. One of the most recent and thoughtful defenses is offered by Darwall in his *Impartial Reason* (1983). Let us examine some of his remarks.

The following is an example offered at the outset which Darwall believes militates mightily in favor of his Kantian position. The example invites quite careful scrutiny because it is specifically designed to illustrate the soundness of the Kantian view. There is the case of Roberta who, after having viewed a particularly vivid film on the struggles of textile workers, is moved to donate a few hours a week to helping their plight (Darwall 1983, 39–42). His claim is that we are not required to explain her being so moved by reference to a desire, writing:

> Of course, it could have been the case that she had some such general desire as the desire to relieve suffering prior to seeing the film, saw this as an opportunity, and formed the desire to relieve *this* suffering, as per an Aristotelian practical syllogism. But this need not be what happened. (Darwall 1983, 40, italics in the original)

Now, it may very well be that Roberta's being motivated to do volunteer work on behalf of textile workers cannot be explained by the film's speaking to some *already existing* desire to relieve suffering; however, if Darwall wishes to convince us that desire does not explain Roberta's being moved to help he must rule out one more possibility, namely that the film did not *cause* Roberta to come to have a desire as a result of which she was moved to help others. After all, even as Kantians conceive of Humeans the latter are not committed to the view that the set of desires which a person has are fixed. Indeed, precisely what worries many Kantians is that on the Humean view the desires which a person has or may come to have can be due to factors which are quite beyond her or his control.

One way in which viewing a film may move a person to action is that it speaks to an already existing desire, however general. But Darwall is right: we need not suppose that this is what happened in Roberta's case. On the other hand, is it not possible that viewing a film can cause a person to come to have a desire as a result of which she is moved to action? Unless this possibility is also ruled out, the example fails to convince. Not only does Darwall fail to rule out this possibility, he does not even consider it.

Since Darwall is a careful thinker, one naturally wonders what explanation there might be for why he failed to consider this possibility. Well, consider. We are told Roberta was in effect moved to act morally; in particular, she was moved to take another's good to heart. Morality here is understood as an altruistic concept; for Roberta is moved to help the textile workers. Now, if one holds a Hobbesean, and thus an egoistic, conception of the motivational structure of persons according to which their desires are basically self-interested, then it would seem well-nigh impossible to explain how a person might be moved to act morally (that is, in an other-regarding and, therefore, altruistic way) simply by watching a film about the suffering of others, because on a Hobbesean conception of the motivational structure of persons there would seem to be no way for altruistic concerns ever to obtain a foothold in a person's life. One would not look to something internal to the person as a way of explaining how she might be moved to act altruistically. By hypothesis, what so moves her must be something other than desires and something internal to her. It must be external to her.

The problem is that when a Humean conception of the motivational structure of persons as being left to the mercy of their desires is combined with a Hobbesean one regarding the content of desires as being self-interested, the desires of persons leave no room for an individual to be moved by internal considerations to desire to act altruistically; hence, they leave no room for an individual to be moved to act morally if doing so is tied to having the desire to act altruistically. I suggest that Darwall implicitly subscribes to a Humean-Hobbesean conception of the motivational structure of persons and that this is the explanation for why he does not bother to consider the possibility that viewing the film might have caused Roberta to have the desire to help textile workers.[3]

By a Humean-Hobbesean conception of the motivational structure of persons, nothing out of the ordinary is intended. I am focusing upon Hume's claim that it is desire and not reason which moves a person to act; and I am focusing upon Hobbes's claim that the desires of persons are essentially self-interested. These are logically distinct claims which can both be true. More often than not, though, when people talk about the Humean conception of the motivational structure of the person it is against the backdrop of a Hobbesean self-interested and so egoistic view of the content of the desires of persons. Thus, in the *Possibility of Altruism* (1970), Thomas Nagel's main concern is to show that conceptually if we take ourselves seriously, then we must take others seriously. The issue is never whether we take ourselves seriously. Of course we do—so Nagel assumes. And contemporary contract theorists, such as Rawls (1971) and Gauthier (1986), invariably start with the premise that the original contractors are essentially egoistic in the way that they conceive of themselves and then, with various kinds of theoretical machinery, endeavor to show that such individuals would consider it rational to accept an altruistic conception of morality.

Now, precisely what the neo-Kantian approach promises is a way of moving persons to act morally despite their motivational structure. And this makes it quite appealing if one is inclined to think that the Humean-Hobbesean conception of the motivational structure of persons is more or less the correct one, since the Kantian approach makes it unnecessary to offer an altruistic account of the motivational structure of persons in order to be able to make sense of persons being moved voluntarily to act morally. This approach enables one to bypass the issue of what our motivational structure is actually like.

Since Charles Darwin's *The Origin of Species,* the idea that the motivational structure of persons is essentially self-interested has no doubt seemed like one of those empirical truths that we might as well elevate to the status of an honorary metaphysical truth. I do not believe that evolution commits us to understanding Darwin, or more generally, evolution in this way, as I shall try to show in section 2.

1.2 The True and the Good

Following Susan Wolf (1980), it would seem that on the Kantian view the connection between the True and rationality is that conceptually to be rational is to assent to that which is objectively true and good, assuming it is available to one as such. *And it will be recalled that as the view is being understood here assenting carries in its wake sufficient motivational force.* In assenting to the truth of a proposition—that is, believing it to be true and accepting it as such—a person does so at least to the extent that his behavior is guided by it (in the ways indicated in the introduction). As is well known, a most significant metaphysical thesis is thought to be a consequence of the view just expressed, namely: because assenting to objective truth is in accordance with our rational nature, it follows that our free will is not threatened by the fact that as rational beings we are, as it were, compelled to assent to objective truth, since no alternative rational choice is available. The free will of persons is no more threatened in these instances than it is by the fact that persons cannot fly—or so the argument goes (Berlin, 1969). What is meant by rationality here needs to be explained, and I shall do so in a moment.

Now, without taking a stand on whether the Good, of which morality is a part, is a subset of the True or not, Wolf suggests that the two are parallel to one another with respect to rational assent; accordingly, she goes on to argue that our free will is no more threatened when we are, as it were, compelled to assent to that which is objectively good than it is when we are compelled to assent to that which is objectively true. If the True and the Good are parallel with respect to rational assent, then there is every reason to believe that she is right on this point, given that the inference about free will can be made. If so, then moral behavior can indeed be rescued from the contingency of desires in a way which does not threaten our free will. I do not want to question whether that inference can be made; instead, I am interested in the prior claim that the True and the Good are parallel with regard to rational assent. I do not believe the Good is like the True in this respect. But first let me say a word about the way in which rationality is to be understood here.

The term 'rationality' can be understood in two ways, neither of which are all or nothing conceptions. There is the maximizing conception of rationality—economic or instrumental rationality. A person's considered and consistent preferences are taken as given and are maximized (Gauthier 1986, 38). If a person truly prefers to live only for today, and acts accordingly, then on this conception of rationality she acts rationally (Gauthier 1986, 37–38). In contrast to this, there is the mental health conception of rationality (Fingarette and Hasse, 1979). Ideally, a person who is rational in this sense is in full possession of his mental faculties and can distinguish between reality and fantasy. It is the mental health conception of rationality which figures in the Kantian view of the connection between the True and rationality. Thus, a person who systematically fails to assent to the True is irrational in the sense of being mentally deficient. Because economic rationality takes considered preferences as given, it simply cannot be the conception of rationality which the Kantian view employs.

There can be no doubt that the Kantian view has a certain intuitive appeal to it. Unequivocally, the following claims are objectively true: 'Supersonic jets travel faster than cars,' and 'Unless protected in some way a person who is struck by a vehicle moving at 100 miles per hour will be seriously injured'. Surely, to be (mental health) rational just is to assent to the truth of these propositions. No one maintains that rational people can disagree about the truth of these propositions; for the different criteria which deliver these propositions to us as true, are quite beyond dispute. Of course, not all criteria are as reliable as the ones which deliver the preceding propositions to us as true, though as in the case of propositions of logic and mathematics some criteria are presumably even more reliable. But the point is not that all criteria which deliver propositions to us as true are equally reliable. It is, instead, that given sufficiently reliable criteria for delivering the truth of a given proposition the rational person will assent to the truth of that proposition. The discussion which follows pertains to mental health rationality.

In regard to contingent propositions, it is important to bring out that a realist conception of the world is presupposed. As (mental health) rationality would suggest: what is true or false is constrained by events that occur in or states of affairs that obtain in the real word. The proposition 'Jones is a widow' is true if and only if, in the order mentioned, the following two events occurred in the real world: she got married; then her husband died. Although it can often be very difficult to ascertain the truth status of a contingent proposition or, more generally, although the various criteria which we rely upon to determine whether a contingent proposition is true may vary in their reliability, we nonetheless hold that in principle the truth or falsity of a proposition can be objectively established in most cases—that there is a fact of the matter which will do so if only we should discover it. Sometimes it is not worth the effort to discover it; sometimes it is too late to do so. But these considerations do not bear one way or the other upon the point being made, to which I shall return in 1.3.

Now, the question is this: Are there sufficiently reliable criteria which deliver to us the Good—so much so that it can be likewise held that the connection between the Good, of which morality is a part, and rationality is such that to be rational is to assent to the Good and act accordingly? I do not believe so. I shall argue the case indirectly from two directions.

The first consideration I should like to raise has to do with negative judgments of character. Roughly speaking, to say that a person has a morally bad character is to say that he does what is sufficiently wrong often enough and, moreover, that *qua* rational person he realizes this. Negative judgments of character are inextricably tied to the assessment that, functioning as a rational person, the agent fully intended to perform this or that set of actions and that he was well aware of the wrongfulness of his actions. If the wrong done is objectionable enough, the person in question does not only have a bad moral character, but an evil one. By definition, it would seem, an evil person is not one who is completely unable to recognize the Good; rather, he is one who refuses to assent to it—at least to the point where he lets himself be moved by it.

To be an evil person is not *ipso facto* to have one's rationality called into question. None of this is to deny that in some cases there can be mitigating factors. The idea rather is that we seem to think that sometimes a person does what is evil and there are no such factors operative—that sometimes a person's doing evil rather than good cannot be attributed to a failure of cognition (such as mistaken inference) or motivation (weakness of will, say) (Foot 1978; Milo 1984, chap. 7).

There is, to be sure, a sense in which we allow that an evil person is so hardened that he is unable to see the Good. Observe, however, that rarely is it supposed that the person was like that from the outset. Again, we are sometimes prepared to allow that a person's environment might favor his coming to have a morally bad character. But what is normally meant here is not that the person was altogether unable to grasp the Good and that is why he failed to assent to it, but that his circumstances understandably prevented the Good from having any motivational force in his life. But, again, this person is not automatically counted among the irrational in terms of mental health.

American slavery and the Holocaust were paradigmatically evil institutions. This is surely a judgment we would have to retreat from to a considerable extent were we to hold that as with the True, persons must assent to the Good, on pain of being irrational. We shall have to retreat because we hold that a person can be held morally responsible for his wrongful actions only if at some level or the other he was rational enough to appreciate their wrongfulness (Fingarette and Hasse 1979). What makes slavery and the Holocaust such evil institutions is not simply that, respectively, blacks and Jews were so badly harmed, but that rational people were intent upon causing the harm despite the fact that they had good reason to believe they were not justified in doing so. Significantly, most of us do not suppose that the perpetrators of these harms were rational in most other aspects of their lives, but were *excusably* mistaken about the nature of their wrongful actions in these instances. A notable exception is Alan Donagan (1977).[4]

Regarding the Nazi mobile units, Hilberg (1985, vol. 1, 289) writes:[5]

These men were in no sense hoodlums, delinquents, common criminals, or sex maniacs. Most were intellectuals. . . . All we know is that they brought to their new task all the skills and training which, as men of thought, they were capable of contributing. These men, in short, became efficient killers.

Regarding American slavery we know the following to be true (Genovese, 1974): (i) some slave masters kept black women as mistresses; (ii) upon occasion the wives of some slave masters were jealous of black female slaves; (iii) slaves cared for and suckled the children of whites; (iv) sexual liaisons between slave master and female slave sometimes resulted in offspring; and (v) slaves were speakers of the language. On the assumption that a person is rational and given what we know about human beings and social interaction, these considerations unequivocally warrant the belief that slaves were human beings. We do not doubt the rationality of slave masters. Accordingly, we do not suppose that they could have really and truly believed that slaves were less than fullfledged human beings; and this is precisely why we take American slavery to have been such an evil institution. We would have a considerably less negative judgment of it if we thought that indeed slave masters were all irrational and for that reason *could* not appreciate the immorality of their deeds. The very negative judgment that we make of both slavery and the Holocaust cannot be made independent of the assumption of rationality on the part of the perpetrators of these institutions.

The moral of the story, needless to say, is that some of our most important judgments regarding the evilness of certain practices would be impossible to make if we hold that the connection between the Good and the rational is such that to be rational was to assent to the Good, where this means that one is moved to act in accordance with it.

I now want to consider the matter from an entirely different direction, namely that of philosophical liberalism. Although the considerations which follow are probably less compelling than those already advanced against the view under consideration, there are two reasons why a look at philosophical liberalism is important. One is that it is such a salient view in the lives of many today. The other is that it unwittingly lends much credibility to our rejection of the view that the connection between the Good and rationality is such that to be rational is to assent to the Good, since it readily invites the interpretation that the ideal is one of harmonious noninterference *because* there is no transcendent view of the Good to which rational people must on pain of being irrational subscribe to. This is disturbing because the political ideal of harmonious noninterference would seem to be a default ideal—that is, an ideal that we have because it would appear that no compelling case can be made for any ideal. This, in turn, would understandably make one suspicious of the Kantian view of the connection between the Good and rationality. One of the most eloquent and sustained defenses of contemporary philosophical liberalism, John Rawls's contemporary classic *A Theory of Justice (TJ)*, can be understood in this way. A brief look at this work will prove to be very instructive in the end.

One very important aspect of Rawls's multifaceted argument for the principles of justice as fairness over utilitarianism is as follows. Equal liberty secures the self-respect or basic good of individuals because each person knows that he will be free to pursue his plan of life whatever it may be, since the worth of plans is not judged by their usefulness to society as with utilitarianism *(TJ,* sec. 29). Instead, the idea is that when priority is given to liberty, then the worth of all individuals is equally affirmed in virtue of all being equally secure in the knowledge that each is free to pursue his plan of life just so long as his plans are not in violation of the principles of justice *(TJ,* sec. 82).[6] The result is, Rawls tells us, that the principles of justice as fairness yield a considerably more stable society than does utilitarianism; and this consideration, called the argument from psychological stability, is one of the most powerful points of reasoning which the parties in the original position have available for preferring the principles of justice as fairness to those of utilitarianism; for the former can affirm the worth of individuals' plans independently of their usefulness to society, whereas the latter cannot *(TJ,* 454–56).

Now, Rawls also eschews perfectionism, so what follows quite interestingly is this. In *A Theory of Justice,* Rawls holds that a very powerful reason for preferring one set of principles of justice/morality over another is that they maximize harmonious noninterference. The two principles of justice as fairness do this by, as it were, declaring all plans equally good just so long as their execution does not require the violation of its principles. Observe, though, that what is scrupulously avoided is a rational assessment of the worth of plans of life, and so of one another's good, from the standpoint of the principles of justice as fairness themselves. Indeed, Rawls is forced to say that from the standpoint of the principles of justice as fairness a plan of life which calls for counting blades of grass is just as good as one which calls for studying Mozart *(TJ,* 432). And as I have said, that this is a consequence of the two principles of justice as fairness is, according to Rawls, one of the most powerful reasons that the parties in the original position have for favoring his two principles over utilitarianism, since the result is said to be a more stable society than utilitarianism would yield. Thus, it would seem that an argument from harmonious noninterference—the principles of justice as fairness maximize such noninterference to a significantly greater extent than utilitarianism—is one of the most powerful of the arguments which Rawls invokes to show that it is rational to favor his principles over utilitarianism.

Before continuing, a caveat is in order. *A Theory of Justice* is an extraordinarily complex work; and the language of harmonious noninterference is mine, not Rawls's. Still, it is important to see that it is hardly implausible to read the most distinguished contemporary defense of philosophical liberalism in this way. And that is significant if, as I have claimed, the ideal of harmonious noninterference does not set well with the Kantian view of the connection between the Good and mental health rationality.

In working out his theory, Rawls invokes the thin theory of the good to account for the list of primary goods *(TJ,* 396), which includes, in order of importance, self-respect and liberty. And his extraordinarily powerful—but from the standpoint of theoretical elegance, simple—motivational assumption is that individuals prefer more rather than less of these goods *(TJ,* 142). And, of course, the parties' deliberations are shrouded in impartiality insured by the veil of ignorance. In this way, Rawls hopes that the arguments of *A Theory of Justice* will have wide appeal; and indeed they do. But when all is said and done Rawls concedes that he does not have any vantage point from which to criticize individuals, independently of their preferences, for not embracing his theory. Five pages before the end of his contemporary classic, Rawls writes:

> Suppose that even in a well-ordered society there are some persons for whom the affirmation of their sense of justice is not a good. Given their aims and wants and the peculiarities of their nature, the thin account of the good does not define reasons sufficient for them to maintain this regulative sentiment. It has been argued [Rawls references Foot (1978)] that to these persons one cannot truthfully recommend justice as a virtue. And this is surely correct, assuming such a recommendation to imply that rational grounds (identified by the thin theory of the good) counsel this course for them as individuals. *(TJ,* 575)

Rawls concedes that the Good as defined by the principles of justice as fairness can be rejected without a person's being open to the charge of economic irrationality. Nor, *a fortiori,* does he think that such a person would be open to the charge of mental health irrationality. Rawls's (1985) latest writings would seem to bear these claims out.

This should come as no surprise. Economic rationality is purely a subjective notion. It is inextricably tied to each individual's own subjective preferences. And impartiality, however guaranteed, is at best a way of arbitrating among competing rational economic preferences. Impartiality may refine our rational preferences, it may very well help us to see more clearly what they are; but it cannot in the end speak to what they morally ought to be—and certainly not to the point where a person's mental health can be called into question if he should fail to follow the prescribed principles of morality. For in the end it does not have an objective vantage point from which the preferences of persons can be normatively assessed, matters of consistency and the like aside.

So much, then, for the idea that to be mental health rational is to assent to the Good. Philosophical liberalism, insofar as it flies under the banner of relentless impartiality, as it is wont to do, does not allow itself to be substantive enough to yield such a connection between the Good and rationality. I have not claimed, nor do I believe, that philosophical liberalism must fly under this banner.

I have argued from two quite different directions against the Kantian view that the Good and the rational are such that to be rational is to assent to the Good. As I have said, I believe the first argument concerning judgments of character is the more compelling one. The second argument is important, however, because it locates the problem in a very important context, namely that of philosophical liberalism.

1.3 Assenting, consequences, and rationality

Here is a proposition belonging to the True: 'Human beings cannot fly (of their own power)'. And unlike the proposition 'The earth is round', which also belongs to the True, failing to believe and to act in accordance with the first has dire consequences—considerable physical harm, if not death itself. Here is a proposition belonging to the Good: 'The gratuitous killing of innocent people is morally wrong and constitutes murder'. Every moral theory which has a serious claim to our attention embraces it. Now, failing to believe and to act in accordance with this proposition of the Good can also have dire consequences. A person who gratuitously kills an innocent person can be ostracized or harmed by those who identified with the victim, imprisoned, or given a death sentence. But there is a difference obviously. Deliberately acting contrary to a proposition of the Good—flaunting it, let us say, has dire consequences only if others inflict harm upon one on account of one's doing so, which requires that one's flaunting behavior be discovered by them. The dire consequences, if there be any, are tied to the intentional behavior of others. And this seems to be so for all propositions of the Good which are moral propositions.

Not so, clearly, with the proposition 'Human beings cannot fly (of their own power)'. A person who flaunts this proposition by jumping off the top of any high building without a parachute or some other device to break his fall is courting death, regardless of who is looking and in the absence of any intentional behavior on the part of others. In matters of every day living, at least, not all propositions of the True are such that a person will suffer dire consequences if he flaunts them. 'The earth is round' is not; but clearly enough are. Flaunting many propositions of the True has natural physical consequences many of which are quite deleterious to a person's physical well-being regardless of who is looking or what people think. And this is altogether unlike any proposition of the Good which belongs to morality. In a world of indifference or disinterest, a person can get away with murder—and quite literally, too.

So what turns on this difference between the True and the Good? The answer is that insorfar as a rational person desires to live and be physically whole, then he has an internal reason (Williams, 1981) independently of who or how many might be aware of his behavior to assent to many propositions of the True. An analogous claim cannot be made for propositions of the Good. Of course, if a person is altogether indifferent to living, then nothing matters to him, including the way in which the world is. If, however, a person desires to live, then that desire makes many aspects of the True important to him in a way that it does not make the Good important to him. From none of this does it follow that it is rational to believe anything, and thus ignore the True entirely, just so long as one does not desire to live. The point, rather, is that if one does desire to live, then *a fortiori* it cannot be rational to ignore the True entirely. Again, this holds independently of who or how many might be aware of one's behavior. By contrast, it would not seem that we can start with this desire and make a parallel claim concerning the Good. These considerations speak to the remark made in 1.2 that the Kantian view concerning the True presupposes a realist conception of the world.

A final comment. It may very well be true that if enough individuals flaunt the Good, then human flourishing or, in any case, social cooperation would be impossible. It does not follow from this, however, that any given individual suffers simply in virtue of flaunting the Good, as Gauthier (1967) showed in his discussion of Baier (1958).

2. DESIRES, EVOLUTION, AND MORALITY

As I observed, toward the end of section 1.1, the view that persons are relentlessly self-interested and, therefore, non-altruistic in their motivational structure might seem to be a consequence of evolutionary theory. One reason for this, surely, is that the theory tells us that natural selection favors behavioral patterns or traits which serve to maximize an individual's gene pool—that is, which will enable a creature to transmit even more of its genes to the next generation. Given this much as true, it is rather tempting to impute selfish motives to individuals. But the temptation should be resisted. The issue before us is to what extent does a full account of human nature yield an altruistic picture of human beings which, in turn, is in keeping with the requirements of an altruistic morality. As we shall see, the answer is far more than one might be inclined to suppose.

At the outset, it is important to distinguish between motive altruism and unwitting altruism. By the former I mean the intentional bestowing of a benefit upon someone at some cost or risk to oneself, without regard to future gain. By the latter I mean those instances where another has benefited from one's behavior, but where the benefit was in no way intended. Motive altruism is what is generally regarded as genuine altruism; it is the kind of altruism required by an altruistic morality. As the stories about calling birds (Trivers, 1971) make clear, the altruism of evolutionary biology is that of unwitting altruism, and not motive altruism.[7] We are not to suppose, for instance, that in issuing a warning, which jeopardizes its life by making its whereabouts more easily determined by its predator, a calling bird reasons to itself that things will turn out better if it, a single calling bird, should put its life in jeopardy than if the life of its neighboring calling birds are endangered. We are not to impute any such intentions or motives to a calling bird. Of course, unwitting altruism is compatible with motive altruism in that beneficial behavioral patterns which have come about because in general they tend to maximize the gene pool of individuals may very well benefit those whom we in fact desire to benefit. This, however, constitutes a happy confluence of circumstances; it does not show that in the final analysis the motives of individuals are self-interested. Before turning to the main task of this section one more clarifying remark.

Let us assume that the theory of evolution can make sense of altruism among kin (family members) via, for instance, the theory of kin selection. The interesting question is whether the theory can yield the view that there is altruism between non-kin. To the extent that it can do this, a Hobbesean conception, and so a self-interested conception of human nature turns out to be false, and is replaced by a Humean-altruistic one. I shall endeavor to make this idea plausible by looking at two matters which are connected with having offspring.

2.1 Wilson on sexual bonding

In his essay *On Human Nature,* E. O. Wilson (1978) writes that:

> Sex is in every sense a gratuitously consuming and risky activity. The reproductive organs of human beings are anatomically complex in ways that make them subject to lethal malfunctions, such as ectopic pregnancy and venereal disease. Courtship activities are prolonged beyond the minimal needs of signaling. . . . At the microscopic level, the genetic devices by which human sex is determined are finely tuned and easily disturbed. (Wilson 1978, 22)
>
> Thus sex by itself lends no straightforward Darwinian advantage. (Wilson 1978, 122)

Wilson (1978, 137ff) goes on to suggest that sexual activity is a powerful bonding mechanism upon the parties involved, which in turn contributes to their being cooperative in the venture of child rearing. And this has an evolutionary advantage, given the length and complexities of human child rearing.

Now although Wilson does not explicitly say so, there is every reason to believe that he takes the type of bond formed to be one of affection, which is unquestionably one of the fountainheads of altruistic behavior. What makes the foregoing considerations of the utmost importance is that sexual bonding among human beings typically takes place between non-kin. In a word, the Wilsonian suggestion is that sexual bonding is a mechanism which triggers altruism between non-kin.[8] Of course, from an evolutionary standpoint the idea is that the altruism triggered between the two individuals serves their gene pool, since the two affectionately bonded parents are thus likely to be more cooperative in the venture of raising their children (the parents each passing on one-half of their genes), which increases the likelihood that the children will in turn reach the point they can raise children. But, for one thing, the altruism can hardly be deemed any less genuine on this account. And for another, the altruism is no less there if it should turn out that the two affectionately bonded adults do not have children.

Insofar as there is talk of a connection between sexual behavior and altruism, the object of the altruism is generally taken to be the offspring rather than the relevant parents. The Wilsonian suggestion is significant precisely because it extends the object of the altruism to individuals who are not genetically related (non-kin), namely the parents. It gives us a purchase on the view that individuals who are non-kin can be altruistically disposed toward one another. And it is this consideration which I am after. For I am interested in the extent to which a full account of human nature yields an altruistic picture of human beings. The more often it is plausible to hold that there can be altruism between non-kin the better, since the altruism that morality calls for is paradigmatically between non-kin.

(It might be objected that the above considerations only show that non-kin who are members of the opposite gender can be altruistically disposed toward one another. I do not believe so, though space does not permit me to argue that here.)

2.2 Parental love

Following a line of thought which I developed in "Love and Morality" (1985): When things are as they should be, parents love their children—not because they are smart or physically attractive or some such thing, but because the children are theirs. This would seem to be especially true of just-born infants. Any just-born infant may become an intellectual giant or a symbol of physical attractiveness, but this is not known at the moment of birth. Thus, to love the just-born is not merely to love a bundle of unrealized potential, it is rather to love a being the nature of whose potential is unknown to one. A just-born infant may even be without a name for awhile. Parents love their just-born children for no other reason than that they are theirs.

So we may think of parental love for the just-born as having a rather referentially transparent character to it. Of course, it is most relevant to the parents that the child being loved is their child. But the possessive adjective here is not a quality denoting attribute, picking out qualities which the child presently possesses or shall come to possess. The attribute functions purely as an indicator of the child's origins; it does not indicate what the child is or shall be like. It applies equally to any just-born who has the same origins. Hold the origins fixed and one just-born is as good as another. It is in precisely this sense that the transparency of parental love mirrors the transparency of reference.

It is very reasonable to assume that the capacity for parental love would be selected for, given the following: (i) a necessary condition for any biological creature passing on its genes is that it succeeds in leaving behind progeny who, in turn, succeed in doing the same;[9] (ii) among homo sapiens, parental care may arguably be regarded as receiving its greatest expression, since the natural parent-offspring relationship is the longest and most complex among any species; and (iii) among the most basic needs of a human infant is the need for continuous love from its parents (or parental surrogate), as parental love provides what we may call basic psychological security, that is, security on the child's part which is in no way tied to its performances.

Now the disposition toward others that an altruistic morality calls for exhibits a transparency which parallels the transparency of parental love to a remarkable extent. Whether or not we should find ourselves attracted to others on account of their attributes, there is a minimum amount of respect which all persons are owed simply in virtue of being such. If all persons have certain rights or are owed certain duties, then they should be treated accordingly regardless of their attributes.

We can get from parental love to a measure of altruism between non-kin in the following way. As I have indicated the just-born require considerable care and attention which, in turn, requires an enormous amount of time and energy. Social cooperation facilitates such endeavors to a considerable extent (recall the considerations of section 2.1); for parents would hardly be able to provide the necessary care and attention if there was little or no social cooperation among human beings and, instead, everyone had to be concerned with protecting himself against one another at every turn. The amount of care and attention that human offspring require necessitates that humans live in harmony with one another to some extent. Thus, from the standpoint of the theory of evolution it is reasonable to assume that natural selection would favor human beings having a motivational structure capable of varying degrees of altruism, with the altruism of parental love being the most basic and generally the richest expression of altruism among human beings. For natural selection favors those patterns of behavior, dispositions, and so forth which enhances a creature's ability to transmit its genes to its offspring; and social cooperation does just that. An important assumption here is that genuine cooperation requires altruism. Gauthier (1986) thinks otherwise. I have tried to show that he is mistaken (Thomas 1988).

3. CONCLUSION

I trust that what the debate is about has been made a bit clearer. It is not just a Humean conception of our motivational structure which neo-Kantians have found unsettling, but a Humean-Hobbesean one. For unlike the Humean-Hobbesean one, the Humean conception (alone) is, strictly speaking, quite compatible with persons being moved to follow the requirements of an altruistic morality, though it would be a matter of chance that anyone does. The Humean conception of our motivational structure is compatible with rigorous moral training making the difference, whereas the Humean-Hobbesean one would not seem to be. Thus, given this latter conception and our commitment to an altruistic morality, it becomes especially urgent to show that reason alone can move a person to follow the precepts of such a morality.

I do not believe that neo-Kantians are likely to succeed in their attempt. And the arguments of section 2 are meant to show that their failure need not be all that disconcerting despite our commitment to an altruistic morality. For as I have tried to show, starting with quite fundamental aspects of evolutionary theory, as it can plausibly be seen to apply to human beings, the theory can be seen to yield a picture of human beings according to which altruism is very much a part of the nature of human nature. The issue, of course, is not whether it can be established that human beings are entirely altruistic, but only whether we are altruistic enough that the requirements of an altruistic morality can sufficiently resonate with our human nature. The arguments of section 2 give us hope that the answer is an affirmative one. Of course, this altruism has to be nurtured. But this is in keeping with what we know about many of our natural endowments, which is that their full realization requires cultivation. The piano prodigy practices in order to realize fully her musical gift. The mathematical genius studies. Thus, if as I have argued the capacity for altruism comes in the wake of our biological make-up, it hardly follows that moral training which realizes this capacity is unnecessary. And history is a painful reminder of what can happen when this capacity is not nurtured sufficiently.

Notes

I am very grateful to Oberlin College for a 1987–88 Research Status appointment; and to Bernard Boxill, Terrance McConnell, and Howard McGary for illuminating comments upon an earlier draft of this essay. McGary, specifically, made a number of instructive comparisons between the views of Baier and Darwall. I have not been able to take all of his suggestions into account. The arguments of section 2 are much developed in Laurence Thomas, *A Psychology of Moral Character* (forthcoming).

1. Respectively, Stephen Darwall, *Impartial Reason* (1983) and David Gauthier, *Morals by Agreement* (1986) are recent representatives of these two approaches, each speaking, respectively, for Kant and Hume on the issue of motivation. I concentrate upon Darwall because his work is the most recent book-length attempt to defend the Kantian view about motivation. In getting clearer about my own view, I am much indebted to the illuminating discussion of these two approaches by Adrian M. S. Piper (1985).

2. Wolf (1980). My thinking here owes a lot to her ingenious attempt to develop this parallel. Allowing even desires into the picture, she attempts to show that free will is possible. The invocation of her name in reference to Kant (section 1.2) is in reference to the view that the True and the Good are parallel with respect to rational assent and not, obviously, with respect to the issue of motivation.

3. The suggestion is not wholly speculative. For Darwall is a student of Kurt Baier whose moral views have their deep roots in Thomas Hobbes (Baier, 1958). And Baier has been much influenced by David Gauthier (who has been much influenced by Baier) whose moral views also have their deep roots in Thomas Hobbes (Gauthier, 1986).

4. Donagan writes: "A graduate of Sandhurst or West Point who does not understand his duty to noncombatants as human beings is certainly culpable for his ignorance; an officer bred up from childhood in the Hitler *Jugend* might not be" (p. 135). If Donagan is right, then we may not move as readily as we normally do from *X* was a Nazi soldier to *X* was an evil person. I believe that one has to tell an extraordinary story, which Donagan fails to do, in order to block this inference here. For a most illuminating discussion on matters pertaining to culpability, see Robert Merrihew Adams (1985), who not only takes issue with Donagan but argues ever so convincingly that we can be culpable for things we do involuntarily.

5. If it makes sense to talk about reason and desire "warring" with one another, where the former is good and the latter is bad, what makes the Holocaust so devastatingly disconcerting is that it turns that idea inside out, in that every imaginable step was taken to ensure that moral sensibilities (morally decent desires) did not get in the way of the destruction of the Jews. Had the intellectual commitment of Nazi leaders lost to squeamish moral sensibilities—had it lost to an uneasiness that "was the product of moral scruples—the lingering effect of two thousand years of Western morality" (Hilberg 1985, vol. 3, 1011)—that would have been a good thing. But

the leaders made sure that that did not happen. See, e.g., Hilberg (1985, vol. 3, chap. 10).

6. "In a well-ordered society then self-respect is secured by the public affirmation of the status of equal citizenship for all; the distribution of material means is left to take care of itself in accordance with the idea of pure procedural justice" (*TJ*, 545, sec. 82).

7. Authors like Richard Dawkins (1976) are surely partly to blame for the confusion here, writing as if genes actually have a mind of their own. Dawkins writes: "I shall make use of the metaphor of the architect's plans, freely mixing the language of metaphor with the language of the real thing" (p. 23). Stephen J. Gould (1977) alerts the reader as follows: "I do not mean to attribute conscious will to creatures with such rudimentary brains [ants]. I use such phrases as "he would rather" only as a convenient shortcut for "in the course of evolution, males [male ants] who did not behave this way have been placed at a selective disadvantage and gradually eliminated" (pp. 264–65).

8. In his work on abortion, my Honors student, Andrew Manitsky, has suggested to me that it is not implausible to think of sexual interaction between lovers (who are non-kin) as contributing to their moral flourishing, since it enhances self-disclosure and trust. This would clearly accord sexual behavior a non-procreative purpose, and is in keeping with the claims which I have made in the text.

9. Some creatures—e.g., salmon—really do leave their offspring behind, since they do not in any way raise their offspring. Salmon lay their eggs and swim off.

References

Adams, Robert Merrihew. 1985. "Involuntary Sins." *The Philosophical Review* 94.

Baier, Kurt. 1958. *The Moral Point of View.* Ithaca, N.Y.

Berger, Alan L. 1982. "Academia and the Holocaust." *Judiasm: A Quarterly Journal of Jewish Life and Thought* 31.

Berlin, Isaiah. 1969. *Four Essays on Liberty.* New York. Reference is to his essay "Two Concepts of Liberty."

Boxill, Bernard. 1981. "How Injustice Pays?" *Philosophy and Public Affairs* 9.

Dahl, Norman. 1984. *Practical Reason, Aristotle, and Weakness of the Will.* Minneapolis, Minn.

Darwall, Stephen L. 1983. *Impartial Reason.* Ithaca, N.Y.

Dawkins, Richard. 1976. *The Selfish Gene.* New York.

Donagan, Alan. 1977. *The Theory of Morality.* Chicago, Ill.

Dworkin, Gerald. 1974. "Non-Neutral Principles." *Journal of Philosophy* 71.

Fingarette, Herbert and Anne Fingarette Hasse. 1979. *Mental Disabilities and Criminal Responsibility.* Berkeley, Calif.

Foot, Philippa. 1978. *Virtues and Vices.* Berkeley, Calif. Reference is to her essay "Moral Beliefs."

Gauthier, David. 1967. "Morality and Advantage." *The Philosophical Review* 76.

_____. 1986. *Morals by Agreement.* New York.

Genovese, Eugene. 1974. *Roll, Jordan, Roll.* New York.

Gibbard, Allan. 1982. "Human Evolution and the Sense of Justice." *Midwest Studies in Philosophy* 7.

Gould, Stephen J. 1977. *Ever Since Darwin.* New York.

Hilberg, Raul. 1985. *The Destruction of European Jews.* 3 vols., revised edition. New York.

Masters, Roger D. 1978. "Of Marmots and Men: Animal Behavior and Human Altruism." In *Altruism, Sympathy, and Helping,* edited by Lauren Wispe. New York.

Milo, Ronald. 1984. *Immorality.* Princeton, N. J.

Nagel, Thomas. 1970. *The Possibility of Altruism.* New York.

_____. 1987. "Moral Conflict and Political Legitimacy." *Philosophy and Public Affairs* 16.

Piper, Adrian M. S. 1985. "Two Conceptions of the Self." *Philosophical Studies* 48.

Rawls, John. 1971. *A Theory of Justice.* Cambridge, Mass.

_____. 1985. "Justice as Fairness: Political not Metaphysical." *Philosophy and Public Affairs* 14.

Thomas, Laurence. 1985. "Love and Morality: The Possibility of Altruism." In *Sociobiology and Epistemology,* edited by James H. Fetzer. Dordrect.

———. 1988. "Rationality and Affectivity: The Metaphysics of the Moral Self." *Social Philosophy and Policy.* Issue on Gauthier (1986).

Trivers, Robert L. 1971. "The Evolution of Reciprocal Altruism." *The Quarterly Review of Biology* 46.

Wilson, E. O. 1978. *On Human Nature.* Cambridge, Mass.

Williams, Bernard. 1981. *Moral Luck.* New York. Reference is to his essay "Internal and External Reasons."

Wolf, Susan. 1980. "Asymmetrical Freedom." *Journal of Philosophy* 77.

Utilitarian Virtue

MICHAEL SLOTE

Whatever would utilitarianism want with a doctrine of virtue or of particular virtues? Such a question may well occur to anyone reading the title of this essay who is aware of the gulf between utilitarianism—especially act utilitarianism—and the recently reviving tradition of virtue ethics, a tradition that is supposed, among other things, to represent the very opposite of the utilitarian approach. But even if present-day utilitarians have no particular interest in developing a theory of the virtues, I hope to show you that the consistent development of a utilitarianism concerned with more than the evaluation of actions calls for, or at the very least strongly suggests, a utilitarian conception of virtue. Recent work on utilitarianism has shown that optimific right actions are not the only means by which the utilitarian concern for good results may be realized; there is a separate and honorable place for the consequentialist evaluation of human motives and dispositions, and the latter naturally leads to a utilitarian view of the virtues of the sort to be introduced and considered here.

I

In this century utilitarians have focused almost exclusively on the evaluation of actions. Even rule utilitarians treat the consequentialist evaluation of rules chiefly as a means to the evaluation of particular actions. But in an earlier era, during classical utilitarianism's apolaustic succession from Bentham through Mill to Sidgwick, considerable emphasis was also placed on the evaluation of entities other than actions, and in recent years there has been a revival of interest in the utilitarian evaluation of motives, dispositions, works of art, and other potential objects of consequentialistic evaluation.[1] Even if, say, motives are not under the immediate control of the will, they can make a difference to overall human happiness and unhappiness, and a utilitarianism that is comfortable conceiving the Principle of Utility as a standard of moral assessment that may not be particularly useful as a practical guide to action needs to be open to the sorts of indirect practical consideration that lead us to evaluate motives, etc., in their own right. But once we start evaluating motives, dispositions, character traits, and the like in utilitarian consequentialist terms, we are well on our way to a utilitarian theory of virtue(s).

Bentham was aware of utilitarianism's tendency in this direction. In *An Introduction to the Principles of Morals and Legislation,* Bentham spends a great deal of time developing a theory of the evaluation of motives and dispositions (what Adams calls "motive utilitarianism");[2] but in the preface to that work,[3] he says that it is quite easy to generate a theory of virtue and vice, and of particular virtues and vices, from his views about pleasure, pain, motives, dispositions, etc. Indeed, he excuses himself from producing such a theory by claiming that given what he does say in the *Introduction,* the production of a theory of virtue(s) would be "little more than a mechanical operation." However, even working with Bentham's views about the evaluation of motives and dispositions, the attempt to elaborate a utilitarian view of virtue and the virtues raises a number of interesting and perplexing issues. And as far as I can tell, no previous attempt has been made to spell out a utilitarian theory of virtue. In the later *Deontology* Bentham dwells at considerable length on virtue and the virtues, but the view offered there is not a (consistently) utilitarian one,[4] and Sidgwick's *Methods* may offer utilitarian justifications for what we ordinarily take to be virtues, but that is a far cry (as we may soon be able to see more clearly) from offering a utilitarian conception of temperance, courage, and virtue generally. I believe, however, that a utilitarian theory of virtue(s) is well worth having, and so in what follows, I shall first sketch a utilitarianism of motives and character traits and then show how a utilitarianism of virtue(s) can naturally go forward on this by now well-marked utilitarian path.

II

In introducing his motive utilitarianism, Bentham says: "With respect to goodness and badness, as it is with everything else that is not itself either pain or pleasure, so it is with motives. If they are good or bad, it is only on account of their effects: good on account of their tendency to produce pleasure, or avert pain: bad, on account of their tendency to produce pain, or avert pleasure."[5] For Bentham a motive is good, rather than bad, if its effects are good on the whole.[6] But he distinguishes between general motives like love or benevolence and particular instances of such motives (in given individuals on given occasions). On Bentham's view, particular (instances of) motives are to be evaluated in terms of their consequences rather than their intrinsic character as motives, and since no motive, not even benevolence, always has good consequences, the particular benevolence with which a person acts on a given occasion may fail to count as a good, and may actually be a bad, motive. General motives like benevolence, on the other hand, can be evaluated only through the evaluation of their instances. If benevolence, general benevolence, counts as a good motive, that can only be because the total effect of all particular instances of benevolence— present, past, and future—is more favorable than unfavorable to human happiness or pleasure. And the same account is supposed to hold *mutatis mutandis* for human dispositions and their particular instantiations.

However, Bentham adds a qualification or *caveat* to the above account, which is absolutely essential to understanding the fundamental thrust of any utilitarianism of virtue(s). He points out that some names for motives strongly imply a positive, and some a negative, evaluation: it strains ordinary language to speak, for example, of (any particular instance of) avarice as a good motive. But Bentham then also claims that we can always find some neutral term to refer to a particular or general motive: avarice, e.g., can be spoken of as "pecuniary interest," and so the issue of whether any motive is a good one cannot, in one sense, be linguistically prejudged independently of consequences. It may be *de dicto* necessary that any instance of avarice be a bad particular motive—no instance of pecuniary interest counts as avarice unless it has long-run overall bad consequences. But of any particular case of avarice, it is not *de re* necessary that it have had overall bad consequences, that it have been a bad motive, that it have been a case of avarice, and this interesting complexity turns out to be very serviceable to the formulation of a utilitarianism of virtue.

Among the cardinal virtues of traditional ethics—justice, temperance, courage, and prudence or practical wisdom—only the first has been given any sort of utilitarian elaboration. And when Bentham discusses justice, somewhat briefly, in the *Introduction,* he seems to be influenced by what he has said, just a few pages earlier, about the positive or negative connotations of ethical terms. He claims that "justice, in the only sense in which it has a meaning, is an imaginary personage, feigned for the convenience of discourse, whose dictates are the dictates of utility, applied to certain particular cases."[7] For Bentham, the dictates of justice are nothing more than "a part of the dictates of benevolence, which, on certain occasions, are applied to . . . certain actions." And clearly on such a conception it is always morally right to perform just actions.

But this is not the only view of justice open to a defender of act utilitarianism. Smart, in his "Outline of a System of Utilitarian Ethics," treats the dictates of justice as opposed to those of the principle of utility; that is, he takes our ordinary or commonsense views about what is just as constitutive of justice, but questions whether it is always right to perform the sorts of just actions that are morally acceptable according to common sense.[8] Where the dictates of justice conflict with those of utility, it is the latter which determine what it is actually right to do.

It is interesting that Bentham takes such a very different line about the dictates of justice, and I believe his position on this issue is influenced, perhaps even determined, by his views about the names of motives and dispositions. It sounds just as odd to speak of an act as right but unjust as to speak of avarice as a good motive, and the desire to placate common sense that led Bentham to reserve the term "avarice" for instances of pecuniary interest whose overall consequences are bad would therefore naturally lead him to reserve the term "unjust" for actions with bad or less than optimal consequences. But this entails making assessments of justice in accordance with the principle of utility, rather than, like Smart, making such judgments in commonsense terms and leaving it an open question whether any particular just action is morally right.[9] Smart's act utilitarianism leaves the commonsense conception (i.e., his own pre-theoretical understanding) of justice intact and as such offers no distinctive utilitarian conception of justice or of virtue generally. It is only with Bentham's approach that utilitarianism comes into its own as a view or theory of justice. Bentham, however, offers no similar treatment of any of the other traditional virtues, and I shall attempt to make up for this deficiency in what follows.

Bentham's insistence on tying (acts of) justice to the principle of utility and his assumption that human motives and dispositions are to be assessed in terms of their consequences for human happiness give justice almost definitionally the status of a virtue and force us to regard as just certain actions that are ordinarily, or intuitively, thought of as unjust.[10] And we shall see in what follows that a distinctively utilitarian treatment of courage, temperance, and prudence leads to parallel conclusions. But such an across-the-board approach also raises some rather interesting questions about utilitarianism generally that no "mechanical operation" can resolve for us.

III

However, before we can proceed with our discussion of courage, temperance, and prudence or practical wisdom (the treatment of other, "minor" virtues being left to another occasion), we need to become somewhat clearer about certain aspects of the utilitarian aproach to justice. Bentham holds that the dictates of justice are those of utility or benevolence, but in the statements quoted above he also indicates that the term "just" applies less widely than the term "right." However, Bentham, in the *Introduction,* never tells us anything specific about such limitations on the applicability of the notion of justice, and it is difficult to see what limitations he had in mind. In the passage quoted, he seems to want to restrict the term "just" to certain actions, which is very odd, considering how naturally it is applied to social institutions. But of course Bentham also restricts the term "right" to human actions/acts, and to that extent no divergence in usage between "right" and "just" has yet been indicated. In the *Deontology,*[11] Bentham says that the dictates of justice apply only where considerations of benevolence and/or utility give rise to an obligation. But even the familiar utilitarian distinction between right and obligatory actions is not much help to us in making sense of the restrictions on justice that Bentham apparently wishes to defend. A non-obligatory right act is certainly not "dictated" by considerations of utilitarian justice, but isn't such an act just *simpliciter* by the utilitarian's lights? I cannot for the life of me see why not, and it is worth noting here that when Rawls gives expression to what he takes to be the utilitarian conception of justice, as it applies both to social institutions and to individual acts, he seems to imply that the utilitarian regards all and only right acts as just. "The striking feature of the utilitarian view of justice," he says, "is that it does not matter, except indirectly, how this sum of satisfactions is distributed among individuals any more than it matters, except indirectly, how one man distributes his satisfactions over time. The correct distribution in either case is that which yields the maximum fulfillment."[12]

Now according to the principle of utility, it is morally wrong for a person not to maximize his pleasure or satisfactions in situations where no one else can be affected by his actions. So if the distinction between just and unjust is to apply wherever the distinction between right and wrong does, then it will in utilitarian terms be unjust for someone to neglect her own (maximal) welfare or utility. Rawls seems willing to accept such an implication of the utilitarian view of justice—after all, it may be no odder to claim that it is unjust to neglect one's pleasures than to claim, as utilitarians clearly must, that it is wrong to do so. But I am inclined to think that Bentham's vaguely expressed restrictions on justice are best defended—assuming they can be defended at all—in terms of the distinction between self-regarding and other-regarding actions. If justice is to be thought of as a species of right action, perhaps it should be understood as right action undertaken in circumstances where the pleasure-pain or happiness-unhappiness of someone other than the agent (alternatively, of more than one person) is at stake.

Even if we adopted such a restriction on the domain of (the virtue of) justice, however, an anti-commonsensical *self-other symmetry* would still hold for the many cases where the notion was applicable. Ordinary intuitive morality is subject to an asymmetry regarding what an agent may permissibly do to herself and what she may permissibly do to others that I have elsewhere described at considerable length.[13] An agent is normally thought of as morally allowed to do harms or avoid goods to herself that it would be wrong for her to do or avoid to others—one is allowed to sacrifice oneself in a way one may not sacrifice others, and this commonsense asymmetry also extends to matters of justice. What it may be unjust to deny to or lo? .' upon others, it may not be unjust to deny to or load upon oneself—the idea that c .e cannot do oneself an injustice goes back all the way to Aristotle.

But act utilitarianism is self-other symmetric in what it regards as permissible or impermissible, and even if we restrict issues of justice to cases where more than one person's interests are at stake, the symmetry of utilitarian justice leads to stark conflict with the deliverances of commonsense talk and intuition. On any utilitarian account of justice, it is unjust to increase the happiness of others when one could have created a greater sum of happiness by enhancing one's own happiness alone, and this and a host of other examples should make it clear that the clash between commonsense morality and utilitarianism on the subject of justice is in no way eliminated—even if it is to some extent limited—by restricting the sphere of justice to certain sorts of action-situations.

In that case, one may well wonder whether there is any reason for a utilitarian to restrict the sphere of justice. Utilitarianism is fairly comfortable these days with its own clashes with commonsense intuition, and the desire to limit such clashes to the greatest extent possible is not, therefore, a very good utilitarian motive for restricting the sphere of justice. Isn't such a restriction really very anti-utilitarian in spirit; and doesn't it make more sense from the utilitarian standpoint—a standpoint from which considerations of simplicity always have their appeal—to identify the right and the just? Perhaps so, but there are other considerations which may incline the utilitarian toward limiting the sphere of justice. Such a limitation, far from being an atypical complicating move, as viewed from a utilitarian perspective, is quite similar to and no worse motivated than other limitations that utilitarians have imposed on their moral conceptions.

Act utilitarianism, for example, reserves the terms "right" and "wrong" for voluntary (human) actions/acts, rather than allowing those terms to apply to other events involving human (or other rational) beings. But consider how act utilitarianism evaluates actions as right or wrong. Something may not count as an action unless it is motivated and/or backed by some sort of intention, but utilitarianism leaves the particular motivation/intention behind an act out of account in morally assessing it.

Only the act's consequences are relevant to that assessment, and on the quite standard utilitarian view that focuses on actual rather than expectable or probable consequences, the rightness of an action may be independent of its agent's ability to foresee its consequences. But if agential motivation and reasonable belief are to be shunted aside in this fashion, so that what is right or wrong can sometimes be entirely a matter of luck (it turns out to be wrong for Hitler's mother not to have killed Hitler), then why should the utilitarian restrict the terms "right" and "wrong" to human *actions*? Why not treat an agent's involuntary slipping on a banana peel as right or wrong depending on that *event's* more or less foreseeable consequences? I think it might be very difficult for act utilitarianism to justify its restriction on the use of "right" and "wrong",[14] but in the light of that restriction, a proposal to limit the sphere of justice and injustice, say, to actions bearing on the happiness-unhappiness of people other than the agent, however difficult it may be to justify, is clearly not without utilitarian precedent. So let us remain neutral on whether the utilitarian account of justice needs to incorporate limitations on the sphere of the just. The distinctively utilitarian character of such an account remains in either case, and we are now ready, I think, to consider how best to frame similarly utilitarian accounts of the other principal virtues.

IV

What would a utilitarian conception of courage be like? From the account previously given of justice, certain conclusions fall naturally into place and certain questions inevitably arise.

First of all, if we want a distinctive utilitarian view of courage, we cannot treat courage in the way in which Smart dealt with the concept of justice: that is, we cannot concede the correctness of commonsense criteria of courage and question only whether courageous action thus conceived is always morally right or acceptable. Such a move would leave us with no specifically utilitarian view of courage—it would give us only a utilitarian position on the rightness and wrongness of (given instances of) courage. To have a utilitarian conception of courage as a virtue, I think we must follow not Smart, but Bentham: we must recognize and accommodate the oddness of speaking of courage as wrong and cowardice as right, by ruling out the possibility of immoral courage or morally good cowardice. And for a utilitarian this can be done only by making the courageousness or cowardice of an appropriate act depend solely on its overall, long-term results.

As with a utilitarian theory of justice, the implications of such a view run headlong into our ordinary notions about courage. Consider, for example, an individual who out of fear runs from the scene of battle to a position of safety. His action will presumably have to count as an instance of utilitarian courage if, for example, his actions mislead the enemy into a fatal underestimation of the courage of his comrades-in-arms and permit his side to win a victory with overall better results than if he had never fled. Or if his flight so angers his fellow soldiers that they fight better and win a less bloody, optimific victory, that act of fleeing will also count as courageous by the utilitarian account. The typical utilitarian indifference to moral motivation when assessing given actions here leads to ignoring the fearfulness of the person who flees and thus to a judgment concerning his courage that is out of keeping with common sense in much the same way that it is to hold that a malevolently intended action may escape wrongness through its unintended good consequences. And the idea that an act may count as courageous because of the optimific way in which it gives others an example of what not to do is very much in keeping with more general utilitarian ideas of right and wrong: cf. Williams's "reservation" of non-utilitarians whose bad example keeps a host of others from deviating from the true utilitarian path and is therefore optimific and morally right according to act utilitarianism.[15] (Our present examples of utilitarian courage also remind one of cases where it is all right in utilitarian terms to kill one person to prevent the killing of many others.)

A utilitarian account of courage has other implications with interesting similarity to what utilitarian accounts of right and wrong have to swallow. Act utilitarianism seems to entail that it can be wrong not to use extra water during a water shortage because one's private actions will not, in fact, produce any bad results; and by the same token it may be cowardly (or at least not courageous) to join the battle and kill one of the enemy, if a victory less costly by that one death would have been achieved without one's participation; as with right and wrong, a utilitarian view of courage and cowardice allows the applicability of these notions to depend on unforeseeable quirks of circumstance and on the accidental results of confluent events. But if the utilitarian is prepared to accept such unintuitive results in morality generally, I can see no reason for her to flinch from similar results concerning the virtue of courage or of justice.

However, we have so far been considering only examples where the issue of courage vs. cowardice naturally arises, examples connected with death and danger. We must now consider whether a utilitarianism of courage should cast its net more widely and take in cases where such issues do not ordinarily arise. The question, that is, is whether judgments of courage are relevant wherever the rightness or wrongness of an action is at stake, or whether we ought, on utilitarian grounds or precedent, to limit the sphere of courage and cowardice.

We have already seen a similar issue raised in connection with justice. But if every utilitarianly right action can be considered utilitarianly just and we make a similarly expansive move with regard to utilitarian courage (and other virtues), then we very quickly end up with a utilitarian doctrine of the unity of the virtues. Very quickly, but also, I think, very uninterestingly by comparison with the way such a doctrine is arrived at within the Platonic and Aristotelian traditions. From the standpoint of the latter, the doctrine of unity (to the extent it really does follow from their assumptions) is the rather surprising fruit of approaches that take seriously the conceptual and moral differences we normally assume to exist among courage, justice, temperance, and prudence. But a utilitarian unity of the virtues would build that unity into its views on justice, courage, etc., in the most painfully obvious way. Let us not make utilitarian virtue uninteresting by such a step. If there is any excuse to think of justice as absorbing all of morality and thus as applicable to any situation of right or wrong, there is much less excuse to conceive courage and cowardice in this fashion. We need an account of courage that is distinctly utilitarian (this rules out Smart's approach), but that avoids the triviality and uninterestingness that result from treating all virtues alike. And we can achieve this by narrowing the sphere of courage in line with common opinion and philosophical tradition, while at the same time applying a rigorously utilitarian self-other symmetric criterion of courageous action with respect to those actions about which the issue of courage properly arises.

If we limit the applicability of courage and cowardice to actions in response to danger, then we can avoid treating every optimific or beneficent action as an instance of courage, and the sphere of courage will be differentiated from that justice, whatever we say about the latter's relation to rightness generally. The limitation just indicated is certainly inadequate to the precise contours of one's commonsense views about courage—e.g., it fails to distinguish courage from what David Pears calls "darage."[16] But given the way utilitarianism typically prides itself in caring more about good consequences than about fine distinctions of ordinary language, I doubt whether the utilitarian would or should feel a need for further narrowing or complication of the above-mentioned conditions for applying the courage-cowardice distinction. And having said as much, I think we have said all we need to or can say about the utilitarian virtue of courage within present limitations of space. It is time to turn to the remaining cardinal virtues.

V

As far as I can tell, the virtue of temperance presents no special obstacles to utilitarian treatment. Just as it seems natural for utilitarianism to limit application of the term "courageous" to acts in response to (or motives and dispositions pertaining to) danger, the utilitarian may wish to think of temperance as including only actions responsive to (or motives and dispositions pertaining to) an agent's (own) appetites. Alternatively—and as Bentham seems to suggest in the *Deontology*—any action having to do with pleasures of the (agent's) senses might be deemed to fall within the sphere of temperance, and where pleasures, say, of sight and sound are not objects of (bodily) appetite, this latter stipulation would diverge from that first mentioned.[17] On either stipulation—and we need not decide between them here—the realm of the temperate (or moderate) and intemperate (or immoderate) will not include all actions and motives which bear on human happiness. However, on any utilitarian account, an action falling within the sphere of temperance and intemperance will be assessed by the usual consequentialist criteria, counting as temperate or intemperate according as its consequences for human happiness are overall good or bad.

Such a view of temperance has, of course, a number of counterintuitive implications. Because a truly utilitarian view must regard effects on others as just as relevant to the assessment of an act as effects on the agents, what would ordinarily be regarded as an act of intemperance will have to be treated as temperate, if its consequences serve overall human happiness—perhaps by giving errant humanity a powerfully instructive example of how certain behavior can harm the person whose behavior it is. But such results will presumably not be disturbing to utilitarians, and we are clearly now in a position to formulate a utilitarian conception of temperance that can take its place alongside similarly utilitarian views of justice and courage. But prudence raises—or appears to raise—some special problems for any attempt to find utilitarian versions of the cardinal virtues. Analogues of these problems can arise in regard to temperance and even courage, but they emerge most forcefully in connection with prudence, and we must consider them next.

As ordinarily conceived, temperance, courage, and, of course, justice, have rather obvious other-regarding aspects. They are not exclusively, or even primarily, valued for the way they serve their possessors; and indeed their status as virtues in good part connects with the good they do for a larger community, for people other than those who possess these virtues. But prudence seems different; it appears to be exclusively concerned or connected with the good of its possessors, and if that appearance is not misleading, then it will be a fundamental error to aim for a utilitarian conception of this virtue that treats the good of other people as directly relevant to whether an agent is acting prudently.

On a utilitarian view, an action may count as imprudent if it best serves its agent's interests but does so at the expense of overall human good, most particularly, the good of others. And this is decidedly odd. But if there is an error involved here, is it a conceptual one? Can a utilitarian account of prudence be ruled out *a priori,* or are we not rather faced here with another sharp moral disagreement between utilitarianism and ordinary ethical intuitions? It also sounds odd to speak of failures to serve one's own ends as instances of injustice, but utilitarianism wants to hold that such talk is not symptomatic of conceptual error, but, rather, of the greater moral clarity and vision that can be achieved by shuffling off the weight of moral tradition, together with its sediment of intuitions, and making moral assessments from a more rational and impersonal standpoint. And I can see no reason why a utilitarian should not say the same about a utilitarian theory of prudence. It may seem odd to conceive of prudence in terms which give so much weight to the interests of people other than its possessor(s), but, according to utilitarians, that may have little or no force against the validity of such a conception.

But are those objecting to a utilitarianism of prudence even correct about the self-regarding focus of prudence as ordinarily or traditionally conceived? (In the ordinary sense of the term, "prudence" connotes a certain kind of long-range playing it safe. This connotation is largely absent when philosophers regard prudence as equivalent to the notion of practical wisdom, and I shall be assuming the latter equivalence in what follows.) In calling an act prudent, do most people, for example, simply mean that it (expectably) serves the interests of its agent? I think not. We do not typically regard it as imprudent when someone acts against his own self-interest in order to do the just or honorable thing.[18] And an act that flies in the face of justice or honesty but serves the interest of its agent is not naturally thought of as prudent (we are not likely to regard it as imprudent either): if a bank teller, knowing he will not be caught, helps himself to a better life by stealing from his bank, we are reluctant to call him or his actions prudent even if we share his assessment of the chances of his getting caught. So other-regarding considerations and moral justifications play a direct role in what is ordinarily regarded as prudent or imprudent. But, of course, the moral claims that affect ordinary judgments of prudence are made from a commonsense moral standpoint, and utilitarianism disputes the validity of commonsense morality. So it should now be clear how the utilitarian can reply to those who object to the idea of a utilitarian account of prudence.

We have seen that the conceptual tie between prudence (practical wisdom) and acting in one's own self-interest is much less direct than might initially be supposed. In ordinary terms, a self-sacrificing act may not count as imprudent if it is morally required and/or praiseworthy, and a successfully self-interested act may not be regarded as prudent if it is seen as dishonorable or otherwise immoral. So the moral justification of an action is *on conceptual grounds* relevant to the question of its prudence, but the moral claims that we ordinarily treat as relevant to such questions are most typically commonsense ones whose validity the utilitarian would dispute. And if we substitute utilitarian moral justifications for ordinary ones in determining what is or is not prudent, we end up with a utilitarian theory of prudence. In summary then: if, as our ordinary judgments about prudence implicitly allow, moral justification is directly relevant to judgments of prudence and imprudence, and if, as the utilitarian holds, the only valid kind of moral justification must ultimately be cast in utilitarian terms, there can be no objection to a utilitarian account of prudence which treats acts as prudent or imprudent depending on whether they serve overall human happiness, and so are morally justified, or oppose such happiness, and so are morally unjustified.

As a result, any act which serves the (maximal) good of its agent but not (maximal) overall human good will then lack a utilitarian moral justification and therefore fail to exemplify the utilitarian virtue of prudence. But the violence this does to our ordinary intuitions is, as we now can see, primarily attributable to the assumptions of utilitarian morality, rather than to any violation of the meaning of "prudence." The relevance of moral constraints and justifications is built into ordinary usage of this term, and cannot be regarded as the alien imposition of a utilitarianism overleaping its proper boundaries. So if act utilitarianism is the correct view of right action, a utilitarianism of prudence and other virtues is entirely appropriate and will bear to more traditional treatments of the virtues something like the relation act utilitarianism bears to commonsense views about right and wrong action. A utilitarianism of virtue and of the particular virtues can be as strong as other forms of utilitarianism, and at this point, therefore, the case for and against utilitarian virtue seems to blend with the case for and against more familiar forms of utilitarianism. In the next, and final, section of this essay, I want to talk about some considerations that threaten commonsense ethical views and may well strengthen the general utilitarian position.

VI

I earlier made brief reference to the self-other asymmetry of the commonsense morality of right and wrong and of justice and injustice. But the discussion we have just concluded allows us to see that the commonsense ethics of *virtue* in fact contains a *pair* of symmetrically related asymmetries. We know that certain ways of failing to help others count against the justice of one's actions in a way that relevantly similar failure to help oneself does not. And so our commonsense understanding of justice is structured by an agent-sacrificing self-other asymmetry. On the other hand, commonsense prudence seems subject to a precisely opposite, agent-favoring asymmetry. For certain ways of failing to help oneself would ordinarily be taken to count against the prudence of one's actions in a way that parallel failures to help others would not. (It is true that morality and justice are ordinarily taken to permit agents to give preference to their own good, but such agent-relative agent-favoring permissions do not give rise to an agent-favoring self-other *asymmetry* with respect to justice, because ordinary justice and morality also allow agents to give preference to the good of *others.*)

By contrast, a utilitarianism of virtue sweeps away both the above-mentioned asymmetries and treats prudence, justice, courage, and temperance as uniformly self-other symmetric. The unity and simplicity thereby achieved is, however, counterbalanced by the many clashes with ordinary intuition such a uniform account entails. And so it might seem at this point that a genuine stand-off exists between utilitarianism and intuitive accounts of the virtues. But I think the situation is actually worse for commonsense ethical views than their defenders have realized. Self-other asymmetry seems irrational and unmotivated, to be sure, from the impersonal perspective of utilitarian ethics, but problems arise for such an asymmetry even from within the perspective of commonsense ethical thinking. Commonsense morality itself has a difficult time making sense of its commitment to a self-other asymmetry of right and wrong (or justice and injustice).

To begin with—and I have argued the point at much greater length elsewhere—the difference between what we may do to ourselves and what we may do to others is not attributable to the factor of consent. It is morally worse negligently to harm another than negligently to harm oneself, but in neither case is consent likely to be present. But apart, for a moment, from whether we can explain or justify the asymmetry—after all, it may represent a ground-floor intuitive assumption—there is the difficulty of *reconciling it with other aspects of commonsense morality.*

Unlike act utilitarianism, ordinary morality treats our obligations to others as dependent on how near they stand to us in relations of affection or special commitment: obligations to our immediate family (other things being equal) being stronger than to our relations generally, obligations to friends and relations being stronger than to compatriots generally, and obligations to the latter, in turn, being stronger than to the people of other countries. To that extent, ordinary morality reflects the normal structure of an adult's concerns. We are naturally more concerned about and have more reason to be concerned about the well-being of friends and relations than of more distant others, and commonsense morality seems to build such differences into the varyingly strong duties it assigns us to concern ourselves with others' well-being. However, by means of its self-other asymmetry, commonsense morality also superimposes an absolute moral discontinuity on the structure of concern in which each agent is normally situated. On the one hand, it encourages the idea that strength of obligation weakens as one gets further from the agent, but on the other hand, and in seeming opposition to the first idea, it assumes that there is no moral obligation whatever (except indirectly) for the agent to benefit *himself.* Once one leaves the agent behind, the agent's obligations vary in proportion to his reason for concern, but where he has greatest reason for concern in the natural course of things, he has no direct obligation whatever. And this appears odd and unmotivated even apart from any utilitarian or consequentialist perspective (though the latter provides a way out of the oddness, the seeming inconsistency or discontinuity).

In fact some well-known attempts have been made to explain away or justify the self-other asymmetry (or some aspects of it), but in the light of what has just been said, those attempts make the picture appear even bleaker for commonsense morality by making it appear impossible to make sense of the above-mentioned discontinuity in commonsense thinking. Let me explain.

Both Butler and Kant point out that one can (attempt to) account for the (apparent) lack of moral duties to provide for one's own good in terms of normal human desires and instincts and plausible assumptions about their influence on our actions. We can be expected to take care of ourselves most of the time, and that, according to the account, is why there is no need for morality to impose obligations or duties to do so.[19] But such an explanation immediately gets into trouble if we consider (as Butler and Kant do not) the facts about our relations to other people that we mentioned above. We can normally be expected to take better care of our spouse and children than of distant others, yet our obligations to the former are stronger than to the latter, and this is just the opposite of what one would expect if the above account were correct about duties to seek one's own good. But it is commonsensically very natural to try to explain and justify the self-other moral asymmetry, and more particularly the absence of duties to seek one's own good, in terms of what is normal and expectable, and I think this is additional proof of how much common sense is at odds with itself in this general area. What seems like the only possible and sensible explanation of the self-other asymmetry makes nonsense out of another aspect of commonsense morality, and these internal difficulties of ordinary thought about right and wrong offer some reason, I think, to favor a utilitarianism or consequentialism that eliminates the difficulties by insisting on complete self-other symmetry in its account both of right action and of particular virtues.[20]

Nor are these internal difficulties the only ones that can be pointed to in commonsense morality. In his recent *The Rejection of Consequentialism*,[21] Samuel Scheffler shows that the most natural and appealing explanation of why it is (ordinarily considered) wrong to kill one person to prevent a greater number of persons from being killed actually undercuts what it attempts to justify. If the wrongness is attributed (roughly) to the sheer badness of killings, then the difficult question arises how it can be objectionable to act in such a way as to minimize the occurence of such bad (or horrible or objectionable) actions. Common sense thus here again seems at odds with itself, because the reasons it is inclined to offer in its own support actually tend to cast further doubt upon it.

Some moral philosophers have recently told us that theory is out of place in ethics and that an intuitive approach to ethics makes more sense than consequentialism or utilitarianism, with their self-styled theoretical aspirations. But this assumes that an entirely intuitive approach can give us what we need in this area, and the situation turns out to be less favorable to such an approach than this attitude presupposes. Rather, the situation in ethics is much more like what we find in the area of confirmation—to take just one example—where our intuitive gropings toward general principles and explanations of our ordinary judgments about what confirms what have been shown (by Hempel) to lead to inconsistency. Such a result is an invitation to philosophical theorizing of a sort empowered *to discard some strong intuitions*. And the situation in ethics seems, in the light of what has been said above, to be somewhat similar. Commonsense ethics, when fully and consistently followed out, leads to inconsistencies and/or glaring inadequacies, and that is an invitation to theorizing about right and wrong and virtue. To the extent utilitarianism takes up that invitation and can avoid commonsense morality's problems it may meet a challenge that common sense itself presents, and to the extent it does not fall prey to similar inconsistencies, its rejection of ordinary intuitions may be vindicated and a strong prima facie case is made for its superiority to the commonsense ethics both of right and wrong and of the virtues.

Notes

1. See, for example, Robert Adams's "Motive Utilitarianism," *Journal of Philosophy* 73 (1976); 467–81; and Slote, "Object-Utilitarianism," *Pacific Philosophical Quarterly* 66 (1985): 11–24. In what follows, I shall assume the correctness of recent criticisms of rule utilitarianism and shall, therefore, be discussing only *direct* consequentialist evaluation.

2. See Adams, "Motive Utilitarianism."

3. See *An Introduction to the Principles of Morals and Legislation* edited by Burns and Hart (London, 1982), 3.

4. On this point, see, of course, the *Deontology* itself (Oxford, 1983), but also Ross Harrison's *Bentham* (London, 1983) chap. 10.

5. *Introduction,* 100. Also see pp. 96ff., 114f., 125.

6. Bentham never considers the possibility that a motive might have to have better consequences than any other (or any relevant alternative) in order to count as good, and such a view does not, in any event, seem very plausible. Bentham uses a criterion of optimificness only for right *action,* and even here he is inconsistent; in some very prominent places he indicates that overall *good* consequences are a sufficient condition of an act's rightness. On this point, see Slote, *Common-sense Morality and Consequentialism* (London, 1985), chap. 3.

7. *Introduction,* 120n.

8. See Smart, "An Outline of a System of Utilitarian Ethics" in *Utilitarianism: For and Against,* edited by Smart and Williams (Cambridge, 1973), section 10.

9. Using Hare's terminology, we can say that Bentham treats the evaluative meaning of "justice" as primary and changes its descriptive meaning so that it accords with his commitment to utilitarianism, whereas Smart gives primacy to the descriptive meaning and, on utilitarian grounds, modifies or seeks to modify the term's evaluative meaning.

Note further that if Bentham wants to avoid the oddness of calling unjust actions right, he may have reason to avoid the frequent utilitarian assumption that right actions may be blameworthy (i.e., right to blame). There are several maneuvers open to him, but I do not want to take up this problem here.

10. I would like to leave open the question whether all good human dispositions can be considered virtues.

11. See *Deontology,* 127, 220.

12. See *A Theory of Justice* (Cambridge, Mass., 1971) 26, also 187. The idea that utilitarian justice and injustice are applicable to every action is more explicit in S. Scheffler's *The Rejection of Consequentialism* (Oxford, 1982), 33.

13. See chap. 1 of Slote, *Common-sense Morality and Consequentialism.*

14. It is much easier for Kantianism and commonsense morality, with their stress on factors of motivation and intention in the evaluation of actions, to justify such a restriction.

15. See Williams, "A Critique of Utilitarianism," in *Utilitarianism: For and Against,* p. 130.

16. See Pears, "Aristotle's Analysis of Courage," in *Midwest Studies in Philosophy* 3, (1978): 273–85.

17. See *Deontology,* 213.

18. On this point, see Foot, "Are Moral Considerations Overriding?" in *Virtues and Vices,* (Oxford, 1978), p. 187.

19. See Butler's "A Dissertation upon the Nature of Virtue" in *The Analogy of Religion,* (London, 1736); and the Preface of Kant's *Metaphysical Elements of Ethics.* Butler is skeptical

about the account, but for reasons which, I believe, are ultimately less telling against common-sense morality than those offered here.

20. It is an interesting question just how much self-other asymmetry Aristotle wishes to admit into his views on justice, practical wisdom, and right action.

21. Scheffler, *Rejection of Consequentialism,* esp. chap. 4. Commonsense morality also seems to be inconsistent on the subject of moral luck. See, on this point, Slote, *Common-sense Morality,* chap. 7, and various works cited there.

How Thinking about Character and Utilitarianism Might Lead to Rethinking the Character of Utilitarianism

PETER RAILTON

I

"One cannot properly judge actions by their outcomes alone. The motive from which an act is performed is independently important, and makes a distinctive contribution to moral assessment not only of the actor, but of the action. Moreover, if morality is to achieve a secure place in individual lives and social practices, it is necessary that agents develop firm characters to guide their choices and to provide others with a stable basis of expectation and trust. Any sensible moral theory therefore must give a central role to the encouragement and possession of virtuous character."

When such thoughts are heard, can it be more than a moment before a condemnation of act utilitarianism follows? Still, many critics of *act* utilitarianism remain drawn to what I will call the guiding utilitarian idea, namely, that the final ground of moral assessment—including assessment of character—must lie in effects on people's well-being.[1] For such critics, a favored strategy has been to turn to indirect forms of utilitarianism, such as rule utilitarianism. And indeed, moral philosophers in general appear increasingly to be convinced that *if* utilitarianism is to be defensible, it will be in an indirect form.

Perhaps, then, with the above remarks about the importance of character fresh in our minds and with some sympathy for the guiding utilitarian idea alive in our hearts, we should consider the possibility of formulating an indirect utilitarianism worthy of the name *character utilitarianism*. And that is indeed what I propose to do, by considering two forms character utilitarianism might take. In the end, however, it will seem doubtful whether either form can satisfactorily accommodate our concerns about character, and this will in a roundabout way tell us something about how utilitarianism has been conceived and about how a reconception of it might better serve the guiding utilitarian idea. Sometimes in philosophy, getting there is half the fun. In the case of character utilitarianism, not getting there will have to be all of it.

II

One form character utilitarianism might take would follow the model of rule utilitarianism and hold that an act is right just in case it would be done by someone having a character,[2] the general possession of which would bring about at least as much utility as any alternative.

To assess this possibility, let us look directly to the model. Rule utilitarianism sometimes is defended along lines that echo the remarks about character voiced at the outset: "We need rules in moral life because it is a poor idea to send moral agents into the world without the guidance they afford. Moral decisions often involve complex problems that call for large amounts of information and stable, coordinated responses. Further, individuals inevitably slant deliberation in their own favor. If moral agents were left to their own devices it would be worse overall than if they were to follow shared rules of the kind that would be chosen on broadly utilitarian grounds."

For present purposes, let us define rule utilitarianism as the moral theory that deems an act right just in case the act conforms to a set of rules the general acceptance of which would bring about at least as much utility as any alternative.[3] Do the above reflections about the need for rules lend support to rule utilitarianism?

Nothing in rule utilitarianism as here defined inherently mitigates against case-by-case deliberation by individual moral agents. Since it is highly unlikely that the rules prevalent in any given agent's society are optimal, it is as much the task of a rule-utilitarian deliberator to figure out which sets of rules would be optimal as it is the task of an act-utilitarian deliberator to figure out which acts would be.[4] In answering such questions the rule-utilitarian deliberator would face essentially similar problems arising from changing or incomplete information, tendencies toward personal bias, and the like. And a society of rule-utilitarian deliberators would have problems of coordination akin to those afflicting act-utilitarian deliberators. Indeed, since multiple sets of rules may be optimal, even well-informed, unbiased, continent rule-utilitarian deliberators could fail to coordinate.[5] Finally, although rule utilitarianism places the question whether an act *would conform to* certain rules at the center of moral evaluation, it characteristically attaches no direct significance to the question whether an act *is in fact done from respect for* a rule.

Rule utilitarianism is a theory of the moral rightness of individual acts, not a moral endorsement of rules or rule-following deliberation or rule-governed action. To be sure, it is an indirect theory, for it applies the test of utility to rules rather than individual acts. But its appeal to rules in giving a criterion of the rightness of acts must not be confused with its according actual, shared rules—and their many benefits—a prominent place in moral life. It might of course turn out that acts promoting the widespread adoption and following of useful rules would be approved by rule utilitarianism; but then equally it might turn out that such acts would be approved by act utilitarianism. The case of rule utilitarianism should make us wary of the idea that if one is concerned about X's, one should be an X-utilitarian.

Similarly, character utilitarianism, if defined as above, is a theory of the rightness of individual acts, and although it appeals to character in giving a criterion of rightness, it no more than act utilitarianism assigns a special place to the cultivation or exercise of character in practice, and it no more than act utilitarianism makes the moral evaluation of an act depend upon the motive from which the act was actually performed.

III

Perhaps, then, character utilitarianism should be built on a different model. We might take its lines from motive utilitarianism, as recently discussed by Robert M. Adams,[6] and adopt as its ultimate concern the moral value of actual possession of character. Suppose we were to define character utilitarianism as the moral theory according to which a character is morally better the higher the utility of general possession of that character. Would this give us what we want?

Not obviously. Once again, let us examine the model before the copy. The characterization of motive utilitarianism that Adams seems to prefer is the following: A motive, among those humanly possible, is morally better the higher the average utility of anyone's having it on any occasion.[7]

Motive utilitarianism begins with the moral evaluation of actual possession of motives—but it also ends there. It does not, for example, tell us whether right action depends upon motive. Indeed, it has no implications, even indirect, for the assessment of actions. The having of a motive is not an action; and though the cultivation of morally good motives normally would involve various sorts of actions, motive utilitarianism is silent on whether we should act in such a way as to encourage good motives in ourselves or others (as Adams notes, p. 481). Moreover, in the assessment of motives it ignores a range of questions that would be central to any discussion of the appropriate role of motives in our moral life, e.g., questions about the cost or likelihood of bringing people to have certain motives, and so on.

Motive utilitarianism is what William K. Frankena has called an *aretaic* theory—a normative theory of moral *value*— and thus stands in contrast with *deontic* theories—normative theories of moral *obligation*.[8] Deontic theories take as fundamental the question what it would be morally right or wrong to do, whereas aretaic theories take as fundamental the question what would be morally good or bad. Among deontic theories are divine command ethics, natural law ethics, Kantian ethics, and act and rule utilitarianism; among aretaic theories, ethics of virtue and motive utilitarianism. Adams draws this distinction in his own way by distinguishing the (deontic) question 'What should I do?' from the (aretaic) question 'Have I lived well?' and he remarks that motive utilitarianism is concerned with questions of the latter sort (p. 474). He in effect observes that an aretaic theory need not be bound by a constraint comparable to the *"ought* implies *can"* restriction on deontic theories, for he notes that one may be liable to the judgment that one has not lived well even though one's life has been among the best of those "causally possible" for one to lead (p. 475). It is, for example, legitimate within an aretaic theory to ask, "Is Jack morally perfect?" where this question is only minimally bounded by the bare constraints of what it takes to be a person.[9] It is legitimate to ask this, and not to worry about whether Jack is actually capable of moral perfection, because an aretaic judgment of perfection does not imply that he *ought* to be perfect, or is *obligated* to be perfect, or is *wrong* for being imperfect.[10]

It comes as something of a surprise, then, when Adams speaks of motives as "right" (p. 471), says that "from a motive-utilitarian point of view Jack ought . . . to have been as weakly interested in maximizing utility as he was" (pp. 471–72), and worries therefore about "incompatibility" between "right action, by act-utilitarian standards" and "right motivation, by motive-utilitarian standards" (p. 475). However, since rightness in action concerns choice among causally possible options, whereas having the best motives (at least, according to motive utilitarianism) does not, it is not obvious that there is a common dimension of assessment along which this incompatibility could arise.

To adapt an example of Adams's: Wretch that I am, I cannot have the best motives humanly possible, and so I could not bring myself to "love righteousness and my neighbors"; instead, "I did my duty out of fear of hellfire for the most part" (p. 475). Act utilitarianism says that if indeed I did do my duty, then I acted rightly, for doing my duty amounted to acting in ways, of those available to me, most conducive to net utility. Motive utilitarianism does not contradict this by telling me I did anything wrong. Rather, it simply says that, whatever I did, I failed to possess the best sort of motives humanly possible. Is there any incompatibility here? (Is there any incompatibility in saying, "Lefty pitches the baseball as fast as he can, as fast as any coach could ask him to, but he still is not the best fastball pitcher humanly possible"?)

Perhaps incompatibility is more likely to arise when we shift from general to specific standards of excellence, and confine ourselves to that which is causally possible for given individuals. We might for example ask not whether Jack has perfect motives, but whether he has the best motives among those possible for him. Here 'best possible' presumably means "bringing about—directly by their possession or indirectly by their effects—at least as much net utility as any others he might actually have had." However, this last phrase is ambiguous. One way Jack might have had better motives is that he might have been brought up differently, had better luck in his youth, and so on. (Lefty pitches as fast as he can, but still is not the best fastball pitcher he could have been, since he might have had better coaching in Little League.) Such possibilities raise no issues about the rightness of Jack's actions, for they are not acts on his part.

Alternatively, Jack might have had better motives as a result of having made different choices or tried harder. Would this show that he did not act rightly? Whenever a choice is made that affects what motives one will have, the utility or disutility of the consequences of this choice will in part be the direct or indirect result of one's possession of these motives. Suppose Jack has made motive-affecting choices in ways that did not bring him to have the best possible motives of those available to him. Still, he may have acted rightly, since the costs that would have been involved in acquiring motives that would subsequently have made the greatest possible contribution to utility—as opposed to more easily acquired motives whose subsequent contribution was less—might have been sufficiently high to offset the gains. Thus an act-utilitarian standard of right action need not recommend choosing in such a way as to have the best possible motives among those causally accessible to the agent.[11] This might be thought to be a kind of incompatibility between act and motive utilitarianism.

Consider now the other direction of comparison. Could it be the case that if Jack had the best possible motives (of those causally accessible to him) he would in some circumstances act wrongly by act-utilitarian standards? It may bring about the greatest utility on the whole if Jack is strongly motivated to be honest, so strongly that he does not even try to deceive—though he would succeed were he to try—in some cases in which this would be optimal. This could come about if the psychological changes necessary for Jack to become more likely to deceive in such cases would inevitably increase Jack's tendency to deceive in many non-optimal cases as well. Thus there is no necessary coincidence between having the best motives by motive-utilitarian standards and acting rightly by act-utilitarian standards. This, too, might seem an incompatibility.

It can be replied that there is no strict incompatibility in either case, since judgments of the rightness of acts and judgments of the goodness of (possession of) motives lack a common subject matter. (Lefty has the best strikeout record in the league, but a mediocre earned-run average.) Motive utilitarianism, even in its individualistic form (p. 480), does not imply that one ought to have the best motives among those available. And act utilitarianism, because it does not until supplemented—e.g., by motive utilitarianism—contain a theory of moral value, does not imply that the moral value of motives is determined exclusively by their contribution to right action.

IV

Yet one who aspires to be a character utilitarian may find this rather beside the point. For, to him, the issue is not one of incompatibility in a logical sense. Rather, he has the concerns about the place of character in morality expressed in the opening paragraph of this paper, and he thinks, "If I accept both character utilitarianism and act utilitarianism, then an evaluative dualism may arise in which what I deem right in action lacks an appropriate connection with what I deem good in character. In a number of cases, the two aspects of evaluation will simply go their separate ways, whereas my hope was to integrate them."[12]

Suppose, for example, that part of the best character available to Mel is a powerful sense of parental responsibility. This is so, we may suppose, because with this sense he will receive great satisfaction from helping his child—a highly useful thing that he is more likely to do, and do well, if he finds enjoyment in it—and because without it he would become more self-absorbed and less motivated to take into account the interests of others in general. Consider now a choice he faces between conferring a smallish benefit upon his young son and conferring a considerably larger benefit upon people unknown to him. Mel could spend an afternoon taking his son and a friend on an outing he knows they would especially like, or he could find a sitter to mind his son at home while he goes out to spend the afternoon canvassing for grass-roots economic development in Central America.

We need not imagine that the sort of parental concern that would be part of the best character available to Mel is one which would dispose him in such cases *always* to elect to spend time with his child—surely there would be room for activities of both sorts. But suppose that on this particular Saturday Mel has just returned home from an extended, utility-maximizing trip. An act-utilitarian computation reveals that it nonetheless would bring about more intrinsic good were he to go door-to-door for agricultural self-help projects. All things considered—including, for example, long-term effects on his character and his relation with his son—it would be wrong according to act utilitarianism for Mel to take his son on the outing, and he accordingly is morally obliged not to do so. Yet it may also be the case that if Mel had the best sort of character available to him he would on this Saturday deliberately sidestep his all-things-considered obligation and go on the outing. And here there is a rub. The normative force of claims about "the best sort of character" available to one is unclear and perhaps unimpressive or unpointed in comparison to claims about one's "all-things-considered moral obligation." It is not unusual in ethics to come across conflicts among duties each of which is weighty, but this case is of a different nature. An all-things-considered duty stands on one side, while on the other there is no duty at all, for motive utilitarianism does not enjoin us to act as someone with good character would. So if, contrary to duty, Mel does go on the outing—either because he has a good character or because he is trying to act as someone with good character would—how is Mel to regard the moral status of what he is doing? And how can Mel really embrace his character in a moral sense? Yet it may be crucial to achieving the good effects of this character that he so embrace it.

An act utilitarian can respond that the impression that judgments of character are inconsequential in guiding action is something like an illusion of perspective. When we broaden our gaze to take in decisions that will affect the sort of character we have—and many of our decisions have such effects—we will find within act utilitarianism all the injunctive force we need to give weight to character. Act utilitarianism does not tell us to maximize episodes of right action; its concern is only and always with maximizing utility.[13] Thus when Mel contemplates his past, and considers choices that would have altered his commitment to his child in such a way as to have made it likely that he would have decided to go door-to-door that Saturday, he will see that, on our hypothesis,[14] he was at the time under an all-things-considered act-utilitarian injunction to act to promote instead a parental commitment that would lead him to favor going on the outing. Here, the act utilitarian argues, is the sought-after normative affirmation of character: the best way to achieve good results almost always involves taking seriously the development of firm character, where "taking seriously" includes embracing a character even though it will sometimes lead to wrong action.

If our would-be character utilitarian complains that what he wanted was an affirmation of the intrinsic rather than strategic value of character, the act utilitarian has two lines of reply. First, to the extent that the character utilitarian has in mind whatever intrinsic *non*moral value character may have, the act utilitarian of course affirms this and allows it to enter directly into his calculations of utility. Second, to the extent that the character utilitarian has in mind whatever intrinsic *moral* value character may have, then he is in effect supposing the falsity of his own view, since the point of character utilitarianism is to give an account of moral value without appealing to any notion of *intrinsic* moral goodness.

Of course, the sorts of character that act utilitarianism would recommend that we develop will not in general be exactly the ones that an aretaic character utilitarian would identify as "best (among those available) to have." For, as we have already noted in connection with motives, act utilitarianism takes into account not only how much utility arises from the having of a character, but also how much is lost or gained in the acquiring, teaching, or encouraging of a character, and how much utility arises from act-affected sources other than character and the consequences of character. However, the value of having a character will certainly figure prominently in act-utilitarian assessment, and so character-utilitarian evaluations will certainly have a place in the scheme. Moreover, one can accept an act-utilitarian account of rightness in action without being (what might be called) a *hegemonic* act utilitarian, that is, without believing that all moral evaluation is based at bottom upon evaluations of the rightness of acts. One could, for example, hold that whenever there is direct concern with moral evaluation of character, character utilitarianism can stand entirely on its own alongside act utilitarianism, fielding whatever questions come its way.

V

Still, the aspiring character utilitarian may have the uncomfortable sense that his concerns have somehow been shoved to the periphery. Perhaps act utilitarianism can issue an endorsement of cultivating firm traits of character, but some of the issues raised by the remarks about character and action with which this paper began remain unresolved.

First, what of the idea that motives make a distinctive contribution to the moral assessment of an act, a contribution in some ways independent of the consequences of the act?

Suppose that Frank has a character that is among the best available to him, and that indeed is among the best humanly possible. But he is human, and in order that he be sufficiently sensitive to, and critical of, unjustified inequality he must also harbor a trace of resentment of just about any inequality. As a result, he finds a certain satisfaction in seeing those of high status taken down a peg or two. An opportunity presents itself for him to facilitate this in the large firm for which he works. He is asked his candid opinion of Richard, a superior in the firm who is being considered for an employee award. Now Frank is honest and cooperative. And his honest opinion is that Richard is worthy, though overrated. Ordinarily, Frank's reluctance to damage a candidate's chances for something as peripheral as an employee award would outweigh his cooperative desire to supply an honest answer to a legitimate question, and he would find some polite way—undamaging to the candidate— to beg off. In this case, however, he reflects for a moment, and then quite deliberately says, "I think he's overrated, though, of course, there is no question of such a choice actually embarrassing you." Frank is giving a candid opinion, and one that he has reason to believe will have good effects, since it seems likely to advance the candidacy of some less senior employees whom Frank believes to be at least as deserving of the award as Richard and also to be more likely to benefit significantly from it. But deep down Frank is also hoping that his carefully chosen remark will tilt the decision against Richard, and what lies behind his hope is largely the idea that this would be something good *not* happening to Richard, to whom so many good things have already happened. However, without realizing it, Frank has said exactly what his questioner wanted to hear—the only thing holding up giving the award to Richard was precisely this person's idiosyncratic fear that the choice would somehow prove embarrassing.

Suppose now that for the award to go to Richard would for complicated reasons do considerably more good than Frank had imagined—so much more that Frank's response turns out to have been utility maximizing. Yet don't we feel a bit queasy about the moral status of Frank's action? Are we content to call it right, as an act-utilitarian standard would indicate?[15] And if the function of a character-utilitarian standard is simply to answer questions about the moral value of character within the realm of what is causally possible for humans, then it too will find nothing to criticize about Frank—he is as good as a human can be. What would seem to be needed is a way of reaching a motivation-related evaluation that applies to individual actions and that is not a function solely of consequences.

Second, we have not fully quieted the earlier worry about chafing between acting from good character and the act-utilitarian insistence that it is always all-things-considered obligatory to maximize the good. The possibility of chafing does not exist because, as it is sometimes said, act utilitarianism requires that agents actually consult the test of utility in deliberating about their choices.[16] Insofar as deliberation is an action, or can be influenced by action, act utilitarianism requires optimality, whether or not this involves distinctively utilitarian deliberation or a resolve to act in an optimal way, and it may on occasion (or even always) involve neither, but rather a tendency to act, say, from character.[17]

Instead, chafing threatens largely because it seems to us so plausible that acting optimally will not infrequently require action that in one way or another goes against good character. The conflict suggested in the case of Mel, between optimal action and the natural action-tendencies of parental concern, arises not only on the odd Saturday afternoon, but daily, whenever he faces a decision about how to make use of his time or money or energy. And it arises not only for parental concern, but for any special relation he might have with other individuals or groups, or with his work or avocations. The ubiquity of such potential for conflict in Mel's life—and in our lives— is the joint product of human psychology and the world in which we and Mel now find ourselves. On the one side, there are many in severe need who could benefit dramatically from reallocation even of small resources. On the other, there are few among those with ample resources who could be unstintingly responsive to this need except at great personal cost. Not all of this cost would be due to selfishness in any narrow or pejorative sense. For some will arise from possible impairment of an individual's ability to have in any deep way the more particular attachments and engagements of family, friendship, and work that anchor the self and supply much of the structure and interest of life.

To be sure, act utilitarianism does not tell us to set out to destroy these attachments in order to clear the way for doing impersonal good. It can recognize that people will be able to act reliably to promote the general good only if they can sustain the integrity and interest of their own lives. Act utilitarianism, therefore, may school us in the importance of acting so as to develop and maintain practices and characters that merge a tendency to promote general well-being with other psychological characteristics that lend integrity and interest to lives. So far so good. But it tells us one thing further: Someone with as good a character as possible in this sense nonetheless does what is morally *impermissible* whenever, owing to such character, he fails to the slightest degree to optimize when given the chance.

There will be cases in which it is uncontroversial that the best character available to an agent can lead to wrong action. Consider the example involving Frank, but remove the supposition that Frank could have had reasonable confidence that his remark would have positive effects overall. Assume, perhaps, that he knows Richard to be aware of being in the running for the award and to be prone to respond in an exaggerated way to anything that hints of failure. Assume that Frank can (correctly) see that these considerations would be just enough to make it optimal in the circumstances to keep his opinion of Richard to himself. And assume that, when voiced, Frank's opinion will—as he hopes—steer the award away from Richard. Thus redescribed, Frank's action would count as wrong by an act-utilitarian standard. And it would probably strike most of us as morally wrong, even though it would stem from the best character available to him.

But there are many cases on the other side. It is rather unintuitive, for example, to judge it morally wrong for Mel to go on the Saturday afternoon outing. In a more general example, the most generous people I know give something like 15 percent of their income to charities and other worthwhile causes. Assume that this approaches the "maximum sustainable yield" for most people. Perhaps anyone who committed himself on a regular basis to giving substantially more, say, 30 percent, would after several years feel so cramped that he would lose interest in the whole thing. Or perhaps he would have so hardened his heart against providing for his own or his family's "less needy" desires as to become a crank whose example leads his children to swear off all but minimal charitable contributions for the remainder of their natural lives. Yet, on any given occasion of making a gift, any of my generous friends could give more than 15 percent without noticeable harm and to considerable good effect. Thus, on each occasion when they give 15 percent they act wrongly, contrary to their moral duty. That is, with regard to charitable giving, they act wrongly almost all the time. In that respect, they act like me, even though I give only a few percent. Wrong is wrong, after all.

But most of us would be inclined to say that they do not really act like me—they act much better. Indeed, it would accord with ordinary usage to say that when they give 15 percent they not only act better, they act rightly, even beyond the call of duty.

This would sit comfortably alongside the idea that they have something close to the best character available to them. But it contradicts act utilitarianism.

Now act utilitarians will rush to tell us that they have the wherewithall to explain the moral distinction between my acts and those of my more generous friends. For example, act utilitarians can distinguish the question whether an act is wrong from the question whether it would be right to blame the agent for it. Yet I may be morally countersuggestive while my generous friends, bless them, respond constructively to moral criticism. If criticized, they would nudge their annual charitable contributions still closer to the sustainable limit and add some further, exceptional gifts from time to time. Thus it could be right in act-utilitarian terms to blame them for giving "only" 15 percent, but not to blame me for giving a paltry few percent. Similarly, to heap praise upon the charitable acts of such people might simply embarrass them and fill the rest of us with envy and self-loathing, making us less charitable out of a mixture of spite and increased consumption as we apply to our wounded self-esteem the balm of luxury.

If indirect act-utilitarian approaches seem not to yield the judgments wanted, an act utilitarian might attempt to generate the judgments directly by introducing a vocabulary of degrees of wrongness in which to say that, for example, while both my giving 2 percent and their giving 15 percent are wrong, mine is wronger. Yet wrongness may not be the concept for the job.

For a start, 'right' and 'wrong' mark a binary distinction—hence the oddness of 'wronger'—and it may be useful in moral theorizing to keep them that way, especially since we already have a serviceable vocabulary of degree in moral assessment: 'better' and 'worse', 'more valuable' and 'less valuable', and so on.

More importantly, the binary character of 'right' and 'wrong' reflects deeper facts about their use. Right and wrong are quasi-juridical notions, linked to requirement and impermissibility, and it is clear why this is usually seen as a dualism— perhaps with a vague boundary—rather than as a matter of degree.

Now it seems inconsistent with anything like our ordinary understanding of 'morally right' to say that the boundary separating the right from the wrong is to be sharply drawn infinitesimally below the very best action possible. 'Wrong' does mark a kind of discontinuity in moral evaluation, but one associated with real unacceptability. For this reason 'right', though not itself a matter of degree, covers actions that are entirely acceptable given reasonable expectations as well as those that are optimal. 'Wrong' comes into clear application only when we reach actions far enough below normal expectations to warrant real criticism or censure.

As quasi-juridical notions, rightness and wrongness are to be found ready-made in some conceptions of the basis of morality, such as those of divine command and natural law. Not so in the case of the underlying conception of utilitarianism, which consists not in laws or commands directed at individuals, but in overall states of affairs that realize varying amounts of value. Individual acts are parts of these states of affairs, and are both bearers and causes of value. But they are not the only parts, the only bearers, or the only causes. Intrinsic good is realizable in human lives through being and doing alike—through experience, acts, characters, institutions, and practices. All of these phenomena interact, and the utilitarian perspective upon them—

and the value they realize—is global rather than local, symmetrical rather than agent-centered. (Perhaps for these reasons, a direct utilitarian standard has always had greater plausibility as a criterion of choice in public policy than in personal ethics.[18]) Obviously a complex treatment will be needed to accommodate within a scheme of global, symmetrical evaluations of continuously valued states of affairs an account of one multiply entangled, discontinuous, asymmetrical, local component of moral evaluation, such as rightness in action.

The utilitarian can—and typically does—pull out one contributor to value and one component of moral evaluation and link them in a fairly simple, direct or indirect way. The act utilitarian does this in giving his account of moral rightness. 'Right' becomes as a result a term of art, and incongruities arise partly because most of us will continue to understand the term as carrying many of its traditional connections—for example, with reasonable expectations, praising and blaming, etc.—and partly, too, because the utilitarian himself continues to draw upon some traditional connections—for example, with all-things-considered obligation. A dilemma may present itself. Either the act utilitarian is also making, say, 'all-things-considered obligation' a term of art—with a change in its role that removes obligation so far from reasonable expectation that we no longer expect most people in our society to come close to carrying out their obligations—or the act utilitarian is retaining our familiar sense of, and role for, 'all-things-considered obligation', in which case most people will be amazed at what is expected of them and at what they are liable to criticism for failing to do.[19]

The source of this dilemma is familiar in contemporary philosophy. Once one accepts a reasonable degree of holism about discourse and practice, one accepts that any attempt to introduce new meanings or roles into this network will involve two complementary processes. First, it will bring about alterations in the meanings and roles of other elements of discourse and practice, and thus run the risk of changing the subject. Second, it will itself be vulnerable to alteration beyond original specification as a result of "backward linkages" from the rest of the network, and thus run the risk of saying something unintended. The utilitarian who is attempting a quite systematic account of ethics must be very careful which part of the network of moral discourse and practice he seizes upon when he begins his reconstruction. It may be inadvisable to proceed as the act utilitarian does, by initially taking up the threads that converge on the notion of moral rightness. Although reconstruction must eventually come to this notion, if a utilitarian ties a tight knot between the goodness of states of affairs and the rightness of individual actions he may find that he is unable to get back the slack he needs for successful reconstruction except by unraveling the strands connecting right action to obligation, reasonable expectation, blameworthiness, and so on—increasingly changing the subject. The importance of where the utilitarian takes—or makes—his slack becomes especially evident when, out of a concern with character, we look up from the traditional focus upon right action and glimpse the multiple dimensions and questions of moral assessment that need to be tied together without creating excessive strain.

VI

What is the alternative to commencing utilitarian reconstruction deontically, with a theory of right action? Some distinctly nonutilitarian philosophers appear to favor outright abandonment of the categories of right and wrong in ethics, but it seems to me that in morality as in law, there is a highly useful function to be served by the particular sort of guidance such notions provide to agents. We thus do have a reason for attempting to give some account of deontic judgments within moral theory, but it is a further question whether moral theory should start with such judgments.

Aretaic theories afford an example of how one might start elsewhere, namely, with assessments of moral value. But as the name suggests, such theories have largely been concerned with virtue, and what is needed is a broader category than *arete*. For want of anything better, I will forego the felicity of Greek roots and introduce the harsh latinate term *valoric* to cover direct assessments of what is better or worse from a moral point of view, whether these assessments be made of acts, agents, characters, institutions, or whatever. When the moral point of view in question bases its assessments ultimately upon an impartial reckoning of the nonmoral good realized, we have what may be called *valoric utilitarianism.*

Valoric utilitarianism starts out from the guiding utilitarian idea that no sort of act or motive or institution has intrinsic moral value and that whatever value it has from a moral point of view depends in the final reckoning upon how it affects human well-being. There are, of course, multiple valoric utilitarian positions, depending upon how well-being is understood and upon whether effects on well-being are evaluated in terms of total amount of utility realized, average amount, distributed amount,[20] or whatever. In what follows I will be concerned only with a maximizing valoric utilitarianism. Although I will not defend this choice here, it must be admitted to be a choice—nothing in the theory of nonmoral value tells us that for purposes of moral evaluation greater total nonmoral value is always superior to lesser, a claim that belongs to the realm of moral theory proper.

Is it therefore a claim about moral value? In a sense, yes, for it is a matter of what is "better rather than worse from a moral point of view." It would however be confusing to appropriate the familiar term 'moral value' for such claims. A maximizing[21] valoric utilitarian assessment of an action or a character would consist in asking directly how much net nonmoral value would be realized by, and as a result of, its occurrence or existence. But notoriously, an act or character can strike us as morally bad even though it happens to bring about very good results. Like 'right' and 'wrong', 'morally good' and 'morally bad' owe their content in part to judgments about *kinds* of actions or characters and about what *characteristically* goes along with them, and in part as well to judgments about the *normal range* of human variation. Moreover, 'morally good' tends in ordinary use to be applied only to the limited range of human thought and action that involves *moral conscientiousness,* and so would not be applied to actions of, say, spontaneous affection that, although highly beneficial, lack distinctively moral motivation.

Valoric utilitarians thus should not assume that their notion of "better or worse from a moral point of view" coincides with our notion of moral value. They will almost certainly have to use complex and indirect means to give an account of judgments of moral value (in the ordinary sense) and thus should insist that they are using 'better or worse from a moral point of view' as a technical term. To emphasize this while at the same time avoiding a cumbersome phrase, let us remint an expression coined by Bertrand Russell, and speak of acts or character traits that are better rather than worse from a moral point of view as more or less *morally fortunate.*[22] Thus one could speak of Frank's unenthusiastic remark (under the original assumptions) as morally most fortunate relative to available alternatives, even if not morally right or morally good as we ordinarily understand these terms. Frank's overall character, too, would be morally most fortunate relative to available alternatives, and here ordinary usage might deem this character morally good. Moreover, valoric utilitarianism would say that it is unfortunate, relative to a perhaps unattainable ideal of character, that Frank's moral outrage at unjustified inequalities must be allied to his rather spiteful resentment of all inequalities, just as ordinary usage would say that owing to this spiteful streak Frank, though good, is not perfect. Put another way, among the motives underlying Frank's act are some which, even though they are part of a character both fortunate and good, are not themselves either fortunate or good.

As this example suggests, valoric utilitarianism has direct application not only to acts, but to any object of moral assessment. In this way it differs not only from familiar indirect utilitarianisms, but also from direct act utilitarianism. One can ask how morally fortunate an individual act is, or how morally fortunate actions of that kind usually are, or how morally fortunate it would be if everyone regularly took such actions, and so on. And one may ask how morally fortunate it is that on a given occasion an individual possesses or acts from a given character, or how morally fortunate a character of that kind usually is, or how morally fortunate it would be if most people had such characters, and so on. And thus far, we have spoken only of valoric utilitarian judgments based upon the *absolute* amount of nonmoral value that is or would be brought about.

In moral practice we have a special interest in judgments based upon the *relative* amount of nonmoral value that acts, characters, etc. would bring about, especially those within the range of alternatives causally accessible to us. For example, we often want to know which acts, among those the agent would succeed in performing if he tried, would bring about at least as much nonmoral value as any others.[23] I suppose one could call the view that such acts are morally most fortunate "act-token valoric utilitarianism," but this view would not as such be a theory of moral rightness, nor would it be in competition with "act-type valoric utilitarianism" or "rule valoric utilitarianism" or "character valoric utilitarianism." "Rule valoric utilitarianism" and "character valoric utilitarianism," for example, are direct views about the fortunateness of rules or characters, not indirect views about the fortunateness of acts.

Consider again my generous friends. According to valoric utilitarianism, (1) it is very fortunate relative to available alternatives that they give 15 percent of their income to worthy causes—since this does a large amount of good compared to most other uses of these funds—but (2) it would be still more fortunate if on occasion or regularly they were to give 30 percent. Yet (3) it is most fortunate relative to available alternatives that they have the characters they do, even though these characters lead them not to give more than 15 percent. For although it would be more fortunate for them to have characters that would lead them always to give 30 percent, such characters are not causally accessible to them, and we have supposed that it would in fact be less fortunate were they to have characters that would lead them to be strongly inclined to try to give 30 percent. Moreover, (4) their acts of donation are more substantially more fortunate than mine, despite the fact that (5) chastising them for not giving more would, owing to their more measured and appropriate response, be more fortunate than chastising me.

Consider, too, Mel's Saturday afternoon. The valoric utilitarian would say that (1) it would be more fortunate were Mel to go off canvassing, but (2) less fortunate were he to have the sort of character that would make it highly likely for him to do so. Valoric utilitarianism would also say that, (3) given the resources available to Mel and the world as it is, it would be more fortunate were his psychology such that he would reliably do more for Central American peasants and others in great need, even if this meant doing less for his kith and kin. Yet valoric utilitarianism would also say that (4) it would be more fortunate were the world and Mel's psychology such that he could live a life in which contribution to his own good and the good of kith and kin were more consonant with maximizing the general good, at least, so long as this were achieved by raising the resources available to others rather than simply lowering the resources available to Mel.

So far the valoric utilitarian's judgments do not strike me as either morally complacent or grossly at odds with our moral concepts. For example, although the value of doing more nonmoral good has been recognized, no claim has been made to the effect that it is always wrong to fail to optimize.

However, the rejoinder will be made: perhaps nothing jarring has been said about right or wrong, but that may only be because nothing has been said about them. And it must be admitted that, as described thus far, valoric utilitarianism is indeed an incomplete, and to that extent unspecific, moral theory. Note, however, that it is also in its own way quite a bit more comprehensive theory than familiar deontic utilitarianisms, for it furnishes assessments of what is better or worse from a moral point of view not only with regard to acts, but also motives, characters, distributions of resources, and so on. Moreover, in its hegemonic form—the form with which we are concerned here[24]—valoric utilitarianism is quite specific in at least one respect about how it is to be completed. For it tells us that all moral evaluation—evaluations of moral rightness, moral goodness, and the like—are to be traced back to assessments of the total amount of nonmoral good realized in the world, i.e., to what is more rather than less fortunate. Upon this base would be built accounts of these other species of moral evaluation, and once the valoric utilitarian moves beyond judgments of what is more or less morally fortunate, about which he is relentlessly direct, he is free to become indirect. Indirect and intricate. For in view of what has been said about the holism of moral discourse, any plausible account of, say, moral rightness can be expected to be quite elaborate, involving not only questions about rules or principles, but also about motivations, dispositions to feel guilt or attribute blame, and so on. Thus a valoric utilitarian account of rightness might deem an action right if it would conform to normative practices—comprising rules, motivations, dispositions, etc.—that would be fortunate.[25] But if it is to overcome some of the difficulties facing existing indirect utilitarianisms, the valoric account may have to avoid certain idealizations and abstractions. For example, it may have to attach primary significance not to the question "Which practices would be most fortunate if generally observed?" but rather "Which practices are most fortunate given circumstances as they are and will be?" And it may also have to attach importance not simply to whether an action *would* be performed if the agent had fortunate motives, dispositions, etc., but also to whether it actually was the result of such causes.

Given the characteristic structure of valoric utilitarianism, it may be able to escape the charge of "rule worship" that has been laid against various forms of deontic indirect utilitarianism. For in an instance in which an act in conformity with fortunate normative practices would lead to bad outcomes, the valoric utilitarian is able to say that it would be morally more fortunate—i.e., better from a moral point of view—if the practice were violated and a more beneficial act performed. This application of direct utilitarian assessment is not, it must be noted, a judgment of rightness. The act in violation of fortunate normative practices remains wrong, and this accommodates the commonsense thought that certain sorts of action—torture, deception, the sacrifice of innocents—are wrong even when, owing to unusual circumstances, they are beneficial.

This may seem puzzling. "What am I to do," an agent seeking moral advice in such circumstances may ask, "that which is most fortunate or that which is right?" Shouldn't there be a definite answer as to which evaluation to follow? There are definite answers, but there is no one question. If the agent wants to know which acts, of those available to him, are most highly valued from a moral point of view, he receives one answer. If he wants to know which acts would be right or wrong, he receives another. It is a familiar feature of ordinary moral life that in doing something right, one is not always doing the best—there is, after all, supererogation. Moreover, in doing something right, for example, in rejecting certain sorts of deception, one may be doing a good bit of harm. Insofar as the moral point of view is concerned, it is preferable if the most fortunate act is performed. But the most fortunate act may be blameworthy by the sorts of standards that ground judgments of right and wrong. This is a bit like the fact that the morally fortunate thing to do may be illegal and appropriately punished. It is a bit more like the fact that the best thing to do from the standpoint of promoting the law itself may be illegal.

Perhaps, however, the agent is asking a different question still. He may want to know whether he has more reason to do what is morally fortunate or what is morally right. This, however, is not a question to refer to moral standards or even to the moral point of view. For it is the office of practical reason to answer questions about the place of morally fortunate—or morally right—action in a rational life.

It would be a very large task to develop a valoric utilitarian reconstruction of the discourse and practice of assessments of moral rightness, or, for that matter, of moral goodness or social justice. Such a reconstruction would have to withstand stresses from several directions at once—from the need to retain continuity with existing language and practice as well as the need to avoid complacency and make appropriate improvements. Whether such a reconstruction could give character and rules a significance in morality closer to roles suggested by the imagined defenses of character and rules quoted in the initial sections of this paper cannot be judged until we have before us a more definite idea of what such a reconstruction might look like.

Still, those drawn to the guiding idea of utilitarianism may wish to consider the possibility that valoric utilitarianism gives the most direct expression of what they find attractive in that idea. And it is possible to say something about what valoric accounts of rightness or goodness might look like. For act and rule utilitarianism could be seen as more or less simple prototypes of how one might develop an account of moral rightness in action within a valoric framework; and motive and character utilitarianism (in the second form discussed) could be seen as prototypes of how one might develop an account of moral goodness of motive or character within such a framework. The difficulties these prototypes have faced in meeting the simultaneous stresses of necessary continuity with existing practices and appropriate reform are instructive, for they show where the valorist needs to work outward from the guiding utilitarian idea with greater sophistication. Of course, if, even after considerable time, more successful prototypes were not forthcoming, then this failure might provide a different sort of instruction, to the effect that the fault lies with the guiding idea itself. Those who are already impatient with utilitarianism may feel they have seen more than enough to reach such a judgment—Is utilitarianism asking for our patience for another century or two? To them I can only say that, by this standard, the grace period of deontology would also have expired.

VII

We have taken a curious route from our starting point. Consideration of how judgments of character might figure in a utilitarian moral theory have led us not to new advancements in utilitarianism, but rather to a new starting point, one further back than where we began. That could be fortunate for utilitarianism. Progress sometimes comes from taking a fresh start. But at the same time, the view from the valoric starting point is not entirely cheering to the utilitarian, since from this vantage utilitarianism as it stands seems to lack a satisfactory account not only of goodness of character, but even of the category of moral assessment with which it has most preoccupied itself, right action. And it will be cold comfort to the valoric utilitarian to learn that, in the eyes of many moral philosophers, that much of valoric utilitarianism is obviously true.[26]

Notes

1. One might expand this guiding idea to include all sentient beings. In this paper it will be restricted to people, though not on principled grounds.

2. Throughout I will speak of having a character rather than having specific traits of character. The view could be formulated in either way, but there may be something to be said for the more holistic notion, just as in contemporary rule utilitarianism reference is usually made not to individual rules, but to sets of rules or "moral codes."

3. Many formulations of the notion of 'general acceptance' exist. Some, for example, ignore questions of teaching or socialization and simply assume widespread—or even ideal—compliance. Others more plausibly incorporate costs of teaching, difficulty of internalization, and so on, in assessing optimality and do not assume anything like ideal compliance. Similarly, rule utilitarians may differ over whether they are recommending *action in accord with optimal rules* or *active consultation of optimal rules in deliberation.* Since there can be no guarantee that the former always requires—or even always permits—the latter, and since in cases of conflict it seems at odds with a broadly consequentialist spirit to treat a form of deliberation as intrinsically required, I have taken for our definition a version of rule utilitarianism that adopts the former line.

4. I mean by 'rule-utilitarian deliberator' to designate, not someone who—in deliberation or action—actually lives up to the requirements of rule utilitarianism, but someone who *tries* to do so in the following sense: he accepts the rule-utilitarian account of rightness and he conscientiously endeavors to determine which acts, of those available to him, would satisfy it. Similarly for 'act-utilitarian deliberator'. It is important to see that neither theory need set forward such conscious, conscientious striving as a moral ideal. We will return to this point below, in connection with act utilitarianism.

5. It is perhaps a defect of rule utilitarianism that it could turn out that agents would escape rule-utilitarian criticism despite their failure to coordinate if each could correctly claim to be conforming to one of the optimal sets of rules. (I suppose any optimal set of rules would somewhere contain an injunction to coordinate, but our example supposes that the injunctions of the equi-optimal sets of rules have already been taken into account.) Actual-outcome act utilitarianism, by contrast, would condemn an agent's failure to coordinate optimally whenever it was in his power to do so. This, of course, would leave untouched the interesting problems of how agents might actually go about achieving coordination.

6. See R. M. Adams, "Motive Utilitarianism," *The Journal of Philosophy* 73 (1976): 467–81, esp. p. 480. Otherwise unattributed page citations in the text refer to this work.

7. For the sake of consistency with the rest of this paper, I have put his definition (p. 480) in terms of actual rather than expected utility.

8. See William K. Frankena, *Ethics,* 2nd ed. (Englewood Cliffs, N.J., 1973), 121, 122.

9. Adams restricts the question of what motives "the morally perfect person" would have to "patterns of motivation that are causally possible for human beings" (p. 470), but we may also wish to consider persons more broadly. A Kantian might, for example, want to say that a morally perfect *person* would have a holy will, while a morally perfect *human* would have at best a good will.

10. But doesn't calling something good entail a claim that it "ought to exist"? Philosophers have indeed often spoken as if this were so, but to whom or what would this 'ought' be addressed in those cases where we speak of the goodness of impossible perfection?

11. Because the difference in question arises from the fact that the act utilitarian casts his evaluative net wider, this situation could arise even if the acquisition of motives were assumed to be effortless. For example, it may be that, of the sets of motives available to me, M would bring about more utility than any other, and *a fortiori* more than N. However, perhaps in order to have motives M, I must also as a matter psychological necessity have beliefs B, which themselves directly bring me a certain amount of utility; on the other hand, in order to have motives N I must have beliefs C, which, we will suppose, directly bring me more utility than B. The beliefs are not caused or otherwise brought about by having the motives, and so their direct utility does not figure in the evaluation of the motives or the effects of these motives. It therefore could turn out that although motives M would bring about more utility than motives N, the motive-belief package $M + B$ would bring about less utility than $N + C$. If we consider a choice among acts that would determine which of these packages I would (effortlessly, we suppose) come to have, an act-utilitarian standard would favor promoting $N + C$.

12. Adams may be expressing a similar concern when he speaks of "the way that the motives, and especially the kind of conscience, regarded as right must be related to the acts re-

garded as right in anything that is to count as a morality" (p. 479), and it may be this concern that lies behind his talk of incompatibility.

13. Contrast here the claim of Bernard Williams that act utilitarianism "contains something which a utilitarian would see as a certain weakness, a traditional idea which it unreflectively harbors. This is, that the best world must be one in which right action is maximized." B. Williams, "A Critique of Utilitarianism," in *Utilitarianism: For and Against,* edited by J. J. C. Smart and B. Williams (Cambridge, 1975), 129.

14. That is, on the assumption that, were Mel's parental attachment to weaken, the result would be that he would bring about less utility in the long run. Note that this assumption is in a relevant sense more inclusive than the assumption that strong parental attachment is among the motives it would be best for him to have. See below.

15. I have tried to formulate the example so that the act would be right on either a prospective or an actualist account of act-utilitarian duty.

16. Williams disagrees, arguing that "There is no distinctive place for *direct* utilitarianism unless it is, within fairly narrow limits, a doctrine about how one should decide what to do" ("A Critique of Utilitarianism," 128).

17. For discussion, see P. Railton, "Alienation, Consequentialism, and the Demands of Morality," *Philosophy and Public Affairs* 13 (Spring 1984): 134–71, esp. 148–56.

18. Presumably the global, symmetrical character of the underlying conception of utilitarianism—which yields "no comprehensible difference which consists just in my bringing about a certain outcome rather than someone else's producing it"—helps account for Williams' criticism that utilitarianism cannot give a plausible account of agency and moreover leaves individuals forever at the mercy of a "universal satisfaction system" ("A Critique of Utilitarianism," 96, 118). Although I would emphasize that these are features of the *underlying* utilitarian conception, and not necessarily of all accounts of right action justified by appeal to that conception, it must be said that Williams' criticism has made vivid an important part of what would be involved in giving a satisfactory utilitarian account of right action.

19. I was guilty of failure to take the full measure of this dilemma when, in a footnote to "Alienation, Consequentialism, and the Demands of Morality," I attempted without saying as much to pick and choose among the connections the expression 'right'—as used by an act utilitarian—would retain with existing usage (p. 160n).

20. The role of distribution here would be distinct both from the role distribution would play if it had intrinsic *non*moral value—which could then be figured directly into a maximizing or averaging scheme without loss—and from the role distribution would play if it had intrinsic *moral* value in the narrow sense. I suppose that a defense of allowing distribution the role in question would have to take the form of showing distributive constraints to be partly *constitutive* of the moral point of view.

21. Hereinafter, this qualification will be dropped.

22. See B. Russell, "The Elements of Ethics," reprinted in *Readings in Ethical Theory,* 2nd ed., edited by Wilfrid Sellars and John Hospers (Englewood Cliffs, N.J., 1970), 12. Russell uses the term for a somewhat different purpose, to pick out those acts that actually (as opposed to prospectively) have good consequences.

23. This is what we would like to know, although of course we seldom do, and so settle instead for some prospective estimation of the value that would be realized. It seems to me that valoric utilitarianism is most plausibly formulated in terms of *actual* nonmoral value realized, although the valorist's account of such notions as moral rightness, goodness, and so on, may well appeal to *prospective* value. It is, I think, because of utilitarians' undue focus upon the question of right action that it has seemed so natural to formulate their view, at base, in terms of prospective value. For how can one say that agents are *obliged* to act as full information would indicate, given that they never will have full information? Once, however, we see the problem of constructing an account of moral obligation from the standpoint of what I have called the guiding idea of utilitarianism, it becomes more plausible that it is actual well-being that matters at bottom, and that prospective value matters because it is predictive of actual value.

24. Just as act utilitarianism could be held in a nonhegemonic way (e.g., in tandem with motive utilitarianism), so can valoric utilitarianism (e.g., in tandem with act utilitarianism). However, since our aim here is to get some idea of what a nondeontic utilitarianism might look like, and in particular to see how an integrated valoric utilitarian approach to the various species of moral evaluation might be made, it will best suit our purposes to focus upon hegemonic valoric utilitarianism, which denies deontic judgments any independent foundation.

25. Compare here Richard B. Brandt's notion of a "moral code," as presented in *A Theory of the Good and the Right* (Oxford, 1979), chap. 9.

26. I would like to thank William K. Frankena for very helpful comments on an earlier draft of this paper.

Aristotelian Justice as a Personal Virtue
DAVID K. O'CONNOR

Justice has not fared well in the revival of virtue ethics. In the first place, justice seems more at home in debates about public policy and social institutions than in descriptions of the moral strengths and weaknesses of individuals. We are much more likely to commend a policy than a person for being just. And when we do praise individuals for justice, they are often being singled out for their performance of specialized roles as judges or arbitrators. To describe a potential colleague as always honest, witty, gracious, tenacious, insightful, helpful, dependable: all of these and many more are specific ways of recommending someone, and conjure up specific expectations about his or her conduct. But except for some special contexts (tenure review, for example), I am more likely to puzzle than enlighten if I prepare you to meet someone by saying, "Professor So-and-So is always just." How often, after all, *can* we be just? Justice does not seem to characterize us in the way other virtues do. Justice may be the primary virtue of social institutions, but it seems a distinctly derivative one of individuals, perhaps being nothing other than a settled resolve to promote and support just institutions and the policies issuing from them. From this point of view, there is little independent interest in justice as a personal virtue.

But even when justice has been of interest within virtue ethics, it has often suffered in comparisons to virtues like love, compassion, and care. Such virtues, with their direct and natural concern for other human beings, can seem to correct or at least complement the indirect and artificial respect required by justice. Justice, it might be thought, is too entangled with a dubious conception of the autonomous individual to reflect the interdependence that is central to (at least some kinds of) moral experience. Justice seems a virtue fit only for cold and distant strangers, like the characters in a Western; and its demands like the verdicts of a hanging judge, cruel but fair. An account of the virtues that looks to forming members of a moral community would naturally be uneasy with a virtue that seems designed for mere co-existence.

Perhaps justice is simply obsolete as a personal virtue, and virtue ethics can get along without it, or at least without giving it a very exalted role. But there is something surprising about this conclusion, and I want to explore a way of understanding justice that avoids it. Where can we look for an account of justice that avoids the two objections that (1) justice is primarily a virtue of social institutions and policies and only derivatively of individual persons, and (2) justice is as a virtue definitely in tension with and probably inferior to directly altruistic virtues such as love and compassion? I will turn for a helpful model to the founding father of virtue ethics, Aristotle himself. Aristotle was certainly concerned with the institutions that embody justice in different kinds of political regime, but his analysis in the fifth book of the *Nicomachean Ethics* is primarily concerned with justice as a psychic state *(hexis)* of individuals. He describes this psychic state independently of his account of just political institutions, and so provides an account that avoids the first objection. Furthermore, Aristotle was not only unaware of a sharp divide between the virtues of justice and love *(philia),* but makes a point of their near-identity.[1] We should then expect his account of justice to have exactly the sort of resources we need to rehabilitate justice as a personal virtue.

But things are not so simple, and in our eagerness to exploit the father's resources we must beware of squandering the patrimony. The Aristotelian model does not provide a direct answer to our questions about the status of justice as a personal virtue. Aristotle's questions are different from ours, and we can learn more by seeing this difference than by precipitously making him address our concerns. I will be more concerned to bring out the framework within which Aristotelian justice finds its place than to exploit Aristotle's views for answers to questions raised from our framework. His questions are interesting and explore parts of moral life that we might otherwise overlook.

I will emphasize two aspects of the Aristotelian account of justice that distinguish it from most contemporary accounts, whether or not within virtue ethics. First, the vice that provides the primary temptation to injustice is not the same in Aristotle and contemporary accounts. Aristotle disagrees with us about the "enemy" that justice must overcome. I will describe this by saying that Aristotle offers an alternative account of the *corrective* aspect of justice. Second, the exercise of Aristotelian justice expresses a kind of personal excellence in social interaction different from the kinds contemporary accounts emphasize. This disagreement over the particular capacity that justice perfects concerns what I will call the *expressive* aspect of justice. The corrective aspect of justice is the virtue's negative side, telling us what it guards against, while its expressive aspect tells us the positive side of what human capacities it brings into play and perfects.

After examining the corrective and expressive aspects of Aristotelian justice, we will be better able to see how Aristotle treats justice as a personal virtue, and why it is closely connected by him to love. Aristotelian justice is primarily concerned with a part of moral life different from what our understanding of justice would lead us to expect, and the problems and rewards of justice are correspondingly different. I will try to illustrate how Aristotelian justice focuses on a kind of selfishness quite different from the egoistic partiality at the heart of our conception of injustice. I will conclude by considering the resources of the alternative Aristotle offers to virtue ethics, and the change in emphasis that this alternative would require.

A. THE CORRECTIVE ASPECT OF JUSTICE

What distinctive moral defect does justice oppose and correct? Philippa Foot has given a lucid description of the typical contemporary answer to this question:[2]

> Virtues such as justice . . . correspond not to any particular desire or tendency that has to be kept in check [as do virtues like temperance and courage] but rather to a deficiency of motivation; and it is this that they must make good. If people were as much attached to the good of others as they are to their own good there would no more be a general virtue of benevolence than there is a general virtue of self-love. And if people cared about the rights of others as they care about their own rights no virtue of justice would be needed to look after the matter.

This picture of justice and its relation to the other virtues implies a fundamental division of virtue into two different kinds. On the one hand, *interpersonal* virtues like justice and benevolence make good our vicious tendency to be partial to our own desires and prerogatives to the detriment of others. On the other, there are *intrapersonal* virtues that moderate and channel various sorts of desires and emotions. For example, the virtue of temperance moderates and controls our desires for bodily pleasures, while courage controls the effect of fear on our actions. These latter virtues confront a set of temptations very different from those connected with justice and the other interpersonal virtues: the intrapersonal virtues are not essentially "other-regarding" and are not opposed primarily by the threat of egoistic partiality. They are instead concerned with the intensity of various desires and the relative priority of the ends reflected in these desires.

In contrast, Aristotelian justice does not primarily involve the control or correction of egoistic motives. Instead, it is like the intrapersonal virtues in opposing misorientation toward or overvaluing of the various sorts of inferior ends. Justice is, of course, concerned with how our actions affect other people.[3] But in Aristotle's picture, what tempts a human being to fall short of a virtue like temperance or courage is just what leads him to be unjust; Aristotle sees no special role even in the interpersonal virtues for egoism and its control. Consider Aristotle's discussion of the motives of unjust people in the following passage:[4]

> The reasons people choose to harm [others] and do base things contrary to the law are vice and incontinence. For when people have either one vice or many, they are unjust with regard to whatever they are vicious. For example, an illiberal person [is unjust] with regard to money, a licentious person with regard to bodily pleasures, a soft person with regard to taking it easy, a coward with regard to dangers (for because of fear he deserts those in danger with him), an honor-lover *[philotimos]* because of honor, a sharp-tempered person because of anger, a victory-lover because of victory, a bitter person because of revenge, a thoughtless person because he is deceived about the just and unjust, a shameless person because of contempt for reputation. In the same way with other [causes of vice], a particular person [is unjust] with regard to a particular underlying [cause of vice].

It is clear here that Aristotle understands injustice to have the same underlying causes as vices we would usually think of as intrapersonal. He sees no fundamental division of virtue because he does not believe that injustice is the result of unrestrained egoism so much as of misorientation.[5]

In the passage above, Aristotle is discussing what in the *Nicomachean Ethics* he calls "universal" or "inclusive" justice. But his discussion of the narrower virtue of "particular" or "partial" justice again shows that misorientation, not egoism, is the threat to justice. The special type of misorientation that characterizes particular injustice is the desire for the pleasure that comes from gain, especially gain concerning the external goods of wealth and honor.[6] Aristotle names the vicious overvaluing of such goods *pleonexia.* As he understands this virtue, a person who is just (in the narrow sense of particular justice) is opposed not to the egoist or the partial person, but to the money-grubber or the ruthlessly ambitious person. With regard to what it opposes and corrects, then, particular justice is much like liberality and magnificence (concerning wealth) or magnanimity and proper pride (concerning honors).[7] There is once again no fundamental division between the focus of interpersonal and intrapersonal virtue.

There are two interesting consequences of taking Aristotle's perspective and treating misorientation rather than unrestrained egoism as the root of injustice. First, the Aristotelian account will not categorize the same set of actions under injustice as the contemporary account with egoism at its core. Bernard Williams' criticisms of Aristotle's account provide a striking illustration of this. Williams has a conception of the virtue of justice very much like Foot's. Injustice is distinguished from other vices, says Williams, by the fact that "this vice, unlike others, does not import a special motive, but rather the lack of one," namely, a lack of concern with promoting just distributions.[8] An act can be characterized as unjust whenever it displays this sort of indifference, whatever else its motives may be. "There are acts that are unjust . . . which are the products of fear, jealousy, desire for revenge, and so on."[9] Williams criticizes Aristotle's claim that an action must be motivated by *pleonexia,* an overvaluing of wealth or honor, to count as unjust. The corrective aspect of justice essentially involves overcoming our tepid commitment to fairness rather than our voracious appetite for external goods.

Given this account of what justice opposes and corrects, Williams will not count some cases Aristotle considers paradigmatic of injustice as injustice at all, and similarly an Aristotelian will not count some of Williams' cases. I will illustrate this by considering two hypothetical cases involving a pair of vicious men, Greedy Greg and Lascivious Larry. The first has a misdirected interest in money, the second too much devotion to the rites of Aphrodite.

For the first case, suppose Greg and Larry are both guilty of seducing a wealthy colleague's wife. Following his lascivious ways, Larry commits adultery out of lust, aiming at sexual pleasure. But true to his name, Greedy Greg aims not so much at the physical pleasure as at the monetary gifts the wife will bestow on him, or perhaps the blackmail she will pay him to keep the affair quiet. On Aristotle's view, Greg is here a paradigm case of an unjust man.[10] His misorientation toward money—and thus his *pleonexia*—has led him to harm another person. Though Larry has also done harm, his motive was not the type that characterizes injustice. Intemperate yes, unjust no. On the other hand, Williams would not count either Greg or Larry as unjust. While both are vicious, neither has displayed injustice's characteristic insensitivity to fairness.

For the second case, suppose both men are judges or arbitrators in a dispute involving the distribution of goods. Greedy Greg accepts a monetary bribe to favor one party in the dispute, while Lascivious Larry accepts sexual inducements. In this case, Williams' view of the virtue of justice implies that both men suffer from the same moral failure: the actions of both display the indifference to fair claims that characterizes injustice. On the Aristotelian view, however, only Greedy Greg displays the vice of injustice: the misorientation behind his action, but not the misorientation behind Lascivious Larry's action, falls within the vice of *pleonexia* that justice opposes.[11]

We can summarize these different ways of categorizing unjust actions in the following table:

		MOTIVE	
		GREED	LUST
ACTION	MISDISTRIBUTION	A W	W
	SEDUCTION	A	

A = Case of Aristotelian injustice
W = Case of Williams' injustice

We see an important disagreement here about which cases should receive a unified explanation and which cannot. From Williams' point of view, the Aristotelian account wrongly separates the acts of misdistribution of Greg and Larry; for both display a special kind of insensitivity to just distributions. Furthermore, it also mistakenly unifies Greg's misdistributing and his seducing, since only the former act involves this special insensitivity. From the Aristotelian view, Williams fails to see that one and the same psychic flaw—an overvaluing of money—is operative both in Greg's accepting the bribe and in his mercenary sexual adventures, albeit in different contexts. Nor would an Aristotelian believe that there is a special indifference that Greg and Larry share when they accept their quite different bribes. He or she would doubt that there is any more of a unified, motivationally relevant "indifference to just distributions" in both misdistribution cases than there is an analogous unified, motivationally relevant "indifference to sexual licitness" in both seduction cases. Either of these special types of indifference looks to the Aristotelian like an empty cause postulated to explain an incidental unity.

This disagreement over the underlying psychic causes of injustice brings us to the second consequence of Aristotelian justice's focus on misorientation rather than egoism: its alternative view of the task of moral education. On the view of justice that Foot and Williams share, the strategy for educating people in the interpersonal virtues will be quite different from the strategy for educating them in virtues like temperance, courage, liberality, and magnanimity. These intrapersonal virtues do not depend on the development of the particular sensitivity to fair claims that justice requires. It is quite possible on this view for the two kinds of virtue to be developed independently: the lustful man or the materialistic man may well be a just man, and the temperate man or the man who does not overvalue money may still fail to be sensitive to the just claims of others. It is no guarantee of justice that we have internalized the proper hierarchy of ends, for high-minded injustice is injustice all the same.

The Aristotelian view is entirely at odds with this. It sees injustice as the interpersonal result of an intrapersonal misorientation. More specifically, the psychic root of injustice is overvaluing the external goods of money and honor, treating them as if they were constituents of happiness rather than the mere equipment of it. The human being whose interest in such goods is not delimited by his orientation to the end of virtuous activity will naturally be led to harm others in his futile and misguided search for satisfaction. For this reason, Aristotle calls external goods like money and honor "goods people fight over" *(perimachêta)*.[12] The education required to combat the temptation to greed and ambition must then focus directly on promoting a devotion to virtuous activity, a devotion that will put wealth and honor in their place and prevent them from becoming divisive motives for injustice. For the Aristotelian, the man of liberality and magnanimity will be the just man; and the misorientation of the greedy and overly ambitious makes them at least potentially unjust. There is no causally independent sensitivity to fair claims that can anchor justice in a sea of disordered interests.

Aristotle's approach is manifest in a passage of the *Politics* where he discusses the institutions required to prevent injustice and civil conflict *(stasis)* from arising in a community.[13] He criticizes one Phaleas of Chalcedon for suggesting that equality of property would remove the causes of civil conflict: "Even if one were to institute moderate property for all, it would not help. One ought to level desires rather than property, . . . for if people's desires go beyond necessities, they will commit injustice to satisfy them." The only effective cure for civil conflict, claims Aristotle, is public education that corrects people's tendency to be grasping *(pleonektein)* of money and honors. Such correction depends mainly on changing people's orientation from valuing money and honors for their own sake to valuing them only for their contribution to virtuous activity. In itself "the nature of desire is without limit," and only by providing a limit in the life of virtue can the pursuit of external goods be prevented from becoming a source of conflict and injustice. Development of the proper orientation, not the development of a sensitivity to fair claims, is the heart of education in justice.

In summary, we can say that Aristotelian justice takes aim at a different kind of moral failing from what we would expect of justice. The unjust man has not lapsed into egoistic partiality, and he will not be improved primarily by becoming more responsive to others. Instead, he needs to re-order his interests, putting first things first. Then he will not be tempted by those goods that prove so divisive when pursued as ends themselves. His injustice is but the outward manifestation of a psychic misorientation, and the cure for the underlying moral disease of misorientation will also clear up the symptom of unjust treatment of others. The corrective aspect of justice is not on this Aristotelian view essentially different from the corrective aspect of the intrapersonal virtues; and so there is not the sharp distinction between the psychic bases of interpersonal and intrapersonal virtues that exists in most contemporary treatments.

B. THE EXPRESSIVE ASPECT OF JUSTICE

Justice is not a virtue characterized merely by the particular kinds of temptation it holds down. An account of justice that spoke only of its corrective aspect would be as incomplete as an account of excellence in swimming that told us only how not to drown. Such accounts will also typically have a more positive side that shows us what psychic capacities justice engages and perfects. This expressive aspect of justice has not, I believe, had as unified a treatment in contemporary moral philosophy as its corrective aspect, so the contrast with the Aristotelian account is somewhat less clear. But a sketch of two approaches within the contemporary perspective will provide a basis for comparison.

One approach might follow Kant in focusing on justice as an expression of autonomy. The idea here would be that acting on a universalizable principle allows the agent to rise above his empirically given desires and drives. By so escaping from the grubbiness of pathology, the agent exercises his capacity for true freedom. Just action expresses this freedom from empirical determination. For the metaphysically less daring, a stripped down version of this idea could focus on rational consistency rather than autonomy.[14] Here the idea would be that rational consistency requires action to conform to certain standards of impartiality, so that failure to live up to the standards convicts one of inconsistency. On this version, the just agent escapes from a practical analogue of fallacy rather than from pathology, and the capacity that finds expression in just action is simply rationality rather than freedom. But either way, the expressive aspect of justice would focus on the capacity for practical rationality, whether or not this is linked with freedom from empirical determination.

A second approach could stress the human capacity for mutuality and reciprocity, focusing more on equality with others than freedom for oneself. Justice might on this view be understood to depend on the ability to see oneself as merely one source of valuation among others. The just person would exercise his or her capacity to be party to a reasonable consensus, and to express his particularly *moral* interest in fairness.[15] Alternatively, the capacity perfected by justice might be more Humean, linked to emotional or sentimental response to the good of others (e.g., through sympathy), though this link would typically be distinguished from the more direct link displayed by benevolence or love. In either case, justice would express a special human capacity for identification and involvement with others' conceptions of the good.

I believe that these two approaches to the expressive aspect of justice, one emphasizing rationality, one mutuality, cover most contemporary conceptions. Either could complement the sort of account of justice's corrective aspect seen in Foot and Williams. But if Aristotelians see no such special capacity, linked to justice and independent of the capacities exercised and perfected in the intrapersonal virtues, how will they explain the positive side of justice? There seems on this model nothing to explain how the praise of an action as just adds to its characterization by an intrapersonal virtue like liberality or magnanimity. The worthwhile human capacities seem to have been exhausted by the intrapersonal virtues, leaving justice with no special excellence of its own to express.

In a way this description of the expressive aspect of justice is true. As there was no type of misorientation peculiar to injustice, so too there is no special type of proper orientation that makes justice valuable. Just actions simply *are* actions of liberality or magnanimity, grounded in the same psychic states and aiming at the same ends. But in praising an action for its justice, the Aristotelian does not focus primarily on the fact of proper orientation. Instead, he or she will focus on the excellence of the action as a contribution to a *common* pursuit of the good, to its fitting into a context of shared life. It is true that when an action is criticized as unjust from the Aristotelian perspective, we can be sure that it is motivated by an inordinate attachment to money or honor. But it is not this attachment which is being criticized so much as the effect this attachment has of making the greedy or ambitious person a bad partner or colleague. Justice has its primary and clearest application within the context of communities pursuing a shared conception of the good.

Aristotelian justice does not directly express, then, a human capacity for altruism or impartiality, but for partnership or collegiality. It applies primarily to our interactions with others conceived as partners (though not necessarily equals[16]), sharing in our conception and pursuit of the good, not to our confrontations with others conceived as independent sources of valuation. One way to appreciate this contrast is to consider the different way that selfishness becomes a threat to and is overcome by justice when conceived as expressing on the one hand a capacity for altruism and on the other a capacity for partnership. On the altruism model, selfishness is caused by a poorly developed sensitivity to the independent good of others, and it is overcome by appealing directly to this capacity for justice. On the Aristotelian model, selfishness is the effect in interpersonal life of misorientation toward divisive goods, and its cure depends on reorienting the agent to higher goods, the successful pursuit of which requires and fosters partnership.

To illustrate these differences, consider an analogy with a case of selfishness on an athletic team. Suppose you are the coach of a girls' grade school basketball team. Most of your players are at about the same skill level, but one is much better than the others. This star athlete can run faster, jump higher, dribble and shoot much more effectively than anyone else on the team. When you watch her working out in the gym by herself, she appears to have mastered all the skills that go into making a fine basketball player. But as soon as you see her in an *interpersonal* context, this rosy picture is destroyed. Like many gifted but immature athletes, your star doesn't use her talents to benefit the team effort. On fast breaks she outruns her teammates and spoils the pattern; on defense she wanders from her own assignment and horns in on someone else's. But worst of all, on offense your "star" hogs the ball, dribbling too much and shooting too often; and when she does bother to pass, she befuddles her slower, less coordinated teammates by bouncing rockets off their shins and foreheads. In short, Coach, you have a selfish basketball player on your hands.

How do you go about turning this playground prima donna into a good basketball player? You might try appealing to her capacities for altruism or impartiality. Perhaps you could take her aside and explain that she should give the other girls a chance, even if they aren't much good. Or you could ask her how she would like it if a more talented girl embarrassed her by throwing passes she couldn't handle, going after her latent regard for the categorical imperative. But I think these approaches have an inappropriate conception of selfishness behind them. Her problem is not that her egoism leads her to ignore the needs and desires of her teammates (though she may do this too). You don't cure her selfishness by developing her sensitivity to the fair claims of others. Instead, you need to change her understanding of success, of excellence in basketball.

Part of this will usually consist simply in getting her to think more about *team* success, about outscoring other teams, and less about how many points she scores herself. Teach her to enjoy winning, and she will probably be less tempted to dominate the action, since this usually hurts a team. But if she is far enough above the level of her teammates, the team might actually win *more* games when she dominates and her teammates simply stay out of the way. Your team may well score more points if on every possession she drives the length of the court and fires away. Your star's increased concern for the team's winning could exacerbate her selfish play rather than cure it.

This puts you in a delicate position as a coach. If all you care about is winning grade school basketball games, then you will let her dominate. But if you want to develop your star's excellence as a basketball player—excellence that might be fully exploited by teammates and rewarded with victories only at the high school level and beyond—you will attack her selfishness in another way.[17] You must go beyond making this talented athlete care about team success and change her understanding of what *individual* excellence is in basketball. The skills she perfects and exhibits in her private workouts, she must learn, do not yet make her a fine basketball player. Until she learns to use these individual skills as a member of a team, they are not excellences of a basketball player, but only of a gym rat. An excellent basketball player, as opposed to someone skilled merely at dribbling or shooting or throwing the ball behind her back, uses these skills in ways that respect the limitations of her teammates and exploit their strengths.

This sensitivity to her teammates may look at first to your star like a *sacrifice* of excellence, as if she were to play down to their level. But this is wrong. An exquisite sensitivity to their teammates is very much a part of what makes Magic Johnson and Larry Bird great players, for example: it makes *them* better *individual* basketball players, and not merely their teams better teams. But this kind of sensitivity to one's teammates is quite different from the sensitivity recommended in the contemporary approaches to justice. It is sensitivity to others *as partners* in the pursuit of a shared goal. Of course, this "interpersonal" excellence would be useless without the developed repertoire of "intrapersonal" skills that your star has developed in the gym. But when at last you can praise her as a fine basketball player, and not merely as a fancy dribbler or accurate shooter, what you have primarily in mind will be something besides these skills. You will have cured her selfishness by helping to change her conception of athletic success from scoring many points and dominating the action to contributing to team success with and through her teammates.

In an analogous way, Aristotelian justice is the virtue of a human being who is a good partner in the pursuit of some worthwhile goal, especially the goal of virtuous action within the context of a political community. The greedy person and the overly ambitious person will not make good partners in this pursuit any more than an athlete bent on scoring as many points as she can makes a good teammate. But their failing, though it involves a type of selfishness, is not primarily a failure of fairness, an indulgence in partiality. Aristotelian justice is more akin to the virtues that make for a good colleague than those that make for a good judge, more directly opposed to the love of honor that leads some academics to monopolize conversations, or stack departments with supporters, than with the indifference to strangers that lets the poor starve. Not that Aristotelians should be indifferent to starving strangers; but that is not the part of moral life with which justice is most concerned.

Given this focus of justice on excellence in partnership or collegiality, it should no longer be surprising that Aristotle links justice closely with friendship. For he thinks of friendships precisely as partnerships in the pursuit of some good, whether pleasure or utility or virtuous activity. In this respect, Aristotle's conception of friendship is quite different from ours, emphasizing the ties of close collaboration rather than of emotional intimacy.[18] It is in the shared life of friendship that the correction of misorientation is most crucial and the expression of partnership most rewarding. Because justice and friendship correct the same vices and express the same excellence (though friendship does so in a tighter and denser nexus of shared activity),[19] there is no hint in the Aristotelian perspective of the Humean distinction between the direct, natural concern for others embodied in benevolence and the indirect, artificial concern for others embodied in justice. For the Aristotelian, love is the perfection of justice, not a modification of it.

We have seen that the Aristotelian approach to justice differs in two important ways from most contemporary approaches. First, it takes a different view of the enemy to be overcome by justice, emphasizing misorientation to inappropriate ends rather than egoistic insensitivity to fair claims. Second, it emphasizes collegial excellence in shared pursuit of a common vision of the good, rather than the respect appropriate between human beings who confront each other as independent sources of value and valuation. As a consequence of these emphases, Aristotelian justice combats selfishness and perfects our interpersonal lives in contexts unlike those most prominent in the contemporary accounts. We are rather unused to confronting in theory the question, "What is required of me and what may I expect as a colleague or partner of others?" even though we confront it often in practice. But the Aristotelian approach gives such questions center stage, and is more concerned in interpersonal life with the quality of the peace than the restraint of war, so to speak.

Some may respond that if this account of Aristotle is right, his approach to interpersonal virtue has little interest for us. For if we think that the most pressing and important moral questions—at least concerning interpersonal virtues—have to do with allowing for and respecting diverse conceptions of the good, Aristotelian interests will seem peripheral, cliquish, and perhaps somewhat elitist. But I prefer to think of Aristotle as pointing toward a part of our moral lives that has great importance for making and unmaking human excellence, perhaps more central than what contemporary accounts point to. For Aristotle locates justice not at the extremities of community, but at its beating heart. Aristotelian justice can characterize a human being in the way that being a good colleague can, because it focuses on our excellence in pursuit of what we hold highest. The shared life of virtuous activity is neither so trivial nor so easy that it cannot profitably be the focus of ethical inquiry into human excellence.[20]

Notes

1. See *NE* 8.1.1155a22–28.

2. Philippa Foot, "Virtues and Vices," in *Virtues and Vices* (Berkeley, 1978), 9.

3. This is why Aristotle says that justice is virtue considered "in relation to others" *(pros heteron).* See, e.g., *NE* 5.1.1130a12–13; 5.2.1130b1–2.

4. *Rhetoric* 1.10.1368b12–24.

5. I have discussed the interpretive issues at length in "The Aetiology of Justice," in *The Foundations of Aristotelian Political Science,* edited by Carnes Lord and Paul Vander Waerdt (Berkeley, forthcoming).

6. See, e.g., *NE* 1130b4.

7. I discuss the relation between particular justice and the virtues of liberality and magnanimity in "The Aetiology of Justice."

8. Bernard Williams, "Justice as a Virtue," in *Essays on Aristotle's Ethics,* edited by Amelie Rorty (Berkeley, 1980), 198.

9. Ibid., 192.

10. Aristotle uses the contrast between a man who commits adultery for sexual pleasure and a man who commits adultery for gain to show the distinctive character of particular justice at *NE* 5.2.1130a22–28.

11. Aristotle's view is reflected, I believe, by the different attitudes we have to judges corrupted by sexual favors and judges who accept monetary bribes. We are more likely to describe the first as morally weak than as unjust.

12. See *NE* 9.8.1169a20–22; *EE* 8.3.1248b27.

13. *Politics* 2.7.

14. I have in mind Alan Gewirth's approach, for example.

15. I am thinking of the John Rawls of the Dewey Lectures, for example.

16. Aristotle's accounts of both justice and friendship are much concerned with the different obligations of partners who are peers and partners who are unequal in some relevant respect. If the inequality is too great (as, e.g., between human and god), no partnership is possible, and hence there is neither justice nor friendship in such relationships either. See, e.g., *NE* 8.7.1159a4–5.

17. If the star athlete can bring a team more success as a selfish dominator than as a sensitive partner even at the *highest* level of competition, can we still say he or she would attain greater basketball excellence by becoming less selfish? In this case, there seems to be no (actual, at least) level of competition to support a preference for unselfishness; yet many will still feel an "aesthetic" preference. The interminable debates about whether Wilt Chamberlain (the dominator) or Bill Russell (the team player) was the greater player seem to me to reflect this issue. Aristotle himself discusses a very similar issue when he explores the legitimacy of a man of outstanding virtue becoming a king rather than taking his turn in a system of rotating rule. See *Politics* 3.14–17.

18. I have defended this interpretation of Aristotle's treatment of friendship *(philia),* and explored the contrast between his approach focused on partnership and our usual conception focused on intimacy, in "Two Ideals of Friendship," a paper delivered in shortened form at the Eastern Division of the American Philosophical Association, December 1987.

19. To say that justice and friendship share *identical* corrective and expressive aspects is not quite true, since on Aristotle's view justice but not friendship has an intrinsic relation to law-abidingness. But this complication does not affect the point at issue here.

20. I would like to thank the University of Notre Dame's Institute for Scholarship in the Liberal Arts for a Junior Faculty Summer Research Grant in support of research on this paper. I would also like to thank Arnold Davidson and W. David Solomon for discussions of some of the main ideas of the paper.

Internal Objections to Virtue Ethics

DAVID SOLOMON

I. WHAT IS AN ETHICS OF VIRTUE?

While there has been much talk recently about the revival of an ethics of virtue (EV), it is not always entirely clear what such a revival might entail. There are three quite different views expressed by contemporary moral philosophers that might be taken to point to such a revival. There is, first, the view that recent moral philosophy has not paid sufficient attention to moral criticism and deliberation that centrally involves virtue concepts. The charge has been often made, for example, that contemporary moral philosophers pay excessive attention to the most abstract terms involved in ethical thought and talk, terms like 'right', 'good', and 'ought', while largely ignoring richer and more concrete terms like 'sensitive', 'compassionate', and 'courageous'.[1] Since these latter terms typically refer to virtue-like aspects of human character, one might regard this charge as a gesture in the direction of an EV.

A second view associated with the "revival" of virtue ethics holds that any developed ethical theory must include a *component* that deals with virtue. The thought here is that an ethical theory will be incomplete in an important sense if it does not have an account of virtue attached to it. William Frankena, for example, has argued forcefully that while an account of the virtues is not sufficient for an adequate ethical theory, any ethical theory which does not embody an account of the virtues will be importantly incomplete.[2] In introducing his own view of the virtues, he defends what we might call a "double aspect theory of morality," according to which a theory of the virtues will always be one feature of an adequate ethical theory, but not the most basic feature. Similarly, John Rawls finds it necessary to incorporate an account of the virtues in his broadly deontological moral theory, but his account of the virtues, like Frankena's, has a decidely inferior position within his overall political theory.[3]

There is, finally, a third and much stronger account of what is involved in the revival of an EV, according to which an EV entails the view that normative theory

428

must have a structure such that assessment of human character is, in some suitably strong sense, more fundamental than either the assessment of the rightness of action or the assessment of the value of the consequences of action. There is much in this characterization of an EV that needs clarification and expansion, but for our purposes we can pass over some of the deeper difficulties. It does presuppose that we can distinguish three features of any human action: that it is performed by some *agent,* that some particular *action* is performed, and that the action has certain determinate *consequences.* It is further presupposed that practical judgments typically take as their subject matter one of these three features of action. Either they are judgments of the agent, e.g., "she is honest and just," or of the action, e.g., "what he did was wrong," or of the consequences, e.g., "the skyscraper that he built is bad for the downtown area." The task of normative ethical theory—broadly conceived—is to order these kinds of practical judgments with the aim of showing that some practical judgments play a primary role in the overall justificatory structure of ethics. One looks for a foundation for ethics, such that foundational claims stand to other adequate moral judgments in a relation of justification or support.[4]

An EV, according to this third view, is a normative theory that takes the foundational moral claims to be claims about the agent, or about human character. It takes judgments of character or of agents as basic in that it construes the fundamental task of normative theory to be to depict an ideal of human character. The ethical task of each person, correspondingly, is to become a person of a certain sort where becoming a person of that sort is to become a person who has certain dispositions to respond to situations in a characteristic way. We recognize differences among persons of quite different kinds. Some people are shorter or fatter than others, some more or less intelligent, some better or worse at particular tasks, and some more courageous, just, or honest than others. These differences can be classified in various ways: physical versus mental differences, differences in ability versus differences in performance, etc. Those features of human beings on which virtue theories concentrate in depicting the ideal human being are states of character. Such theories typically issue in some list of virtues for human beings where these virtues are states of character which human beings must possess if they are to be successful as human beings, i.e., to reach the appropriate telos of human life.

Given this general characterization a virtue ethics will typically have three central goals:

(1) to develop and defend some conception of the ideal person;
(2) to develop and defend some list of virtues that are necessary for being a person of that type;
(3) to defend some view of how persons can come to possess the appropriate virtues.

One can also characterize a virtue ethics by contrasting these sorts of goals with the goals typically attaching to normative theories that take judgments of each of the other two types as basic. A normative theory that takes judgments of *actions* as basic, a deontological theory, will typically have as its goals:

(1) to formulate and defend a particular set of moral rules, or to defend some procedure for generating appropriate moral rules;[5]
(2) to develop and defend some method of determining what to do when the relevant moral rules come into conflict.

A normative theory which takes judgments of *consequences* of actions as fundamental, a consequentialist theory, will attempt:

(1) to specify and defend some thing or list of things which are good in themselves;
(2) to provide some technique for measuring and comparing the amount of the relevant good thing (or things) that might be brought about;
(3) to defend some procedures for those cases where one is not in a position to determine which of a number of alternative actions will maximize the good thing or things.

The third view of what is entailed by a concern with virtue in ethics is clearly much stronger than the first two. It suggests not only that moral philosophers should "pay attention" to virtue concepts and include a virtue component in a complete normative theory, but that the concept of a virtue is in important respects a more fundamental notion than the concepts of 'the right' or 'the good' where the good is seen as attaching to objects as possible consequences of our action. It is the third view of the importance of virtue in ethics that I will attend to in what follows.

II. OBJECTIONS TO VIRTUE ETHICS

The most striking feature of virtue ethics is the near universality of its rejection in contemporary ethical theory and in modern ethics generally. For the most part, the field has been left to broadly deontological normative theories and their consequentialist opponents. Both of these types of theories, while differing in many respects, find themselves in agreement on the inadequacy of an EV. There are undoubtedly a number of reasons for the widespread rejection of an EV but there is an important distinction among these reasons which I will mark by dividing them into two classes, *external* objections and *internal* objections.

By an external objection to an EV, I mean an objection that comes from outside ethics proper. Typically, such objections will raise broadly epistemological or metaphysical difficulties with an EV. The primary external objection to an EV claims that an EV cannot be sustained because a necessary condition for the success of such a theory is a certain metaphysical or theological underpinning which, given the rise of distinctively modern science and the decline of classical theology, is implausible.

From the metaphysical side it is argued that what is required to sustain a virtue ethics is a broadly teleological view of nature—a view according to which explanations in terms of final causes are legitimate and, indeed necessary, for understanding nature. Such a view underpins an EV in that it can provide a justification for supposing that normative questions about human action are ultimately to be settled by appealing to the contribution action may make to the movement of persons toward their metaphysically fixed end or telos. Character is a way a human being can *be,* and such a teleological view of nature underpins an EV in that it supports the view that human beings should *be* a certain way.

The rise of distinctively modern natural sciences is supposed to show that such a teleological view of human nature is implausible in that the history of science is alleged to show that the mysteries of nonhuman nature have only been revealed when such a teleological conception has been set aside. Modern science has mounted a relentless assault on such a teleological conception, and natural teleology has been defeated in every encounter. Since a large part of the justification for a teleological conception of human nature was always that such a conception was necessary for the understanding of nature in general, its failure in this latter respect makes it implausible to take it seriously in the former.

Some have attempted to salvage virtue ethics by substituting for natural teleology a theological account of teleology according to which the teleological structure of nature can be guaranteed by the purposive nature of God's creative activity. The difficulty with a theological underpinning for ethics is not so much that it has been undermined by modern conceptions of nature and our powers to uncover its mysteries (although this is part of the story); the main difficulty is that if we must rely on a particular theological account of human nature, then any ethical view which is based on this account will not have the universal appeal that we expect of a *moral* view. The theological account will support virtue ethics only for those who accept the relevant theological beliefs, but it is frequently alleged that an appropriate foundation for ethics must make a more general appeal. It is the hope of most people who do normative theory that ethical discourse will allow persons from different theological traditions to talk across these traditions—to rise above their theological differences. But if the structure of moral argument is itself grounded in one of these traditions then this goal will not be able to be satisfied.

Internal objections to virtue ethics differ from external objections in that they come from within ethical reflection itself. They claim that there are general considerations connected to the *point* of ethical theory or to the structure of the moral point of view that make a virtue ethics untenable. As a consequence of being internal they ultimately depend upon arguments that support the claim that ethics really is the way they say it is. There is always the possibility, given their internal character, that these objections can slip into being question-begging.

In setting out the most important of these objections, I am not going to locate them in particular writers. They seem to me, however, to be found in many modern ethical theorists of otherwise quite different persuasions. I think all of them, for example, are found in Kant, although some of them are more obviously there than others, and utilitarians also frequently have recourse to them. They express a set of assumptions which are taken seriously by many contemporary writers and thinkers about ethics.

There are three central internal objections to virtue ethics. The first objection, which I will call the "self-centeredness objection," alleges that an EV tends to focus too much attention on the agent. As we noted in discussing the structure appropriate to an EV, such theories demand a focus on the character of the individual agent. What gives point to the task of acquiring the virtues is that one supposes that one should become a person of a particular kind. One wants to change one's character from "the way it is" to "the way it ought to be," in the language of Alasdair MacIntyre.[6] This view demands that the moral agent keep his or her own character at the center of his or her practical attention. To many persons this requirement that each agent keep his or her character as the central focus of practical thought seems to import an unjustifiable degree of self-centeredness into ethics. If one supposes that the point of moral reflection essentially involves a concern for others (or at least a concern that the interests of others be taken into account in practical thought, or that one move away from a narrowly prudential view of one's action) then it may appear that an EV cannot satisfy this requirement.

This attitude toward an EV is reflected in the claims frequently made that Aristotle, Plato, and other classical virtue theorists are ethical egoists of some sort. The thought behind such claims seems to be that for classical virtue theorists, it is *rational* for an agent to acquire the virtues only insofar as it is a good for that agent that he or she acquire them. But if the rationality of virtue acquisition is thus grounded in the needs of the agent, so the argument goes, the needs, wants, and desires of others have, from the point of view of morality, an insufficiently prominent status. Many twentieth-century Kantians have argued that this agent-centered feature of classical virtue theory makes it impossible for such theories to account for genuine moral obligation.[7]

The second internal objection, which I will call the "action-guiding objection," alleges that an EV lacks the capacity to yield suitably determinate action guides. Normative ethics is undoubtedly supposed to have a practical point. We engage in it partly out of a disinterested pursuit of truth, but like cookery and engineering, it would be misunderstood if its theoretical point were allowed to exclude all others. An important part of the practical aim of normative theory is that it guide our actions in situations where we find ourselves in moral conflict because we feel required to perform each of two incompatible actions. Also, guidance seems appropriate in situations of moral indeterminacy where we are unclear what we should do because our deliberative apparatus does not appropriately cover a new case in our experience. Moral life sometimes seems almost exhausted by cases like these where we are plagued by moral conflict or moral indeterminacy. It is alleged by proponents of the action-guiding objection that normative ethics should help in each of these cases by providing principles or rules (action-guides generally) of a suitably algorithmic character which will help deliver us from our perplexity. Both deontological theories and consequentialist theories of the modern sort, it is argued, fare much better in this respect than do virtue theories. An EV, with its emphasis on the development of states of character, lacks the capacity for precision or determinateness found in the two alternative views. Critics of virtue ethics, in this respect, point to the failure of classical virtue theorists even to attempt to provide determinate guides to action. We are reminded that Plato and Aristotle seldom discuss moral quandaries and when they do the advice forthcoming (such as the advice to feel certain emotions "at the right times, with reference to the right objects, towards the right people, with the right motive, and in the right way"[8]) has seemed egregiously unhelpful. The conclusion is drawn that it is in the very nature of an EV that it cannot provide the kind of determinate guidance for action that is required in an adequate normative ethics.[9]

The third type of internal objection, which I will call the "contingency objection," is the most deeply Kantian objection of the three. It alleges that the moral goodness of an agent should be within his or her control at the moment of action. The spirit of this objection permeates much modern ethical thinking, I think, and it is largely responsible for some of the more notorious features of Kant's treatment of the concept of moral worth in the first section of the *Groundwork*. It is particularly evident in his discussion of naturally benevolent persons—persons who act benevolently solely because they are moved by feelings of care and concern for their fellow creatures.[10] Kant is quite clear that persons so motivated should get no moral credit for their otherwise morally praiseworthy benevolent actions. Kant does not mean, of course, as he is sometimes taken to mean, that we should seek to extirpate such feelings on the grounds that they may interfere with moral goodness. His view is rather that such feelings are, from the point of view of a moral evaluation of the agent, neutral. They count neither for nor against the moral goodness of the agent. And the reason they are morally irrelevant features of the agent is that they lie outside his rational control. Benevolent feelings toward others (as a species of what Kant called pathological desires) may have either of two sources—biological or social. Some persons, biologically or genetically, may be naturally disposed to care for others; others may have had inculcated in them by social training, either of an explicit or implicit sort, a tendency to have certain benevolent feelings toward others. In either case, the agent does not have it within his power upon the occasion of action to call up such feelings if they are not already there. If the presence of such feelings, or the disposition to have such feelings on certain occasions, is used as a determinate of moral goodness, then an agent's level of moral goodness will be, at least partly, a matter of luck. Perhaps Kant's deepest insight (or prejudice as it may seem) was that morality should not, in this respect, be a matter of luck.[11]

This argument is relevant to an EV in that moral character, if conceived as a bundle of dispositions to act or to have certain feelings about action, would surely be outside the control of the agent at the moment of action. Indeed, many aspects of an agent's character are surely not within his or her control at all. This contingency of moral goodness is reflected in a number of features of classical virtue theory, especially in the pessimism about moral conversion expressed by Aristotle and Plato and in their emphasis on moral education as a matter of forming habits in the service of shaping character. If the achievement of moral goodness must be within the power of every moral agent upon every occasion for action, then surely the critic here is right. An EV cannot satisfy that constraint.

III. RESPONSE TO THE OBJECTIONS

The objections to an EV set out above constitute a formidable challenge to anyone who hopes to revive an EV. It seems to me, however, that there is an important difference between the challenge set by the central external objection, and that set by the three internal objections. Any response to the external objection will have to involve one of two strategies, either of which will involve philosophical work on a grand scale. One might respond by attempting to resurrect Aristotelian natural teleology as a comprehensive theory of nature. I am skeptical about the prospects for the success of such a project, but am willing to wish those well who may want to attempt it. More promisingly, one might attempt to give an account of human social activity that, after the manner of A. MacIntyre or C. Taylor, aims to establish a teleological account of rational action.[12] The defense of such a "local" teleology will surely present far fewer philosophical difficulties than the more ambitious Aristotelian project, but, as the recent work of MacIntyre and Taylor suggests, it remains a formidable project. Whatever strategy one might adopt in responding to the external objection to an EV, however, it is clear that the issues raised are of a level of complexity that makes it impossible to address them here.

Things seem to me otherwise, however, with regard to the internal objections to an EV. Although these objections have been widely used by the deontological and consequentialist opponents of an EV, each of them seems to me to fail to damage seriously the prospects for an adequate EV. And in the case of each of these objections, the failure is largely of the same nature. Each places demands on an EV which neither deontological nor consequentialist normative theories can satisfy. So while it may be true that an EV cannot meet the standards for a normative theory demanded by these objections, neither will the standard theoretical alternatives to an EV be able to meet these demands. While this "partners in crime" strategy, if successful, will not show that these demands should not be placed on normative theories, it will at least place those defenders of consequentialist or deontological alternatives to an EV who wish to use them in a rhetorically awkward position. In the remainder of this paper, I would like to sketch briefly how this strategy can be used with regard to each of these objections.

1. The self-centeredness objection

It may appear that there is a quick response to the self-centeredness objection available to the virtue theorist. He may point out that the objection fails to take account of an important distinction between two features of an EV. There is, first, the feature that the objector notices: the central place that one's own character plays in the practical thinking associated with an EV. But there is also within an EV the set of virtues that each agent aims to embody in his character. While the first feature of an EV may appear to render it excessively self-centered, the second feature is surely able to counteract that danger. The particular virtues characteristic of an EV may be as other regarding as one might wish. While each agent may be expected to devote primary practical attention to the development of his or her own character, that attention may be required to turn the agent into a person fundamentally concerned with the well-being of others. Classical virtues like justice, Christian virtues like love or charity, and Alasdair MacIntyre's favorite modern virtue, Jane Austen's amiability, all have a predominantly other-regarding character.[13] They both restrict the attention I am allowed to pay to my own wants, needs, and desires, and force me to attend to the wants, needs, and desires of others.

This response may still appear insufficient, however, in that it allows the self-centeredness objection to arise at a deeper level. At this deeper level, the objection points to an asymmetry that arises between an agent's regard for his own character and his regard for the character of others. The question raised here has this form: Since an EV requires me to pay primary attention to the state of my own character, doesn't this suggest that I must regard my own character as the ethically most important feature of myself? But, if so, and if I am suitably concerned about others, shouldn't my concern for them extend beyond a mere concern that their wants, needs, and desires be satisfied, and encompass a concern for *their* character? Shouldn't I indeed have the same concern for the character of my neighbor as I have for my own?

Consider an example here. Suppose that I hold a virtue theory according to which Christian love or charity is the primary virtue. I believe, that is, that my fundamental ethical task is to become the sort of person who has toward others the attitudes we associate with Christian love. Then, it would seem that I must hold the view that my having this virtue is the most important thing for me; practically I must subordinate everything else to this. But—and this is the problem—Christian love does not require of me—that is, the developed virtue does not—that I bring it about that others around me possess Christian love. Rather Christian love requires me to attend to the wants, needs, and desires of others. But doesn't this suggest that I regard others as less morally important than myself? Satisfying their needs is good enough for them, but I require of myself that I become a loving person.

This asymmetry between my attitude toward my own character and my attitude toward the character of others is, it seems to me, ineliminable within virtue ethics. And this is why the virtue theorist must simply look for partners in crime—if, indeed, this is a crime. And, it can surely be shown that theories of the other two sorts equally fall prey to it. Consider Kant's claim in the Introduction to the *Doctrine of Virtue* that the distinction between duties to myself and duties to others lies in the fact that while I can only seek to make others happy, I must primarily seek to make myself good.[14] His claim here is that it is not a proper object of my action to try to bring it about that others do the right thing. (The Kantian slogan here might be, "rightness for me, happiness for you.") And it is surely not merely an accidental feature of Kant's particular deontological theory that an asymmetry similar to that characteristically found in an EV between concern for self and concern for others is found there. Deontological theories characteristically require that each agent regard his or her own actions in a different light from the actions of others.

Consider, for example, the fact that deontological theories typically forbid agents to perform one morally bad action, A_1, in order to prevent some other agent (or agents) from performing two or more actions, A_2-A_n, which are morally indistinguishable from A_1. The justification for this is surely not that deontological theories regard A_1 as somehow morally worse than A_2-A_n taken together. Even the deontologist might be forced to admit that from a "purely objective" standpoint, it is a morally "worse" thing that several morally bad actions occur than that a single morally bad action occur. The reason deontological theories require the agent to avoid morally bad actions in these cases is that an agent's relation to his own actions is special in a way that his relation to the actions of others is not. We need not inquire here into the nature of this "special relationship," since merely recognizing that deontological theories are committed to it is sufficient to show that such theories will suffer from the same sort of "self-centeredness" that was alleged to be so damaging to an EV.

A similar kind of difficulty bedevils the history of utilitarianism.[15] In classical utilitarianism there is a tension between the kind of universally benevolent character I am required to develop in myself and the kind of requirements that constrain my activities toward others. The point is not that I am required to make myself benevolent, but only required to make others happy. Classical utilitarianism surely does require me (at least under normal conditions) to attempt to make others benevolent too. The point is rather that my concern for their benevolence can be at most an instrumental concern, while my concern for my own benevolence cannot be, at the deepest level, of this character. The benevolence of others is only of instrumental concern to the utilitarian, because all of his concerns with regard to others are guided ultimately by the single requirement to maximize human happiness. Under normal circumstances, inducing benevolence in others is a useful way of promoting that end. But the utilitarian's concern for his *own* benevolence cannot be in the same way a matter of merely instrumental concern. His own benevolence is, as it were, the perspective from which the benevolence of others attains a kind of (instrumental) moral significance; but his own benevolence cannot, itself, attain moral significance from this perspective, because it *is* the perspective. It is in this way that even for a utilitarian one's own character has a special status that is denied to others.

One might attempt to respond to this claim about utilitarianism by pointing out, what is surely true, that a utilitarian possessed of a suitably benevolent character may have good utilitarian reasons to change his character in such a way that he or she is no longer benevolent. For example, a utilitarian may decide that human happiness will be maximized if everyone, including himself, comes to have a character that is thoroughly selfish and mean-spirited. In such a case, a good utilitarian should set to work to root out his benevolent character and to replace it with a suitably selfish set of dispositions. This possibility may seem to suggest that, after all, the benevolent character of the utilitarian is only of instrumental concern to himself or herself after all. But this conclusion would be too hasty. What remains true is that there is never a moment at which the agent in question is both a utilitarian and such that he can regard his benevolence as a matter of merely instrumental concern. If he succeeds in his moral transformation, one can only conjecture what his attitude might then be toward his former benevolence. But his attitude after the transformation will, of course, be of no relevance to this argument, since after the transformation, he will no longer be a utilitarian.

These remarks about utilitarian and deontological theories are intended to suggest that while an EV may require an asymmetry between an agent's attitude toward his own character and that of others, similar asymmetries are found in the two other types of normative theory. Both deontological theories and consequentialist theories require agents to treat their own actions or motivational structures differently from those of others. In this respect, it is difficult to see that the special features of the asymmetry in the case of an EV should constitute a serious objection to theories of that type.

2. *The action-guiding objection*

The virtue theorist's response to the action-guiding objection involves three claims. First, that an EV can guide action more successfully than the objection seems to recognize. Second, that the deontological and consequentialist alternatives to an EV are *less* successful at guiding action than the objection alleges. Third, that the demand for determinate action-guidingness as spelled out by these opponents involves more than one dubious claim about the relation between ethical theory and action.

With regard to the first point, it is important to note that it is simply false that virtue theories do not provide *any* guidance for action. Rather, they provide it at a place and in a manner that seems inappropriate to many modern ethical theorists. Virtue theorists suggest that the primary focus of moral evaluation is human character, and since character is a dynamic phenomenon, the focus is on the whole life of a person. The moral life is not, on this view, best regarded as a set of episodic encounters with moral dilemmas or moral uncertainty (although anyone's moral life will certainly contain moments of this kind); it is rather a life-long pursuit of excellence of the person. The kind of guidance appropriate to such a pursuit will be quite different from that envisioned by many modern ethical theorists. An EV primarily helps us to answer questions like: What features of human life contribute essentially to human excellence? What character traits should one strive to develop? In taking such questions as primary, it will, of course, fall short of providing determinate guidance of action for the whole range of problematic situations in which human beings might find themselves. But it does not take this as its goal. The task of an EV is not determinately to guide action; that task is left to the virtues. Virtue theories do not propose algorithms for solving practical difficulties; they propose something more like a fitness program to get one ready to run a race. This does not mean, of course, that an EV is completely without resources in guiding particular actions. A just person does not seduce a good friend's wife or husband; a charitable person does not refuse to extend help to the needy; and a courageous person does not run when the first shot is fired.

This kind of guidance in what some might regard as "easy" ethical cases is unlikely to satisfy the opponent of an EV, however. They will point out that their claim is not that a virtue theory is *useless* in guiding action; rather, it is that in the genuinely tough cases where we demand rules or principles, a kind of algorithm for right action, virtue ethics is found wanting. It does not provide what is provided by consequentialists in the principle of utility or by broadly deontological theories in principles like Kant's universal law formulation of the categorical imperative. But here the opponents of an EV have surely gone too far. If one examines the algorithmic moral principles put forward by philosophers of a consequentialist or deontological stripe, one seems always to find difficulties in applying these principles. Some of these difficulties are of a broadly theoretical sort like those utilitarians have in making sense of interpersonal comparisons of utility. But others involve more down to earth problems in applying principles to cases. These problems are reflected in the fact of practical disagreement among ethical theorists who agree on the alleged algorithmic principles. Many contemporary Kantians, for example, while largely agreeing with Kant's formulation of the fundamental principle of morality, are horrified at some of the conclusions he drew from it. Nor do they necessarily agree among themselves on what the results of such applications should be. Utilitarians similarly find themselves frequently in theoretical agreement, but practical disagreement. Both utilitarians and Kantians are frequently found on both sides of all of the most controverted moral issues in contemporary discussion. Positions on ethical theory do not typically fix practical attitudes on controversial issues involving abortion, the use of nuclear weapons, affirmative action, or the details of schemes for distributive justice.

The conclusion to be drawn from this ubiquitous practical disagreement is, I think, that the claims for the determinate action-guiding power of deontological and consequentialist normative theories are overstated. What seems to be the case is rather that each of these putative algorithmic principles requires a quality of judgment, not too unlike what classical virtue theorists called *phronesis* for its application. Easy moral cases are easy for everyone—virtue theorists, deontologists, and consequentialists; hard cases are also hard for everyone, demanding on all views, as it may seem, an exercise of practical wisdom that eludes being captured in a formula.

It still may be argued, of course, that deontological and consequentialist alternatives to an EV fare better with regard to action-guidingness than does an EV; and that to the extent that they do so they are to be preferred to an EV. To assess this claim, it would be necessary to get clearer both on what it is for a normative theory to be determinately action guiding and also on why it is a good thing that normative theories should strive to maximize their action-guiding power. Both of these topics are enormously complicated and also much neglected in recent discussions of normative ethical theory.

With regard to the first topic, it is important to note that action-guidingness as a property of a normative theory is hardly a simple property. Although it seems clear that action-guidingness in this sense involves some relation between a normative theory and particular normative problems, the relation will involve a number of different aspects. For example, in attempting to measure the overall action-guiding power of a normative theory, one needs to distinguish at least three different senses in which one theory, NT_1, might be regarded as being more determinately action guiding than another theory, NT_2. First, with regard to *breadth* of action-guiding power, NT_1 might yield solutions to a wider range of normative problems than does NT_2. Second, with regard to *specificity* of action-guiding power, NT_1 might yield more specific, or more narrowly circumscribed, solutions to particular normative problems than NT_2. Finally with regard to *decisiveness* of action-guiding power, NT_1 might yield more decisive solutions, in the sense of solutions recommended with a higher degree of probability that they are correct, than NT_2. It is also important to see that these criteria could conflict in the case of comparisons of particular normative theories. Thus, in comparing NT_1 and NT_2, one might discover that NT_1 resolves a wider range of normative problems than NT_2, but that NT_2 resolves the problems it resolves either more decisively or more specifically. Other kinds of conflicts could also arise.

These distinctions are important in their own right, but they are especially important to the topics under discussion here because they point to difficulties in addressing the question of how to measure the overall action-guiding power of a normative theory. If there are a number of different senses in which one normative theory might be said to be more powerfully action guiding than another, then it seems appropriate that the question about the relative action-guiding power of different types of theories will have to be asked with regard to each of these senses. In comparing the action-guiding power of an EV with the powers of its deontological and consequentialist opponents, then, one must compare them *at least* with regard to breadth, specificity, and decisiveness.

Here I can only suggest what seems to me the likely outcome of such a comparison. With regard to breadth of action-guiding power, there seems no reason to suppose that the opponents of an EV will fare better than an EV. An EV can yield a set of virtues that will be relevant to choice in virtually every situation of choice in which an agent might find himself. If EVs are capable of such maximal breadth, then they are hardly likely to suffer in this regard from comparison with deontological and consequentialist theories. I suspect that opponents of an EV would agree with this point, and concentrate on deficiencies of an EV with regard to specificity and decisiveness. But at this point it is important to recall a point made above: that within an EV it is not the theory of the virtues which is supposed to be primarily action guiding, but rather the virtues themselves. It is not the theoretical account either of the point of the virtue of justice or of its role in the overall economy of practical thought that is supposed to guide action, but rather the virtue of justice itself. With this point in hand, however, the proponent of an EV can argue that it is not implausible that such a developed virtue can guide action with at least as much specificity and decisiveness as any rule or principle. An agent who embodies the virtue of justice may discern the justice of particular actions, projects, or institutions as specifically and decisively as some impersonally formulated rule or principle. Indeed, one might suppose that virtues might fare better than rules or principles with regard to specificity and decisiveness. It is because they embody a more complex capacity for discernment than do rules and principles that they defy formulation in rules or principles. In support of this claim, one can point to many examples of powers of discernment (e.g., in wine-tasters or art critics) where we do not suppose that inability to formulate powers of discernment in rules or principles need lead to lack of either specificity or decisiveness.

These general remarks about the relative action-guiding power of normative theories, of course, are of the most preliminary sort. Much more needs to be said both about the precise nature of the various measures of action-guiding power and about the structure of virtues which allows them to embody the relevant powers of discernment. But I hope that even these preliminary remarks make it clear that an EV is not without resources, and considerable resources at that, in combatting the claim that it suffers in a comparison of action-guiding power with deontological and consequentialist theories.

3. The contingency argument

We can again use a partners in crime strategy in formulating an initial response to the contingency argument. It can be shown, I think, that neither consequentialist nor deontological theorists can escape the charge that moral goodness on their view too is tainted with contingency. For utilitarianism, the argument is straightforward. Moral goodness, on this view, must be given either an objective or a subjective reading. If it is given an objective reading, then moral goodness will be determined by the value of the *actual consequences* of an agent's actions. But surely nothing could be less under the control of an agent. Typically the actual consequences of an action are influenced not only by the intention of the agent, but also by all of the natural contingencies of the world that intervene between the intention and the consequences. Efforts may be made by the agent, of course, to control these intervening factors, but no amount of effort can insure that the actual consequences of an action match the original intention.

For this reason, the utilitarian may reject the objective reading of moral goodness, and substitute a subjective view. But a subjective view fares little better. According to a subjective view, moral goodness will be determined by the *intended consequences* of an action. But surely whether one has sufficiently benevolent intentions to satisfy the strong requirements, say, of utilitarianism, is frequently going to be outside the control of the agent at the moment of action. I may, of course, frequently have it within my power to intend an action that is required by the principle of utility. But the subjective account of moral goodness requires more than this. It requires that I intend the action in question *as a means* to the greatest happiness of the greatest number, and it is surely far from clear that this intention is always within my power.[16]

Since Kant was so insistent on the contingency argument, one might suppose that his view, at least, escapes the charge. But it is far from clear that this is the case. Although Kant's account of the moral goodness of an agent is too complicated to discuss in detail here, the central idea of it is that an agent is morally good just in case he wills right actions because they are right. One's belief that an action is right need not be the sole motive for performing the action, but it must be a sufficient motive in the sense that if it were the sole motive then, other things being equal, it would move the agent to perform the action. Kant seems to think that his own account of moral goodness escapes the contingency objection in that he believes that agents always have the power to act conscientiously, where conscientious action is right action motivated by the belief that it is right. Kant admits, of course, that we may not always be able to call up feelings or desires for the end of our morally required action, but the bare ability to will what is right, because it is right, is supposed always to be available to us. Given the variety of ways in which human powers of choice may, however, be impaired, this view seems literally incredible. Kant seems never to have fully appreciated that the capacity for conscientious action is subject to the vagaries of socialization and explicit training in a way similar to the capacity for benevolent action, although he implicitly admits this when in his metaphysical view he removes the will to the noumenal realm where it must be located if any taint of contingency is to be removed.

This brief attempt to demonstrate some difficulties both utilitarians and Kantians may have in removing contingency from attributions of moral goodness surely settles very little. It may be possible for the opponents of an EV to develop an account of moral goodness that escapes the difficulties above, and then one would have to examine such a view to determine if contingency does not sneak in in some other way. My suspicion is that it always would, but I know of no general argument to establish this. A more fruitful line of inquiry, I suspect, would pursue the question of why so many moral philosophers have sought an account of moral goodness that is free of contingency. Perhaps an understanding of the reasons for this quest would free us from the need to continue it.

Notes

1. This charge has been made by a number of philosophers, but it is especially powerfully made in Elizabeth Anscombe, "Modern Moral Philosophy," *Philosophy* 33 (1958), and in Julius Kovesi, *Moral Notions* (New York, 1967).

2. William Frankena, *Ethics* (Englewood Cliffs, N.J., 1973), 65–67.

3. John Rawls, *A Theory of Justice* (Cambridge, Mass., 1971). The inferior position Rawls attributes to the virtues is evident from his characterization of virtues as "sentiments, that is, related families of dispositions and propensities regulated by a higher-order desire, in this case a desire to act from the corresponding moral principles" (192).

4. I do not intend to suggest, however, that an EV need be a foundationalist theory in the sense in which such a theory is contrasted with a coherence theory. There is surely no reason why an EV could not be ultimately supported by a form of argument that is broadly coherentist.

5. This characterization may need to be modified in certain respects to account for "act deontological" views.

6. Alasdair MacIntyre, *After Virtue* (Notre Dame, Ind., 1984), 67.

7. Perhaps the most powerful arguments of this sort are still to be found in Prichard's "Does Moral Philosophy Rest on a Mistake" reprinted in his *Moral Obligation* (New York, 1950).

8. Aristotle, *Nicomachean Ethics,* Ross translation (London, 1966), 38.

9. This alleged inability of an EV to provide determinate action guides is one of the main motives of those who have claimed that an account of the virtues can at most provide one component of a normative ethical theory. Frankena, for example, is quite explicit in taking this as the main justification for his "double aspect" normative theory.

10. Kant's discussion of the naturally benevolent person is found in chap. 1 of the *Groundwork of the Metaphysics of Morals.*

11. One can arrive at this same Kantian thought, I think, by reflecting on the implications of his views on "ought implies can."

12. Cf. MacIntyre, *After Virtue,* and Charles Taylor, *The Explanation of Behaviour* (London, 1964).

13. MacIntyre, *After Virtue,* 127.

14. Kant argues there that there are two ends "which are at the same time duties": "one's own perfection and the happiness of others. One cannot invert these and make, on the one hand, our own happiness and, on the other, the perfection of others, ends which should be in themselves duties for the same person," *The Metaphysical Principles of Virtue,* translated by James Ellington (Indianapolis, 1964), 43.

15. Although I develop this argument only in connection with classical utilitarianism, I think similar results would follow in considering any consequentialist view.

16. I do not mean to suggest here that classical utilitarians were unaware of these difficulties. Mill, indeed, goes to some lengths to combat them. He says in *Utilitarianism,* "The multiplication of happiness is, according to the utilitarian ethics, the object of virtue: the occasions on which any person (except one in a thousand) has it in his power to do this on an extended scale— in other words, to be a public benefactor—are but exceptional; and on these occasions alone is he called on to consider public utility; *in every other case, private utility, the interest or happiness of some few persons, is all he has to attend to,"* emphasis added (J. S. Mill, *Utilitarianism* [Indianapolis, 1957], 25.) The question that Mill's position raises is, however, whether it can be reconciled with other features of his utilitarianism. I suspect it cannot.

Contributors

Felicia Ackerman, Department of Philosophy, Brown University

Robert M. Adams, Department of Philosophy, University of California, Los Angeles

Kurt Baier, Department of Philosophy, University of Pittsburgh

Marcia Baron, Department of Philosophy, University of Illinois

Lawrence A. Blum, Department of Philosophy, University of Massachusetts

Richard B. Brandt, Department of Philosophy, University of Michigan

Sarah Conly, Department of Philosophy and Religion, Bates College

Michael Davis, Center for the Study of Ethics in the Professions, Illinois Institute of Technology

Cora Diamond, Corcoran Department of Philosophy, University of Virginia

Fred Feldman, Department of Philosophy, University of Massachusetts

R. Z. Friedman, Department of Philosophy, University College, University of Toronto

John Kekes, Department of Philosophy, State University of New York

Joel Kupperman, Department of Philosophy, University of Connecticut

Alasdair MacIntyre, Department of Philosophy, Vanderbilt University

David L. Norton, Department of Philosophy, University of Delaware

Martha C. Nussbaum, Department of Philosophy, Brown University

David K. O'Connor, Department of Philosophy, University of Notre Dame

Peter Railton, Department of Philosophy, University of Michigan

Richard J. Regan, S. J., Department of Political Science, Fordham University

Amelie O. Rorty, Department of Philosophy, Radcliff College

Nancy Sherman, Department of Philosophy, Yale University

Michael Slote, Department of Philosophy, University of Maryland

David Solomon, Department of Philosophy, University of Notre Dame

Robert C. Solomon, Department of Philosophy, University of Texas

Gabriele Taylor, St. Anne's College, Oxford University

Richard Taylor, Department of Philosophy, Union College

Laurence Thomas, Department of Philosophy, Oberlin College

James D. Wallace, Department of Philosophy, University of Illinois

David B. Wong, Department of Philosophy, Brandeis University

Peter A. French is Lennox Distinguished Professor of Philosophy and chairman of the philosophy department at Trinity University in San Antonio, Texas. He has taught at the University of Minnesota, Morris, and has served as Distinguished Research Professor in the Center for the Study of Values at the University of Delaware. His books include *The Scope of Morality* (Minnesota, 1980), *Ethics in Government* (1982), and *Collective and Corporate Responsibility* (1984). Theodore E. Uehling, Jr., is professor of philosophy at the University of Minnesota, Morris. He is the author of *The Notion of Form in Kant's Critique of Aesthetic Judgment* and articles on the philosophy of Kant. Howard K. Wettstein is associate professor of philosophy at the University of Notre Dame. He has taught at the University of Minnesota, Morris, and has served as a visiting associate professor of philosophy at the University of Iowa and Stanford University. He is the author of *Has Semantics Rested on a Mistake? and Other Essays* (Stanford University Press, forthcoming).